THE
STONE-CAMPBELL
MOVEMENT

THE STONE-CAMPBELL MOVEMENT

The Story of the American Restoration Movement

LEROY GARRETT

Library of Congress Catalog Card Number: 94-69389
International Standard Book Number: 0-89900-415-6

PUBLISHER'S PREFACE

College Press is pleased to publish this thoroughly revised edition of Leroy Garrett's history of the churches whose common roots are in the Restoration Movement. Those who are familiar with previous editions will note significant rearrangement and additions to the older material including some helpful updating. This version of the unique challenge to Christian unity will inspire its readers to keep the Restoration ideal alive until the Lord Jesus returns to claim His church. At one time the fastest-growing and most evangelistic effort in American history, the Stone-Campbell Movement in reality was an appeal for the vitality of the first church. History has recorded the beginning of the American Restoration Movement in the early 1800s, and those members of the movement insist that it all began with Christ in the early years following His resurrection.

Let there be no mistake, Jesus will always have a church and will always work with those who love Him and are called according to His purpose. Let this volume on church history be a wake-up call to revitalize the church, to fan the flame of evangelism, and to exercise a relentless effort at uniting all Christians in love. To this bold venture this volume, *The Stone-Campbell Movement*, is dedicated for the glory of Christ's church, in heaven and on earth.

Chris DeWelt
President

TABLE OF CONTENTS

1

INTRODUCTION
THE MOVEMENT AND THE CHURCH

*This I regard as history's highest function, to let no worthy action
be uncommemorated, and to hold out for the reprobation
of posterity that which is notorious for infamy.*
— Tacitus, Roman historian

The value of history is variously appraised, from Henry Ford's insistence that history is bunk to Montaigne's view that history is the window through which we look out upon our world. If Hegel saw history as the story of mankind's struggle to be free, Thucydides saw the study of the past as a means of interpreting the future. Harvard's George Santayana spoke to us all when he warned that those who ignore history have to repeat its mistakes. And we can all probably agree that there is at least some truth in that line engraved on the cornerstone of the National Archives in Washington, D.C.: *The Past Is Prologue.*

But it is Tacitus, who saw the study of history as having a moral purpose, who especially speaks to us as we begin our study of the Stone-Campbell Movement. There is much in the Movement's history that qualifies for what Tacitus referred to as "conspicuous for excellence," and this we want to highlight.

We should like to follow his advice and "let no worthy action be uncommemorated," and yet hold out for "the reprobation of posterity" anything that was not right and should never have happened. This means that we draw the picture of our heritage as it is, warts and all. There is no other acceptable way to do history.

This is anecdotal history in that we are storytelling. The Movement that dreamed of uniting the Christians in all the sects did not intend to become still another church, much less three more, which it eventually did. We are telling that story as objectively as possible, realizing that complete objectivity is an illusive goal. But we are determined that it not be a "house" job, slanted in favor of any one of the three churches that have emerged from the Movement, whether the Christian Churches (Disciples of Christ), Churches of Christ, or Christian Churches (Independent).

1

It is understandable that the historians in each of these churches would be inclined to see their own segment as the true heirs of the Movement, and it is reasonable that they would write their histories from the perspective of their own church. While I have no quarrel with this, it is my intention to tell the story as an outside observer might tell it, even though I am a third-generation member of the Churches of Christ.

Having served as an editor for forty years, I assigned myself the task of telling the story of the Movement as a journalist would tell it, objectively and anecdotally. I have sought to move inside the sources and write as an "on sight" reporter would write, more as a storyteller than a historian. It is my intention to take the reader there and allow him to see for himself rather than to tell him what to think.

It may be evident that I have a quarrel with some of the unfolding events, but I hope it will be equally evident that it is a lover's quarrel. And that I have laid out the facts as they are, some of which are not nice. As Tacitus advised, I have sought to preserve what is excellent and hold up to censure what is notorious. It will be evident that both the sublime and the ridiculous are there.

I can lay some claim to reasonable objectivity in that I have moved among all three of the branches of the Movement, probably more than any other living person. I have visited extensively among all three churches, both at home and abroad. My friends and contacts are among all three, almost equally, probably because I draw no lines, accepting them all as equals. Not fully agreeing with any but loving them all! I have either taught regularly or lectured occasionally in colleges of all three, and I have written in the journals of all three. I have been involved in agencies that are open to and serve all three, particularly the Disciples of Christ Historical Society, the World Convention of Churches of Christ, and the European Evangelistic Society which sponsors the Institute of Christian Origins in Tübingen, Germany.

A Sense of History

From the early days of the Movement its leaders were conscious that they were making history. Both Barton W. Stone and Alexander Campbell were aware of the importance of preserving data and records for the benefit of some future historian. By 1833 the Stone and Campbell forces had united and were some 30,000 strong, and the Movement was nearing the end of its first generation, but Campbell considered it far too soon even to begin to chronicle the events..

"Let us first see a reformation in fact – a reformation in sentiment, in practice — a reformation in faith and manners, before we talk of writing a history of it," he told an inquirer. He revealed that he saw his work as only having begun when he went on to say that any history written then would have to be "the history of a *struggle for reformation* rather than the history of a reformation."[1] He was too busy making history to be writing it!

In the same article Campbell assured his people that he was preserving the documents for such a history, and that once the story was told it would reveal that many obscure souls, who would not want their names mentioned, played significant roles. He noted that only his father would be able to recall the early days of their struggle when only two other men shared their views.

Campbell appeared uneasy about what judgment history would make of his efforts: "It would be exceedingly incongruous to do more than preserve the documents till we ascertain, or posterity ascertain, in what, or how far, we have restored the apostolic institutions."

As aware as Campbell was of the importance of saving data, the historian today can only wish that he had been more successful in preserving some key documents. We wish, for instance, that more of his letters to his first wife Margaret had survived. (Some theorize that his second wife Selina destroyed them!) We also wish we had the document in which the Brush Run church, the first of the Campbell congregations, set forth the conditions by which it would be a part of the Redstone Baptist Association. If Campbell had saved but one document, it should have been that one.

By 1848 Campbell was ready to share some of his historical notes with the readers of his journal, which provide us with vital source material on the early days of the Movement, from 1809-1829. In six installments he provides rare glimpses into such things as the worship of the Brush Run church and the evangelistic fervor of Walter Scott. Concerning Scott's role he wrote, "A great company, increasing from year to year, still occupies the theatre of the great achievements of the years of 1827, 1828, and 1829." This is reflective of Campbell's conviction that through Scott's preaching the primitive gospel was restored during those years, which we shall recount later.

In this data Campbell reveals that he and Walter Scott had agreed that when one made an inquiry of what he should do to be saved they would tell him what Peter told the inquirers on the day of Pentecost, "Repent and be baptized in the name of the Lord Jesus in order to the remission of sins." In recounting Scott's preaching and the hundreds that he baptized in a single year, Campbell noted, "It was a glorious time!"[2]

As years passed there was a growing concern that a history be prepared. Isaac T. Reneau of Kentucky, who prepared numerous obituaries for Campbell's paper through the years, told the editor in an obituary of Nancy Haggard, wife of Rice Haggard, that "This present Reformation cannot escape History; that its history is destined to future generations, all must see."

Reneau wanted a history of the Movement to be impartial, and so it must, he insisted, be mindful of its earliest pioneers, such as Rice Haggard. He told Campbell how Haggard united with Barton W. Stone in 1804 and wrote a pamphlet on the name Christian, thus preparing the way for reformation "according to the light they then had."[3]

Reneau's plea that Rice Haggard not be lost in obscurity has gone unheeded by the Movement's historians. We are pleased, due to recent research on Haggard, that in this history we can lift this significant pioneer from his undeserved obscurity.

In 1863, when Reneau appealed to Campbell for a history, the Movement still did not have a historian. But Dr. Robert Richardson, who eventually in 1868 published a history in the form of Alexander Campbell's biography, began a historical series of nineteen installments called "Reformation" in Campbell's paper as early as 1847. This account of the Movement had Campbell's blessing, who extolled Richardson as one uniquely qualified to interpret what had happened, and it can be looked to even today as representing the true character of the Stone-Campbell Movement.

It is this series, for instance, that the doctor observes that the character of a thing can be judged by that which gave it birth, and then says, "This reformation was born of the love of union, and Christian union has been its engrossing theme." Its design, he goes on to say, has been to urge two important truths: there can be unity of faith and at the same time liberty of private judgment.

To reconcile these two has troubled Protestants for three centuries, Richardson conceded, but he was sure that "the present reformation" had discovered the principles that would reconcile them. One of these principles, he noted, was that the divine basis of union is in the acceptance of the great fundamental truths of the Christian faith. He commended Campbell for basing his plea for unity upon those essentials of the faith to which all parties can accede.

In this series Richardson also pointed out that the pioneers had no intention of starting another sect. It was in fact abhorrent both to their feelings and their principles, and he thought this was evident in their earliest efforts to associate themselves with some denomination while preserving their own freedom. He noted that the pioneers had learned that Protestantism had failed in two important respects: by an overemphasis on doctrinal details and making these details the basis for fellowship; and by making matters of opinion into matters of faith.

The essence of the Movement, he allowed, was to correct these errors by recognizing that people can never agree on details but only on generals. "It is as essential to unity that there should be a universal faith," he observed with typical discernment," as it is to diversity that there should be an individual opinion." He thus recognized that the only unity possible is unity in diversity.[4]

Another young associate of Campbell that went on to survey the Movement's history was C.L. Loos, who as a professor of math and science at Bethany College led the prayer at Campbell's funeral in 1866.

As a keen observer of his people's history he wrote an extended series on "The Nineteenth Century Reformation" in *The Christian Evangelist* in 1899. His introduction to the two-volume abridgement of the *Millennial Harbinger* (1901) also reveals his grasp of the story of the Movement.

In his chronicle Loos reveals that he himself presided over the Baptist/Disciples unity conference in Pittsburgh in 1866, and then reported on its results to Campbell, who was on his deathbed. Over prospects of unity between the two churches, Loos quotes Campbell as saying, "I have always regretted that the Baptists and we had to part; it ought not to have been so." Moved to tears by the good news that Loos had brought, the dying reformer went on to say, "I had hoped that we and that great people could have stood together for the advocacy of apostolic Christianity. They are worthy of such a mission."[5]

Barton W. Stone was not as reluctant as Campbell to write a history of the Movement early on, as soon as 1827. In his own journal, the *Christian Messenger*, he wrote nine installments on "History of the Christian Church in the West" at the urging of "A Member of the Church of Christ," which shows how those names were used interchangeably. It covers the first two decades of the Stone movement.

Stone used the historical series not only to show that "the world might be able to form a correct judgment respecting our course," but as a teaching tool as well. In one installment, for instance, he reveals that it was his discovery of the nature of faith and how it is produced, especially as revealed in John 20:30-31, that led him to launch his movement. The Calvinists of his day believed that regeneration precedes faith, and that faith can come only as a miraculous act of God.

Stone's history was personal, not only because it was written in the first person but also because it candidly revealed his anxieties amidst the turmoil of his changing world. When he tells how three of his associates, who had left the Presbyterians with him, defected to a new sect called Shakers, he admits that "this was the first serious check to our progress, and it was humiliating in the extreme."

The defections, however, helped the future of his movement, he surmised, in that they served to curb speculations and bring its people closer to the Bible. Undaunted by the loss of part of his leadership, Stone labored on against great difficulties for the next two decades. He could at last record that "our numbers from a handful have swelled to many thousands, and many churches have doubled their numbers every year for some time past."[6]

The Genius of the Movement:
Restoration or Reformation?

One will notice in the foregoing data that the Movement was nearly always referred to as a Reformation, often with the capital R as in "the present Reformation." A term often used by the rank and file was "the current Reformation" as in the above quotation from Reneau. As we have seen, both of Campbell's young associates, Richardson and Loos, used "Reformation" in the title of their early histories of the Movement. When Barton W. Stone yielded the leadership of the Movement to Alexander Campbell, he acknowledged him to be "the greatest promoter of this reformation as any man living," while Campbell himself sometimes referred to the Movement as "the New Reformation."

While the terms "restore" and "restoration" were sometimes used, especially in the context of Campbell's early essays on "The Restoration of the Ancient Order of Things," it was not the usual way of describing the Movement. Early on they were called "Reformed Baptists" and they called themselves reformers or simply "the Reformation," but never restorers, and the term "Restoration Movement," while current in recent generations, was apparently never used.

The earliest historians, who began to write as the Movement approached its first centennial, called their chronicles a history of the Disciples of Christ. So it was with B.B. Tyler (1894), Errett Gates (1905), W.T. Moore (1909), and W.W. Jennings (1919), while J.H. Garrison, in the tradition of Loos and Richardson, called his history *The Reformation of the Nineteenth Century*. M.M. Davis was the first to call his work a history of the Restoration Movement (1913), but in the next edition two years later he returned to the tradition of the Movement's historians by changing the title to *How The Disciples Began And Grew*.

It is only in recent generations, with the emergence of Churches of Christ and Christian Churches as separate churches, that the term "Restoration Movement" has become dominant. It is their historians that have popularized the term "the Restoration Movement." For example, all these historians use that term in their titles: H. Leo Boles (1932), P.H. Welshimer (1935), Earl I. West (1949), Harold Ford (1952), Homer Hailey (1952), J.D. Murch (1962), Bill Humble (1977), Max Ward Randall (1983), J.M. Powell (1987), Henry E. Webb (1990), and James B. North (1994).

That all these writers among the Churches of Christ and Christian Churches describe their histories in terms of "the Restoration Movement," while the Disciple historians never have (except for M.M. Davis in one edition), reflects how differently the Movement has been interpreted. It is not as much a difference between "liberal" and "conservative" as it is a divergence of viewpoint as to the genius of the Movement. Was it (and is it) a restoration or a reformation, or was it both? Was the emphasis restoration or unity? These motifs have been in tension through much of the Movement's history. Those who emphasize restoration tend to neglect unity. Those who make unity dominate usually eschew restoration.

This history is the first to use the title "The Stone-Campbell Movement," and this is because it is not only deemed more descriptive but also because the title is impartial. This is not a history of the Disciples of Christ, Christian Churches, or Churches of Christ in particular, but of all three in general. It is not written from the perspective of any one of these churches. It is rather a history of a movement within the church at large, the Stone-Campbell Movement.

It is granted that the title questions whether the Movement should be seen as "the Restoration Movement." One reason for this is that there have been many restoration movements throughout the history of the church; the Mormons, who use the idea with abandon, being one of them. In its May 18, 1992 issue, *Christianity Today* had an extensive treatment on "The Restoration Movement" which deals primarily with Pentecostal movements, and mentions the Stone-Campbell Movement only in passing. So, in identifying this history in such a way one runs the risk of being asked which Restoration movement he has in mind. Another reason we avoid any reference to restoration in the title is that we question whether restorationism, as that term has come to be understood, was the real genius of the Movement.

Our abandonment of the title "Restoration Movement" in the first edition of this book in 1981, and our thesis that the Movement was a unity movement and a reformation more than a restoration movement, received a cool reception from some quarters. Our accompanying thesis that restorationism by its very nature has been divisive throughout the history of the church, spawning scores of sects, and was a major cause in dividing the Stone-Campbell Movement, also received much negative response.

It is deemed appropriate, therefore, in this second edition to state our case more fully and to weigh the question more deeply, *What was the genius of the Movement?* Was it restoration or reformation, or in some manner both? To what extent has this question contributed to the tension that has long prevailed between restoration and unity?

Restorationism (sometimes called primitivism) generally has these characteristics: (1) the true church apostatized and ceased to exist; (2) the various denominations that emerged are false churches; (3) the New Testament provides a blueprint or prescription for the exact character of the true church; (4) each restorationist sect believes it has "restored" the true church in its pristine purity.

Some use this colorful illustration to explain restorationism: Should the game of baseball become extinct for centuries, some future generation could "restore" the game in its original character by following the pattern set forth in the old book, "The Game of Baseball," turned up by the spade of an archeologist; the rules of the game, the shape of the field, the position of the players are all prescribed, and so the game could be restored precisely as it was played centuries earlier. So it is with the church, the argument goes on to say, for even though the true New Testament church ceased to exist it can be restored by following "the pattern" set forth in the New Testament.

Restorationism tends to be ahistorical. It claims that only the source of the stream, original Christianity, really matters. When one can leap backward to primitive Christianity and recover the original church, the intervening centuries do not matter. Even the Protestant Reformation is irrelevant since it led only to a proliferation of sects and did not restore the true church.

Primitivism thus assumes a simplistic hermeneutics that likens the New Testament to a rule book that clearly spells out the nature of the Church of Christ upon earth. That there have been scores of restorationist sects, each claiming to be the true church and each insisting it has correctly followed "the simple pattern," makes such a view of the New Testament suspect.

It may also be questioned whether the Stone-Campbell Movement was restorationist in this sense. The following evidence may help to show that it was primarily a unity movement, by means of reforming the church, while the restoration motif, though present, played a subordinate role.

1. There are at least five founding documents of the Movement, all of which are unity documents, calling for the unity of all Christians in one way or another. Only one of the documents, the *Declaration and Address*, makes any reference to restoration. But it is evident that Thomas Camp-

bell, author of the document, was not a restorationist as above defined, for it was in that same document that he made the statement that has become the most famous quotation in the Movement's history: "The Church of Christ upon earth is essentially, intentionally and constitionally one." He wrote that in 1809 before he launched his movement and before he had his first congregation. His reference to "The Church of Christ upon earth" was his testimonial that the church then existed and always had since the Spirit of Pentecost breathed it into existence, and that he had no illusion of restoring the true church that did not exist.

Campbell may appear to be a restorationist when he includes as his purpose to "come firmly and fairly to original ground, and take up things just as the apostles left them" and to stand upon "the same ground on which the Church stood at the beginning." But this is hardly an appeal to a prescribed pattern for a restored church, for in the Appendix of the same document he allows for "variety of opinion and practice," noting that such was the case even with the primitive churches, "without any breach of Christian unity."[7]

2. Barton W. Stone, the founder of the Movement if only one person is named, regularly referred to the movement as a reformation, such as when he wrote of Alexander Campbell, "I am constrained, and willingly constrained, to acknowledge him the greatest promoter of this reformation than any man living."[8] He apparently never referred to their work in terms of restoration or a Restoration Movement. He always saw himself as a reformer who continued in the great tradition of Martin Luther. Like Thomas Campbell, he believed in the inviolability of the church. Unity was his constant theme, his motto being "Let Christian unity be our polar star."

3. Alexander Campbell, as we have noted, sometimes referred to restoration, but not in the way restorationism is defined above. He rather used the term as a synonym for reformation or as a means of effecting reformation. This is evident in such references as "this great and good cause of Reformation, or restoration, of the ancient order of things",[9] and "A reformation, or a restoration of primitive Christianity, in letter and in spirit, in word or in deed," which he wrote to the president of Georgetown College in 1858.

In the same letter he explained that he was advocating

> a reformation, not so much in doctrine, but for the advancement of the best interests of mankind, for the honor of our Lord and Master, for the good of his people, for the union of Christians, and for the conversion of the world, and all this on a catholic basis, broad as the foundation on which the Lord said he would build his church.[10] (Emphasis his)

That statement of Campbell's intention goes far in identifying the genius of the Movement: *a reformation for the union of Christians and for the conversion of the world*. Robert Richardson provides a more extended statement of the Movement's intent when he described Campbell as "a pioneer on the road to peace and Christian union," and went on to summarize his goal as: "to take the Bible as the only rule of faith and morals, to unite upon those facts and principles which are commonly received by all parties, and to obtain deliverance from a set of quarrelsome opinions by setting them at liberty."[11]

It should be noted that Campbell insisted in the letter to the college president that his reformation was "not so much in doctrine" but on "a catholic basis." Hardly anything could be more antithetical to restorationism, which is both doctrinaire and parochial.

Campbell usually referred to restoration in terms of restoring "the ancient order," which especially referred to such "institutions" and "ordinances" as baptism, the Lord's day, and the Lord's supper. He had an extended series on this subject in his *Christian Baptist* days, and in an essay in the *Millennial Harbinger* he said, "The restoration of the gospel institution has been our theme for many years," and goes on to refer to "the brethren who are zealous for the restoration and the reformation, etc. upon themselves, that they may learn, understand how far they are restored, reformed, and blessed with the pure unadulterated institution of Jesus Christ."[12]

These references suggest that Campbell made reformation and restoration, which he even applied to one's spiritual life, to mean the same thing. While he wrote of restoring ordinances and the ancient order to the church, as well as to restoring the ancient gospel and primitive Christianity, he apparently never wrote of restoring the church itself, as if it had disappeared from history. He believed, like his father and like Stone, that the church has always survived upon the earth, as Christ promised that it would, but has always been in need of reform.

4. If any of the founding fathers would appear to be a restorationist it would be Walter Scott, for he often referred to "the Restoration" and to the "Restoration of the Ancient Gospel." But he was referring to his own "five finger exercise" by which he preached baptism for the remission of sins and baptized one William Amend in 1827, the first in recent history to be so baptized, Scott supposed.

Even Alexander Campbell supported this view for a time, referring to the gospel being restored in 1827, though he later backed away from such a daring claim. Scott himself tempered the claim a few years later by explaining that it was "the practical exhibition and application of the

Gospel" that was restored, not the gospel itself, which he granted had always been proclaimed by the church.[13]

When Scott referred to the Movement in general he, like the others, called it the reformation, such as referring to Alexander Campbell as "the leader in the present famous Reformation."[14] And when he referred to his own contribution of simplifying the place of baptism, he used restoration the way the Campbells did: "the church of God on that day, had restored to it publicly and practically the ancient gospel."[15]

Scott made the crucial distinction between restoring to the church that is already a reality something that is lacking and the notion of restoring the church itself as if it had ceased to exist.

5. The rank and file out in the churches consistently referred to the Movement as "the Reformation" or "the current Reformation," as is evident from the correspondence of the times. There are scores of such instances, especially in the letters sent to Campbell's *Millennial Harbinger*. A letter from a woman in Buffalo, N.Y. in 1839 is a case in point. She begins a long letter to Campbell by saying she is reporting on "the progress of the reformation" from her region. She goes on to refer to a Baptist she believes to be ready to "advocate with us the principles of reformation," and to a union meeting that had been recently held as promising much for "the cause of reformation."[16]

In a paper published in Indiana an obscure evangelist, John Longley, referred to his 47 years in the work, part of it with the "now sincerely lamented father in Christ, Barton W. Stone." He writes, "At the dawn of the present Reformation, I saw its beauty and embraced it at once." He reports baptizing more than 3,000 persons.[17]

Letters from abroad expressed the same concept, such as one from J. Wallis in Nottingham, England in 1837, who reported to Campbell on the progress of "the reformation" in his country, and goes on in his letter to use such descriptions as "brethren of the reformation" and "principles of the reformation."[18]

The most compelling witness is Robert Richardson, whose *Memoirs of Alexander Campbell* (1868) is the earliest definitive history of the Movement. On the title page he described his work as "A View of the Origin, Progress And Principles Of The Reformation Which He Advocated." In his chronicle of 1217 pages he consistently refers to the Movement as "the Reformation." He referred to the new church at Wellsburgh, Va. as "the second church of the Reformation." (Vol. 2, p. 69). He described Phillip Fall of Nashville as being "fully engaged in the reformatory movement." (Vol. 2, p. 168). He even quotes Campbell's critics as using the term, accosting him with, "Is this your boasted Reformation?" (Vol. 2, p. 440). He referred to "the cause of Reformation making better progress than before" (Vol. 2, p. 498). Early on he wrote, "The Reformation was as yet but imperfectly developed or established" (Vol. 1, p. 493).

While Richardson never used the term "Restoration Movement," he did sometimes use "restore," as when he described Campbell and Walter Scott as seeking "to emulate each other in their efforts to restore the pure primitive apostolic gospel to the world" (Vol. 1, p. 512). He used "restoration" when he explained why Campbell chose to be immersed: "It was the restoration of the Christian faith to its original simplicity" (Vol. 1, p. 410). Like Campbell, Richardson would sometimes refer to reformation in terms of "restoring the ancient order of things."

In reading Richardson it is clear that he is telling the story of "the Reformation," as when he refers to Brush Run as yet "the only church in the Reformation" (Vol 1, p. 489), and when he quotes from a Campbell letter to the effect that he was "scattering the seeds of reformation in the West" (Vol. 2, p. 252). In comparison to the almost exclusive use of "Reformation" the term restoration barely appears, and when it does it is in reference to restoring ordinances to the church, not to restoring the church itself.

A Movement Within The Church

The leaders of the Movement have always suffered a certain embarrassment for being a separated people while pleading for Christian unity. Their image as a unity people especially suffers in the 20th century when they are themselves divided into three separate churches with numerous subdivisions. The problem of pleading for unity while being separatists, however much unintended, has plagued them from the beginning.

The problem has recently been posed by Robert O. Fife in the form of a question: "How may a people who exist as a distinct community within the Church, for the sake of witness unto the unity of the Church, avoid the negation of their witness by their very existence?"[19] Fife says this can be done by the concerned community functioning as a movement within the church rather than as a separate church or denomination. A movement is a movement, he says, and the church is the church. It is appropriate, he says, for there to be movements for various causes within the church, but their distinction can exist only *within* the church. A movement is not the same thing as the church.

Fife defines a movement as "a community of understanding and concern which exists and serves within the Church, and for its edification." It is an action group within the church but not the church itself. He illustrates the nature of this distinction by noting that we are not baptized into a movement, nor do we commune as "members of a movement." A movement, he concludes, is to identify its distinctiveness in terms other than the church and yet in a way that relates to the church.

The pioneers of the Movement we are studying may not have made this distinction as clearly as Fife does, but it is evident that they made the distinction in that they saw their efforts as a movement within the church at large. It certainly was not their mission to add still another church (much less *three!*), for they believed there were too many already.

This volume tells the story of the Republican Methodists, led by James O'Kelly and Rice Haggard, who in 1794 resolved to be "Christians simply" and take the Bible as their only rule of faith and practice, thus anticipating the Stone-Campbell effort. It was first of all a freedom movement in that it sought liberty in Christ apart from clerical domination. They did not intend to add still another denomination, but to be an action group within the church, a movement working for freedom and eventually the unity of all believers.

In his "History of the Christian Church in the West" (1827), the earliest account of the Movement, Barton W. Stone said time and again that he had no intention of starting another church. While he was excluded by the Synod of Kentucky (but not before he had withdrawn himself from that body), he insisted that he had not really left the Presbyterians. Like Luther, who had not actually withdrawn from the Roman church but only that part of it that considered the pope infallible, he had not really withdrawn from the Presbyterians but only from that part that sought to restrict him unduly. He separated (without really leaving!) so as to be free to read, study, and explain the word of God for himself.

It is odd that Stone would still claim to be a Presbyterian twenty years after he had left that church, but it is reflective of his sensitivity to the contradiction he sought to escape, being both a separatist and a unitist. He was not only trying to be ecumenical at a difficult time, but he was in essence saying that he wanted to be a movement within the church, which of course he had not left when he ceased being a Presbyterian. He said as much when he wrote, "The Synod takes it for granted that a separation from their reverend body is a separation from the church," and again, "We only withdrew from the judicatories with which we stood connected, and not from the church."[20]

The desire to be a movement within the church is particularly evident in Thomas Campbell's beginnings, for when he organized the Christian Association of Washington he made it clear that "This society, by no means considers itself a church, nor does it at all assume to itself the powers peculiar to such a society." He went on to say that the members of the society did not consider themselves a church, "but merely as voluntary advocates for church reformation."[21]

So, Campbell's Association was to be a society or movement within the church, working for its peace and unity. While this society eventually "became the Brush Run church," the first Campbell congregation, as historians usually describe it, it could be argued, as Fife does, that it did not *become* the Brush Run church but was "subsumed *within* the Church." Brush Run was thus a movement within the church witnessing to the divine mandate for Christian unity. Fife goes on to say, that "voluntary advocates for church reformation often have to separate from other Christians in order to worship according to their conscience does not mean that they are 'separatists' in any sectarian sense."

Alexander Campbell not only agreed with his father and Stone that their work was to be a movement within the church and not a separate church, but added the principle of catholicity to the equation. In his debate with N.L. Rice the Presbyterian he insisted that his movement was not sectarian because: "Our doctrine is catholic, very catholic. Not Roman Catholic nor Greek Catholic, but simply catholic." He referred to his people's catholic name, catholic creed, catholic baptism, catholic book, catholic table.

When Mr. Rice suggested that he was only creating another sect (and the most schismatic one!), Campbell retorted by pointing to the Westminster Confession of faith and saying, "I thank the Lord that my charities extend far beyond the contents of that little book lying on the table." He then turned to Rice and said, "Yes, sir, while I go for only one true catholic, apostolic church, and while I cannot find it in any of these Pedobaptist 'branches,' I can find Christian people among them all!"[22]

It is clear that while Campbell had no heart for creating another "branch" church, he saw his work as a movement dedicated to catholic principles within the church that had existed since the days of the apostles.

Some of Campbell's people today might be surprised that he would identify himself and his movement as catholic. Such ones are to be advised that Campbell not only referred to himself as "very catholic," but went so far as to propose catholicity as "the rule of union" among believers. In 1839 he called for "a congress of all Protestant parties," and he was willing to invite the Greek and Roman sects as well, suggesting that the basis of unity should be whatever is admitted by all parties to be catholic or universally accepted.[23] Such a gathering was called two years later by John T. Johnson in Lexington, Ky. at which Campbell set forth the resolution that Christians unite upon the catholic principles that they held in common.[24]

It is noteworthy that in his 1839 series on unity Campbell stated that while his passion for unity went back many years "it was sometime before we could clearly see the ground on which all true Christians could form one visible and harmonious union."[25] For thirty years, he was saying, he did not "clearly see" what he finally saw in 1839, that Christians can unite upon catholic principles or the things they hold in common.

It is appropriate to ask whether Campbell's followers have ever "clearly seen" or understood or appreciated the depth and breadth of his plea for unity on catholic grounds. It is evident that he saw his work as a reformation, a movement within the church pleading for unity on catholic grounds, and not as a separate church competing with other churches. He believed in only one church – holy, apostolic, catholic – and that is where he was doing his thing.

There was one historian of the Movement, however, who early on recognized the catholic nature of the Campbell plea. In 1906 W.T. Moore wrote in his "The Plea of the Disciples of Christ":

> The Disciple movement unquestionably furnishes a common ground, or a ground that is thoroughly catholic in every respect. A careful examination of the principles of the movement will reveal the fact that there is nothing in these principles that may not be accepted by every evangelical denomination in Christendom.[26]

A Faded Dream

The genius of a cause can sometimes be seen in the complaints of its leaders in reference to unreached goals. John Rogers, a leader among the Stone churches who helped to effect the union with the Campbell churches in 1832, related to Walter Scott, editor of *The Evangelist*, that he was hearing complaints from "leading brethren in the reformation." They were saying, "We profess to be Reformers; but it is much to be regretted, that thus far our reformation has consisted more in theory than practice, more in talking than acting." Rogers went on to tell Scott that the reformation itself must be more united and show more brotherly kindness. "We must act on our principles," he said, "and show their superiority over sectarian principles."[27]

Rogers indirectly identified the burden of the Movement. It was to be a reformation within the church, effectively advocating unity principles superior to sectarian principles. He was fearful that they were not succeeding.

Walter Scott himself complained in a letter to P.S. Fall, one of the leaders in the South, about the Movement, which reveals that Fall also was troubled with the way things were going:

> When you express your doubts of the matters connected with the recent Reformation I sympathize with you, for the thing has not been what I thought it would be by a thousand miles. We are indeed "a sect" differing but little, of anything that is good, from the parties around us. Alas! My soul is grieved everyday.[28]

Whether the Movement was "a sect" in Scott's day or even today can be questioned, but Scott, who was given to emotional overstatement, makes it clear that such was not its intention. Alexander Campbell always insisted that "You cannot make a sect of us" because of the catholic principles advocated. But practice is obviously another matter, and even Campbell conceded that "There is a great deficiency, not in the system we advocate, but in the practice of many congregations."[29]

But Campbell was usually sanguine about the Movement's progress and its future, insisting that it would never divide if it was true to its principles. In 1846 he reported that "the reformation of the 19th century," while "yet in its infancy," had been promulgated throughout the United States and its territories and into some parts of Europe.[30]

A few years later he exulted that the time was when the principles of "this great and mighty movement" were discussed but by a few, but now the number was between 200,000 and 300,000.[31] In his earlier years he referred to "the millennial church" and "a new age is soon to be born; and the great regeneration is at hand,"[32] which at least meant an end to sectarianism, a united church, and the triumph of the gospel throughout the world.

After all, Campbell did not name his journal "Restoration Herald" or even "Reformation Gazette" but the *Millennial Harbinger*, which expressed his conviction that he was a catalyst, along with the new American republic which he idealized, for a coming millennium. But in his latter years, with the approaching tragedy of the Civil War, these postmillennial views waned, and his hope turned more to what lies beyond "the present material universe."[33]

In time, however, it became evident that the ideal envisioned by Stone and Campbell had been lost, especially when that Movement which had been launched "to unite the Christians in all the sects" itself fractured into two churches, then three, then numerous splinter groups. J.H. Garrison, editor of the *Christian Evangelist*, when speaking of the catholicity of the Movement in 1897 had to concede that the dream had faded: "That there have been among us, at times, manifestations of the party spirit quite inconsistent with the catholicity of our position, we are compelled to admit."[34]

A.T. DeGroot, Disciples historian, spoke for many when he surveyed the scene in 1940 and concluded, "This spectacle of *divided unionists* is the most obvious indication that somewhere in the program of the Movement is to be found a cause for schism."[35]

By 1979 the Movement had become so fractured that Reuel Lemmons, a Church of Christ editor, spoke in even more tragic terms:

> A movement which began on the glorious note of uniting the Christians in all the sects has degenerated in a mere century and a half, into subdividing that unity into narrow, sectarian camps. Each splinter splinters further. This very obvious fact is evidence that something is basically wrong in the attitude and aim of the movement.[36]

It is to Lemmons' credit that he saw the glory of the original dream of the Movement along with the agony of the divisions that eventually came. If there was much that went wrong, there was much that remained right. Perhaps Jacob Creath, Jr., back in 1873, sized up the character of the Movement when he wrote, "We as a people are in a transition state, like caterpillars, passing from their rude state into the butterfly state."[37] A Movement in transition! There was the dream and the ideal of unity, a heritage to be prized. Then in the transition stages came the rude reality of a divided unity movement.

The dream need not forever fade; the ideal need not always be lost. The principles that the pioneers forged on a rugged frontier can be revived. If indeed the Movement is in transition and like a caterpillar awaiting its butterfly stage, there is hope for tomorrow. The dream can live on.

This is the story of that Movement. The unfolding events may show that the states were mixed, sometimes rude, sometimes on the verge of becoming a butterfly.

ENDNOTES

[1]Alexander Campbell, "History of the Reformation," *Millennial Harbinger*, 1833, p. 94.

[2]Alexander Campbell, "Anecdotes, Incidents, and Facts," No. 6, *Mill. Harb.*, 1849, pp. 46f.

[3]"Obituary Notices," *Mill. Harb.*, 1863, p. 94.

[4]Robert Richardson, "Reformation," *Mill. Harb.*, 1848, p. 36, 74. This series begins in 1847, p. 275.

[5]C.L. Loos, "The 19th Century Reformation," *Christian Evangelist*, Jan. 12, 1889, p. 41.

[6]Barton W. Stone, "History of the Christian Church in the West" (No. 9), *Christian Messenger*, Vol. 1, 1827, p. 269.

[7]Thomas Campbell, *Declaration and Address*, p. 64.

[8]John Rogers, *Biography of Elder Barton Warren Stone*, Cincinnati, 1847. p. 76.

[9]Alexander Campbell, "Preface," *Mill. Harb.*, 1850, p. 1.

[10]Alexander Campbell, "Dr. D.R. Campbell," *Mill. Harb.*, 1858, pp. 471f.

[11]Robert Richardson, "Decline of Partyism," *Mill. Harb.*, 1841, p. 243.

[12]Alexander Campbell, "Reformation and Restoration," *Mill. Harb.*, 1835, p. 24.

[13]Walter Scott, "Restoration of the Ancient Gospel," *The Evangelist*, 1833, p. 16.

[14]*Ibid.*, p. 59.

[15]*Ibid.*, p. 162.

[16]"Communication from Sarah H.C. Gardiner," *Mill. Harb.*, 1839, p. 419.

[17]*Christian Record*, Aug. 1851, pp. 33f.

[18]"News From The Churches," *Mill. Harb.*, 1839, pp. 238f.

[19]Robert O. Fife, *Celebration of Heritage* (Los Angeles: Westwood Foundation, 1992), pp. 265f.

[20]Barton W. Stone, "History of the Christian Church in The West, No. 5" *Christian Messenger*, 1827, p. 169.

[21]Thomas Campbell, *Declaration and Address*, p. 4.

[22]*Campbell-Rice Debate*, Lexington, 1844, p. 491.

[23]Alexander Campbell, "Union of Christians No. 1," *Mill. Harb.*, 1839, pp. 211f.

[24]Alexander Campbell, "Union Christian Meeting," *Mill. Harb.*, 1841, pp. 258f. Cf. *Ibid.*, p. 445 where he calls for unity on the basis of "common Christianity."

[25]Alexander Campbell, "Union of Christians No. 1," *Mill. Harb.*, 1839, p. 212.

[26]Quoted in Ronald Osborn, "One, Holy and Apostolic Church," *The Reformation of Tradition* (St. Louis: Bethany Press, 1963), p. 337.

[27]John Rogers (Letter), *The Evangelist*, 1832, p. 113.

[28]Quoted in Ralph G. Wilburn, "A Critique of the Restoration Principle," *The Reformation of Tradition* (St. Louis: Bethany Press, 1963), p. 231.

[29]Alexander Campbell, "Preface," *Mill. Harb.*, 1832, p. 4.

[30]Alexander Campbell, "Preface," *Mill. Harb.*, 1846, p. 1.

[31]Alexander Campbell, "Preface," *Mill. Harb.*, 1850, p. 1.

[32]Alexander Campbell, "Preface," *Mill. Harb.*, 1833, p. 1.

[33]Alexander Campbell, "The Gospel," *Mill. Harb.*, 1865, p. 517. In this the last article he ever wrote he expresses hope of a heaven that "no living man, however enlightened, however enlarged, however gifted, ever formed or entertained one adequate conception."

[34]James H. Garrison, "A 19th Century Movement," *Christian Quarterly*, 1897, p. 165.

[35]A.T. DeGroot, *Grounds For Division Among The Disciples of Christ* (Chicago: Privately published, 1940).

[36]Reuel Lemmons, "Fragmentation," *Firm Foundation*, Vol. 96, No. 29, 1979, p. 450.

[37]*Gospel Advocate*, Vol 15, 1873, p. 60.

2

PHILOSOPHERS AND THEOLOGIANS
EUROPEAN INFLUENCES ON THE MOVEMENT

*He that takes away Reason to make way for Revelation
puts out the light of both.* – John Locke

William Jones, a leading figure of the Movement in Great Britain, once wrote to Alexander Campbell in America: "May I hope for pardon, sir, if I add that even 'the Reformation' in the United States owes something in the way of gratitude to our Scotch Churches."[1] He might have said that the Movement was indebted not only to Scotland and all of Great Britain, but to Europe's intellectual and religious history.

But Mr. Campbell did not have to be urged into an awareness of his European heritage, for he often spoke of the debt he owed. In his debate with Robert Owen, for example, in 1829, he spoke at length of this heritage:

> While we are grateful to all, who have labored in the cause of the emancipation of the human mind from the shackles of kingcraft and priestcraft; and while we are mindful of our more immediate benefactors, we are not to forget the praises due to those who have long since died, and whose victories were more efficient, and salutary in their consequences, though less boisterous, and less noisy, than those achieved by the sword or the cannon.[2]

He was wide-ranging in his praises. He saluted old Solon, one of the seven wise men of ancient Greece, for his "Know thyself" philosophy, insisting that Mr. Owen's skepticism had nothing to offer man in reference to his origin, mission, or destiny.[3] He pointed to Cicero's appreciation of Socrates for being the first to call philosophy down from the heavens and place it in the cities and to introduce it into private houses.[4]

Campbell reminded Owen that despotism took its first shock from the Reformation, but he also had high praise for "our own revolutionary heroes and statesmen," and he often named Jefferson and Franklin among his heroes. He also saluted "the labors of Milton, the poet" and acknowledged his debt to the inductive philosophy of Francis Bacon and the principles of investigation as laid down by Sir Isaac Newton, and he suggested to

Owen that the principles of Bacon and Newton might well guide them in their debate.

Campbell indicated that civil and religious liberty owed its debt to John Locke, "the Christian philosopher," who laid the foundation of a new order of society by his *Essay on Toleration*. That little essay, he observed, "first burst the chains that held England and Europe fast bound under a religious and civil despotism," and it gave the first impulse to the spirit of free inquiry and laid the foundation of our present liberties, referring apparently to his own movement for religious liberation as well as the freedoms of the new republic that was now his adopted country.

It should be widely heralded, Campbell thought, that John Locke had done more for civil and religious liberty than all the skeptics who have written from the days of Pyrrhus to those of Robert Owen.

The purpose of this chapter, therefore, is to identify both the philosophical and theological influences upon the Stone-Campbell Movement that came from the Old World, particularly as they affected the thinking of Alexander and Thomas Campbell.

Isaac Newton

The Campbells approached the mysteries of the Bible much like Newton and Bacon approached the mysteries of the universe, *in search of facts and of principles to interpret those facts*. The modern world ushered in by Copernicus, Kepler, and Galileo was completely different from the ancient and medieval ages it displaced. The big difference was the rise of science, which achieved its triumph in Newton (1642-1727). The scientific method was so different that there was no way for the old world to understand the new. Bertrand Russell says it well when he points out that Plato and Aristotle could not have made head or tail of Newton.[5] The method used by the Campbells in biblical interpretation seemed as strange to the religious leaders of their day as Newton's method was to the people of his day. The Campbells were among the forerunners of a scientific approach to Scripture.

While Newton is remembered for his law of gravitation and the three basic laws of motion, it was his new way of thinking and solving problems that brought on the age of science. In his search for facts he drew upon all possible sources. He is reputed to have said, "If I have seen a little farther than others it is because I have stood on the shoulders of giants." When asked how he had managed to learn so much, he replied, "By applying my mind to it."

By applying my mind to it! That would serve as an excellent summary of some of Alexander Campbell's rules for interpreting the Bible. In the debate with Owen he drew upon one of Newton's principles of investigation:

> Everything, says the great teacher, is to be submitted to the most minute observation. No conclusions are to be drawn from guesses or conjectures. We are to keep within the certain limits of experimental truth. We first ascertain the facts, then group them together, and after the classification and comparison of them, draw the conclusion. There are generic heads or chapters in every department of physical or moral science. We are never to shrink from the test of those principles.[6]

He went on to set a Newtonian standard for himself, which was to influence all his polemical and literary efforts, and to make his Movement vulnerable to the charge of being directed more to the head than to the heart: "Any argument, therefore, which we may offer, we wish to be examined by the improved principles of the inductive philosophy, by those very principles which right reason and sound experimental philosophy have sanctioned as their appropriate tests." This became Campbell's way of studying the Bible.

Francis Bacon

Francis Bacon (1561-1626) was a full century before Newton and was at the twilight of the new age of science. He had a passion for language, its symbols and its fallacies. His investigative mind earned him the title of "the father of induction," for he lived in a world rooted in deductive assumptions. It was his concern for language that most influenced Alexander Campbell. Bacon wrote in his *Novum Organum* of "the Idols of the Mind," those fallacies from tradition and faulty thinking that blind people to facts.

"Idols of the tribe" stem from the sluggish mind that is satisfied and too lazy to think, and that accepts only those things that support its superstitions and traditions. "Idols of the Cave" relate to the habituated mind that finds security in the way it has always believed and acted; it wants things kept simple, even if they be erroneous, so that its preconceptions are kept intact. "Idols of the Market Place" are the pet words and phrases that are invented to shade one's view of reality; it specializes in blurred, indistinct meanings. "Idols of the Theatre" are fanciful theories and exotic philosophies that only confuse the real facts.[7]

Campbell found such fallacies in the sectarian creeds and theological speculations that hindered one's effort to understand the facts of the Bible. He was impressed with Bacon's definition of a fact as "something said or something done" and his emphasis upon observation. Facts are gathered by observing the things that are either "said" or "done" and by applying such rules of induction as to verify them as true.

Campbell applied this to the Bible, which was an inductive (or scientific) approach, something as new in his day in regard to Scripture as it was in Bacon's time in reference to general knowledge. "All revealed religion is based on facts," he wrote in 1830, and drawing upon Bacon's conclusions he went on to say, "By facts we always mean something said or done. The works of God and the words of God, or the things done and spoken by God, are those facts which are laid down and exhibited in the Bible as the foundation of all faith, hope, love, piety, and humanity."[8]

He goes on to lay down a Baconian principle that undergirded his whole reformation theology: *All true and useful knowledge is an acquaintance with facts.* He went on to show that facts have the higher purpose of touching the heart: "He that made the heart of man and gave him an intelligent spirit knows that facts alone can move the affections and command the passions of man." Campbell thus saw the gospel as a love story made up of facts that God had given to man. He even rooted his appeal for unity in facts, pointing to "the seven facts of Ephesians 4" as the ground for the church's oneness: one body, one Spirit, one hope, one Lord, one faith, one baptism, one God.

As Bacon was with science so Campbell was with Scripture, for both were suspicious of anything that goes beyond what is observable. This made for suspicion toward theological systems and creedal confessions, and gave place to the "faith vs. opinion" theme that has always been basic to the Movement's plea. Faith is belief in testimony (facts), drawn from what the Scriptures explicitly say, while opinions are what one supposes those facts imply. Bacon thus helped Campbell to develop an inductive approach to the Bible, in which one draws conclusions only in terms of what is observably evident, rather than the traditional deductive approach of having one's conclusions already in hand and using the Bible to support them.

John Locke

It impressed Campbell that the great John Locke (1632-1704) spent the last years of his life reading almost no other book but the Bible. The day before he died Locke exulted in the love that God had shown to man in justifying him by faith in Christ, and he thanked God for having called him to the knowledge of the Savior. When asked about the shortest and surest way to the true knowledge of the Christian religion, he replied, "Let him study the Holy Scriptures, *especially the New Testament.*"[9] Locke had, after all, written a treatise on the reasonableness of Christianity, and he had paraphrased the epistles of Paul with attending notes (published posthumously).

Locke's simple trusting faith moved Campbell to refer to him repeatably as "the Christian philosopher," a faith that he found all too rare in his considerable reading in the history of philosophy. He had a different view of David Hume, the old Scottish skeptic who had himself borrowed much from Locke: "How preposterous, then, was it for the learned and ingenious author of the *Treatise on Human Nature* to elaborate an essay to prove that no man could rationally believe the testimony of any number of persons affirming a supernatural fact; because, as he imagined, their testimony was contrary to universal experience."[10]

Campbell was impressed that though a philosopher Locke was a believer. When he died in 1704 Locke was surrounded by devoted friends to whom he declared that he left the world "in perfect charity for all men and in sincere communion with the whole church of Christ, by whatever names Christ followers call themselves." Though a faithful Anglican the philosopher referred to "the church of Christ" much like Thomas Campbell did in the *Declaration and Address* a century later.

Locke's plea for freedom, toleration, and for a better understanding of the nature of knowledge was not without its price. He had to hide from the law under an assumed name to do some of his writing. Part of his life was spent in exile away from his native London. In 1702 the University of Oxford formally condemned his *Essay Concerning Human Understanding* even after it had gained acceptance in intellectual circles both at home and abroad. This led him to write to a friend, "I take what has been done there rather as a recommendation of the book." He wrote *A Letter Concerning Toleration* while hiding from his enemies, and then published it anonymously, admitting only in his will to have written it.[11]

This *Letter* was revolutionary in a country where the church was aligned with the state and where dissenters were persecuted. In the first paragraph he nails the authorities of the persecuting state church with: "I esteem that toleration to be the chief characteristic mark of the true Church," and reminds them that Jesus told his disciples, "The kings of the Gentiles exercise lordship over them, but ye shall not be so." True religion is not for pomp or oppression, he told them, but for virtue and piety. Locke further chided the authorities with: "It is vain for any man to usurp the name of Christian, without holiness of life, purity of manners, benignity and meekness of spirit." He pointed to the glaring inconsistency of tolerating whoredom, fraud, and malice and yet not allowing for conscientious dissent. It is better, he insisted, to root out immoralities than to extirpate sects.

He was among the first to call for a separation of church and state, which even the Reformation had not called for. The care of souls does not belong to the magistrate and the affairs of state is not the business of the church, he declared. He gave a definition of the church, which is echoed in Campbell's writings: "A church, then, I take to be a voluntary society of men, joining themselves together of their own accord in order to the public worshipping of God in such manner as they judge acceptable to Him, and effectual to the salvation of their souls."

He even questioned infant baptism when he said that the church as "a free and voluntary society" would preclude anyone being born a member of it, for otherwise the religion of parents would descend to the children by right of inheritance. Everyone would hold his faith by the same tenure he does his lands!

When one reads the following paragraphs from Locke he can understand why W.E. Garrison would say that it is difficult to distinguish them from what Thomas Campbell says in the *Declaration and Address:*

> Since men are so solicitous about the true church, I would only ask them here, by the way, if it be no more agreeable to the Church of Christ to make the conditions of her communion consist in such things, and such things only, as the Holy Spirit has in the Holy Scriptures declared, in express words, to be necessary to salvation. I ask, I say, whether this be not more agreeable to the Church of Christ than for men to impose their own inventions and interpretations upon others as if they were of Divine authority, and to establish by ecclesiastical laws, as absolutely necessary to the profession of Christianity, such things as the Holy Scriptures do either not mention, or at least not expressly command?
>
> Whosoever requires those things in order to ecclesiastical communion which Christ does not require in order to eternal life, he may, perhaps, indeed constitute a society accommodated to his own opinion and his own advantage; but how that can be called the Church of Christ which is established upon laws that are not His, and which excludes such persons from its communion as He will one day receive into the Kingdom of Heaven, I understand not.[12]

The principle of unity, therefore, that has been prevalent from the beginning of the Stone-Campbell Movement, that *nothing is to be made a test of communion that God has not made necessary to salvation,* goes back to John Locke in 1689.

Equally influential upon the Campbell movement was Locke's *Essay Concerning Human Understanding* in which he sets forth his empiricism, which is the view that all our knowledge (with the possible exception of logic and mathematics) comes through experience. The child's mind is at birth a *tabula rasa*, a blank tablet, and so all ideas that he comes to have are through impressions and sensations by way of the five senses. Locke thus rejected innate (inborn) ideas, a notion that was as old as the ancient Greeks and more recently taught by the influential Descartes, the father of modern philosophy.

This meant that even the idea of God was not in man in some "natural" way, but that he knows of God only by God revealing himself to man. He thus rejected "natural religion" as having any valid source of religious knowledge. Nature may confirm what God reveals about himself, but is not itself a means of knowing God.

This was a revolutionary point of view, but it was part of the new scientific way of thinking. Theologians and philosophers from Anselm to Thomas Aquinas to Descartes had contended that God could be known through reason and that his existence could be proved by logic, which was the essence of "natural religion," summarily rejected by both Locke and Campbell. Campbell followed Locke not only in rejecting innate ideas, but in negating feelings and mystical experiences as valid sources of religious knowledge.

They both believed that a knowledge of God has its source only in God's disclosure of Himself through revelation. Those who supposedly found God through reason or nature, such as Socrates, were actually drawing upon tradition about God that is traceable to the patriarchs or the Jewish prophets.

When O'Conner says that Locke "swept away a lot of metaphysical lumber,"[13] he is saying that Locke gave the world a clearer view of how knowledge comes. Man knows by observing particulars, not by deducing from a cluster of universals that are subjectively inspired, as Plato concluded.

Locke says we know an object by studying its qualities, not by speculating about its "substance," which the philosophers admitted to be unobservable, whatever it is. If all the qualities of an object (its size, color, sound, temperature, etc.) are different from another object, they have to be different things. And never mind about some mysterious, identical "substance" that supposedly makes them the same.

The distinction that Campbell drew between the Old and New Covenants exemplifies the influence of Locke's theory of knowledge. If the qualities between the two are different — given at different times to different people with different purposes, and having different institutions and commands — then they cannot be an identical covenant, as most theologians of his day contended. They pointed to some spiritual "substance" that made them one.

Campbell reasoned the same way about the church, which he called "the New Institution," and about baptism and the Lord's day. These are to be seen in the light of their context, with all the facts about them allowed to speak for themselves. They are not to be identified in some mystical way with such Old Covenant institutions as the Sabbath or circumcision.

Locke also helped Campbell in his view of reason and revelation, a pairing that has often found expression in the Movement.[14] While revelation is always the source of our knowledge of God, reason is the faculty by which we reflect upon the ideas that come through tradition and Scripture. They both concluded that reason cannot have creative power; it cannot make ideas out of nothing. Reason to the soul is what the eye is to the body. "It is not light, but the power of perceiving and using it," as Campbell put it.

In good Lockean terms Campbell criticized the philosophers for their view of reason: "Some philosophers have almost deified reason, and given it a creative and originating power. They have so eulogized the light of reason and the light of nature that one would imagine reason to be a sun rather than an eye; a revelation rather than the power of apprehending and enjoying it."[15]

Beyond all this was Locke's attitude toward truth, especially what Bertrand Russell calls his "lack of dogmatism." Since truth is hard to ascertain one should hold his opinions with some measure of doubt. Locke made the important distinction between a love for truth and a love for some particular doctrine which is proclaimed as the truth. In his *Essay* he gives the one unerring mark of love for truth as "not entertaining any proposition with greater assurance than the proofs it is built upon will warrant." Campbell put this noble idea into his own words by saying that one's faith in something should be no stronger than the evidence that supports it.

Locke's influence on the thinking of the Movement reached beyond the Campbells. In his recent study on Walter Scott, William A. Gerrard notes that Locke "strongly influenced the Movement's greatest evangelist. He points to Scott's motto from Scripture, "Come now, let us reason together," and sees the evangelist's emphasis upon reason and revelation as drawn from Locke, whom he quotes as saying, "He that takes away Reason to make way for Revelation puts out the light of both."[16] It was common not only for Scott but for many of the evangelists to carry three books in their saddlebag: a Bible, a hymnal, and a copy of Locke's *Essay Concerning Human Understanding*.

Locke might well have influenced the Movement's important distinction between faith and opinion as expressed in the motto "In essentials unity, in opinions liberty, in all things charity." To "the Christian philosopher" the essentials were clear and simple: faith in Jesus Christ as Lord and obedience to his explicit commands. All else is opinion.

This is not only the way to unity, Locke allowed, but the only means of avoiding malevolence among Christians. In this respect he differed from the Puritans, who as restorationists had an extended list of essentials drawn from their view of the primitive church. But Locke nonetheless defended the Puritan right to dissent.

Leonard Allen sees Locke's "social compact" theory, a kind of covenantal agreement between people and their ruler, as an influence upon Alexander Campbell's view of the Kingdom of God, which led him to see the church in precise constitutional and monarchial terms. This in turn led Campbell and his heirs, Allen reasons, to treat the New Testament as "the statute-book of Heaven" and made it "a book of case law."[17]

If this is a fair appraisal, it surely reaches beyond what either Locke or Campbell intended. Given their emphasis on the centrality of Christ and the grace of God, it can be questioned whether either Locke or Campbell made good "lawyers" when it came to handling holy Scripture.

But one conclusion appears certain: the Enlightenment in general and John Locke in particular had a telling influence on the Campbells and the Movement they launched.

Scottish School of Common Sense

The Common Sense philosophy of Scotland, of which Thomas Reid was the chief spokesman, has had substantial influence upon American thought, especially in the nineteenth century. Perry Gresham thinks the Stone-Campbell churches share some of this influence:

> The Christian Churches would do well to study the Scottish sources of the rational philosophy which Campbell brought with him from Glasgow. There is a strong measure of Adam Smith in the political ethics of the communion. Thomas Reid exercised a substantial influence over the thought of the pioneers who set the norms whereby the congregations have developed. The reasonable approach to worship and Bible study came from the mood of common sense which dominated the University of Glasgow at the turn of the century when Thomas and Alexander Campbell were students.[18]

When Gresham addressed the World Convention of Churches of Christ in Edinburgh in 1960, he spoke on "Proud Heritage from Scotland," in which he emphasized the influence upon his church of the Common Sense school. Daniel Sommer Robinson, who was named for one of the Movement's pioneers and himself a philosopher, suggests that the Movement's favorite slogan, "Where the Scriptures speak, we speak; where the Scriptures are silent, we are silent," first stated by Thomas Campbell, was inspired by the Scottish philosophers who traced all valid religious knowledge to the divine revelation in the Scriptures.[19]

The Common Sense school arose as a protest to the skepticism of David Hume, who was also a Scot but not usually included in "the Scottish school." Hume had taken empiricism so far as to question the principle of cause and effect, dismissing it as sheer speculation. He even doubted that there is a real world apart from human consciousness, and if there is, its existence cannot be proved, just as God's existence can be neither proved nor disproved.

Thomas Reid (1710-1796), who was a pastor as well as a professor, succeeded Adam Smith at Glasgow University. Reid was at Glasgow, the university attended by both of the Campbells, when he created his Common Sense philosophy, the purpose of which was to justify the ordinary man in believing in what his five senses tell him about the world. It was intended as a balanced view in that it rejected metaphysical speculation, as did both Locke and Hume, and yet appealed to "common sense" in interpreting the world, lest doubt lead one to the point of being ridiculous.

Common Sense philosophy has been defined as "the power of knowledge in general, as it is possessed and employed by a man of ordinary development and opportunities." It is the view that the common man has the power to know the external world and its relations through his senses. Thus in his *Inquiry into the Human Mind on the Principles of Common Sense*, Reid contends that the things which we perceive do exist and they are what we perceive them to be. Common sense dictates that nature will continue to behave as it has in the past, and that whatever exists must have a cause which produced it.

Moreover, common sense sees in the law of cause and effect as expressed in the order and design of the universe sufficient grounds for one to believe that an intelligent Being caused it to exist. Reid observed that the rule of cause and effect was so widely accepted that there was no one that did not act upon it, including David Hume! And such popular opinion, Reid insisted, stands on a higher authority than philosophy, and philosophy had better get with it or make itself contemptible.

Reid concedes that the common man may need help from philosophy on the deeper speculations, but as for those things that are within the reach of every person's understanding, and upon which the whole conduct of human life turns, the philosopher had best follow the multitude or make himself look ridiculous. After all, he points out, when the common man smells a rose for the first time he *knows* that it is a new fragrance to him, and the next time he meets that smell he *knows* that it is a rose that he is smelling. Common sense for common people!

The Campbells had high regard for ordinary folk. Their plea appealed to the common people because they could understand it and they saw something in it for them. Alexander Campbell applied Reid's emphasis on "general understanding" to what he called the *consensus fidelium*, which was the faithful consensus of common folk who sincerely and studiously apply their minds to a problem. If they come up with the same answer they are probably right. This supported a claim he often made, that the essentials for which he pled for a united church were generally agreed to by all denominations.

This "Common Sense" view of Scripture convinced Campbell that people can understand the Bible alike on things that really matter, and these are the basic facts of the Bible. Concrete facts, not abstract deductions! The information that God has for us is in the Bible, and we can understand it like we understand anything else, *By applying our minds to it!* as Newton would say, and as the Common Sense school would say. This is applying the scientific method to the study of the Bible, bequeathed by the Enlightenment.

But Campbell's favorite Common Sense philosopher was not Thomas Reid but Dugald Stewart (1753-1828), who had the distinct honor of succeeding his own father at the University of Edinburgh, where he was lecturing when young Campbell was a student at nearby Glasgow. In 1840 Campbell told an assembly of American teachers that Dugald Stewart was "the greatest of metaphysicians," and proceeded to give his favorite quote from the professor who was hailed in his native Scotland as "one of the greatest of didactic orators."

The quote was about philosophy itself and originated with Seneca: "Philosophy forms and fashions the soul, and gives to life its disposition and order, which points out what is our duty to do, and what is our duty to omit. It sits at the helm, and in a sea of peril directs the course of those who are wandering through the waves."[20]

Stewart, a follower of Reid, sought to defend Common Sense against the charge of being little more than Mother-wit, so he substituted the term "fundamental laws of human belief." These "essential laws of faith" are those that every person follows in the normal pursuits of life, and anyone who would call them into question would be thought insane. These consist of such things as knowing that one exists, that he is distinct from the world around him, that the laws of nature behave as they always have, and that there are intelligent beings beside oneself.

If there is certainty in these areas, as common sense dictates, then a much larger body of knowledge is also certain. Man can know about himself, about God, and about the revelation that God has given of Himself. This was to challenge the sceptical philosophy that influenced much of Europe at the time.

It may also be called the inductive method, a term Campbell often used. It calls for careful observation, experimentation, and trial and error. What now seems commonplace, studying a passage in context and considering the who, what, why, when and where, was rare on the frontier. But Campbell made it a rule for interpreting the Bible.

Campbell insisted that since we read a newspaper or a letter *naturally* (not necessarily *literally*), we ought to read the Scriptures that way, guided by the same rules of interpretation that we would follow in reading anything else. One does not need to "speculate" in reading the Bible anymore than he would in reading any other book, and thus allow the *natural* conclusions to follow. It was what Locke, Reid, and Stewart had been saying about human knowledge in general. Common Sense interpretation!

Advocates of Unity

There are numerous instances since the Reformation of concern either for the unity of the church or for the restoration of primitive Christianity, but it was only in the Stone-Campbell Movement that these concerns were blended into a common plea: *the unity of the church through a restoration of primitive Christianity*. History has demonstrated, however, that such a plea has the problem of sincere people interpreting "primitive Christianity" differently. We observed in the previous chapter that because of this weakness the plea was in time given a more catholic base. It is also unique to the Stone-Campbell Movement that it is the only church (as opposed to mere individuals) that has made unity its business.

The voices that have pled for the union of all believers have been few, and the results modest, at least until the dawning of the ecumenical movement in the 20th century. Typical is the case of one Abraham Van Dyke, a lawyer of Coxsackie, N.Y., who published in 1835 an impressive little volume on *Christian Union or An Argument for the Abolition of Sects*, in which he said that the bond of union is love and that divisions within the church are a violation of its constitutional unity. While he wrote much like the Campbells at a time when the Movement was coming into its own, he was apparently influenced only by the impelling nature of the subject in the Scriptures.

This was the case with the Europeans who wrote and worked for unity with such diligence, each in his own little corner. They were moved by such factors as Jesus' high priestly prayer for the unity of his church and the apostolic insistence that division is a sin.

One obvious influence upon the Stone-Campbell Movement was a statement that first appeared in a Latin treatise in Germany about 1625. Published secretly, pseudonymously, and without reference to date or place, it pled for peace in the church between Lutherans and Calvinists. It suggested a way for the peace to come: "If we would but observe unity in essentials, liberty in non-essentials, charity in all things, our affairs would certainly be in the best possible situation."

The idea became a slogan and was used by Richard Baxter (1615-1691), the Puritan minister who sought to reform the morals and religion of his parish, who put it this way: "In fundamentals unity, in non-fundamentals (or doubtful things) liberty, in all things charity."[21]

It has long been current in the Movement, worded to read "In matters of faith, unity; in matters of opinion, liberty; in all things, love," or "In essentials, unity; in non-essentials, liberty; in all things, charity." For years the *Christian Evangelist* used the slogan as part of its front-page logo, giving it still a different slant: *In faith, unity; in opinions and methods, liberty; in all things, charity.*

Richard Baxter, who wrote extensively on Christian union, surely made the most ambitious use of the slogan when he submitted his plan of unity to none other than King Charles II of England. Archbishop James Ussher, the Anglican primate of Ireland who gave his now famous chronology to the church makes the honor's list of those who advocated unity in the seventeenth century, suggesting union between Anglicans and Presbyterians.

Edward Stillingfleet, an Anglican minister, published his *Irenicum* in 1661 in which he sounded like John Locke (and Thomas Campbell) when he expressed concern that the church of his day should not require more than Christ himself required as conditions for communion, and that it is this imposition of opinions that causes divisions in the church.

Another slogan on unity that goes back to the seventeenth century comes from George Calixtus, a Lutheran who dared to advocate unity with the reformed Roman Catholic Church, calls for oneness on the basis of "what has been believed always, everywhere, and by all." We cannot be sure that Alexander Campbell knew of Calixtus' motto when in a union meeting in 1841 in Lexington, Ky. he proposed, "*Resolved*, That the union of Christians can be scripturally effected by requiring a practical acknowledgement of such articles of belief and such rules of piety and morality as are admitted by all Christian denominations."[22] Enough to say that both Calixtus and Campbell were ahead of their time by advocating such a broad basis for unity among Christians.

Hugo Grotius wrote on *The Way of Ecclesiastical Peace* about 1640, amidst severe sectarian feuding, and Christoph Pfaff, a Lutheran, issued his *Pacific Address* to the Protestants in 1720, in which he contended that all Protestant communions were basically one, which was a very unpopular view. Still others suggested that councils be called for purposes of union, an idea that goes back to Luther and Calvin, who were always sensitive about a divided church and never lost hope that unity could be realized.

The most indefatigable unionist of all, however, was John Durie (Dury), a Scot, who spent more than a half century working for the union of Protestants, and eventually included Roman Catholics in his efforts. He issued pamphlets and travelled widely in quest of a united church, even if the results were something less than successful.

Kenneth Scott Latourette, who recounts these efforts for unity, concludes, "How much of these efforts for unity carried over into the nineteenth and twentieth centuries and contributed to what eventually came to be called the Ecumenical Movement we cannot certainly know. That some connection existed is clear."[23]

Restorationists

As we have noted, there was hardly any interest at all in these unity efforts for a restoration of primitive Christianity, but there were nonetheless developments of this point of view in the post-Reformation church. One of the most interesting is that of Michael Servetus, who was executed for heresy by Calvin in 1553, who was one of the first persons ever to write a book on *The Restitution* (Restoration) *of Christianity*, the doctrines of which cost him his life. A typical restorationist, he believed that the primitive church went into apostasy when it eventually aligned itself with Rome under Constantine and became doctrinally corrupt through the teachings of Augustine and other fathers of the church. His task was to restore the true church.

As a child of the Reformation and an associate of Calvin, Servetus was disenchanted with the direction that reform had taken and became aggressive in opposing what he considered to be highly speculative views, especially in reference to the Trinity. In his *Restitution* he set forth an elaborate theology of baptism in which he insisted that only believers' baptism by immersion is scriptural. Pedobaptists, he complained, have only a ceremonial washing but not the healing or illumination that comes with immersion into Christ.

Servetus taught that baptism is the ordained Christian ark, "rescuing man from the abyss of perdition." It is not a mere external washing but an inner gift. When critics argued that this was too much stress on an external, Servetus supplied many examples from both Testaments of faith being linked to some action, such as Noah and Naaman, who were not saved by faith alone but by building an ark and dipping in the Jordan. One cannot be saved without both faith and baptism.

Many a Campbellite preacher was to make similar points and to use the same illustrations. They would have also appreciated the emphasis that Servetus placed upon the Lord's Supper in his *Restitution*, contending that the Christian cannot live without the communion with Christ that it makes possible. If one is born again in baptism, he must find regular nourishment in the Supper. He believed one should prepare himself for it by repentance, prayer, fasting, and even by giving to the poor as an expression of thanksgiving.

These views do not sound so reckless as to cause one to die at the stake, but one must remember that the Protestant reformers were often as oppressive and intolerant as those against whom they rebelled. Besides, anabaptism (second baptism as an adult) was only one charge against Servetus when he was brought to trial in Calvin's Geneva. He was also charged with rejecting the doctrine of the Trinity as set forth in the Nicene Creed.

The court ruled that Servetus should die by fire. Calvin, who carried on an extended debate with him at the trial, mustered enough mercy to recommend a less painful form of execution. But the court was adamant. As he died amidst the flames he cried out "O Jesus, Son of the eternal God, have pity on me!" If he could have prayed, "O Jesus, *eternal Son of God*, have pity on me!" and thus satisfied the Nicene Creed, he could have lived![24]

Servetus' doctrinal aberration and Calvin's hangup in reference to it is reminiscent of a similar controversy between Alexander Campbell and Barton W. Stone almost three centuries later. Stone held views on the preexistence of Christ similar to those of Servetus and would certainly have demurred from the Nicene Creed on the Trinity. Campbell, always more Calvinistic, was more orthodox on that doctrine, even if he avoided the term Trinity. They too debated the question at length and it may have put some strain on their relationship (see chapter 4), but no one called for a fagot.

Campbell accepted Stone as his Christian brother because he acknowledged Jesus as Lord, but this was not sufficient for Calvin in regard to Servetus. There is a greater difference here than three centuries, for it means that the church had learned much more about religious liberty, and it was coming to the place, at least in the Stone-Campbell Movement, where its people were judged more by their Christian character than by their opinions.

What historians call "the restoration motif" or primitivism was strong in the sixteenth century church. We have referred to Servetus' book on restoration, which was in 1553, but there were several others. John Campanus wrote his *Restitution* in 1532, in which he pled for a "Catholic restitution" that would seek truth "among the sects and all the heretics."

It was the loss of the apostolic view of God and man that caused the church to fall away, Campanus believed, and he always insisted that he was "orthodox" because he was apostolic. Bernard Rothmann and William Postel also wrote on the restoration of the primitive church. Rothmann's book called for a restoration of baptism and the Supper and it was also eschatological in nature.

The prevalence of the restoration ideal at this point in history has led George H. Williams to write:

> So widespread was restoration (restitutionism) as the sixteenth century version of primitivism that it may be said to be one of the marks of the Radical Reformation, over against the (institutional, ethical, and partly dogmatic) Reformation on the Magisterial side."[25]

He finds some traces of restoration, however, in the leading Reformation leaders, especially Calvin. But it was the Radicals, especially the Anabaptists, that he describes as "a radical break from the existing institutions and theologies in the interrelated drives to restore primitive Christianity, to reconstruct, and to sublimate."[26]

Heirs of the Stone-Campbell tradition, who often refer to themselves as the Restoration Movement, are therefore not to be surprised when Leonard Verduin's book, *The Restitutionist Movement*, referred to in Williams' account, does not refer to them, but to the restorationists of the underground Reformation. This illustrates why I chose not to call this book a history of the Restoration Movement.

Franklin Littell has suggested that the best term to describe the movement of the Anabaptists would be "the Restitution." But the Anabaptists were not only restorationists but exclusivistic restorationists, believing that they had restored the only true church. As Littell puts it: "The Anabaptists proper were those in the 'Left Wing' who gathered and disciplined a 'True

Church' upon the apostolic pattern."[27]

They thus withdrew to themselves, repudiating the established churches. Like most restorationists, they believed that the primitive church of the apostles had lost its purity and had ceased to be the church, and that they and only they had restored it.

As restorers or restorationists the Anabaptists were not reformers, and were therefore willing to ignore the intervening centuries since the primitive church, as if history had nothing to say to their age. William R. Estep observes that this really began when Conrad Grebel, one of the fathers of Anabaptism, was exposed to the Greek New Testament under Erasmus and Zwingli. The study of the Greek text led him and his disciples to be rebaptized by "believer's baptism." It was the first time in the history of the Reformation that anyone had dared to form a church on what was conceived to be the New Testament pattern.[28]

While the restoration motif was present in the Stone-Campbell Movement, it was different from the Anabaptists in that it was defined in terms of reformation and its mission was unity. Unlike the Anabaptists, its leaders considered themselves part of the reformed tradition, their goal being to continue and complete the reformation begun by Luther. Restoration was thus a means of reformation. They called themselves reformers, not restorers. This puts them in a different tradition from the Anabaptists and the Radical Reformation.

Because of persecution the Anabaptists and other restorationist sects of the Radical Reformation were virtually eliminated by the end of the sixteenth century, except the Mennonites. But what C.C. Morrison calls "the illusion of restorationism" continued through the seventeenth and eighteenth centuries, finding a home in scores of denominations.

Morrison counts 176 restorationist sects, and asks the embarrassing question "What kind of book is our Bible that it could yield 176 different conceptions of the Church of Christ, each deemed of such importance that it required a separate church to be founded upon it?"[29] He names his own Disciples of Christ as one of these. But the question remains as to whether the Stone-Campbell Movement was, in the main, restorationist in this sense, even if the exclusivistic, sectarian element did eventually emerge within it.

Glas and Sandeman

Among those restorationist groups referred to by Morrison that are the most interesting to us are those of the 18th century that broke away from the Church of Scotland. One of these was led by John Glas (1695-1773), who, like the Anabaptists, believed it was wrong for the church to be aligned with the state, and that the church should be governed by the simple order in the New Testament rather than by synods and councils. His quarrel with the Church of Scotland had more to do, therefore, with procedures than with doctrine. He soon decided that each congregation should not only be autonomous, but that it should be directed only by the Scriptures and should pattern itself after the primitive churches.

The Glasite churches, perhaps as many as thirty in Great Britain, eventually had practices that made their way to America and into the Stone-Campbell Movement, such as: (1) weekly communion; (2) plurality of elders in each church; (3) scriptural names only, mainly Church of Christ; (4) the Lord's day of the New Testament made distinct from the Sabbath of the Old Testament. While Glas did relate baptism to the remission of sins, he did not believe that its only mode is immersion, and he did not repudiate infant baptism. He also taught, as did the Campbells, that faith begins with intellectual assent and leads to simple saving trust, and is not miraculously or subjectively induced.

But the most important feature of the Glasite movement was its passion to restore New Testament Christianity. They searched the New Testament for the minutest detail on the life of the church. They found an "order of worship" in Acts 2:42: "They continued stedfastly in the apostles' doctrine and fellowship, and in breaking of bread, and in prayers."

Interpreting the first part to refer to the instruction that the church receives when it assembles, and fellowship as meaning the collection of funds, they came up with this necessary procedure: teaching, giving, the Supper, prayers — in that order. This illustrates what Morrison meant by the "illusion of restorationism," for each sect has a different interpretation of what constitutes the primitive pattern.

There still exists in Great Britain a few Glasite churches that follow this set order. One such meetinghouse in Edinburgh, which I have visited, is marked with a small sign that reads: *Church of Christ (Commonly Called Glasites or Sandemanians)*, and along with the hours of worship there is a quotation of Acts 2:42!

There are yet a few churches in the Movement in the United States, non-instrumental, one-cup Churches of Christ, that are influenced by the Glasites on this point and meticulously follow the four items outlined in Acts 2:42. This group represents a separate fellowship among non-instrument churches, further illustrating the divisive tendency of restorationism.

The Glasites were no exception, for Glas' own church in Dundee, Scotland divided while he was away, the point of issue being whether only ordained ministers may serve the Supper. The movement also split over baptism after a few years, some of them becoming immersionists. Once the Glasite movement reached New England its divisions continued, one church splitting over the possession of worldly goods and another over the erection of an "expensive" meetinghouse.

Historians are agreed that John Glas had an impact upon the Movement. Lynn A. McMillon, in a Ph.D. thesis at Baylor, put it this way: "The thought and practice of John Glas also bears a striking similarity to that of the nineteenth and twentieth century American Restoration movement. With the exception of the doctrine of infant baptism and the order of worship, they exhibit a marked likeness."[30]

After all, seven years before Barton W. Stone was born "the first Church of Christ in North America was constituted May 4, 1765, at Portsmouth, New Hampshire"[31] by Robert Sandeman (1718-1771), Glas' son-in-law. He was probably the ablest leader of the movement, having migrated to America in 1764. This first Church of Christ probably practiced foot washing and the holy kiss as well as weekly Communion and mutual edification.

The Portsmouth church, however, may have to yield its place as the first Church of Christ in this country to Danbury, Conn., for a congregation was started there a year earlier by Ebenezer White, a follower of Sandeman. But White differed with Sandeman sufficiently that the latter would have started a church of his own in Danbury had it been opportune.[32]

The church at Danbury came to have special ties to the Campbell movement, which makes it the oldest of all the Campbell churches, if its Sandemanian origin is allowed. Joseph Moss White, son of Ebenezer, separated some of the disciples from his father's church and started a Church of Christ of his own in late 1764, which makes it but a few months younger than "the first Church of Christ" at Portsmouth. Since the father could not whip the son, in the matter of churches at least, he joined him and again they had one church, but only for awhile. It soon split again over the building of a meetinghouse.

After a few more years the Danbury church split still again, this time over infant baptism now that some of them had come to accept only adult baptism by immersion. One of their number, John Osborne, who had refused to baptize his infant daughter, heard of a Scottish Baptist Church in New York City that believed as he did about baptism. There he met Henry Errett, the pastor, who was a friend to the Campbells and the father of Isaac Errett, and was immersed at his hands in 1817. Upon his return home he in turn immersed others, and the Danbury church became an immersionist congregation.

It was Henry Errett's tract on baptism that also brought Walter Scott to New York for a visit and helped to turn his life toward the Movement. But Errett's church had a problem with petty issues, which we have found to be typical of the Scottish churches. They actually carried on a serious correspondence with a church in Edinburgh as to whether the service of worship should be opened with a hymn or a prayer.[33]

The Sandemanian churches in New England enjoyed modest growth, with six or eight congregations by the time of Sandeman's death in 1771, and at least one in Canada. Had it not been for his premature death at 53 and his controversial political position of advocating loyalty to the British crown, which once caused him to be arrested and fined, his movement would probably have been much more effective.

His practice of weekly Communion, rejection of creeds and reliance only upon the Scriptures, wearing the name Church of Christ, the rule of elders in autonomous congregations, mutual ministry, rejection of titles for preachers, and especially his passion for restoring the church of the New Testament made him a precursor of the Stone-Campbell Movement.

Alexander Campbell was often called upon to deny that he was not unduly influenced by that Scottish triumvirate of "Glas, Sandeman, and the Haldanes," while at the same time expressing his appreciation for them, especially the Haldanes. A Baptist minister, long after Campbell's death, accused the Movement of being "an offshoot of Sandemanianism." G.W. Longan replied that Campbell disagreed with Sandeman more than he agreed.[34]

While the Movement was hardly an offshoot of the Glas-Sandeman-Haldanes restoration effort, there is no question but what Campbell was influenced by it. When accused of being "substantially a Sandemanian or Haldanian," Campbell replied that he considered Sandeman "as condescending as any man this age has produced" and as "a giant among dwarfs," and admitted a prejudice against him until he spent a winter reading him.

Campbell admitted he was well acquainted with their work "since John Glas was excommunicated by the high church of Scotland for preaching that Christ's kingdom is not of this world." He conceded that he was in debt to them, just as he was to Luther and Calvin, as much for their errors as for the truth they taught. But he had not read them for ten years, he said, for he was then giving most all his time to a study of the Scriptures themselves.[35]

Sandeman's theological contribution to the Movement, as distinguished from the more practical ones that we have listed, was his view of the nature of faith, which was read widely and admiringly by those who had no interest in his sect. The common view, which Sandeman challenged, was that faith comes only as a special act of grace on God's part and not by any initiative on man's part.

He contended that faith in Christ is not all that different from any other faith that man has, for all faith is based upon testimony and comes through man's assent to facts. This of course satisfied the Lockean minds of Thomas and Alexander Campbell and Walter Scott, and it reflects the basic doctrine of faith of the Movement from the outset.

The Haldanes

While we meet the Haldanes again in chapter six, we should notice in this context that they too were determined to restore the primitive church in polity, ordinances, and worship. Like Glas and Sandeman, they withdrew from the Church of Scotland and started their own movement. Being wealthy laymen they gave liberally to evangelistic efforts, organizing Sunday Schools, building tabernacles and seminaries, all for the purpose of making the decadent church more spiritual. Their first independent church was in Edinburgh in 1799, and while their growth also was modest they eventually had churches scattered over Great Britain and a few in America.

They were like the Glas-Sandeman folk in that they believed in the sufficiency of the Scriptures, congregational independence, rule of elders, and weekly Communion, but differed in that they were immersionists. They made the reading and teaching of the Bible central in their public worship, and they wore no particular name, referring to themselves simply as Christians or disciples. They made no distinction between clergy and laity, and the holy kiss and footwashing were not as prevalent as with the Glas-Sandeman churches.

Above all else the Haldanes were determined to restore the primitive faith by preaching the apostolic gospel, and it is especially here that they were forerunners of the Movement we are studying. James Haldane put it this way when he set up a society for the promulgation of the gospel: "It is not our desire to form or extend the influence of any sect. Our whole intention is to make known the evangelical gospel of our Lord Jesus Christ."[36]

When Alexander Campbell visited Europe in 1847 he addressed churches throughout England, Scotland, and Ireland. At their annual cooperative meeting that year in Chester, England there were representatives from 29 churches to hear him. James Wallis of Nottingham, England in his *Christian Messenger* described these churches as "advocating original Christianity, and contending for the ancient order of the church of God —

the doctrines and institutions delivered to the faithful by the holy Apostles."[37]

These were now part and parcel of the Movement. Many if not most of these churches were Sandemanian or Haldanean, and Sandeman and the Haldanes could not have agreed more with Wallis' description of them.

The Haldaneans that migrated to America had some influence upon the beginning of the Movement, especially in the persons of James Forrester and William Ballentine, both Scots. Forrester settled in Pittsburgh and started a school and a church. He taught and baptized Walter Scott, and died shortly afterwards, leaving Scott to care for the church, and from there Scott helped start the Movement. Ballentine, who directed the Haldane seminary in Elgin, Scotland, migrated to Baltimore and Philadelphia in the late 1820's, where he helped build new churches.

The Haldaneans in general and Ballentine in particular were adamant for mutual ministry, and this Scottish influence was strong in the American congregations. Richardson says it was Ballentine who introduced mutual ministry into the Scottish churches, and it was his influence that caused it to be practiced in the church at Pittsburgh, made up mostly of Scots.

In that church the practice was a problem in that debates and dissensions often accompanied it. Scott and Campbell, even though they agreed in principle to mutual ministry, were repelled by what went on in that church, insisting that "none should teach publicly except those capable of edifying the church."[38]

This illustrates once again the problem that all these restorationist groups had with divisiveness. From the Anabaptists and their sub-groups to the Glasites to the Sandemanians to the Haldanes, they all had a proclivity to divide. Ballentine, for instance, who is described by Richardson as an excellent man, brought with him from Scotland the view that a plurality of elders must preside over each congregation.

Since the Haldane churches practiced a one-man rule, this issue, insisted upon by Ballentine, divided the Haldane churches. The Stone-Campbell Movement was blessed by much of its heritage from Scotland, but it also had to absorb this divisive tendency of being pushy about opinions.

The Scottish heritage included a vigorous concern for the recovery of the ancient order, a reverence for the divine ordinances, and a reaffirmation of the authority of the Scriptures as opposed to clerical or ecclesiastical domination. There was the implication that each person can understand the Scriptures for himself and that each congregation can take care of its own affairs and determine for itself the nature of the primitive church that it accepts as its pattern.

The problem was they never seemed to be able to get along with each other and divided over what they conceived to be "the pattern" for the church. There was a total absence of unity consciousness.

This was the important difference with the Stone-Campbell Movement. Of all the restorationists they were the only ones to plead for the unity of all believers. This led Garrison and DeGroot to say: "When Thomas and Alexander Campbell adopted the familiar formula of restoration, they combined it with the almost forgotten ideal of union and thus produced a strikingly different result.[39]

The strikingly different result was that to the extent the Movement was truly a unity movement it avoided the internal fissions that characterized their Scottish forebears. But whenever it allowed restorationism to dominate over the plea for unity it too became divisive, not unlike its European counterparts.

ENDNOTES

[1]Lancelot Oliver, *New Testament Christianity*, Birmingham, Eng.: Publishing Commission of Churches of Christ, 1911 (Reprinted by College Press, Joplin, MO), p. 206.

[2]*The Evidences of Christianity*, A Debate Between Robert Owen and Alexander Campbell, Cincinnati, 1829; McQuiddy Printing Co.: Nashville, 1946, p. 281.

[3]*Ibid.*, p. 101.

[4]Alexander Campbell, *Popular Lectures and Addresses*, Bethany, Va., 1861, Nashville: Harbinger Book Club, n.d., p. 104.

[5]Bertrand Russell, *History of Western Philosophy*, New York: Simon and Schuster, p. 525.

[6]*The Evidences of Christianity*, p. 282.

[7]For an interesting discussion of Bacon's "Idols of the Mind" see Emil Brehier, *The 17th Century*, University of Chicago Press, 1938, pp. 31f.

[8]Alexander Campbell, "The Confirmation of the Testimony," *Millennial Harbinger*, 1830, p. 9.

[9]Alexander Campbell, "Religious Anecdotes of Dying Professors," *Millennial Harbinger*, 1833, p. 427.

[10]Alexander Campbell, *Popular Lectures and Addresses*, p. 118.

[11]D.J. O'Conner, *John Locke*, New York: Dover, 1967, pp. 21f.

[12]*A Letter Concerning Toleration* is readily available in most libraries in such reference works as *The Harvard Classics* and *Great Books of the Western World*.

[13]D.J. O'Conner, *John Locke*, p. 216.

[14]Robert Milligan, for example, published *Reason and Revelation* in 1868.

[15]*Popular Lectures and Addresses*, p. 117.

[16]William A. Gerrard, *Walter Scott: American Frontier Evangelist*, (Joplin, MO: College Press, 1992), p. 93.

[17]C. Leonard Allen, *The Cruciform Church*, 2nd Edition (Abilene, TX: ACU Press, 1990), p. 46.

[18]D.S Robinson, *The Story of Scottish Philosophy* (New York: Exposition, 1961), p. 8.

[19]*Ibid.*, p. 22.

[20]*Popular Lectures and Addresses*, p. 101.

[21]See John R. W. Stott, *Christ the Controversialist* (Downers Grove, IL: InterVarsity, 1970), p. 44. The slogan was originally credited to one Rupert Meldenius, which may have been a pseudonym.

[22]"Union Christian Meeting," *Millennial Harbinger*, 1841, p. 259.

[23]Kenneth Scott Latourette, *A History of Christianity* (New York: Harper and Brothers, 1953), p. 893.

[24]For extended references to Servetus that makes use of most recent research see George H. Williams, *The Radical Reformation* (Philadelphia: Westminster, 1975).

[25]George H. Williams, *The Radical Reformation.*, p. 375.

[26]*Ibid.*, p. 846.

[27]Franklin H. Littell, *Anabaptist View of the Church*, Starr King Press, p. 47.

[28]William R. Estep, *The Anabaptist Story* (Grand Rapids: Eerdmans, 1975), p. 11.

[29]C.C. Morrison, *The Unfinished Reformation* (New York: Harper and Brothers, 1953), p. 156.

[30]Lynn A. McMillon, *The Quest for the Apostolic Church: A Study of Scottish Origins.* An unpublished Ph.D. thesis, Baylor University, 1972, p. 92.

[31]*Ibid.*, p. 119.

[32]*Ibid.*, p. 118.

[33]*Ibid.*, p. 119.

[34]W.E. Garrison and A.T. DeGroot, *The Disciples of Christ, A History* (St. Louis: Bethany Press, 1948), p. 48.

[35]Alexander Campbell, "Reply," *Christian Baptist*, Vol. 3, (1827), Gospel Advocate Edition, p. 182.

[36]Robert Richardson, *Memoirs*, 1, p. 160.

[37]Alexander Campbell, "Letters from Europe No. 32," *Millennial Harbinger*, 1848, p. 567, quotes the Christian Messenger.

[38]Robert Richardson, *Memoirs*, 2, p. 126.

[39]Garrison and DeGroot, *Disciples of Christ*, p. 53.

3

JAMES O'KELLY AND RICE HAGGARD
THE AMERICAN PRELUDE TO THE MOVEMENT

We are Christians simply.

By a stroke of the pen and $15,000,000 Thomas Jefferson doubled the size of the United States in 1803 by the purchase of the Louisiana Territory from France. Within a century the purchased territory became thirteen states whose farm lands alone were worth seven billion dollars. It was a capital gain of hundreds of times the original purchase price. Besides wanting the port of New Orleans, the philosopher President could tell that America was destined to move west.

While the entire population of the young nation in its first census in 1790 was barely four million and only five percent of that number lived west of the Allegheny Mountains, the western expansion had nonetheless begun and Jefferson could foresee that the prospects were limitless.

In 1769 Daniel Boone, "ordained of God to settle the wilderness," made his way through the Cumberland Gap into what is now Kentucky (then part of Virginia). He was followed by thousands of pioneer farmers so that by 1800 there were upwards of 225,000 of them. Almost half that many were then in Tennessee and nearly 50,000 in Ohio, which became a state in 1803. Indiana became a state in 1816, followed by Alabama in 1817, Illinois in 1818, and Mississippi in 1819. Missouri was still a territory in 1812, but nine years later it had grown enough to be eligible for statehood. The five states that were originally known as the Northwest Territory, the heart of the midwest, multiplied sixfold from 1810 to 1830.

The conquest and settlement of the West is one of this country's greatest achievements. In the first census in 1790 there were only two states west of the Alleghenies (not counting western Virginia) with a total population of 110,000. By 1850 there were twenty-nine states and the population had increased by ten million, which was almost half the population of the entire nation. They migrated from the eastern states by any means possible, many of them on foot, pulling carts filled with their meager belongings.

One observer remarked that it seemed that all of America was breaking up and moving westward. As they moved west religion moved with them.

W.E. Garrison expressed it romantically when he described the phenomenon as "religion follows the frontier."[1]

Winthrop S. Hudson describes the westward migration as "a stampede" and notes that it created two fears for the people in the East. One being that the move west would lead to an imbalance of political power, and the other that the West, being far removed from the civilizing influences of the East, would revert to barbarism and subvert the moral order of society.

Hudson quotes a Roman Catholic bishop, who saw the crucial importance of what was to become the heartland of America, as saying, "Give us the West, and we shall take care of the East." He points out that as the churches followed the frontier they were not only resolved to conquer the West but to reconquer the East.[2]

It was amidst this western surge that the Stone-Campbell Movement began and grew, following the frontier. Barton W. Stone launched his movement the same year that Ohio became a state, and Alexander Campbell was rebaptized by immersion after "the primitive order" in 1812, the same year Louisiana became a state. A new frontier gave birth to a new movement.

More than ninety percent of the people on the frontier made no profession of any religion. It seems that as they made their way west they were not only trying to get away from the eastern states where they had not done well financially, but as far away from Europe and its religious tyranny as possible.

Freedom of religion had come to mean freedom *from* religion. The frontier was wild and rugged, attracting those especially of an independent spirit who had little interest in the traditional forms of religion.

Even from the early colonial period religion in America was basically nonconformist if not radical. The Puritans, Quakers, Mennonites, Tunkers, and the Amish were all a part of the colonial scene. Even the Baptists were hardly more than a curious sect back in England before they migrated, and the Presbyterians were notorious for their opposition to the established church. While the Anglican church existed in all the colonies, preserving a semblance of orthodoxy, it was the radical and independent spirit of nonconformity that was to prevail.

The Great Awakening

Nonconformity did prevail for several decades, finding fertile soil in a land that was conducive to independency, but by the early 1700's there was a serious decline in religious interest. After a full generation of religious deprivation, there was another period of spiritual enthusiasm, called the Great Awakening, dating from about 1735.

The revival found its origin in the fervent oratory of Jonathan Edwards of Northampton, Mass., but reached its apex in the fiery preaching of George Whitefield, lately come from England, where people gathered by the thousands to hear him and where he gained the reputation of being the greatest preacher of the century. Whitefield preached up and down the colonies from New England to Georgia, causing great religious excitement everywhere he went. Under the spell of his moving oratory students at Harvard wept, women fainted, and hundreds were converted.

Edwards so excited his audiences that he would sometimes have to request that they be quiet so that he might continue. In his famous "Sinners in the Hands of an Angry God," preached in Enfield, Conn. in 1741, the people were so stirred that they held on to benches and tree trunks lest the ground open up and they be swallowed by hell.

The revival swept from New England through the middle colonies into the South. In most any town religion was the topic of conversation and the churches grew rapidly. In New England alone there were upwards of 50,000 converts out of a population of 300,000. Whitefield was a precursor of Stone-Campbell in that he worked enthusiastically with all churches and was nonsectarian in his preaching. He sounded like a "Campbellite" when he said the likes of this in a sermon in Philadelphia:

> Father Abraham, whom have you in Heaven? Any Episcopalians? "No." Any Presbyterians? "No." Have you any Independents or Seceders? "No." Have you any Methodists? "No, no, no!" Whom have you there? "We don't know those names here. All who are here are Christians — believers in Christ — men who have overcome by the blood of the Lamb and the word of his testimony." Oh, is this the case? Then God help us, God help us all, to forget party names, and to become Christians in deed and in truth.[3]

There was fire in what he had to say, such as complaining that the gospel was not being preached in the churches, and that the Church of England was in good order only outwardly. Benjamin Franklin, the patriot, admired Whitefield's fiery spirit, and was led to help subscribe the funds to erect a building for his ministry, once the established church refused him theirs. That building eventually became the University of Pennsylvania.

But it was Edwards more than Whitefield that gave the Great Awakening its theology. Edwin S. Gaustad, who describes Edwards as "New England's most brilliant theologian," explains that it was Edwards who gave the Awakening its "deep emotion," which Edwards saw as the essence of true religion.

Edwards insisted that a change of mind was not the same thing as a change of heart, and it is the change of heart that makes for a change of life. Faith is more than propositional and religion more than knowledge, he avowed. Religion must touch the affections if it has real meaning.[4]

Both Stone and Campbell would agree with this emphasis upon heart religion, and often said things similar to what Edwards said. Campbell, in fact, included "education of the heart" in his educational philosophy, insisting that head knowledge is not enough. It is unfortunate that this emphasis did not influence the Movement more than it did. In time the Movement became more rationalistic after the order of Locke than deeply emotional after the order of Edwards.

Even a balance between the two was hardly realized, though Stone and Campbell were both deeply pious men. But the Great Awakening, by making the young nation more religious, nevertheless helped prepare the soil out of which the Movement emerged a half century later.

The Second Awakening

Religion held its own in American life through the Revolutionary War, but it reached a new low during the fifteen years following the war. In the early 1800's, however, there was another significant revival that swept the country known as the Second Great Awakening. It came just in time, not only because the moral condition of the nation had become deplorable, but also because the churches were struggling for survival.

This revival had no leaders of the stature of Edwards or Whitefield. While it was less dramatic, it was equally effective. It was more imperceptible than the first awakening, emerging throughout the young nation almost simultaneously, while beginning, like the first, in the East.

The heroes were a new church in America, the Methodists, having migrated from England, bringing the piety and revivalism of John Wesley with them. Wesley had introduced the circuit system in England with some success, and it proved even more effective on America's frontier, especially in the stewardship of the indefatigable Francis Asbury, the church's first bishop in this country.

The Methodist circuit rider, a common sight on the frontier, was an itinerant minister, preaching under trees, in saloons and log cabins, as well as an occasional meetinghouse. He was always an evangelist, for he was not only eager to minister to any Methodists he might find, but to win sinners for the Lord from the raw material he found out on the edge of civilization. In the early period of the move westward the Methodists were the most successful of any church in reaching the masses. Their zeal was so thorough that the frontier folk would describe the severity of the weather with, "There's no one out but crows and Methodist preachers."

The Baptists also made ideal western immigrants in that they were in search of cheap land. In those early days before 1800 their preachers were nearly all farmers, so they were of the people and with the people in the move west. Their form of church government also fit folk who were suspicious of episcopacy and inclined to democracy and individuality. They formed many churches across the edge of the new nation, most of them very small, averaging no more than 20 members.

Since most of the immigrants to this country before the Revolution were Scotch-Irish, it was the Presbyterians who had the most strength in the colonial states, and it was they who could with less difficulty move across the Alleghenies and form still more churches. They had twelve churches in Kentucky as early as 1785, and in time they took over 2,000 churches by merging with Congregationalists. They were out on the frontier "firstest with the mostest," and they took their passion for education with them, which explains the abundance of Presbyterian schools and colleges throughout the Midwest.

The Anglicans represented the older and richer families in New England who were not inclined to venture westward, and so the church did not follow the frontier but waited for a more developed civilization. But not so with the Roman Catholics. While they were later than the other churches in the westward move, having only a sprinkling of people in the decade following the Revolution, they finally grew so rapidly that by 1814 they had 10,000 in Kentucky alone.

The Second Awakening, therefore, not only shored up the sagging churches in the East, but it also inspired the western expansion with the spirit of revival. Camp meetings were in vogue, with preachers from most every denomination using this method, and sometimes the revivalists would cooperate in preaching to the masses that gathered.

James McGready, a Presbyterian, was an outstanding revivalist who not only converted thousands but stirred up such excitement in his meetings that the people behaved in strange ways. He was accused of so distracting people as to divert them from their occupations, and at one of his meetings the opposition against him was so fierce that his pulpit was torn away and burned, and he received a threatening letter written in blood, which is one more example of how frontier life was wild and wooly.

Peter Cartwright, a famous Methodist circuit rider, tells how Logan county, Kentucky, the scene of some of McGready's revivals, was called "Rogues' Harbor" in that it was a haven for escaped murderers, horse thieves, highway robbers, and counterfeiters.[5]

It was at a McGready revival that Barton W. Stone, one of the founders of the Movement, first began to associate the revivals with the need for moral reform and church renewal. As the revivals moved throughout Kentucky, Tennessee, the Carolinas, western Virginia, Pennsylvania, and even into Northwest Territory, they came to Stone's home church in Cane Ridge, Bourbon County, Kentucky.

Stone was preaching at Cane Ridge what McGready was preaching elsewhere. In August of 1801 Stone was joined by dozens of other preachers, including 18 Presbyterians, in conducting the greatest of all revivals of the Second Awakening, attracting as it did upwards of 25,000 people and producing fantastic results. It was out of this Cane Ridge revival that came the raw materials for the beginning of the Christian Church under Barton W. Stone and others, the first half of the Stone-Campbell Movement. We tell this part of the story in more detail in the next chapter.

The Frontier Mind

Frederick Jackson Turner (died 1932) was the first American historian to set forth the "frontier thesis," which pictured the frontier as "symbol and myth" and credited it with nurturing a distinctive religious character. He did not see the West as a place as much as a mindset which created the conditions for the emergence of a new order of institutions.

Turner equated the West with "free land" and this created primitive economic and political conditions that made for a distinct America, separating it from Europe as the East had not done. He saw the West as breaking the bonds of tradition, escaping from the past, scorning older societies, and as indifferent to the lessons of history.

The character of the frontier mind influenced the nature of frontier institutions, or to put it another way, only those institutions flourished on the frontier that could consistently communicate with the frontier mind. There is a reason, for example, why Mormonism, born in the East, would never have survived had it not moved west, and why the Presbyterians and Methodists prospered in the West when the Episcopalians could not. An understanding of the frontier mind also explains why the Stone-Campbell Movement emerged amidst the drama of the expansion of a new republic, and why it flourished only as it was a part of that religion that followed the frontier.

The frontier mind can be rather specifically identified:

1. *Individualism.* The view that religion lies solely "between man and his God," insisted on by Jefferson, and not the business of any hierarchy, was commonly held, and it was part of the larger fabric of the rugged individualism that permeated the frontier. If it was man for himself against the wilds and the Indians, then it was man for himself when it came to religion.

This accounts for an almost wholesale rejection of the orthodox religions they had known. Edwin Scott Gaustad notes that a stress on the competence of the individual soon led to scorn for those areas where all men were not competent, and this included theology. As he put it: "Dismissed as a professional, artificial activity, theology grew simpler and simpler until it was a question whether any existed at all."[6]

2. *Freedom*. Westward Ho! was a call to the free, adventurous, curious spirit. Arthur K. Moore suggests that their free spirit made them both energetic and aggressive, for even a Joshua cannot lead an apathetic people to the land of Canaan. He thinks curiosity moved them westward and that they may have had an unconscious hostility toward the mountainous barriers that separated them from the wide-open spaces. The fact that the frontier was there was their challenge to attack.

Moore goes on to explain why the frontier mind would not respond normally to traditional religion and ethics: "Reckless, exuberant, lawless, violent, brave, the frontiersman of Kentucky acted the part of the utterly free agent and by word or gesture expressed a lively contempt for artificial ethical prescriptions."[7]

This passion for freedom will be evident in all the documents composed by the founders of the Stone-Campbell Movement in their break from traditional religion.

3. *Sense of destiny*. They were indeed pioneers, not refugees or displaced persons. A sense of destiny propelled them on and on, despite almost unbelievable hardship. Gaustad calls it a manifest destiny, explaining: "Like ancient Israelites following a cloud by day and fire by night, America's explorers, colonists, and citizens were steadied in their journey by the vision ahead. And for them, as for their predecessors approaching Canaan, the hand that led them was the hand of God. Providence knew and Providence directed."[8]

Some scholars argue that the frontier mind is understood only in reference to their warlike heritage in their Scotch-Irish background, for even those who migrated from Ulster had lived in a state of constant watchfulness. This led R.C. Buley to conclude that "the Kentuckians who opened that part of the Old Northwest on the Ohio River were distinguished by a restless energy, freedom of thought, and a sense of destiny, all attributable to their military heritage."[9]

Perhaps this will help answer the oft-asked question as to why Alexander Campbell was so belligerent! But the sense of destiny is also present. While Charles Finney was predicting that the millennium would come to America by 1838 and William Miller was prophesying that Christ would come by 1843, Campbell was writing 26 essays on his postmillennial position, in which he insisted that the Jews will be converted, the world will be won to Christ, the church united, and righteousness will reign over the earth, all before Christ comes – with America in the center of it all.[10]

These traits of the frontier mind lent more power to the laity in the church, and being removed as far as they were from ecclesiastical centers they found a place for local autonomy. Voluntary church membership was more acceptable than arbitrary membership by birth. Episcopacy had come upon hard times, even among the Episcopalians in the East.

It is understandable that Francis Asbury would have difficulty making the new Methodist Episcopal Church truly a church ruled by bishops, especially since it was not advocated by Wesley and was not even practiced in England. We shall now see that this difficulty set the stage for the formation of the Christian Church in America, destined to become an important part of the Stone-Campbell Movement.

James O'Kelly
"We are Christians simply."

"I must preach the gospel wherever a door is opened, but I have no intention of a separate party," replied James O'Kelly, then 58 years old, when asked what he was going to do now that he had separated himself from the Methodist Episcopal Church. *I have no intention of a separate party.* It was a refrain that characterized the beginnings of the Movement.

Barton W. Stone did not intend a separate party, and Thomas and Alexander Campbell were adamant in having only a society dedicated to peace and unity within the church at large and not another denomination. But it did not work out that way with either O'Kelly, Stone, or the Campbells. History reveals that a dissenting group that separates hardly ever avoids crystallizing into a sect.

Such was the case even with the Methodists, with whom O'Kelly had been a minister for over 30 years. John Wesley, like Thomas Campbell, only wanted "clubs" or societies that would work for the spiritual reform of the Church of England. As the clubs spread from their place of origin at Oxford University and became numerous, Wesley found that he had a "church" on his hands, whether he intended it or not. Because of the methodical nature of their pious practices they were dubbed "Methodists," but the name was not official and the societies did not formally become a denomination until Dec. 25, 1784, in Baltimore, Maryland.

John Wesley, who disliked the term bishop, ordained Thomas Coke to be "superintendent" of the Methodist movement in America. Coke in turn created the Methodist Episcopal Church by ordaining Francis Asbury as the first "bishop." John Wesley was himself suspicious of both episcopacy and separatism. He made legal arrangements before his death for the formation of the Methodist denomination, but chose himself to remain within the Church of England and was buried in the clerical garb of that church.[11]

Not a bishop himself and unable to persuade an Anglican bishop to ordain a bishop for his separated people, Wesley reluctantly ordained a "superintendent" for his Methodist society in America, who would in turn ordain clergy. It was a dubious beginning for the Methodist *Episcopal* Church in this country, its first bishop being created by men who were not themselves of the episcopal order.

The English counterpart became the Methodist Protestant Church, which has never had bishops. This curious turn of events lay at the root of the defection of James O'Kelly and the formation of the Republican Methodist Church and finally of the Christian Church.

No one is sure where and when James O'Kelly was born, but it was probably in Ireland, though some say Virginia, and the date was about 1734. It is known that he lived to be 92, dying about 1826, after an incredibly hard life. He settled in Surry county, Virginia at an early age and afterwards moved to North Carolina. There was a tradition that he worked his way to colonial America on a boat, but nothing is certain. Tradition also has it that O'Kelly was an able boxer and fiddler and that he grew up with little thought of religion. We do know that he married Elizabeth Meeks, whose family settled near Jamestown during the early days of the colony, and that they had two sons and enjoyed a long life together.

O'Kelly's wife was the first to join the Methodist society, then one of his sons, who in turn helped to convert his father, who was slow in coming around. He afterwards wrote that it was not by the blessed means of preaching but by the kind illuminations of the Spirit that he was brought to God. His was a moving, fearful conversion, and he was apprehensive in approaching God in prayer.

"With the Bible in my hand," he was afterwards to write, "I besought the Lord to help me, and declaring that during life that sacred Book should be my guide."

That was a prophecy as well as a prayer, for it was his devotion to the Bible as the sole guide in religion that eventually brought him into confrontation with the Methodist clergy. Once forsaking everything not religious and burning his fiddle, he joined the Methodist circuit riders, who are described by one historian as "freedom-intoxicated."

O'Kelly loved John Wesley, whom having never seen he trusted as an interpreter of the Scriptures. It impressed him that Wesley honored only the Scriptures as authoritative in matters religious, and that he had a way of saying, "We will be downright Christians." That was close to what O'Kelly and Haggard were to say as founders of the Christian Church — "We are Christians simply," which in the Movement's history was to be refined to *We are Christians only.*

He was licensed to preach by "the holy preachers," as the circuit riders were called, piety being their hallmark, when they gathered for one of their conventions. They were actually "lay preachers," farmers for the most part, and none of them were ordained by one having taken holy orders. As we have seen, the Anglicans had put a ban on Wesley's Methodists, and so they had to work with what they had.

O'Kelly was about 40 years old when he started preaching, and it was about two years before the outbreak of the Revolutionary War. Technically, he was at this time a "lay preacher" in the Church of England, where the Methodists were then uneasily bosomed. Ten years later when the Methodist Episcopal Church was officially created, he was ordained a clergyman in that new church by "Bishop" Thomas Coke.

As a preacher O'Kelly was earnest in prayer and powerful in exhortation. People flocked to hear him, to the consternation of the Anglican clergy, who questioned his right to preach, especially in their chapels. He was a man of great natural talent, and he soon became an outstanding preacher. As one of "Asbury's Ironsides" he was now among the Methodist leadership.[12]

Asbury's circuit riders had a hard time of it, politically as well as financially, especially in Virginia where a Thomas Jefferson had not yet risen to bring freedom of religion. The Church of England was the established church. Taxes had to be paid to the church and attendance was compulsory. Dissidents could be jailed and sometimes were, especially if they published their ideas, and they were not allowed to preach.

But O'Kelly did his thing anyway, as did others of "the holy preachers," and he was loud in his protests against such oppression. Such conditions encouraged "freedom-intoxicated" people to migrate into "Kentucke country" and the Old Northwest Territory. When Daniel Boone found a gap about a thousand feet wide in the Cumberland Mountain and ventured into Kentucky, the preachers were not far behind.

These Methodist preachers were not free to serve the sacraments, celebrate the rites of matrimony, baptize, or even to perform burial rites, for they were still within the Church of England and only its ordained clergy could do such things. Even Asbury himself would not perform such rites. This changed in 1784 when they had a church of their own.

But the new Methodist Episcopal Church was headed for trouble. Francis Asbury, who came to America in 1771 with the blessing of John Wesley, was in complete control of the Methodists, and with some justification in that it was through his indomitable will against frightful difficulties that the movement grew. When Coke arrived, having been made "Bishop" by Wesley, he knew very well that Asbury would remain *the* leader, even if the lesser is to be blessed by the greater.

Asbury not only ruled the new church, but he did so with an iron hand. He had presiding elders that were to advise with him on ministerial appointments, but they knew better than to offer any advice, for Asbury listened to no one except God. Methodist historians describe him as autocratic and domineering; Luccock and Hutchinson going so far as to have a sub-heading of a chapter on him entitled "Asbury the Dictator." They point out that it is amazing that he was able to do what he did in the new republic where the watchword was democracy since he had not the slightest idea what the word meant.[13]

Dictator or not, it would be difficult to find anyone in the entire history of the church who suffered greater privations and hardships for the cause of Christ than Francis Asbury. He crossed the Appalachians, which he referred to as "the Lord's dirtiest trick on the horseback rider," forty times. He recorded in his diary that they were bad enough when they were dry, but virtually impossible when wet. One entry reads: "When we had ascended the summit of the mountain, we found it so rich and miry, that it was with great difficulty we could ride along; but I was wrapped up in heavy, wet garments, and unable to walk through weakness of body; so we had to pitch, slide, and drive to the bottom."

If it was not mountains it was swamps, or river bottoms, or unblazed trails through a wilderness. In western Virginia he not only encountered mountains on horseback but "We have had rain for eighteen days successively, and I have ridden about two hundred miles in eight or nine days; a most trying time indeed."

His horses were always running away, falling from exhaustion, or going lame. His notes indicate that he suffered from boils, fevers, inflammatory rheumatism, sore throat, weak eyes, bronchitis, asthma, toothache, ulcers, neuralgia, and intestinal disorders. On the frontier where he helped carve a civilization there was no such thing as comfort. Winter or summer he slept in the wilds, or in barn lofts – or, if in a frontier cabin, in a bed with at least two others! No wonder that he would write: "O, how glad should I be of a plain, clean plank to lie on, as preferable to most of the beds; and where the beds are in a bad state, the floors are worse."

Asbury was as undaunted in devotion as in travel, rising at 4:00 a.m. for two hours of prayer and meditation and two hours of study before beginning the day. He knew the New Testament nearly by memory and would study Hebrew on horseback. He fasted regularly. He was an example for his band of "holy preachers," and until they became too numerous he would pray for each one by name every day. Since he had the heart of a shepherd toward them, it was perhaps not inappropriate for him to ask them to address him as bishop.[14]

It was risky for James O'Kelly, a man of only moderate influence among his people, to challenge the judgment of Francis Asbury, one who had earned the loyalty and admiration of the Methodists. O'Kelly was also pious and dedicated, and he too suffered hardship in the wilds of the new republic, as did all the itinerant preachers, but no one equaled Asbury. O'Kelly was an abler preacher, but he was no bishop, and apparently had no desire to be, Asbury's charges to the contrary notwithstanding.

It was in 1792, only eight years after the new church had begun, at the General Conference in Baltimore that O'Kelly introduced a resolution that challenged the extent of Asbury's episcopal authority. He had apparently accepted the idea of episcopacy, even with reluctance, and had enjoyed a friendly relationship with Asbury, even to the point of gaining his highest commendation as a dedicated preacher. But O'Kelly wanted the church to be more democratic and wanted the preachers to have more freedom than Asbury allowed.

His resolution thus read: "After the bishop appoints the preachers at Conference to their several circuits, if any one thinks himself injured by the appointment, he shall have the liberty to appeal to the Conference and state his objection, and if the Conference approve his objection, the Bishop shall appoint him to another circuit."[15]

The motion was innocuous enough, and it was consistent with what was practiced in England under Wesley, where the preacher had what was commonly called "the right of appeal." It simply meant that a preacher who feels that the bishop has been unjust in his treatment of him can circumvent the bishop's authority by appealing directly to the Conference, which may or may not uphold the judgment of the bishop. But it was too much for the autocratic Asbury, and, while he excused himself from the debate since it concerned his authority, he let it be known that he believed the motion, if passed, would destroy the authority of the bishop.

O'Kelly appeared to have the majority on his side during the early stages of the debate, but the Asbury forces eventually prevailed and the motion was lost. Before the vote was taken O'Kelly, convinced that the preachers were too much influenced by Asbury, stood before the assembly with his New Testament held aloft, and said: "Brethren, hearken unto me, put away all other books and forms, and let this be the only criterion and that will satisfy me." He thought such an appeal would sway the freedom-loving preachers, but he was wrong.

This was too much for O'Kelly, so he withdrew from the Methodist Episcopal Church, and, while it was not his intention to do so, soon formed the Republican Methodist Church, *republican* meaning to him what it means in the dictionary, "one who believes that the supreme power rests in all the citizens entitled to vote and is exercised by representatives elected."

Within only a few months O'Kelly lured 10,000 Methodists away from Asbury, who was bitter, accusing O'Kelly of being ambitious for power. But modern Methodist historians probably have it right when they say: "O'Kelly felt that the church had been delivered into the hands of a one-man autocracy, and that he could not abide." They add: "We feel that he made a mistake in withdrawing, but we are judging with the advantage of more than a hundred years."[16]

A number of those who left with O'Kelly eventually returned to the Methodists, and Asbury himself made kindly overtures to O'Kelly, sending him word that in losing him he was losing his right eye, right hand, and right foot. The bishop also sent him ten British pounds, which in those days was enough to buy a horse, because he had suffered so much for the cause of truth and liberty. One Conference went so far as to offer O'Kelly forty pounds a year to travel and preach wherever he pleased, making him accountable directly to them and not the bishop.

But the die was cast. When one takes up his saddlebags and walks out, it is not easy to turn back. There is no evidence that O'Kelly ever desired to. He wanted a free church or none at all. He did, however, make overtures for peace with the Methodists before he finally formed a church of his own. At one of the new church's conferences in 1793 they went on record to the effect that they wanted to be united with the Methodists and made a personal appeal to Asbury "to consider our distress." Inasmuch as they also requested that he examine the episcopal order in the light of the Scriptures, the overture came to naught.

The new church was formed on Christmas Day, 1793 in Manakintown, Virginia amidst humble circumstances. They had no meetinghouses and the prospect of supporting their preachers was poor, but in a matter of days they could count a thousand members. In time entire Methodist churches became Republican, a fact that haunted Asbury, causing him to make negative references to O'Kelly now and again in his journal.

Christians Only

They met in August, 1794, in Surry County, Virginia, in the Old Lebanon Church, formerly a Methodist church, to consider how they should be governed. It was an uneasy experience for them, as it always seems to be for people committed only to the Scriptures since they differ on what the Bible authorizes. They did agree that the church is made up of "all real Christians in the world," and that there is but one office in each congregation, that of elders, the apostolic office being limited to "those extraordinary days."

They were especially concerned about what name they should call themselves. Even if they had, for the moment, called themselves the Republican Methodist Church, they could hardly go around calling themselves Republicans. Neither were they Methodists anymore.

It was at this point that Rice Haggard, who for years had been a Methodist alongside Asbury and had joined O'Kelly's walkout, stood before the group with the New Testament in his hand and said: "Brethren, this is a sufficient rule of faith and practice, and by it we are told that the disciples were called *Christians*, and I move that henceforth and forever the followers of Christ be known as Christians simply."[17]

The motion was unanimously adopted, and it was henceforth the name by which they were called, and their church was subsequently called the Christian Church. At the same meeting they also resolved unanimously that the Bible itself would be their only creed, and without a dissenting voice they acknowledged Jesus as King and Head of their people. While they were at it they renounced all human institutions in the church as being a species of popery. With all this done they proceeded to ordain elders.

Thus the Christian Church was formed in August, 1794. It eventually produced "Cardinal Principles of the Christian Church," which reflected the sentiments expressed when it first began, as well as the ideal of the Stone-Campbell Movement generally which it antedated by a decade or more. The principles are:

1. The Lord Jesus Christ is the only Head of the Church.
2. The name Christian to the exclusion of all party and sectarian names.
3. The Holy Bible, or the Scriptures of the Old and New Testament our only creed, and a sufficient rule of faith and purpose.
4. Christian character, or vital piety, the only test of church fellowship and membership.
5. The right of private judgment, and the liberty of conscience, the privilege and duty of all.
6. The union of all Christians to the end that the world may believe.[18]

It is remarkable that these frontier people, so soon emerging from an austere sectarian situation, should come up with a document as thoroughly ecumenical as this one. It could be argued that this document states the ideals of the Movement more effectively, and certainly more concisely, than either the *Last Will and Testament of the Springfield Presbytery* or *The Declaration and Address*, which we are yet to consider. To say the least it deserves a place alongside them. But this document has been neglected by the historians, if not ignored, just as James O'Kelly and Rice Haggard have not been accorded their proper place.

The document is persuasively positive, stating with disarming brevity what the Christian Church is for more than what it is against. Its first words focus on the Lord Jesus Christ as the only head of the church. It did not have to put down popes, councils, or even Bishop Asbury. If one accepts Christ as Lord how can he object to wearing the name Christian rather than a sectarian name? Its third principle states what virtually every creed in Christendom has recognized, the sufficiency of the Scriptures, even if it has not always been practiced.

The fourth principle would be questioned by some heirs of the Movement today in that it does not explicitly recognize baptism as the door into the church, a judgment that would have to be made about all the early documents of the Movement since none of them mention baptism. But this is to overlook what this early Christian Church discerned to be the vital mark of the Christian and consequently of the church, *Christlikeness*. Their Wesleyan background had bequeathed to them the ideal of vital piety. They would likely say that baptism itself is not sufficient for fellowship in the church, but clear evidence of Christian character as well.

Since they practiced baptism by sprinkling, as they had done as Methodists, they would probably say that their fourth principle takes baptism for granted. They eventually accepted baptism by immersion to the extent that they became associated with Barton W. Stone's movement. The fourth principle says that there can be no true Christian Church and no real fellowship in Christ apart from vital piety and Christlikeness, and if there is to be any test made for membership and fellowship in the Body, this should be it.

Perhaps more than any other ideal the fifth principle came to be the hallmark of the Stone-Campbell Movement, articulated especially by Alexander Campbell, and here it was set forth and acted upon by people in the 1790's who for the most part did not live even to hear of Alexander Campbell, who was then a seven-year-old lad back in Ireland. Opinions may be freely held, the leaders would readily grant, but they cannot be imposed upon others or made tests of fellowship.

The Movement would soon have a motto, *In essentials unity, in non-essentials liberty, in all things love.* O'Kelly and his people wrote the prelude to that motto. The principle of the right of private judgment and the liberty of conscience was born of uneducated, frontier people in the throes of religious depotism.

James O'Kelly lived on to a ripe old age, ever serving the Christian Church. He travelled mostly by gig, planting new churches and confirming old ones. Many of his preachers and churches came from the Methodists in the years immediately following 1794, but by no means all. The church's periodical, the *Herald of Gospel Liberty*, estimated its membership in 1808 at 20,000 in the southern and western states, which by this time would have included some of the Stone churches.[19]

O'Kelly wrote an Apology, which is similar in name and purpose to one later produced by Barton W. Stone and his fellow Presbyterians, a large part of which is reproduced in MacClenny's biography of O'Kelly. The book also has samples of O'Kelly's other writings, including some pungent remarks on Christian unity.

Surprisingly, MacClenny finds evidence of friendship between O'Kelly and Thomas Jefferson. He reports that Jefferson arranged for O'Kelly to preach in the House of Representatives. The sermon was so moving that "Mr. Jefferson arose with tears in his eyes, and said, that while he was no preacher, in his opinion James O'Kelly was one of the greatest preachers living."[20]

In his *Apology* O'Kelly stated that "God hath showed me what is good; and I have striven to do justly, love mercy, and walk humbly," and in his will he bequeathed his body and soul back to God who had given him his sojourn upon the earth "in full assurance of a resurrection and a comfortable hope of acceptance."

The church O'Kelly formed eventually joined forces with the Stone movement and became known as "the Christian Connection." The Methodist historian is therefore wrong who says that O'Kelly's church divided and subdivided until they did not know what they believed.[21] Insofar as we know there was never any personal contact between O'Kelly and Stone. The most important influence on Stone from the Christian Church leadership was in the person of Rice Haggard.

Rice Haggard
"Let none be expelled but for a breach of the divine law."

Should you ask Rice Haggard what would be Satan's most effective device against the church on earth, he would have a ready answer: "To me it appears, that if the wisdom and subtlety of all the devils in hell had been engaged in ceaseless counsels from eternity, they could not have devised a more complete plan to advance their kingdom than to divide the members of Christ's body."

He also pointed to the principle of "In opinions liberty" in trenchant terms: "One thing I know, that wherever non-essentials are made terms of communion, it will never fail to have a tendency to disunite and scatter the church of Christ."[22]

These pungent lines come from a 31-page booklet by Rice Haggard in 1804, which was lost to historians until it was discovered by John W. Neth of Milligan College in 1953. Republished by the Disciples of Christ Historical Society in 1954, it now takes its rightful place as one of the most important documents in the Movement's history. We have seen how Haggard persuaded O'Kelly's new church to take the name Christian, and we shall see that he later had the same effect upon the Barton W. Stone people.

The *Address* sets forth his reasons for urging the adoption of the name Christian. It is also an appeal for unity, setting forth some of the same principles that were afterwards proposed by the Campbells.

These facts show that the O'Kelly-Haggard movement not only held primacy over the Stone and Campbell movements in terms of time, but that it was also first in producing an ecumenical document of substantial import, and one that set forth the principles of reformation that came to characterize the Movement.

While the *Address* is a plea for unity, its purpose was to persuade the "different religious societies" to adopt the name Christian. The way to unity, according to Haggard, is for all parties to discard their sectarian names and to wear the name that God gave his church. In recovering the name, he said, the churches might also recover "the thing," that is, what it really means to be a Christian.

He makes several arguments for the name Christian: (1) it is a patronymic name in that it descends from Christ himself; (2) it is a catholic name in that it is the one name that all can agree to wear, for as Haggard put it, "He who broke down the middle wall of partition has taken away partition names, and united all his followers in his own name, as one common denomination; (3) it was given by divine authority as indicated in Acts 11:26: "The disciples were called Christians first in Antioch."

He also referred to Acts 26:28, where Agrippa said to Paul, "Almost thou persuadest me to be a Christian," and to 1 Pet. 4:16, "If any man suffer as a Christian, let him not be ashamed; but let him glorify God on this behalf." It is therefore "the ancient and proper name for the church." He explained how sectarian names came about: "Each party liked the other so little, they were not content to be known by the same name. Hence it came to pass that each espoused the name by which they chose to be distinguished from the rest."[23]

As Haggard accounted for the rise of partyism, he expressed surprise "that things which will be granted not essential to the salvation of the soul should so long have been made terms of communion." It may be granted that the person is true to *the faith* and exemplary in character, and yet he cannot be accepted into the church, or if he is in the church, he may be excommunicated because he has not complied with "all the punctilious of our party," he complained.

As Thomas Campbell was to do later, Haggard pinpoints the evils of partyism, which he found evident in his day. Some of these are: (1) each party supposes that while others may be partly right it is altogether right, which fosters pride and ambition in itself and a disdain for others; (2) a great deal of time is spent in "inventing and vending" arguments so as to draw people from one party to another; (3) a party puts more importance on conforming to its distinctive features, such as its form of government or discipline, than to Christian character, so that drunkenness and lying are more likely to escape the censure of the church than infractions of party standards; (4) one tends to support only his own party and to weaken the rest, even to forbidding them to do good; (5) in a given town there are several struggling assemblies at variance with each other, when they should be together, and each supposes that it has God on its side to the exclusion of all the others.

Again like Thomas Campbell in the *Declaration and Address*, as we shall note in chapter 5, Haggard treats the cause of division, showing how it can be removed. He observes that there is no instance of "the church of Christ" ever dividing when each side strictly adhered to the word of God. If that sounds like begging the question, he goes on to say: "It is a fact confirmed by history and observation that the more closely any body of Christians adhere to the word of God as the only standard of faith and practice the more firm and lasting will their union be."[24]

In appealing to the Bible as "the only standard of faith and practice," which became a hallmark of the Movement, Haggard antedated both Stone and the Campbells. He also outlines a plan for unity that is strikingly similar to that of Thomas Campbell:

1. We are to worship one God, for to do more is idolatry.
2. Acknowledge one Savior, Jesus Christ, for there is no other.
3. Let the Bible be the one and only confession of faith.
4. Let us have one form of discipline and government, and let this be the New Testament. The Old Testament is necessary as a guide to

our faith, and it leads us to the New Testament, which is the constitution of the Christian Church.

5. Let all Christians consider themselves members one of another, for
   they are knit together by joints and bands, with Christ himself as
   head.

6. All Christians ought to be members of one church, for there is but
   one foundation, which is Christ. And the name of this body origi-
   nates from its head, which makes it "the Christian Church or the
   Church of Christ."

7. Let us all profess one religion. If that be the religion of Jesus Christ,
   then let it be called by his name.

8. Let none be received as members of the church but such as are
   made alive in Christ, for the Lord's temple is built of lively stones, a
   spiritual house.[25]

He concludes his plan of unity by urging: "Let none be excommunicated from the church but for a breach of the divine law." Since each one
is grafted into the vine by faith, it is only sin that can separate him from
God. He challenges those who would draw lines of fellowship on other
grounds: "Where is the man or set of men who hold a divine charter to
forbid communion, or cut off from the church militant, those who hold
communion with God and are fit candidates for the church triumphant?"

Thomas Campbell was soon to emphasize the same in his *Declaration
and Address*: "No man has a right to judge, to exclude, or reject his professing Christian brother, except insofar as he stands condemned or rejected by
the express letter of the law." Both men came to see that it was the imposition of opinions (non-essentials) as if they are the express word of God,
making them terms of fellowship, that causes division. This call for freedom
of opinion and a communion based only upon what the Scriptures expressly
teach was to become the genius of the Stone-Campbell Movement.

The heirs of that Movement had no way of realizing, until this *Address*
was found in 1953, that this insight goes all the way back to the obscure
Rice Haggard. And to see how he put his finger on the problem of division:
*Whenever non-essentials or opinions are made terms of communion it
always tends to divide the church of Christ.* It not only serves to lay bare
the nature of division in Haggard's own day, but it helps to explain its
persistent presence in every generation of the church.

Haggard had a way with words and conciseness was one of his virtues,
as for example: "Nothing is a sin but what the Scriptures forbid, and nothing a duty but what they enjoin." This may be a debatable hermeneutics
and is more Calvinistic than Lutheran, but it is certainly a call for a more

inclusive fellowship. He is saying that judgments must be drawn from what the Scriptures actually teach, not deductions based upon presumptions.

Haggard did not put his name or even a *nom de plume* to the *Address*, which made its discovery all the more difficult, but he did say a word about himself in the preface: "(The author) considers himself connected with no party, nor wishes to be known by the name of any — he feels himself united to that *one body* of which *Christ is the head*, and all his people fellow members." The lone clue that such a document existed appeared in Stone's autobiography where, in explaining how his people eventually took the name Christian, says: "We published a pamphlet on this name, written by Elder Rice Haggard, who had lately united with us."[26]

This self-imposed obscurity did not allow for the preservation of much information about him. From the outset historians have credited Rice Haggard with providing the name Christian for O'Kelly's new church, garnered from the Methodists, in 1794, and that ten years later he did the same for Stone's new group, which emerged from the Presbyterians.

Haggard has therefore the distinction of naming two new groups of believers, thus establishing himself as one of the founders of what came to be known as the Christian Connection, a fusion of the different Christian Churches under O'Kelly and Stone. The discovery of his *Address* enhances his role in history all the more. Even though there has been considerable research in recent years on his life and work, the information remains slim.

The late Colby D. Hall of Texas Christian University, motivated by the finding of Haggard's tract, published in 1957 a study of Rice Haggard, "the frontier evangelist who revived the name Christian." This little volume summarizes several research projects on Haggard back through the years, the most notable being J.P. Barrett's *The Centennial of Religious Journalism* in 1908.

This is a study of the *Herald of Gospel Liberty*, the first religious newspaper in America, edited by Elias Smith, which has tucked away in its faded columns some information on Rice Haggard. It was here that John Neth first discovered Haggard's *Address*, republished in its volumes for 1808-09, which enabled him eventually to find a copy of the original pamphlet.

These sources reveal that Haggard was born in Virginia about 1769, and at age 22 was ordained by Bishop Asbury himself. He became one of Asbury's circuit riders, with all its attending hardships. He was a companion of James O'Kelly and stood by him in his break with Asbury, which led to the formation of the Republican Methodist Church.

We have observed that it was Haggard who stood before the new church and pointed to the New Testament as the only sufficient rule of faith and practice, and how he moved that they call themselves "Christians simply." His motion was unanimously adopted, thus creating the first Christian Church in America, August 4, 1794.

In 1804 Haggard was with Stone at Cane Ridge, Ky. where he named his second church "the divine name," but not for long, for in 1807 he was back in Norfolk, Va., near where he was born. Since he died at age 50, he had but twelve more years to live. He spent those years laboring among Christian Churches. His widow survived him by 43 years, and at her death in 1862 Isaac T. Reneau wrote an obituary for Campbell's journal, in which he said that Rice Haggard, one of those pioneers to be remembered, along with his wife, "held quite a conspicuous position in this part of Kentucky."

Reneau further reveals that Haggard was well educated for his time, and that he united with Stone so as to "prepare the way for reformation." He not only refers to Haggard's essay on the Christian name but also says that he was the first among the reformers to publish a hymnal (1818).[27]

Colby D. Hall concludes his study of Haggard with this assurance:

> Above all, we know that he aroused his generation to the genuineness and value of his "big idea," the exaltation of the name Christian. We know he was faithful to "the name that is above every name." True it is that this name has been slow of general acceptance. How Rice Haggard would have rejoiced if he could have lived into the twentieth century when the name is gradually coming into its own![28]

Elias Smith and Abner Jones

Robert Richardson refers to the Smith-Jones movement as "the Eastern branch of the Christian Connection,"[29] the other branches being the O'Kelly-Haggard and the Stone movements. This cannot mean, however, that there was ever a "connection" in the sense of union or cooperation, or even that there was substantial contact between the Eastern effort and the other two.

We have learned that the O'Kelly Christian Churches influenced the Stone group through Rice Haggard, and we may conclude that many of the O'Kelly churches gradually became identified with Stone and ultimately with Campbell. But there is no evidence that this was the case with the Smith-Jones movement.

Smith (1769-1846) and Jones (1772-1841) were Baptists who rebelled against Calvinism and led their churches into independency in 1801, Smith in New Hampshire and Jones in Vermont. They took the name Christian and called their congregations Christian Churches, which eventually numbered fourteen. While they remained immersionists, they did not come up with a new interpretation of baptism. While it is significant that they called themselves Christians and their congregations Christian Churches, they had little else in common with the other groups. They were not a unity movement and there is no evidence that their concern was to restore primitive Christianity.

Campbell corresponded with some of their leaders and concluded that his efforts and theirs had little in common.

The freedom and independence of frontier religion encouraged separatism, and there are numerous instances of one church or several breaking with the establishment, some of these taking the name "Christian" or "Church of Christ" who had no connection with the Stone-Campbell Movement or its forerunners. Some Baptist churches in Indiana and North Carolina became "Churches of Christ" in their search for "original ground," but nothing ever came of it. An association of twelve Baptist churches in Kentucky were "constituted on the Bible," but they did not become a movement such as we are describing.

We find no distinctive kinship between such groups and the Stone-Campbell Movement unless they were either a unity effort, a movement to restore the primitive faith, or a people resolved to reform the church and its institutions, such as baptism and the Lord's Supper. There was, for instance, a single Baptist church in Indiana, which was the oldest in the state (1798), that became The Church of Christ on Owen's Creek, and went on to accept the teachings of Alexander Campbell and to become part of the Movement.

But there was a nominal connection with the Smith-Jones churches. We have noted that Elias Smith republished Haggard's essay on the Christian name in his *Herald of Gospel Liberty*. And in 1828 Barton W. Stone estimated "the sect called Christians" to have 150,000 members and 1,500 churches, which must have included all three Christian groups, albeit, as we have seen, his figure was excessive.[30] It reveals, however, that the three groups saw themselves as involved in the same enterprise.

So we conclude with W.E. Garrison that there was "very little mutual acquaintance" between the Smith-Jones churches and those of O'Kelly-Stone and that despite the efforts of some historians to make it otherwise there was nothing that approximated an organic union between them. But still they were aware of each other and there were some meaningful contacts.

As Garrison notes, William Guirey, who became a zealous immersionist and separated a group known as "Independent Christian Baptist" from others of the Connection in Virginia who still practiced affusion, was influenced by the New England Christians. Guirey in turn made an immersionist of Joseph Thomas, the "White Pilgrim," who started Christian churches in Virginia that eventually identified with the Movement.

There is also evidence of some influence on the Stone people by New England evangelists who travelled in the South, but when Stone invited them to share in the union with Campbell, the response was negative.[31]

Part of what is now the United Church of Christ was previously the Congregational Christian Church, and part of that was the Christian Church of the old Christian Connection that did not identify with the Campbell movement. Stone led a substantial part of the Christian Connection into union with Campbell, but those who considered such a union a mistake continued as a separate Christian Church. In 1908 this group published a *Centennial of Religious Journalism*, a book by J.P. Barrett that celebrated a century of Elias Smith's journal. This book included a biography of Rice Haggard by J.J. Summerbell.[32]

This indicates that after a century the remnant of the old Christian Connection felt an historic affinity with Elias Smith and the New England Christians, as well as with Rice Haggard and the Kentucky Christians. But these people were always cool toward the Campbell movement, believing that it had corrupted and decimated the Christian Churches.

ENDNOTES

[1]See his book by that title, (New York; Harper & Bro., 1931).

[2]Winthrop S. Hudson, *Religion in America* (New York: MacMillan, 1987), pp. 128-129.

[3]William Warren Sweet, *The Story of Religion In America* (New York: Harper, 1935), p. 206.

[4]Edwin S. Gaustad, *A Religious History of America*, New Revised Edition (San Francisco: Harper, 1990), p. 58.

[5]*Ibid.*, p. 325.

[6]*Ibid.*, p. 145.

[7]Arthur K. Moore, *The Frontier Mind* (Lexington: University of Kentucky Press, 1957), pp. 48, 67.

[8]*Ibid.*, p. 154.

[9]R.C. Buley, *The Old Northwest*, Vol. 1 (Bloomington: University of Indiana Press, 1951), p. 139.

[10]The essays, entitled "The Coming of The Lord," were in response to Miller's views and published in the *Millennial Harbinger* from 1841-43.

[11]Halford E. Luccock and Paul Hutchinson, *The Story of Methodism* (New York: Methodist Book Concern, 1926), p. 178.

[12]The most important source on O'Kelly is W. E. MacClenny, *The Life of Rev. James O'Kelly and the History of the Christian Church in the South*, originally published in 1910, republished by Religious Book Service, Indianapolis, 1950.

[13]*Ibid.*, p. 246.

[14]On Asbury see especially L. C. Rudolph, *Francis Asbury*, Nashville: Abingdon, 1966.

[15]W. E. MacClenney, *James O'Kelly*, p. 88.

[16]Luccock and Hutchinson, *Story of Methodism*, p. 323.

[17]W. E. MacClenney, *James O'Kelly*, p. 116.

[18]*Ibid.*, p. 121. See also William T. Scott, "A Brief History of the Christian Denomination," *Christian Sun* (Richmond, VA), April 26, 1956, p. 3.

[19]*Ibid.*, p. 148.

[20]*Ibid.*, p. 171.

[21]Buckley's *History of Methodism*, Vol. 1, p. 343.

[22]Rice Haggard, *An Address to the Different Religious Societies on the Sacred Import of the Christian Name*, Nashville: Disciples of Christ Historical Society, 1954 (Originally published in Lexington, KY, 1804).

[23]*Ibid.*, p. 18.

[24]*Ibid.*, p. 23.

[25]*Ibid.*, pp. 23-25.

[26]John Rogers, *Biography of Barton W. Stone*, Cincinnati, 1847, p. 50.

[27]*Millennial Harbinger*, 1863, p. 94.

[28]Colby N. Hall, *Rice Haggard* (Ft. Worth: T.C.U. Press, 1957), p. 46.

[29]Robert Richardson, *Memoirs of Alexander Campbell*, II, p. 474.

[30]*Christian Messenger*, Vol. 3(1828), pp. 189f.

[31]Garrison and DeGroot, *The Disciples of Christ: A History*, pp. 114, 216, 270. On William Guirey see James B. North, *Union In Truth* (Cincinnati: Standard, 1994), pp. 19f.

[32]Colby N. Hall, *Rice Haggard*, p. 40.

4

BARTON W. STONE
THE MOVEMENT BEGINS

Let Christian unity be our polar star.

If the events up to this point have been prologue, then we can say that the Stone-Campbell Movement actually began with Barton W. Stone. If but one person is named, then it was he who was the founder of the Movement. If two persons are named, then Stone and Alexander Campbell were the founders. If multiple persons are named, then Thomas Campbell, Walter Scott, along with James O'Kelly and Rice Haggard would be listed, along with others whose stories are told in this book. To put it another way, there would have been no Movement such as we are recounting had it not been for Barton W. Stone and the events growing out of the great Cane Ridge Revival in 1804.

"I do, as far as I see it consistent with the word of God," answered the 26-year-old Barton W. Stone when he was asked by the Transylvania Presbytery of Kentucky if he received and adopted the Westminster Confession of Faith as containing the system of doctrine taught in the Bible. Even though it was an unorthodox answer, it was accepted by the Presbytery and Stone was ordained to the ministry in the fall of 1798.[1]

Born in Port Tobacco, Maryland on December 24, 1772, life had been difficult for young Barton. He recalls how as a lad he watched his older brothers leave home to fight in the Revolutionary War, and of hearing the sound of artillery as General Green and Lord Cornwallis met in mortal combat only 30 miles from his home. He was a frontiersman. He eluded marauding Indians as he crossed unexplored wilderness country in North Carolina and Tennessee. He made himself vulnerable to wild beasts as he bedded down at night far removed from civilization. When he passed within a few miles of Nashville in 1796, he noted that it was "a poor little village, hardly worth notice."[2]

It was unlikely that Stone ever made it to his own ordination service, for he backed out of being a preacher at least twice. He first resolved to be a member of the bar, entering Guilford Academy in North Carolina, now Guilford College, in 1790. From a boy he had one thing going for him, a

71

love for books. Wealth was not among his blessings, poverty stalking him all the days of his youth. When the small inheritance from his father, who died when Barton was a baby, was exhausted it looked as if he would have to quit school, but the schoolmaster, recognizing his potential, saw him through, allowing him to pay later.

It was while he was at Guilford that religion began to lay claim on him, which he strongly resisted, resolving at one point to slip away to Hampden-Sidney College in Virginia to escape it. Instead he associated with those students who made light of divine things, and joined with them in making fun of the pious. But his conscience would allow him no peace.

A year passed before Stone was at last converted, for even the great James McGready, who came to Guilford for a revival, failed to reach him. It was a young preacher, William Hodge, who spoke on "God is love" that supplied what was needed. He had heard so many preachers who "thundered divine anathemas" that Hodge's thesis on the love of God appeared to Stone as some new doctrine. E.E. Snoddy suggests that it was that sermon by Hodge that became "an anchor of his soul through his period of doubt and uncertainty, and was the formative factor in his attitude toward all men" and was partly responsible for Stone becoming an ambassador of the love of God.[3]

Moreover it led Stone to come to terms with the one concept that was destined to make him a reformer, the notion that man can believe upon hearing the gospel without waiting for a miracle to make it possible, which was then common in Calvinism. "I now saw," he observed after hearing Hodge, "that a poor sinner was as much authorized to believe in Jesus at first, as at last — that now was the accepted time, the day of salvation."[4]

But Calvinism almost did him in nonetheless. Embarrassed over what he called "many abstruse doctrines," he broke off his study of theology and resolved to engage in some other calling. Then came a siege of illness, including a fever he contracted while traveling home, now in Georgia, that might have been fatal save for the kindness of a stranger who bore him down from his horse unconscious and nursed him back to health.

After spending 1795 teaching languages in an academy in Washington, Georgia, his compulsion for the ministry was rekindled, though he continued to resist it. He nonetheless made his way back to North Carolina where he was licensed to preach by the Orange Presbytery and accepted an assignment to minister in the southern part of the state.

But again he backed off from it, supposing he was not qualified for such a solemn work. He slipped away, hopefully to some place where he would be a perfect stranger, leaving his preaching partner alone, only to be told by a pious old lady that he was doing a Jonah.

72

Stone did not really find himself as a preacher until he went to Kentucky, where he accepted two charges in Bourbon county, Concord and Cane Ridge, and resolved to settle down as a pastor and cease his wanderings. He applied himself more closely to reading and study. He enjoyed some needed success with some 80 additions in the two churches in the first few months. After some two years in this ministry the time came for him to be ordained by the Presbytery of Transylvania.

All along the Confession of Faith had been a problem to him, but now he renewed his study, trying to make himself accept its doctrines. Not only did he stumble at the doctrine of the Trinity, but he also had trouble with election, reprobation and predestination. In his preaching he had ignored the Confession, confining himself to the practical aspects of the faith. But now he had to face his superiors in the Presbytery, and he was supposed to believe things that he could not conscientiously accept.

He decided not to accept ordination, confiding his misgivings to two pillars of the Presbytery. When they were unsuccessful in removing his doubts, they asked him how far he was willing to go in accepting the Confession. When he stated that he would accept it insofar as it conformed to the word of God, they decided that that would do and went on with the ordination. When the moment of truth came and he was asked the big question before a large congregation, as to whether he would accept the Confession, he answered loudly so they could all hear him: "I do, as far as I see it consistent with the word of God."

That was not the way it usually went. Stone had crossed his Rubicon. He was a budding reformer within the established order, a fully ordained clergyman in the Presbyterian Church.

Cane Ridge Revival

If the biggest thing in Stone's life in 1801 was the great Cane Ridge revival, the event that must have been a close second was his marriage to Elizabeth Campbell. He was now 28, and this is the first evidence of any romance in his life. He had been too busy eluding robbers, Indians, poverty, and Calvinism to have had any time for girls in his life. He was so preoccupied in his autobiography with the revival that he gave only one unexciting line about Elizabeth: "My companion was pious, and much engaged in religion."

But it was more exciting than it sounds. He had managed to save $500.00 with which he had bought 100 acres of land some five miles from Cane Ridge. As was typical in those days, the neighbors had "lifted" a log cabin for him, perhaps in a single day, and it was to this humble abode that he brought his wife, straight from her father's house.

Here Elizabeth died nine years later after giving birth to Barton W. Stone, Jr., who also died. Her four daughters lived. Stone later married Celia Wilson Bowen, who bore him six more children. He had a total of 49 grandchildren, two of whom were playmates of Mark Twain in the streets of Hannibal, Missouri. One of Stone's sons was an officer in the Confederate army.[5]

The revival at Cane Ridge was as ecumenical as anything that had ever happened on the frontier, which was commonly marked with sectarian bigotry. Presbyterian, Methodist, and Baptist clergy, perhaps as many as 30 or 40, not only worked together "with more harmony than could be expected," but they forgot their confessions and creeds and preached the gospel. It was a suitable climate for the emergence of a unity movement, especially since it was the people themselves who were demanding a united effort.[6]

The size of the revival was estimated from 12,000 to 20,000, with Stone himself going as high as 30,000, a figure given by military men. The crowd was said to have been made up of all kinds, from the governor of the state to prostitutes, blacks as well as whites, the blackleg and the robber as well as the devout worshiper. It was a large open air meeting, or several meetings spread over an extended area, with several preachers discoursing at one time.[7]

The woods were filled with hundreds of vehicles and tents, creating a vast campground. It was an occasion for excitement and fervor, and for several days there were many phenomenal, incredible manifestations. Stone called them miracles, insisting that if they were not miracles, they had the same effects in that they caused many unbelievers to accept Jesus as the Christ.[8]

These "exercises," as they were called, consisted of laughing and singing, the jerks, dancing, falling, and even screaming and barking. Stone was impressed with their authenticity. While he did not personally experience any of them, he describes them in detail. The falling and screaming would sometimes go together, leaving the subject as if he were dead. The jerks was mostly a head movement, which sometimes agitated the whole body.

Stone reported that some of the people became amazingly acrobatic, for they would stand in one place and jerk backward and forward with their head almost touching the ground. He says the dancing was heavenly, as if accompanied by angels, and would continue until the subject fell over exhausted.

"Barking" was a description given in derision, for it was actually grunts that accompanied the jerks. Witnesses would see people on hands and knees in the woods, making this noise with uplifted hands, and would report that "they barked up trees like dogs."

It was the singing exercise that Stone considered the most inexplicable, for it came not from the mouth or nose but from the breast, the sound emanating from deep within, and it was heavenly. When he and a doctor friend attended one pious lady thus affected, they agreed that it was the most unusual thing they had witnessed in all of nature. Such exercises were done by the devout and unbelieving alike, the devout manifesting a concern for the lost and the unbelievers testifying to their repentance. It was a revival where the gospel was preached and where sinners turned to God, and it was this that gladdened Stone's heart most of all.

Stone was convinced that the "miracles" attested to God's presence and approval. Thirty years later in his *Christian Messenger* he recounted what the great revival had meant to him, explaining that it enabled him to see the effects of the religion of Jesus in people's lives more than ever before.[9]

The Cane Ridge revival was part of the Second Awakening or Great Western Revival that had its roots in the Great Awakening in New England under Jonathan Edwards a half century earlier. But one historian likens the earlier revival to "a backyard bonfire" in comparison to the conflagration that swept through Tennessee and Kentucky in the early 1800's. Another has called it "America's Pentecost."[10]

It was a spiritual face lift to the frontier churches who were struggling for existence amidst a rapidly growing population in which only a small percentage professed church membership. Sensualism and secularism permeated society in general while sectarianism and indifference blighted the churches in particular. Preachers like Barton W. Stone longed for a revival, and it came with a vengeance and with the thunderous cries of the likes of James McGready.

The revival not only meant spiritual renewal for the churches, but their numbers increased significantly, some congregations gaining hundreds of new members. Moreover the revival served as a catalyst in initiating a movement to unite the Christians in all the sects.

Apology of the Springfield Presbytery

Cane Ridge not only had ecumenical implications in that ministers of all faiths preached the same gospel and reaped the same harvest, but there was anti-Calvinism in its appeal that "Christ died for all men" and not only for "the elect." This brought opposition from orthodox circles of Presbyterians, and some of their ministers, who were caught up in the spirit of Cane Ridge, soon found themselves in trouble, Richard McNemar and John Thompson in particular, though there were several "revival men" who were suspect.

Charges against McNemar began in the Presbytery of Washington, Kentucky and slowly made their way to the Synod of Kentucky, sitting at Lexington in 1803. By that time John Thompson of Springfield, Ohio became implicated in the charges. The case against them was that they were teaching contrary to the Confession of Faith, and the first step for the Kentucky Synod to take was to bring them to trial.

While the question of bringing McNemar and Thompson to trial was being debated on the floor, the two men withdrew to draw up a protest over what was taking place. They were now joined by three other Presbyterian ministers, Robert Marshall, John Dunlavy, and Barton W. Stone. These five were the most eminent among the "revival men" and were respected by their peers, Marshall being the clerk of the synod.

The "Protest" that they delivered to the moderator, in which they withdrew themselves from the jurisdiction of the Kentucky Synod, later became part of *The Apology of the Springfield Presbytery*. It stands as the first of the important documents produced by the Stone-Campbell Movement. This "Protest," which was signed by these five men on September 10, 1803, may be even more significant than *The Last Will and Testament of the Springfield Presbytery*, which was composed almost a year later.

This is true not only because the "Protest" is the Movement's first declaration of freedom from ecclesiastical control, but also because it proclaims the right of free men to interpret the Scriptures for themselves and to base their faith upon the Bible alone, apart from the opinions of men.

The document is also significant in that it reveals the irenic spirit these men manifested amidst controversy. In revealing both the temper and principle of the Movement, the "Protest" is second in importance only to Thomas Campbell's *Declaration and Address*. It is not as well known as it should be.

Even though *The Apology of the Springfield Presbytery* consumes 100 pages of Stone's autobiography, the "Protest" itself takes barely two pages, and it was this that the five men prepared while the synod recessed and then presented to the moderator. It began by saying:

> "*Reverend Sir*: We, the underwritten members of Washington and W. Lexington Presbyteries, do hereby enter our protest against the proceedings of Synod, in approbating that minute of the Washington Presbytery which condemned the sentiments of Mr. McNemar as dangerous to the souls of

men, and hostile to the interests of true religion, and the proceedings therewith connected; and for reasons which we now offer, we declare ourselves no longer members of your reverend body, or under your jurisdiction, or that of your Presbyteries."

They go on to assert their right to interpret the Scriptures for themselves, even as the Confession of Faith itself allows, and that the Supreme Judge must be the Spirit speaking in the Bible rather than the decrees of councils or the opinions of men. Referring to the judgmental action of the synod, they add: "From the disposition which Synod manifests, it appears to us that we cannot enjoy this privilege, but must be bound up to such explanations of the word of God, as preclude all further inquiry after truth."

They affirm their loyalty to those "doctrines of grace" which have inspired every revival since the Reformation, but they add, so as not to neglect the creed in question, that these doctrines are "darkened by some expressions in the Confession of Faith, which are used as the means of strengthening sinners in their unbelief, and subjecting many of the pious to a spirit of bondage."

Like Socrates on trial before the Athenians, they suggest that they should have been supported in their efforts to resolve the difficulties of the Confession, but that they have instead been hauled into court as disturbers of the peace. They conclude that their only recourse is to relieve the synod of the disagreeable task of trying them by withdrawing themselves from its control.

These were, of course, fighting words, and it may not have helped much when they added: "Our affection for you, as brethren in the Lord, is, and we hope shall be ever the same: nor do we desire to separate from your communion, or to exclude you from ours."

They went on to set forth a principle for unity between people who disagree that was to become a hallmark of the Movement: "We ever wish to bear, and forbear, in matters of human order, or opinion, and unite our joint supplications with yours, for the increasing effusions of that divine Spirit, which is the bond of peace."

They expressed hope that in the providence of God the synod would soon adopt a more liberal plan in reference to creeds and confessions. They then bade them adieu. The synod afterwards sent a committee to confer with the dissidents in an effort to reclaim them, but one of the committee was converted to their side. After other efforts proved futile the synod finally suspended the five ministers. It sent committees to their churches to read the bull of suspension and to declare the pulpits vacant.

Since Stone was not ordained upon an unconditional acceptance of the

Confession, he claimed that it was unfair to defrock him for teaching things contrary to it. The other four likewise considered the synod's action invalid in that they had already removed themselves from its jurisdiction.

The "Protest" reveals that these founding pioneers of the Movement had no intention of being separatists. They did not presume themselves to be right and everyone else wrong. They were not even withdrawing fellowship from anyone. They simply wanted to be free to interpret the Scriptures for themselves without threat or reprimand. That it still pleased them at this juncture to be Presbyterians is evident from the fact that they proceeded to organize a presbytery of their own, which they called the Springfield Presbytery.

It is important to see that Stone and his colleagues would have never gone independent if diversity of interpretation had been allowed. *Theirs was a protest against a demand for conformity based upon a creed.* Still they were irenic and cooperative. Stone revealed years later that they offered to return to the jurisdiction of the synod if they were allowed to function as a separate presbytery, to which there was no reply.[11]

Their short-lived presbytery was hardly a presbytery in terms of Presbyterian judicatory. It was never formally organized, having neither structure nor officers. There were not even any member churches or representatives from churches. It was no more than a small group of Presbyterian ministers who were bound together by common purposes.

The only thing they did of significance was to produce two documents. Besides *The Apology of the Springfield Presbytery* there was *The Last Will and Testament of the Springfield Presbytery*, which was the document that laid to rest the presbytery they had created.

The first document was sent out in pamphlet form to the churches as an explanation and a defense of their withdrawal from the synod. The names of all five men appeared on the pamphlet, but it was written by only three of them, Marshall, Thompson, and Stone. The document anticipates some of those principles that came to characterize the Movement, such as its rejection of creeds. It predicts that creeds will eventually be given to the moles and bats. The document makes it clear that the five men do not make their objections to the Confession a test of communion, which is expressive of the more open view toward fellowship that the initiators of the Movement always took.

The document also stated Stone's position that faith is produced by hearing the gospel, along with his rejection of the doctrine that the sinner must be miraculously regenerated before he can believe. This was strikingly similar to what Alexander Campbell was to say a few years later.

The Apology was widely circulated, creating both support and opposition for the fledgling reformation. Stone informs us that "The presses were employed, and teemed forth pamphlets against us, full of misrepresentation and invective and the pulpits everywhere echoed their contents." It was the kind of advertising they needed. The opposition was so bitter that it created sympathy for the dissenters, and the curious were eager to find out what it was all about.[12]

In Virginia the Methodists republished *The Apology* since it was against the Presbyterians, but they omitted the section against the creeds! The reformers began to enjoy some success, especially when David Purviance, another influencial Presbyterian minister, came over to their side. His name will be found as the sixth signature on the second document they produced.

The Apology has had some influence in recent history in that W.W. Sweet included the "Protest" as selective reading in his *Religion on the American Frontier.*[13]

Last Will and Testament of the Springfield Presbytery

Soon after his separation from the synod, Stone went before his congregations to explain why he could no longer preach among them as a Presbyterian. "My labors should henceforth be directed to advance the Redeemer's kingdom, irrespective of party," he told them, and proceeded to relieve them of their salary obligation to him, tearing up the contract in their presence. But he assured them that he would continue to preach among them, though not on the same basis as before.[14]

This radical change in his life also led him to emancipate his slaves. Now without either salary or laborers, he turned to his little farm as a means of livelihood as he continued to preach far and wide, almost as much as before. Often when he returned home he would find the grass getting ahead of the corn, and he would work in the field at night in order to redeem the time. He was a poor man, but he was free.

There is some ambiguity as to why the Springfield Presbytery was laid to rest in less than a year after its creation. F.D. Kershner's explanation that "its proponents soon discovered that the New Testament contains no more reference to a presbytery than it does a creed" is not adequate, even though the six men in their *Address* stated that they could find neither precept nor example in the New Testament for the likes of presbyteries and synods.[15]

They had already stated their willingness to remain in the synod as a presbytery if allowed to interpret the Scriptures for themselves. It is, therefore, unlikely that they so soon objected to such organizations *per se*, but to their sectarian character.

As they stated in the *Address*, that while the presbytery they had created provided unity for themselves, it nonetheless made them "a party separate from others." This confirms what Stone wrote in his *Biography* afterwards, that "we had not worn our name more than one year, before we saw it savored of a party spirit." So, as he put it, "With the man-made creeds we threw it overboard and took the name Christian."

So, the early demise of the Springfield Presbytery was further expression of their passion to shed all marks of sectarianism, lest they be "a party separate from others." Now wearing only the name Christian, which they saw as the way to unity, they could plead in their *Address* for the universal spread of the gospel and the unity of the church while saying "We heartily unite with our Christian brethren of every name."[16]

This gave birth to *The Last Will and Testament of the Springfield Presbytery*, June 28, 1804, the date Stone chose for the beginning of his reformation and a suitable one for the origin of the Christian Church and the beginning of the Stone-Campbell Movement. The document is as important for the circumstance that called it forth as for what it said, for it was a charter for a new kind of church, one that based its faith and order upon the Bible alone.

It was when they denounced human names and creeds, Stone tells us, that persecution became intense. But they grew rapidly and came to be known as the Christian Church or the Church of Christ. *The Last Will and Testament*, along with the "Protest" and Haggard's pamphlet on the Christian name, points up the theological literacy of the new church.

Garrison says the document was "whimsically phrased"[17] and Kershner describes it as "delightfully ironical."[18] It is true that one might miss the nuances if he does not recognize in some of its lines a playful attitude. This paragraph, for instance, has a touch of both humor and sarcasm:

> We will that the Synod of Kentucky examine every member, who may be suspected of having departed from the Confession of Faith, and suspend every such suspected heretic immediately, in order that the oppressed may go free, and taste the sweets of gospel liberty.

The opening paragraph may be intentionally overdrawn, making it appear that their small group is enacting some great unfolding drama, which may be intended as a put-down of the pomp and arrogance of ecclesiastical structures:

> THE PRESBYTERY OF SPRINGFIELD, sitting at Cane-ridge, in the county of Bourbon, being, through a gracious Providence, in more than ordinary bodily health, growing in strength and size daily; and in perfect soundness

and composure of mind; but knowing what it is appointed for all delegated bodies once to die: and considering that the life of every such body is very uncertain, do take, and ordain this our last Will and Testament, in manner and form following, viz.:[19]

But nothing could be more serious than their *Imprimis,* meaning "in the first place," which reads: "We will that this body die, be dissolved, and sink into union with the Body of Christ at large, for there is but one Body, and one Spirit, even as we are called in one hope of our calling." This stands as one of the great unity principles in the history of the Movement. It indicates that almost from the outset the Stone people had a concern for the oneness of the church, even though it was not this concern that originally motivated them to be reformers.

It also shows that they understood, as Thomas Campbell soon afterwards did, that the Church of Christ upon earth already existed and was by its very nature one, apart from their own efforts. They began as a *freedom* movement, not a unity movement. But the influence of Cane Ridge with its ecumenical emphasis was such that the unity of all believers came to be a corollary to their thinking on Christian liberty.

This is indicated not only by their *Imprimis* but by the "Address" that they issued along with *The Last Will and Testament.* In it they expressed their desire to unite with Christians of every name, persuaded as they were that such unity would "terminate in the universal spread of the gospel." If they began with a passion to be free, they soon had a passion to unite. They were saying that if the church is free of creedalism and partyism it will become a united church.

These sentiments also reveal that while they now chose to be Christians only, they had no illusion of being the only Christians. They readily acknowledged "Christian brethren of every name" and sought to be one with them, though this was not yet a major objective. Another impressive line in the document that would be relevant to any age was: "We will that preachers and people cultivate a spirit of mutual forbearance, and pray more and dispute less."

Two of the items in *The Last Will and Testament* reflect their commitment to congregational polity: "We will that the church of Christ resume her native right of internal government — try her candidates for the ministry," and "We will that each particular church, as a body, actuated by the same spirit, choose her own preacher, and support him by a free will offering . . and never henceforth *delegate* her right of government to any man or set of men whatever." This aversion for ecclesiasticism and passion for self-rule came to characterize the Movement in all its persuasions for all time to come.

Stone had his problems with the new church almost before it got started. Of the five ministers who walked out on the Presbyterians and created the Springfield Presbytery, he was the only one left by 1811. In 1805 McNemar and Dunlavy joined the Shakers when they invaded Kentucky with a flair of new doctrine, an intrusion that disturbed Stone more than it needed to since the losses were not great.

In 1811 Marshall and Thompson publicly repudiated their "errors" and returned to the Presbyterians. All this caused Stone to double his efforts to save his reformation, working harder than he had in all his life, as he put it, even to the point of stalking the Shakers wherever they went, debating them into defeat.

He was well rewarded, for he continued gaining in both preachers and members, growing at least as rapidly as other churches on the frontier. In 1804 he had but a few hundred members in 15 congregations in Kentucky and Ohio. By 1826 he could count 15,000 members in 300 congregations.

Stone and Alexander Campbell

Beginning in 1823 Alexander Campbell made 14 trips to Kentucky during his long traveling ministry. On his second visit in 1824 he met Stone for the first time, and from then on they saw each other frequently. When together they conversed at length; when separated they carried on a vigorous correspondence, often disagreeing. In afteryears Stone handed Campbell an impressive compliment: "I will not say there are no faults in brother Campbell; but that there are fewer, perhaps, in him than any man I know on earth; and over these my love would throw a veil and hide them from view forever."

He goes on to say of Campbell: "I am constrained, and willingly constrained, to acknowledge him the greatest preacher of this reformation of any man living. The Lord reward him!"[20] This provides a clue as to why the Stone and Campbell people were able to join forces and present a united front for their common cause. Though Stone was 15 years older than Campbell and had begun the Movement while Campbell was yet a teenager back in Ireland, he nonetheless relinquished his right of leadership to the man he considered abler than himself. Richardson says that Stone's reformation was "almost identical" with that of Campbell's, and that the two men formed a warm, personal attachment to each other that lasted through life. He concludes that it was their friendship that made possible the subsequent union between the two movements.[21]

Yet there was some unevenness in their relationship, as could be expected between two strong leaders of separate energetic movements.

This was disconcerting to some of their colaborers. An editor in Tennessee complained that "There seems to be an unnecessary jealousy existing among some of our brethren in regard to whom credit is due in commencing the present Reformation, father Stone[22] or brother Campbell."[23]

The claim to priority was however the least of their disputes. One practical difference was whether those within the Movement should be called Christians, which Stone adamantly insisted upon, or Disciples, which Campbell strongly favored. The dispute resolved itself by the use of both names.

Another serious difference was the practice of open Communion, though they did not then call it that. Stone believed that Communion was for all believers, while Campbell, even though he professed a "We neither invite nor debar" position, believed that only immersed believers should take the Lord's Supper. While this issue was never resolved and has been a point of conflict throughout the Movement's history, it too was practiced both ways in the early days.

Behind the Communion question was a more fundamental difference, baptism by immersion as a test of fellowship. Both men repudiated their infant sprinkling by being immersed as adults, but Stone was unwilling to make immersion a test of church membership and Communion while Campbell was, at least in his earlier years. Stone believed that baptism by immersion was ordained of God, but he was unwilling to make it the *sine qua non* (absolutely essential) of the Christian faith, as Campbell appeared to.

As for the practice of rebaptizing those who were not consciously baptized "for the remission of sins," which some of the Campbell people insisted upon without his approval, and which continues to be an issue to this day, Stone wrote:

> To assert that none but such as have been immersed for the remission of sins are members of the Church of Christ is to assert that Christ has had no church on earth for many centuries back: for but a few years ago had the old apostolic doctrine of baptism for remission been revived.[24]

Stone urged forbearance toward those who remain unconvinced of the truth of baptism by immersion, a position that Campbell later took in his now famous Lunenburg Letter (1837). But in those years leading up to the union of the Stone and Campbell churches in 1832 it was a serious point of difference. The Stone churches simply did not make as much of baptism as did the Campbell churches. The Campbell people in turn considered the Stone churches too "latitudinarian," one of their big words in those days, on what they saw as a command of God.

This issue was resolved by the Stone churches eventually accepting

Campbell's position on baptism, albeit they were never as adamant on the subject as he. Stone tells how he stumbled upon the idea of baptism for remission of sins almost by accident when he was preaching in a large meeting in Concord, Ky. With sinners gathered at the mourner's bench praying, he suddenly cried out to them like Peter did on Pentecost, "Repent and be baptized for the remission of sins, and you shall receive the gift of the Holy Ghost." But there was no response and he soon let it slip from him. He explains that he never came to understand this doctrine on baptism until it was revived some years later by Alexander Campbell.[25]

Stone tells how those Presbyterian ministers who signed *The Last Will and Testament* with him decided that they should be immersed, but only after they had agreed together that it should remain an open question and not be made a test of fellowship. But they had no one to immerse them who was himself an immersed believer. The Baptists would not do it unless they cast their lot with them. Concluding that if they were authorized to preach they were authorized to baptize, even if they themselves were not yet immersed, they proceeded to immerse each other.[26]

While they did not actually preach immersion from their pulpits for some time, most of those in their congregations were immersed over the next several years. In 1827 Stone wrote in his paper that "There is not one in five hundred among us who has not been immersed. From the commencement we have avoided controversy on the subject."[27]

The question has been raised by some in recent years as to whether Stone himself was ever immersed. This stems from the fact that in his autobiography, where he tells the story of his people being immersed, he never explicitly states that he was immersed, though he does say that he, like the others, was dissatisfied with his infant sprinkling. John Rogers, who put the autobiography together and supplied chapter headings and who knew him for 40 years, understood Stone's account of the immersions to include himself, for he supplied the heading "Is Himself Immersed."

In a later account Stone removes all doubt as to what happened:

> There are many pious Christians, who from ignorance of immersion as their duty, have neglected it, and yet are accepted of God with all their ignorance. . . . For twelve years I thus lived without immersion, and believe I lived under the smiles of heaven. But when I became acquainted with my duty, I submitted to it.[28]

The differences between Stone and Campbell surveyed thus far anticipated what has long been an oddity in the Movement: *disputation over methodology more than theology.* While the Movement has had a tragic history of internal fission, virtually all of the disputes have been over methods.

There was, however, at least one weighty theological difference between these two founding pioneers. It had to do with the doctrine of the Trinity, particularly in reference to the preexistence of Christ. While both men saw the term Trinity as unbiblical and speculative, Campbell was the more orthodox in that he was inclined to defend the doctrine while avoiding the term Trinity. Stone rejected the concept of the Trinity, maintaining that while Christ as "the Word" was the "instrumental cause" of creation but not the First Cause, which in effect made him a created being.

Stone was also unorthodox on the Holy Spirit, seeing it as power or energy from God but not a third person in the Godhead. There might be three persons in God, he allowed, but only in essence, not as separate beings. God and Christ were separate beings in that they had separate wills, he concluded. He further claimed that the Scriptures do not reveal the mode of God's existence and that there is therefore no way for us to know. Since Jesus said things like "I came down from Heaven not to do my own will, but the will of him that sent me," he concluded that only the Father is God and that Jesus is His Son. Jesus is therefore to be honored as the Son but not to be worshiped as God.[29]

To Stone's antagonists, including Campbell, this was shades of the old fourth century heresy known as Arianism, and thus he and his followers had to bear the epithet of Arians. But this was unjust, for Arianism denied both the eternity of Christ and his incarnation (that is, Jesus was not the preexistent Christ or Logos), while Stone affirmed both that Jesus was the Christ and that Christ was eternal with God.

Campbell was all too aware that the Christians in the West were tainted with Arianism, and it is likely that this, more than anything else, explains his lack of enthusiasm for the union that was eventually effected. He wrote to Stone:

> I am truly sorry to find that certain opinions called Arian or Unitarian, or something else, are about becoming the badge of a people assuming the sacred name of Christian and that some peculiar views of atonement or reconciliation are likely to become characteristic of a people who have claimed the high character and dignified relation of the Church of Christ.[30]

It so happens that this was in response to a letter that Stone had sent to Campbell, criticizing *him* for being too speculative on the preexistence of Christ! Both of the Campbells remained Calvinistic in much of their theology, Thomas more than Alexander, especially in reference to the atonement, while Stone was strongly anti-Calvinistic. He refered to Calvinism as "a chilling, repulsive doctrine that has led many to infidelity and thousands to stubborn insensibility."[31]

He exchanged arguments with Thomas Campbell on the atonement, rejecting the view of vicarious suffering, that Jesus was the sacrificial Lamb in the hands of an angry Father. These exchanges with the Campbells disturbed the rank and file leadership, causing Stone to withdraw from the debate. He was later to give credit to Alexander Campbell for causing him to become less speculative in his teaching. He had no doubt become too engrossed in such theories, giving over a large portion of his *Christian Messenger* to them during its first three years.[32]

When the controversy between Campbell and Stone was injected by Rice into the debate he had with Campbell in 1843, friends of both men were persuaded that Campbell had treated Stone less than charitably. Rice used the disagreement "to show how fundamentally the two most prominent men in this reform church differ from each other on two of the most important doctrines of the gospel — the character and the work of Christ."

Rice quoted from Stone at length to show that his views were unorthodox, while Campbell's were acceptable. He then said: "If there is union in a body of men composed of materials so utterly discordant, most assuredly it is not Christian union." He strengthened his point by references to the unorthodox views of Aylett Raines and Dr. John Thomas, two other associates of Campbell, which will be noted in other contexts.[33]

Campbell responded to Rice by charging that if Barton Stone had been in the hands of the Westminster divines they would have either cut off his head or hanged him. He conceded that "Unitarian" or "speculator" might be just descriptions of Stone, and then said: "I do not approve of all that Barton W. Stone has written and said, yet I believe our society has been and is pursuing a most salutary and redeeming policy."

He went on to make reference to Stone's past, which Stone's friends found offensive: "Whither has fled the Newlightism of former days? How long will its speculations be remembered that floated on the winds of thirty years?"[34]

Leaders of the Movement in Kentucky, including John T. Johnson, did not like it, and they told Campbell in no uncertain terms that the things he had said and published to the world were calculated to produce a wrong impression with reference to his new brethren in Kentucky. They considered it slanderous to be called such as New-Lights, Arians, or Stoneites. They reminded Campbell that when the two groups united "Neither considered the other as holding views subversive of Christian faith and practice" and that they preached the same great principles.

The complaint was signed by four evangelists and eight elders and deacons. In a separate letter Johnson informed Campbell that many brethren in Kentucky were grieved over the injustice done to Stone in the debate, and that Campbell had further erred in omitting Stone's paper from the list of journals he had published that were advocating reform based upon the Bible alone, which appeared to be deliberate. The Kentuckians clearly believed that Campbell should have defended Stone against Rice's attacks.

Campbell made no response to this except to publish their letters and explain to Johnson that the omission of Stone's *Christian Messenger* was an oversight, which he corrected in a subsequent list of the journals favorable to the reformation.[35]

But in the debate Campbell made it clear to Rice what he conceived to be the basis of unity, which allowed for such differences as existed between Stone and himself, as well as numerous others that Rice kept referring to, which in this context happened to include Dr. James Fishback, a prominent Baptist who had come over to Campbell's side, but who held some different opinions.

> Our bond of union is not opinion, nor unity of opinion. It is one Lord, one faith, one baptism, one Spirit, one hope, one God and Father of all. These we all preach and teach. We have no standard opinions amongst us. We have no patented form of sound words drawn up by human art and man's device, to which all must vow eternal fidelity. It is our peculiar felicity, and perhaps, it may be our honor, too, that we have been able to discover a ground so common, so sacred, so divinely approbated, so perfectly catholic and enduring, on which every man, who loves our Lord Jesus Christ sincerely, may unite, and commune, and harmonize, and cooperate in all the works of faith, in all the labors of love, and in all the perseverance of hope.[36]

As to Stone's response to Rice's accusation that he was a Unitarian and believed that Jesus was a mere man and a created being, he said: "Now I reply for the last time (so now I think) that at no time of my long life did I ever believe these doctrines. I never taught them either publicly or privately, from the pulpit or press. How Mr. Rice obtained his information I can only conjecture." As for the problem this created for Campbell, he wrote: "Brother Campbell has to suffer on my account what I have had long to suffer for him. He is malevolently assailed for holding me in fellowship . . . and I have been with equal malevolence assailed for holding him in fellowship, because of his supposed errors."[37]

There can be no question that Campbell held Stone in high esteem. When Stone died in Hannibal, Mo. in 1844, he wrote of him as "the honored instrument of bringing many out of the ranks of human tradition and putting into their hands the Book of Books as their only confession of faith and rule of life."[38] The next year he was in Hannibal, in the home of Stone's daughter where the reformer had died, and wrote of his pleasure of being in the residence where "the venerable Barton W. Stone" had departed this life.[39]

During their extensive correspondence, which sometimes became theologically overloaded, Campbell would assure "brother Stone" that he was his brother, in spite of their differences, because he too believed that Jesus is Lord. They agreed to disagree and went on with their work. They thus became a paradigm of the Movement's plea for unity in diversity.

As for other differences between these founders of the Movement, Campbell was wealthy, "a pioneer in broadcloth," which allowed him leisure for study and travel, while Stone was a poor, hands-on man of the soil, which limited his work as a reformer. Campbell was blessed with incredible energy and good health, never going to bed ill except to die at 78. Stone was frail, often ill, lived a difficult life, and died at 72.

While both were editors and preachers, Campbell was abler and more versatile, equally at ease as a college president and a statesman. Stone was reserved, introverted, self-effacing; Campbell was aggressive, precipitous, dominating. Stone was the quiet teacher, Campbell the engaging debater. Stone was a passable speaker, Campbell an impressive orator. Wherever Campbell was he dominated the scene, while Stone was more laid back.

Stone was a man of the Spirit, known for his Christlikeness, forgiving and forbearing, and not given to confrontation. Campbell too was a pious man, but he loved a fight and was known to hold grudges. Stone had a greater passion both for evangelism and unity than Campbell. While Stone's plea for unity was based on love, forbearance, and humility, Campbell's was more structural, based upon what he called "the ancient order," at least in his earlier years.

William G. West, who did a Ph.D. at Yale on Stone, sees substantial cultural differences between the two men. He notes that Campbell studied at Glasgow in Scotland while Stone attended frontier schools in Virginia and North Carolina. Campbell read the philosophers and theologians while Stone read only compilations of such men. Campbell relished debates while Stone distrusted them. Campbell was able to build a brick study in his yard where he spent long hours, while Stone carried books to the field where he sought snatches of time for study.

West sees it as significant that while both men broke with Calvinism, Campbell's was more superficial, having to do with such issues as baptism, Communion, conversion, and ministerial calling, while Stone was concerned with predestination, total depravity, the Trinity, and the nature of Christ.[40]

Stone's Polar Star

In the garden of the Disciples of Christ Historical Society in Nashville stands a cenotaph in honor of four founding pioneers of the Stone-Campbell Movement. The likeness of Barton W. Stone is engraved in marble, along with Thomas and Alexander Campbell and Walter Scott. Under Stone's likeness is carved "Let the unity of Christians be our polar star." To him it was more than a slogan, for it was an interpretation of Jesus' prayer in John 17 for the unity of all believers.

Stone saw the church as the old ship Zion that must be guided by the polar star if it is to fulfill its mission of winning the world for Christ. If the world is to be *won* the church must be *one*. So, the Lord's prayer, "May they be one, even as we are one, so that the world may believe,' will be answered, Stone held, only if the church is guided by the polar star, which is its unity. It was more than an impressive metaphor, for to Stone it was the essence of the Movement he had launched.

In 1835 Stone wrote in his journal, "For 32 years of my ministry I have kept in view the unity of Christians as my polar star." In doing so, he said, he had "suffered reproach, persecution, privation of ease, and the loss of friendship, wealth and honor from men."[41]

Richardson grants that a passion for unity marked Stone's movement more than Campbell's. He notes that "the idea of uniting all men under Christ" was dominate in Stone's ministry, while Campbell's emphasis was upon "an exact conformity to the primitive faith and practice." Stone was more a unitist, Campbell more a restorationist, while both were reformers, Richardson allows.[42]

Stone's favorite sermon on unity was "Four Different Kinds of Union," which reveals his view of how unity can be realized. First, there is Book Union, which is based on authoritarian creeds of men and therefore unacceptable. Second, is Head Union, founded on human opinion, which is no better than the first. Third, is Water Union, based on baptism, which is still an unstable compact. Fourth, is Fire Union, a unity created by the presence of the Holy Spirit in the life of the believer, which is what Jesus prayed for.

He worked for unity as if his life depended on it, insisting that when Christians are united with Christ and filled with his Spirit they will be united to one another. The Holy Spirit is thus the bond of union. It is love and trust more than doctrine that unites us. Division among Christians is sinful and scandalous; it "makes heaven mourn and hell rejoice."[43]

In his doctoral study, William G. West was impressed that Stone called for a national convention on unity long before there was an ecumenical movement, urging unity as the only means of converting the world to Christ. But Stone thought of unity between individuals more than between churches, which might take too long, he figured. West recalls another of his slogans, "Let every Christian begin the work of union within himself."

West further observes that while Stone pled for unity on the basis of trust and love, others in the Movement conceived of unity only on the grounds of a hard and fast biblical pattern. He notes that this "biblical primitivism" view has prevailed since the time of Stone, leaving the Movement to suffer one division after another. He draws this conclusion as to what might have been if Stone's view of unity had prevailed:

> Had the Disciples of Christ or Christian churches followed Stone's emphasis, it is highly probable that they would not have divided into three major wings and some twenty-three other groups, each stressing one or more divisive issues. It is almost equally certain that they would have been closer to the main bodies of Protestantism and more influencial in the American religious scene.[44]

West could have also said that if Stone's more open view of things had prevailed, the Movement would have been more inclusive and less sectarian, as it eventually became. In 1831, when the character of the Movement was taking shape, Stone made this plea: "Let us acknowledge all to be our brethren who believe in the Lord Jesus, and humbly and honestly obey him as far as they know his will and their duty. Let us not reject whom the Lord has received."[45] It was a view of brotherhood that struggled in vain to prevail.

It is ironic that a people emanating from such an ecumenical soul as Barton W. Stone would not only have a problem in accepting other believers but even a problem in accepting each other. It is tragic that what Luther A. Weigle, onetime dean at Yale Divinity School, said of Stone could not be said of his followers in general: "He was a 'grass roots' practioner of Christian unity rather than a debater about it."[46]

Other Contributions

Stone's contribution to the Movement, first of all, is that he gave it approximately half of its initial resources, in personnel, ideas, and action. Second, he gave the Movement its passion for Christian unity in that he was its first true ecumenist. But there was more. He built a religious community that became one of the largest in Kentucky. He was an effective leader, preparing evangelists and sending them throughout Kentucky, such as Samuel Rogers, who baptized over 7,000. Rogers tells how Stone ordained him, gave him a Bible, and said: "Preach its facts, obey its commands and enjoy its promises."[47]

Stone went on record as saying that the noblest work of his life was the union of the Stone-Campbell movements in 1832. It is safe to conclude that the Movement would never have united except for his genial spirit.

John R. Howard, a Missouri editor, saw Stone as a harbinger for the more effective ministry of Campbell: "If brother Campbell has been mainly instrumental in stripping the gospel of the human appendages, additions and glosses by which it was clogged and obscured, it must be acknowledged that father Stone was greatly instrumental in preparing a people for its reception."[48] Like John the Baptist, he prepared a people. A Tennessee historian claimed that the people Stone prepared were a better people than the Campbellites.[49]

Be that as it may, Stone gave his people both spirit and structure, providing for an ordained ministry and intercongregational organizations, as well as a sense of mission and destiny. When he finally left Kentucky and moved to Jacksonville, Illinois, shortly after the union of the two movements, he found two churches, one Christian and the other Disciples. At his insistence they became one church, almost immediately, which well illustrates the point that Howard made. He prepared a people, a unity-conscious people.

There is a renewed interest in Barton W. Stone among the heirs of the Movement today. While almost totally eclipsed by Campbell all these years, he is being lifted from obscurity by more recent research. Henry E. Webb, in a history of the Movement from the Independent Christian Church perspective, treats Stone at length. He concludes that the union of the Christians and Disciples in 1832, without which there would not have been an ongoing Movement, could not have occurred without Stone.[50]

In a recent history for the Disciples, Mark G. Toulouse tells his readers that they were "Born in America," and that there are four founding fathers whose names they should remember. Barton W. Stone heads the list. He is careful to point out that Stone had a unity movement of his own with at least 10,000 followers before he had even heard of the Campbells.[51]

For Churches of Christ readers, Leonard Allen writes of "Distant Voices" that lie in obscurity in their history. Barton W. Stone is introduced as offering "The Only Hope for Unity." That hope is not in taking "the Bible alone," as his readers might suppose. Allen points to all the divisions created by those who claim to take the Bible alone. Stone's "great secret" for unity is the indwelling of the Spirit in each believer. The "want of the Spirit" is "the grand cause of division."[52]

Bill Humble, director of the Restoration Center at ACU, has prepared a four-part VCR presentation of the life of Barton W. Stone. Entertaining as well as resourceful, it features vignettes on Stone's contribution from scholars and archivists from all three churches of the Movement. These include J.M. Powell, R.L. Roberts, Jerry Rushford, and Adran Doran from Churches of Christ; Sam Stone, Henry Webb, and James North from Christian Churches; and James Seale and Franklin McGuire from Disciples of Christ. It is one more encouraging instance of all three churches working together in probing their common heritage.[53]

Another recent joint study of Stone is in a book published by the Disciples of Christ Historical Society in celebration of the 200th anniversary of the erection of the Cane Ridge meetinghouse. The log building is today well preserved by being encased in a larger structure, and is open to visitors. The book contains presentations on Stone and Cane Ridge by scholars of all three churches, with each presenter telling how his church remembers Stone.

Speaking for the Disciples of Christ, Anthony Dunnavant tells how their historians at first treated Stone's movement as only a "tributary" to the Campbell movement. In time, however, Stone was viewed as a "founder," along with the Campbells and Scott, and his movement the earlier of "two main streams." But in recent years Stone has become an "icon" to the Disciples — "from precursor to icon" as Dunnavant puts it. This is because the Disciples "needed a different founder, a liberal founder, an *ecumenical* founder," and Alexander Campbell did not meet that criteria. Since Campbell was a restorationist and Stone a unitist, the Disciples adopted Stone. The other two presenters found no substantial "memory" of Stone in their churches.[54]

Richard Hughes, a Churches of Christ scholar, in still another recent study, surprisingly traces the origins of his church more to Barton W. Stone than to the Campbells. Even more surprising, he identifies Stone as an apocalypticist and argues for "apocalyptic origins of Churches of Christ." Members of Churches of Christ might be persuaded that the New Jerusalem has apocalyptic origin, but it will be a hard sell to convince them that their church has such origin, even in what Hughes calls Stone's "apocalyptic primitivism."[55]

What is important in all these recent studies is that the significance of Barton W. Stone is being revived. The benefit of such a revival will be to give the Stone movement its proper place alongside the Campbell movement and its role in the unity of the Movement. The risk of such a revival, as some of the studies suggest, is that Stone will be set more at variance with the Campbells than he was. The fact remains that the two movements had so much in common that they became a united unity movement, which was quite a feat for the American frontier.

The people Barton W. Stone prepared may have eventually become a denomination, but we may conclude that it was *a denomination in protest.*

With his eye on the polar star, which was the unity of all believers, Stone could never have accepted denominational status except provisionally, *in protest*, until God's church on earth could be one in reality.

ENDNOTES

[1]John Rogers, *Biography of Elder Barton Warren Stone*, Cincinnati, 1847, p. 30.

[2]*Biography*, p. 22.

[3]C.C. Ware, *Barton Warren Stone* (St. Louis: Bethany Press, 1932), p. xiv.

[4]*Biography*, p. 11.

[5]C.C. Ware, *Barton Warren Stone*, p. 103.

[6]*Ibid.*, p. 108.

[7]*Biography*, p. 37.

[8]*Biography*, p. 38.

[9]Vol. 5 (1831), p. 165.

[10]R.H. Gabriel, *The Course of American Democratic Thought*, New York: Ronald Press, 1956, p. 35; Paul K. Conkin, *Cane Ridge: America's Pentecost* (Madison: U. of Wisconsin Press, 1990).

[11]*Christian Messenger*, Vol. 1 (1826), p. 100.

[12]*Biography*, p. 49.

[13]See Vol. 2, *The Presbyterians*, New York: 1936, p. 318.

[14]*Biography*, p. 49.

[15]F.D. Kershner, *Declaration and Address* (St. Louis: Mission Messenger, 1975), p. 15.

[16]*Biography*, p. 50.

[17]W.E. Garrison and A. T. DeGroot, *The Disciples of Christ: A History* (St. Louis: Bethany Press, 1958), p. 108.

[18]Kershner, *Declaration and Address*, p. 15.

[19]Stone makes it clear in his journal, *Christian Messenger*, Vol. 1 (1826), p. 241, that he was not the author of this document and did not approve of the manner in which it was written, but did approve of the content.

[20]*Biography*, p. 76.

[21]Robert Richardson, *Memoirs of Alexander Campbell* (Cincinnati: Standard, 1897), Vol. 2, p. 118.

[22]It was common to refer to those men as "Father" when they became aged. "Elder" was the usual title for preachers, so as to avoid clerical titles and to preserve the idea that they were all the laity.

[23]C.C. Ware, *Barton Warren Stone*, p. 310.

[24]*Christian Messenger*, Vol. 8 (1834), p. 28.

[25]*Biography*, p. 61.

[26]*Ibid.*

[27]*Christian Messenger*, Vol. 1 (1826), p. 267.

[28]*Christian Messenger*, Vol. 12 (1841), p. 38.

[29]"Answer to Samuel Brown" in *Christian Messenger*, Vol. 3 (1828), p. 58f.

[30]Richardson, *Memoirs*, Vol, 2, p. 204.

[31]C.C. Ware, *Barton Warren Stone*, p. 309.

[32]"To Elder Thomas Campbell," *Christian Messenger*, Vol. 7 (1833), p. 230.

[33]*Campbell-Rice Debate*, Lexington, 1844, p. 853.

[34]*Ibid.*, p. 865.

[35]The list includes 13 journals and appears in *Millennial Harbinger*, 1844, p. 143. The corrected list that includes Stone's paper is on p. 427. On the Kentucky correspondence, *Mill. Harb.*, 1844, pp. 414-416.

[36]*Campbell-Rice Debate*, p. 505.

[37]C.C. Ware, *Barton Warren Stone*, p. 314.

[38]*Biography*, p. 107.

[39]"Our Tour to the West," in *Millennial Harbinger*, 1846, p. 72. The story Mark Twain tells of encountering Alexander Campbell in his print shop in Hannibal is apocryphal. See L. C. McAllister, "Fact and Fiction in Disciples History," in *Discipliana*, Vol. 39(1979), p. 511.

[40]William G. West, *Barton Warren Stone: Early American Advocate of Christian Unity* (Nashville: Disciples of Christ Historical Society, 1954), p. 133.

[41]*Christian Messenger*, Vol. 9 (1835), p. 285.

[42]Robert Richardson, *Memoirs*, Vol. 2, p. 198.

[43]*Christian Messenger*, Vol. 11 (1840), p. 128.

[44]William G. West, *Barton Warren Stone*, pp. 129-130.

[45]*Christian Messenger*, Vol. 5 (1831), p. 21.

[46]West, *Barton Warren Stone*, Introduction.

[47]Richardson, *Memoirs*, Vol. 2, p. 332.

[48]*Christian Reformer*, 1836, p. 819.

[49]John Carr, *Early Times in Middle Tennessee* (Quoted in C.C. Ware, *Barton Warren Stone*, p. 262).

[50]Henry E. Webb, *In Search of Christian Unity* (Cincinnati: Standard, 1992), p. 62.

[51]Mark G. Toulouse, *Joined in Discipleship* (St. Louis: Chalice Press, 1992), pp. 22f.

[52]C. Leonard Allen, *Distant Voices* (Abilene, TX: ACU Press, 1993), pp. 15-20.

[53]Bill Humble, *Like Fire in Dry Stubble: The Life of Barton W. Stone*, VCR,

1991, Abilene, TX: ACU Restoration Center Library.

[54]Anthony L. Dunnavant, "From Precursor of the Movement to Icon of Christian Unity: Barton W. Stone in Memory of the Christian Church (Disciples of Christ)," *Cane Ridge in Context: Perspectives on Barton W. Stone and the Revival* (Nashville: Disciples of Christ Historical Society, 1992).

[55]Richard T. Hughes, "The Apocalyptic Origins of Churches of Christ and the Triumph of Modernism," *Religion and American Culture*, 2, (Summer 1992), pp. 181f.

5

THOMAS CAMPBELL AND
THE DECLARATION AND ADDRESS
THE MOVEMENT'S FOUNDING DOCUMENT

The Church of Christ upon earth is
essentially, intentionally, and constitutionally one.

It was probably as uncommon back in 1851 as it would be now for a minister to deliver a valedictory sermon. But Thomas Campbell's family and friends decided that his ministry of 60 years was about over, and that it would be appropriate for a formal service to be held in recognition of this milestone. A large congregation gathered on Sunday, June 1, 1851 at the Bethany church, including students from Bethany College and McKeaver's Female Seminary in nearby West Middletown, Pennsylvania.

Thomas Campbell was now 88, having been born in Newry, Ireland on February 1, 1763. He had both a university and seminary education, having spent three years at Glasgow in Scotland, which was founded in 1451, and five years at Whitburn, a seminary of the Anti-Burgher Seceder Presbyterian Church, which he had joined after having been reared in the Church of England.

Having come to America in 1807, he had helped to initiate the Movement that now claimed upwards of 200,000 followers, and he was rightly considered one of its four founding fathers, along with his son Alexander, Barton W. Stone, and Walter Scott. It had been only 30 years since his efforts numbered no more than 200 people in six congregations.[1] Now it was a force to be reckoned with in the life of the young republic that had begun to move west.

For three years the old man had been blind. Now widowed and enfeebled he had spent the last years of his life at his son's home in Bethany, but he was vigorous enough to converse with the many visitors that came from all over the world. He knew so many hymns and Scriptures from memory that he never lacked in resources, even for a valedictory address. If he lacked recall, he would ask one of the family or a visitor to read to him.

When he was unable to get into a buggy for the trip to the church, they improvised a low-slung, horse-drawn sled, usually resorted to during the winter snows. To add dignity to the occasion two deacons met the venerable patriarch out in the yard and led him down the aisle to his place before the congregation. The sermon, drawn from Matt. 22:37-40, was transcribed by W.K. Pendleton, a professor at Bethany and twice son-in-law to Alexander Campbell, and preserved both in the *Millennial Harbinger* of 1854 and in Alexander's *Memoirs of Elder Thomas Campbell*, published in 1861.

In giving what he called his "last public service of my long-protracted life," he apologized for not being able to read to them from the Scriptures, "for it has pleased my merciful heavenly Father — ever blessed be his name — in the wisdom of his Providence, to take from me my sight." For his last sermon he spoke on the greatest commandment of all: "Thou shalt love the Lord thy God with all thy heart, and with all thy soul, and with all thy mind, and thy neighbor as thyself." It impressed him that Jesus did not call for some marvelous deed as the greatest commandment, or for animal sacrifice or painful penance; but simply to love God with all that we are.

Love had been his theme throughout his long ministry, and John 3:16 had been his favorite passage. Lester McAllister describes Thomas Campbell as "the Man of the Book," which is the title of his study, for he was so absorbed by the Scriptures — teaching them, writing about them, meditating upon them, as well as extensively memorizing them. He could just as well be called "the envoy of love," for love was not only his constant theme, but he saw it as the only means of accomplishing the purpose of his ministry, the unity of all believers.

He saw love as the essence of the Christian faith: "Christianity is emphatically, supereminently — yea, transcendently, the religion of love."[2] When he grew concerned over the direction that the Movement had taken after its first generation he blamed a loss of love they had at first, which he described as their "divine badge of discipleship."[3]

Declaration and Address

Thomas Campbell's *Declaration and Address*, published in 1809, was the founding document of the Stone-Campbell Movement. The late W.W. Sweet, a dean among American church historians, recognized it as one of the great documents of the American church,[4] and ecumenical leaders have acknowledged it as "one of the great milestones on the path of Christian unity in America."[5]

F.D. Kershner observed that while it was written during the Napoleonic wars "it proclaimed what came to be known later as the Ecumenical Program nearly a century and a half before the World Council meeting at

Amsterdam."[6] H.E. Johnson saw it as setting the stage for Alexander Campbell's life's work, that "Alexander's primary purpose was to give practical application to the principles of the *Declaration and Address.*"[7] The document thus became the design for the Movement, particularly in the Campbell wing.

Moreover, the leaders of the Movement through the years have looked back to the writing of this document as their beginning, in spite of the fact that the Stone wing of the Movement had primacy in terms of time. When the Disciples celebrated their Centennial anniversary, it was not in 1904, which would have recognized Barton W. Stone and his *Last Will and Testament of the Springfield Presbytery* as the founding event, but in 1909, in Pittsburgh, which honored both the place and the time of the origin of the Campbell movement.

On that occasion the Disciples issued a special edition of the *Declaration and Address* in which they said, "September 7, 1809, is universally accepted as bearing the same relation to the people now known as Disciples of Christ, Christians, or Churches of Christ, that July 4, 1776 holds to the United States of America,"[8] with only a passing reference to Barton W. Stone. This interpretation of the origin of the Movement, which in terms of historical fact may be questioned, illustrates the dramatic role that the *Declaration and Address* has played in the history of these people.

It was C.L. Loos, however, who gave this document its most meaningful description. Longtime professor of Bethany College and a junior colleague to Alexander Campbell, he was well acquainted with Thomas Campbell, and he lived not only long enough to celebrate the Centennial anniversary of the Movement but also to write his reflections on its history. He saw the *Declaration and Address* as "a prospectus of the reformation."[9]

A study of the document's subsequent influence shows Loos' estimate to be true. While the Stone forces had the primacy in time, they did not provide a prospectus or design to sustain a reformation movement. It is reasonable to conclude that without the *Declaration and Address* the Stone-Campbell Movement would not have made it.

In defining the role of the Campbells, father and son, Loos sees Thomas as the inaugurator and Alexander as the executor. "The inceptive thought and first scheme of this extraordinary movement had their origin with Thomas Campbell," he says, and he describes him as "a man of large brains, of superior natural endowments, and what was notable in him in this respect was the well balanced adjustment of these gifts. The form of the head at once indicated this (he was no *roundhead*), and familiar acquaintance with the man confirmed it."[10]

Background To The Document

Roundhead or not, Thomas had come to the new world in 1807 seeking his well-being: health, freedom, adventure, opportunities for his young family. It was what many of his Irish friends had done before him. Back in Ahorey, Ireland he was both a pastor and a schoolmaster, a dual profession that he continued in America. Leaving his family behind so that he could make proper arrangements for them to join him later, he came to Washington, Pennsylvania, which was then frontier country in a nation of less than five million population. Presbyterians from Ireland favored that part of Pennsylvania, causing that area to be referred to as "an American Ulster," but only a few of these were of Thomas' particular sect.

He was soon greeted by old friends, given a seat in the synod of his church, and assigned to minister on the farflung frontier in the environs of Washington. He was given $50.00 to launch him on his circuit-riding mission. Partly due to his Irish friends in the community who knew of his ministerial excellence in Ulster, but also due to his irenic spirit, he was soon one of the most popular preachers among the Seceders. But as is often the case with genial and irenic souls amidst partyism, Thomas Campbell was headed for trouble.

The Presbyterians on the American frontier were even more sectarian than they were in Ireland and Scotland where Thomas had made modest attempts to give them a broader view of fellowship. In an effort to preserve doctrinal soundness his synod had ruled against any fellowship with other Christians. Since Seceder Presbyterians were so few on the farflung frontier, it was necessary for them to mingle with those of other denominations, including other kinds of Presbyterians, if they were to have any church life.

It was consistent with Campbell's nature to encourage this and to minister to all believers alike. His fellow ministers soon became suspicious of his ministry. Since he was almost alone as a cultured and educated minister, some of the opposition might have been prompted by professional jealousy, especially since he was so popular.

Among his offenses was serving Communion to those other than of his sect, even to other Presbyterians. It was this at last that led to his being brought before the presbytery to give an account. Here was a man of peace, who had been involved in no controversy during his sixteen years as a minister in Ireland, but who was now so controversial in America that preachers of his own denomination would have no fellowship with him.

The presbytery selected a committee to look into the question of his orthodoxy. In the meantime Campbell was to cease his ministerial functions. The committee eventually brought seven written charges against him, all rather obtuse points having to do with Calvinistic doctrine and church polity. His practice of open communion was not mentioned.[11]

The answers he was allowed to make to these charges reveal some of the ideas, at least in embryo, that later found expression in the movement he launched, such as faith being the result of testimony rather than mystical experience, the question of whether creeds should be the basis of fellowship, and the right of elders to function equally with ministers. His answers indicated that he was still a Calvinist in theology, which continued to be the case for the rest of his life. It was mostly his desire to be free of ecclesiastical domination and his preference for a more open fellowship that led to his eventual break with the Presbyterians. Lester McAllister summarizes the conflicts:

> Campbell was in revolt against the authority of the presbytery and its limitation of fellowship to those who belong to their particular sect. In these charges and in Campbell's answers clear evidence is presented of Campbell's growing impatience with the sectarian spirit so apparent in his section of the American frontier.[12]

The presbytery used his answers as a cause for suspending his right to preach indefinitely. Thomas appealed to the synod, the next highest court in Presbyterian judicatory. The synod found his trial before the presbytery "irregular" and reversed its sentence of suspension, and then proceeded to deal with him on their own. After considerable sparring between the two parties, the synod finally "rebuked and admonished" him for his unsatisfactory answers to the charges, insisting that he should be suspended from office if he could not do better, which was not all that different from what the presbytery had done to him.

But the synod had removed his suspension, leaving him free to return to Washington and minister as he had done before as part of the Chartiers presbytery. While he was disappointed by the way he had been treated by his fellow ministers, he was still determined to remain with his church and to work peacefully among his people. But it was not to be.

The presbytery, its decision now reversed by the higher court, remained cool and uncooperative toward Thomas, and always found some reason for not giving him an assignment. When further controversy ensued over what had transpired before the synod, Thomas decided he had had enough, and proceeded to withdraw from the presbytery and the Seceder denomination, renouncing all such ecclesiastical authority in the process.

They subsequently suspended him from ministerial office, but since he was already out on his own, it was meaningless except as a vindictive gesture. Campbell dramatized his break by returning to the synod the $50.00 tendered him shortly after his arrival in Pennsylvania. It was at about the same time that his son Alexander had dramatically indicated his break from the same denomination by walking out of a Communion service, which is recounted in the next chapter.

Similar to the case of Stone and the "revival men" in Kentucky who produced "The Apology of the Springfield Presbytery" as a result of their confrontation with Presbyterian authorities, Thomas Campbell also wrote an important essay that he called a "Protest and Appeal" which he placed before the synod during their debates. It is relevant in that it anticipates some of the ideas later expressed in the *Declaration and Address*. It also reflects a development of some of the principles that became basic to the Movement, especially the determination to accept only the Bible as authoritative in matters of faith and practice. The paper was presented to the Associate Synod of North America on May 18, 1808, and it contained such revolutionary ideas as:

> It is therefore because I have no confidence, either in my own infallibility or in that of others, that I absolutely refuse as inadmissable and schismatic the introduction of human opinions and human inventions into the faith and worship of the Church.
>
> It is therefore because I plead the cause of the Scriptural and apostolic worship of the church, in opposition to the various errors and schisms which have so awfully corrupted and divided it, that the brethren of the Union should feel it difficult to admit me as their fellow laborer in that blessed work?
>
> And all this without any intention on my part to judge or despise my Christian brethren who may not see with my eyes in those things which, to me, appear indispensably necessary to promote and secure the unity, peace, and purity of the Church.
>
> For what error or immorality ought I to be rejected except it be that I refuse to acknowledge as obligatory upon myself, or to impose upon others, anything as of Divine obligation for which I cannot produce a "Thus saith the Lord."

But Thomas Campbell was rejected, not for violating a clear "Thus saith the Lord," but for deviating from a party creed. This fact was to change his life. He was now out of the established church, a circumstance he had no way of anticipating. Now he was a freelance minister, at liberty to move among his people, to do and to teach as he pleased. It was not, however, the kind of freedom he desired, separated as he was from wife and family, still a stranger in a new world, and through no fault of his own, as he saw it, alienated from his church and fellow clergy. He had sent word for his family to join him, but this was to be delayed due to their shipwreck at sea.

From the fall of 1807, when the conflict with the presbytery began, until the summer of 1809, when his family at last arrived from Scotland, Thomas was engaged in a new ministry: *a plea for the unity of all Christians upon the Bible alone.* He preached wherever he had opportunity, always speaking out against partyism in the church, which was seldom done in those days. He rarely had access to a church, his meetings being in the open air or in barns or homes.

There is no evidence that Campbell gave any consideration to starting a church of his own. He still considered himself a Presbyterian minister, if not a Seceder, and he was now ministering to Regular and Associate Presbyterians, as well as to those of other denominations, and he could have had an independent church of his own since his following was now substantial. It was his desire to work *within* the existing churches as much as possible, sowing seeds of peace and unity.

He came to see the need of some kind of an organization through which to do his thing, not a church as such but a society that would rally support for the goals he had in view, one that could involve concerned people from all the churches. Such auxiliary societies had functioned successfully in his homeland. The large numbers that supported his views and attended his meetings convinced him that something substantial could be done.

Christian Association of Washington

After some discussion with his closest associates, Campbell organized the Christian Association of Washington, with 21 people serving as a steering committee. Their first decision was that a document should be prepared setting forth the ideals and intentions of the society. This led to the creation of the *Declaration and Address*, which was written in the attic of a home that still stands between Mt. Pleasant and Washington, Pennsylvania, then owned by a physician named Welch, who was a supporter of the society and host to Thomas until his family arrived from Europe.

The society met on a weekly basis to hear Campbell preach and to discuss their common goals. Since they were not a church, each one remained in his or her own denomination. After a few months of meeting in homes they erected a log cabin a few miles out of Washington, which doubled as a schoolhouse for the community. The old building has long since disappeared, lost to history, but the site where it once stood, now a vacant lot, has been identified.

In one of their early gatherings in the home of Abraham Altars, who was not a church member, Thomas set forth the motto, which was to be the rule of their new society, "Where the Scriptures speak, we speak; and where the Scriptures are silent, we are silent." It is one of the most quoted sayings in the history of the Movement, and is viewed by some as the essence of its plea. It was apparently original with Campbell.

When he laid it out as the guiding principle of the society, one of his friends made an immediate application: "Mr. Campbell, if we adopt *that* as a basis, then there is an end to infant baptism." "Of course," replied Campbell, "if infant baptism be not found in Scripture, we can have nothing to do with it." Some discussion followed in which some became upset over the possible abandonment of a venerable practice of long standing, but the motto was nonetheless adopted as the society's guideline. But for some time to come Thomas chose to make the question of infant baptism a matter of private judgment.[13]

Once Thomas Campbell had completed the *Declaration and Address* and presented it to the Association for its approval, it was unanimously adopted and was at once ordered to be published, September 7, 1809. It was not until the end of that year that it was ready for circulation. In the meantime Alexander Campbell, having joined his father, read the galley proofs and was in complete accord with the intentions of the document and with the principles set forth.

As originally published it consisted of 56 closely spaced pages and was made up of four parts: a short Declaration, an introduction that set forth the purpose of the Association; an Address that scored the evils of a divided church and set forth principles for the unity of the church; an Appendix that commented further on what had been set forth and which dealt with possible criticisms; a Postscript calling for steps to be taken immediately.

It was not what a modern printer would call "good copy" in that the paragraphs were too long, the sentences cumbersome, and there were no subdivisions or topical arrangement. But it was typical for the times and was not difficult to read, even though it was largely ignored by the very ones for which it was intended, the clergy. It would be of interest to the Baptists that among the few reactions from the Presbyterian clergy to the principles set forth was, "Sir, these words, however plausible in appearance, are not sound. For if you follow these out, you must become a Baptist."[14] The Declaration reads as if it were written by a freedom fighter, or as if it were taking its cue from the Declaration of Independence, which must have influenced its title as well as some of its sentiments. It begins with:

From the series of events which have taken place in the churches for many years past, especially in this Western country, as well as from what we know in general of the present state of things in the Christian world, we are persuaded that it is high time for us not only to think, but also to act, for ourselves; to see with our own eyes, and to take all our measures directly and immediately from the Divine standard; to this alone we feel ourselves Divinely bound to be conformed, as by this alone we must be judged.[15]

He goes on to call for "a thorough reformation in all things, civil and religious, according to his word," which led Ronald Osborn to conclude that Campbell "clearly affirms the consistency of freedom in the church with freedom in the state."[16]

The Declaration or Introduction also emphasizes what might be called the principle of non-judgment. "We are also persuaded that no man can be judged for his brother, so no man can judge for his brother," it reads, concluding that "no man has a right to judge his brother, except insofar as he manifestly violates the express letter of the law." With the cry of a prophet it also sets forth in no uncertain terms the purpose of the new society:

Being well aware, from sad experience, of the heinous nature and pernicious tendency of religious controversy among Christians; tired and sick of the bitter jarrings and janglings of a party spirit, we would desire to be at peace; and, were it possible, we would also desire to adopt and recommend such measures as would give rest to our brethren throughout all the churches: as would restore unity, peace, and purity to the whole Church of God.

Campbell states that the purpose of the Christian Association of Washington was to promote "simple evangelical Christianity, free from all mixture of human opinions and inventions of men." While the society "by no means considers itself a Church," it included in its mission the support of "a pure Gospel ministry" and the distribution of the Scriptures to the poor. Most noteworthy was its desire to encourage the formation of similar societies with like purposes.

He must have envisioned his movement, *within* the church, spreading across the country, carrying on its unity efforts in many societies, their manifesto being the *Declaration and Address*. As Kershner puts it: "Thomas Campbell expected his *Declaration and Address* to produce a religious revolution within a few years. In this he was doomed to disappointment. Like every great leader he was ahead of his age."[17]

Principles of the Document

The verbosity of the Address section, where some paragraphs run for several pages, subjects the document to the risk of not selling for what it is worth. It is therefore helpful to provide some outline to the ideas set forth, such as follows, which faithfully summarizes the thought, as the quotations will indicate.

1. *Division is terribly sinful, obstructing the mission of the church.*

He refers to divisions within the church as sad, evil, awful, woeful, and accursed. The party spirit breaks up churches and neighborhoods alike, and as for unevangelized areas they "remain to this day entirely destitute of a Gospel ministry, many of them in little better than a state of heathenism, the Churches being either so weakened with divisions that they cannot send ministers, or the people so divided among themselves that they will not receive them." At length he scores the evil of partyism, such as: "What awful and distressing effects those sad divisions produced! what aversions, what reproaches, what backbitings, what evil surmisings, what angry contentions, what enmities, what excommunications, and even persecution!!!"

2. *It is the responsibility of Christians to be more sensitive to the divisions within the church and do something about them, however insurmountable the task may appear.*

"Is it not then your incumbent duty to endeavor, by all scriptural means, to have these evils remedied," he writes, and then adds this special word to the clergy: "And does it not peculiarly belong to *you*, who occupy the place of Gospel ministers, to be leaders in this laudable undertaking?" He criticizes those who are complacent and who think the task too difficult, or who argue that the time is not ripe. The prayers of Christ and the church both in heaven and on earth are with those that make the effort to unify the church, and so "We judge it our duty to make the attempt, by using all due means in our power to promote it." And he asks why it should be thought incredible that the Church of Christ cannot resume its original unity, peace, and purity.

3. *Divisions, for the most part, are over matters of private opinion, not over the essentials.*

The churches are agreed, not only on the great doctrines of faith and holiness, but on the positive ordinances of the Gospel institution, "so that our differences, at most, are about the things in which the kingdom of God does not consist, that is, about matters of private opinion or human invention."

4. *Christ is the only source of unity, his word the only terms.*

"You are all, dear brethren, equally included as the objects of our love and esteem. With you all we desire to unite in the bonds of an entire Christian unity — Christ alone being the *head*, the center, his word the rule; an explicit belief of, and manifest conformity to it, in all things — the *terms*." He points out that for the sake of unity neither can require more than this of the other.

5. *The call to unite the church is not unreasonable, the time is not unseasonable.*

"We hope, then, what we urge will neither be deemed an unreasonable nor an unseasonable undertaking. Why should it be thought unseasonable? Can any time be assigned, while things continue as they are, that would prove more favorable for such an attempt, or what could be supposed to make it so?" He recognizes that there will always be those in the church that will support its divisions, and that Satan will not be idle in preserving them. He observes that men do not hesitate to act when their secular interests are at stake.

6. *Since Jesus prayed for the unity of his church, it must follow that adequate means can be found. We can do it!*

"That such a thing, however, will be accomplished, one way or other, will not be questioned by any that allow themselves to believe the commands and prayers of our Lord Jesus will not utterly prove ineffectual. We believe then it is as practicable as it is eligible. Let us attempt it. 'Up, and be doing, and the Lord will be with us.' Shall we pray for a thing, and not strive to obtain it!!"

7. *Since we will be one in heaven, we must be one on earth.*

"There are no divisions in the grave, nor in that world which lies beyond it," he says. "There our divisions must come to an end! We must all unite there! Would to God we could find in our hearts to put an end to our short-lived divisions here; that so we might leave a blessing behind us; even a happy and united Church."

8. *We must begin to associate with each other and be less interested in our own party, or unity will never be achieved. United we shall prevail!*

The task of uniting the church cannot be done if we "run every man to his own house and consult only the interests of his own party." He lays down a practical rule: "Until you associate, consult, and advise together, and in a friendly and Christian manner explore the subject, nothing can be done," and so he lays on them "the obvious and important duty of association." Again and again he states his willingness to unite with the Christians in all the sects. "United we shall prevail!," he assures them.

9. *With nations being ravaged by war, how can we remain a divided church?*

Here Campbell looks beyond his own new frontier to a world wracked by the Napoleonic wars, "these awful convulsions and revolutions that have dashed and are dashing to pieces the nations like a potter's vessel." He poses a sober question that could be asked of most generations of Americans: "Have not the remote vibrations of this dreadful shock been felt even by us, whom God has graciously placed at so great a distance?" Then he cries like a prophet to a dispassionate people: "Is it time for us to sit still in our corruptions and divisions when the Lord, by his word and providence, is so loudly and expressly calling us to repentance and reformation?"

10. *Our efforts for unity are but a humble beginning, so we solicit the help of others, for the collective graces of the whole church will assure us success.*

He praises "that dear-bought liberty" that has set him free from "subjection to any authority but his own in matters of religion," and because of this the Association is seeking to promote peace and unity, "the mite of our humble endeavors." The propositions he sets forth, he allows, are but preliminary, and he seeks "the collective graces that are conferred upon the Church" so that what is sown in weakness will be raised in power. He sought the counsel and cooperation of all Christians, "however unhappily distinguished by party names," in promoting "the unity, purity, and prosperity of his Church."

Propositions of the Document

Following these principles are thirteen propositions that form the heart of the *Declaration*, several of which are a repetition of the foregoing principles. The first proposition is probably the most quoted and most influential paragraph ever written in the Movement's history:

> That the Church of Christ upon earth is essentially, intentionally, and constitutionally one; consisting of all those in every place that profess their faith in Christ and obedience to him in all things according to the Scriptures, and that manifest the same by their tempers and conduct, and of none else as none else can be truly and properly called Christians.

This has served as the basis of the Disciples' theology of the church, *that the church by its very nature is one, and that it is a contradiction to speak of a divided church.* Unity is somehow there, as God's gift, however hidden by partyism. Ronald Osborn, quoting this paragraph from Campbell, writes: "From the outset Disciples have emphasized the insight so often repeated in ecumenical circles today concerning the givenness of unity among all Christians,"[18] but Ralph Wilburn may capture the meaning more pointedly when he sees the unity of the church as "real but not adequately realized."[19]

It should be noted that when Campbell penned these lines he did not yet have a congregation of his own, and yet he spoke of the church as a reality upon earth. It is apparent that he did not conceive of his movement as an effort to restore the church that did not exist.

Thirty-five years later Thomas combined this line on the church's unity with his ever consuming theme, love, in a letter written from his son's home in Bethany: "The church of Christ upon earth is constitutionally and essentially one: therefore, the first relative duty of every member of it is to preserve this unity by loving each other as Christ has loved them."[20] Those combined principles, *The church is one, therefore love,* form the essence of Thomas Campbell's teaching.

His third proposition points to a practical way of restoring unity, one that he considered especially relevant since he was to refer to it now again throughout his ministry:

> Nothing ought to be inculcated upon Christians as articles of faith, nor required of them as terms of communion, but what is expressly taught and enjoined upon them in the word of God. Nor ought anything to be admitted as of Divine Obligation, in their Church constitution and managements, but what is expressly enjoined by the authority of our Lord Jesus Christ and his apostles upon the New Testament Church, either in express terms or by approved precedent.

This principle grows out of what he had already referred to as a point of concern, that differences are nearly always over "things in which the kingdom of God does not consist." The church generally has had a proclivity to divide over things of which the Scriptures are silent, and the heirs of Campbell's own movement have, in the words of W.E. Garrison, "quarreled more about what they do, than about what they *think*."[21] Campbell's solution is that nothing is to be made a test of fellowship except what is expressly taught or enjoined in the Scriptures.

The last phrase "in express terms or by approved precedent" seems to compromise this since an approved precedent (or example) is often subject to varying interpretations. This was the only point that Alexander Campbell questioned when he studied the document for himself. Since examples in the Scriptures often point to methods, which may be affected by time and circumstance, young Alexander supposed that the safer course would be to make nothing a test of communion except what is expressly enjoined (period).

The *Christian Evangelist* used this principle by slightly altering a well-known motto, which it carried on its masthead for many years: "In faith, unity; in opinions and methods, liberty; in all things, charity."

His sixth proposition may be the most discerning of all since it gets to the very heart of so many theological differences:

> Although inference and deductions from Scripture premises, when fairly inferred, may be truly called the doctrine of God's holy word, yet are they not formally binding upon the consciences of Christians farther than they perceive the connection, and evidently see that they are so; for their faith must not stand in the wisdom of men, but in the power and veracity of God. Therefore, no such deductions can be made terms of communion, but do properly belong to the after and progressive edification of the Church. Hence, it is evident that no such deductions or inferential truths ought to have any place in the Church's confession.

Campbell tells his Christian brothers that they may be right in their theological deductions – their views may truly be the doctrine of God's holy word – but they still have no right to impose such views upon others *until they perceive the connection*. This is reflective of the law of love that ruled in all of Campbell's thought, for love demands that we allow to another that which we claim for ourselves: that one be held responsible for only what he has come to accept after due consideration.

He is saying that deductions (opinions and interpretations) cannot be made terms of fellowship. It is an affirmation that became basic to "the Plea" of the Movement for generations to come.

His son Alexander was to express the principle in a different way: "No man can be saved by the belief of any theory, true or false. No man will be damned for disbelief of any theory. To make *new* theories is the way to make *new divisions*. To contend for the *old* is to keep up the old *divisions*."[22]

Thomas recognizes that theological differences are to be worked out, if possible, *within* the fellowship, and that unanimity of viewpoint is not to be made a condition to fellowship. Such things belong to the "after and progressive edification of the church." Agreement, if it is realized, must therefore come through education from within and not by imposition from without.

The seventh proposition recognizes that individual differences must be considered in making judgments relative to fellowship, a principle long recognized in educational circles.

> Although doctrinal exhibitions of the great system of Divine truths, and defensive testimonies in opposition to prevailing errors, be highly expedient, and the more full and explicit they be for those purposes, the better; yet, as these must be in a great measure the effect of human reasoning, and of course must contain many inferential truths, they ought not to be made terms of Christian communion; unless we suppose what is contrary to fact, that none have a right to the communion of the Church but such as possess a very clear and decisive judgment, or are come to a very high degree of doctrinal information; whereas the Church from the beginning did and ever will consist of little children and young men, as well as fathers.

Campbell here recognizes that the scriptural injunction "it is according to what a man hath and not according to what he hath not" applies to one's acceptance into the fellowship of the church as well as to his ability to give. He stresses this principle further in the eighth proposition by saying, "It is not necessary that persons should have a particular knowledge or distinct apprehension of all Divinely revealed truths in order to entitle them to a place in the Church." He further insists that they should not be required to make a profession more extensive than their knowledge.

Two decades later his son Alexander indicated that he had been influenced by this principle when he wrote: "We never did, at any time, exclude a man from the kingdom of God for a mere imbecility of intellect; or, in other words, because he could not consent to our opinions."[23]

Pervading the document is the implication of a law of unity and fellowship, which, when violated, is as great a sin against God and man as any other law that God has given for man's good. Division is not merely an evil, but it is "a horrid evil, fraught with many evils," and he brands it as anti-Christian, anti-scriptural, and even anti-natural in that it obstructs man's most noble impulse, to love and accept his fellows. From the *Address* can be lifted those ideals that read like laws, laws that are so weighty in their implication and consequence that Campbell appears bewildered that the church can go on ignoring them. Such as:

> No man has a right to judge, to exclude, or reject his professing Christian brother, except insofar as he stands condemned or rejected by the express letter of the law.
>
> The great fundamental law of unity and love ought not to be violated to make way for exalting human opinions to an equality with express revelation, by making them articles of faith and terms of communion.

The first and foundation truth of our Christianity is union with Christ, and the very next to it in order, union with each other in him — "that we might receive each other, as Christ has also received us, to the glory of God."[24]

That Scripture, Romans 15:7, which is alluded to several times in the document, became to Campbell what may be called "commandment by metaphor." It is not simply "Receive one another," but "Receive one another as Christ has received you, to the glory of God." This Scripture, along with John 13:33, which has a similar metaphor: "Love one another as I have loved you," also referred to in the document, became his mandate for an urgent plea for the unity of all believers.

One criticism he deals with in the Appendix is the charge that he is guilty of latitudinarianism, which he dubs "a gigantic term," and which we would call liberalism. He insisted that he took no greater latitude than the divine law allows, either in judging persons or doctrines, and he only hoped that such latitude would pervade the whole church. It is a great evil, he ventured, for men to determine *expressly*, in the name of the Lord, when the Lord has not *expressly* determined, and thus judge their brothers because they have a different opinion. Latitudinarianism would lessen that evil![25]

Unity and Restoration

Disciples historians find two motifs running throughout the Movement's existence, unity and restoration, and these have been seen as in tension with each other, if not contradictory, and consequently the source of faction within the Movement. Ronald Osborn sees this as early as the *Declaration and Address* itself: "My own study of the *Declaration and Address* convinces me that union and restoration are inextricably intertwined in the thought of Thomas Campbell."[26]

The restoration motif is viewed as possibly contradictory to the unity plea in that it calls for an exact or detailed recovery of primitive Christianity in doctrine, worship, and organization, which, if insisted upon, calls for a uniformity that is at variance with the principles laid down by Thomas Campbell.

There are grounds for Osborn's conclusion that unity and restoration are inextricably intertwined, but the question is what Campbell meant by restoration. He says, for instance that the cure for divisions is "by simply returning to the original standard of Christianity, the profession and practice of the primitive Church, as expressly exhibited upon the sacred page of New Testament scripture." He even urges: "Let *us* do as we are there expressly told *they* did, say as *they* said; that is, profess and practice as therein expressly enjoined by precept and precedent, in every possible instance after *their* approved example."[27]

This reads as if Campbell sees restoration as patternism, which allows for no latitude in what one conceives to be the ancient order. If this is what he means it would contradict the principles set forth in the Address, where he insists that real unity must necessarily be diverse. In view of what he says elsewhere in the document, we may conclude that Campbell is here referring to the *essentials* of the primitive faith as the bond of union, not the myriad of details that may or may not be relevant.

In the Appendix, for instance, he says that each Christian will do his best to interpret and practice the will of God, but in following this general rule there will be "some variety of opinion and practice." Then he says, "This, we see, was actually the case in the apostolic Churches, without any breach of Christian unity; and if this was the case at the erection of the Christian Church from among Jews and Gentiles, may we not reasonably expect that it will be the same at her restoration from under her long anti-christian and sectarian desolations."[28]

This is one of the few times he uses *restoration* in the entire document, and here he is saying that in the restored church of his day there will be "some variety of opinion and practice" just as there was in the primitive church, and if they could be diverse and yet united, so can we. We conclude, therefore, that it is the unity motif that pervades the *Declaration and Address*, not restoration. And it is a plea for the unity of all Christians, based only upon loyalty to Christ as Lord rather than human opinions, that stands as Thomas Campbell's contribution to the Movement and to the church at large.

A half century after the publication of the *Declaration and Address*, Alexander Campbell stated that he had never seen in print nor heard from a human lip one objection, plausible in the least degree, to a single position set forth in the document. "It, indeed, assumes," he went on to say, "the only plausible ground or basis of that union, communion, and co-operation, for which our Savior prayed, and for which all earnest Christians ever pray."[29] Thomas Campbell himself, after 24 years, wrote to Barton W. Stone that no one had offered any objections to the principles set forth in the document, which he considered "a complete scriptural reformation, urged and defined."[30]

Other Contributions

As for his other contributions to the Movement, W.E. Garrison says that Thomas Campbell after the *Declaration and Address* "never wrote a line, delivered a speech, or made a decision which had any marked effect on the faith or fortunes of the movement which he had started."[31] This is hardly the case, for he did go on to serve as a trusted adviser to his son, who soon emerged as the leader of the Movement, and he was involved in decision-making, such as Alexander's decision to publish a new translation of the New Testament.

He not only wrote for his son's publications, but now and again served as editor *pro tem.* He was an inveterate letter writer, and these letters, sometimes penned anonymously, appear throughout the years in the *Christian Baptist* and the *Millennial Harbinger.* They are replete with sage advice from the patriarch of the Movement.

Alexander interrupted his series on "Reformation" in 1836 in order to present a lengthy letter from his father, for it spoke urgently to their current efforts for reform. The father feared that the Movement had become far too controversial in character, and that it was being retarded by its own advocates who did not really understand what it was all about. He warned that a people could attain "the purest orthodoxy" and still miss the point of "practical Christianity."

In this letter the older Campbell urged that most controversy could be avoided by simply teaching "the express declarations and dictates of the sacred oracles," for people are disinclined to argue over what the Bible actually says. He also advised that troublesome opinions could best be handled by showing their irrelevancy rather than their falsity. His voice through the years was one of moderation, and it is evident that his people never attained the spiritual maturity that he had and that he wished for them.[32]

While he was not a debater, he sometimes used his letters to rebuke those who erred, such as Sidney Rigdon, a leading Disciple that converted to the Mormons. He described Rigdon as "the professed disciple and public teacher of the infernal Book of Mormon" and himself as "the professed disciple and public teacher of the supernal books of the Old and New Testaments of our Lord and Savior Jesus Christ, which you now say is superseded by the Book of Mormon."[33]

Uncharacteristically, he challenged Rigdon to a debate on the all-sufficiency of the Bible, but Rigdon did not accept. Thomas once went into Mormon country, the environs of Kirkland, Ohio, to stave off any influence Rigdon and the Mormons might have on his own people.

Apart from his own contribution as an apostle of unity and an envoy of love to the strife-ridden church of his day, Thomas Campbell's greatest gift to the Movement was his own son. If he was its initiator who laid out the design, his son was its executor. Alexander had his father to look to, not only for the wisdom of his disciplined mind, but for his pious and exemplary life as well. In the *Memoirs* of his father he stated that he walked more closely with God than any man he knew, and that he would often find his father in his room, unaware of anyone's presence due to his blindness, praising God with great joy.[34] Walter Scott also esteemed him as the most exemplary person he had ever known.[35]

But there was fire in his piety, which manifested itself at such times as to spare the Movement any schisms while aborning. A notable instance was in 1828 in his defense of young Aylett Raines, who was on the verge of being expelled by the Mahoning Association for his espousal of Universalist notions. "The devil has brought this question into this association to sow discord," fumed the genial Campbell.

He went on to say, "Brother Raines and I have been much together for the last several months, and we have mutually unbosomed ourselves to each other. I am a Calvinist and he a Restorationist; and although I am a Calvinist, I would put my right arm into the fire and have it burnt off before I would raise my arm against him."[36] This gesture saved Raines for a lifetime of effective ministry within the Movement.

Thomas was appealing to a law of unity and brotherhood that he had given expression to twenty years earlier: *No man has a right to judge, to exclude, or reject his professing Christian brother, except insofar as he stands condemned or rejected by the express letter of the law.*

Thomas Campbell labored to make this law the rule of a Movement and the practice of the church, which he saw as "essentially, intentionally, and constitutionally one," a unity that was real but not adequately realized.

ENDNOTES

[1]Alexander Campbell, *Memoirs of Elder Thomas Campbell*, Cincinnati: 1861, p. 131. Alexander Campbell estimated that in 1850 the Movement had 2,000 churches with an average of 100 each, for a total of 200,000 (*Millennial Harbinger*, 1850, p. 231).

[2]Thomas Campbell, "A Synopsis of Christianity," *Millennial Harbinger*, 1844, p. 481.

[3]Thomas Campbell, "An Address to All Christian Brethren," *Millennial Harbinger*, 1844, p. 199.

[4]"Campbell's Position in History," *Christian Evangelist*, Vol. 57, No. 76 (1938).

[5]D.H. Yoder in *A History of the Ecumenical Movement*, edited by Ruth Rouse and S. C. Neill, London: 1954, p. 237.

[6]F.D. Kershner in Thomas Campbell, *Declaration and Address* (St. Louis: Mission Messenger, 1975), p. 10.

[7]H.E. Johnson, *The Declaration and Address for Today* (Nashville: Reed and Co., 1971), p. 7.

[8]*Declaration and Address* (Centennial Ed., 1909), Introduction.

[9]C.L. Loos, "History of the 19th Century Reformation," *Christian Evangelist*, Vol. 18(1899), p. 104.

[10]The reference to shape of the head was influenced by phrenology, a fad in those days that many people took seriously, including the Campbells.

[11]W.H. Hanna, *Thomas Campbell: Seceder and Christian Union Advocate* (Cincinnati: Standard, 1935), pp. 39f.

[12]Lester G. McAllister, *Thomas Campbell: Man of the Book* (St. Louis: Bethany Press, 1954), p. 83.

[13]Robert Richardson, *Memoirs of Alexander Campbell*, Vol. 1 (Cincinnati: Standard, 1897), pp. 236f.

[14]*Ibid.*, p. 250.

[15]A useful text with helpful introduction is Thomas Campbell, *Declaration and Address* (St. Louis: Mission Messenger, 1975).

[16]Ronald E. Osborn, *Experiment in Liberty* (St. Louis: Bethany Press, 1978), p. 24.

[17]F.D. Kershner, *Declaration and Address*, p. 14.

[18]Ronald E. Osborn, "The One Holy Catholic and Apostolic Church," in *The Reformation of Tradition*, The Renewal of the Church, Vol. 1, Edited by W.O. Blakemore (St. Louis: Bethany Press, 1963), p. 345.

[19]Ralph Wilburn, "The Unity We Seek" in *The Revival of the Churches*, The Renewal of the Church, Vol. 3, Edited by W. B. Blakemore (St. Louis: Bethany Press, 1963), p. 345.

[20]Thomas Campbell, "Extract of A Letter," *Millennial Harbinger*, 1844, p. 104.

[21]W.E. Garrison, *A Fork in the Road* (pamphlet) (Indianapolis: Pension Fund of Christian Churches, 1964), p. 6.

[22]Robert Richardson, *Memoirs of Alexander Campbell*, Vol. 2 (Cincinnati: Standard, 1897), p. 153.

[23]Alexander Campbell, "Millennium No. II," *Millennial Harbinger*, 1830, p. 146.

[24]*Declaration and Address*, pp. 53, 55.

[25]*Ibid.*, p. 72.

[26]Ronald E. Osborn, *Experiments in Liberty*, p. 87.

[27]*Declaration and Address*, p. 77.

[28]*Ibid.*, p. 64.

[29]Alexander Campbell, *Memoirs of Elder Thomas Campbell*, Cincinnati: 1861, p. 111.

[30]Thomas Campbell, "Letter to Barton W. Stone," *Millennial Harbinger*, 1833, p. 421.

[31]W.E. Garrison, *Religion Follows the Frontier: A History of Disciples of Christ* (New York: Harper and Row, 1931), p. 88.

[32]Thomas Campbell, "To the Editor of the *Millennial Harbinger*," *Millennial Harbinger*, 1836, pp. 214-218.

[33]A.S. Hayden, *History of the Disciples of Christ on the Western Reserve*, Cincinnati: 1875, p. 217. Walter Scott said Thomas Campbell frequently offered propositions for debate. See *Memoirs of Elder Thomas Campbell*, p. 277.

[34]*Memoirs of Elder Thomas Campbell*, p. 232.

[35]Ibid., p. 279.

[36]A.S. Hayden, *History*, p. 168.

6

ALEXANDER CAMPBELL
THE MOVEMENT IN DESIGN

A restoration of the ancient order

In 1809 when Alexander Campbell was only 20 years old, he went before the elders of the Anti-Burgher Seceder Presbyterian Church in Glasgow to obtain a metal token that would allow him to participate in the upcoming semiannual communion service. Being a member of the Secession Church in Ireland and having no letter, he was required to go before the session in Glasgow and be examined. He was accordingly examined by the session and received the token. This was common practice in the churches of that day, and it was typical for a pastor to have his own tokens struck according to his design and preference.[1]

When the hour came for Alexander to commune with his fellow Seceders, there was serious doubt in his mind as to whether he should do so. Some 800 communicants were served in shifts as they gathered around eight or nine tables at a time. Alexander kept postponing his decision, hesitating to enter by the door into the Communion room, allowing the others to go on ahead of him as he dropped farther back in the waiting line. Finally he made his decision. Once he was seated at one of the tables, he dropped his token into the plate, but declined to partake of the elements when they passed before him. He walked out a free man, realizing that life would never be the same now that he had turned his back upon the church of his youth.

If Robert Richardson could say of that experience, "The ring of the token, falling upon the plate, announced the instant at which he renounced Presbyterianism forever, the leaden voucher becoming thus a token not of communion but of separation,"[2] one could also see it as the beginning of the reformation he would soon launch in the new world.

Being mature for his years, Alexander did not allow youthful impetuosity to lead him to speak or to act in ways that he would later regret. He kept his resolutions to himself and was thus able to leave Scotland with the usual certificate of good standing from his elders.

His doubts at the time of the Communion can be traced to the influence of the Glasite Independents and the Haldane brothers in general, which we have recounted in chapter two, and to one Greville Ewing in particular. Ewing was an associate of the Haldanes who had left the Church of Scotland in 1798 after giving his farewell sermon in Lady Glenorchy's Chapel in Edinburgh one wintry Sunday. When the Haldanes set out to form their first "Congregational Church" in Edinburgh, in which James Haldane served as pastor, it was Greville Ewing that designed its form of government, which allowed for a lay ministry, a free observance of the ordinances, and the Bible as the only guide in religion.

When the first Haldane church was formed in Glasgow on old Jamaica street (which remains much the same today and bears the same name) in a large building once used for a circus, in about 1801, Ewing was its pastor. This is where Alexander Campbell found him when he came to the city to study at the University of Glasgow in 1807.

Ewing conducted a seminary for Presbyterians in both Edinburgh and Glasgow, but this was closed by the time Alexander came to the city in 1807. Ewing was giving all his energies to his large and wealthy congregation. It was both at Ewing's home and at his church that Alexander was led to take the issues of reformation seriously. After going to his own Seceder Church on Sunday mornings, he attended Ewing's Congregational Church in the evenings, to which the vivacious pastor would sometimes attract as many as 2,000. He had what he called "discussion groups" for university students in his home, and it was here that he and Campbell became trusted friends.

The Glas-Sandeman influence on Campbell can be better understood when it is realized that Ewing was much closer to these reformers than were the Haldanes. Indeed, one reason why the Haldanes closed down Ewing's seminary in Glasgow was that he had introduced the works of Glas and Sandeman. The Haldanes were less inclined to break away from the Church of Scotland than were the earlier reformers, and their original intention was simply to awaken the church to greater zeal and piety and not to introduce doctrinal changes. When they were finally compelled to go independent, it was Ewing, influenced more by Glas and Sandeman, who directed their efforts toward doctrinal and organizational reform.

For instance, it was Ewing who first introduced the celebration of the Lord's Supper every Lord's Day in his Glasgow church, a practice eventually adopted by the Campbell movement in America. Yet when the Haldanes finally rejected the practice of sprinkling infants and began to baptize by immersion only, Ewing insisted that sprinkling and the baptism of infants were scriptural, which may help to explain why Campbell himself was reluctant to yield on these ideas.

Besides an emphasis on weekly Communion, Ewing's influence on Campbell included these elements of reform, which were rarely practiced at that time: (1) a devotion to the Scriptures themselves rather than the creedal emphasis of the clergy; (2) an independent or congregational form of government; (3) an emphasis upon the rights of lay ministers and a rejection of clerical privileges; (4) a plurality of elders in each church; (5) the practice of mutual edification (Ewing's church had a meeting each week for this purpose); (6) the view that faith is not supernaturally induced but based on the belief of testimony, the appeal being to the intellect as well as the heart.

The Haldanes and Ewing also thought of reformation in terms of a restoration of primitive Christianity. In earlier years the emphasis was upon evangelism, but now they sought a pure and simple evangelical Christianity based upon the exact practices of the primitive church. Only three years before Alexander's arrival in Glasgow, James Haldane had published his *View of the Social Worship and Ordinances of the First Christians.*

This book, along with those of Glas and Sandeman, along with the conversations with Greville Ewing, gave young Campbell an inclination toward reform and armed him with much of the raw material with which he would soon launch his own search for the ancient order on a new frontier in a new world.

A passion for the unity of the church was not, however, part of the raw material gathered at Glasgow. As we have seen, the plea for a restoration of primitive Christianity goes far back into history and was not new to the Scottish reformers, and certainly not afterwards with the Campbells, but it was left for the Campbells, along with the Stone movement, to relate the restoration of primitive Christianity to the unity of the church. This was to be its unique feature: *the unity (and reformation) of the church through a restoration of the ancient order.*

That the Scottish influence on young Campbell was real and lasting can hardly be questioned. While he was not often inclined to reflect upon these experiences, he did afterwards recall that "he imbibed disgust at the popular schemes, chiefly while a student at Glasgow."

This may be the most important ingredient in the making of a reformer, *disgust*. It was disgust for a sectarian view of the church, we may say, that caused him to drop his token and walk out of that Communion service, a service that he realized would exclude the likes of Greville Ewing. It was a disgust for "the janglings and jarrings of sectarian strife" that led him and his father to launch a movement for peace and unity.[3]

The academic influence on Alexander at the university was not as significant as the religious influence of the city. Since his birth at Balleymena, County Antrim, Ireland in 1788, he had been schooled almost entirely by his father, which had been so well accomplished by them both that university studies were not all that much of a challenge.

Along with his course of study, he found time to make his living by conducting private classes in Latin and English, try his hand at poetry, keep a diary, study the Scriptures, and engage in extensive self-examination, as well as to socialize rather extensively with bright young men from all parts of Great Britain.

It must have been satisfying for him to study with two professors that had taught his father 25 years before. His studies for that one year at Glasgow were Greek, including a course in the Greek New Testament, literature and logic, French and experimental philosophy. In order to do all this he retired at 10 p.m. and rose at 4 a.m., a schedule he was to follow during most of his productive years. Glasgow classes in those days began at 6 a.m.!

Since he arrived at the university with facility in Greek as well as Latin, he was able to present his professor with his own translation of Homer and Sophocles. He also submitted various essays in both prose and verse. It was this ability to coast through his college studies that enabled him to cultivate the friendship of Greville Ewing.

Despite his erudition there was one thing that Campbell could not do. He could not sing! His biographers recognize his "deficiency in the musical faculty." He did, however, make an effort to sing and eventually published a hymnal, for which he authored at least four of the hymns, which reflect his poetic talent. Nor did he have the slightest interest in fiction.

But Glasgow was still more. Alexander had lived only in small villages in rural areas. Now he was in a city of 114,000, the industrial capital of Scotland, and in an academic setting of 1500 students. This new adventure of 300 days in Glasgow prepared him in more than one way for the new world that awaited him.

Journey to America

When on July 31, 1809 Campbell set sail for America on the *Latonia*, it was not the first time he had tried it. In October of the previous year, having received word from his father that the family should join him in Pennsylvania, he had set sail from Londonderry, Ireland only to suffer shipwreck a few days later along the rocky coast of the Irish sea. While his life was not in real danger, it served to make him more introspective and led to his decision, which was probably inevitable, to devote his life to the

Tragedy's
Affection
Faith

ministry. That the wreck was not unduly perilous is evident by the fact that he had time to save both personal effects of the family and a boxful of books. Some of the books, mostly in the classics and theology, are still preserved in the Campbell Room at Bethany College.

It was this interruption that led him to Glasgow. On the island of Islay, where he lodged temporarily following the shipwreck, he made friends with a man who was acquainted in Glasgow. Since Alexander was going to spend the winter there, this man wanted him to meet a good friend of his, and so wrote for him a letter of introduction to one Greville Ewing!

Young Campbell did not fare too well by sea in those days, for even on this second journey a leak in the hull of the ship led him to urge the captain to return to Scotland. Deciding that it was less risky to continue the journey than to attempt to return, the captain sailed on toward America, while every able-bodied man, including Alexander, spent several hours each day running the pumps so as to stay even with the incoming water. They also came upon a storm which raged for days, the fiercest that anybody on board had ever witnessed, including the hardened sailors, and they all feared certain destruction.

Once the sea was calm, Alexander wrote in his diary: "Such was that dreadful storm, and such its effects, but thanks be to that God who raises the winds and quells the tumults of the seas, that it did not prove fatal to us all."[4]

This diary, which he entitled "Journal of a Voyage from Ireland Towards America, 1808," (the first attempted voyage was in 1808, the second in 1809) was eventually laid away in a trunk that was removed from Bethany to Adelaide, Australia in 1920 by Julian Barclay, a grandson to Alexander. This forgotten trunk was discovered in 1964, and the diary, along with other valuable manuscripts, including scores of sermons preached by Alexander in his early 20's, were found, providing Campbell scholars with a real find in primary sources.[5]

Finally, on September 29, 1809, the old *Latonia* cast anchor in New York harbor, and Alexander and his family, after 55 days at sea, set foot in the new world. Thirty-eight years later he was to recall the most delightful moment of that experience, which was the pleasure of drinking a glass of cold, fresh milk![6]

After a week visiting New York, Alexander conveyed the family to Philadelphia by stage coach. There they hired a waggoner to bear them across Pennsylvania to Washington, which was to be their new home, a distance of 350 miles. They made about 30 miles per day, sometimes riding in the wagon, sometimes walking. Alexander found the vast expanse of forests different from his native Ireland, which was almost destitute of woods.

He was also impressed with the way Americans trusted each other, for he never found lock or bolt on any door of the inns along the way, not even the bedroom doors. The inns in those days were commodious and comfortable, with dining room, carpeted parlor, and always a bar. Along the main roads one could be found every ten or twenty miles.

Word being sent ahead, Thomas Campbell met his family with spare horses some three days from their destination, after a separation of two years. They had lots to talk about, including the religious change of both father and son. Each feared his own account to the other would prove embarrassing, but now they discovered they were of one mind, not in spite of, but because of, all that had happened to them both. Thomas told of the trials he had suffered from his superiors, suggesting that he might well have been killed except for the law of the land.

Even before they reached their destination father and son talked of the need for a plea for Christian union based upon the Bible alone. W.E. Garrison refers to the legend that Alexander read the *Declaration and Address* there on the road from proof sheets that his father had in his saddlebags, and presumes it to be true. But Alexander, writing of the event in 1848, makes it clear that while he read the documents in proof sheets, the first he had ever seen, it was after his arrival in Washington, Pennsylvania.[7]

Both men marvelled over a providence that had brought them to the place, though by different experiences, where they could think of pursuing a common goal in reference to the reformation of the church.

Transition Years

The next few years of Alexander's life were transitory. He moved from an unknown young pioneer preacher to a controversial figure of some notoriety and the leader of a fledgling reformation among Baptist churches.

He was first of all a student, preparing himself in the Scriptures, languages, and history as if he knew what the future would demand of him. One study device was to memorize ten verses of Scripture each day, read them in the Greek or Hebrew, and then see what commentators said about them. But he was not a member of any denomination, and he had not yet preached his first sermon, even though he was going on 22.

His first sermon came on July 15, 1810 in a private home, which called for a bit of daring since he was not ordained or authorized by any church or clerical organization. It was one more assumption against clerical prerogatives on the part of the Campbells that brought them first into suspicion on the part of the clergy and finally into disrepute. Alexander was born full grown as a preacher in that he was never a novice. He appeared to be a veteran from his very first effort, and he went on to give some one hundred sermons that first year.

The Australian manuscripts, referred to above, reveal unusual maturity and insight in the handling of Scriptures and ideas in these early sermons, and a theology of some substance. From the start his eloquence was conversational in tone, and he spoke as if his only intention was to be understood. This set him apart from most of the clergy of his day. While that first sermon had its text, Matthew 7:24-27, it was more expository than textuary, which was consistent with his lifelong suspicion of "textuary sermons" and "textuary divines."

Even here in this first discourse, which was written and then memorized, the pattern begins to emerge for which he was to become famous: a linguistic-historical treatment of the passage, within the framework of basic principles drawn from extensive resources. He addressed the head as much as the heart, and spoke with reverence and unaffected simplicity. His voice was distinct and commanding, and he rarely made a gesture of any kind.

It was about this time that he was offered a seminary (boys' school) to teach, but turned it down on the ground that he was to devote himself to the budding reformation effort. He resolved first, however, with his father's encouragement, to give himself over to six months of intensive study of the Bible, "divesting himself of all earthly concerns."

But he was soon ready to marry, and did so on March 12, 1811. His bride was the lovely Margaret Brown, 18-year-old daughter of a carpenter that Thomas Campbell had met while out calling. Promising Mr. Brown some books, he sent them along by Alexander. Legend has it that when Margaret saw him from an upstairs bedroom coming through the front gate that she then and there pegged him as her man.

That same spring the Brush Run church was organized, and on New Year's Day, 1812, Alexander was ordained to the ministry by that church, with his father officiating. Even though Brush Run joined the Redstone Baptist Association in 1815, after being turned down by a Presbyterian association, Alexander was not yet to make any inroads into Baptist churches. His various preaching opportunities were mostly in homes friendly to the ideals of the Christian Association of Washington. He was still unimmersed, as were all the Brush Run church, and could hardly be considered a "Baptist" in any sense.

Once when asked why he had joined no party, he replied, "Which party would the Apostle Paul join if he were on earth?," and he insisted that he could not be a party man "Because no party will receive into communion all whom God would receive into heaven."[8]

It was in these days that Campbell resolved that he would always preach the gospel at his own expense, accepting nothing from the churches for his labor. His father predicted that he would wear many a ragged coat if he pursued such a course. He grossly underestimated the financial genius of his son, who was destined to become one of the richest men in Virginia. This rise to wealth began when his father-in-law deeded the family farm over to him and Margaret, which was designed to keep the young couple at home. The entire Brush Run church seriously considered at one time migrating to Ohio.

The Campbells Are Immersed

During these transition years Alexander gave more than passing attention to the place of baptism. He and his father alike, because of the principles they had espoused, were challenged by one and then another in reference to the baptism of infants, but they passed this off as not all that important. After all, they had been baptized, and the thought of going out of the church only to come back in again was repugnant to them. Alexander had even given a sermon on Mark 16:15-16, where believer's baptism is made part of the great commission. He was later to say of that sermon, "As I am sure it is unscriptural to make this matter a term of communion, I let it *slip*. I wish to think and let think on these matters."[9]

Once he had a baby of his own, he could not let it slip any longer. Already he had gathered those books that were for infant baptism, and he had been studying the Greek New Testament in search of an answer. But now his study of the subject reached beyond diligence to the point of becoming a passion. He must decide if his baby Jane, named for his mother, should be sprinkled.

He first concluded that the Scriptures do not authorize infant baptism. But is it to be rejected as a human invention? Are those baptized as infants actually unbaptized? Once he checked every use of the Greek words rendered *baptize* and *baptism* in the New Testament, he was satisfied that believers, and believers only, are the proper subjects of the ordinance. Not only did he decide not to baptize little Jane, but he resolved that he himself should be immersed.

Not being one to delay what he saw to be his duty, Campbell set out at once to obey what he now saw as a positive divine command. He prevailed upon one Matthias Luce, the only Baptist minister he knew, to perform the rite according to the pattern given in the New Testament. Alexander did not want to recite any "religious experience," which was a common practice, but to be immersed simply on the basis of his confession that Jesus is the Son of God. Luce, realizing he might be censured for acting contrary to Baptist practice, at first objected, but finally agreed to do it because he thought it was right.

While Alexander was making these plans, his sister Dorothea confided in him her doubts about her infant baptism and her desire to be immersed. He then revealed to her his plans and included her in them. Dorothea wanted him to get the blessings of their father, which they both considered unlikely since he had adamantly insisted that baptism should not be made an issue and that they could not go around "dechristianizing" the whole Christian world.

Thomas Campbell had immersed three members of the Brush Run church, but they had not previously been baptized by any mode. To their surprise, father Thomas said little more than "You must please yourself." They were even more surprised when later, on the day of the immersion, he casually mentioned to them on the way to the creek that Mrs. Campbell had brought along a change of clothes for the two of them.

They agreed that, because of their position, the baptismal service should be made public. So a large crowd gathered at David Bryant's farm, alongside Buffalo Creek, where they conducted a service that lasted for seven hours, most of the time being taken by Thomas Campbell, explaining why he was taking such a step after so long a delay. One of David Bryant's sons had time to leave the service, go into town, and be mustered into the War of 1812, and then to return and still hear an hour's preaching and witness the immersions!

Thomas pointed out that he had hoped to avoid any question about baptism so as not to hinder their plea for Christian unity. This had led him to overlook what he now considered the plain and obvious teaching of the Scriptures. Alexander followed his father with an extended treatment on what the Scriptures teach about baptism, quoting Acts 2:38 in particular: "Repent and be baptized, every one of you, in the name of Jesus Christ, for the remission of sins, and you shall receive the gift of the Holy Spirit." This led still others to respond, so that on June 12, 1812, seven persons were immersed into Christ in the old Buffalo for the remission of their sins. Thirteen more were immersed at the next meeting of the Brush Run church.[10]

When Alexander wrote of this experience 38 years later he explained why he considered it so significant:

> This company, as far as I am yet informed, was the first community in the country that was immersed into that primitive, simple, and most significant confession of faith in the divine person and mission of the Lord Jesus Christ, without being brought before a church to answer certain doctrinal questions, or to give a history of all their feelings and emotions, in those days falsely called "Christian experience," as if a man could have Christian experience before he was a Christian.[11]

127

The occasion of their immersion was a watershed event in the lives of the Campbells, not only because it set them apart as immersionists, which moved them even further from their Presbyterian heritage and in the direction of the Baptists, but also because it eased Alexander into the leadership of the Movement in the place of his father. While Thomas was only 50 years old at this time, this event marks the point at which the leadership of the reformation shifted to Alexander.

Once the son chose to take that daring step that formally and publicly separated him from pedobaptists, when it appeared that his father would not, it was from that time on a matter of father following son. As Richardson puts it: "From this hour, therefore, the positions of father and son were reversed, and each tacitly occupied the position allotted to him. Alexander became the master-spirit, and to him the eyes of all were now directed."[12]

It was also the beginning of persecution. The Brush Run church was ridiculed, sticks and stones were sometimes thrown at the Campbells when they baptized their converts, and Alexander found himself becoming increasingly controversial, especially among his erstwhile Presbyterian friends. On one occasion he took refuge from a storm on a woman's porch. When she learned that he was Alexander Campbell, she sent him on his way, storm or not.

More than all this, Campbell's immersion marked a new beginning in his approach to biblical interpretation. Baptism was but part of a larger system, and as a symbol it was related to other symbols. As he put it: "I must know now two things about everything, its cause and its relations." In applying this to baptism he came to speak of the whole Christian system as exhibited in three symbols, baptism, the Lord's Supper, and the Lord's day, and these became his constant themes. So, in explaining the significance of his immersion he wrote in 1848:

> It was not a simple change of views on baptism, which happens a thousand times without anything more, but a new commencement. I was placed on a new eminence — a new peak of the mountain of God, from which the whole landscape of Christianity presented itself to my mind in a new attitude and position.[13]

The Sermon on the Law

It could be added that the immersion of the Campbells brought them and the Brush Run church into what Walter Scott called "the bosom of the Baptist churches." While Alexander makes it clear that "I had no idea of uniting with the Baptists more than with the Moravians or the mere Independents,"[14] he nevertheless soon found himself itinerating among Baptist churches so extensively and with such acceptance that he was asked by them to bring the Brush Run church into their Redstone Association.

In response to the invitation the Brush Run church prepared an eight or ten page document in which they set forth the conditions under which they would join the Baptist association. These included the freedom to preach and teach the Scriptures as they understood them apart from the demands of any creed. Campbell was to regret in afteryears that this historic document was not preserved.

With or without this document it remains clear that Brush Run in no wise relinquished its sense of a unique mission in joining the Baptists, and that they were hardly "Baptist" in either doctrine or practice even though they were in the Association. Immersion was about the only common ground, as compared with the other sects, and they differed on this in regard to its import, for to the Baptists baptism was a mere command, while to Brush Run it was a discovery that led them to readjust their whole view of the Christian religion.

Campbell's reputation with the Baptists grew steadily, so that in 1816 when the Redstone Association met at the Cross Creek Baptist Church, only ten miles from his home, there was strong support for his being a key speaker. The pastor of that church, who nursed prejudice against Campbell, managed to block the move and put in his own man. But when that man turned ill, which Campbell afterwards described as "providential," even the pastor agreed that Campbell should speak.

This set the stage for the most famous and influential sermon he ever delivered, known simply as the "Sermon on the Law." It proved to be so momentous that B.L. Smith, who included the sermon in his two-volume abridgment of the *Millennial Harbinger*, hailed the occasion as the actual beginning of the Restoration Movement.[15] Campbell himself was to say 30 years later that had it not been for this sermon and the opposition it aroused he might never have launched his reformation.[16]

He also described the sermon as "rather extemporaneous," for he had but short notice. He asked that the other speaker for the day might go first so that he would have time to collect his thoughts. When one now reads the sermon, which is included in the 1846 *Millennial Harbinger*, where Campbell republished it a generation later because of the continuing demand, he marvels that such a weighty treatise could ever have been given on a moment's notice. It but shows the erudition of Alexander Campbell, even at age 28.

The sermon caused such a furor, even to the point of threatened excommunication from the Association for "damnable heresy," that Campbell decided to commit it to writing from the notes he had made and issue it as a pamphlet. He was then censured for its written version and had to stand trial at the next meeting of the Redstone Association, only to have the charge dismissed for not being within its jurisdiction.

The sermon itself, the text being Romans 8:3, was Alexander's declaration of freedom from the Old Testament system in favor of the new institution brought by Christ and his apostles through the gospel. The clergy of his day made no real distinction between the Old and New Testaments, and such ideas as "identity of the covenants" were common. This means that the Scriptures were indiscriminately applied to man's need, with little effort made to interpret a passage in the light of its context.

Thus no distinction was drawn between "the law" and "the law of faith," which led to a false synthesis of two systems, imposing upon the church a mixture of Mosaic and Christian elements. At the outset Campbell dwelt upon this distinction: "the law," without any restrictions, which occurs about 150 times in the New Testament, always refers to the law of Moses; whereas "the law of liberty," "the law of faith" or "the law of Christ" refer to the new order.

So as to select from the Old Testament what it desired and discard the rest, the clergy had long divided the law of Moses into three parts, the moral, the ceremonial, and the judicial. Campbell rejected this as unsupportable by Scripture, and insisted that "the whole law of Moses" stands or falls together. If we are "not under the law but under grace," then we are not under any of the Mosaic law.

At the same time he contended that "the moral law" — such as the Ten Commandments — was not part of the law of Moses as such, even if recorded there, for it existed long before the Mosaic dispensation, just as the first and second greatest commandments as given by Jesus (love of God and love of neighbor) are not part of that law but rather the very foundation for it.

God is a covenant-making God, Campbell was saying, and He deals with man through a succession of covenants. The law of Moses, serving its purposes, gave way to the new covenant under Christ. So the Christian dispensation is not merely an extension of the Mosaic legal system, as was commonly taught. He urged the "law preachers" to realize they were under a mandate to preach the gospel, not law, and to hearken to Jesus' words: "Teach the disciples to observe all things whatsoever I command you," and not to Moses' words. It was the Pharisees, he told them, that insisted that "We are Moses' disciples, but as for this man we know not who he is."

It was too much for some of the "law preachers." The pastor of the church, who was already opposed to him, looked for any advantage against him. When a woman fainted in the audience, he used it to delay the service and, if possible, to unnerve the speaker. Once Campbell had finished, the pastor assembled the powers that be out in the yard, insisting "That is not Baptist doctrine," and that it should be exposed as heresy before the meeting closed. Wiser heads cautioned that such a move would only be to Campbell's advantage and that the people should be left alone to decide for themselves.

This sermon was the beginning of a "seven year's war," as Campbell described it, between him and the Association, which ended only when he spoiled their plans of excommunicating him. By surreptitiously leaving Brush Run, which belonged to the Redstone Association, and joining his new congregation at Wellsburg, which did not, he left them, as he put it, "like hunters foiled by their quarry."[17]

The site of the old Cross Creek church can still be seen three miles north of Wellsburg, West Virginia, though the meetinghouse has long since disappeared. A marker identifies the spot where this memorable sermon was preached. But the visitor will get a better picture if he realizes that the sermon was probably given under a tent alongside the building, for in his reference to the event 32 years afterward Campbell casually refers to the tent.[18]

The "Sermon on the Law" meant a new hermeneutics. The Movement would henceforth contend that all efforts to justify infant baptism (in the place of circumcision), tithing, observing holy days and sabbaths, and the uniting of religion with civil law from the Old Testament are unwarranted. The Brush Run church could now defend itself for not calling Sunday "the Sabbath," for they could show that the old Hebrew law has nothing to do with the Lord's day of the new institution under Christ.

This interpretation of the Old and New Testaments as successive but distinct covenants had been set forth by Johannes Cocceius, a Dutch theologian who died in 1669. His views found wide support in Great Britain and America in the following century. Since Campbell quoted him at least once in the *Millennial Harbinger*, albeit unapprovingly, he was no doubt acquainted with his views.[19] But it is unlikely that young Campbell in the "Sermon on the Law" was influenced by anyone or anything except his own dogged determination to interpret the Scriptures aright.

Farmer And Educator

The years following the "Sermon on the Law" could be described as the lull before the storm. The eight years since the writing of the *Declaration and Address* had seen little progress for the Movement. It had but two

131

churches, counting the tiny congregation that Thomas Campbell gathered into the school he taught in Pittsburgh. Alexander was not itinerating as much, mainly because of opposition from the Redstone Association. These proved to be years of personal preparation for Alexander, financially as well as biblically. For some years now he had been a farmer, and he gave considerable time to putting his farm in shape and to extending his holdings. He was soon to own nearly all of what is now Bethany, some 2,000 acres, and he eventually reached as far west as Ohio and Illinois to buy land.[20]

He knew how to work as well as to study. With his own hands on one occasion he put up in one day one hundred panels of rail fence. He could plow the fields as well as the next farmer, but when he rested his horses in the shade, he would take from his overalls' pocket a New Testament, which he always had with him, and pursue his incessant study of the word. He also found time to socialize with his neighbors, showing a lively interest in their affairs. Though they knew him as a scholar and a preacher, he both charmed and disarmed them with his plainness and simplicity. He was warmly appreciated as friendly, hospitable, cheerful and witty. Life was fun to him, whatever he was doing.

He loved his newly adopted country. He became a naturalized citizen as quickly as time limitations allowed. To an uncle back in Ireland he wrote in 1815: "No consideration that I can conceive of, would induce me to exchange all that I enjoy in this country, climate, soil and government, for any situation which your country can afford. I would not exchange the honor and privilege of being an American citizen for the position of your king."[21]

In 1818 he started Buffalo Seminary, a school for boys, in his own home, using the main floor for classrooms and the upstairs for a dormitory, while he, Margaret and the babies repaired to the basement. This enterprise he was later to regret, not only because the dampness of the basement may have hastened Margaret's premature death, but also because he found himself the caretaker of a lot of boys who did not share his interest in spiritual things.

Some of his students became doctors and lawyers and were forever grateful to Campbell for the experience, but he was hopeful of preparing co-workers in the task of reformation. Being a vivacious teacher, he made even a school like that exciting, and he soon had more pupils than he could accept, but nonetheless he closed it after four years. With room and board at $1.50 a week and tuition $5.00 a quarter, it was not calculated to add materially to his wealth, even in the economy of that day.

Walker And Maccalla Debates

In our time it is unlikely that gentle Presbyterian ministers would go around challenging Baptists to debate, but it was not all that unheard of on the American frontier of 1820. The problem with the Baptists was that they were not as well educated as the Presbyterians, and so they had no one that could take up these challenges with any prospect of victory. No one, that is, except Alexander Campbell.

While the "Sermon on the Law" had established him as a different kind of Baptist and even as a dangerous man, he was considered nonetheless sound on baptism and as one who could champion their cause against the best of the pedobaptists. So Alexander was urged upon by the pastor of the Baptist Church in Mt. Pleasant, Ohio to accept the challenge being made by one John Walker, a Seceder Presbyterian preacher of the same village.

Managing to overcome what he called a "natural aversion to controversy," which many who knew him would question, Campbell moved into a new experience, debating. It was destined to catapult him into fame and provide him the means of promulgating his basic principles of reform. By the time he had his second debate he was on record as saying: "We are fully persuaded that a week's debating is worth a year's preaching, such as we generally have, for the purpose of disseminating truth and putting error out of countenance."[22]

The most important thing about the Walker debate, his first one, is that it ever happened, for it was a watershed event in Campbell's life. He came to enjoy such skirmishes. The first one was barely over before he issued a challenge for another one. He was temperamentally qualified for these forensic confrontations, having as he did an instinct to go for the jugular. His anti-clericalism at this time made it inevitable that he would be at odds with the professional ministry in one public way or another.

John Walker was the least competent of the five men that Campbell eventually met on the forensic platform, and was in fact almost a washout, due in part perhaps to the probability that he did not realize what he was getting himself into. The rules allowed for 40 minutes for each speech and for the debate to continue as long as seemed proper. Walker's first speech was but two minutes and he was ready to call it quits after only two days. His own moderator, who was probably an abler disputant, was to later excuse Walker's performance on the ground of insufficient preparation.

But Walker set forth the usual arguments by the pedobaptists of that day, one of which was that baptism comes in the place of circumcision as practiced by the Hebrews, which of course included infants. Campbell, with his eye on the jugular, observed that the pedobaptists do not really believe that argument, for if they did they would baptize only boys, and would do it only on the eighth day. Another was based upon household baptisms. If Lydia and her household and the jailer "and all his house" were baptized, as the Scriptures indicate, then this would include infants. Campbell rejoined that since the jailer's house *rejoiced* and *believed* and Lydia's house was *comforted as believers*, it is evident that no infants were included.

Walker made the old argument that the identity of the covenants placed baptism in the place of circumcision. This gave Campbell the opportunity to repeat what he had done in the "Sermon on the Law" and thus liberate the Christian system from the legalism of the Mosaic dispensation. The Baptists were so suspicious of this doctrine that they had second thoughts as to whether their victory over the Presbyterians was as glorious as it first appeared.

In this first debate Campbell referred to Acts 2:38, pointing out to Walker that baptism is "for the remission of sins" and not therefore for infants who know no sin. It was only in connection with the argument against infant baptism that he used the passage, and he did not yet see the broader implications of Acts 2:38 and the doctrine of immersion for remission of sins. This discovery was to await the debate with Maccalla. At this point Alexander did not connect even his own baptism with the remission of sins.

The Maccalla debate came three years later, in 1823, and was held in Washington, Ky., resulting from Campbell's own challenge to meet any pedobaptist of reputation. This time he had an opponent much more respected among the Presbyterians, and one known for his argumentative powers, being trained for the bar as well as the pulpit.

The Ohio ran too low for steamboat travel that October, so Alexander rode horseback the entire 300 miles from Bethany to Washington, Ky. At his side was Sidney Rigdon, who was to sit with him during the debate and take notes for its publication. Rigdon was an able Baptist minister that Campbell had persuaded to tend the church at Pittsburgh, begun by his father. He moved there from the Western Reserve where he had been influential in the reformation. His association with the Movement at this time is noteworthy since in a few more years he would join the Mormons and become the right hand man to Joseph Smith, their prophet. At this time Rigdon was held in high esteem by Campbell.

After eleven days on horseback he wrote to his wife back in Bethany, one of the few letters to his first wife that was preserved:

My Dear Margaret: Through the mercy and kindness of our heavenly Father we have arrived in safety and in health at the ground of debate. . This is a healthy and fine country, and everything is cheerful and animating. I have no news relative to the debate. Great expectations on all sides, and much zeal. Too much party spirit. I hope and pray that the Lord will enable me to speak as I ought to speak, and cause the truth to be glorified. Your loving husband, A. Campbell[23]

It was in this debate that Campbell first dealt with the the design or purpose of baptism. Already he had identified penitent believers as the proper subjects and immersion as the proper mode. Now he was to show that the immersion of the penitent believer is *for the remission of sins*, as set forth in Acts 2:38. This was the first time in the history of the Movement that this doctrine was set forth. Campbell presented it in such a way that it was unlikely he would ever be accused of teaching "water salvation," "a gospel of water," and other such charges that were eventually made against the reformers.

Campbell, for instance, said to Maccalla: "I know it will be said that I have affirmed that baptism 'saves us,' that it 'washes away sins.' Well, Peter and Paul have said so before me. If it was not criminal in them to say so, it cannot be criminal in me." He goes on to recognize that the gospel is such that it calls for an explanation to say that any external act done by man can be said to save him. This is the context in which he sets forth his distinction between *real* and *formal* remission of sins: one is *really* saved when he believes, *formally* saved when he is baptized.

The blood of Christ *really* cleanses those who believe, he says, while baptism is the formal proof and token of it. "The water of baptism, then, *formally* washes away our sins. The blood of Christ really washes away our sins," he concluded. Using the apostle Paul as an illustration, he notes that if Paul's sins had already in every sense been washed away when he believed, he would never have been told to "Arise and be baptized and wash away your sins." While this argues the case for baptism, it also concedes that in *some sense* Paul was saved before he was baptized. He was really saved when he believed, he was saying, but formally saved when he was baptized. Yet Campbell stresses that baptism is an ordinance of God and *necessary* "for a formal and personal remission of purgation of sins."[24]

Maccalla did not press Campbell on what attitude an immersed believer should have toward one who is really saved by faith but whose sins have not been formally washed away in baptism. In afteryears Campbell did not say much more about this distinction between real and formal remission, but it was implied in the now famous Lunenburg Letter in which he addresses the question of whether there are Christians among the sects. He there acknowledges as Christians those who believe in Christ but have mistaken the proper form of baptism, and he sets forth his definition of a Christian: "Everyone that believes in his heart that Jesus of Nazareth is the

Messiah, the Son of God; repents of his sins, and obeys him in all things according to his measure of knowledge of his will."[25]

Beginning with Campbell's apparent equivocation, the question of the design of baptism has found no final answer at anytime in the Movement's history. While some of Campbell's own followers claimed that he changed his mind about the distinction between real and formal remission as set forth in the Maccalla debate, Campbell himself insisted in his latter years that it was a distinction he had consistently made throughout his ministry. When he was 52, seventeen years after the Maccalla debate, he issued this complaint:

> Some of my brethren, with too much ardor, through the force of strong feeling, and without all the premises before them, have transcended this view and these bounds and given to baptism an undue eminence – a sort of pardon-procuring, rather than a pardon-certifying efficacy. But such has never been my reasoning or my course.[26]

He goes on in the same essay to say, "I appeal to my speeches in the Maccalla debate in proof of this; and these contain the first promulgation of these views in America, or anywhere else known to me in the present century." When Campbell finally, at age 64, issued a book on baptism, he repeated the position taken in the Maccalla debate nearly 30 years before:

> The influence which baptism may have upon our spiritual relations is, therefore, not because of any merit in the act as our own; not as a procuring cause, but merely as an instrumental and concurring cause, by which we "put on Christ," and are united to him formally, as well as in heart.[27]

These debates served to popularize the name of Alexander Campbell and the cause of reform that he represented, especially among the Baptists, to whom he was now something of a hero, even if a dubious one. In printed form the Walker debate quickly moved through two editions and 4,000 copies. The Maccalla debate also enjoyed a substantial circulation, especially in Ohio and Kentucky, where the Movement was soon to find new impetus.

A Nonsectarian Stance

During this transition period Campbell completed making a clean break from his sectarian past in the Anti-Burgher Seceder Presbyterian Church. If he was now a reformer he was a nonsectarian reformer, eager to cooperate with other Christians. Once he broke from his sectarian past he was never again a separatist. From the outset he opted for his young churches at Bethany and Wellsburg, the first two, to belong to Baptist associations, and for years he himself identified himself with the Baptists. When his movement was at last separated from the Baptists, he referred to his people as "We, as a denomination, are as desirous as ever to co-operate with all Christians on the broad and vital principles of the New and ever-lasting covenant."[28]

While he now and again conceded that his new church was a denomination, he was adamant about not being a sect, thus making a vital distinction between a denomination and a sect. While he admitted that he had tried both "the pharisaic plan and the monastic," he made it clear that he had renounced sectarianism once for all:

> I was once so straight a Separatist that I would neither pray nor sing praises with any one who was not as perfect as I supposed myself. In this most unpopular course I persisted until I discovered the mistake, and saw that on the principle embraced in my conduct, there never could be a congregation or church upon the earth.[29]

In the same context he said, "I was once so straight that, like the Indian's tree, I leaned a little the other way." He went on to describe "making our own nest and fluttering over our own brood" and "confining all goodness and grace to our noble selves" as "the quintessence of sublimated pharisaism." He blasted sectarianism as the offspring of hell!

Young Campbell was now free of the old sectarian spirit that he had come to loathe. He would soon be saying, "I declare non-fellowship with no man who owns the Lord in word and in deed. Such is a Christian."[30] He was now saying even to his dissenters, "I will esteem and love you, as I do every man, of whatever name, who believes sincerely that Jesus is the Messiah, and hopes in his salvation."[31]

Such openness took on a further dimension in an imaginary conversation he created between Martin Luther and a monk named Erastian. The monk asked Luther what he thought had come of his parents who died in the Roman church. Luther was confident that his parents were in heaven, as well as his grandparents, for they all died pious Catholics. Erastian is amazed and asked why then he had caused such a fuss all over Europe and the world if one could be saved in the Roman church.

Campbell has Luther explain that while his parents could be saved in the Roman church he could not be, for he had more light than his parents had. He has Luther say, "They lived in conformity to all they knew, and died in the church; I live in conformity to what I know, and have left the church." He then has Luther state what is sometimes called the principle of available light: "The ratio of piety is the ratio of conformity to the revealed will of God." He also has Luther say, "No man can be justified today by living in accordance with the knowledge he had yesterday," and "As the brain grows the heart should grow."[32]

This liberating view that one is responsible only for the light given him and that it is disbelief that condemns one, not unbelief, gave Campbell a more tolerant attitude toward those who have never heard. He often distinguished between wilful ignorance, which he found inexcusable, and unwilful ignorance, and he found errors of the heart far more serious than errors of the intellect.

The Design In Place

The design was now in place. The debates brought Campbell's reformation to its budding stage. It was left for publication ventures and evangelistic endeavors to bring the bloom. The particulars of the design would include:

1. They would be a movement *within* the already existing churches, with no intention of starting still another sect. They had only three congregations by 1823 (Brush Run, Pittsburgh, Wellsburg) and each of these belonged, or made an effort to belong, to a denominational association. While this intention was eventually abandoned, there is no question but what this was part of the design from the outset.

2. It was basically to be a reformation, designed to bring the existing churches closer to "the ancient order," a term that will now be current among them. There is no indication that they supposed that the church itself had to be restored to earth, as if it did not exist, or that they themselves were *the* church to the exclusion of others. They rather wanted to do something important for the church and for "the Christians·among the sects."

3. They would be a unity movement, based upon the principle of reform as enunciated by Luther. The church will be united as it becomes what it ought to be. The principles of unity were already set forth in the *Declaration and Address*.

4. Their plea would be for a unity and fellowship based only upon the Scriptures, apart from human creeds. Up to this juncture and for decades yet to come, this would be a central theme. "Where the Scriptures speak we speak, where the Scriptures are silent we are silent" was an effort to capsule this emphasis. Campbell's writings and debates were largely in opposition to creedalism. He believed that the surrender of creeds and acceptance of (and a *knowledge* of) the Scriptures alone would turn the tide.

5. This intense opposition to creeds was coupled with a suspicion for all opinions (theology) in religion. While opinions may be held as private property, they are not to be imposed upon others as matters of faith.

6. Their call for reform was to emphasize three "institutions" or "ordinances," as Campbell called them: baptism, the Lord's Supper and the Lord's Day. The doctrine of "baptism for remission of sins" was now in place, and it would continue as a unique and controversial feature of the Movement. All three congregations of the Movement were now immersionists and their leaders were champions of this mode of baptism, and they all now celebrated the Supper each Lord's Day.

7. They would increasingly come to emphasize personal piety and the cultivation of the Christian virtues, especially a knowledge of God's word, as essential to the reformation of the church.

8. They had forever renounced sectarianism. A sect they would not and could not be. Perhaps a denomination, but only in protest, until the Lord's prayer for the unity of all his people upon earth is realized.

As he rode alongside Sidney Rigdon en route to the Maccalla debate, Campbell had several issues of his new publication, the *Christian Baptist*, in his saddlebags, which he began on the Fourth of July of that same year, 1823. He had deliberately withheld it from circulation in Kentucky lest it compromise his chances for an effective entree with leading Baptist ministers who had gathered for the debate.[32]

The die was cast.

ENDNOTES

[1]The late Joseph Dampier of Emmanuel School of Religion, Johnson City, TN, entertained visitors with an impressive collection of such tokens of British pastors of this period.

[2]Robert Richardson, *Memoirs of Alexander Campbell*, Vol. 1 (Cincinnati: Standard, 1897), p. 190.

[3]Thomas Campbell, *Declaration and Address* (St. Louis: Mission Messenger, 1975), p. 24.

[4]*Memoirs*, Vol 1, p. 198.

[5]For a description of this material see Alger Morton Fitch, *Alexander Campbell: Preacher of Reform and Reformer of Preaching* (Austin: Sweet Publishing Co., 1970), pp. 7-16.

[6]"A. Campbell's Departure," *Millennial Harbinger*, 1847, p. 351.

[7]Alexander Campbell, "Anecdotes, Incidents, and Facts No. 1," *Millennial Harbinger*, 1848, p. 280.

[8]*Memoirs*, Vol. 1, p. 353.

[9]*Memoirs*, Vol. 1, p. 392.

[10]*Memoirs*, Vol. 1, pp. 395-403.

[11]Alexander Campbell, "Anecdotes, Incidents and Facts," *Millennial Harbinger*, 1848, p. 283.

[12]*Memoirs*, Vol. 1, p. 402.

[13]Alexander Campbell, "Anecdotes, Incidents and Facts No. 2," *Millennial Harbinger*, 1848, p. 345.

[14]*Ibid.*

[15]Benjamin Lyon Smith, The *Millennial Harbinger* Abridged, Vol. 1 (Rosemead, CA: Old Paths Publishing Co., 1965), p. 409.

[16]Alexander Campbell, "Sermon on the Law," *Millennial Harbinger*, 1846, p. 493.

[17]Alexander Campbell, "Anecdotes, Incidents and Facts No. 4," *Millennial Harbinger*, 1848, p. 556.

[18]*Ibid.*, No. 2, p. 348.

[19]Alexander Campbell, "Tracts for the People No. 3," *Millennial Harbinger*, 1846, p. 21.

[20]He traded merino sheep for land in the West. Part of the campus of Illinois State University (Bloomington) was given to the school by Campbell.

[21]*Memoirs*, Vol. 1, p. 466.

[22]*Memoirs*, Vol. 2, p. 90.

[23]*Memoirs*, Vol. 2, p. 71.

[24]W.L. Maccalla and Alexander Campbell, *A Public Debate on Christian Baptism*, London: 1842, Reprinted by Old Paths Book Club, 1948, p. 116.

[25]Alexander Campbell, "Any Christians Among Protestant Parties," *Millennial Harbinger*, 1837, p. 411.

[26]Alexander Campbell, "Mr. Meredith on Remission," *Millennial Harbinger*, 1840, p. 545.

[27]Alexander Campbell, *Christian Baptism, with Its Antecedents and Consequents* (Bethany, VA: published by author, 1851), p. 219.

[28]"To An Independent Baptist," *Christian Baptist*, Vol. 3, No. 9 (April 3, 1826); College Press reprint (1983) of D.S. Burnet's abridged edition (1835), p. 238.

[29]*Millennial Harbinger*, 1840, p. 556.

[30]*Christian Baptist*, Vol 7, No. 11 (June 7, 1830); College Press reprint edition, p. 651.

[31]*Christian Baptist*, Vol. 3, No. 8 (March 6, 1826); College Press reprint edition, p. 223.

[32]"Dialogue: Between Martin Luther and the Monk Erastian," *Millennial Harbinger*, 1837, p. 539.

[33]"Preface," *Christian Baptist*, Vol. 1 (1823). He purposely prepared the preface on July 4; all Commencement exercises at Bethany College for the first decades were held on this national holiday, expressive of Campbell's consummate patriotism.

7

ALEXANDER CAMPBELL AND
WALTER SCOTT AMONG THE BAPTISTS
THE MOVEMENT IS FORCED OUT

We rested uneasily in the bosom of the Baptists.
— Walter Scott

There was a reason for those copies of the *Christian Baptist* that Alexander Campbell had stashed away in his saddlebags during the Maccalla debate. He met one evening during the debate in the home where he stayed with a number of distinguished Baptist ministers. Fearing that their profuse praise for his part of the debate meant that they presumed he was closer to their own position than he really was, he decided to level with them:

Brethren I fear if you knew me better you would esteem and love me less. For let me tell you that I have almost as much against you Baptists as I have against the Presbyterians. They err in one thing and you in another; and probably you are each nearly equidistant from original apostolic Christianity.[1]

They wanted to know what he had against the Baptists. He then went to his room and brought back the copies of his journal. After telling them of the new publication, he proceeded to read to them from it, articles on the "Kingdom of the Clergy" and the "Call to the Ministry." The more he sought to alert them to his heterodoxy the more enthusiasm they showed toward him. They wanted to hear more and more. At this he distributed the copies of the journal to the most influential preachers present, asking them to examine the contents at their leisure during the debate.

This episode probably advanced Alexander's cause more than the debate itself, for these preachers, mostly from Kentucky, went back to their churches and opened the windows to the fresh air of reformation blowing their way from a tiny village in Virginia.

Jeremiah Vardeman, the most influential Baptist minister in Kentucky, was especially helpful in opening up opportunities for Campbell throughout the state. It also served to give an extensive circulation to the *Christian Baptist* throughout Kentucky. It proved to be the breakthrough that the Movement needed. Kentucky was soon to belong to Alexander

Campbell, a state destined to have the largest number of adherents to the Movement of any state in the union.

This set the stage for a three months' foray into Kentucky in 1824, the first of many trips he would make into the state in the ensuing years. Here he met men who were to become leaders in the Movement, including Raccoon John Smith, Barton W. Stone, and Jacob Creath, Sr. His ministry filled the daylight hours and spilled over into the night. For some 60 days he spent five hours an evening in intimate exchange with church leaders across the state who were eager to hear him expound upon the Scriptures in reference to their own problems. This enabled him to become well acquainted, both with the general state of religion in the state, and with many of the leading clergy.

The contacts that he had with P.S. Fall, pastor of the Baptist Church in Louisville, led that congregation to become the Movement's fourth church. It was considered "reformed" when it resolved to give up its creed and confession of faith and be directed only by the Scriptures, and to celebrate the Supper on every first day. Being Baptist, it was of course already immersionist.

Campbell's influence among the Baptists of northeastern Ohio, then known as the Western Reserve, was also growing substantially. The Mahoning Baptist Association had organized only since the Walker debate in 1820, and it consisted of some seventeen churches that were already permeated with Campbell's teaching. One of these, as we have noted, was Wellsburg, Alexander's own church that joined the association in 1823 after being formed out of the Brush Run church.

It is interesting that among the 30 members that left Brush Run for Wellsburg there was not only Margaret Campbell, but also Miss Selina Bakewell, close friend to Margaret, who in just five more years was to become the second Mrs. Campbell.

The churches of the Mahoning Association were, more or less, like Brush Run and Wellsburg, though they were still "Baptist" churches, at least outwardly. The few strictly Campbell churches wore no party name. When Thomas Campbell issued a "letter of dismission" for the work at Wellsburg he wrote: "Be it known to all whom it may concern, that we have dismissed the following brethren in good standing with us, to constitute a church of Christ at Wellsburg."[2]

The Mahoning churches were still Baptist in name, but they were now referred to as "Reformed" Baptists. This was the case in Kentucky as well as Ohio. There gradually came to be scores of churches that were dubbed either "Reformed" Baptists or "Campbellites." Those within the Movement, even the Campbells, referred to themselves simply as *Reformers*, to distinguish themselves from other Baptists. They were not yet known as Christians or Disciples. It was these "Reformed" Baptist churches that soon became known as the Disciples of Christ.

As late as 1827 Campbell was unequivocal about his intention to remain a Baptist: "I do intend to continue with this people so long as they permit me to say what I believe."[3] In the same essay he made it clear that he had no idea of adding to the catalogue of new sects, but that he would rather labor to unite the Christians in all the sects and to abolish sectarianism.

From the outset the Campbells sought to avoid separation. Their Washington Association was to be a society *within* the church working for peace and unity, its members remaining in their own churches. When this proved infeasible and the Brush Run church resulted, it became a part of a Baptist association, as did their church at Wellsburg. They also sought membership for their church in Pittsburgh, but were turned down. Even when rejected by his own Presbyterian synod, Thomas sought in vain for ministerial status with another, and Alexander could comfortably refer to his "union with the Baptist denomination."

It is evident, therefore, that they did not choose to be separatists, even though this was at last thrust upon them. It is equally clear that they did not want to start a new denomination, but to launch a movement of reform among the existing churches. While they did not rest easily within the bosom of the Baptists, they were prepared to make it work. In the preface of his first volume of the *Christian Baptist* Campbell doubted if a reformer among any party could survive or if a journal such as the one he was launching could make it. But after three years of apparent success and acceptance among the Baptists, albeit with some vigorous opposition, he was prepared to say of them:

> In one thing they may appear, in time to come, proudly singular and preminently distinguished. Mark it well. Their historian, in the year 1900, may say, "We are the only people who would tolerate, or who ever did tolerate, any person to continue as a reformer or restorer among us.'[4]

But it was not to be so, for the "Reformers" were doomed to be expelled by the Baptists, not that it was to be all their fault. Campbell's earlier fears were well grounded, after all. The story of the separation cannot be properly understood without an acquaintance with him who came to be known as "the voice of the Golden Oracle."

Walter Scott
"The rose of Sharon has no thorns."

When on April 11, 1861 the Confederates fired on Fort Sumter, it was apparent to the already divided nation that civil war could not be averted. Few agonized over the tragedy as much as Walter A. Scott, one of the nation's most devoted adopted sons. Born in Scotland in 1796 and coming to this country in 1818, he wrote to one of his sons a few days before the fall of Fort Sumter: "I can think of nothing but the sorrows and dangers of my most beloved adopted country." Once the war began he wrote plaintively: "Oh, my country! my country! How I love thee! how I deplore thy present misfortunes!"[5]

In a few days he was dead of typhoid pneumonia, even though his health had been good. Whether the tragedy of war precipitated his death cannot be known. Being an unusually sensitive person, he was terribly grieved that brothers in the Lord would soon be killing and maiming each other on the field of battle.

John Rogers, a fellow minister, was at his side. "Is this death?," he asked Scott, who replied, "It is very like it." Rogers then asked, "Do you fear death?," to which Scott replied, "Oh, no, I know in whom I have trusted." In those hours, as during his ministry of 40 years, Scott looked to Jesus as the Golden Oracle, and being the ardent orator and evangelist that he was, he became known as "the voice of the Golden Oracle."[6]

When Alexander Campbell received word of Scott's death, it only added to his own grief in the nation's darkest hour. Travelling by gig toward Richmond, he had immediately turned homeward upon hearing the news of Fort Sumter. As he passed through towns and villages, he witnessed his countrymen preparing for war. He realized that things would never be the same for him and his church.

Then came the news that his closest friend and most devoted colaborer was dead. He was soon to write:

> I knew him well. I knew him long. I loved him much. We might not, indeed, agree, in every opinion nor in every point of expediency; but we never loved each other less because we did not acquiesce in every opinion and in every measure. By the eye of faith and the eye of hope, methinks I see him in Abraham's bosom.[7]

Campbell described him as "Next to my father my most cordial and indefatigable fellow-laborer in the origin and progress of the present Reformation," and he mentioned that he often took counsel with him in matters affecting their work. He also honored him as "truly eloquent in the whole import of that word." Not only did he consult with Scott on the design of baptism prior to the Maccalla debate, but it was also Scott who suggested that he add *Baptist* to the name of the journal that Campbell intended to call simply *The Christian*. Scott believed this gesture would open doors since their work was then mostly among the Baptists.

Educated at Scotland's famed Edinburgh University, Scott was destined to be a teacher for much of his life. Coming to this country through the kind offices of an uncle, he spent his first year at an academy on Long Island teaching Latin. He then went to Pittsburgh where he taught for a fellow Scot, George Forrester, who was to change the course of his life. Forrester had a church as well as a school, and he was influenced by the teachings of Robert Sandeman and the Haldanes.

In its efforts to restore the primitive pattern, Forrester's church not only practiced immersion but foot washing and the holy kiss as well, which caused them to be dubbed "kissing Baptists" by their neighbors. Influenced by Forrester's knowledge and piety, Scott began a search of the Scriptures to determine for himself the terms of pardon. At home with Greek as well as Latin, he made his way through the New Testament in the original. Convinced that the sprinkling he received in his native Church of Scotland was not scriptural, he submitted to immersion at the hands of Forrester and joined his congregation.

When Forrester was accidentally drowned shortly afterwards, Scott found himself the pastor of a church as well as principal of an academy. The academy was distinctive in that the New Testament itself was a textbook, while other schools of Presbyterian background studied the Westminster Confession of Faith. The gospels in particular absorbed Scott's attention, and he taught them so thoroughly in the original language that he came to know them virtually by memory in the Greek. One theme came to dominate his thought, *Jesus is the Christ.* He was not satisfied that this truth be engraved in his heart, for he also inscribed it above the door of the school. This was to him "the Golden Oracle."

His work in Pittsburgh was interrupted by a visit to a Scotch Baptist church in New York that he felt compelled to make. This church had issued a tract on baptism that led Scott to suppose that there was much he could learn from them. The tract taught baptism for the remission of sins, and even questioned the discipleship of anyone who was not so baptized. It anticipated the design of baptism that Scott and Campbell were later to teach.

The visit proved to be a disappointment in that Scott did not see in the personal life of the church what he supposed was implied by the tract. While he stayed with them for three months, he decided that he was unable to bring them to his own understanding of the primitive faith, despite their position on baptism, and resolved to return to his ministry in Pittsburgh.

On his return to Pittsburgh he visited still another church in Washington D.C. that was reputedly of the primitive faith, but he found them so steeped in sectarianism that he was left disconsolate by the whole experience. He then did a rather strange thing: "I then went to the Capitol, and, climbing up to the top of its lofty dome, I sat myself down, filled with sorrow at the miserable desolation of the Church of God."[8]

This melancholic trip to New York illustrates the brooding disposition that was to characterize Scott all his life. These traits led Campbell to say of him, even in his eulogy of the man: "He had his moods and tenses as men of genius generally have." Earl West, commenting on a recently-discovered letter that Scott wrote in 1851, says of him: "While Scott had a keen analytical mind, he was a moody individual, and there were times when he felt as though he were completely left out of brotherhood activities and walked around as if in a trance."[9]

In the letter Scott likened himself to David, "like a dead man out of mind," and complained that no one wrote to him except "creditors and dunners" and that he was forgotten by almost all his former friends. While it may be true that Scott early on faded from the main flow of events, it is hardly the case that he was forgotten.

Once again with his school and church in Pittsburgh, he was to meet men who would change the course of his life. Robert Richardson, whose wealthy father was the chief patron of the school, was one of his pupils. Richardson, who became a physician, was a co-laborer with Scott and Campbell, and eventually served as the Movement's first historian, authoring the resourceful *Memoirs of Alexander Campbell*.

In the *Memoirs*, which is far more than the story of Campbell, Richardson tells how he and Scott would walk in his father's garden in the evening (which is now downtown Pittsburgh!) and enjoy the beauty of nature. Scott's mind would frequently revert to his ruling thought, the Christ. On one occasion when young Robert handed Scott a rose, he asked his pupil if he knew why Jesus is called "the rose of Sharon," and explained that it is because that particular rose has no thorns. Richardson, who had also studied under Thomas Campbell as a boy, tells how Scott was enraptured with the simplicity of the gospel, how he devoted every spare moment to a study of the Bible, and how his heart burned with a desire to communicate the plan of redemption to lost humanity.

It was in the Richardson home that Scott first met Alexander Campbell in 1821, when Scott was 25 and Campbell was 33. Had they met sooner nothing might have come of it. Both men had by now imbibed the spirit of reformation from the writings of Glas, Sandeman, and the Haldanes, but Scott only recently from the library of George Forrester. Scott was at this point as far advanced in the idea of a faith apart from human creeds as Campbell was, but Campbell, due to the influence of his father, was more advanced in his views on church reform and unity. Scott, influenced more by the Haldanes, thought more in terms of an exact restoration of the primitive church based upon the pattern of the New Testament.

Richardson, who knew both men from the time they first met, describes Campbell as fearless, self-reliant, and firm, while Scott was naturally timid, diffident and yielding. Campbell was always positioned, like the North star, unaffected by terrestrial influences; Scott, like the magnetic needle, was often disturbed and trembling on its center, though always seeking to return to its true direction. While both were uniquely gifted with rational powers, Campbell was given more to reason and Scott more to emotion. Campbell was livelier and more cheerful, even in repose, while Scott was more abstract, meditative, and sometimes sad.[10]

Scott's Plan of Salvation

Scott not only helped to name the *Christian Baptist*, as we have seen, but using the pen name of Philip he joined Campbell as one of the writers. In the very first issue he began a four-part series on the plan for preaching the Christian faith. No one in the Movement had thus far attempted to be so definite as to call for "the plan" of how one becomes a Christian, and even in this series Scott did not develop "the five finger exercise" which he was later to make famous.

But already he is conscious of "one uniform and universal plan of teaching the religion" which he believed stood over against the sectarian schemes devised by the clergy. In the first essay he uses "the plan" nine times, and goes on in the second essay to say: "There exists a certain, uniform, authorized plan of preaching Jesus, a plan consecrated by the high examples of all the heavens, and the holy apostles and prophets."[11]

The plan is to preach the one glorious fact that Jesus is the Christ, the Son of God. This is to be attested to by events of his life, prophecies, and miracles. He lays down two basic principles: (1) Members of the church of Christ are united to one another by believing the one grand fact that Jesus is the Christ; (2) The proclamation of this fact is the only way to increase the church.

He stresses all through these articles that "The bond of union among Christians is the belief of a matter of fact, that Jesus of Nazareth is the Son of God," and this is the only condition to being saved. As he puts it: "One has only to believe in this name, and his is eternal life" (second essay), or to be even more emphatic: "Let no one think that any thing more is necessary to our salvation than to believe this fact" (fourth essay).

All this was different from the kind of preaching one heard among the numerous sects on the frontier in the 1820's. The "five points of Calvin-ism" were made a test of fellowship, as well as various tenets from this creed or that confession of faith. Scott complained that the preachers ranted about everlasting fire rather than to proclaim the one glorious fact, and they harangued and sermonized more than they preached the gospel, which he identified simply as the one grand truth that Jesus is the Son of God.

The articles he wrote for Campbell also emphasized that faith comes through testimony (the gospel) rather than through some subjective or mystical experience. Rather than using various emotional techniques, the preacher should show that sinners are blessed when they believe and confess like Peter: "Thou art the Christ, the son of the living God." Scott contended that Peter then knew little else, but he was blessed for his faith. The sinner needs no more, whether the mourner's bench or some emotional experience.

This quotation shows how he sought to displace the appeals of sectari-anism with the simple plan of preaching Jesus as the Christ:

> Passing by, for the present, the various stupid schemes, all different and all wrong, pursued by Roman Catholics, Socinians, Arians, Covenanters, Seced-ers, Presbyterians, High-Churchmen, Baptists, Independents, and so forth, let us attend to the plan of teaching the truth pursued by God — by the Lord Jesus Christ — by the Holy Spirit, in presenting it to all men in the scriptures and by the apostles and all who first preached it — a plan founded in the very nature of the saving truth itself, and into which ignorant missionaries feel themselves driving when every human scheme failed.[12]

Even though Scott had come up with the idea of "the plan of salva-tion," a concept that has gained wide acceptance throughout the Move-ment's history, he yet allowed no place for baptism, even though he himself had been immersed at this time. Not only does he not mention baptism throughout these four essays, he avoids reference to it even in those contexts where one would expect it to be included. His reference to Mark 16:16 is an example: "He that believeth (that he is the Son of God) shall be saved, he that believeth not shall be damned."

His treatment of Acts 2 in the fourth essay is even more conspicuous for its lack of any reference to verse 38 where baptism "for the remission of sins" is clearly set forth, a doctrine that he was afterwards to emphasize. He brings the story of the pentecostians right down to verse 37, where they ask, "Men and brethren, what shall we do?" Then he says: "We see that in this most primitive of all Christian speeches, there are just two things that are essentially obvious — the fact of the Saviour's resurrection, and the testimony of God which proves it."[13] He goes on to insist that only one thing is necessary to salvation, to believe that Jesus of Nazareth is the risen Christ. Both Scott and Campbell were later to expand this bare minimum to belief in the one fact and submission to the one institution (baptism).

The New Evangelism

Scott stayed with his church and academy in Pittsburgh until 1826, at which time he moved to Steubenville, Ohio, which put him closer to Bethany and Alexander Campbell. By this time Campbell's views had permeated the Baptist churches of the Mahoning Association, which now numbered 16, one of these being the church at Wellsburg, Va., which was represented in the Association by Campbell himself, along with his father-in-law, John Brown. Scott was a visiting speaker at the annual meeting of the Association for that year, though he was neither a member nor a Baptist. Scott's church back in Pittsburgh was simply called "Church of Christ," as were some of the reformed churches of his native Scotland, and while they were immersionists they were not Baptists.

He was later to explain that when he first joined that church in 1819 it was the only one of its kind that he knew of in this country.[14] Even though the Campbell churches at Brush Run and Wellsburg were also called "churches of Christ," they were counted as Baptist churches and thought of themselves as such, albeit as something less than orthodox.

Scott had no intention of visiting the gathering of the Mahoning Association in 1827 until his neighbor, Alexander Campbell, came by his home and persuaded him to go along. It was a momentous occasion in the Movement's history, and Garrison and DeGroot are right in concluding that if it were not for Scott's work with the Mahoning Association "there would probably never have been occasion to write a history of the Disciples."[15]

The minutes of the Association for that year reveal that the Braceville, Ohio church had moved that an evangelist be chosen to preach among the churches. A committee was chosen to act upon this, and it recommended "That Bro. Walter Scott is a suitable person for the task, and that he is willing, provided the Association concurs in his appointment, to devote his whole energies to the work." The committee further recommended that a fund be created for Scott's support through "voluntary and liberal contributions" from the churches of the Association.

It was a remarkable turn of events for this to happen to Scott. He was not at that time recognized as a successful evangelist. He was neither a Baptist nor a member of the Association and he was known to have views quite different from those who were leaders in the Association. Adamson Bentley and Sidney Rigdon were both known as dynamic preachers, and at least two other preachers among them were successful evangelists. Then there was Alexander Campbell who might have been chosen, but the lot fell on Walter Scott. It came to be recognized as the most significant thing the Mahoning Association ever did.

Scott later wrote in his journal, *The Evangelist,* how he personally responded to his appointment and the sacrifices it entailed:

> I never made one objection to the nomination, nor to the appointment, but saw in it a providence. I believed no mortal then understood but myself. I immediately cut all other connections, abandoned my projected Editorship, dissolved my academy; left my Church, left my family, dropt the bitterest tear over my infant household that ever escaped from my eyes, and set out under the simple conduct of Jesus Christ, to make an experiment of what is now styled the Ancient Gospel.[16]

His evangelistic mission was an "experiment." This is explained by the fact that, as he himself put it, "I had consulted no mortal on the topic of the Ancient Gospel, the very phrase was unknown." He goes on to say, not unlike the apostle Paul, that what he did was prompted by no man and what he preached came from no man. The truth is that at this time Scott was not sure what all he would preach or just how he would go about it.

As we have seen, he had decided upon "the plan" in his essays in The *Christian Baptist,* which was simply the proclamation that Jesus is the Christ. His "experiment" was not only to test this position but to probe further both into the Book and into the heart of the sinner.

He admits that his first effort, which was somewhere beyond the pale of the churches of the Association, was a dismal failure. Perhaps he intended it literally when he wrote that "the people fled." Baxter, his biographer, explains that his preaching sounded like a new religion to his auditors, being so radically different from what they were used to hearing. He came across as sincere but deluded, and he excited wonder, pity, and even scorn. But it was not all fruitless, even if there were no responses, for he was experimenting, finding his way, creating "the plan."[17]

His first response came in his visit with the Baptist church in New Lisbon, Ohio, the town in which the Association had named him their evangelist a few months before. He spoke long, first on Peter's confession that Jesus was the Christ in Matthew 16, and then on Peter's proclamation on Pentecost in Acts 2. He outlined the great facts about Jesus as given by the apostle, and then showed how the people cried out, "Men and brethren, what shall we do?" Unlike the omission in his essay four years before, he echoed in his brilliant oratory the response of Peter, "Repent, and be baptized, every one of you, in the name of Jesus Christ, for the remission of sins, and ye shall receive the gift of the Holy Spirit."

He spoke with great force and power, insisting that what saved those on Pentecost would save the sinner today, that the word of God meant what it said, and that it should be obeyed now as it was then. There was only one response. One William Amend made his way through the crowded meetinghouse to take Scott's hand and to be baptized for the remission of his sins. Since Scott went on to convert thousands more, this first response took on historic significance. He later wrote to Amend to ascertain from him just what the circumstances were that led him to become his first convert. Amend's response remains one of the most valuable letters in the archives of the Movement, and it tells an interesting story.

The letter revealed that Amend was not in the audience at all that day, except as it filled the house and spilled over into the yard. He was listening to Scott from a distance. For some time Amend had resolved if he ever heard anyone preach the gospel like Peter did on Pentecost that he would obey it. After searching the Scriptures for years in an effort to learn what one is to do to be saved, he spent years more trying to find someone to baptize him on the terms set forth in Acts 2:38.

A Presbyterian, Amend sought his pastor's help, but he did not want any man to baptize him who did not believe in what he was doing. He wrote to Scott: "To this scripture (Acts 2:38) I often resorted. I saw how Peter had opened the kingdom, and the door into it, but, to my great disappointment, I saw no man to introduce me, though I prayed much and often for it."[18]

Amend had waited for years when Scott came to town. He had been disappointed in so many preachers that it was with reluctance that he listened to one more, and then only at the edge of the circle. But as Scott spoke he moved closer in, and finally he was down front ready to be baptized. In the letter he reminded Scott of his closing words that memorable day: "The Scriptures no longer shall be a sealed book. God means what he says. Is there any man present who will take God at his word, and be baptized for remission of sins."

When Amend heard that, he told Scott, "At that moment my feelings were such that I could have cried out, 'Glory to God! I have found the man whom I have long sought for.'" While Amend found his man, Scott found his plan. From that moment on there was what the Movement's historians have chosen to call "the new evangelism."

Richardson concedes that it was Scott and not Campbell who made "a direct and practical application" of the doctrine of baptism for remission of sins, securing for it a conspicuous place in the history of the reformation.[19]

Campbell also, in 1831, gives Scott credit for "restoring the Ancient Gospel" in the fall of 1827 by arranging the several items involved as faith, repentance, baptism, remission of sins, the Holy Spirit, and eternal life.[20] These six items were often reduced to five, enabling the preacher to count them off on the fingers of one hand, by combining the last two.[21]

Scott would ride into a new community in the afternoon and, attracting a group of children going home from school, he would engage them in conversation. Having a way with children, he would have them count the five steps off on their fingers: faith, repentance, baptism, remission of sins, gift of the Holy Spirit. He would have them to make a fist of their fingers, put it in their pocket, and when they got home to take it out and tell their parents what they had on their fingers.

He would tell the children to urge their parents to come to the school-house that night and hear a man talk about those five points. It was one way an evangelist in those days had of getting the word out that he was in town. Since there was little else for people in those days to do in the evenings, it only took a word for them to have a crowd. On one occasion when Campbell arrived in Zanesville, Ohio unannounced, he hired a lad to go from house to house and announce: "Alexander Campbell will speak tonight in the court house at candle lighting." That night he had his crowd.[22]

This five-step plan has remained current among heirs of the Movement, but it has undergone some interesting alterations. Some who honor the five steps have them arranged: hearing, faith, repentance, confession, and baptism, which is a radical departure from Scott's plan in that it lists only what man does, while Scott laid emphasis on what God does in response to man's obedience, the remission of sins and the Holy Spirit.

His earliest biographer, William Baxter, reports phenomenal results of Scott's first year as an evangelist — "not far from one thousand new converts." New churches had been formed and new life infused into old ones, some doubling their membership. This was unbelievable, for in the years before Scott was sent out the Mahoning churches did well to hold their own or to enjoy modest growth.

It is understandable that at their next annual meeting they had little interest in conducting routine business. They rather rejoiced over the results of the new evangelism. More important, preachers from several sects had begun to preach the "Restored Gospel," as Scott preferred to call it, including some from the "Christian Churches," which proved to be the first substantial contact between the Stone and Campbell churches.

The Campbells became concerned over what Scott might be doing in the Western Reserve, once reports began to come in of his unprecedented success. Thomas went over to look in on what was going on and reported back to his son that Scott had found a practical way of applying what they held in theory but had not been able to effect. Even though it had been 15 years since the Campbells themselves had been baptized, and longer than that since the Movement was launched, they had up to the time of Scott baptized very few people.

They had made headway in gaining support for their cause among the Baptists, but since these people were not rebaptized but accepted as Christians already, they were not converts in the sense that Scott was converting people. Scott moved people as few evangelists could with his power and fervor, some of his hearers likening him to Peter on Pentecost.

Scott's power over an audience was compared to the power of the wind over the sea. It was said that his hearers would sometimes sway when he swayed, and if he lifted his eyes heavenward they would do likewise. He sometimes caused a ripple of laughter, but more often he moved them to tears. Even Campbell, who was usually unemotional outwardly, came under the spell of Scott's oratory on one occasion, crying out from his seat, "Glory to God in the highest!"[23]

From 1830, the year the Mahoning Association was dissolved, until 1861, the year of his death, Scott was busy as an evangelist, educator, editor, and author, even though he never came anywhere near sharing Alexander Campbell's prominence in the Movement. He baptized an average of 1,000 a year for 30 years, far more than anyone in his generation. He conducted various academies. He served for one year as the first president of the Movement's first college, Bacon College in Georgetown, Kentucky (1837). He edited several journals, the most influential being *The Evangelist*, 1832-1844, with some interruptions in publication. He was also co-editor with John T. Johnson of *The Christian* for one year.

Scott authored five books, the most important being *The Gospel Restored* (1836) and *The Messiahship* or *The Great Demonstration* (1859). He now and again had a seminary going in his own home in which he trained men for the cause. He is also to be remembered for his close association with virtually all the leaders of the Movement of that day. He has been hailed throughout the years as one of "the big four," along with Barton Stone and the Campbells. He lived the last ten years of his life in Mayslick, Kentucky, where he died and was buried.

While Scott often insisted by both voice and pen that the "restored Gospel," as he conceived it, was the only means for the unity of all Christians, there is evidence that he came to see that the Movement he helped launch and "the Plan" that he gave to it were not as inherently irresistible as he supposed they would be. In a letter to P.S. Fall in 1840 he made the startling statement: "When you express your doubts of the matters connected with the recent Reformation I sympathize with you, for the thing has not been what I hoped it would be by a thousand miles. We are indeed 'a sect' differing but little, of anything that is good, from the parties around us. Alas! my soul is grieved every day."[24]

Separation from the Baptists

The title of this chapter indicates that the Reformers among the Baptists were forced out. Whether that is what happened depends on how one interprets the available facts. It is arguable that they brought the separation upon themselves, and that if they had behaved differently it could have been avoided.

Speaking of Scott's three-year mission as an evangelist among the Mahoning Baptist Association, Dwight E. Stevenson, one of his biographers, makes this judgment:

> When Scott reached the end of 1831, he, by the genius of his analytical mind and his infectious enthusiasm, had completed the creation of the Disciples, given them an evangelistic method, separated them beyond all return from the Baptists, and set them on their independent course. Without him there may never have been a multitude of converts presenting the problem of organization and pastoral care. A measure of chaos is the price of all creation, and he was pre-eminently a creator.[25]

With Scott, then, according to Stevenson, comes "the creation of the Disciples," while up to this point they were but reformers resting somewhat uneasily in "the bosom of the Baptists." We have seen that it was Campbell's intention to remain with the Baptists so long as he could teach his convictions. But he did not remain, not so much because he could not freely teach, but because of the nature of the Movement itself. It was a reformation, designed to change churches from within, an effort to be nonsectarian while in a sectarian context. Campbell and Scott *did* change from within an association of some 20 churches, which became their beachhead for a broader operation.

By providing a home for them the Mahoning Baptist Association brought the Reformers to a fork in the road. They could remain within the Association and work for reform among the Baptists and other denominations. Or the Association could serve as the nucleus for a new denomination, separated from the Baptists. While it was not planned that way, it was the latter fork of the road that was taken. It may be that they had no choice, circumstances being what they were.

While Campbell later said that he was "forced out" by the Baptists, it was a separation that was probably inevitable, even if the reformer insisted that it was unnecessary. The Reformers were able to make inroads among the small Mahoning Baptist Association because of a few key leaders who espoused the Campbell cause, but most of the associations were antagonistic, making Baptist strongholds impregnable.

W.E. Garrison notes that these associations, while supposedly voluntary, assumed legislative and judicial powers, which enabled them to disfranchise the Reformers at will. He points to an instance in 1825 when ten orthodox Redstone Baptist churches excluded thirteen of their number, which included the Brush Run church, when they refused to adhere to the Philadelphia Confession. They in turn created their own association, one sympathetic with the Reformers.

While this illustrates the role played by the Baptist associations in the separation that was crystallizing by 1825, the break was not complete until Walter Scott's evangelism further agitated Baptist leaders. In the preface to his 1843 *Harbinger* Campbell dates the "excision and repudiation" from 1828, and accounts for it on the basis of "the fervid spirit and glowing eloquence of Elder Walter Scott."

The seeds of separation were sown when Baptist associations expelled churches that were inclined toward Scott and Campbell, and when churches withdrew fellowship from their own members who were so inclined. These altercations led to the independence of the Reformers who were soon to be known as Disciples of Christ. When the Baptist associations and churches rejected their maverick members, it was an invitation for them to become Disciples. By the time the separation was an accomplished fact, the Reformers had captured scores of Baptist churches and thousands of members.

It was a separation that Campbell would live to regret. In hindsight, a generation later, he believed the differences could have been resolved. Even up to the time of Scott's evangelism Campbell believed he could work with the Baptists. But by the late 1820's the climate was such that division appeared inevitable. By 1831 Campbell seems to have lost all hope of reconciliation:

> Proscription and exclusion have done their utmost: and the Baptists, once thought to be the most tolerant, clement, and opposed to persecution, have gone farther than any sect in the New World in excluding persons for differences in opinion. No sect in this union has published more proscriptive, illiberal, and unjust decrees, than we can furnish from Baptist journals, associations, conventions, etc. against us. . . For our part, we cannot fight under Baptist or Paidobaptist colors. We think a sin in a Baptist is just as condemnable as in a Paidobaptist.[26]

Clearly the battle was joined. Campbell no longer talked about how future historians would praise the Baptists of his time for tolerance toward those among them who would reform them. The Baptists on the other hand became more and more critical of Campbell and his followers. The attitude of one Baptist minister, Garner McConnico, who once argued with Campbell for twelve hours with hardly a break, was not atypical:

> Campbellism has carried away many whom I thought firm. These wandering stars and clouds without water, ever learning and never able to come to the knowledge of the truth, make proselytes much more the children of the devil than they were before. O Lord! hear the cries and see the tears of the Baptists; for Alexander has done them much harm. The Lord reward him according to his works .. See them dividing churches, and spreading discord, and constituting churches out of excommunicated members. Such shuffling — such lying — such slandering — such evil speaking — such dissembling — such downright hypocrisy — and all under the *false* name of reformation.[27]

A similar spirit was shown by a Baptist minister of Youngstown, Ohio, who persuaded some 80 members of the Mahoning Association to withdraw and start the Beaver Association. This Association made history by drawing up "the Beaver Anathema" in 1829, an infamous list of charges against the Reformers that became the basis upon which other associations denounced them. The Tate's Creek Association in Kentucky excluded seventeen reforming churches, adding to the list of Beaver charges.

The charges had to do mostly with conversion: the Reformers teach that there is no promise of salvation without baptism and that baptism procures salvation and the Holy Spirit, that one is to be baptized on his profession of faith apart from any further examination, that there is no direct operation of the Holy Spirit before baptism, that one's obedience is the means of God's election.

They also charged that the Reformers taught that there is no special call to the ministry and criticized "experimental religion." They also believed that the law of Moses was abolished and that there is no "mystery" in the Scriptures.

Other associations in Kentucky adopted the Beaver anathema: Sulphur Fork in 1829; Goshen and Long Run, which included Louisville, in 1830, though the Baptist church in Louisville had already divided on rather friendly terms, dividing the property between the two groups and continuing as two churches in relative peace.

In Virginia the Appomattox Association subscribed to the Beaver excommunication in 1830, insisting that none of its churches should have a preacher of Campbell's persuasion. The same year the Dover Association adopted the Beaver measure and then set forth its own denunciation and list of errors. Known as "the Dover anathema," it served to exclude several reforming preachers. Campbell responded to this in the *Millennial Harbinger*, describing the Dover decree as "the Rubicon is passed."

In his next issue was an "Address to the Virginia Baptists" in which he chided them for betraying their own heritage as peacemakers, for it was in Virginia in 1787 that dissident groups of Baptists became the United Baptists of Virginia in that "they conceived it better to bear with some diversity of opinion in doctrines than to break with men whose Christian deportment rendered them amiable in the estimation of all true lovers of genuine godliness." Once he had reminded them that their own recent history gave them cause to behave more magnanimously, he laid it on them with the likes of "Alas, for the degeneracy of Virginia Baptists!"[28]

The Reformers Become Separatists

By 1832 the Rubicon had been crossed. The Reformers were a separate people, a rather large separatist group for frontier country. A reasonable estimate would be from 12,000 to 15,000 members in upwards of 200 congregations. Only about half of these came from the Baptists, for since 1824 in Kentucky and 1827 in Ohio thousands were brought into the Movement by baptism from the world.

This rapid growth is accounted for by the success of such pioneers as Raccoon John Smith, homespun preacher in Kentucky, who was quoted as saying he had *baptized* 700 sinners and *capsized* 1500 Baptists.[29] Then there was Jeremiah Vardeman, another Kentucky evangelist, who baptized 550 in less than a year. In Ohio, Adamson Bentley, Walter Scott, and Sidney Rigdon reported 800 baptisms in only six months.

The cause of the separation is not easily identified. While the Beaver and Dover decrees listed Baptist grievances against the Reformers, these were not likely the real issue. As late as 1831 Campbell was insisting that the Reformers and Baptists were in substantial doctrinal agreement, and that the problem was that the Baptists would not practice what they preached. "They say that faith, repentance, immersion, and the Holy Spirit are all necessary to constitute a Christian; and so we say," he wrote.

He also listed as points of agreement the nature of Christ's kingdom, baptism as a seal to the believer, the honoring of the Lord's day and the Lord's supper according to the New Testament, the holy life, the change of heart, the necessity of the blood of Christ, and the Fatherhood of God. Then he asked, *What is the controversy about?* His answer: "because of not living according to, and carrying out these principles, and because, in numerous instances, they have made them of non-effect by their tradition."[30]

While traditions may have hindered the Baptists in being more open, Campbell here understates the case, for there were substantial differences, especially in that the Baptists were often rigidly Calvinistic and the Reformers strongly anti-Calvinistic. Too, the Baptists observed the Supper periodically, while the Reformers believed they should do so each Sunday. The Reformers believed that baptism was for the remission of sins, while the Baptists did not. The Reformers did not want to wear any sectarian name; the Baptists were reluctant to surrender the name they proudly wore.

Both agreed that no organization should control local churches, but the Baptists did have their associations to which the Reformers objected. The Reformers rejected the idea of a special call to the ministry and an ordained ministry, which the Baptists practiced. The Reformers received members by confession and baptism, while the Baptists asked for a personal testimony and congregational vote. They also made the Philadelphia Confession of Faith a test of fellowship, to which Campbell particularly objected.

And yet Campbell believed there was sufficient common ground to avoid separation. The Reformers were soon to unite with Stone's Christians in Kentucky, but they were not all that much more unanimous in doctrine and practice with them than they were with the Baptists.

The real culprit in the separation was the sectarian spirit, perhaps from one side as much as the other. But it is to the credit of the Reformers that they never expelled anyone from their congregations for holding Baptist views, while there were numerous instances of Baptists withdrawing from Reformers. In one case a man was forced out for simply reading the *Millennial Harbinger*. When eighteen other members prepared a remonstrance for such action against an exemplary brother, they too were summarily withdrawn from.[31]

In another instance two people declared themselves "the church" and proceeded to withdraw from 128 Reformers within the congregation. The charge was that they were not true to "what is common among the Baptists."[32]

Only rarely did the Reformers walk out on the Baptists and start their own church. It did happen, however, in the formation of what is now the Vine Street Christian Church in Nashville.

The separation from the Baptists was something the Reformers, now Disciples of Christ, had to live with for generations to come. It appeared contradictory to their plea for unity.

Under the aegis of John T. Johnson the Disciples invited all the denominations, especially the Baptists, to a unity meeting in Lexington, Kentucky in 1841, but only one leading Baptist showed up. In 1866 another effort was made in Richmond, Virginia, and after several days of consultation it was agreed that the time for a union of the two groups had not yet come.

Alexander Campbell always regretted the separation. Joseph King, who was a student under Campbell at Bethany, reported in his memorial sermon on the occasion of Campbell's death that when he was told of the Disciples-Baptist union effort in Richmond that the old reformer wept with joy, saying, "This is one of the happiest moments in my life," which happened to be the last day of his life.[33]

In emerging as a distinct group the Reformers had to do but two things: stop calling themselves Baptists and dissolve the Mahoning Baptist Association. The first of these was a matter of course. The second took place in 1830, to the delight of Walter Scott, who opposed associations as contrary to the ancient order, and to the consternation of Alexander Campbell, who saw that his people needed such annual gatherings. McAllister and Tucker are, therefore, correct in their "Timeline of the Christian Church (Disciples of Christ)" when they name 1830 as the beginning of the Disciples of Christ.[34]

Campbell's New Version

Among the grievances that the Baptists had against the Reformers was their use of *The Living Oracles*, a new version of the New Testament published by Alexander Campbell in 1826, which is hailed by Edgar J. Goodspeed, the eminent New Testament scholar and Bible translator, as the first of the "modern" versions in the United States.[35] Among the resolutions passed by the Appomattox Association, for example, was "to discourage the use of Campbell's new translation of the New Testament." Among the charges against those who were expelled from Baptist churches was that they made use of the new version.

Since Campbell actually translated, and not merely transliterated, the Greek term *baptizein* into "immerse," one would suppose that the Baptists would have gone for it, challenged as they were by the paidobaptists. But this caused John the Baptist to become "John the Immerser," which challenged the source of the Baptist name. A still greater offense was the absence of the sacrosanct *thy, thou* and *thine*, along with *goes* for *goeth* and *know* for *knowest*, of the King James Version. This was like uprooting them from their literary culture, or like asking them to repudiate apple pie.

It was "modern" also in that it imposed a new vocabulary on the reader. The word *church* does not appear even once. The reader sees instead: "On this rock I will build my congregation." *Holy Spirit* displaced

Holy Ghost, and there was *reform* instead of *repent* and *proclaim* instead of *preach*. It departed from the usual breakdown of chapters and verses and arranged the narrative into paragraphs instead.

Luther A. Weigle, chairman of the translation committee for the Revised Standard Version when he was at Yale, credited Campbell with being honest in handling the Greek text and courageous in presenting its meaning, and that he was aware of the basic principles of interpretation and translation. But he saw in Campbell's version one obvious defect, and this was his English diction. "He tended to substitute ornate words of Latin derivation for the ordinary words of common use," Weigle noted, citing examples.

He saw Campbell's "A city situate on a mountain must be conspicuous" as a needless elaboration of "A city set on a hill cannot be hid." And whoever reads "Whosoever commits murder shall be obnoxious to the judges" will almost surely misunderstand what is meant, Weigle insisted, even though it is a correct statement in archaic legal language.[36]

Weigle was also impressed that Campbell's version "strikingly resembles" his own Revised Standard Version in many particulars. Cecil K. Thomas' definitive study of Campbell's version, for which Weigle wrote the introduction, lists a number of cases where Campbell anticipates the RSV in correcting the King James, such as "be anxious" for *take thought* in Matthew 6:25; "bankers" for *exchangers* in Matthew 25:27; "morsel" for *sop* in John 13:26; "overlook" for *wink* at in Acts 17:30; and "faint-hearted" for *feeble-minded* in I Thessalonians 5:14.[37]

Campbell did this work for the sake of clarity, realizing that English as a living language changes through usage, making it necessary to revise the English Bible every two centuries or so. In the preface to his new version he contended that even if there were no mistakes in the *King James* it would be necessary to have a new translation because of the evolution of language. To help the reader along he included over 100 pages of critical notes and appendices.

The translation itself was not original with Campbell and was not intended to be. He borrowed it from three Scottish scholars, George Campbell of Aberdeen (the Gospels); James Macknight of Edinburgh (the Epistles); and Philip Doddridge of the Congregational Church in Scotland (Acts and Revelation). He filled in with various other translations, especially one by Charles Thomson, published in Philadelphia in 1808. He felt free to make changes in the sources he used, drawing heavily upon his own knowledge of the original Greek, using Griesbach's Greek New Testament, 1805 edition.

Some thought that Campbell took undue liberties in a version purported to be the work of others. One of his critics leveled this barb: "Out comes a prospectus for another New Testament, which was to be taken from Doctors Macknight, George Campbell, and Doddridge. Well, I took the new book and read it attentively, and what did I see? Behold a New Testament made up of scraps from these men, and when neither of them suited, he puts his own rendering. And this Testament is handed to the public, well suited to the religious infidelity of the Unitarian compiler."[38]

While Campbell's version went through several editions and revisions even after his death, it had a comparatively limited circulation, being used mainly by some Disciples and a few Baptists. It came to be known as "the immersionist version," which marred its image and limited its circulation.

Charles Clayton Morrison in his book *The Meaning of Baptism* is convinced that this one error, of rendering *baptizein* as immersion, was the undoing of Campbell's version, causing it to be rejected even by the Baptists themselves and only mildly accepted by the Disciples. Morrison argues that *baptizein* means something like "initiation," which happened to be by immersion in apostolic times.

While the etymology of the term would be *to dip* or *to immerse*, it did not necessarily have that meaning in the New Testament, just as words in all languages come to mean something different from their etymological meaning. Morrison thinks Campbell especially erred in rendering Eph. 4:5 as "one Lord, one faith, one immersion," and that his New Testament would have received wide acclaim had he used better judgment in reference to this one term.[39]

Two significant events, both in 1829, lifted Campbell from a rather provincial reputation as pioneer preacher and reformer to a highly respected gentlemen of wide acclaim, "a defender of the faith" and a protector of the rights of the people. These were his debate with Robert Owen, the famous socialist of both New Lanark, Scotland and New Harmony, Indiana, in Cincinnati, and his role as delegate to the Virginia Constitutional Convention in Richmond, where he sat with the likes of James Madison and James Monroe, former Presidents, and John Randolph, the nation's Chief Justice. By the close of the decade Alexander Campbell was as well known "in the West," and especially from Pittsburgh to Cincinnati, as Billy Graham would be known in those parts today.

The Owen Debate

Campbell recognized that his reformation was directed as much against infidelity as against sectarianism. It is a matter of history that infidelity poured into America from Europe during the 1820's like a flood, and much of it was part and parcel of the socialism advocated by Owen. It was necessarily anti-religion, for it contended that religion was an obstruction to man's welfare and happiness and to his escape from ignorance, poverty, and superstition.

Hoping for a complete renovation of society, enthusiastic socialists had established communities in various places in America, which proved to be especially popular to foreigners in this country. Like his father-in-law, David Dale, who conducted a successful socialistic enterprise in Scotland, Robert Owen started a similar community in New Harmony, Indiana, which was never to attain the glory of the Scottish enterprise. But Owen's community flourished for a time, attracting theorists and skeptics in large numbers, and it issued a publication that not only taught its principles of socialism but also declared war on religion.

Infidel or not, there were things about Owen that Campbell appreciated. He saw that Owen had a deep commitment for the improvement of society, and that he pursued his goals at his own expense and with no intention of profiting financially from his efforts. He admired him for his talents, education, fortune, and zeal, but he was at a loss to understand how one could be "educated in the kingdom of Scotland" and benefit so little from its advantages. He predicted that Owen's efforts, however well-intentioned, would come to naught on the ground that man simply cannot be happy in this world without the hope of immortality beyond the grave.[40]

Calling on Campbell at his home in Bethany to arrange the preliminaries for debate, Owen found his disputant not only affable and pleasant but also quick with repartee. On one occasion while they were out walking Campbell showed his visitor the family cemetery, which some Bethanians today call "the Westminster Abbey of the Disciples," whereupon Owen observed that he had one advantage over the Christian in that he had no fear of death.

"Well," answered Campbell, "you say you have no *fear* in death; have you any *hope* in death?" After a solemn pause Owen admitted that he had no hope in death. "Then you are on a level with that brute," Campbell rejoined, pointing to a nearby ox. "He has fed till he is satisfied, and stands in the shade whisking off the flies, and has *neither hope nor fear in death*." At this Owen could only smile, and seemed willing to admit the justice of Campbell's logic.[41]

Owen entered the debate with everything going for him. Mexico had just offered him a large portion of what is now California for the purpose of establishing his social scheme on a grand scale. In Austria Prince Metternich listened intently to his social philosophy and had his clerks copy his documents. It was known that his views had influenced the educational system of Prussia, and he influenced our own trend toward educating the very young in nursery and kindergarten.

But the debate was hardly a debate, for the two men, with such diverse philosophies, moved along parallel lines and hardly ever came to the issue to be discussed, which was that religion is founded on ignorance and is opposed to the immutable laws of human nature. In fact, Owen spent most of his time for the nine days reading a 200-page manuscript that he had prepared for the occasion, giving only passing notice to anything Campbell said. He set forth "twelve facts" about human nature that he reverted to again and again.

Campbell accepted the "facts" insofar as they went, but rejected them as an adequate description of man in that they viewed human nature as strictly mechanistic and naturalistic, ignoring man's moral and spiritual nature. Several of the propositions would satisfy such modern behaviorists as B.F. Skinner, just as Owen's utopia at New Harmony would strongly resemble Skinner's mythical community in his *Walden Two*.

Campbell's concluding words of his opening address are among the most impressive in the history of the Movement. Pointing to the real issue of the debate, he said: "It is not the ordinary affairs of this life, the fleeting and transitory concerns of today or tomorrow; it is not whether we shall live all freemen or die all slaves; it is not the momentary affairs of empire, or the evanescent charms of dominion – nay, indeed all these are but the toys of childhood, the sportive excursion of youthful fancy, contrasted with the question, *What is man? Whence came he? Whither does he go?*"

He went on to ask an audience of 1200 that had packed Cincinnati's Methodist Church, people from many states, after many had been turned away:

Is he a mortal or an immortal being? Is he doomed to spring up like the grass, bloom like a flower, drop his seed into the earth, and die forever? Is there no object of future hope? No God – no heaven – no exalted society to be known or enjoyed? Are all the great and illustrious men and women who have lived before we were born, wasted and gone forever? After a few short days are fled, when the enjoyments and toils of life are over; when our relish for social enjoyment, and our desires for returning to the fountain of life are most acute, must we hang our heads and close our eyes in the desolating and appalling prospect of never opening them again, of never tasting the sweets for which a state of discipline and trial has so well fitted us?

This was the real question, he insisted. "It is not what we shall eat, nor what we shall drink, unless we shall be proved to be mere animals; but it is, shall we live or die forever?" Witnesses reported that there were tears on many faces as Campbell concluded with:

> Shall spring ever visit the mouldering urn?
> Shall day ever dawn on the night of the grave?

Campbell effectively employed the old ontological argument, first enunciated by St. Anselm, combined with the argument from First Cause, popularized by St. Thomas Aquinas and Descartes. All our ideas are the result of sensation and reflection, he argued, showing also his dependence on Locke's *tabula rasa* theory, so man's mind is by nature a "blank tablet" with no innate idea of God. Since man has the idea of God, it had to be given to him by God, by revelation, and, man's nature being spiritual, he readily accepts the idea from God, the great First Cause.

When he challenged Owen to explain how man has the idea of God, the infidel replied, "By imagination." Campbell retorted that the principles of philosophy (which then embraced psychology) prove that imagination cannot create ideas but only rearrange the ideas that are already in the mind.

Owen was clearly unprepared to *reason* with Campbell. Once he had read his long manuscript, in sections day by day, he at last turned it over to his disputant to conclude the debate and continue to say what he would. Campbell went on to talk for twelve hours, though this was broken into several sessions over the next two days. He talked about the divine philanthropy, the gospel, and the principles of love which fulfill every moral precept. Since Owen had said so much about the evils of sectarianism, Campbell exposed creedalism as being responsible for all partyism and pointed to the primitive faith as the answer.

Since his opponent had strong humanitarian concerns, Campbell expressed his own faith in the future happiness of man, which he was sure could come only through the universal spread of the primitive Christian faith. He emphasized throughout the debate that there is no way for man to be happy in this world without the hope of immortality. Since Owen allowed for no hope in his community at New Harmony, Campbell predicted that it would come to naught, which it did after a few years.

Campbell and Owen had such rapport in their personal treatment of each other, and the audience responded to the infidel with such courtesy, that Campbell feared this might be interpreted by Owen as at least a partial endorsement of his position. This led Campbell, as he closed the debate, to ask all those who favored the spread of the Christian faith over the world to stand. Most everyone did. He then asked those to stand who were opposed to the spread of the Christian faith. Three people stood.

Thomas Campbell, who was on hand to hear his son debate, used the occasion to baptize several converts, including several of skeptical views, including Dr. M. Winans, who became one of the Movement's brightest minds in that generation and who wrote stimulating articles for Campbell in the *Millennial Harbinger*.

The published debate, which went through several editions, including one in London that was widely read, was destined not only to bring acclaim to Campbell from the believing community, but respect and admiration from the skeptics and infidels as well. For the rest of his life Campbell was often invited by the skeptics to address their gatherings. This was due as much to the magnanimity with which he treated Owen and all skeptics as to his challenging addresses. The skeptics were not used to being treated so graciously by preachers, and it is not evident that Campbell showed the same graciousness toward the clergy that he showed the skeptics. He was destined to reach many disbelievers over the years. Richardson thought it safe to conclude that no one was ever known to have converted as many skeptics as did Alexander Campbell.[42]

Some thought that he at least clipped the wings of Robert Owen, for as the debate wore on the infidel would equivocate more and more, such as denouncing Christianity "as at present taught," a qualifier he did not use at first. He remarked to people after the debate that there were "difficulties on both sides." He clearly admired Campbell, describing him as manly, honest and fair as well as learned and industrious. In later life Campbell esteemed Owen as the most gentlemanly opponent he ever met in debate.

The debate caught the fancy of Frances Trollope, the English author then living in Cincinnati, who wrote about it in detail in her *Domestic Manners of the Americans*. What impressed her most was that the disputants never lost their cool and would even go out to dinner together after blasting away at each other's doctrines on the platform. She also referred to Campbell's power over his audience and the people's admiration of him.

Most of all the debate gave prestige and visibility to the new church that was emerging and to its movement for peace and unity. In defeating Owen, Campbell had put to flight a common foe of all believers. There is nothing he could have done at that time that would have enhanced his stature more or more greatly advanced his cause.

Virginia Constitutional Convention

The Owen debate was hardly over before Campbell became involved in politics, which proved to be his first and last venture into public office. He served as a delegate from his district to the Virginia Constitutional Convention of 1829-30, which was an elective office that he did not at first seek. Being a minister, he was reluctant to become involved in any political activity, and it was only when his friends assured him that as a delegate to the convention he would be above the ordinary sphere of politics, and that the dignity of the office was such that his position as a religious leader would not be compromised, that he consented. He was also assured that the occasion would give him opportunity to extend his principles of reformation to some of the most influential leaders of the state.

He was, after all, to sit in the convention with two former Presidents, James Madison and James Monroe, as well as Chief Justice John Marshall and the governor of the state, William B. Giles, and numerous other eminent men from throughout the state. Even so, Campbell accepted the overture of his friends with the understanding that he would not have to campaign personally.

But it did not turn out that way. Challenged by a distinguished lawyer in nearby Wheeling for the office, he felt compelled to go out in search of votes. On one occasion he and the lawyer confronted each other before the electorate. The lawyer made the mistake of talking too long and of telling the people that a preacher had no business serving in such an office.

Realizing that the audience was weary, Campbell spoke briefly, and mixing humor with sincerity he appealed to what interested them most of all as farmers, his intention to represent the agricultural community at the convention, identifying himself as one of them, "a practical farmer" who held the plough with his own hands. He won the election hands down!

The issue at the convention was whether representation was to be based upon all the white population, as Campbell and the western districts desired, or upon the white population plus the slaves owned by the whites, as preferred by the eastern area and which had long been the practice.

The Tidewater residents owned far more slaves than those in the west, something like 40,000 to 50,000, while the white population was about the same. So the easterners insisted that representation and suffrage be based upon wealth and property, the "property" including the slaves that the whites owned. This always gave the easterners the political leverage. The problem was never solved and eventually led to the formation of West Virginia in 1863.

Campbell was one of the leaders in defending the cause of the west. He argued from principle, much like he did in the Owen debate:

> Suffrage is not a right derived from or conferred by society, for it is a right which belongs to him as a man. Society may divest him of it, but it cannot

confer it. But what is the right? It is that of thinking, willing and expressing his will. A vote is nothing more nor less than the expression of a man's will. God has given to man the power of thinking, willing and expressing his will, and no man ever did, as a free agent, enter into any society without willing it . . It is a right natural and underived.[43]

He proposed to the convention that the constitution should allow that "Every resident, free, white male of 21 years of age shall have the right of suffrage." It was rejected. He also proposed: "Representation shall be uniform throughout the state, that as individuals suffrage should be equal, without respect to disparity of individual fortune, so an equal number of qualified voters are entitled to equal representation, without regard to aggregate fortunes." It also was rejected.

It was evident to the 96 delegates that slavery was the underlying issue. This led to an exchange between Campbell and John Randolph, who defended slavery on the grounds that the system had produced great men. "I have lived in a country that produced great men, learned and powerful," rejoined Campbell, referring to his native Ireland, "but how were they created, sir? For one noble lord there were 10,000 ignoble paupers, and for one great scholar, there were 10,000 ignoramuses."

He went on to say to Randolph: "That is the secret, sir. I never wish to see this mode of making great men introduced into this Commonwealth. I trust, sir, that we will rather strive to make many middling men than a few great and noble men."

Again and again through the long convention Campbell addressed the chair in behalf of freedom, human rights, suffrage, and general welfare. At one point he told the delegates that it was the God of heaven who was the author of suffrage in that He gave Israel the right to express their will in reference to the covenant at Sinai. And that covenant was a constitution, so God gave His people a constitution long before the Virginia constitution and it had the guarantee of general suffrage!

In reading the record, one sees that the delegates from the Tidewater resented these critiques against their system from an immigrant clergyman. One of them blurted out during one session: "Mr. Chairman, even the God of heaven cannot satisfy this man, for he has a Bible all his own!" But the man from Brooke County joined battle for what he believed a just cause, insisting that "I am a man, sir, and as such I cannot but feel interest in everything which concerns the prosperity and happiness of man." He went on to say that it was principles that had brought him there, and that if he lived in Northampton he would feel the same way.

Campbell lost every measure he fought for. His noblest effort was for general education and common schools as part of the constitution, believing as he did that suffrage and education go hand in hand. Gov. Giles repudiated general suffrage on grounds that it would be chaos if the slaves were freed and allowed to vote. But Campbell argued that an *educated* populace could be trusted with their own destiny, and so he wanted the new constitution to make the legislature responsible for educating the masses. The motion was printed in the record, but the delegates never acted upon it. One wonders if the delegates could have ignored this plea for common education if Thomas Jefferson had been there.

At that time Virginia's lower court justices appointed their own successors. Campbell wanted this changed, believing it to be dangerous. He boldly asked Chief Justice Marshall if he felt competent to select his successor. Marshall remained silent. The motion was rejected. Once the new constitution was placed before the people for their approval, Campbell wanted them to have the right to answer this question: *Shall the basis of representation in both branches of the legislature be the white population exclusively?* This too was rejected.

When the delegates finally completed their new constitution, Campbell proposed that some of the grammar be tidied up here and there. Even this was rejected! When the people of Campbell's district came to vote on the new creation, it was turned down unanimously, leaving the rift between east and west deeper than ever.[44]

Campbell was preacher as well as politician during the four months he was in Richmond for the convention. He spoke in various pulpits on Sundays and lectured on other occasions throughout the city, and many of the delegates heard him often. People interested in his plea for unity came from various parts to visit with him, some of whom became leaders of the Movement.

Former President James Madison was one who often heard Campbell during his stay in Richmond. He spoke highly of Campbell's role in the convention, and then added, "But it is as a theologian that Mr. Campbell must be known. It was my pleasure to hear him very often as a preacher of the gospel, and I regard him as the ablest and most original expounder of the Scriptures I have ever heard."[45]

ENDNOTES

[1] Robert Richardson, *Memoirs of Alexander Campbell*, Vol. 2 (Philadelphia: J. B. Lippincott, 1868), p. 88.

[2] Richardson, *Memoirs*, Vol. 2, p. 69.

[3] *Christian Baptist*, Vol. 3 (1825), p. 320.

[4] Richardson, *Memoirs*, Vol. 2, p. 235.

[5] William Baxter, *Life of Elder Walter Scott* (Nashville: Gospel Advocate, n.d. orig. pub. c. 1873), p. 445.

[6] Dwight E. Stevenson, *Walter Scott: Voice of the Golden Oracle* (St. Louis: Christian Board of Publication, 1946).

[7] Alexander Campbell, "Elder Walter Scott's Demise," *Millennial Harbinger*, 1861, p. 297.

[8] Baxter, *Life of Elder Walter Scott*, p. 55.

[9] Earl I. West, "A Letter from Walter Scott," *Gospel Advocate*, Vol. 92 (1950), p. 829. The letter is deposited with Disciples of Christ Historical Society.

[10] Richardson, *Memoirs*, Vol. 1, p. 510.

[11] Walter Scott (as Philip), "On Teaching Christianity, No. 2," *Christian Baptist*, Vol. 1 (1823), Gospel Advocate Edition, p. 66.

[12] *Ibid.*, p. 31.

[13] *Ibid.*, p. 137.

[14] Walter Scott, "Three Divine Institutions," *The Evangelist*, Vol. 1 (1832), p. 93.

[15] W.E. Garrison and A.T. DeGroot, *The Disciples of Christ: A History* (St. Louis: Bethany Press, 1948), p. 182.

[16] Walter Scott, "Three Divine Institutions," *The Evangelist*, Vol. 1 (1832), p. 94.

[17] Baxter, *Life of Elder Walter Scott*, p. 103.

[18] The letter appears in full in Baxter, *Walter Scott*, p. 112.

[19] Richardson, *Memoirs*, Vol. 2, p. 84.

[20] Alexander Campbell, *Millennial Harbinger*, 1831, p. 480.

[21] One publisher used this five-finger exercise as the logo on the cover of a book on Scott. See John W. Neth, *Walter Scott Speaks*, Milligan College, TN, 1967.

[22] Alexander Campbell, "Incidents on a Tour to Nashville, Tennessee, No. 1," *Millennial Harbinger*, 1830, p. 556.

[23] Dwight E. Stevenson, "Walter Scott and Evangelism," *Voices from Cane Ridge* (Edited by Rhodes Thompson) (St. Louis: Bethany Press), pp. 175f.

[24] W.W. Fortune, *The Disciples of Christ in Kentucky*, Convention of Christian Churches, 1932, p. 170.

[25] Dwight E. Stevenson, *Walter Scott: Voice of the Golden Oracle*, p. 118.

[26] Alexander Campbell, "Conclusion to Volume 2," *Millennial Harbinger*, 1831, p. 567.

[27]Alexander Campbell, "Abner W. Clopton, Garner McConnico, Etc.," *Millennial Harbinger*, 1830, p. 542.

[28]Alexander Campbell, "The Dover Decree," *Millennial Harbinger*, 1832, p. 574; "Address to the Virginia Baptist, Part 1," *Millennial Harbinger*, 1832, p. 583.

[29]John A. Williams, *Life of Elder John Smith* (Nashville: Gospel Advocate, 1956, orig. pub. 1870), p. 385.

[30]Alexander Campbell, "Conclusion to Volume 2," *Millennial Harbinger*, 1831, p. 568.

[31]A.S. Hayden, *History of the Disciples of the Western Reserve* (Cincinnati: Chase and Hall, 1875), p. 352.

[32]Alexander Campbell, "Extracts," *Millennial Harbinger*, 1830, p. 479.

[33]Joseph King, "A Memorial Sermon On the Occasion of the Death of Alexander Campbell," *Millennial Harbinger*, 1866, p. 206.

[34]Lester G. McAlister and William E. Tucker, *Journey in Faith: A History of the Christian Church (Disciples of Christ)* (St. Louis: Bethany Press, 1975), p.16.

[35]Edgar J. Goodspeed, *As I Remember* (New York: Harper and Bros., 1953), pp. 167, 177. Goodspeed in defending himself against a mass of criticism for rendering the Lord's Prayer in its shorter form, appealed to the fact that Alexander Campbell did the same thing as early as 1826!

[36]Cecil K. Thomas, *Alexander Campbell and His New Version* (St. Louis: Bethany Press, 1958), pp. 13-14.

[37]*Ibid.*, pp. 41-42.

[38]Garner McConnico, "Mr. Clopton's Review of Campbellism, No. 6," *Millennial Harbinger*, 1830, p. 540.

[39]Charles Clayton Morrison, *The Meaning of Baptism* (Chicago: Disciples Pub. Society, 1914), pp. 16-20.

[40]Richardson, *Memoirs*, Vol. 2, pp. 234-235.

[41]*Ibid.*, pp. 242-243.

[42]Richardson, *Memoirs*, Vol. 2, p. 284.

[43]Richardson, *Memoirs*, Vol. 2, p. 311.

[44]Campbell's speeches, etc. are preserved in *Proceedings and Debates of the Virginia Constitutional Convention of 1829-1830* (Richmond, 1830).

[45]Richardson, *Memoirs*, Vol. 2, p. 313.

8

JOHN T. JOHNSON, RACCOON JOHN SMITH AND JOHN ROGERS THE MOVEMENT UNITES

Let us no longer be Campbellites or Stoneites.
— Raccoon John Smith

The two wings of the Movement, the Christians, principally in Kentucky, and the Reformers or Disciples, mainly in Ohio, united their forces in the winter of 1831-32. Within three years the union was generally accepted among the Stone churches, though some remained "New Lights" or "Christian Churches," ultimately uniting with the Congregationalists in 1931.

Though at first reluctant, the Disciples became a part of the merger, and it was virtually complete within a few years. When Barton W. Stone moved from Kentucky to Jacksonville, Illinois in 1834, he found both a Christian and a Disciples church in the same town. He insisted that he would identify with neither of them until they united, which they did forthwith.[1] For him to be able to make such a demand and for it to be vigorously acted upon shows how the urgency for union had taken hold in only two or three years.

The two groups combined numbered 20,000 to 30,000, with about half from the Stone churches.[2] Campbell was initially fearful that the union was premature. That they were able to effect it without his help shows that it had a broad base of support. While it did have the enthusiastic support of Stone, it took more than this to bring it about. It had to have grass roots support, and this came from several Kentucky leaders, on both sides, who had the ears of the people.

The contributions of three of these, John T. Johnson, Raccoon John Smith, and John Rogers are especially significant. What the Movement was at the time of the union in 1832 is reflected in the spirit of these frontier preachers. If the two movements, both of which already had a generation of history, were likened to rivulets flowing in parallel lines, occasionally moving near to each other but never becoming one stream, it was these three men, and a few others like them, who served as engineers to bring

173

the tributaries together into one impressive stream. Once the union was effected the new church was the largest in Kentucky.

John T. Johnson

"I feel the spirit of evangelism burning within me."

It is rare for one to move from the U.S. Congress to the work of an evangelist, but this was the case with John T. Johnson. He grew up in a political family. His brother served as Vice President under Martin Van Buren, and he himself served in the Kentucky legislature as a young man. Educated at Transylvania University, he was admitted to the bar when only 21. He was married two years later to 15-year-old Sophia Lewis and settled on a Georgetown farm until he volunteered for the War of 1812.

He was an aide to General William H. Harrison, who later became President, and once had his horse shot out from under him. He himself was shot while standing but a few feet from the general, who was cognizant of his heroism and once spoke to him of the incident of having his horse killed from under him. He returned from the war a sick man and almost died of a fever.

By 1819 he had served four years in the state house and had become wealthy in real estate, but in the financial crisis of that year he lost all he had, which amounted to $50,000. He was still able to be elected to Congress in 1820 and reelected two years later. He considered his most important vote in Congress to be the one he cast for Andrew Jackson for President, the election being decided by the House of Representatives since the popular election was not decisive.

Since Jackson was the people's choice, Congressman Johnson passed by Henry Clay of his own native Kentucky to become one of the four legislators whose votes proved decisive for Jackson. To him it was a matter of whether the people could be trusted to elect their own leaders. He described that vote as "one of the proudest acts of my life." The people returned him to Congress in 1828 for still another term, after which he withdrew from political life in preference for quiet farm life and the practice of law. Born in 1788, the same year as Alexander Campbell, he was now 42 and on the verge of becoming a preacher.

Johnson had joined the Great Crossings Baptist Church near his home in 1821, but being involved in politics in the ensuing years, he gave only passing attention to religion. In 1829 he became interested in the teaching of Alexander Campbell, whose writings had influenced the preaching of the pastor at Great Crossings, Jacob Creath, Jr., who became well known in the Movement's history.

When Creath was brought to trial by his church and removed from the pulpit for teaching Campbellite heresies, Johnson was led to study the principles of the reformation for himself. Once convinced, his soul caught fire, and it remained aflame for the next 25 years, during which time he gave his life to evangelism.

"I feel the spirit of evangelism burning within me!," aptly describes the fervor with which he preached. The reports on his labors indicate that he baptized upwards of 500 annually during his 25-year ministry. He thus became known as "the evangelist of Kentucky," and it was largely his successes that caused the Disciples to number 30,000 in Kentucky by 1840.

The artist that painted the gallery of pioneer preachers, which is on display at the Disciples of Christ Historical Society in Nashville, assigned Johnson his appropriate role. He has Thomas Campbell serving the Lord's Supper. Alexander Campbell, Robert Richardson, and Walter Scott are standing before an open Bible. Isaac Errett and W.K. Pendleton also have conspicuous places. The artist places Johnson in the most prominent place of all, out in front of the entire gallery. He is baptizing!

Some of Johnson's methods indicate that the Disciples even in this early period were moving toward cooperative efforts between churches. Johnson's congregation in Georgetown, in cooperation with two others, set up a fund to sustain him in the field. The officers of one congregation supervised the fund and made regular reports to the others. Whatever money Johnson received in the field he turned in to the evangelistic fund, and the officers in turn paid him his salary.[3]

He also contended that there should be order and authority behind those who represent the church as evangelists, and that every preacher entering a strange town should be able to produce letters of credit to the effect that he is acting with authority from the church. Since the Movement was plagued with men who were "wholly unsent and uncalled," as Campbell described them, Johnson and Campbell exchanged views on what might be done about freelance preachers.

Johnson reported to Campbell on some of the ordination services in which he had participated, which included prayer, fasting, and imposition of hands, and it was his view that no one should minister among the churches who had not been duly authorized in some such manner. Campbell dealt with this problem now and again through the years, writing on one occasion: "These comets of which you speak belong not to our system. . . . Our system is not a system of comets, or wandering stars, though one or two may now and then appear amidst the regular planets as omens of what may be expected should we depart from the ancient order of things."[4]

But there were wandering stars among the preachers. It was a problem the Disciples would not readily solve. Johnson anticipated some Disciples of later generations in his reasoning on cooperation and confederation. While suspicious of all such arrangements, he argued that they do no violence to the Scriptures so long as each church is free to participate or not participate, and when each church has a voice in the decisions made.

Johnson thought an evangelist should be responsible only to the church that sends him forth, not to a cooperative agency. Johnson also expressed concern to Campbell over the paltry income an evangelist usually received, again identifying such problems as illness, old age, and death that Disciples of a later age would attempt to solve for their ministers through various agencies.

He preached with a sense of urgency and moved men to repentance as few preachers could. While strongly Biblical, he was also a fervent exhorter. It was typical for him to cry out with great earnestness and sincerity, "Will you serve God and live forever, or serve the devil and perish everlastingly? Oh, let the goodness of God lead you to repentance — the dying love of the Savior reconcile you to God!" He built churches upon the Bible alone, and the great appeal of the Movement to him was that it freed people from sectarian creeds and encouraged them to accept each other on the basis of faith rather than opinion. This was his constant theme.

His success was phenomenal. It was common for him to baptize from 30 to 100 in a protracted meeting, and his patience and persistence seemed unlimited. He preached two full weeks in Richmond, Virginia without a single response. Undaunted, he continued on, and there were finally 55 additions to the church. After this meeting in Richmond in 1846, he went to Bethany to visit with Campbell and to preach at his church, which was the only visit he ever made there. Since it was summer there were but few students around, but he nonetheless baptized six of those who were there. This profoundly impressed Campbell, who made no claim of being an evangelist. It was said of Johnson that it was difficult for one to listen to him and not accept what he said. Campbell obviously admired this persuasive power, especially in a preacher who was promoting his own principles of reform.

Campbell tried to explain the man in the next issue of his journal:

The great secret of brother Johnson's success is his evident sincerity, honesty, and great earnestness — gifts of transcendent value, superadded to good sense and a clear perception of the gospel facts, arguments, precepts, and promises, and a plain, clear, and emphatic expression of them in a familiar and intelligible style.[5]

Campbell also described Johnson as "one of the most laborious, useful, exemplary, and successful evangelists in America."[6] While Campbell described him as self-sufficient and bold, L.L. Pinkerton reported that he appeared timid and embarrassed when he first began to speak, which was caused, he thought, by his "unaffected diffidence." Johnson was no shouting revivalist, Pinkerton said, and he showed no affectation. His spoke in an earnest conversational tone and never clowned. It never occurred to him to be an orator.

One got the impression, Pinkerton observed, that Johnson was talking to him rather than delivering a sermon. He describes him as five feet ten inches in stature, slender and erect, and his hair, once jet black, was now sprinkled with gray. His conversation was always easy and chatty, his manner chaste and dignified, and in meeting him one was impressed at once that he was in the presence of a well-bred gentleman.[7]

While Johnson baptized thousands, he never immersed those already immersed, the practice of which was later to become a matter of controversy in the Movement. His many reports from the field show that he distinguished between immersed believers and unimmersed believers, always receiving the former without further baptism and always immersing the latter. Such as:

> For five days we labored hard twice each day publicly; also from house to house. Two volunteered from the world, and four worthy members united from the Baptists.[8]

> The result of the meeting was 25 additions; of these 18 were from the world, one from the Baptists, and six of the brethren living in the vicinity.[9]

> We had the unspeakable pleasure of receiving four persons among the King's friends. One was an aged, most respectable and intelligent leader of the Methodist congregation, who had been previously immersed. Two females of the same sect united with us and were immersed.[10]

The evangelist was also sympathetic with cooperative efforts between the denominations, especially in regard to the unity of believers and the translation and dissemination of the Scriptures. He addressed the Bible Revision Association, made up mostly of Baptists, in 1855 and encouraged them to issue a translation of the Scriptures that would correct the many deficiencies of the King James version.

He arranged for the first known unity meeting between the Disciples and other churches in Lexington in 1841. While it was poorly attended by denominational leaders, including the Baptists, for whom it was especially intended, it gave Alexander Campbell the chance to underscore the ecumenical character of the Movement.

Johnson was also supportive of cooperative efforts among his own people, whether it was raising support for Bacon College, the first Disciples college, which he helped to found, or in leading in state and national conventions, which had begun during his prime. His biography is replete with instances of his raising money for this or that agency or society. He was probably more organization-conscious than any other of the pioneer leaders.

Printer's ink flowed in his veins as it did with most all of the early leadership, though he never had a publication all his own. His co-editor assignments placed him alongside the Movement's most eminent men: with Barton W. Stone, *Christian Messenger*, 1832-34; with B.F. Hall, *Gospel Advocate*, 1835-36; with Walter Scott, *The Christian*, 1837; with D.S. Burnet, *The Christian Preacher*, 1838; and with Benjamin Franklin, *Monthly Review*, c. 1852.

Still he did not write extensively. His most informative writings are his many reports to Campbell, covering the entire period of his ministry, published in *Millennial Harbinger*. He reported to Campbell the number he had baptized, and would sometimes add "and organized a church with elders and deacons."[11]

This was at the heart of restoring "the ancient order"— congregations presided over by elders and deacons. Instances of discipline also show up in the reports: "The church yesterday withdrew her fellowship from one of the brethren who was engaged in retailing ardent spirits, and thus saved him from ruin; for he immediately repented, declined the business, and was restored."[12]

Johnson collaborated with Barton W. Stone in the publication of a hymnal in 1832. Campbell had also issued a hymnal in 1828, and in 1835 the two were combined, with Campbell becoming the sole owner. This went through at least five editions and enjoyed extensive use among the churches. Richardson reports that Campbell received considerable income from its sale through the years, and in 1862 he willed the proceeds to the American Christian Missionary Society.[13] There is no evidence that either Johnson or Stone made anything from it. Walter Scott's name also appeared as a compiler in the combined edition.

While he enjoyed a close relationship to most of the early leaders, Johnson felt a special affinity to Alexander Campbell. It was, after all, his teaching that jarred him into spiritual consciousness, causing him to write in later years:

The public mind was much excited in regard to what was vulgarly called Campbellism, and I resolved to examine it in the light of the Bible. I was won over, and contended for it with all my might in the private circle. I was astonished at the ignorance and perversity of learned men, who were reputed pious, and otherwise esteemed honorable. My eyes were opened, and I was made perfectly free by the truth. And the debt of gratitude I owe to that man of God, A. Campbell, no language can tell.[14]

It bothered him that Campbell was the object of so much abuse and persecution, much of it coming from the clergy who "seem to hate Alexander Campbell with a hatred that should only be directed against the arch fiend of the lower regions." He was certain that their "envenomed shafts" would fall harmless at his feet, and that "His piety, his goodness, and his greatness, will be properly appreciated by the good and the great of succeeding generations."[15]

Johnson proposed that the churches unite and send Campbell to England, believing that he could do for that country what he had done for America. When Campbell finally went to England, Johnson observed that while he was slandered by his enemies in America he was esteemed by the people abroad, and he was especially delighted when the *Millennial Harbinger* began in a British edition.[16]

As for the attacks on Campbell, Johnson thought he knew what the outcome would be: "His goodness and his greatness will outlive all the malice of his enemies. His fame defies the insidious attacks of envy. And the mighty work he has accomplished will constitute one of the greenest spots in the world's history, when his opponents are dead and forgotten."[17]

His enthusiasm for Campbell knew no bounds. In addressing the Bible Union, which was made up of some of Campbell's critics, he dared to say, in honoring those who had pioneered in Bible translation: "I trust it will not be considered indelicate or out of place to name Alexander Campbell as one of those distinguished pioneers of this century, who risked all that was dear to him of worldly interest, at a most perilous crisis. His life and labors are on record here and in heaven."

As if it were not enough to leave such praise on a positive note, Johnson went on to say: "Snarlers may snarl, infidels may gnash their teeth, false professors may defame, and the envious may scowl at him with green-eyed hate and malice. He stands erect and as firm as the Rock of Gibraltar, defying Ocean's foaming, dashing billows. He is on the rock." Some no doubt considered it indelicate![18]

It was Campbell's magic touch that had led Johnson into the ministry. In his notice of Johnson's death in 1857, Campbell recalls the occasion. After one of his discourses in Georgetown, to which Johnson, still a lawyer, gave "concentrated and deeply interested attention," he invited him to a walk in the yard around the meetinghouse.

"Brother Johnson, you are aware that the Baptists are occasionally wont to say that they sometimes 'feel a deep and solemn impression on their minds.' I now feel such an impression on my mind, and it is concerning not myself, but you," Campbell said to him as they paused in the churchyard. They were quiet for a moment, and then Johnson asked, "And what is it?" Campbell responded: "It is that you should abandon politics and the law, and go and preach the gospel."

Johnson promised that he would give the proposal grave and solemn reflection. Campbell goes on to relate how he passed through Georgetown a few months afterwards and asked a brother how things were going. The reply was: "Nothing remarkable, save that John T. Johnson has given up politics and is now preaching the gospel."[19]

But the thing that impressed Campbell the most about Johnson was something he noticed while dining with him in his home — the piety and devotion with which he offered thanks at the table!

Johnson And Stone: Vision of Unity

Richardson states that Johnson probably had more to do with the union of the Stone and Campbell churches than any other person, and it is likely that it would never have occurred without him. He was the right man at the right place at the right time. In 1831 he found Barton W. Stone, who also lived in Georgetown, Ky. at the time. Each had inspired a concern for unity in his respective church.[20]

Having left the Baptists and starting a church "on the Bible alone," as he liked to put it, Johnson became closely associated with Stone, who had long been of similar persuasion. Being 16 years Johnson's senior, Stone also had long nourished a passion for unity. Stone shared his concerns with his new friend who came into town from his country church to visit with him.

Johnson came to have deep sympathy for Stone's efforts to unite the church on the Bible alone, and this subject soon engrossed much of his attention. As the two men came to see that their own people had so much in common, they began to pray and to talk about the possibility of union. So as to promote their internal unity Johnson joined Stone as co-editor of the *Christian Messenger*.

In recounting the union of the two groups, which Stone described as "the noblest act of my life," he refers to Johnson as "there is no better man," and says: "We lived together in Georgetown, and labored and worshipped together. We plainly saw that we were on the same foundation, in the same spirit, and preached the same gospel. We agreed to unite our energies to effect a union between our different societies."[21]

Raccoon John Smith, in explaining his own interest in the union, expressed the conviction that Johnson and Stone had been called of God to the work of uniting the two brotherhoods. He looked to them as leaders in the effort, even though he himself played a prominent role. He tells how an informal and private conference was held in Georgetown to discuss the prospects of the union. It was decided that two unity meetings would be held, four days each, the first in Georgetown, embracing the Christmas weekend, and the second in Lexington, over the New Year's Day weekend, 1831-32.[22]

At the unity sessions themselves Johnson moved into the background, leaving it to Smith, representing the Reformers or Disciples, and Stone, representing the Christians, to be the spokesmen. Once it was resolved that the union should be effected, they realized that it would be possible only by direct contact with the churches. They therefore decided to send Smith and Samuel Rogers, one from each communion, on a visitation tour among the churches, to tell what happened at Lexington.

This turned out to be a three-year ministry, and it was Johnson's leadership that kept the men at their mission. He raised money and served as secretary and distributor of the fund that supported them.

As these men did their work Johnson reported in Stone's paper of the "astonishing change in Kentucky" and urged the readers to promote the union. "The success of the brethren this year – their indefatigable industry, their devotion to the cause – should rouse us to action and dispose," he advised the readers, and then added with his characteristic optimism, "We hope every Christian will feel it his high privilege to assist in this glorious reformation."[23]

In his latter years Johnson gave considerable thought to the direction the Movement had taken, which he referred to as "the reformation." Unlike the flighty Scott who was disillusioned, Johnson saw the results as phenomenal and entertained the highest hopes for the future. In his essay on "Triumphs and Defense of the Reformation," published in the *Christian Journal* of 1846, he refers to the struggle through which the pioneers had passed: "We have had to contend and toil hard for every inch of ground we have gained; and we have been unfeelingly reproached because we have gained no more. The conquest, however, has been unparalleled, except in the primitive age!"[24]

He had no doubts as to what had happened: "The ancient apostolic gospel has been restored in all its purity . . and the Christian is led infallibly to the true Church." The reformation now had 200,000, he figured, and this in only 18 years. He appreciated what Luther and his reformation had

done, but this came up short of the goal. It was the Stone-Campbell reformation that had restored the true gospel and given to the world the true
apostolic church.

The reference to 18 years is especially interesting, and he refers to this
number twice in the essay. This means he dated the beginning of "the
restored gospel" in 1827, not at the time of Thomas Campbell's *Declaration
and Address* in 1809, or the baptism of the Campbells in 1812, or the dissolution of the Mahoning Association in 1830, all possible dates for the beginning. He rather looked back to when Walter Scott first preached baptism
for the remission of sins and baptized William Amend, which was in 1827.

Generations later another leader in the Movement published a book in
which he argued that the prophecy in Dan. 8:13-14 concerning the cleansing of the sanctuary, was fulfilled in 1827 when Scott began to preach
baptism for the remission of sins.[25]

Johnson believed that posterity would vindicate their controversial
efforts: "Our efforts may be derided; we may be insulted, mocked, and
scoffed at; the most vulgar epithets may be applied to us; the pen of detrac-
tion and slander may subject us to the hatred and odium of many; but the
impartial historian will award ample justice in transmitting to posterity a
faithful service."

The heirs of his efforts, who now have a Movement divided several ways,
may well be chastened by his confidence in the future that he bequeathed
to them: "These divine principles, acted out by our children, will redeem
our names and motives from temporary obloquy; and the advocates of this
Reformation will be hailed as the benefactors of the 19th century."

But if the heirs of Johnson's reformation have failed him, his hope did
not end there. It extended beyond future generations, and this time
perhaps with more assurance: "But the most delightful reflection of all is
that the Savior will award the plaudit, 'Well done,' at the great day, before
an assembled universe."

Raccoon John Smith: Two Churches Unite

In 1868 when Raccoon John Smith was 84 years old, he attended a
district meeting in Chillicothe, Missouri, where he continued to manifest
much of the preaching power of his younger years. During the occasion he
was asked about his association with John Rogers, who had died the year
before, a picture of the old pioneer being placed before him. Raccoon took
the likeness in his palsied hand and silently studied it. "I knew him well,"
he said. "We labored together in bringing about a union of the Reformers
and those called Christians. He was one of the purest men I have ever

known in this Reformation. I have never allowed any man to say aught against the character of John Rogers. He's gone to his reward and I will soon follow him."[26]

It had been 36 years since the union of the Stone and Campbell churches in Lexington in 1832. It was a fragile union at the outset. If Barton W. Stone and John T. Johnson were the catalysts that effected the union, Raccoon John Smith and John Rogers were the implementers.

It could be argued that it was in a unity meeting, in which the Lord's prayer for the oneness of his people was the dominate theme, that the Stone-Campbell Movement really began. It was at least the beginning of the Movement as a union of two unity movements. Lexington, 1832, must therefore be seen as the pivotal year in the Movement's history, and perhaps its greatest and most unique accomplishment.

It was a festive occasion with the spirit of Christmas and New Year's in the air, along with the dream of a united church. Earlier unity efforts by Stone and Johnson had set the stage for Lexington. The site was the Christian meetinghouse on Hill street, which should have been preserved as a historic shrine, but is now the location of a business enterprise.

Since the house was full we may presume the presence of a few hundred people. It was well advertised and was described as "a mass meeting of the brethren," and not only for elders and preachers. The called purpose was to discuss the possibility and practicability of a union, talk about their differences, and to determine upon what basis, if any, unity could be effected.

The differences between them, which will be listed in detail later, were substantial, and there were those on both sides that considered them insurmountable. But there was the one principle, that they all accepted, and it was this that made them one people: *They were all of one Lord, one faith, and one baptism.*[27]

This principle, drawn from Ephesians 4:5, continued for a long time to influence the internal unity of the Movement. Jesus' prayer for the unity of believers was also foremost in the thoughts of those that gathered, according to the records, and we may conclude that it is only in such an atmosphere that unity between diverse parties can be realized. They certainly had not gathered to debate and quarrel over differences.

It was agreed that one from each party should deliver an address, setting forth, as he saw it, the scriptural ground of unity, without referring to points of difference between them. Raccoon John Smith and Barton W. Stone were selected. The two of them met privately to decide how they would proceed, neither of them knowing what the other planned to say. Stone asked Smith to go first.

Raccoon saw the Lexington meeting as the most important event in the Movement's history. The leaders had been saying and writing a great deal about unity, and Raccoon himself had been in prayer sessions with Johnson and Stone for the unity of God's people. This unity meeting would determine whether all this was for real, and "whether the teachings of Campbell were only the speculations of a graceless and sensuous philosophy," as Raccoon put it.[28]

Raccoon had often been criticized for believing that Christians could be united upon the Bible alone, apart from any creed. The proof of his teaching was to be in this Lexington meeting. For him there was much at stake.

When Raccoon John Smith stood up to speak, it might well have been the most dramatic moment in the Movement's history. His biographer captured the drama in this moving paragraph.

> Smith arose with simple dignity, and stood, prayerful and self-possessed, before the mingling brotherhoods. He felt, as no one else could feel it, the weight of the responsibility that rested on him. A single unscriptural position taken—the least sectarian feeling betrayed — an intemperate word — a proud, unfraternal glance of the eye — might arouse suspicion and prejudice, and blast the hope of union in the very moment when it was budding with so many promises. Every eye turned upon him, and every ear leaned to catch the slightest tones of his voice.[29]

He spoke concerning the desirability and practicality of unity. It is desirable because Jesus prayed for it and the apostles enjoined it. It is practical in that God has but one family upon earth and that family is to be united upon the one Book. But union in Jesus is not an amalgamation of sects, and a union of sects would never bless either the church or the world. Since unity upon any system of human invention is both impossible and undesirable, the only union that is practical and desirable must be based upon the Word of God as the only rule of faith and practice.

Raccoon showed how speculations and opinions, when contended for and made terms of communion, are always divisive. This can be avoided, he insisted, if believers would simply allow the Bible to speak for itself. Illustrating his point, he noted that the church has argued about the nature of the Atonement for centuries and was never able to resolve the issue, eventually dividing over it.

He said he resolved questions like that by simply setting forth what the Bible actually says, such as "My Father is greater than I." He said when he quoted such passages he would not stop to speculate upon the inferiority of the Son. Or, when he says "Being in the form of God, he thought it not robbery to be equal with God," he does not offer opinions upon the consubstantial nature of the Father and the Son. "I will not build a theory on such texts and thus encourage a speculative and wrangling spirit among my brethren," he told his Lexington audience.

Here is the genius of the Stone-Campbell Movement enunciated by a backwoods preacher. Union among Christians can be practically realized when opinions are not imposed upon others as tests of communion. Only what the Bible clearly and distinctly teaches can be required of all believers.

Opinions may be held as private property, but not imposed upon others. As Smith laid it before the unity meeting: "Whatever opinions about these and similar subjects I may have reached, in the course of my investigations, if I never distract the church of God with them, or seek to impose them on my brethren, they will never do the world any harm."

He went on to identify the gospel as a system of facts, commands, and promises, and insisted that no deduction or inference drawn from them, however logical or true, forms any part of the gospel of Jesus Christ. Our *opinions* about the gospel are not part of the gospel and therefore cannot be held as a threat over those who may deny them, he added.

Speaking for himself, he said he was willing to surrender any opinion for the sake of unity, but he would not surrender one fact, commandment, or promise of the gospel for the whole world. "While there is but one faith," he told them, "there may be ten thousand opinions; and hence if Christians are ever to be one, they must be one in faith, and not in opinion."

He concluded by saying, "Let us, then, my brethren, be no longer Campbellites or Stoneites, New Lights or Old Lights, or any other kind of *lights*, but let us all come to the Bible, and to the Bible alone, as the only book in the world that can give us all the Light we need."[30]

Smith's biographer says Stone responded to Raccoon with "a strain of irresistible tenderness." He agreed that Christians could never unite upon their speculations, even though he himself was given to speculation. Mysterious and sublime subjects may interest the Christian philosopher, but they hardly edify the church, he conceded. He confessed that even though he had delivered speculative sermons from time to time that they had always left him with barrenness of soul. He agreed with Smith that speculations should be left out of the pulpit and that one should teach only the words of inspiration.

Agreeing with Raccoon on the basis of unity, Stone at last said, "I am willing to give him, now and here, my hand." As they shook hands they pledged each other their fellowship, which became a symbol of the unity achieved on the occasion. Those assembled were urged to express their willingness to unite by giving each other their hands, which they did amidst joyful and tearful greetings.

A song spontaneously arose among them, further confirming their oneness. The next day was the Lord's day, on which occasion they broke the loaf together and again pledged to each other their brotherly love. It was a handshake that shook the frontier.

Raccoon John Smith was prepared by tragic circumstances for the sensitive role assigned him by Providence on this occasion. Reared in abject poverty, he struggled not only for what education he could get but in some instances for survival itself. He married Anna Townsend in 1806 when he was 22 and went on to acquire enough land and money to make him ambitious for more.

Dissatisfied with his chances in Wayne County, Ky., he made his way to Huntsville, Alabama, which was then but a village of a few houses and scattered farms. There he was able to purchase with small payments 10,000 acres from the government. Then a budding Baptist minister, Raccoon had visions of himself as a rich man with a southern mansion and scores of slaves to work his land.

Then tragedy struck. While he was absent from home one night, his log cabin burned to the ground, killing two of his children. His wife Anna, who was on a visit of mercy to a nearby home when the fire struck, could not forgive herself of the unintentional neglect and could not be consoled. She took sick and soon died. Raccoon himself then came down with a fever that laid him low for four months. His neighbors who watched after him expected him to die at any moment. He despaired of life itself, praying not only that he would die but his surviving babies as well, who had to be cared for by others. Because of a local prejudice in regards to his particular fever, he was given no water to drink lest it kill him. One night a tearful neighbor, in response to Raccoon's agonizing cry for water, decided to give him all the water he desired since he was dying anyway. He fell into a peaceful sleep, not death as his friends supposed. From that point on he began to rally.

Convinced that the Lord had chastened him for his proud ambitions, he made his way back to southern Kentucky, back to his home and kin, and with hardly anything of this world's goods. He was now 32, an ordained Baptist preacher of considerable talent and education for one of his humble background. It was by dogged determination that he had improved himself. But he was so smitten by tragedy and so humbled by God's chastening hand that he was now bereft of both drive and ambition.

His friend Jeremiah Vardeman, who himself was to become a leading figure in the Movement in Kentucky, encouraged him to attend the meeting of the Tate's Creek Association, where a large number of ministers and their people would gather. He showed up so ungainly attired, with homespun pants that were too short and an old faded coat, that he was not recognized by those who knew him and was ignored by the others.

While the leaders of the Association met for business in the meetinghouse, two young, inexperienced preachers were appointed to address the hundreds who gathered outdoors. One of the ministers who finally recognized Raccoon urged him to follow the young men in addressing the audience. Still downtrodden, he was reluctant to do so, but when the young men faltered and fumbled, waiting for the Spirit to speak through them, and finally sat down speechless, Raccoon's spirit stirred within him and he became his old self again.

Once before the audience, he was of such uncouth appearance that the people, already disappointed in the performance of the two young men, began to disperse. "Stay, friends, and hear what the great Augustine said!," he cried out to them. They paused to listen, and he told of how Augustine wished to see three things before he died: Rome in all her glory, Paul preaching on Mars Hill, and Jesus in the flesh.

As the people still hesitated to return to their seats, he cried out again, "Stay and hear what the great Cato said." As he went on to quote Cato and then Thales, the ancient Greek philosopher, it was apparent that the crudely dressed stranger had something to say and knew how to say it.

Once the audience was his, he went on to deliver a stirring message on the redemption that is in Christ, with oratorical skill and Calvinistic orthodoxy. Someone hurried to the building to tell the ministers that a man was preaching the like of which he had never heard. It was the rebirth of an almost destroyed Raccoon John Smith.

They called him Raccoon because he lived amongst the coons along the South Fork of the Cumberland River and because he often wore a cap of raccoon's skin. He was also as crafty as a coon with his repartee. There is the time when he sat with a Methodist divine in a tavern ready to enjoy a mug of wine. The divine insisted that they should thank God for the blessing. As he continued to pray on and on, Raccoon finished his mug and then proceeded to drain the divine's as well, placing the empty mug back before the preacher's closed, uplifted eyes. Once the preacher saw to his amazement that his wine was already consumed, Raccoon reminded him that the Bible does not say pray, but to *watch* and pray!

Once while walking in the woods he came upon some boys, who, when they saw how strange he looked in his rough attire and raccoon cap, proceeded to poke fun at him. "Maybe he is Abraham," chided one. "Or maybe Isaac," said another. "Or is he Jacob?," asked another, all of them having fun at Raccoon's expense. Appreciating that they had some Sunday school knowledge, he nonetheless laid it on them: "Boys, I'm neither Abraham, Isaac, nor Jacob; but I am Saul the son of Kish out looking for his father's asses, and I didn't know that I would find them so soon!"

Raccoon was once baptizing his converts in some stream when he nudged a paedobaptist preacher, who was watching the immersions with studied curiosity, toward the water, insisting that he was going to immerse him. Protesting vehemently that it would do him no good if it were against his will, he begged Raccoon to turn loose of him. "You say it would do you no good if it were against your will, but did I not see you the other day sprinkling an innocent babe when it was against its will?"

Marked as his life was by inexplicable tragedy, perhaps he had a special need to laugh and have fun. But it was always in such a way as to endear himself to people. He was both liked and appreciated by the humble folk with whom he lived in the boondocks. But behind his cheerful countenance and dry wit was a restive spirit, one made uneasy by the theological dogmas of his Calvinistic faith.

He was troubled by the doctrine of election and reprobation, especially since the fiery death of his children. He could hardly bear the thought that his babies could pass from a burning cabin to a burning hell, which had to be their destination should they not be of the elect. It also bothered him to realize that according to his Calvinistic religion the multitudes that are lost were decreed by God to be lost even before they were born, and there is nothing that they can do about their condition. Faith saves, and faith alone, he believed, but Calvinism taught that sinful men can do nothing to have faith, for even this is a gift of God and comes only when God chooses to bestow it upon the elect.

He began to express his doubts about Calvinism, which was widely accepted by the churches on the frontier. On one occasion in March, 1822 he was urging sinners to repent and believe the gospel. "Jesus died for you," he said, "but if you believe not, you must be damned." In his confusion he became silent. "If the elect who hear me should not believe, what I am preaching is false, for they are to be saved anyway," he said to himself, "and if the non-elect should believe me, my preaching is false, for they are to be lost in any event since Christ did not die for them."

He was both too honest and too confused to continue, so he closed his address. But he went on to tell them, "Something is wrong. I am in the dark. We are all in the dark. But how to lead you to the light, or to find the way myself, before God, I know not."[31]

The crowd dispersed, and he went silently home to his second wife,

Nancy, whom he had married on Christmas Day, 1816. To her he poured out the confusion of his thoughts, hoping for some ray of light to dispel the darkness from his mind. They knelt down and prayed together. He asked God for light. He promised both the Lord and his wife that he would now take only the Bible as his oracle, that he would study it carefully and follow it faithfully, wherever it might lead him.

From the hour of that prayer and pledge Raccoon pursued a search of the Scriptures that sometimes kept him up all night, even after working in the field all day. He weighed Calvinism in the light of an open Bible, point by point, and finally concluded that its entire superstructure was based on the notion that man's death in sin denies him of his freedom to act. What then does "death" mean? he asked himself, believing that the peace of a hundred churches that his ministry touched depended on the answer.

Christians are also said to be dead, he told himself, dead *to* sin. If they can be dead *to* sin and yet still have the power to sin, then the sinner, who is dead *in* sin, may have the power to believe. Once this conclusion was firmly fixed, he was persuaded that the system he had so long preached was without substantial basis.

Such was the state of his mind when someone placed in his hands the prospectus of a new religious journal named *The Christian Baptist*, edited by Alexander Campbell. Raccoon became an avid reader, albeit a critical and suspicious one. As he read on, month by month, he was impressed with the editor's erudition and style, but he supposed that he must be a wholly unregenerate man, writing as he did about "Experimental Religion." Some of his neighbors in "the hollow" cancelled their subscriptions, including Raccoon's own brother, but Raccoon kept on reading, insisting that he would remain a subscriber, even if Mr. Campbell be the devil himself, just for the manner of his saying things.

It was about this time that Campbell made his first trip into Kentucky, the spring of 1824. He was to speak at Flemingsburg, some 20 miles from Mt. Sterling, where Raccoon then had a farm, having moved from southern Kentucky a few years before. He urged his brethren to invite Campbell to come on to Mt. Sterling, as a matter of courtesy, but the prejudice against him was too strong for that. Raccoon set off for the 20 miles on horseback alone to hear him.

In the town he met William Vaughn, a Baptist preacher that he knew well, who had been travelling with Campbell for eight days through two counties. Raccoon wanted to know if the controversial figure was a Calvinist, Arminian, Arian, Trinitarian, or what. Vaughn said that he did not know, that he did not seem to be any of these things. Raccoon assured his friend that he could tell what he was, once he heard him.

He asked Vaughn if Campbell knew anything about heartfelt religion. His friend told him that Campbell was the most pious, godly man he had ever been around. "What does he know about Christian experience?," Raccoon asked. At this Vaughn told Raccoon that he was taking him to meet Campbell so that he could determine these things for himself.

Raccoon was often to relate through life the occasion when he first saw Alexander Campbell. The reformer was taking off his sherryvallies, for he had been riding that morning in the mud. As Campbell arose to greet him, Raccoon recounted, his nose seemed to stand a little to the north! But apart from any introduction, what Raccoon wanted to do most of all was to sit down and have a long look at the man that he had heard so much about, the man whose writings had put so many new thoughts into his mind.

That night he heard Campbell speak out in the yard, for the meeting-house was too small to accommodate the crowd. He gave an exposition on Galatians, with a special treatment of the allegory of the two women in chapter 4, distinguishing as he often did between the two covenants.

Afterwards Raccoon complained to Vaughn that he did not ride 20 miles to hear a man preach for just 30 minutes. Vaughn suggested that he look at his watch. Raccoon was surprised to see that Campbell had spoken for two and a half hours. "I have never been more deceived," he admitted. "Two hours of my life are gone, I know not how, though wide awake, too, all the time." Vaughn wanted to know what measure he took of the man. "Be he saint or sinner," said Raccoon, "he has thrown more light on that Epistle, and on the whole Scriptures, than I have received in all the sermons that I have ever heard before."[32]

John Rogers: Messenger on Horseback

John Rogers, who was 16 years younger than Raccoon, was also a Kentuckian, having been born near Winchester, which was near Cane Ridge where Barton W. Stone was conducting his own reformation. While Rogers was deprived of religion in his youth, having never heard a sermon until he was 17, he was baptized by Stone in 1818 and became a member of the Christian Church. In those early years he came to know some of the leading preachers of the Christian Church, the most notable being Moses Dooley and his two sons, Thomas and Reuben.

Moses and Reuben fulfilled their ministry and passed on before they ever heard of the Campbell movement and long before the union of the two parties in 1832. Thomas Dooley, whom Rogers remembered as the sweetest singer he ever heard, lived until 1847, but he did not follow Stone into the union, choosing to stay in that Christian Church that remained separate from the Campbell influence.

Rogers began preaching when he was 19, and the anecdotes from his early life reflect a life of poverty similar to that of Raccoon John Smith. Poverty was, of course, common in those days, not only preachers but for those who would support them. Rogers' friends raised $18.00 to help him buy a horse. Now in need of only bridle, saddle, and saddlebags, he worked as a carpenter for bridle and saddle, and a friend gave him some old saddlebags. He was now able to go forth preaching.

He studied for a time under Barton W. Stone. His biographical notes reveal that the Christian Churches had long had district conferences and were both licensing and ordaining ministers long before any of them had heard of the Campbells. Stone himself wrote Rogers' certificate of ordination, the service itself being solemnized by prayer and laying on of hands by the presbyters. It read as follows:

> The elders of the Christian Church assembled at Minerva, April 10, 1820, have unanimously ordained our brother, John Rogers, to the ministry of the Gospel, according to the will of God, our Savior, by the commendation of the Christian Church at Georgetown, in which he has lived and labored for some time past.
>
> Signed by order of the Elders.
>
> Barton W. Stone, E.C.C.[33]

The initials E.C.C. meant Elder of the Church of Christ or Christian Church. They used both names for the church but always called themselves Christians. At this time they had only a few meetinghouses of their own, most gatherings being in homes, though it was common for them to use a Baptist building. Rogers preached for 40 years, remarking afterwards that he hardly ever entered the pulpit without being embarrassed. There is no evidence that he ever had any contact with Raccoon John Smith prior to the Lexington meeting.

Like both Smith and Stone, who considered the union of the two churches as the most significant thing they ever did, Rogers was gratified with the achievement and went so far as to say: "The importance of that union has never been appreciated, and perhaps cannot be yet. It will be hereafter, when we who were the actors in it shall have passed away. It was and is such a union as the world never witnessed before, nor since." He also said that it was a union that had not been severed and he hoped it never would be.[34]

Both Raccoon and Rogers lived to attend the General Convention held in Cincinnati in 1866, the year Alexander Campbell died. They dined

191

together on one occasion in the presence of the younger generation of Disciples as well as their own. They reminisced on the old days, recalling pioneers of the faith they knew personally: the Campbells, the Creaths, Stone and Scott. Rogers told how he once sang one of his own hymns to Alexander Campbell and was disappointed when the reformer referred to it as a soliloquy, even if intended as a compliment.

Raccoon and Rogers were both hymnologists. Raccoon asked the group at the Convention to sing one of his songs. When a brother started it, others soon joined in:

> There's a region above,
>   Free from sin and temptation,
> And a mansion of love
>   For each heir of salvation.

As the group sang on the two old men, now grown feeble, walked about the room embracing their brothers and sisters in the faith. Finally the two of them shook hands and them embraced, weeping for joy, while the group sang on:

> There shall friends no more part,
>   Nor shall farewells be spoken;
> There'll be balm for the heart
>   That with anguish was broken.[35]

John Rogers made a unique contribution to the Movement in that he helped effect a union that may have otherwise come to naught. Along with Raccoon John Smith, he rode horseback to visit scores of Stone and Campbell churches. For three years in church after church their message was the same: *We are now a united people!* That they were able to effect such a union is a testimonial to the unity-mindedness of the people. The unity appeared to be so solidified in Rogers' declining years that he was persuaded it would long endure.

Unity in Diversity

It was unity in diversity. We have seen that the Disciples and Christians had much in common at the time of their union. They both gave high priority to the unity of all believers and were separate unity movements. They both made faith and obedience to Christ the only basis of fellowship, rejecting human creeds and human names as divisive. They both looked to the Bible as their only rule for faith and practice. They had a common enemy, Calvinism, and they both rejected its principal doctrines with abandon.

They both practiced baptism by immersion for believers only, and the founders of both parties had the common experience of rejecting sprinkling and being immersed. But there was by no means conformity of viewpoint in either doctrine or practice, the differences being rather substantial.

1. The most notable difference was in evangelism, both in theory and practice. The Christians were zealous and emotional, even to the point of using the mourner's bench, which was then common, and they had numerous evangelists. The Disciples, who had only Walter Scott in the field at the time of the union, had neglected evangelism.[36] Too, they were more rational in their approach, far less emotional, and rejected the mourner's bench.

2. While they were both immersionists, the Christians did not emphasize it like the Disciples did, believing that one can be saved without being immersed and that it is not necessary to Christian communion. Like Campbell, Stone taught baptism for the remission of sins, but he did not press the point and admitted to an inconsistency in application.

3. The Christians had an ordained ministry and a higher concept of the ministerial office, and insisted that only the ordained may baptize and preside over the Lord's supper. The Disciples were actually anticlerical and believed in the priesthood of all believers in the sense that any believer may baptize and serve Communion.

4. Those in the Stone movement were adamant in wearing the name Christian, believing this to be a divinely-appointed name, while the Campbell followers preferred Disciples. Campbell himself concluded that "Christian" was given in derision by outsiders and not divinely given at all. In the first years following the union the name Christian was more widely used, but eventually the name Disciples prevailed, though both names have always been used in identifying both the church and the members.

5. From the very first Sunday at Brush Run the Disciples served the Supper every first day, influenced as they were by Scottish reformers. The Christians observed it on an irregular basis up to the time of the union.

6. The Christians had a broader view of the ministry of the Holy Spirit, both in the conversion of the sinner and in the life of the believer. The Disciples were inclined to limit the Spirit's influence to the Scriptures and the preaching of the word.

7. While both were unity-conscious, the idea of uniting all men in Christ was more predominate with the Christians. The Disciples were more

concerned for a restoration of the ancient order. This difference caused Richardson to think of the Stone people as preachers and the Campbell folk as teachers.[37]

These differences do not take into account the rather serious conflict between Stone and Campbell over the doctrine of the preexistence of Christ, which led one Disciples historian to conclude that it was the risk of being identified with Arianism that caused Campbell to be less than enthusiastic about the union.[38]

The differences were formidable, certainly as much so as those that fractured the Movement generations later. Still they were united in that they became one church; they were diverse in that there were differences. Unity in diversity. It was a concept that would continue to characterize the Movement. They were free to differ but not to divide, they were often to say.[39]

We have seen that it was Johnson and Stone that set the stage for the union, and that it was Smith and Rogers that ratified it with the people. It remains to be said that it was evangelistic success that actually consolidated the union, for as evangelists like Rogers and Smith baptized hundreds of converts each year, they brought them into a *united* unity Movement, and the growth during the 1830's was phenomenal.

The misgivings and suspicions that existed on both sides concerning this unlikely union were allayed only by the wise counsel of leaders on both sides, especially the editors who had regular contact with the people. We have seen that Johnson joined Stone as an editor of the *Christian Messenger* for the express purpose of solidifying the union. Stone's "Address to the Churches of Christ," wherein he made that great plea, *Let the unity of Christians be our polar star*, was helpful in persuading his people to accept the Disciples.[40]

Raccoon John Smith's *Address*, a privately published pamphlet, which enjoyed an extensive circulation among the Disciples, went far in satisfying those people that they should unite with the Christians. This was crucial since there was so much prejudice against Stone and his speculative views.[41] Smith's *Address*, which Rogers acclaimed as a fair and clear statement of the principles of the reformation, may be considered among the most significant documents of the Movement's history.

Alexander Campbell also encouraged the union once it was effected, which was most important. It was even more important that he did not discourage it during its formative stages. It says something for the depth of the leadership of the two parties that they were able to achieve such a union without the help of the most influential man among them. It also says something for their independence of mind, an ingredient for good or ill that the Movement has never lacked.

ENDNOTES

[1]John Rogers, *Biography of Elder Barton W. Stone*, Cincinnati, 1847, p. 79.

[2]Robert Richardson, *Memoirs of Alexander Campbell*, Vol. 2, p. 370, numbers the Christians with Stone at 10,000 to 12,000; W.W. Jennings, *Origin and Early History of the Disciples of Christ*, p. 193, numbers both groups at 20,000 to 30,000.

[3]John Rogers, *Biography of Elder J.T. Johnson* (Nashville: Gospel Advocate, 1956, orig. pub. 1861), p. 193.

[4]Alexander Campbell, "To Epaphras No. 3," *Millennial Harbinger*, 1832, p. 502.

[5]Alexander Campbell, "News from the Churches," *Millennial Harbinger*, 1846, p. 477.

[6]Rogers, *Biography*, p. 298.

[7]Rogers, *Biography*, p. 329.

[8]"The Campaign in Mason County, etc.," *Millennial Harbinger*, 1841, p. 210.

[9]Rogers, *Biography*, p. 253.

[10]*Ibid.*, p. 106.

[11]Rogers, *Biography*, p. 277.

[12]*Ibid.*, p. 360.

[13]Richardson, *Memoirs*, Vol. 2, p. 658.

[14]Rogers, *Biography*, p. 21.

[15]*Ibid.*, p. 236.

[16]"News from the Churches," *Millennial Harbinger*, 1843, p. 377.

[17]Rogers, *Biography*, p. 241.

[18]Rogers, *Biography*, p. 400.

[19]"Letter from Brother R.C.R.," *Millennial Harbinger*, 1857, p. 110.

[20]Richardson, *Memoirs*, Vol. 2, p. 379.

[21]John Rogers, *Biography of Elder Barton W. Stone*, pp. 78, 79.

[22]John A. Williams, *Life of Elder John Smith* (Nashville: Gospel Advocate, 1956, orig. pub. 1870), p. 368.

[23]Rogers, *Biography of Stone*, p. 59.

[24]Rogers, *Biography of Johnson*, p. 244.

[25]J.W. Chism, *The Cleansing of the Sanctuary* (Rosemead, CA: Old Paths Book Club, 1962, orig. pub. about 1910).

[26]W.C. Rogers, *Recollections of Men of Faith* (Rosemead, CA: Old Paths Book Club, 1960, orig. pub. 1889), p. 206.

[27]Williams, *Life of Elder John Smith*, p. 369.

[28]*Ibid.*, p. 370.

[29]*Ibid.*, p. 371.

[30]*Ibid.*, p. 372.

[31]*Ibid.*, pp. 115, 116.

[32]*Ibid.*, pp. 131, 132.

[33]W.C. Rogers, *Recollections of Men of Faith*, p. 179.

[34]*Ibid.*, p. 164.

[35]*Ibid.*, p. 204.

[36]Richardson, *Memoirs*, Vol. 2, p. 199.

[37]*Ibid.*, p. 199.

[38]A.W. Fortune, *The Disciples in Kentucky*, Convention of Christian Churches In Kentucky, 1932, p. 117.

[39]W.T. Moore, *Comprehensive History of the Disciples of Christ* (New York: Revell, 1909), see Preface.

[40]Barton W. Stone, "Address to the Churches of Christ," *Christian Messenger*, 1832, p. 263.

[41]Williams, *Life of Elder John Smith*, p. 382.

9

PIONEERS OF THE FRONTIER
THE MOVEMENT MOVES WEST AND SOUTH

The Campbellites are spreading like a prairie fire.

By 1848 the Movement had made such a place for itself on the American frontier as to be included in the second edition of *A History of All Denominations in the United States.* Under the title "A History of the Disciples of Christ," it had an extensive chapter all its own, including a handsome lithograph of Alexander Campbell.

It was written by Robert Richardson, the Movement's first historian, who, oddly enough, told the story strictly from the Campbell perspective, not even mentioning Barton W. Stone or the Lexington union. But he includes the Stone churches when he numbers the members as "but little short of 200,000" in 1848.

Still in its first generation, it is noteworthy that Richardson referred to the new church as a denomination. While praising its biblical literacy, he wrote, "It may be safely affirmed, that no denomination in our country is so familiar with the Bible." Alexander Campbell was also by now referring to his people as "our denomination."[1] This is interesting since the heirs of the Movement in later generations have been adamant about not calling themselves a denomination, reverting to such euphemisms as "our fellowship."

In the historical sketch, which ran some 12,000 words, Richardson named the purpose of the Movement as: "Thus, having for their object to unite all Christians together in the common faith, without regard to difference of opinion; and in the full enjoyment of the common salvation, without respect to sectarian distinctions."[2]

Since Thomas Campbell's *Declaration and Address* in 1809 and Raccoon John Smith address in Lexington in 1832 this had been the plea of the Movement: *Unity on the grounds of the common faith, not in matters of opinion.* And as Richardson put it in his historical sketch, it was assumed that Christians could unite on "the claims of that common Christianity in which most parties are agreed." He thought it was this simple plea that accounted for the dramatic growth of the Movement, from only 25,000 to 30,000 in 1832 to some 200,000 by 1848.

This means that many people did lots of work in a multitude of places as the Movement followed the frontier, mostly west but also south. The farmer-preachers, lawyer-preachers, doctor-preachers, and schoolteacher-preachers were too many to number. And "the pioneer woman" was at their side making enormous sacrifices. The vast majority of men and women who "won the West" was never known to recorded history.

In recounting the experiences of some of them we are to realize that they are but a sampling of the stories that could be told. Starting with Reuben Dooley, born in 1773, who travelled with Stone in the wilds of Kentucky, and continuing to Pardee Butler, born in 1816, who labored in the "new West" as far as Kansas, we have a representation of two generations from both the Stone and Campbell backgrounds, extending to the ends of the frontier. Then there were the women pioneers.

"New Light" Preachers

"They were bold and daring, as pioneers had to be."

In his research on the "New Lights," a term applied to the Stone movement, Colby D. Hall found scraps of information in various documents on 54 preachers. The number surprised him since frontiersmen were not given to record-keeping. He found them rough and ready and usually with meager education. They were bold and daring, as pioneers had to be.[3]

Reuben Dooley was another of those Presbyterians who rebelled against Calvinism, resigning himself to a fate of being eternally lost, until Samuel Findlay, of Stone's Christian Church, converted him and instilled within him a desire to preach. The scanty information on him indicates that he was a most remarkable character, a great preacher who baptized hundreds. Samuel Rogers describes him as "a man of great physical endurance, plain in attire, and, in his address, humble as a child; but zealous, prayerful, hopeful and untiring in his labor of love."[4]

He goes on to say that Dooley was an effective exhorter, and that it was he who led him to Christ, which was contribution enough for any man, as we shall see in our study of Rogers' ministry. Dooley was an intimate friend of Stone and travelled with him extensively. Dying in 1822, he contributed much to what the Movement finally became, and it is noteworthy that he never as much as heard of Alexander Campbell.

William Kinkaid, born in 1783, grew up as an Indian fighter and a woodsman, and then went on to study under Stone and became a preacher in the Midwest. He became a student of both Latin and Greek, and he studied Hebrew under a Jewish scholar, finally publishing a book on Biblical doctrine, all of which was rare for a frontiersman. Typical of the Stone preachers, he went on record for fellowshipping all believers of every name, however much they differed from him, but, he insisted, "I refuse to call myself by any other name than that of Christian," which made him a good "New Light."

Sprinkled a Methodist, Elijah Goodwin was but a boy when he decided to preach, practicing on the trees and cattle. The "New Lights" reached him with their emphasis upon the love and grace of God. Once immersed, he served mostly in Indiana. He had a way of saying, "I will give two errors for one truth any time." Like so many of the preachers, he worked for nothing, receiving only one dollar during one seven year period of his life. As an evangelist he sometimes travelled as many as 3,000 miles a year, all on horseback, where he preached to those who had never heard the primitive faith. Many churches through the Midwest owe their beginning to him. He was also among the earliest editors of the Movement, joining J.M. Mathes of Bloomington, Indiana, in publishing the *Christian Record* in 1847.[5]

John Secrest, born about 1795, should be mentioned because of his early contacts with the Campbells, forming one of the links between the two groups. Richardson recognizes that it was due to the success of Secrest and other preachers of the Stone movement that led the Mahoning Association in 1827 to send out Walter Scott as an evangelist. He reveals that Secrest was present on that occasion and addressed the Association.[6]

He had by that time baptized 3,000 in Ohio alone, while the Reformers had reached but few. His success was due in part to what Alexander Campbell, whom he frequently visited in Bethany, had taught him about baptism. He was effectively practicing what the Reformers held as theory. He motivated the Campbell people to greater efforts and at the same time was a catalyst in bringing them and the Stone people together.

In fact it may have been John Secrest and not Walter Scott who first preached "the restored gospel." We have seen that Campbell gave Scott credit for this, when he baptized William Amend in New Lisbon, Ohio on Nov. 18, 1827, and this has been generally accepted. But Nathan Mitchell, another New Light preacher, records in his autobiography that Secrest immersed him on Aug. 6, 1827, at Barnesville, Ohio "on a profession of my faith in the Divine Redeemer."

Mitchell makes it clear that later that same year or early in 1828 Secrest "preached boldly and fearlessly faith in Christ, repentance unto life, and immersion by the authority of Christ into the name of the Father, Son and Holy Spirit in order to the remission of sins." Mitchell explains that this was not the practice of the Stone churches, even if Stone held it in theory, but that it was learned from Alexander Campbell. He says the Stone preachers at this time did not even require baptism for church membership, even though they did immerse.[7]

Samuel Rogers

"My Master first, then others."

Once when passing through Baltimore, Samuel Rogers paused at a beautiful spring in quest of a drink of water. At the same time a silver-mounted carriage halted nearby, from which a slave alighted, bearing a silver pitcher and cup. Meeting him at the spring, Rogers asked for a drink. "If you please, sir, when I have served my master." Sensitive of the just reproof, he waited until the slave returned, whereupon he was courteously served a cup of cool water. Rogers both thanked and tipped the slave, not so much for his courtesy, but for teaching him a lesson that he never forgot, how to serve *his* Master. "My Master first, then others" became Samuel Rogers' lifetime motto.[8]

He learned the lesson well. Though reared in poverty and ignorance, with only three months' of schooling, he braved the rigors of the frontier through sixty years of ministry. He helped forge both a new republic and "the new Reformation." For the first he fought in the War of 1812, for the second he added over 7,000 converts and scores of churches, all in the name of "the Sun of Righteousness," as he often referred to his Master.

In the war against the British he fought under Major John T. Johnson, who was later to be his fellow evangelist. He came through the war unscathed, though after one encounter he counted seven bullet holes in his clothing. As an evangelist he suffered incredible hardship in bearing "the ancient faith" into virgin fields. He followed the frontier through Ohio, Indiana, Illinois, and Missouri, his message always being "the Bible and the Bible alone as the only rule of faith and practice."

Born in 1789 in Charlotte county, Virginia, Rogers was christened a Methodist by Bishop Francis Asbury himself. His father migrated to "Upper Louisiana" or "New Spain," which is now Missouri, in 1801. Young Samuel was living alongside the Missouri river, twenty miles above St. Louis, when the Lewis and Clark expedition camped in the neighborhood in 1809.

He was in such primitive country that he was in his teens before he saw either a preacher or a teacher. When his family moved to Kentucky he married a girl who lived near Cane Ridge, where she and her family were "liberated from the shackles of Presbyterianism" by Barton W. Stone. He too was immersed into Christ under the preaching of Stone and Reuben Dooley in 1812, after which he took up arms against the British. It was the same year that the Campbells were immersed up in Virginia, and for similar reasons, but it would be a decade or more before they would even hear of each other. Rogers indicates that even at this early date there were "thousands" who had joined the Stone reformation.

The Stone people had few meetinghouses in those days, so the churches met outdoors when the weather permitted or in homes, where the women prayed and exhorted almost as much as the men. Rogers was ordained by an aged woman as well as by Reuben Dooley. Ordination was the general practice among the Stone churches, more so than among the Campbell churches. Thomas Campbell, however, ordained his son Alexander at their first church at Brush Run in 1812, as well as other preachers.

The mourner's bench was also common in the Stone meetings, even though the mourners were finally immersed. Writing fifty years later, Rogers expressed mixed feelings over its abolishment: "We had mourners' benches in those days, and they were things unauthorized by the Word of God. We long since abolished them, and we did right in so doing; but I almost fear that we did it in such a way as to abolish the mourners too."[9]

Their idea of preaching was "forsaking all and taking a journey," and Rogers was no exception. While he lived in Clinton county, Ohio for twenty-four years, he travelled extensively over much of the Midwest, especially Missouri, where he would labor from six months to a year at a time, baptizing hundreds on each mission and planting numerous churches. It bothered him to leave many churches with no one to care for them, a situation that became a serious problem in the missionary efforts of the Stone-Campbell Movement.

In towns Rogers would use the courthouse or some other public building. In the country logs or planks were laid out in the woods for seats, and meetings were often in the larger cabins or in barns. He helped to erect the first house ever owned in his part of Ohio by those who wore the name Christian. He named it Antioch, after the city where the disciples were first called Christians, according to Acts 11:26.

He was awed by the vastness and beauty of the untouched frontier. He sometimes traversed country where no one could be found for many miles in any direction. Our great western cities were then but tiny villages if they existed at all. He tells how his father was offered 150 acres of land in Paincourt, Missouri for his fine horse, which he did not accept. Paincourt is now St. Louis and the acreage is now part of the downtown metropolis. But it was above Paincourt in the illimitable expanses of the western frontier that this pioneer preacher was touched by the grandeur of it all. After spending the night on the ground, using his saddle for a pillow, he wrote:

At the break of day I was up, and, soon having my tea ready, I ate a hearty breakfast; unspanceled Paddy, saddled him, and was off. I entered a vast prairie just as the sun was rising. The scene overwhelmed me. I stopped my horse to gaze with awe and delight upon it . . The god of day seemed to come up out of the very ground, and to be struggling to free himself from the tangled meshes of grass.

From this grand scene I saw by faith one far more sublime: when the King of Eternal Day – not the center of the physical system, but the center of the spiritual universe – arose from Joseph's tomb. I gazed, and wondered, and adored, while my poor soul was filled with unutterable delight. Looking back through the clouds of fifty years the scene of that morning rises vividly to view, and I seem to catch again the inspiration of that hour.[10]

The prairie grass in a dry autumn, which sometimes stood six feet high, resembled the waves of the sea when the wind blew over it. Prairie fires were always a present danger to the traveler. In the afternoon of the day described above, Rogers saw the smoke of such a fire. They were known to sweep across the plains as fast as a horse could run. He had no way to flee the danger. Knowing his way like an Indian, he unhurriedly eased out of his saddle, took pieces of flint and steel from his saddle bag, and skillfully struck them together so as to ignite the dry grass with the dancing sparks. His life depended on it!

But there was no problem. In the event the grass was damp, he had dry-rot in his saddlebags, which he also used to start camp fires. As horse and rider stood on the windward side of the backfire, a place of refuge was soon burned off. There they stood and watched an ocean of fire pass them by, and then continued their journey across a charred wilderness.

Not only were there no inns, but the humble cabins of new settlers were usually far apart. They served as oases of hospitality for the weary sojourner. Rogers arrived after dark at one such abode one wintry night. Having forded swollen streams, his clothes were frozen upon him. His host met him in the yard, invited him into his little log cabin where a fire burned in the fireplace, and bedded and fed his horse in the barn. The wife was cooking a pot of stew at the hearth.

Once inside, the warm fire not only dried his clothes and thawed his bones, but its light revealed that his hosts had black faces. The Southern-born preacher decided it was no time for nice distinctions. It so happened that his hosts were also members of the Christian Church. After a hot meal he bedded down for the night amidst prayers and thanksgiving.

A roaring fire and a big breakfast awaited him the next morning. His host had his horse ready for him, fed and saddled, waiting at the door. He mounted and rode off into the dark, well before dawn. He was a pioneer preacher amidst pioneers.

Rogers' long ministry reveals how the preachers of his day suffered financially. He tells of a three-month mission into Pennsylvania in which scores were converted, but his labors did not earn enough for him to buy a pair of boots. On another occasion he had to sell his Bible and hymnal for money to get home on. He described preaching as "a starving business," and went on to say, "I never knew more than two or three of the preachers in our ranks, at that day, who supported themselves by preaching exclusively. Yet no class of men ever labored more faithfully or constantly than they for the salvation of souls."[11]

He says the people were embarrassed to give money to preachers, and the preachers were made to feel like felons for taking it. Most gifts came from individuals rather than churches, and the donor would awkwardly slip a pittance into the preacher's hand while bidding him farewell. The preachers were ready to jump out of their boots, he says, if anyone should hear money jingle in their pockets.

There was not this awkwardness in sharing other things with the preachers' family. Rogers was always assured that his family would not be left to starve during his long absences. It was by common consent more than by agreement that when brethren took their corn or wheat to the mill they would drop off some meal or flour at the preacher's house, at hog-killing time the preacher would get his share, and at sugar-making there was an extra "stirring-off" for him who bore the gospel to remote places.

The sisters remembered the children with a few extra yards of cloth when they prepared the web for the loom, linsey for the girls and jeans for the boys. In the face of such generosity Rogers supposed that he was blessed with "creature comforts," even if he had but little money. There was always enough tea, dried beef and cold cornbread for his saddlebags, to sustain him on his extended journeys.

Samuel Rogers was a preacher's preacher in that he had a way of winning men to the ministry. He thought that his greatest contribution to the church may have been Elder Benjamin Franklin, whom he baptized and urged into evangelism. But there were several others, including Elijah Goodwin and Winthrop H. Hopson. Many a "farmer preacher" found his encouragement from "Uncle Sam," as he was often called. In one revival alone seven preachers were sent out from among the converts.

He always had a word of encouragement, as well as sundry admonitions ("Don't forget that God is the great Disposer"), for the young preacher. And he was ready to help his fellow preacher who was poorer than himself. One such was William Rogers, a Kentucky mountain preacher who had twenty-two children, all by one wife. Since his talents as an evangelist were hampered by poverty, Samuel went before the state's missionary board and pled for his support.

In his *Autobiography* Rogers does not forget the pioneer woman. He tells of Ben Franklin's mother shouting praises to God when her son obeyed the gospel, and of the old Negro mammy who baptized a dying girl, who had heard him preach, when no one else could be found to do it. His favorite was the poverty-stricken wife of William Rogers, who taught her husband to read, helped to prepare him as a preacher, and then encouraged him to carry the gospel to the poor mountaineers, while she remained home and cared for the children. She made preachers of six of her sons!

Samuel looked upon William Rogers (they were no kin) as the most interesting and effective preacher he ever heard, and he had heard Aylett Raines, Ben Franklin, John T. Johnson, Walter Scott, and Thomas and Alexander Campbell, all of whom he highly esteemed. While nourished only on the one book that his wife taught him to read and never having left the Kentucky mountains where he was born, William nonetheless had a knack for "accommodating his discourses to the capacity of all his hearers," as Samuel put it.

He recalls how William Rogers answered the charge that his people did not believe in the Old Testament. Taking in hand one of the rifles that the frontiersmen had brought with them to the meeting, he pointed to its foremost and hindermost sights, explaining that the two Testaments were like that. They have to go together to hit the mark, and each is useless without the other, he explained.

He built his sermon around this homely illustration, showing how the Old Testament, with its types, shadows, and prophecies, is the hindermost sight that might be lined up with the New Testament, the foremost sight. The object is Jesus Christ, which can be seen more clearly when one looks through both sights, for one is the fulfillment of the other.

Samuel Rogers was never able to put his own life and preaching together until he met Alexander Campbell in 1825 at age 37. He had relied too much on feelings, dreams, and vague impressions, and not enough on the testimony of Scripture itself, which is what Campbell gave to him. He heard him the first time in a two-hour discourse in Wilmington, Ohio, and as he spoke "cloud after cloud rolled away from my mind, letting in upon my soul, light and joy and hope, that no tongue can express."[12]

Campbell thus delivered him from a subjectivism that had tossed him upon the billows of doubt and into a whirlpool of skepticism, as he put it. He saw Campbell's work as the Reformation more than Stone's, and he was convinced that the Stone churches would never have made it without a union with Campbell. Rogers accused his own Stone people of being preoccupied with speculation and theorizing, and it was really the Campbell influence that made them "a Bible people."

Rogers told Robert Richardson that he would have gone crazy but for

Alexander Campbell, comparing him to Ezra, who restored the law of God. Stone gave him the Bible, he said, but it was Campbell who taught him how to read it in its connection.[13]

As part of the Stone movement, Rogers was a Christian only, accepted the Bible as his only creed, preached the gospel, and baptized by immersion. For fifteen years he carried the message across a rugged frontier, immersing thousands and forming them into congregations. All this before he even heard of Alexander Campbell. But still he left hundreds of perplexed mourners at the bench because of his subjective approach to religion. He was like a cook with the essential ingredients who did not know how to put them together. Campbell enabled him to do that.

Rogers was convinced that Alexander Campbell's coming to America was by "the direction of a gracious providence of God." People were waiting to hear Campbell in the new world that would never have heard him in the old, he surmised.

Rogers provides us with an eyewitness account of the case of Aylett Raines before the Mahoning Association in 1828, which we recounted in chapter 5. He tells how Raines, after being baptized by Walter Scott, went on to baptize many of his former associates among the Universalists. While he proved himself an effective preacher among the reformers, the Association was hesitant to receive him since he still held to the Universalist premise that everyone will eventually be restored to the fellowship of God. We related how Thomas Campbell came to his defense, insisting that such an opinion cannot be made a test.

Rogers tells how profoundly impressed he was by Campbell's defense of Raines. He expressed regret that it was not preserved, for "that speech sounded the key-note upon the subject of Christian union and communion." He remembers that the elder Campbell told the Association that it might as well exclude him since he had spent the prime of his life preaching Calvinism and was still philosophically a Calvinist. But he held his Calvinism as private property, he explained, just as Raines held his speculations as opinion.

Campbell went on, according to Rogers' account, to draw a distinction between matters of faith, which are enjoined upon all in order to the enjoyment of Christian fellowship, and matters of opinion, which may be held as private property. Rogers was impressed that Campbell went so far as to say that he had no hope of ever getting completely rid of his Calvinism, except it be by the slow process of perspiration, for if he attempted to vomit it all up at once it would choke him!

This speech caused the Association not only to receive Raines but to resolve that opinions are private property and are not to be made tests of fellowship. This led Rogers to state what became the essence of the Movement's plea for unity: "Unity in matters of faith, liberty in matters of opinion." He further concluded:

> On that ground, and on that alone, can we ever hope to see the Christian world united. Men can never agree on opinions – they have no binding authority, and should not have. But in matters of faith, tens of thousands have been united, and millions more may be. All that is needed for the accomplishment of this end, is a high regard for the plain teachings of God's Word.[14]

At one point in his autobiography Rogers refers to his own venturesome spirit, which always bore him further west: "I determined to get out of the old ruts – to change my location – to go further West."[15] This passion to move on explains the westward reach of the Movement. The preachers followed the frontier west. In some instances Rogers and others of like devotion captured virtually the entire community for "the Plea." There was some justification for the complaint that "the Campbellites are taking the country like a prairie fire."

B.F. Hall
"I found the keystone of the arch."

B.F. Hall is another of the pioneer preachers that was ordained by Barton W. Stone and labored among Christian Churches for years before he became acquainted with the Campbells. Ordained in 1825, he did much of his work in Tennessee and Alabama, and it was there that his impressive preaching won the heart of Tolbert Fanning, whose conversion made a big difference in the history of the Movement in the South.

Like Rogers, Hall too was troubled by the theological implications of the mourners' bench, which, as we have seen, was of common use among the Stone churches. Rogers tells how the mourners' bench troubled Stone himself. "Something is wrong," Stone would lament, in the presence of mourners who never found relief.

On one occasion Stone addressed the audience: "On the day of Pentecost, those who 'were pierced to the heart' were promptly told what to do for the remission of their sins. And 'they gladly received the word, and were baptized.'" He went on to quote: "he that believeth and is baptized shall be saved." This not only confused the audience, who had not heard it that way before, but his own preachers as well. Rogers, who was present, thought that the dear old brother was beside himself.[16]

An incident in Hall's life dramatizes the trauma experienced by these pioneers over the doctrine of baptism for remission of sins. He stopped one evening on a trip to Tennessee in 1826 to visit with friends. His eyes fell by chance upon a book he had heard about but had never seen, *The Campbell-Maccalla Debate*, which had been published three years before.

When he read Alexander Campbell on the design of baptism, he sprang to his feet, dropped the book, and exclaimed: "Eureka! Eureka! I have found it! I have found it! I have found the keystone of the arch." He said he had seen the empty space of the keystone a hundred times, and that he had some idea of its shape and size, so when he read Campbell on baptism for remission he knew that it would fit the space exactly. He said it was like being converted again, and that it made him happier than when first converted.[17]

Hall goes on to tell how he discussed the doctrine of baptism for remission, as set forth in Campbell's writings, with Barton W. Stone. Stone told him of his experiences with the doctrine, that he had preached it many years before, and that it so chilled the audience that he had completely abandoned it. When Hall insisted that it was nonetheless the word of God and that he intended to preach it, Stone asked him not to do so in his presence.

At this point in the history of the Stone churches Hall says that Samuel Rogers was the only other preacher that agreed with him that baptism for remission should be preached. As we have seen, however, Stone and the Christian Churches, for the most part, finally came to adopt Campbell's position.

Hall was a significant pioneer preacher, not only in his own right, but also because of his association with the pillars of the Movement. In 1835 he and John T. Johnson started a periodical in Georgetown, Kentucky known as the *Gospel Advocate*, which is not to be confused with a paper of the same name that started in Nashville two decades later by Tolbert Fanning. He travelled and preached with both of the Campbells, and often wrote to Alexander Campbell relative to his labors and the problems of the growing Movement.

In 1889 when W.C. Rogers published a book on the pioneers he had known personally, B.F. Hall was one of the eleven he selected, but the account is less than flattering. Comparing him to John T. Johnson, Rogers assures the reader that he expects to see Johnson in heaven, but he is not so sure about Hall!

Rogers described Hall as having a problem with his pride. He tells of Hall holding an audience in Nashville "spell bound" by his eloquence. But there was not the usual response. Hall turned to Tolbert Fanning, who was part of the audience, complained of the results and asked for an explanation. Fanning candidly observed that the people were so impressed with the splendor of the sermon and the masterful elocution that they had no occasion to think of the salvation of their souls.[18]

Rogers also tells how Hall's estimate of his own talents led him to suppose that he was greater than Alexander Campbell. Travelling with Campbell from Bethany to Richmond, rotating the preaching as they visited churches along the way, it seemed to him that he was the better preacher. But once they reached Richmond where Campbell had a full house on a Sunday morning, the reformer spoke so forcefully and knowledgeably that Hall was ashamed that he had ever compared himself to him, and from that time on he was reluctant even to speak in Campbell's presence.

But B.F. Hall, who was also a dentist, made his name as one of the great preachers of the reformation. Standing at least six feet tall and weighing no less than 200 pounds, he made an imposing figure to see as well as hear. He entertained the children by leading his own hymns with great enthusiasm, and his illustrations were so apt that the black slaves would gather in the back of the building to hear him with great delight. He was known widely as a power in the pulpit. And his letters to Campbell from the field indicate that he was tuned in to the problems.

In one letter he identified a problem in Kentucky: "There are but few churches that meet every first day to keep the ordinances. They are too much in the monthly system."[19] He agreed with Campbell that "the ancient order of the church" implies that congregations should assemble each first day and break bread. He also complained about the poor pay given the evangelists. The people love to hear preaching, but they do not want to pay for it, he told Campbell.

But the preacher dentist had his hangups. While he could take off occasionally and hunt big game in Texas, he had a thing about cats. A little feline followed someone into his service one evening in Carlisle, Kentucky. Upon entering the pulpit he espied the critter, and with much ado ordered that it be expulsed forthwith, for he could not preach with a cat in the house, even if it be hid from his sight. Once the cat was ousted, he began his sermon, but showed concern that it might reappear, which it did. Insisting that the devil had sent the abominable cat to ruin his discourse, he urged the brethren to dispose of it once for all!

Like other preachers on the frontier, Dr. Hall suffered hardship in order to bear the message of reform to the outer edges of the young republic. He was one of the master builders of the Movement. And he gave to it Tolbert Fanning, which was gift enough for any man.

Tolbert Fanning

"I am sorry that I ever saw a paper or heard of a college."

Tolbert Fanning was the prince of the Movement in the South, and he exemplifies how the early leaders made effective use of two devices, the paper and the college, which have played a strategic role throughout the Movement's history. As Fanning's story unfolds it seems unlikely that he would ever express sorrow for editing a paper or building a college. The events that caused such a remark are not only interesting but reflect what has always been an Achilles' heel to the progress of the Movement: *an apparent inability of editors and founders of colleges to get along with each other.*

Born in Cannon County, Tennessee in 1810, Fanning grew to have such strength that at barn raisings he was expected to man one corner by himself. Standing six feet six and weighing well over 200 pounds, he was well endowed for the rigors of pioneer farming and preaching. Two years after he was converted by B.F. Hall's preaching in 1827 he set out as a preacher.

It must have been a humble beginning, for several who heard him told him to his face that his prospects were hopeless, that he would never make a preacher. But it was not long until he was holding audiences spellbound by his plain and simple manner of presenting the Scriptures. He eventually baptized hundreds in Tennessee, Alabama, and Mississippi and founded numerous congregations.

Nashville became Fanning's base of operation, and it was there that he began the *Christian Review* in 1844 and the *Gospel Advocate* in 1855, which is today the oldest journal published by the Churches of Christ wing of the Movement. It was also there that he founded Franklin College in 1844, on property now occupied by the Nashville International Airport.

While Fanning had his own church in nearby Franklin, he was also active in the Church of Christ in Nashville, which became one of the most influential congregations of the Movement. Founded in 1820 by Baptists influenced by Alexander Campbell, it eventually withdrew from its Baptist affiliation, formally repudiated human creeds, and became a Church of Christ in 1827. While its practice of weekly Communion helped to identify it as part of the Movement, it became known in Nashville as a church concerned for the city's poor.

By the 1840's it was one of the Movement's most progressive churches. It had 500 members, half white and half black, and an organized Sunday school. It had as many as three services on Sunday for teaching and evangelism, and then the members assembled in the afternoon for the Lord's supper. It had able elders who took care of the church without the services of a hired preacher. This enabled it to send its evangelists to plant new churches, one of which was Tolbert Fanning, whose relationship with the church dates back to 1830 when he was a student at the University of Nashville.

The church was host to the Movement's most prominent preachers through the years, including Alexander Campbell, whose first visit was as early as 1827. He baptized his converts in the Cumberland River at the foot of Main street.

In 1846 the Nashville church hired the most gifted young minister in the Movement, Jesse B. Ferguson, who also became one of the most controversial due to his bizarre heresies. His story is told in chapter 11. In time the church was not only decimated in numbers, but its building burned and its reputation marred. Through these vicissitudes Tolbert Fanning was at its side as its alter ego.

Convinced that it was a mistake for the elders to hire Ferguson, Fanning sought in vain to dissuade them. The church's success, he believed, was due to its Scripture-centered, elder-oriented ministry, which at the time was the general practice within the Movement. While Fanning cooperated with Ferguson, he was convinced that the speculative theology that he brought to the pulpit was responsible for the decline of the congregation.

This experience confirmed Fanning in his conservatism and caused him to resist anything "liberal." It eventually influenced David Lipscomb, Fanning's protege, who became the conscience of the church in the South in the generation following the Civil War. It solidified the conservatism of the southern church. James R. Wilburn, Fanning's resourceful biographer, reminds us that Fanning's battle cry became, *Remember Nashville — and Lot's wife.*[20]

Fanning brought to his native South and to the Churches of Christ the Campbellian view of education. While he was not educated at Bethany, which was only four years older than his own college, he did travel with Campbell and was influenced by his writings and his educational philosophy. As was the case at Bethany, Fanning's Franklin College (named for the American revolutionary) offered a program from the juvenile level at age five through college. While the Scriptures were taught at all age levels, it was a liberal arts program rather than a Bible college.

Fanning went further than Campbell in avoiding any alignment between a college and the church. While Campbell put into Bethany's charter that theology could not be taught, Fanning insisted that his college was not a "school for preachers." He claimed that it was the Franklin church that trained the preachers while they were enrolled in the college, pursuing a general education.

The relationship that a Christian college sustains to the church has thus been a sensitive issue from the early days of the Movement. It has been considered "Campbellian" for such a school to be a liberal arts college in which the Bible is taught rather than a Bible college as such.

That Fanning was a pioneer in the Movement's educational ventures is evident in the fact that Franklin was only the third college to have begun, antedated only by Bacon College in 1836, with Walter Scott as president, and Bethany College in 1840, with Alexander Campbell as president. Better located than either of the other two and offering a wider variety of courses, Franklin soon had 150 students.

Fanning encouraged them to work and learn a trade as well as to study, and so some became blacksmiths or shoemakers or saddlers. This fit well with his opposition to a fixed salary for preachers, which to him encouraged indolence. Franklin must be the only college ever that had no contractual arrangement with its teachers. At the end of each year the faculty would evaluate its work and determine its own pay accordingly.[21]

Franklin may have been the most influential of the earlier colleges, and its effect upon the southern church cannot be questioned. It educated such southern leaders as E.W. Carmack and J.E. Scobey, as well as David Lipscomb and E.G. Sewell, longtime editors of the *Gospel Advocate*. Sewell was a great preacher in Tennessee, persuading thousands to be baptized. David Lipscomb once sent Sewell to resume a revival that he had conducted for two weeks with no responses. After a few days he had baptized sixty. Franklin College was respected for its quality of education, Lipscomb said that after fifty years in education he had never seen a school that did better work.[22]

It was as an editor that Fanning had his greatest influence upon the thinking of the Movement, especially in the South. Journalism was the heart of his life's work, spanning thirty years of his ministry, while the time given to Franklin College was only half that. He founded both the *Christian Review* and the *Gospel Advocate* in hopes of clarifying in the mind of the public the nature of the Movement.

As an editor he searched the New Testament diligently for "the perfect pattern" for the church, believing that no party had yet found it. This led him to question the biblical basis for the Movement's first national missionary society (1849): "Did the missionaries of the New Testament ever hold a missionary meeting; ever form a society; ever preach a missionary sermon; ever take a collection for missionary purposes; raise a subscription for that purpose?"[23]

This presumption that the New Testament not only mandates an ancient order but prescribes a fixed pattern has long pervaded the Movement. It has served to make it vulnerable to internal dissension and division as it did in Fanning's era.

As an editor Fanning treated those themes that had been common to the Movement since Campbell's *Christian Baptist*. He was "anti-sectarian, anti-partisan, anti-denominational," and he echoed the slogan *Union and peace on the Bible alone.* And like Campbell he conceded that there were Christians in "the denominations," calling them "Christians in confusion." His biographer says that "Fanning would most certainly agree with his brethren who were fond of saying, 'Though we are not the only Christians, we are Christians only.' "[24]

Dying in 1874, he was not around for the eye of the storm over instrumental music, though it was becoming an issue in the search for a fixed pattern. But in what little he did say about the instrument he branded it as a "mockery of all that is sacred," putting it in the same class with choirs, fashionable church buildings, and "hired preachers."

Fanning was in the eye of the storm over the missionary society, but his position was ambivalent in that he was first an ardent supporter and then a bitter critic. The Tennessee churches before the Civil War were more organized for cooperative action than any state in the South, and Tolbert Fanning was largely responsible for this. As early as 1842 twenty-nine churches were involved in "unity for action" in evangelizing the state and in educational endeavors, with the Church of Christ in Nashville serving as the agent for the other churches "to receive, manage and disburse all the funds that may be collected."

Fanning found in the New Testament a pattern for such cooperative efforts in that the New Testament churches did cooperate. Such matters as the ordinances of the gospel are settled questions, he reasoned, but in the matter of churches using their resources to advance the cause of Christ they are "required to exercise their worldly wisdom." Here Fanning takes a position that has never been fully accepted by the more conservative elements of the Movement: *Since the Scriptures teach that churches should cooperate, human judgment or worldly wisdom must dictate the methods employed.* Fanning himself had trouble abiding this rule.

Such reasoning led Fanning to support David S. Burnet's American Christian Bible Society in 1845, serving as a vice-president, even when Campbell did not; and to help organize the Tennessee Evangelizing Association in 1852, acting as its secretary. In between those dates in 1849 he accepted a vice-presidency of the American Christian Missionary Society in Cincinnati, though he was not present. It proved to be a tenuous relationship.

Fanning was soon opposed to such societies, to the one in his own state as well as the national one, becoming one of their most effective critics. Wilburn concludes that Fanning did not change his mind about the appropriateness of societies per se, but became disenchanted by their formalities and official resolutions. He saw the ACMS as an unscriptural ecclesiasticism that was no longer a "cooperation of churches" but a "human organization," something distinct from the church, that sought to preempt the function of the local congregation. As a "separate body" it detracted from the church itself.[25]

One might suppose that it was the "war resolutions" by the ACMS in 1861 and 1863, during the Civil War, that caused Fanning to change his mind. The resolutions branded southerners as "armed traitors" and urged all churches to sustain the cause of the Union. But these only confirmed his suspicions of the society's presumed political and ecclesiastical power.

The war resolutions caused Herman Norton, a Tennessee historian of the Movement, to say: "The approval of the resolution made a few realize, for the first time, the potential power inherent in a missionary society." But Fanning would say that he had seen the handwriting on the wall a decade earlier.[26]

Always a Christian gentleman, Fanning sought a reconciled diversity with his society brethren. His answer to the society question was to hold consultation meetings of delegates from the churches where problems would be studied and methods of cooperation determined. While resolutions and constitutions would not be introduced, they could serve to resolve such differences as the society. Such consultations could and should be on the national level. It is odd that he could have such progressive ideas while holding to a patternistic hermeneutics.

Fanning saw a division on the horizon and he sought to avert it. Continuing his fellowship with the ACMS, he attended the convention in Cincinnati in 1859. He was once more with Raccoon John Smith, Moses E. Lard, Benjamin Franklin, David S. Burnet, Walter Scott, Samuel and John Rogers, and about 300 others. To his *Gospel Advocate* readers he described them as "a mighty host of strong and earnest men."

He was eager to warn them of the direction the society was taking, even though Isaac Errett, always an ardent society man, was just as eager to keep him quiet. Fanning's chance came when he was invited to the floor to report on the work in Tennessee. He conceded that there was much good in missionary societies, but told them how the churches in his state were sending out missionaries without one.

The church, is after all, "the pillar and ground of the truth" and is its own missionary society, he insisted, and is sufficient for all of a Christian's labor of love. He also spoke of love, peace, and unity among brethren. It must have been impressive when he concluded his remarks, disagreeing with them as he did, with words of reconciliation: "But I am happy to say, that from what I have heard on the floor, we are one people."[27]

We have here far more than an episode in the life of a leading pioneer minister, for it reveals how frail the fabric was that held a unity movement together. Delicate as a glass menagerie, it only needed a more belligerent and bombastic spirit than the gentle and loving Tolbert Fanning to make pieces of it instead of peace. Such leaders were sure to come.

It is well to ask at this point about the nature of the Movement's unity. To Fanning his people were still one, despite what he considered a serious difference. If unity means agreement on such issues as the society, then they were already divided. Fanning found room in the church for disagreement over such peripheral areas as methods. *We are one people!* was a bold affirmation of unity in diversity. Others would rise with a different spirit.

Fanning's first love was preaching, and he was at his best as an evangelist. He believed that his first responsibility was to the unsaved. Since he once edited a farm magazine and was an authority on farming techniques, he had excellent rapport with farmers who might otherwise have been prejudiced against him as "a Campbellite."

When his carriage broke down in Russellville, Alabama, delaying a trip to Mississippi, he spread word to the agricultural community that there would be preaching "at candle lighting." By the time his carriage was repaired he had baptized forty people, and things were going too well for him to leave. He finally baptized over one hundred, providing Russellville with a Church of Christ, made up of more than two-thirds of the heads of families in the community. He then proceeded to Columbus, Mississippi where he baptized a like number, starting a church there as well.[28]

This was not atypical, for he started scores of congregations throughout the Deep South, often taking with him the young men studying at Franklin College, who in turn did a similar work when they went out as evangelists. His style was typical of the more successful preachers of the Movement: simple, direct, bold, logical, and persuasive. His messages were distinctly biblical, and they were so clear and articulate as to hold people's attention. Like Campbell, he stressed the need to interpret the Scriptures responsibly and objectively rather than emotionally and speculatively, and his constant themes were the primitive faith and the ancient order.

Fanning's most trying crisis was not the Civil War, as traumatic as that was for him, but a controversy involving the man he most admired, Alexander Campbell, and his associate editor of the *Millennial Harbinger*, Dr. Robert Richardson. In historical retrospect the dispute appears as wholly unnecessary, but it may be accounted for in the light of the problem that J.B. Ferguson had caused the church in Nashville by his speculative philosophy, a tragedy that Fanning could not forget. His motto of "Remember Nashville and Lot's Wife" was a constant reminder of what "philosophy false so-called" could do to the church.

He saw Ferguson-like tendencies in a series of essays by Dr. Richardson, which began in the 1856 *Millennial Harbinger*. The series, which began as "Misinterpreting the Scriptures" and continued as "Faith vs. Philosophy," were calculated to move people from a "letter" approach to Scripture to a "spirit" approach. To Richardson many of the Movement's preachers viewed the Bible as "a system of external or outward communication, terminating upon the ordinary understanding," thus ignoring the spiritual in both man and the Scriptures.

While the "letter" of the Bible, by which he meant its words and forms, is "the mere vehicle of truth," it is the spirit of man alone that can "perceive or contemplate the truth presented." Borrowing from 1 Cor. 2:14, 15, the doctor insisted that Scripture is spiritually discerned and that the most precious truths are foolish to the natural man and he cannot understand them. He concluded by saying that the Bible to a spiritual man is not engraved on tables of stone or "merely imprinted upon the pages of a book," but rather written upon the living heart and inscribed upon the discerning mind.[29]

While this may appear innocent enough, Fanning remembered Nashville when he read it. He saw this as a repudiation of the Scriptures as the only source of God's revelation, and as subjective and speculative, making man's "spirit" the final arbiter rather than the Bible itself. He branded it as "Natural Theology," which to him was a form of atheism, and he proceeded to attack it in the pages of the *Gospel Advocate*. In their exchanges from month to month in their respective journals, the dispute concerned the place of Natural Theology.

Fanning saw Richardson as making shipwreck not only of his faith but that of the entire Movement, which was based upon the Bible. To him Natural Theology was man's ingenious effort "to know God by the exercise of his own faculties and to serve him by a worship and a law of his own discovery."

The doctor was astounded that Fanning associated Natural Theology with atheists like Robert Owen, and explained that Campbell had been teaching Natural Theology at Bethany College for years. He pointed out to Fanning that Campbell believed that man could not *originate* the idea that there is a God, for this must be revealed by the Creator himself. But since the days of Adam the fact of God's existence has been revealed and the idea lives on through tradition. In nature God *confirms* what he has already revealed, providing proof of his divinity through the things he has created (nature), and this is what Rom. 1:19-20 is saying and this is the point of Natural Theology.[30]

This was too much for Fanning. He avowed that he preferred to become a beggar in the street than to learn that Alexander Campbell taught Natural Theology. He made a trip to Bethany to see Campbell so as to determine for himself the truth of the matter. He learned to his dismay that the old reformer was now senile, as he saw it, and that he could not talk with him without his wife being on hand to coach him. He left convinced that Campbell's greatness had passed and that he was now unduly influenced by younger men like Dr. Richardson. One would have supposed that the gentle and irenic Fanning would have called on the doctor, who also lived at Bethany, and talked the problem out, but it was not to be.

In the end Campbell, senile or not, took pen in hand and rebuked Fanning for his attitude, suggesting that the real problem was his prejudice against the *Millennial Harbinger* and Bethany College in favor of the *Gospel Advocate* and Franklin College.[31] Richardson in the meantime chides Fanning for making a "bugbear" out of Natural Theology and breaks off any further discussion with him. He even charged that Fanning was too ill-equipped in both attitude and mind to carry on such a discussion.

Fanning was crushed. He felt so close to Campbell that it was almost too much when he, of all people, impugned his motives. Campbell's judgment may well have made Fanning look bad to the church generally, for when J. W. McGarvey met him for the first time he was surprised to find such a courteous Christian gentleman.

It was at this point that Fanning was so depressed that he expressed sorrow that he had ever seen a paper or heard of a college. Being a pacifist, he suffered persecution during the war both from his fellow southerners and the Union army when it moved in to occupy Nashville. The war left both his college and his home in ruins, and he suffered from severe poverty, even to the point of going hungry. But nothing hurt him like the senseless altercation with Richardson and Campbell.

This sad affair was not the work of small men. One could not name three leaders in the Movement's early history who were more gentlemanly and exemplary. Fanning and Richardson were widely appreciated for their conciliatory attitude, and if Campbell had been belligerent in his earlier years, he was no more as he neared 70. And yet they called each other names, impugned motives, and made mountains out of molehills. How could three eminent leaders violate the very principles of unity and brotherhood they had long advocated?

Beyond human depravity the answer may lie in the incredible power that editors came to have among the churches, a power that tended to corrupt well-intentioned men who felt compelled to protect their power base.

The Movement did not have bishops but it did have editors. It was as an "editor bishop" that Alexander Campbell had no qualms about calling upon the missionary society in Tennessee to discipline Jesse B. Ferguson, or to call upon all the churches to build an edifice in Washington, D.C., specifying not only the time for the donation but the amount that each was to give.[32] And it was as an editor that Fanning's influence among southern churches was not unlike that of a bishop.

Lord Acton's famous dictum, "Power tends to corrupt and absolute power corrupts absolutely," may not only help to explain the altercation between these early editors, but why the Movement eventually divided again and again. The Movement never had its despotic bishops, but it has not been without its ambitious editors.

Editor bishop or not, Tolbert Fanning's irenic spirit prevailed. As war clouds gathered that would pit brother against brother, he was grieved. Like two-thirds of those in the South, he hated slavery and never owned a slave. He saw South Carolina secede from the Union, then Mississippi, then Alabama, and at last there was the Confederacy. It was 1861 and due to the crisis he had to shut down his *Gospel Advocate* for the duration. His parting words were, "Brethren, we are one, and have but one work to perform."[33]

There would be editors with a different spirit.

Pardee Butler

"If I live anywhere, I shall live in Kansas."

If Tolbert Fanning was the prince of the Movement in the South, Pardee Butler was its prince in the West, in the far West, for when Butler migrated to Kansas in 1855 it was a Territory and known as part of "the great American desert." It would be six more years before it would become the Union's 34th state.

J.B. McCleery, who worked alongside Butler during part of his 35-year ministry in Kansas, described him as a certain kind of prince: "Pardee Butler was the Moses to the church in this wilderness, and for years following he was in some sense like Paul, 'having the care of all the churches.'"[34]

In urging the Disciples' fledgling missionary society to support his efforts, he complained that the Methodists had 120 workers in Kansas, the United Brethren nine, the youthful Missionary Baptists four, while only he represented "the primitive faith." But one man like Butler was enough to make a difference, for within a few years he had formed seven churches and organized them with both a missionary society and a state convention, such as they were. Within five years Kansas had twenty congregations and about a thousand members.

More than any of the pioneers, he involved himself in the social issues of his day, being strongly antislavery and a prohibitionist. A gentle and humble preacher, he sought to allay the racial prejudices of white Christians who had migrated to Kansas by teaching the parable of the Good Samaritan. He showed how Jesus taught that the most despised races are our brothers. He pointed to Peter's vision in Acts 10 as to how God taught the apostle that he should not call any man or nation common or unclean.

Among the few blacks that moved to Kansas some became members of the Christian Church. It was the custom to receive new members with the "right hand of Christian fellowship." On one such occasion a white sister managed to go forward with the others to welcome a cultured black man into the church, but only by wearing gloves, lest she be forced to "touch a nigger's hand." This was the prejudice that Butler sought to remove from the church.[35]

Born in 1816 in New York, he migrated with his parents to Ohio when he was a baby, and he grew up in an area where "Alexander Campbell and Walter Scott had been preaching the union of Christians on the Bible alone, and there was great enthusiasm." In his youth he heard both Campbell and William Hayden, and he was baptized by a Baptist preacher who had been swayed by Campbell's teaching.

After preaching his way across Illinois and Missouri, Butler went into Kansas just after the Kansas-Nebraska Act of 1854 ruled that the people of the two territories should decide whether they be slave or free. This came to be called "squatter sovereignty." On the eve of Kansas' decision, *pro* and *con* forces rushed there, making "bleeding Kansas" a place of virtual civil war.

Butler was a willing participant in the controversy in that he wanted to help make Kansas free of slavery as well to capture it for Christ. He was well prepared in heart and mind for the task. He made his living teaching school and herding sheep, during which time he memorized the New Testament. His spare time was given to reading the Bible, church history, and the writings of Alexander Campbell.

He was really a pioneer on the frontier, for when he passed through St. Joseph, Mo. there was not so much as a small inn, and Kansas City did not exist. Once he crossed the Missouri River, he felled trees for a rude log cabin for his family. As he moved on into Kansas he laid out his own town and named it Pardee, after his mother's family, though it is no longer on the map.

He had one big disadvantage as a frontiersman. He could not swim! This was almost his undoing in fording creeks and rivers, making him too dependent on his horse. And it was most hazardous when his pro-slavery enemies chose to "raft" him, which consisted of isolating one on a rude, narrow raft and escorting him down the river and out of town. In his case the river was the turbulent Missouri, and he might not have made it to shore miles away had he not converted into a paddle the flagstaff that his enemies had erected in derision.

The flag billed his "vehicle" as the *Eastern Aid Express* and its occupant as "Rev. Mr. Butler agent for the underground Railroad." It pictured him on a horse with a black riding double with him, and it had him saying, "Greely to the Rescue. I have a Nigger." The reference was to Horace Greeley, who founded the New York *Tribune* as a crusading newspaper, who was then fighting for the abolition of slavery and for a free land policy in the West, prompting him to make his famous statement, "Go West, young man, go West!"

Butler was Greeley's kind of man in that he went West and built houses, churches, and towns, and he was an avowed "free soiler," which was different from an abolitionist, a term Butler did not like, even though he was anti-slavery. As a Free-Soiler he wanted all new territories and states of the Union to be free of slavery. This got him into lots of trouble in "bleeding Kansas" where houses were burned, towns plundered, and people murdered by rebels on both sides of the slavery issue. Folk who came across from Missouri insisted that "Our niggers won't be worth a dime" if Kansas went free. To the pro-slavery people an abolitionist was a rogue ("They steal our niggers"), and so when one was "rafted" as Butler was, there must be a big R lettered on his forehead, identifying him as a rogue.

The mob in Atchison, who did the rafting, could bear Butler as a preacher but not as a Free-Soiler. It would be all right if he just left Kansas and never returned. As they circled him with guns in hand, he assured them with unflinching courage that, "If I live anywhere, I shall live in Kansas." Defying their orders never to return to Atchison, he did return not only to preach but to avow his Free-Soil politics. This time, after a motion to kill him was overruled, they chose to tar and feather him, which meant to strip one to the waist, cover his body with tar, and then apply feathers, though in his case they had to substitute cotton.

Butler had difficulties with his own church for his "involvement in politics." Isaac Errett, representing the missionary society and eager to support the gospel in Kansas, urged him to "ignore" the issue of slavery so that this would be possible. With characteristic conviction and courage, he wrote to the society's secretary, "I would not make this 'Reformation of the nineteenth century' a withered and blasted trunk, scattered by the lightnings of heaven, because it took part with the rich and powerful against the poor and the oppressed." He went on to remind Errett of those cherished principles of free discussion that their people had so "ostentatiously heralded to the world."[36]

Support from the society or not, he lived on in the state of Kansas that he helped make free for thirty more years, preaching and building churches, and if he was not appreciated by the officials of his own church, he was by others. By the time of his death in 1888 he was honored as one of Kansas' great pioneers, and his turbulent career was the subject of editorials in many newspapers.

A former governor of Kansas hailed him as having the kind of stuff that martyrs are made of, and the pastor of the First Presbyterian Church in Atchison wrote to a newspaper editor: "I am moved to lay a wreath of tribute upon the grave of the old hero. He was a man of most invincible courage. Earl Morton, by the open grave of John Knox, said, 'Here lies one who never feared the face of man.' Mr. Butler was a John Knox sort of man."[37]

The "John Knox" of the Movement preached on many themes, and one of his favorites was the unity of Christians. His judgment as to how unity will eventually come is both engaging and practical: "The protestant denominations will all become one yet, not by other churches coming to any one church, but their differences will almost imperceptibly disappear, and they will all melt into one, and no one will be able to tell how it was done."[38]

Pardee Butler stood virtually alone among the Movement's pioneers as a radical social activist. It may appear odd to us that the likes of Isaac Errett and Alexander Campbell could make slavery a political issue rather than a moral one, and urge their fellow preachers to preach the gospel and not get involved in "politics." This may explain how the Movement averted an open split over slavery, but it also explains why Pardee Butler was persecuted.

If we multiplied these stories tenfold, it would still not be a tithing of what might or should be told. There was, for instance, Knowles Shaw, an Ohioan, "the singing evangelist," who authored "Bringing in the Sheaves" and practiced it by bringing ten thousand people to Christ. J.M. Barnes took a degree under Campbell at Bethany and then returned to his native Alabama where he established hundreds of congregations in that state and throughout the South. W.H. Fleming represents hundreds of farmer-preachers who preached on Sundays during "crop time," riding horseback twenty miles on Sunday morning to an appointment and back again the same day. After harvest all their time would go to preaching, baptizing, and building churches, with meager remuneration. Fleming never left the county in Tennessee where he was born, except for something very special, such as to join the Confederate army.

Whether in winning the West or in winning the South, they had one thing in common as they consolidated the Movement: a commitment to build the church upon the Bible alone. While they were at it, they were building a new republic as well.

Women Pioneers
"Shapers of a Movement"

While today 76% of the U.S. population accepts the idea of women preachers and in some seminaries, including Disciples institutions, upwards of one-half are women, it has not always been that way. While women have always done more than their share of "the work of the church," their ministry has been confined mostly to the quiet corners behind the scenes. Women, especially before the Civil War, were not unlike children in that they were to be seen but not heard.

The time was when they could not get an education, conduct business, or even have legal control of their children. They could not manage their own money, even when they had inherited it. Any influence they had in the church was indirect, as wives and daughters. When they served as missionaries it was under the aegis of some man.

This began to change after the Civil War, perhaps because of the more assertive roles of women during that time. In the post-Civil War period women began to form their own denomination-wide organizations, both benevolent and missionary, some of which had substantial influence. Within a decade or so following the War most every Protestant denomination, including the Disciples, had a national woman's organization. This inevitably led to other public roles of ministry. In time there were women teachers, preachers, evangelists, authors, editors, and reformers. By 1918 there was actually an International Women's Preacher Association, in which Disciples ministers served as officers. Their number was not legion, but they were there and are to be numbered among the pioneers.

From the earliest days of the Movement women were vigorously involved in preaching and starting churches. The "Three Marys" of Somerset, Pa. were the most notable. Mary Graft, Mary Morrison, and Mary Ogle were all baptized as adults, and early on they resolved to reject creeds and make only the Bible their rule of faith. By writing letters and calling from house to house they soon taught classes and held prayer meetings. While at first loosely associated with the Redstone Baptist Association, they joined no sect. When Thomas Campbell came to Somerset in 1828, they resolved to call themselves Disciples of Christ.

The three Marys evangelized their community, baptizing converts, and building up the church. By the 1840's the Christian Church in Somerset had 500 members. All three lived beyond their threescore and ten and served the church for some 40 years. Many came to look to them as "Our Mothers in Israel" and they gained a place in the Movement's history as "the Three Marys of Somerset, Pa."

Even earlier than the three Marys were women preachers in Elias Smith's New England movement. While always a Freewill Baptist, Nancy Cram's heart was with the Christian Church. Doing evangelistic work in upstate New York, including work among the Oneida Indians, she won converts not only by preaching but also by her fervent prayers. One such prayer was impromptu, at a funeral, and was so moving that she was invited to hold a revival. The revival was protracted, in fields and barns, until hundreds were converted and the community transformed. She converted several men who became preachers in the New England movement, and her preaching built up Christian Churches.

Cram also converted Abigail Roberts, who preached in Elias Smith's movement as early as 1816, converting hundreds and starting at least four churches. She suffered not only as a "female preacher" but for being part of what was considered an heretical movement, especially since it rejected creeds and sectism. She was once threatened with tar and feather.

Nancy Towle, a schoolteacher, was probably the most-traveled of New England's female preachers, itinerating 10,000 miles in a decade, suffering incredible hardship. She worked with numerous other women preachers, who were more abundant in New England than in any other part of the Movement. Some were singing evangelists and others Sunday school evangelists.

It is probable that the first woman to be ordained to the ministry in the Movement was Clara Hale Babcock. She was ordained at age 39 in 1888 or 1889 and became pastor of the Christian Church in Erie, Illinois. She eventually became an evangelist and over a period of three decades conducted revivals in Illinois and Iowa and gained some 1400 converts. She baptized over a thousand more as the pastor of several churches. She was extolled for her strong intellect and for her ability to expound the Scriptures.

There were numerous others. Jessie Coleman Monser, ordained in 1891, not only held several pastorates in Illinois but helped to produce a cross-reference Bible. Marinda Lemert not only felt her own call to the ministry, but became an apologist for other women who wanted to enter the ministry. In 1888 she wrote articles defending the call of women and labeled "the doctrine that seals woman's lips" a heresy. She insisted that those who make gender a test make Paul contradict himself. A black woman, Sarah Lue Bostick, challenged both racial and sexual prejudice when she became a prominent preacher in both black and white Christian Churches in Arkansas in the last half of the 19th century.

Clara Hazelrigg was ordained at age 37 in 1897 after a career in education. She evangelized in eight states in the West and served as pastor to the West Side Christian Church in Topeka. Her most noted convert was Jesse Bader, who not only became a famous evangelist but the founder of the World Convention of Churches of Christ. She too defended the woman's call to preaching, noting that it is preparation and consecration, not sex or previous condition of servitude, that determines the call.

Some women, like Bertha Mason Fuller who was ordained in 1896, became ministers when they assumed the pulpit at the illness or death of their husbands. Others, like Gustine Weaver, pioneered by taking classes at a divinity school. She studied under J.W. McGarvey at the College of the Bible in 1895, but only by entering class late, by sitting on the back seat next to the door, by not speaking to the men, and by exiting early when the prof nodded to her! But it was Ellen Moore Warren who was the first woman to take a degree from a Disciples seminary, the College of the Bible in 1916.

Barbara Kellison was more aggressive in her defense of women's rights in ministry. In 1862 she wrote a long essay on the question, arguing that it should be settled by the Bible. She painstakingly answered the objections to women preaching and pointed to the inconsistencies of those who opposed it. She observed that freed male slaves had more rights in the church than women, and pointed to the way some would have women enter heaven only long enough to sing or be segregated in a corner to themselves!

Some women became writers and editors, a notable instance being Jane Errett, daughter of Isaac Errett, who served the *Christian Standard* for 61 years in various capacities, longer than any other person. When Isaac Errett founded the journal in 1866, Jane was at his side as assistant editor. Debra B. Hull, in her brilliant study of Christian Church women, says that when Isaac Errett died in 1888 his daughter would have become editor had her name been John instead of Jane! But "Miss Jennie," as they called her, would hardly have been an editor bishop. If a woman filled that role it was Bess Sommer, wife of Daniel Sommer, who took over the *American Christian Review* from her husband and would not let him write for it! She had no little influence among the "Sommerite" Churches of Christ.

Other women served the *Standard* as writers and columnists, including the poignant Persis Christian, who did not hesitate to debate "the women's issue" in her column. In one column she noted that while the male clergy debated the issue there were 722 women in the U.S. (up to 1890) who had already settled the matter by responding to God's call to preach the gospel. When the *Standard* began the 20th century it announced that five talented writers would serve as special contributors. Four of them were women!

Jessie Pounds, who died in 1921, wrote several children's books, 600 hymns, and over 1,000 poems. She was also an exhorter, encouraging good works in numerous areas. An endowed chair at Hiram College is named for her. If there was a theologian among the women writers it was Mattie Boteler (died 1929), who taught an innovative Bible class at Central Christian Church in Cincinnati for 35 years in which she trained lay evangelists, men as well as women. She wrote Bible commentaries for classes and served as editor of *The Lookout*. She was known to be uniquely perceptive not only in the Scriptures but the nature of the Movement as well.

Eliza Davies heard Alexander Campbell in her native Scotland and attended him while he was in jail in Glasgow. She was so impressed that she followed him to America. She ministered to his distressed family at Bethany for several years, taught at Midway orphanage in Kentucky, and served as a missionary teacher in the back country of Australia. Her engaging 570-page autobiography, *The Story Of An Earnest Life* (1881), is one of the most important books in the Movement's archives. It provides intimate portraits of such leaders as J.W. McGarvey and Robert Richardson as well as rare glimpses into Campbell family life. It is also the story of a Christian woman's triumph over incredibly difficult circumstances.

Then there were the women educators, not the least of which were within the Campbell family. Jane Campbell McKeever, Alexander's sister, founded Pleasant Hill Female Seminary in West Middletown, Pa., near Bethany, first in her home and then in 1842 on its own campus. Offering a Mistress of Arts degree, it was roughly equivalent in curriculum to the men's colleges, including Bethany. It educated some of the Movement's most influencial women, including Jane Errett and Decima Campbell, Alexander's tenth daughter. While she was at it, Mrs. McKeever and her husband reared 20 children, natural and adopted.

Alexandrina Campbellina Pendelton ("Miss Cammie") was the precocious daughter of Lavinia and William Pendleton and the granddaughter of Alexander Campbell, who doted over her. She not only became a lifelong professor of modern languages at Bethany College, but helped pull the college through difficult times. She was an effective fund raiser as well as an exacting teacher. Three of Campbell's daughters were also influencial in the Movement. While Lavinia and Clarinda, both of whom married William Pendleton, died as young mothers, they travelled with their father and became articulate exponents of his reformation. They also provided moral support for the founding of Bethany College.

Decima, a child of Campbell's old age, survived her father by 54 years, thus providing witness to the next two generations. She lived on in the Campbell Mansion and helped to preserve it along with the Old Meeting House. Selina Campbell, Alexander's second wife, survived her husband by 27 years and was a witness of the Campbell era to the next generation, including a book of reminiscences of her husband's homelife. She was also a fund raiser for various causes.

Emily Tubman (born 1794) is honored as one of the influential women of the Christian Church because of her philanthropy. A Georgian and a former slave owner, she supported the Confederacy during the Civil War. She was a charter subscriber to the *Millennial Harbinger* and often entertained Alexander Campbell on his trips to the South. She helped start the Christian Church in Augusta. She became a very rich widow when her husband, an Episcopalian, died in 1836. For a half century she doled out large sums for the Movement's causes, including missions. She not only gave money to Bethany College but recruited students from the South. At her funeral it was said she did more good by her exemplary life than by the money she gave away.

Other women in the South served as presidents or de facto co-presidents of colleges with their husbands. Charlotte Fall was a teacher at Nashville Female Academy before she married Tolbert Fanning in 1836. They ran several schools together, evangelized together (though she did not preach), and finally founded Franklin College (for men) and an attending school for women in 1845. The schools were in effect one school and they were sort of co-presidents. When Campbell visisted Charlotte's school he gave it high marks. They said that she would teach all day and then do domestic chores at night. This was typical of the pioneer woman.

Luela St. Clair's husband became president of Christian College in Columbia, Mo. in 1893 and died a few months later. She was named to succeed him. She was joined later by Emma Moore as co-president. For a time the two women actually owned the college. Two other women, one white and one black and both preachers, were instrumental in starting Jarvis Christian College in Texas in 1913. Many Disciples women were active in the temperance movement, including Carry Nation herself, who was married to a Disciples minister. She and her cohorts destroyed saloons with hatchets in the name of the Lord!

Women also organized the Christian Woman's Board of Missions in 1874, which eventually had an African-American auxiliary, and the National Benevolent Association in 1887 which had special concern for widows and orphans at home and abroad. Women's leadership in these organizations brought them to the attention of the Christian Church as a whole.

Finally, there were the deaconesses (Why not simply deacons?) who have been more generally accepted than women preachers, at least in theory. Even Alexander Campbell, who said he stood with Paul when it came to women speaking in church, saw women deacons as part of the ancient order. Tolbert Fanning, editor of the *Gospel Advocate* in Nashville also called for women to serve as deacons, as did Robert Milligan in his influencial *Scheme of Redemption*, insisting that "The Diaconate of the primitive Church was not confined to the male members."

Still, women deacons have been rare, virtually non-existent in some segments of the Movement. But as early as 1833 the Christian Church in Baltimore had "three Elders, three Deacons, and three Deaconesses." There were other instances of women deacons, but such a role for women never materialized, which is odd since it had leadership sanction. But the leaders never promoted it, perhaps because of the Victorian role women were expected to fill, especially in the South. But one Churches of Christ minister made a point when he said, "We have many women deacons. We just don't call them that!"

Louanna McNeil Bawcom, a Churches of Christ missionary, did research on women in missions in her church up to 1969. She found over 200 who were serving or had recently served in 40 different countries, including nine African nations.[39]

This survey of women among the pioneers is but a tiny sampling of those who served. The vast majority served in the shadows, not only keeping the family together while their men were out as evangelists, but nurturing the church as well. They not only taught the Sunday school and went calling, but they prepared the Communion, stoked the fire, and kept the meetinghouse. When there was a shortage of men they conducted worship, often from their seats lest they offend. They are the unsung heroes of the Movement, even "Shapers of a Movement" as Debra B. Hull puts it.[40]

ENDNOTES

[1]Alexander Campbell, *Millennial Harbinger*, 1840, p. 556.

[2]Robert Richardson, "A History of the Disciples of Christ" in *A History of All Denominations in the United States* (Harrisburg, PA: J. Winebriner, pub., 1848), p. 231.

[3]Colby D. Hall, *New Light Christians: Initiators of the Nineteenth-Century Reformation* (Ft. Worth: TCU Press, 1959), p. 124.

[4]John I. Rogers, ed., *Autobiography of Samuel Rogers* (Cincinnati: Standard, 1880), p. 21.

[5]H. Leo Boles, *Biographical Sketches of Gospel Preachers* (Nashville: Gospel Advocate Co., 1932), p. 135.

[6]Robert Richardson, *Memoirs of Alexander Campbell*, Vol. 2 (Cincinnati: Standard, 1897), p. 205.

[7]Nathan J. Mitchell, *Reminiscences and Incidents in the Life and Travels of a Pioneer Preacher*, Cincinnati, 1897, p. 311.

[8]Rogers, *Autobiography*, p. 68.

[9]*Ibid.*, p. 30.

[10]*Ibid.*, p. 48.

[11]*Ibid.*, p. 109.

[12]*Ibid.*, p. 111.

[13]Richardson, *Memoirs*, Vol. 2, pp. 332, 333.

[14]Rogers, *Autobiography*, p. 118.

[15]*Ibid.*, p. 131.

[16]*Ibid.*, p. 56.

[17]Richardson, *Memoirs*, Vol. 2, p. 388.

[18]W. C. Rogers, *Recollections of Men of Faith* (Rosemead, CA: Old Paths, 1960), p. 94.

[19]"Extracts from Letters," *Millennial Harbinger*, 1834, p. 472.

[20]James R. Wilburn, *The Hazard of the Die* (Austin: Sweet Pub. Co., 1968), p. 144.

[21]*Ibid.*, p. 90.

[22]H. Leo Boles, *Biographical Sketches*, p. 241.

[23]Jacob Creath, Jr., *Gospel Advocate*, Vol. 8 (1866), p. 41.

[24]Wilburn, *The Hazard of the Die*, p. 69.

[25]*Ibid.*, pp. 190-192.

[26]Herman Norton, *Tennessee Christians* (Nashville: Reed and Co., 1971), p. 108.

[27]Tolbert Fanning, "Annual Meeting of the American Christian Missionary Society," *Gospel Advocate*, Vol. 5 (1859), p. 333.

[28]Wilburn, *The Hazard of the Die*, p. 104.

[29]Robert Richardson, "Misinterpretation of Scripture No. 1," *Millennial Harbinger*, 1856, p. 505.

[30]Robert Richardson, "President Fanning's Reply," *Millennial Harbinger*, 1857, pp. 433-448.

[31]Alexander Campbell, "Faith Versus Philosophy," *Millennial Harbinger*, 1858, p. 86.

[32]Alexander Campbell, "A Loud Call to Our Brethren," *Millennial Harbinger*, 1857, p. 646.

[33]Tolbert Fanning, "The Gospel Advocate," *Gospel Advocate*, Vol. 7 (1861), p. 380.

[34]R.B. Hastings, *Personal Recollections of Pardee Butler*, Cincinnati: 1889, p. 339.

[35]*Ibid.*, p. 306.

[36]*Ibid.*, p. 321.

[37]*Ibid.*, p. 345.

[38]*Ibid.*, p. 357.

[39]Louanna McNeil Bawcom, *Journey With Joy* (Abilene, TX: Quality Printing, 1969).

[40]For recent research on women in the Movement see Debra B. Hull, *Christian Church Women: Shapers of a Movement* (St. Louis: Chalice Press, 1994); C. Leonard Allen, *Distant Voices* (Abilene, TX: ACU Press, 1993); Peter M. Morgan, editor, *Disciples Family Album: 200 Years of Christian Church Leaders* (St. Louis: Chalice Press, 1990).

10

ALEXANDER CAMPBELL IN AFTERYEARS
THE MOVEMENT MATURES

He was the showpiece of the Movement.
— Louis Cochran

On a summer evening in 1854 a stranger arrived unannounced at "the Mansion" in Bethany, Virginia, hoping to see Alexander Campbell. The visitor had been traveling for 80 days, all the way from Adelaide, Australia. When Mr. Campbell came to the door, he explained the purpose of his mission: he had come to unite with "the church of the Disciples" and he wanted Campbell to baptize him. After his visit in Bethany he returned to Australia by way of England and left an account of his sojourn with the editor of the *British Millennial Harbinger.*

After appearing in that journal it was reproduced in Campbell's paper. It is not only one of the most interesting documents preserved in the archives of the Disciples, but its intimate narrative is reflective of the coming of age of both a man and his Movement.[1]

Campbell's writings had reached faraway Australia, convincing the visitor, whom Campbell calls "Brother Hussey," that he should leave his native Church of England and become a Disciple. When he arrived in New York he attended a Disciples church. He found Disciples in Canada as he journeyed west. In Cincinnati he chose to hear Elder Benjamin Franklin, but he had the choice of four congregations, all with commodious buildings, with a combined seating capacity of 2,000. In England the Movement was gaining such ground that the Disciples had a *Millennial Harbinger* of their own, the purpose of which was to republish the writings of Alexander Campbell.

Mr. Hussey was impressed that from "this quiet village shut in on almost every side by high hills there issues forth into almost all parts of America and the world, thousands of pages annually, which have produced no little excitement and embarrassment in the Christian world." Campbell told him how the first church started at Brush Run, and how in his first sermon he likened their work to the acorn that had produced the stately oak under whose shade they had spread the Lord's Supper for the first time. He had predicted on that Lord's day in 1811 that though their beginning be small they would one day be very great. Hussey numbered the Movement in 1854 at 300,000, at home and abroad.

The Australian must have set some kind of record in traveling halfway around the world to be baptized. He wanted "the Bishop," as Campbell was called around Bethany, to baptize him, and he was willing to pay the price of a long journey. Once the arrangement was made to baptize him the first Lord's day morning he was there, he explains: "I accompanied him to a place in the creek used for baptism. We went both down into the water, as did Philip and the Eunuch of old. After putting the usual questions to me, he immersed me into the name of the Father, Son, and Holy Spirit."

The preposition *into* in the ceremony was most important to Campbell, for he often wrote of how baptism is the act by which one formally enters *into* a relationship with God, Christ, and the Spirit, and that this is how the Greek term in Mt. 28:19 should be rendered and not by *in*. The evangelists in the field who learned this lesson well would report their additions to Campbell as did W.T. Moore: "A goodly number of the Methodists came out upon the Lord's side, and were immersed *into* the name of the Father, Son and Holy Spirit," always italicizing the preposition![2]

Hussey reports that Campbell talked with him at length on the one theme that consumed his thinking, *Christianity* — "its foundation is facts, not theory; its design, the conversion of the world; and its great moving principles, faith and love." This was his all-embracing theme, whether he was conversing at Bethany or preaching in Louisville. The visitor had heard "on the road to Wellsburg" that he would find the Bishop "venerable, amiable, and affable," and he reported that it was so, and he added, "his humility is as great as his learning is profound."

He tells of going to the Bethany church one Sunday morning with Campbell, who was then 66. Arriving well ahead of the others, he and the Bishop sat down along the bank of the Buffalo, and here Campbell embarked upon another of his favorite themes, "admiring the beauties of nature and extolling the goodness of God." Here Hussey joins many others in describing Campbell as a conversationalist: "He has a never-failing treasury of things new and old, of psalms and hymns, explanations and illustrations of passages of Scripture, of the choicest description; and which he uses to interest and instruct those who may chance to be in his company."

Once in the assembly, Campbell conducted the service in the same simple and fervent manner as if he were in the bosom of his family. Hussey says he prayed as if he were well acquainted with Him whom he addressed. He took no text for his sermon, but again spoke generally of Christianity, speaking of the wisdom and benevolence of its Author and Founder, and the blessings of receiving it. He spoke as a friend without any attempt at eloquence, and he told the people that he delighted being in their company and that he expected to be with them in eternity. He spoke of what it means to be a Christian and of the glory that awaits the believer. He then gave "the usual invitation" to anyone who would come forward and confess Christ.

As he uncovered the loaf he spoke of "a friend who had said, 'Do this in remembrance of me.'" He then gave thanks for the loaf and afterwards the cup. Hussey reports that *before* breaking the bread Campbell introduced him to the believers, announcing that he would address the assembly that afternoon on Sunday schools, a subject in which he had expertise, which came as a complete surprise. That evening Hussey got to hear James S. Lamar, who was also visiting in Bethany from his field of labor in Georgia.

We learn from this that the Bethany church had three assemblies on Sunday. Hussey also refers to a Wednesday evening meeting. Since Campbell once wrote to Robert Milligan that he preached each Sunday that he was at home,[3] we may conclude that he spoke at one of the services, leaving the other two for visitors and other preachers in the congregation, such as Prof. W.P. Pendleton and Dr. Robert Richardson.

Hussey tells how on one Sunday he rode with Campbell in a buggy a few miles out of Bethany to a gathering that was too large for the meeting-house since the word was out that Campbell was speaking. When Campbell took such pains to make sure his horse was well watered, he thought of the proverb, "A good man is merciful to his beast," and he was impressed at the long stretch of buggies, gigs, and wagons at the place of meeting. Campbell spoke at length on the first chapter of Hebrews, pointing to the Author of salvation, the nature of that salvation, and the danger of neglecting it.

The Showpiece of the Movement

At the time of the Australian's visit Campbell had long been what Louis Cochran descibed as "the showpiece of the Movement." He attracted large crowds wherever he went. In the mid-frontier his name was as well-known as Billy Graham's is today. He was rich, famous, and brilliant, and was wined and dined by the great and near great. Those who heard him described him as "the master of assemblies," and felt they were in the presence of a great man. A man who watched him pass on a London street was heard to say, "There goes a man with the brains to rule all Europe."

It amazed audiences that he could speak for hours without notes, and a Presbyterian divine reported after hearing him exalt Christ from Psa. 24

that it was the most impressive display of divine eloquence that he had ever heard. Others noted how at ease he was before a vast audience, as poised as if he were in his own parlor. Auditors became unconscious of time, however long he spoke.

This is to say that he was indeed the Movement's showpiece, its best advertisement. While multi-talented, it was as a preacher and a religious reformer that Campbell was known. It was therefore appropriate when U.S. postal officials recently rejected a request to honor him on a commemorative stamp, noting that he was primarily a religious figure, who cannot be honored on U.S. stamps, rather than a frontier publisher and editor, founder of a college, politician, lecturer, farmer, world traveler, or even postmaster!

James Madison, former President, realized this back in 1829 at the Virginia Constitutional Convention where he was a delegate with Campbell. On the final evening of the Convention he told Campbell that while he had talents as a statesman, his real calling was preaching, assuring him that he was the best expositor of the Scriptures he had ever heard.

It could be argued that Alexander Campbell was the Movement, certainly its best PR. This is evident not only in that "Campbellite" soon became a synonymn for the Movement, and not always derogatory, but also because it was widely assumed, especially by informed critics, that the Movement would not survive his death. J.B. Jeter, one of Campbell's antagonists, charged that the Movement was held together by "the magic of a name, and by a leader whose authority they have indignantly denied, and implicitly followed." He went on to predict that following Campbell's death the divisive tendencies in the Movement would assert themselves and its unity would be shattered.[4]

Campbell lived in his little village for 56 years, naming it in fact. When he was made its postmaster (which enabled him to mail all his publications free!) there was already a Buffalo, Virginia, so he called it Bethany. That could mean "house of the poor," but almost certainly he did not have that in mind when he chose that name, for in tilling its soil and raising sheep in its hills he made himself one of the richest men in Virginia.

He may well have set a record for franking privileges for a country postmaster in that he sent out a million copies of the *Christian Baptist* and *Millennial Harbinger* over a period of 45 years, plus several editions of his hymnal, five public debates, and several theological works. As a preacher, educator, editor, publisher, translator, and debater Alexander Campbell made a place for himself in the sun. By the middle of the nineteenth century he had solidified that Movement that was launched to unite the Christians in all the sects.

Campbell's message was unequivocal, rooted in the tradition of the Reformation and historic Christianity, centered as it was in Jesus Christ. While he was pious, humble, and mild-mannered, he was conscience of his influence in an ever expanding reformation Movement. Yet he delighted in the simple things of life, especially conversation around the hearth, and was at ease in the bosom of his small home congregation.

He talked and behaved as one who knew what he was doing and where he was going. He was a confirmed optimist, turning almost everything he heard and saw to some good account. He had a cheerful disposition and a rosy outlook. He was often heard to say, "Attempt great things, expect great things, and great things will follow."[5]

Bethany College

"It has been a perpetual incubus and trouble."

Since *incubus* means a nightmare, this is strong language for a college founder-president, and he wrote this *before* the college burned and had to be rebuilt and *before* the student uprising over the slavery question. But he went on to say that he had done it for the cause of education — "literature, science and religion." And he made it clear that the college was a part of his reformation: "It was in its conception, is now in its existence, and will ever be in its fortunes, identified with the cause of the Reformation, and essential to its prosperity."[6]

Since he waited until 1840 to start the college, one-third of a century after his branch of the reformation had begun, it could be questioned whether it was "essential" to his cause, but there can be no question but what it reflected his educational philosophy.

That philosophy was basically very simple, not unlike those who describe a good school as Mark Hopkins on one end of a log and a student on the other.

Once past his threescore and ten, he wrote: "My father, though I say it, was the best educator of young men I ever knew. He caused me, when a boy, to memorize largely many selected passages from the most celebrated English poets, amongst whom were Milton, Young, Cowper and Shakespeare — the latter only in very select passages." This helps to explain why "literature" is mentioned first in his plans for a college.

He explained further: "But primary to these were the Psalms of David, the Proverbs of Solomon, and the Ecclesiastes. In the New Testament, Paul's Epistles to the Romans, and that to the Hebrews, were made as familiar as family worship, with many other selections."[7] This explains why he referred to Bethany as "the only College in the New World, or in the

Old World, known to me, founded upon the Holy Bible and our common humanity."[8] It is evident that he saw the Bible not only as basic to education but as the watershed of all knowledge.

During Campbell's lifetime most colleges were segregated, being either for men or for women, and so Bethany did not admit women until long after Campbell's day. He once named Antioch, Hiram, and Oberlin as colleges that were educating men and women together, but he was left unconvinced that such an innovation was properly adapted to "the genius and development of the sexes."[9]

A rather imposing list could be drawn up of those men who went out from Bethany College in behalf of the Movement, such as Moses E. Lard, a valedictorian at Bethany who went on to become an author and editor. It was he that Campbell called upon to answer J.B. Jeter's *Campbellism Examined* (1855), which was a responsible critique by a highly respected Baptist minister. In the book Jeter conceded that Campbell's views had "exercised an extensive influence on the religious sentiments of the country."

Before Tolbert Fanning started Franklin College in Tennessee, many in the South came to Bethany, such as J.M. Barnes, who evangelized successfully in Alabama. From the West came the likes of John F. Rowe, who graduated with honors in 1854 and went on to become an editor and author of influence. J.W. McGarvey, who became a noted scholar, was not a Christian when he entered Bethany. He was immersed in Buffalo creek while a student and went on to deliver his valedictory in Greek.

The list of preachers goes on and on, the known and the unknown, such as James S. Lamar, O.A. Burgess, Robert Graham, Alexander Proctor, C.L. Loos, F.D. Power, John Shackleford, Charles Carlton, William Baxter, W.H. Woolery. There were those who became statesmen, such as Senator George T. Oliver of Pennsylvania, and Champ Clark, who served as Speaker of the House. Joseph L. Lamar became a justice of the Supreme Court. James A. Garfield, one of our martyred Presidents, served on the board of trustees.

This was consistent with Campbell's educational philosophy:

Men, and not brick and mortar, make colleges, and these colleges make men. These men make books, and these books make the living world in which we individually live, and move, and have our being. How important then, that our colleges should understand and teach the true philosophy of man! They create the men that furnish the teachers of men — the men that fill the pulpit, the legislative halls, the senators, the judges and the governors of the earth. Do we expect to fill these high stations by merely voting or praying for men? Or shall we choose empirics, charlatans, mountebanks, and every pretender to eminent claims upon the suffrages of the people? Forbid it, reason, conscience and Heaven![10]

Campbell believed education must touch the heart as well as the mind, and prepare one for eternity as well as this world: "The whole world within him, as well as the whole world without him, should not only be defined and developed, but cultivated, matured and perfected in full harmony with his origin and destiny, not only as it pertains to the present world, but also as relates to the future and the eternal world."[11]

A man is not really educated, he believed, if he is not religious. "His head may be large and crowded with ideas, but his heart dwarfed and cold to God and man," he wrote. So he wanted an *educational* reformation as well as a religious one: "One item of that reformation, for which we will always contend, is that religious and moral culture must be first, last, midst, and without end, in every school in which man is moulded for the high ends of destiny."[12]

In a recent study on Campbell's educational philosophy, John L. Morrison notes that Campbell perceived all education as moral, and based upon the nonsectarian teaching of the Bible. "Moral culture" is, therefore, to be the aim of all education, whether public or private. He saw education as "the art of living," not preparation for life, but life itself.

Along with Horace Mann, a contemporary and a fellow Disciple, Campbell lost his bid for nonsectarian Bible teaching in public schools, leaving him to rely on such private institutions as Bethany College. But the Bible can and should be taught in public schools, he insisted, in the same way any other book is taught, with the common sense rules of interpretation, leaving it to the students to make the moral application.[13]

After building Bethany College on his own farm, donating to it its first $10,000, and committing his life to it as its president, treasurer and fund raiser, he was satisfied that it was accomplishing what he intended: "We have already in the field some of its first fruits, and they are an offering most acceptable to the aggregate of all who hear them. We want a thousand men in the field of the world, and another thousand in the vineyards of the Lord."[14]

After Campbell's death, Dr. Richardson reported that the college had fully equalled its founder's expectations since so many talented young men had gone out from its halls into the world and among the churches, adding: "The churches, which in many places had long suffered for want of an efficient ministry and competent teachers, began to be supplied, and a new impulse was given to the cause of the primitive gospel."[15]

The Rice and Purcell Debates

"A splendid specimen of eloquent reasoning."

It was appropriate that Henry Clay, who at 66 was known as "the Great Pacificator," should serve as moderator in the Campbell-Rice debate in his own hometown of Lexington, Ky. in 1843. The two debaters had such conflicting personalities, it was supposed, that it took someone with the ability to create the Missouri Compromise to keep the peace.[16]

As moderator Mr. Clay was to be objective and show no partiality, but at one point in the debate he had difficulty doing this, according to one report. During Campbell's first address on the work of the Spirit, Mr. Clay became unusually attentive. He leaned forward and began to bow assent, waving his hand at the same time, in his graceful, approving manner. As Campbell's argument unfolded it was apparent that Clay was carried away by the power of the presentation. Suddenly finding himself, he drew back and looked to see if anyone had seen him off guard.[17]

An Episcopalian divine was also impressed with that particular speech, hailing it as "one of the most splendid specimens of eloquent reasoning I ever remember to have read." The address dealt with a subject basic to the Movement's teaching: the tyranny of theological language and the need to be made free of it. He pointed out that a proper definition of terms would have prevented more than half of all the debates in history, and he called for "a much more simple and scriptural vocabulary."

Illustrating what theological system-builders have done in confusing matters, he pointed to the terms regeneration, conversion, justification, and sanctification, showing the nice distinctions and processive order that are assigned them. He then gave this impressive illustration:

> A foreigner, in becoming a citizen, is sometimes said to be naturalized, some-times enfranchised, sometimes adopted, sometimes made a citizen. Now, what intelligent citizen regards these as parts of one process? Rather, who does not consider them as different metaphors, setting forth the same great change under various allusions to past and present circumstances? From such a statement, none but a simpleton would imagine that a foreigner was first naturalized, then enfranchised, then adopted, and finally made an American citizen: yet such a simpleton is that learned Rabbi, who represents a man, first regenerated, then converted, then justified, then sanctified, then saved.[18]

One wonders if the two men had as much to say on only three subjects, baptism, the Holy Spirit, and creeds, as to require a book of 912 pages. More than half of these are given to baptism, with Campbell affirming that immersion is the only proper mode and that it is for the remission of sins, and Rice affirming that infant baptism is scriptural and that baptism can be performed only by an ordained minister. Campbell affirmed the other two propositions, that the Spirit in conversion operates only through the word of truth, and that human creeds are schismatic.

As to the significance of the debate and its effect on the progress of the Movement, the most noteworthy fact is that it occurred at all. While Campbell was not all that eager, the Presbyterians, sensing that orthodoxy was suffering in Kentucky as a result of the Movement's influence, pressed him for the debate. As J.J. Haley puts it: "This debate in Lexington was the supreme effort of Calvinistic paedobaptists, in that community, to break the influence and stop the progress of the religious reformation."[19]

While the Presbyterians claimed victory far and wide, it did not seem to bother Campbell, who immersed Presbyterians between sessions of the debate and published reports of conversions across the country of those who had heard or read the debate. The sources indicate that the debate was read widely, especially in intellectual circles, and was the occasion of many mini-debates.

Bill J. Humble explains its impact in terms of more open doors: "The prestige which Campbell won for the Restoration Movement through his debates was greatly beneficial in obtaining a more sympathetic study of its plea . . The debates were attended by thousands of interested auditors, and when published the arguments were weighed by thousands more."[20] To one who reads the debate today, especially on baptism, he is impressed that the differences were not all that significant.

W.B. Blakemore sees the Rice debate, which lasted sixteen days, as an occasion of massive "adult education," though that pedagogical term was not then known, and he thinks it remarkable that the Christians and Presbyterians got along as well as they did, despite the bitterness between the debaters. He sees a touch of ecumenicity in it, for "even though the Christian Churches have debated sharply with other Christians, they did not separate themselves from them, but established a variety of cooperative relationships."

He thinks the most positive thing in the debate was an assertion by Campbell that personal commitment to Christ is the only requisite to church membership, and therefore the ground of Christian unity.[21] Some who heard or read the debate concluded it promoted unity in that it discredited creeds as a basis of fellowship and predicated unity only upon the facts of the gospel.[22]

In the discussion on creeds Campbell made it clear that he did not oppose them *per se*, for a church has the right to publish its tenets and opinions to the world. It is that creeds make sects and sects make creeds, and these are substituted for the Bible and made terms of fellowship. And so his proposition read: "Human creeds *as bonds of union and communion* are necessarily heretical and schismatical."[23]

It was generally conceded that Rice did well for himself in the debate, especially by his skillful use of Campbell's writings, making it appear that Campbell was woefully inconsistent. Rice had the advantage of never having written a book! Two women in the balcony, who did not bother to keep their partiality a secret, were overheard discussing that aspect of the debate. One of them, pointing to the pile of books on Rice's table and the lack of any on Campbell's, observed that Rice must be of superior intelligence. The other woman reminded her that the books on Rice's table were *written* by Mr. Campbell![24]

Rice laid on Campbell what he had said in the Maccalla debate to the effect that Paul's sins were *really* pardoned when he believed and *formally* pardoned when he was baptized. He also reminded him of what has come to be known as "the Lunenburg letter," where a Christian is defined as one who believes in Jesus as the Christ and obeys him in all things according to his understanding.

In that letter Campbell said he would make no one duty an absolute standard for being a Christian, not even immersion. He granted that the unimmersed, who have mistaken the form of baptism but have obedient hearts, are Christians.

Rice also reminded Campbell of saying, "I do admit that a person who believes the Gospel, and *cannot* be immersed, may obtain remission." Rice insisted that such admissions were fatal to the proposition that baptism is for the remission of sins. Campbell rejoined by noting that his position emphasized "general obedience," which, when applied to a believer who understands what the Scriptures teach, calls for baptism for the remission of sins.[25]

However much baited by Rice, Campbell refused to take an extreme position on baptism, and rather than do so, turns the table on Rice: "I do not make baptism absolutely essential to salvation in any case, while he makes the knowledge of Christ absolutely necessary in all cases."[26] He refers to Calvinism's damnation of the heathen. He goes on: "The man who never heard the gospel, cannot disobey it; and he who, through any physical impossibility, is prevented from any ordinance, is no transgressor. . . . None suffer, in our views, but those who are wilfully ignorant, or negligent of their duty."[27]

Campbell's apparent ambiguity on baptism is a reminder that the leaders of the Movement, even in the early period, did not view the ordinance alike, as a recent study has clearly demonstrated.[28] Rice was thus in a position to use Campbell's own leaders against him, such as Dr. James Fishback, the prominent Baptist who became a Disciple but never accepted the doctrine of baptism for remission. Even Barton W. Stone was slow of heart to accept it. It was a doctrine, especially in its most rigid form, that would eventually be an occasion of division within the Movement, for there would be those who could never say, as Campbell did to Rice, "I do not make baptism absolutely essential to salvation in any case."

The debate was not above personalities, as were both the Owen and Purcell debates. When Campbell talked about the clergy being "venal," Rice fired back that there was not one Presbyterian preacher in the country that had one-tenth of the wealth Mr. Campbell had. And when Campbell implied that the position he had taken was with some sacrifice in terms of the plaudits of men, Rice assured him that he had gained far more popularity than he would have had he remained a Presbyterian!

It was Campbell's debate with a Roman Catholic bishop in 1837 that established him as both a representative and a defender of Protestantism, but it made for an interesting contradiction. While it ingratiated the new church to the Protestant denominations, it placed Campbell in the awkward position of pleading for unity on the one hand and representing a divided Protestantism on the other.

When Campbell argued against apostolic succession, Bishop Purcell quoted Protestants who defended it. When he leveled criticism against the papacy from Gibbon's *Decline and Fall of the Roman Empire*, Purcell noted that Gibbon had been driven to a hatred of Christianity by his Protestant parents who would not abide their son joining the Catholic Church, as he wanted to do. But whatever merits the debate had otherwise, the disputants came out of it with a high opinion of one another. While Campbell viewed Purcell as a gentleman and as one of the fairest men he had debated, Purcell described Campbell as "a most lovable character who treated me in every way and on all occasions like a brother."

In afteryears Purcell was interviewed by former Indiana governor Ira D. Chase, who was also a preacher in the Christian Church. Purcell was impressed that "Campbell's church . . as a lusty youth has certainly distanced all its rivals in the race for popular favor." He wondered what gigantic proportions it might attain in another quarter of a century, noting that its success had exceeded the fondest dreams of its founder. As for Campbell himself, he thought history would be kind to him, according him a place alongside Luther, Calvin, and Wesley.[29]

Tour of Great Britain

Rumors had it that Henry Clay was himself immersed as a result of the Rice debate. However that may be, he volunteered a handsome letter of introduction to the eminent folk of Great Britain when Campbell journeyed there four years after the debate, in 1847. "Dr. Campbell is among the most eminent citizens of the United States," wrote the Senator, "distinguished for his great learning and ability, for his successful devotion to the education of youth, for his piety and as the head and founder of one of the most important and respectable religious communities in the United States."[30]

The letter gave him access to the American ambassador in London, who in turn introduced him to both the House of Lords and the House of Commons. He was able to hear Lord Broughham orate from the floor, a man he had long admired for his persuasive powers.

He visited more than a dozen English cities, addressing huge crowds in their halls and churches. In Leicester he visited the Abbey where Cardinal Wolsey begged for a place to be buried after living a life of luxury with a king who finally deserted him. He recalled Wolsey's sad words, "Had I served my God with half the zeal I have served my King, he would not thus have deserted my gray hairs."

In Sunderland he was the guest of a shipbuilder who had named one of his ships "Alexander Campbell." In Nottingham he visited with James Wallis, who edited the *British Millennial Harbinger*, a journal that had begun in 1835 when Campbell's influence first began to reach England.

In Chester he presided over the second conference of British Churches of Christ, where 80 churches reported a membership of 2,300. Many of these could be traced to the Glas-Sandeman and Scottish Baptist influence that went on to accept Campbell's teaching, while others emerged on their own, similar to the way the Campbell churches started in America. But there were many others throughout Great Britain, Anglicans and nonconformists, who knew of "the great American reformer," as they called him, who were eager to hear him.

Campbell was at this time, according to Thomas Chalmers, the most famous American outside politics in all of Great Britain. Other Americans lectured in these places, such as Henry Ward Beecher, but they were not known like Campbell, and being a controversial figure only added aura to his presence.

Chalmers, writing in 1892, raised the question as to why Campbell's great renown was allowed to die, while Luther's, Wesley's, and even Bunyan's have not. In fact, he points out, Campbell was more famous in *his* day than these others were in theirs, and that their names have been made great by the loyalty of their followers, whereas Campbell's people have been so uneasy about being "Campbellites" that they themselves have allowed a great name to go into virtual oblivion.[31]

There was such keen interest in Scotland in Campbell's views that some clergy were fearful of the influence he might have in their churches. They plainly did not want their people to hear his plea for reformation, so they formed a conspiracy to do what they could to discredit his name. Learning that he was a wealthy landowner from the slave state of Virginia, they supposed he was a slaveholder, and since Scotland was generally abolitionist this was the ideal ruse to use to turn away the people's ears.

When they learned that Campbell did *not* own slaves and that he had liberated the ones he once owned, they were still resolved to use the slavery issue, supposing that he must have some sympathy for the system. They thus formed a committee to call upon the American visitor in Edinburgh to ascertain his position on slavery, disguising their real intent. One of the preachers later revealed that "We were all intent upon the same aim, to shut Alexander Campbell out of Scotland."[32]

The conspirators framed their questions so as to lead Campbell into an approval of slavery, but he did not fully cooperate. He said that slavery was the "largest, blackest spot upon the American escutcheon," and that he had always advocated the emancipation of slaves by the owners themselves and that he had set an example by freeing his, once he had educated them in the gospel and good citizenship.

But he expressed disapproval of the tactics of abolitionists in both Britain and America, explaining that they did more harm than good and would only lead the country into war and perhaps destroy it. He even ventured that the relation between master and slave was not in itself sinful and that the Scriptures did not condemn it but recognized and regulated it. Even though it is lawful, he told them, it is not expedient and he opposed it on moral, political, and social grounds.[33]

There were soon posted all over Edinburgh, and everywhere that Campbell dared to lecture, placards that read in huge letters: *Citizens of Edinburgh! Beware! Alexander Campbell of America has been a slaveholder himself, and is yet a defender of man-stealers.* Passions were so stirred that Campbell thought it wise to lecture elsewhere in Scotland for awhile. When he finally did return to Edinburgh to speak in the Waterloo Rooms, it must have been the most emotionally-charged experience of his life. Seven thousand had gathered to hear him, and most all of them were suspicious of him, if not adamantly opposed to him.

A witness to the event reported that once the huge audience got its first look at the controversial American, studying him as he took his seat on the stand before them, that there was an immediate response to the effect that he was not what his enemies had caricatured him as being. When he first spoke, there were disturbances, which he ignored, but after a three-hour address he had won the hearts of the Scots.[34]

In Jail In Glasgow

His enemies pursued him still. When they, as leaders in the anti-slavery society, challenged Campbell to debate, he accepted the challenge through the *Edinburgh Journal*, agreeing to meet anyone the society selected so long as it was not the Rev. James Robertson who had to be expelled from the Baptist church in Dundee for molesting his own mother. James Robertson was the name of his archenemy, the one who led the committee that placarded him all over Scotland, but apparently not the man expelled by the Baptists.

Robertson filed suit for libel, and Campbell was soon a prisoner in the famous Bridewell prison in Glasgow. His friends insisted on posting bond and freeing him, but Campbell would not have it, desiring to meet in court the leaders of a society who claim to believe in freedom and yet treat a visitor to their country in such a way.

After ten days in jail a judge released Campbell, ruling that the charge was illegal, but the plaintiff appealed to a higher court, causing the prisoner to be detained still longer. The appeals judge, sensing the injustice of it all, hurried the case along and at last freed Campbell, but not before he was wracked by a deep chest cold, which ended his ministry in Scotland.

Yet his prison life was far from oppressive, for at least four women doted over him, sprucing up his cell and caring for his every need. An indulgent jailer allowed visitors into his small cell to overflowing, as many as eleven at a time, and they came from all of Scotland, the small and the great alike. This allowed him to teach for hours on end his principles of reform.

As for the accuser, he fled the country after being charged with false arrest, forfeiting the equivalent of $10,000 that his friends had posted for his security. This was assessed as a fine and offered to Campbell, who chose to give it to Scottish charities.

One of the women who ministered to Campbell in prison, Eliza Davies, first heard him at a Baptist church in Paisley, Scotland, and the address so impressed her that she resolved then and there to cast her lot with the Disciples. A native Scot, she had migrated to Australia and had married a psychopath who almost ruined her life. She followed Campbell to America, spent a few years in his home at Bethany attending his sick and burying his dead, and then taught several years at the Disciples' orphanage in Midway, Kentucky.

Returning to Australia, she took the plea of the Disciples with her, along with boxes of Campbell's books, and was instrumental in furthering the reformation in that country. She made two voyages around the world, and with the encouragement of Dr. Robert Richardson she wrote a lengthy book on her experiences, which provides many rare insights into the Movement's development on three continents.[35]

She provides information on how those of the Movement identified themselves in these places during the 1840's. When Campbell was freed from prison with a bad cold and needed rest, she tells how one of the brothers said to him, "I hold you prisoner in the name of the Church of Christ," and yet she frequently uses "Christian Church" in her narrative, showing how the names were used interchangeably. Her book gives insights into Campbell's private life, both in Scotland and Bethany, that can be found nowhere else.

She pictures him as sometimes frolicking, as in Scotland when he bounded down the stairs singing as he came, *The Campbells are coming, Aha, Aha!*, in spite of all the problems he was having. She was convinced that he had unusual psychic powers, and her reasons for so thinking are persuasive.

In telling about the first time she heard him at Paisley, when he spoke for three hours on 1 Cor. 13:13 — one hour each on faith, hope, and charity — to the amazement of an audience that was wary of him, she reveals that it was then that she resolved to go to America and be a part of his people.

Eliza said to herself as did Ruth to Naomi: "Whither thou goest, I will go; and where thou lodgest, I will lodge: thy people shall be my people, and thy God my God." After the service they both received various invitations to dine, being visitors, and there was a question as to which one Campbell would accept. Upon meeting Mrs. Davies he resolved the problem by saying: "Where this lady goes, I will go; where she dines, I will dine." Eliza was mesmerized!

Even more impressive was Campbell's revelation to her on Sept. 4, 1847 that he felt terribly depressed, as if some great calamity was hanging over him, which was unusual for him since he was not of a despondent nature. Eliza shared this with a sister and made note of the date. It was the very day that Campbell's beloved son Wycliffe drowned back home in Bethany while swimming on the family farm, which Campbell did not know about until weeks later when he arrived in New York.[36] Such instances in Campbell's life led Arthur Ford, a Disciples minister who became a renowned medium, to claim for him clairvoyant powers.

Travel Among The Great And Small
"The philanthropy of God"

Campbell might well have been the most traveled American of his day. Starting in the early 1820's and continuing well into the 1860's, he traversed the country in every direction and in all kinds of weather. He grew up with the nation, moving from horseback and stagecoach to steamboat and railroad. He was away from home months at a time, and the scores of travel letters that he prepared for his journals are resourceful as Americana as well as for history.

He tells of being lost in a stagecoach one dark night near Springfield, Illinois and of riding a sleigh through the snow-covered streets of Chicago when it was but a village. He was impressed when "the cars" were able to move him along on steel tracks at the clip of 40 miles per hour, and he mentions that he rode the first railway ever built in this country. He also tells of his accidents, on railroad and steamboats alike, once suffering injury.

By 1850 one Campbell watcher, a former president of Amherst College, conceded that "Mr. Campbell has for more than twenty years wielded a power over men's minds, on the subject of religion, which has no parallel in the Protestant history of this country, nor the Romish either." No other person ever made such inroads into other denominations, he allowed, explaining that this was due to Campbell's rare combination of talents, which he listed as: a great knowledge of human nature, a superior education, smooth and captivating eloquence as a preacher, a skilled debater, an untiring industry of his pen and press, and his vast personal acquaintance in his wide circuits.[37]

His wide circuits placed him among the high and the lowly, whether in homes, churches, schools, courthouses, legislative halls, jails, or conventions of sundry types. Such contacts helped his cause to "struggle into life," as he once put it. He only needed to be present in a community to attract both attention and a crowd. When the presiding judge in Ravenna, Ohio in 1831 heard that Campbell was in town, he invited the reformer to address the court, recessing the procedures for the occasion.[38] When he was in Baltimore in 1850 he was invited by a committee of both houses of Congress to speak in the House of Representatives.

The visit with Congress was not an "official" visit before the two bodies in parliamentary session, as some historians have supposed. Campbell's explanation that it was an invitation from "members of both Houses of Congress" is misleading. It was rather a "congressional church," something like the "White House Church" in the days of President Nixon, which assembled on Sundays and heard clergymen of reputation. It did however assemble in the House of Representatives.

Campbell made the nature of the gathering clear when he described the Hall as overflowing with lawmakers, their families, and many citizens on Sunday morning. The myth that Campbell addressed both houses of

Congress led one scholar to search in vain for the speech in official sources. He could not even find a reference to it in nine Washington papers! But the speech was covered by a political reporter and published in a Baltimore paper the next day, which Campbell saw as complimentary.[39]

His subject before the nation's leaders, based on John 3:16, was his constant theme, the philanthropy of God. Starting with creation he reviewed what God has done for man all the way to redemption in Christ. While it was an appropriate subject for a nation on the brink of war, it was always the heart of his message, to the great and the small alike. Whether he preached to presidents, leaders of Congress, governors, industrialists, or the rank and file of the masses, his plea for reform was based on the love of God. He was most at home among obscure saints gathered to celebrate the ordinances of the Lord, as he was on that Sunday in Washington, moving from Capitol Hill to an upper room to break bread with his own church.

A Mid-Course Review
"One Lord, one faith, one baptism"

In an 1843 essay that reviewed the history of the Movement's first generation, Campbell sought to clarify its purpose and intent. He regretted the break with the Baptists, conceding that it was unnecessary. They needed reformation, he insisted, but this may have been effected "without the necessity of a new denomination," admitting as he often did that his new church was a denomination.[40] His heirs have not done as well!

In this review he seemed willing to base it all upon a restoration of the ordinances that God gave to the church. After all, his new organization was founded upon the New Institution alone, and this might enable his people to work better for the union of all Christians than if they had remained with the Baptists. As if to state the essence of the Movement, he named its "one grand characteristic," which is *a restoration of the ordinances of the New Institution to their place and power*. Defining an ordinance as a mode in which divine grace acts upon human nature, he identified the Christian ordinances as "the power of the gospel of the grace of God." This makes every ordinance of the gospel a specific demonstration of divine grace in reference to some effect that can be obtained in no other way.

He first named the study of the Bible as an ordinance, so the first task in restoration is to give the Scriptures back to the church, unmolested by opinions and party creeds. Baptism, the Lord's Supper, and the Lord's day are others. He referred also to "a thorough church organization" with its elders, deacons, and evangelists.

He insisted that the church is to be founded upon the Bible and not the creeds of men. It is to be made up of people who are immersed into Christ, who celebrate the Lord's Supper each first day, who are cared for by its duly appointed elders and deacons, and who send out evangelists to preach the gospel to the lost. His plea always included a call for the unity of all believers.

Near the end of his ministry, in 1862, he was still pleading for a unity based on what he called "the seven superlative facts" in Eph. 4: one Body, one Spirit, one hope, one Lord, one faith, one baptism, one God, and Father of all. He made these the essence of the Disciples' plea and the basis of Christian union. There can be diversity of doctrine and differences of opinion, but Paul's seven facts, when believed and obeyed, unite all of God's church.

Early in his ministry he had named what he considered "the essential attributes" of his plea.[41] While basically the same as the foregoing, he included other ideas he considered crucial to reformation, such as "The restoration of a pure speech, or the calling of Bible things by Bible names" and "The right of private opinion in all matters not revealed in contradistinction from the common faith, without the forfeiture of Christian character or Christian privilege."[42]

He also stressed the importance of understanding the nature of the gospel, which, he contended, is not a theory, a doctrine, or a system of philosophy. It is not even the theory of faith, repentance, and baptism. The gospel is rather the proclamation of remission of sins and eternal life through the sacrifice of Christ to all who obey him.

Campbell and his people were often heard to reduce their plea for unity to the least common denominator, which was "one Lord, one faith, one baptism." This called for no theorizing, but an acceptance of facts and an obedient response to those facts. The gospel first addresses the mind, but goes on to touch the heart.

Robert Richardson: Campbell's Alter Ego

"This reformation was born of a love of union,
and union has been its engrossing theme."

The most articulate interpreter of Campbell's plea was his family physician and biographer, Dr. Robert Richardson, who may be thought of as his alter ego. Of a highly cultured Episcopalian background, Richardson came into the Movement by way of his contact with Walter Scott. He served on the faculty of Bethany College and as an associate editor of the *Millennial Harbinger*, along with being a trusted friend and adviser of the man he most admired, Alexander Campbell.

He may well have been the most perceptive thinker and most lucid writer of the early period. In 1853 he published an 88-page book on *The Principles and Objects of the Religious Reformation, Urged by A. Campbell and Others, Briefly Stated and Explained*. Richardson's biographers think it deserves to be called the "Disciple Manifesto" and describe it as "a model of brevity, comprehensiveness, and clarity." It was a revision of essays that had appeared in the *Millennial Harbinger*, and it is here that they are readily available today.[43]

On the eve of the book's appearance Campbell wrote in his journal that its author had been associated with the reformation for a quarter of a century and was well posted on its history. He hailed it as "a well proportioned miniature" of the plea. He further said it was written in a lucid and chaste style and was worthy of both the author and the cause. He might have added that it provided for both the church and the world the most attractive *apologia* yet set forth as to what the Movement was all about.[44]

At the outset Richardson placed the Movement within the "Reformed" tradition, showing that its purpose was to continue what the reformers of the sixteenth century began. *Reformed* cannot mean that the job is complete. Reformation by its very nature is gradual and progressive. Not only is truth slowly learned, but conformity to it is also slow. However acute a reformer's mind may be, he cannot, when first aroused from the lethargy of ages, at a glance comprehend the whole of divine truth.

The Movement's mission is not, therefore, to disparage the labors and learning of past reformers or to renounce the leading doctrines of Protestantism, but to advance in Christian knowledge and make larger discoveries of divine truth. In the Protestant standards themselves are truths and principles of reform that are neglected, and it is the Movement's task to recover these and other truths and thus restore "a pure primitive Christianity in form and spirit, in principle and practice."[45]

Such a restoration can be realized only when believers are left free to study and think for themselves and not be bound by human authority. He thus speaks of "liberty of conscience and the right of private judgment" as necessary for an ongoing reformation. This is hindered by the imposition of creeds, and anything that obstructs man's progress in divine things must be wrong. "With what consistency," he asks, "can we reject a decision of the Pope and yet submit to one of the primate?"[46]

He gets to the heart of the plea when he contends that unity can come only through "the generalization of Christianity," and that it is in particularizing and in contending for microscopic details that the church has divided into a multiplicity of sects. It is both vain and hopeless to expect the world to accept any particular set of opinions or system of doctrines. People can agree on the general truths and facts of Christianity, and it is only here that unity is possible. He has a neat way of saying "That alone which saves men can unite them."

The doctor reminds his readers of the difference between the Bible and the gospel. The early Christians did not unite upon the "Bible alone," for they did not even have the Bible, but upon the "gospel alone," and they certainly did not have to understand the Bible alike. In those days the gospel possessed identity and distinction in that it was God's power to save, not the whole of revelation. The church thus unites upon *the gospel.* "Let the Bible be to us every thing designed by its author," he says in pointing the way to unity, "but let 'Christ crucified' be not only our peace with God, but our peace with one another."[47]

"This reformation was born of the love of union," he said, "and Christian union has been its engrossing theme." The basis of such a union is in the confession of the great fundamental truth of Christianity, that Jesus Christ is the son of God, which is the *common* faith. He observes that all through its history the church has sought to reconcile unity of faith and liberty of opinion, and he was convinced that his people had found the solution.

There is a way for all believers to unite in the one Body without retrenching from the principle of liberty of opinion. This is to unite upon the facts of the gospel while allowing diversity of opinion in doctrine. It is the "restless zeal for *purity* of doctrine" that has given us all the creeds, he avowed. The church has never really questioned the gospel, and so it is always a *theory* of religion that is made to justify or condemn. It is a creed that makes one a saint or sinner, not the gospel.

He hastened to add that in making the gospel itself the basis of unity the Movement has not deprecated the value of purity of doctrine, but has simply recognized that unity is possible only in the truth of the gospel and not in uniformity of doctrine. So, love of theory must give way to love of Christ. He saw *furor doctrinalis* as the congenital disease of Protestantism. Human nature has a need for certainty, which comes through the gospel, not through doctrinal theories.[48]

Richardson noted that the big question in religion is not the one Pilate asked, "What is truth?," but rather "What is *the* truth?" He granted that while all truths are true, *all truths are not equally important.* "To expect entire uniformity of sentiment in the whole minutiae of Christian doctrine is utterly visionary and futile," he avowed. He identified the truth as "the simple gospel facts" and as the basis of unity. He claimed that Campbell's reformation is the only instance in all Protestantism that draws this important distinction.[49]

Quoting from the *Declaration and Address* to the effect that fellowship must be based upon gospel truth and not upon a proper understanding of all doctrinal matters, the doctor pointed to the vital distinction that had always characterized the Movement:

> Thus in the very beginning of this effort to reform religious society, the subject matter of a saving or essential faith was distinguished both from the uninspired deductions of human reason, and from those divine teachings which, however necessary to enable the believer to make proper advances in Christian knowledge, are by no means necessary to the Christian faith.[50]

The beloved physician, a familiar figure on horseback around Bethany with his top hat and long tails, thus emphasized the important distinctions that the Movement had discovered. But no distinction was more important than the one he drew between faith that is personal over against faith that is doctrinal. He affirmed that the faith that saves is faith in a Person, not in some system of doctrine. Doctrines are not the subject matter of faith, but a Person, the Lord Jesus Christ himself. Biblical faith begins with the acceptance of certain facts, but it goes on "to trust him as our Saviour, to walk with him as our teacher, our friend; to realize his gracious presence with us, and to discern his foot steps in the path we tread."[51]

Unlike most of the other leaders at that time, including Campbell, Richardson emphasized the role of the Holy Spirit in the life of the believer, which he described as "a fountain from within." To the sinner the Spirit is an outward witness to the truth through the gospel, while to the Christian it is a witness from within.[52]

It is evident, therefore, that by the 1850's the Movement was maturing in leadership, outreach, and message. It had reached out to several continents with some 2,000 churches and 200,000 members.[53] Its "Plea," as it came to be called had no uncertain sound, and it was being heard by the multitudes and responded to by many. Alexander Campbell was far and away its outstanding leader, and at this time it could be called his Movement, but this would soon change.

Absent From This Planet

The reformer lived on for another decade or so. Some have said that he was never the same after the occasion of his European tour, which included the death of the son of his old age. But the facts are that following that traumatic year of 1847 he traveled extensively under demanding circumstances, rebuilt a college destroyed by fire, and did some of his most exacting work as an editor and publisher. It was rather the Civil War, which desecrated his adopted country and threatened the peace of his church, that took its toll on Alexander Campbell.

In learning to live with death and tragedy, he found his answer for the untimely passing of Wycliffe. "How often do we see the sinner living to his three score years and ten, while many a pure and excellent strippling is cut down as the green and tender herb, in the very morning of his existence?," he asked shortly after his son's death. His answer was that there is "the strong probability" that God drafts pure and noble spirits from our little world to serve Him in a rapidly increasing ministry in other parts of the universe.[54]

As he grew older he spoke and wrote more about hope and heaven. "Heaven is not a mere state of repose," he ventured. "Its raptures and ecstacies of bliss are all activities of the soul, in wonder, love and praise expressed."[55] The last paragraph that he ever penned spoke of how the present material universe will be fully regenerated into new heavens and a new earth, which will bring new tenantries, new employment, and new joys. "There is a fullness of joy, a fullness of glory, and a fullness of blessedness, of which no living man, however enlightened, however enlarged, however gifted, ever formed or entertained one adequate conception," he wrote, wrapping it up after 43 years as an editor.[56]

Dr. Richardson says that the last time Campbell was at church he momentarily returned to his former glory as he gave his final discourse, on the glory of Christ as set forth in Ephesians 1. When he took to bed to get up no more (He was 60 years old before he ever spent a day in bed sick!), his wife assured him that the Savior would lead him peacefully across Jordan. He replied, "That he will, that he will!" When the day came for him to be "absent from this planet," as he described death, which was Sunday, March 4, 1866, the sun came pouring into his room, and once more he quoted his favorite passage, "The sun of righteousness shall rise with healing in its wings."

Besides the simple service at the Bethany church, where Robert Richardson spoke after the congregation sang, "We've here no abiding city," there were memorial services in various parts of the country. One was given by Joseph King, pastor of the First Christian Church in Allegheny City, Pa., who revealed in his discourse that when he visited Campbell on his deathbed and told him of an effort to unite the Baptists and the Disciples, that the old reformer wept for joy and said that that was one of the happiest days of his life.[57]

Another memorial was given by David S. Burnet, pastor of the Christian Church in Baltimore, who said, when he received the dispatch that Alexander Campbell was dead, "I cannot break the spell."[58]

He had to break it, for if Campbell's mantle was to fall on anyone, it would fall on David Staats Burnet. But not for long.

ENDNOTES

[1]"A Visit to Elder A. Campbell at Bethany," *Millennial Harbinger*, 1854, p. 642.

[2]"Progress of Reform," *Millennial Harbinger*, 1857, p. 598.

[3]"Letter From Brother R. Milligan," *Millennial Harbinger*, 1861, p. 294.

[4]Quoted in Dwight E. Stevenson, "Concepts of the New Testament Church," *The Revival of the Churches*, edited by W.B. Blakemore (St. Louis: Bethany Press, 1963), p. 50.

[5]Eliza Davies, *The Story of An Earnest Life*, Cincinnati, 1881, p, 532.

[6]Alexander Campbell, "Brother B. F. Perky," *Millennial Harbinger*, 1851, p. 715.

[7]Alexander Campbell, "Preface," *Millennial Harbinger*, 1862, p. 3.

[8]Alexander Campbell, "Notes On a Tour to Illinois," *Millennial Harbinger*, 1854, p. 44.

[9]Alexander Campbell, "Notes On a Tour in Iowa," *Millennial Harbinger*, 1858, p. 29.

[10]Quoted in Perry E. Gresham, *Campbell and the Colleges* (Nashville: Disciples of Christ Historical Society, 1973), p. 54.

[11]Alexander Campbell, "An Address on Education," *Millennial Harbinger*, 1856, p. 637.

[12]Alexander Campbell, "Schools and Education—No. 2," *Millennial Harbinger*, 1839, p. 279.

[13]John L. Morrison, *Alexander Campbell: Educating the Moral Person* (Joplin: College Press, 1991), p. 217.

[14]Robert Richardson, *Memoirs of Alexander Campbell*, Vol. 2 (Cincinnati: Standard, 1897), p. 591.

[15]*Ibid.*, p. 536.

[16]A political friend of Clay's remarked: "I should have thought Henry Clay could have made a much better judge of a horse race or good whiskey than a religious debate." See J.J. Haley, *Debates That Made History*, p. 249.

[17]Richardson, *Memoirs*, Vol. 2, p. 514.

[18]Alexander Campbell, *Campbell-Rice Debate*, Lexington, 1844, p. 612.

[19]J.J. Haley, *Debates That Made History* (St. Louis: Christian Board of Pub., 1920, reprint edition by College Press), p. 15.

[20]Bill J. Humble, *Campbell and Controversy* (Rosemead, CA: Old Paths Book

Club, 1952), p. 261.

[21]W.B. Blakemore, *The Discovery of the Church* (Nashville: Disciples of Christ Historical Society, 1966), pp. 20f.

[22]J.J. Haley, *Debates*, p. 236.

[23]*Ibid.*, p. 224.

[24]Richardson, *Memoirs*, Vol. 2, p. 511.

[25]*Campbell-Rice Debate*, pp. 516f.

[26]*Ibid.*, p. 519.

[27]*Ibid.*, p. 556.

[28]For a brilliant study on this see Joseph Belcastro, *The Relationship of Baptism to Church Membership* (St. Louis: Bethany Press, 1963).

[29]J.J. Haley, *Debates.*, p. 248.

[30]Thomas Chalmers, *Alexander Campbell's Tour in Scotland*, Louisville, 1892, p. 30.

[31]*Ibid.*, p. 37.

[32]*Ibid.*, p. 53.

[33]Roberts Tibbs Maxey, *Alexander Campbell and the Peculiar Institution* (El Paso, TX: Spanish American Evangelism, 1986). A compilation of Campbell's writings on slavery, including sections on "In Scotland" and "Letters From Prison."

[34]Thomas Chalmers, *Alexander Campbell's Tour of Scotland*, pp. 76f.

[35]See Eliza Davies, *The Story of An Earnest Life*, Cincinnati, 1881.

[36]*Ibid.*, p. 246.

[37]"Dr. Heman Humphrey's Letters, No. II," *Millennial Harbinger*, 1850, p. 305.

[38]A.S. Hayden, *History of Disciples on the Western Reserve*, pp. 371f.

[39]For the address on Capitol Hill, *Millennial Harbinger*, 1850, p. 406; for research on this event, C. Barry McCarty, "Alexander Campbell's Address to Congress," *Discipliana*, Vol. 39 (1979), p. 19f.; for Campbell's further reference to the event, *Millennial Harbinger*, 1850, p. 429.

[40]Alexander Campbell, "Preface," *Millennial Harbinger*, 1843, pp. 1-7.

[41]Alexander Campbell, "Union, Union, Union," *Millennial Harbinger*, 1862, pp. 49f.

[42]Alexander Campbell, "Synopsis of Reformation Principles and Objects," *Millennial Harbinger*, 1837, p. 530f.

[43]Cloyd Goodnight and Dwight E. Stevenson, *Home to Bethphage: A Biography of Robert Richardson* (St. Louis: Christian Board of Publication, 1949), p. 152.

[44]Alexander Campbell, "Principles and Objects Of the Reformation," *Millennial Harbinger*, 1853, p. 117.

[45]Robert Richardson, "Reformation No. 1," *Millennial Harbinger*, 1847, p. 279.

[46]*Ibid.*, p. 376.

[47]*Ibid.*, p. 509.

[48]Robert Richardson, "Reformation No. V," *Millennial Harbinger*, 1848, p. 32; "Reformation No. VI," p. 73; "Reformation No. VII," p. 253.

[49]Robert Richardson, "Reformation No. X," *Millennial Harbinger*, 1848, p. 620.

[50]Robert Richardson, "Reformation No. XI," *Millennial Harbinger*, 1848, 1848, p. 698.

[51]Robert Richardson, "Principles and Purposes of the Reformation," *Millennial Harbinger*, 1852, p. 606.

[52]*Ibid.*, p. 704.

[53]Campbell said these figures were "within the boundaries of our vision," while others gave larger numbers, *Millennial Harbinger*, 1850, p. 231.

[54]Alexander Campbell, "Mysteries of Providence," *Millennial Harbinger*, 1847, p. 709.

[55]Alexander Campbell, "Christianity Adapted to Man," *Millennial Harbinger*, 1854, p. 125.

[56]Alexander Campbell, "The Gospel," *Millennial Harbinger*, 1865, p. 517.

[57]Joseph King, "A Memorial Sermon on the Occasion of the Death of Alexander Campbell," *Millennial Harbinger*, 1866, p. 206.

[58]David S. Burnet, "A Memorial Discourse on the Occasion of the Death of President Alexander Campbell," *Millennial Harbinger*, 1866, p. 301.

11

HERETICS AND DEFECTORS
THE MOVEMENT SEEKS A NORM

What is expressly enjoined . . .

If words might be better understood by their antonyms and political parties by their mavericks, religious movements might be better interpreted by a study of their heretics and defectors. We call them heretics advisedly, for throughout the Movement's history heresy has defied definition. But there were those leaders who left or were forced out because they departed from an illusive "norm" which they helped to define by their deviancy. In other words, the occasional heretic helped the Movement to clarify what it believed and where to draw the line.

That the Movement's progress was not seriously affected by these deviations, and that there were no early major schisms, indicates a stability that is rare in reformation efforts. Fledgling movements are often decimated by internal strife and division.

These defectors were viewed as heretics more for their behavior than for their doctrine. The principle of "In opinions liberty" allowed for considerable latitude so long as one did not become pushy. From the outset the Movement bore patiently with almost any speculative view from the most opinionated man so long as it was held "incidentally," as one British leader put it, and not made the means of creating a sect.

If Thomas Campbell could admit to being a Calvinist and Aylett Raines a universalist without serious rupture, then the Movement had a high level of tolerance early on. If an unwritten rule emerged, it was something like, "Opinions and speculations are allowed, but don't be pushy about them." Raines, who was persuaded not to be pushy about his, afterwards wrote to Alexander Campbell that he was impressed that so few "disciples of the ancient gospel" depart from the faith, and that they abhorred apostasy more than those in other churches.[1]

Raines named the norm of the Movement in his reference to "the ancient gospel." Any departure from it was apostasy, not speculations sincerely held. Opinions could be held as private property, but it was considered heretical to impose them upon others, even if the opinions were true. This is why they held heresy to be more of a behavioral problem than a doctrinal one. It is why Thomas Campbell could remain a Calvinist and Raines a universalist and be accepted leaders. They did not misbehave in the opinions they held.

This liberal approach was pragmatically effective in that it encouraged one to forget his speculations and get on with what mattered most. It was the case with Raines, who went on to serve with excellence for 50 years in Ohio and Kentucky, and he helped to effect the union between the Stone and Campbell people. Along the way he assured Alexander Campbell that the prediction he had made about the fate of his opinions had come true, for "they have been slowly and imperceptibly erased from my mind."[2] But it did not always turn out that way.

Charismatic Sedition

The story of two other young preachers had unhappy endings. Walter S. Russell, highly respected for his culture and piety, graduated from Bethany in 1856. He immediately became president of Berean College in Jacksonville, Illinois and minister to the local Disciples church, which had been founded by Barton W. Stone. Still in his 20's, he began to teach speculative ideas about the Holy Spirit, becoming something of a "charismatic" in today's terminology. While he did not speak in tongues, he did believe the Holy Spirit exercises "special influence" in working miracles and saving the sinner, "without the intervention of secondary instrumentalists."

While this was a Disciples heresy in reference to the work of the Holy Spirit, it was not an unbearable speculation had not young Russell divided the church over it. Campbell saw him as teaching that "The Holy Spirit himself makes a special visit to the sinner and by an actual impact indelibly prints or writes the gospel upon his understanding, his conscience and his heart; and thus regenerates him by a special influence."

But it was Russell's behavior that led Campbell to rule, not unlike a bishop: "He is evidently now a schismatic, and, as such, cannot be esteemed and regarded as a brother in communion with us." Only two years earlier, after a visit with the young president of Berean College, Campbell had commended him as "admirably qualified for the responsible position he occupies," but that was before he had "turned aside into vain janglings." Campbell did not often say "He is not one of us," but he did in this case.[3]

If Russell was a problem to the Disciples, it was not for long. He died in Vicksburg three years later while caring for sick and wounded soldiers.[4]

The first "heresy trial" came in the late 1850's in the case of I.N. Carman, pastor of the Disciples church in Ashland, Ohio. The charge was that he put forth an uncertain sound in reference to the ministry of the Holy Spirit. The three judges, which included famed evangelists A.S. and William Hayden, reached a guilty verdict but refrained from passing a sentence. They ruled that his teaching was "speculative, schismatic, and unprofitable, and the agitation of them tends only to strife and division."

Another charge against Carmen was that he exchanged pulpits with other ministers in town without consulting with his elders. It is noteworthy that the judges did not fault him for fellowshipping other churches, but for discourtesy in not consulting with his church.

The most serious charge against him was that he conducted meetings in the courthouse, apart from his own church's services, calculated to promote his special interests. Here the judges rebuked him for heresy: "It was schismatical in its tendency, painfully discourteous and unkind toward the church, and destructive of the interests of the cause of Christ at large, and especially in Ashland."

As a result of the judges' conclusions the church made a public announcement that "Carman had voluntarily withdrawn from the church, and was no longer a member of our brotherhood." He quietly dropped out of the picture.[5]

These two cases led Robert Richardson, now an associate editor with Campbell, to comment upon the nature of heresy. He pointed out that to his certain knowledge many of the most devoted and able preachers in the Movement believed that in every real conversion there is a direct influence exerted by the Spirit upon the sinner's heart.

So this was not what made Russell and Carman heretics. It was rather that they imposed their views upon others to the point of division. The faithful preachers, Richardson notes, "had too much good sense and too much regard for the principles of the Reformation" to do that.[6] He could have added that he was one such preacher who believed such about the Spirit's ministry!

W.K. Pendleton, another of Campbell's associates, referred to the Russell and Carmen cases by a reference to the renowned George Campbell's position that error alone, however gross, is not heresy. It is rather malignity or perverseness of disposition, a behavioral problem rather than a doctrinal one. Pendleton pointed to Augustine as saying, "I may err, but I will not be a heretic." Heresy is thus "the tyranny of opinionism," the dogmatism that says you must accept my opinion, Pendleton concluded.[7]

If Russell and Carmen were lesser lights, there were some big time heretics, able leaders with substantial influence, who were seen as threats to the survival of the Movement.

Sidney Rigdon and Mormonism

"Every person who receives the book of Mormon is an apostate from
all that we ever professed." — *Alexander Campbell*

Sidney Rigdon did not read all of Thomas Campbell's letter to him on
February 4, 1831 before he hastily committed it to the flames.

Becoming a preacher within the Movement as early as 1821, Rigdon had
been a friend and a co-worker of both of the Campbells for almost a decade
and was admired among the Disciples for his unusual talents. But now he
was a "Mormonite," and was challenging the world to disprove the claims of
the Book of Mormon. Thomas Campbell wrote to him in response to that
challenge, but rather than accept it Rigdon cast the letter into the fire.

After remembering him as a courteous friend and a beloved fellow-
laborer in the gospel, Campbell greeted him as one who was now "the
professed disciple and public teacher of the infernal book of Mormon"
while he himself was still "a professed disciple and public teacher of the
supernal book of the Old and New Testaments of our Lord and Savior
Jesus Christ, which you now say is superseded by the book of Mormon."

In accepting his challenge, Campbell said he was prepared to prove the
Scriptures to be all-sufficient for salvation and Christian work, which
would be enough to disprove Mormonism and every other ism. Moreover,
he would expose the visions and claims of Mormonism as being no more
valid than those of the Shakers or any other pretentious sect. Inasmuch as
the Mormons were rebaptizing those already immersed, including Disciples, he included among his charges "That rebaptizing believers is making
void the law of Christ." Rigdon had no interest in debating his old friend.[8]

The influence of the Movement first touched Rigdon in 1821 when as a
Baptist minister in Ohio he read Alexander Campbell's debate with John
Walker. In company with Adamson Bentley, the most prominent Baptist
preacher in Ohio, he called upon Campbell in Bethany. In recounting the
occasion in 1848 Campbell revealed that the three of them talked all night
long! Campbell explained his views of the covenants, dispensations,
passovers and pentecosts, the law and the gospel, and especially the
ancient order of things. When Rigdon departed he remarked that if he had
taught one error from the pulpit he had taught a thousand.

It was Rigdon and Bentley who opened up Ohio and the Mahoning
Association to Campbell's influence. Campbell described Rigdon as "the
great orator of the Mahoning Association." The two men were so eager to
push forward with the principles of reformation that Campbell had to
caution them to restrain themselves lest they lose their influence with the
people.[9]

In 1822 Campbell encouraged Rigdon to accept a call from a Baptist church in Pittsburgh that was sympathetic with the reformation. In relating this, Richardson describes Rigdon as a man with more than ordinary ability as a speaker, possessing great fluency and "a lively fancy" that gave him great popularity as an orator. Campbell hoped in vain that Rigdon might be able to bring about a union between the Baptist church and the Movement's second church, next to Brush Run, in Pittsburgh, then presided over by Walter Scott.[10]

Rigdon next appears as Campbell's traveling companion to Washington, Kentucky for Campbell's debate with W.L. Maccalla. The Ohio was too low for steamboat navigation so the two men set out on horseback for the three hundred mile journey, which took them ten days. Sitting up together all night and riding together all day, the two men must have become well acquainted as well as very tired, and Rigdon must have been well schooled in reformation principles. It was Rigdon who transcribed the debate for publication.

In 1825 he returned to Ohio from Pittsburgh and the following two years he was a key speaker at the annual meetings of the Mahoning Association. As we have noted, the 1827 meeting was crucial in that it was the occasion when Walter Scott was selected to serve as an evangelist for the Association. If Rigdon had been selected instead, as he could well have been, there might never have been a Mormon church. This was the eve of the rise of Mormonism, and Rigdon would not have been around to give it its initial surge had he been given an assignment commensurate to his needs at the time.[11]

In his history of the Movement, Richardson gives an extended treatment of the rise of Mormonism, the origin of which he attributes not to Joseph Smith but to Sidney Rigdon. He traces the Mormons through Ohio, Missouri, and Illinois to their new home in Salt Lake City, and he observes that "by incredible industry and the marvelous power of communism" they created, as if by magic, a magnificent city in the midst of an arid waste sown with salt. He goes on to describe it as "the strange spectacle of a social, political and religious absolutism in the midst of a free republic, and of an open, legalized licentiousness in the bosom of a Christian nation."[12]

While Richardson too referred to Rigdon's oratorical gifts, he also described him as given to exuberant fancy and that he depended on superficial endowments for popularity and success. In private he was insolent, unreliable, ungovernable in his passions, and had a wayward temper. He was too ambitious for distinction and was jealous of the reputation of others. This is why he had not succeeded among the Disciples.

He caps off his profile of a heretic by observing that "Floating upon the tide of popular excitement," Rigdon was disposed "to catch at anything which, without demanding labor, might serve for his advancement, and was naturally led to seek in deception the success which he found denied to indolence."

Richardson adopted the Spaulding Manuscript theory of the origin of the Book of Mormon, which is that Rigdon obtained a copy of said manuscript while loitering in a printshop during his Pittsburgh days and revamped it into what eventually became the Book of Mormon. Writing in the style of biblical history, Spaulding for his own pleasure had created a fictional account of nations inhabiting Canaan before the time of Joshua, and how the lost ten tribes became the American Indians.

The theory is supported by the fact that Rigdon spent two months with Joseph Smith shortly before the book's appearance and by the testimonials of people who heard Spaulding read his manuscript, who testified to its similarity to the Book of Mormon. It is also supported by the fact that when the manuscript came up missing from the printshop, where Spaulding had deposited it for safe keeping, Rigdon was suspected of the theft.

Since 1914, when Charles Shook published his *True Origin of the Book of Mormon*, the theory has been generally held by non-Mormons that the new Mormon Bible owed its origin to the Spaulding manuscript. In a more recent study the theory is treated as a virtual fact and Rigdon is named as the founder of the Mormon Church and the one who appointed Joseph Smith as its prophet.[13]

The most impressive research, however, conducted by Fawn Brodie, a lifetime Mormon who was excommunicated for the book she published, dismisses the Spaulding-Rigdon theory as unsupportable. She concludes that it was Joseph Smith himself who wrote the Book of Mormon, which she describes as colorful frontier fiction. She traces Rigdon's life like a Scotland Yard detective and finds no place where he could have contrived the hoax.

While it has been generally assumed that Smith was too ignorant to have perpetuated such a fraud, Brodie not only concludes that he did, but points to Alexander Campbell as the first to give a responsible review of the new Bible. She notes that Campbell recognized without any question that Smith was the author. She says in effect that the author of the Book of Mormon was who Alexander Campbell said it was, Joseph Smith![14]

Under the caption "Sidney Rigdon," Campbell expressed both regret and surprise that his co-laborer had become a Mormon and had "renounced the ancient gospel." He was amazed that Rigdon had stated that he had been hypocritical as a Disciple. Referring to Rigdon's proclivity for signs and omens and the angelic visit that he eventually experienced,

Campbell observed: "He who sets out to find signs and omens will soon find enough of them. He that expects visits from angels will find them as abundant as he who in the age of witchcraft found a witch in every unseemly old woman."

But his attitude toward Rigdon was more matter-of-fact than vindictive. Those turning to the delusions of Mormonism reminded him of the saying of Jesus: "I have come in my Father's name, and you do not receive me: if another come in his own name him you will receive." He saw in the rise of Mormonism a need for his people to be better instructed in the foundations of their faith.[15]

Campbell reviewed the new Bible in his journal and then issued the review as a booklet for wider circulation. His judgments against it were both literary and biblical. He finds the Mormon prophets preaching "baptism unto repentance" and making Christians and forming churches hundreds of years before Christ. He points to the bizarre claim that three of the American prophets were never to die, and while they were seen four hundred years after Christ no one knows where they might now be, walking among us, *thousands* of years old! He notes that the angel Moroni preached that Jesus was "very Christ and very God," concluding that he somehow heard of the Arian controversy!

While naming Joseph Smith as the book's real author, Campbell finds him "as ignorant and as impudent a knave as ever wrote a book," and insists that he bases the entire book on a fallacy that makes God a liar. He refers to the doctrine of the priesthood, which is basic to Mormonism. He points out that the Scriptures make it clear that the priesthood in the Old Testament was given only to Aaron and the Levites, with an attending penalty of death upon anyone from any other tribe that would presume upon the priesthood. The Book of Mormon, however, establishes an entirely new priesthood upon the family of Joseph. The new Bible also impugned the land covenant that God gave to Israel and Judah in that it has God promising America to a pious Jew instead of the land of Canaan.[16]

While Campbell saw Brigham Young as responsible for Mormonism's eventual success, it was Rigdon that provided its initial survival. He was their only man with any influence at the outset, the only one with a church and a following. Until Rigdon entered the scene Joseph Smith had but six followers. It was Rigdon's Disciples church in Kirkland, Ohio that afforded Smith his first mass conversions. Seventeen of the members were rebaptized into the new religion, as was Rigdon himself. Rigdon's popularity in northern Ohio enabled him to reach other Disciples, especially in Hiram.

Mormon historians take note of the fact that many of their first converts were Disciples. But the number of defections was not great, due

261

THE STONE-CAMPBELL MOVEMENT

in part to the quick response of the Campbells.

When Thomas Campbell heard of the Disciples defections, he wintered in Mentor, Ohio and called house to house, warning against the damnable intrusion. And when Rigdon came through issuing his challenges in behalf of a new Bible, the old man, who had never conducted a debate in his life, was there to take him on.[17]

Rigdon was never formally excommunicated. In defecting to the Mormons the Disciples universally viewed him as apostate, and the doors were quickly shut against him in spite of his considerable influence.

The Mormon story, having its beginnings within the shadow of the Stone-Campbell Movement, reveals how soundly orthodox the Movement's leaders were. If it was their heresy, they made it their fight. Their response was the response that the church at large would eventually make against Mormonism. While Sidney Rigdon's new church was a cult, the Disciples church that he left was now a part of mainstream Protestant Christianity.

Some of the enemies of the Movement took advantage of its plight, judging the defections to Mormonism as the legitimate result of "Campbellism." To this Campbell had his reply: *Every person who receives the book of Mormon is an apostate from all that we ever professed.*

Dr. John Thomas and Reimmersion

"A mule is a fit and proper symbol for the character of Alexander Campbell."

The young English physician was in the home of Dr. Robert Richardson in Wellsburg, Virginia in 1833 when Alexander Campbell was pointed out to him, walking down the street toward the house. Having only recently been baptized into Christ for the remission of his sins by Walter Scott in Cincinnati, he had heard so much of Campbell as to be insatiably curious. He was expecting to see a man with clerical bearing, dressed in broadcloth, silk, and fine linen. But here came a man who looked the part of a farm hand, shabbily dressed in an old drab coat and a slouching white hat. While Campbell presented a rough exterior, the doctor soon realized that he had met a new friend, warm and pleasant. It was destined, however, to be an uneasy relationship.[18]

Dr. John Thomas, born in London in 1805, migrated to America at age 27. Quite materialistic at the time, he might not have been "searching for the truth" had it not been for a frightening storm at sea that led him to take the claims of religion more seriously. No sooner had he landed in New York and told friends of his intention to proceed to Cincinnati that he heard that the West was "very much infected with reformation."

After a tedious journey to Cincinnati in a day before there were any railroads, he chanced to be in the home of Major Daniel Gano, who was clerk of the U.S. Supreme Court. Gano embraced the views of the Movement as the result of presiding at the Campbell-Owen debate. He took his conversion so seriously that he forfeited the $500.00 he had bet on a horse in a forthcoming racing classic in Lexington.

Gano pressed the principles of the reformation upon the doctor, and took him to hear Walter Scott, who happened to be in the city at the time. Scott, as was his custom, laid the claims of Acts 2:38 upon him, stressing baptism for the remission of sins in his irresistible way, and before the night was over baptized him in the Miami Canal by the light of the moon. Thomas was to say later that this placed him in the "Campbellite" party at a time when he sought to avoid all partyism.

This brought him eventually to Wellsburg and Bethany where he first met Richardson and Campbell. As eloquent as he was educated, he impressed both Scott and Campbell as having the qualities of leadership that the Movement badly needed. Scott urged him to begin preaching at once, while Campbell advised that he should pursue his medical career while serving with some congregation. They both grossly underestimated the potential of Dr. John Thomas, who would one day have his own church, known as the Christadelphians, made up in part of ex-Campbellites, if he was to have his way.

He visited a full month with Campbell in Bethany, impressed by his 2,000 acres of rich pasture land and the 1,000 sheep that grazed there. But he noted that Campbell lived a simple life despite his opulence, and it was there at the Bethany Church of Christ that the doctor did his first preaching, at Campbell's insistence. The reformer, impressed by his talents and zeal, urged him to prepare himself for "general usefulness" through a study of the Scriptures, providing him directions as to how he should proceed. Campbell urged him not to be an editor, but a physician and a preacher.[19]

But there was something in the chemistry of the Movement that attracted printer's ink, for most all the leaders chose to be editors. Dr. Thomas was an editor within a year after his visit with Campbell, who observed with amazement that he "vaults right into the center of the Apocalypse" in his very first number!

A young editor like Thomas would launch his effort by circulating a prospectus in search of subscribers and by asking other editors to run notices of his proposed publication, as did Campbell, with appropriate commendation. The first number might run a thousand copies, as was the case with the doctor's *Apostolic Advocate*, with many of them circulating as samples. Many such papers would have only a few hundred subscribers and were short-lived. The doctor's paper lasted six years, which was above average, but he was to publish still others. He soon began to lose subscribers due to an odd kind of heresy.

Dr. Thomas promoted the idea that one must understand that baptism is for the remission of sins in order for it to be valid. He insisted that baptism entails "an intelligent faith on the part of the subject at the time of the immersion," and that he should see the baptismal water as dyed with the blood of Jesus.[20]

The target of this interpretation was the thousands of Baptists that had come into the Movement without being reimmersed, including many leading preachers. Thomas laid down the principle that "the terms of admission into the Baptist Church are not adequate to a reception into a Church of Christ," and proceeded to reimmerse all the Baptists that he could persuade.

A correspondent who signed her letter "Susan" informed Campbell of what the doctor was up to, of how he was reimmersing members of the Richmond, Virginia church where he then resided. She was no little disturbed, for she herself believed in Jesus, assuming that at that point she received remission of sins, after which she was buried with him in baptism.

Since the doctor's position made her an alien, she asked Campbell pointedly: "Have we any authority from the New Testament to be immersed because of our education, and could we now come to the water with any assurance that baptism would be to us what it was to the Pentecostian converts?"

Campbell's reply was unequivocal:

> To require of every such applicant a statement of his views of each and every fact and ordinance in the Christian Institution; or to command every such person, without examination, to nullify his former profession and to be baptized for the remission of his sins, is, indeed, to paganize all immersed persons, and to place the world, the whole world, Jew, Gentile, and Christian, just as it was on the day of Pentecost.[21]

In this context Campbell makes it clear that he did not believe that the true gospel first began with him or his Movement. "I thank God that his promise has not failed," he told the sister in Richmond, "that even at this present time there is an election – a remnant – and that this remnant did not commence either in 1827, 1823, or in 1809." The first date was the year that Scott "restored the gospel," the second the year Campbell began the *Christian Baptist*, while 1809 was the date of his father's *Declaration and Address*, which is the year usually given for the beginning of the Campbell movement.

He also answers her question as to who is a citizen of the kingdom of heaven. His answer could appropriately take its place alongside the now famous Lunenburg Letter, which answered a similar question as to who is a Christian, under similar circumstances and at about the same time in his life.

The Richmond Letter thus reads in part:

> And I am asked, Who is a citizen of the kingdom of heaven? I answer, Every one that believes in his heart that Jesus of Nazareth is the Messiah the Son of God, and publicly confesses his faith in his death for our sins, in his burial and resurrection, by an immersion into the name of the Father, the Son, and the Holy Spirit. Every such person is a constitutional citizen of Christ's kingdom.[22]

Richardson explains that it was the Baptists who originated the practice of reimmersion, having required it of some who had been baptized by the Reformers. He explains that Campbell always opposed the practice, however uninformed the person might have been at the time of his baptism with regard to the nature of the ordinance. He says Campbell insisted that reimmersion is never in order "except a consciousness on the part of the individual that at his first baptism he was destitute of faith in Christ."[23]

Campbell first treated the Thomas affair with silence, but as the doctor's influence grew and he persisted in rebaptizing all he could persuade, he felt compelled to act. It especially alarmed Campbell that Thomas urged the churches to reimmerse all Baptists who had joined them, which was contrary to what they had always practiced. The doctor also speculated on the state of the dead and the immortality of the soul.

Campbell finally conceded that "an important crisis has occurred in our community which calls for prompt and decisive measures." He proceeded to publish a twelve-page "Extra" to his monthly issue of *Millennial Harbinger* on the Thomas apostasy.[24]

The essay provides further insights into Campbell's view of the place of opinions and the nature of heresy. He allowed that Dr. Thomas could have held any or all these speculative views *as private property*, but he had no right to propound them with authority or impose them upon the consciences of others. "Liberty of speech and of the press is not with me licentious extravagance nor disregard for the opinions of others," he said.

He also insisted that the openness that he and his people stood for did not require them to support every restless demagogue who would be contentious over something, *anything*. It is in this essay that he makes the statement that "The spirit and soul of all reformation is free discussion," which is engraved under his likeness on the cenotaph in the garden of the Disciples of Christ Historical Society in Nashville.

"We say that it is abhorrent to the reformation for which we plead," he went on to say, "to propagate mere opinions and speculations; and that it is entirely off the ground we occupy to favor those who devote their tongues and pens to build up any theory ancient or modern, original or borrowed." This was Dr. Thomas' sin and this was heresy. One may speculate or opinionize "in passing" but not manufacture issues through dogmatizing.

Dr. Thomas had become to Campbell "an infallible dogmatist" who was out to form his own party, like Sidney Rigdon of Mormon memory. Campbell saw them both as exceedingly fond of new ideas and always boasting of originality, one arrogating to himself a new Bible and the other a new system of doctrine that challenges both Testaments. He saw Thomas as schismatic in charging that Baptists were immersed into the Antichrist and insisting that they must be reimmersed.

Thomas went on with what Campbell called his "untaught speculations" to include such ideas that man does not have an immortal soul and that the righteous will sleep in their graves till Jesus comes. Campbell challenged him with "Why not build a no-soul party?"[25]

There was, however, a place within the Movement for one as opinionated as Dr. John Thomas, provided he would temper his attitude and behavior. This is evident in the response made by David King, a leader of the Movement in England, who assured the doctor, when he made his appearance in that country in 1848, that the churches would be pleased to hear him "if he would proclaim the gospel, and not more than *incidentally* introduce his favourite topic."[26]

But it was too much to ask Dr. Thomas to hold his views "incidentally," for such men are persuaded that their conclusions are not mere opinions but the word of God. At the invitation of concerned brethren, he and Campbell discussed their differences for ten hours in Painesville, Va. in 1838. Campbell's only stipulation was that the proceedings not be published, lest it bring disrepute upon the cause.

The brethren pled with Campbell to settle the matter on the principles of forbearance and forgiveness, so as to save Thomas for the Movement, which he was willing to do. They asked Thomas to sign a resolution that he would cease any discussion of his speculative views "unless in his defense, when misrepresented."[27]

But it was not to be. The controversy went on for fifteen years. Campbell's writings alone in the controversy, which included two "Extras" of the *Millennial Harbinger*, would make a sizeable volume. His essay on "Life and Death," which covers 46 pages and never mentions the doctor by name, is not only an exposure of Thomas' speculations but a brilliant presentation of Campbell's view of the destiny of the soul.[28]

266

After a long, frustrating journey to England, where he was first accepted and then rejected by the leaders of the Movement, Dr. Thomas returned to America and was at last completely isolated from the Disciples. Even he was never excommunicated by a congregation. He died in 1871, leaving behind a tiny sect known as the Christadelphians, who hailed him, even on his tombstone, as the one who "made manifest the nature of the long-lost faith of the apostles."[29]

A fascinating by-product of the Campbell-Thomas controversy was the role played by phrenology, now regarded as a pseudo-science, which determined a person's character by the shape and protuberances of his skull. It was more than a fad in those days, for many people, including both Campbells, had implicit faith in its value. Campbell frequently referred in his writings to his confidence in phrenology, which is surprising.

We learn from one of Dr. Thomas' editorials, not from Campbell, that Mrs. Campbell persuaded her husband to have a "phrenograph" taken by a famous New York phrenologist, the results of which somehow fell into Thomas' hands, which was all he needed to expose Campbell for what he really was, a man as stubborn as a mule! The phrenologist's analysis of Campbell was accepted by his friends as both agreeable and accurate, one Disciple insisting that the phrenologist must have known Campbell intimately, which was not the case. Dr. Thomas provided his readers with a full account of the reading.

The phrenologist saw in the contours of Campbell's head that he was from a long-lived family, had a strong constitution, was very industrious, fond of both mental and physical exercise, worked long hours with ease, was seldom if ever sick, disposed to independency, anxious to excel, had a self-directing mind that leaned on no one, cared little for the opinions of men, had fully developed moral faculties, and his language was more forceful than flowery.

But the phrenograph also revealed what Dr. Thomas seemed to be looking for: that Campbell's conscientiousness was not strong enough to modify his ambition, and that firmness was the strongest trait in his character. Being a rationalist, said the reading, he had no faith unless it be given him by grace. While he enjoyed humor, his own jokes were neither witty nor amusing, but rather sarcastic. Moreover, he was emphatically a utilitarian, a matter-of-fact man in need of the warning influences of adhesiveness.

One can see that the phrenologist ventured into details that modern palmists and fortune tellers seek to avoid. Dr. Thomas assured his readers that the eminent phrenologist had stripped off the fictitious guise that popular credulity had hung around Mr. Campbell, exposing him for what he really was.

He took undue liberties with what the phrenologist actually said. "A mule is a fit and proper symbol of the man," he surmised from the text. It was ambition that placed Campbell the head of a sect, where he courts popular prejudice and ignorance, and his ambition is unmanly and undignified. Moreover, he is faithless and purely political in his friendships!

Selina Campbell, who was the one who ordered the phrenograph in the first place, almost certainly read it in a different light. She probably teased her husband over the phrenologist saying that he had great argumentative powers and a strong appetite!

Dr. Thomas, pleased to find phrenology on his side, proceeded to have his own phrenograph made by the same expert, which he also published. It should have settled the dispute between the two of them once for all, for the doctor found no fault with the phrenologist's summary: "the most prominent points in your character area: energy, perseverance, determination, independence, strength of intellect, moral courage, and vividness of imagination."[30]

Phrenology or not, one may conclude that Campbell pursued his adversaries with uncommon intensity, and he seemed to enjoy a good fight, perhaps because he always won. In the Thomas affair he seemed to indulge in overkill, cranking out reams of controversial material. Conscious that he might appear to be overdoing it, he explained that there were thousands of new converts in the Movement who might be misled by Thomas' speculations.

Campbell's zealous pursuit of heretics is consistent with Robert Richardson's assessment that Campbell put the Movement above everything else, even before his family and himself. His intense opposition toward these dissenters indicates how engrossed he was in the effort. Campbell seems to have feared anyone who might have influence enough to adversely affect the progress of his reformation. It is to his credit that the heretics were unable to draw away any substantial number of disciples. Dr. Thomas was a problem, but he had to leave empty handed.

Jesse B. Ferguson and Spiritualism

"The world is my church."

When Jesse B. Ferguson died in Nashville in 1870 at only 51 and as a virtual recluse, David Lipscomb described him as at one time the most popular preacher in the South.[31] A minister at only 19, he moved up fast in Disciples ranks. When only 27 he was in the pulpit of the largest and most influential congregation in Tennessee, the 500-member Church of Christ in Nashville, which was about half white and half black.

He had all the marks of being sound in the faith. He was a debater for the cause, and in one debate he converted his opponent, a Methodist, to the Christian Church. And what would make one sounder than to serve as an editor of *The Heretic Detector*? He also served as an editor with Tolbert Fanning and finally edited a journal of his own, *The Christian Magazine*. In his first report to Campbell's paper he urged brethren everywhere to avoid "foolish questions" and attend only to the Living Oracles.[32]

He was a speaker in demand among the churches and was highly regarded by leaders who were many years his senior, including Alexander Campbell. He was on the committee that set in motion the American Christian Missionary Society.

It was hardly predictable that he would become a heretic of such magnitude that Campbell would use more than one hundred pages of his journal exposing his "crude and undigested speculations" and branding him as an apostate who must retract his position if he is to have any standing among the churches.

Campbell considered the situation so serious that he called upon the Nashville congregation and the church cooperative that sponsored Ferguson's journal to repudiate him. Determined to ruin his influence, Campbell warned the entire brotherhood of "this leprous spot, this gangrene" down in Nashville. He published letters of repudiation from such leaders as John T. Johnson and Isaac Errett. One such letter from Samuel Church referred to Ferguson's "damnable heresy" and to "a maggot in his brain."[33] There was apparently no question in the mind of the leadership that the Movement had a first-rate heretic on its hands, sitting in high places. But it is a story with two sides, for young Ferguson was convinced that he was faithful to the principles of the Movement.

It is understandable that Ferguson was surprised by this impassioned response to what was being called his "Post-mortem Gospel." First, he had expressed his belief in a second chance after death in Fanning's *Christian Review* back in 1845, and it caused not even a ripple. Why should it cause such a storm seven years later? Second, he sincerely believed that the genius of the Movement was that everyone had a right to his opinions so long as he did not try to impose them upon others.

Since he had set it forth as an opinion, he considered it a violation of the principles of the reformation for him to be denounced as a heretic. "I have uttered and stated an opinion," he pointed out, *"that men who have not heard the gospel will hear it before they are condemned by it.* THIS IS THE SUBSTANCE OF THE WHOLE MATTER."[34]

Ferguson was to learn that what he had to say underwent more scrutiny the more influential he became. Once he became a popular preacher with a big church, and a widely-read editor, his unorthodox views could not so easily pass unnoticed by the likes of Alexander Campbell. We have seen that Aylett Raines was arraigned by his brethren in the Mahoning Association back in 1828 on similar charges, and that the Campbells saved him for the cause through brotherly solicitation. Had they treated Ferguson similarly, it might have saved the Movement one of its most tragic episodes.

In his study of this controversy Enos E. Dowling points to Campbell's inconsistency in this regard: "In 1853 Alexander Campbell was horrified at the thought of fellowshipping 'Universalists and Restorationists'; in 1828 he fought for the privilege." He added in reference to the Raines' case: "That which Raines feared might have happened to him under adverse treatment and criticism happened to Ferguson; for 'he made shipwreck of faith and a good conscience and became a castaway.'" Dowling asks the kind of question that history forces upon us: "Would a more generous course, a kindlier attitude, have saved Jesse Ferguson for a useful and continuing ministry in the Christian Church? We wonder."[35]

Ferguson's position on "The Spirits in Prison," as he entitled the essay in the April, 1852 *Christian Messenger,* may not have been as irresponsible as Campbell made it out to be. Surely one can be mistaken without being schismatic and speculative without being a heretic. True, if he had heeded his own wisdom, given as a very young man, and avoided "foolish questions," he would have spared himself and others a lot of grief.

But then again, does not freedom in Christ allow one to theorize on questions that hold promise of yielding truth, even if ambiguous? Ferguson thought so, admitting that his opinion was not the "usual" interpretation of 1 Pet. 3:18-20 and 4:1-6, but he was searching for truth. He has not been the only one to take these verses to mean that Jesus, while his body slept in the tomb, went "in the spirit" and preached to the dead, to those that did not obey God back in the days of Noah.

Ferguson reveals that he had read "most expositions of modern and ancient critics" and disagreed with them. He gave his readers his own translation of the passages and an exposition. He said he had held the views for eight years, but that he hesitated to express them except in private to a few personal friends, and he then spoke publicly only because several of his readers had asked for his views on those passages.

The most controversial part of his position was that those who die without Christ may yet gain a knowledge of him. This left him open to the charge of believing in a "second chance" theory and even Universalism. But this was hardly fair, for the essay recognized that some would be lost, but not for what was unavoidable on earth. As we have noted, he believed that men will first have to hear the gospel before they will be condemned for not believing it. He was supposing that some might reject the gospel even in death.[36]

Ferguson had begun his paper with the resolution to avoid all "party spirit and bickering," and he waited five years before he presented his theory to the public. He might have said no more about it had his initial essay been ignored, which had been the case with a similar article eight years before in another journal. Even when Campbell took it up with him and billed it as a "posthumous gospel," Ferguson sought to avoid any controversy, waiting several months before making any reply. But once it started, it became bitter.

Campbell would have been consistent with his views on opinionism had he ignored Ferguson's theory. "Let men think as they please on any matters of human opinion, and upon 'doctrines of religion,' provided only they hold *THE HEAD* Christ, and keep his commandments," he had said in the Rice debate. He went on to say, "I have learned, not only the theory, but the fact, that if you wish opinionism to cease or to subside, you must not call up and debate every thing that men think or say. You may debate anything into consequence, or you may, by a dignified silence, waste it into oblivion." He went on to say that "the Philosophy of letting them alone" had been effective in reducing some speculations into oblivion.[37]

GOOD POINT

While discussing another speculative subject, the millennium, he made his position on holding opinions crystal clear: "We do not ask them to give up their opinions. We ask them only not to impose them upon others." On what grounds, then, would he reject an opinionated brother? His answer: "If he will dogmatize and become a factionist, we reject him — not because of his opinions, but because of his attempting to make a faction, or to lord it over God's heritage."[38]

This is the ground upon which Campbell at last rejected Ferguson. His theories were far more than "mere speculation;" they were a denial of the gospel. As Campbell saw it, the young Nashville preacher's contention "places the vilest rebels on earth under a new dispensation of mercy after death, and opens the door out of hell to the vilest inmate that ever died." To give the sinner "a second chance" after death was to deny plain teaching of Scripture, Campbell insisted.[39]

Moreover, Ferguson's translation of 1 Pet. 3:19 interposed the term *now* so as to make it fit his theory — "he went and preached to the spirits *now* in prison," thus making it refer to the spirits that were *then* (at the time of Christ's death) in Hades. Campbell gave a persuasive argument to the effect that the "spirits in prison" were Noah's contemporaries, and that the eternal Word of God, Christ, preached to them through the Holy Spirit that was in Noah. But the *now* would change all that. Campbell saw this as an effort to compromise the sacrificial death of Christ.[40]

That at least one modern version, the *New American Standard*, has "the spirits *now* in prison," as did Ferguson, suggests that such a rendition is not necessarily diabolical. And Ferguson insisted that all his views were within the confines of reasonable differences, and that he certainly was not denying the essentials of the gospel.

If Campbell's opposition toward a fellow preacher and editor only half his age appears immoderate and unnecessary, especially in the light of his own proclaimed openness toward opinions, Ferguson's subsequent behavior vindicated him. He eventually turned to spiritualism and split the Nashville church. Once he tried to turn it into "A humanitarian Church," it took court action to reclaim it as a Church of Christ. Before the Disciples could take possession it was burned to the ground.

Ferguson admitted in a book he wrote on spiritualism that he had been communicating with the dead and conducting seances since 1849, well before his confrontation with Campbell. If Campbell had known this all along, which might have been the case since he had long acquaintance with the Nashville church, it explains his unrelenting pursuit of the young minister. He charged all along that Ferguson did not believe the gospel.

Ferguson, joined by his wife, did not only talk to the dead but received letters from them! When Campbell came to Nashville in 1855 to confront his antagonist face to face, Ferguson claimed to have received a letter from the late Dr. W.E. Channing, the famous Boston Unitarian, that contained a positive command *not* to attend any of Campbell's meetings. Campbell explained that his intention to debate Ferguson, who would presumably defend his theory with anyone, was thwarted by a ghost![41]

Campbell's first address in Nashville during this crisis was in the Methodist Episcopal Church, the largest church edifice in the state. The huge crowd was made up of many denominations and their ministers, including the Methodist bishop. His theme was *Faith, and not feeling nor imagination, is the Divinely constituted basis of all genuine Christian piety and humanity*, based on Hebrews 11. The public realized that the heresy that Campbell had come to oppose concerned all the churches of Nashville. Campbell afterwards addressed the Christian Church, which was the beginning of the end for Ferguson.

Ferguson tried preaching in a theater for awhile, but soon quit preaching altogether. He wandered here and there, dabbled in politics for awhile, and finally returned to Nashville, where he lived in seclusion until he died. Once the most popular man in town, he was no longer even recognized when he occasionally ventured forth.

As Campbell reflected upon what he called "The Fall of Jesse B. Ferguson," he penned one of his most majestic paragraphs ever, words that are still appropriate so long as the occult is a threat to the Christian faith:

> Why should any one, believingly immersed into Jesus Christ as the word, the oracle of the one only Living and True God — the great Teacher sent from God — the Prophet of prophets — "the Sun of Righteousness" — the *Light* of the world — the *Wisdom* of God, by whom, and for whom, all things were created and made — the *Alpha* and the *Omega* — the *First* and the *Last*; — I say why, in the name of reason, or in pretense of more light, consult the spirits of dead men, as if *more reliable, more credible, more enlightened, better informed* of the things spiritual, divine, eternal, than were Jesus the Messiah and the Twelve Apostles of the Lamb!![42]

The Ferguson apostasy forced the young Movement to draw a firm line somewhere on the limits of fellowship. Campbell himself refused to make immersion absolutely essential and the notion of "In opinions liberty" was generally applied rather broadly. But with Ferguson the line was clearly drawn.

When Campbell arrived in Nashville and learned that Ferguson was communing with familiar spirits, he no longer referred to him as a brother, even though he was still the minister at the Christian Church. Campbell did not mince words, branding anyone as "an infidel at heart" who seeks familiar spirits and practices the arts of necromancy.

There was widespread repudiation of Ferguson, who was the first distinct heretic who attempted to stay within the Movement. Campbell described the brotherhood's rejection of him as uniform, spontaneous and universal. As for Ferguson's spiritualism, "it implies a view of the remedial economy which, in its legitimate bearings, essentially entrenches not upon our faith alone, nor on that of all Protestant Christendom, but on the whole evangelical economy."[43]

Opinions, therefore, that threaten "the evangelical economy" do not fall within the category of "In opinions liberty." To Campbell they would not be mere opinions but denials of the gospel, and it is here that he draws the line of fellowship. Campbell is here the defender of the evangelical faith, apart from which people cannot be considered Christians.

The Ferguson case also points up the Movement's vulnerability to influential editors. "The Disciples of Christ do not have Bishops," it came to be repeated, "they have editors!" If Aylett Raines was not rejected in an earlier day with theories as potentially dangerous as Ferguson's, it is to be remembered that he was not an editor.

Campbell was *very* conscious of young Ferguson's popularity and influence as an editor, causing him to question the way men rise to positions of leadership within the Movement, especially as editors. "As a community we have been most reckless in choosing our editors, our scribes, our elders and our preachers," he complained, adding that "We have had a brood of periodicals the most voluntary and irresponsible that I have ever known." Referring to Ferguson's "flattering reputation" as an editor, he said: "The current reformation has had more to fear from its friends and advocates than from its enemies," which is reminiscent of Luther's prayer that he could take care of his enemies if only God would deliver him from his friends.

Campbell may have been indicting his own Movement more than he realized when he went on to refer to the "unlicensed press" as the most fearful omen in his horizon. This may have been a premonition of those debilitating decades yet to come in which "editor bishops" would be largely responsible for divisions within a Movement intended to unite.

"We have editors just out of the shell of conversion," he complained, "a youth converted this year, the next a *preacher*; the next a *scribe*, then an *editor*!!" He went on to say that there should be but three journals: one weekly, which would be for news and announcements; one monthly, which would be general; one quarterly for book reviews and extended studies.[44]

Is Campbell here calling for denominational structure that could both license and limit the *approved* publications? Or is he suggesting that any such reformation movement within the church can be sufficiently mature and disciplined as to impose such restrictions upon itself? If any such movement within the church is to be truly free, the things that bothered Campbell may be part of the price. After all, it has been the "unlicensed press" that has led all reformations, Campbell himself being in that number. Ferguson charged that Campbell's *Millennial Harbinger* served as an ecclesiastical court to try the faith and character of every man who does not mouth its shibboleths – that is, anyone who gains sufficient importance to command its notice! He granted that Campbell had the right to review and criticize anything he wrote, even if in a "magisterial and dogmatic" manner, but that he had no right to pass judgment upon his faith and character and to call for his confession.[45]

If Ferguson was saying that Campbell behaved like an editor bishop, he had some basis for the charge.

Among Ferguson's last words to his congregation were "My church is the world!" And that is the way he went. The people that he left behind chose not to follow him.

If the Movement survived these instances of "the tyranny of opinionism," to use one of Campbell's phrases, it was not for long, for its own leaders, particularly its editors, were soon to be embroiled in such controversy that it could not escape unscathed from schism and open division.

The factious spirit of these earlier heretics was present in the Movement almost from the outset, but there was "one who restrained," and until he be taken out of the way open division would not come. Alexander Campbell was hardly in his grave before the divisive spirit began to take its toll. The next three chapters, which take us through the nineteenth century and into the first decade of the twentieth, is a story of both triumph and tragedy. If it was a period of internal strife, it was also, oddly enough, the period of the Movement's greatest numerical growth.

The Movement had found its norm and had tested it in the vagaries of its heretics and defectors. The norm was stated by Thomas Campbell in the *Declaration and Address*: unity and fellowship were to be based upon "what is expressly enjoined by the authority of our Lord Jesus Christ and his apostles upon the New Testament Church, either in express terms or by approved precedent."

It was a norm with an uncertain future.

ENDNOTES

[1]"Progress of Reform," *Millennial Harbinger*, 1832, p. 513.

[2]W.C. Rogers, *Recollections of Men of Faith* (Rosemead, CA: Old Paths Book Club, 1960, orig. pub. 1889), p. 37.

[3]Alexander Campbell, "Philosophy, Dogmatism, Schism, No. 1," *Millennial Harbinger*, 1860, p. 13.

[4]Nathaniel S. Haynes, *History of the Disciples in Illinois* (Cincinnati: Standard, 1915), p. 62.

[5]"Affairs in Ashland, Ohio," *Millennial Harbinger*, 1860, p. 28.

[6]Robert Richardson, "Doubtful Disputations, No. 1," *Millennial Harbinger*, 1860, p. 25.

[7]W.K. Pendleton, "Walter S. Russell and I. N. Carman," *Millennial Harbinger*, 1860, p. 6.

[8]A.S. Hayden, *A History of the Disciples on the Western Reserve* (Cincinnati: Chase and Hall, 1875), p. 217.

[9]Alexander Campbell, "Anecdotes, Incidents, and Facts," *Millennial Harbinger*, 1848, p. 523.

[10]Robert Richardson, *Memoirs of Alexander Campbell*, Vol. 2, p. 47.

[11]*Ibid.*, pp. 71, 173.

[12]*Ibid.*, pp. 344f.

[13]George Arbaugh, *Revelation in Mormonism* (Chicago: University of Chicago Press, 1932).

[14]Fawn Brodie, *No Man Knows My History* (New York: Alfred A. Knopf, 1967).

[15]Alexander Campbell, "Sidney Rigdon," *Millennial Harbinger*, 1831, p. 100.

[16]Alexander Campbell, "Delusions," *Millennial Harbinger*, 1831, pp. 85-96.

[17]A.S. Hayden, *A History of the Disciples of Christ on the Western Reserve*, pp. 211f.

[18]Robert Roberts, *Dr. Thomas: His Life and Work*, Birmingham, England, 1925, p. 17.

[19]Alexander Campbell, "Extra, No. 1," *Millennial Harbinger*, 1837, p. 579.

[20]Robert Roberts, *Dr. Thomas: His Life and Work*, p. 34.

[21]Alexander Campbell, "Reply," *Millennial Harbinger*, 1835, p. 418.

[22]*Ibid.*, p. 419.

[23]Robert Richardson, *Memoirs of Alexander Campbell*, Vol. 2, p. 444.

[24]Alexander Campbell, "Extra, No. 1," *Millennial Harbinger*, 1837, pp. 577f.

[25]Alexander Campbell, "Dr. Thomas," *Millennial Harbinger*, 1844, p. 214.

[26]Robert Roberts, *Dr. Thomas: His Life and Work*, p. 211.

[27]Alexander Campbell, "A Narrative of My Last Interview with Dr. John Thomas," *Millennial Harbinger*, 1843, p. 226.

[28]Alexander Campbell, "Life and Death," *Millennial Harbinger*, 1844, pp. 529f.

[29]Robert Roberts, *Dr. Thomas: His Life and Work*, p. 253.

[30]*Ibid.*, p. 178f.

[31]David Lipscomb, "Death of Jesse B. Ferguson," *Gospel Advocate*, Vol. 12 (1870), pp. 881f.

[32]James R. Wilburn, *The Hazard of the Die* (Austin, TX: Sweet Co., 1969), p. 124.

[33]Alexander Campbell, "Elder Jesse B. Ferguson's Extra," *Millennial Harbinger*, 1853, p. 149; "The Spirits in Prison," *Millennial Harbinger*, 1852, p. 414.

[34]*Christian Magazine*, Vol. 5 (1852), p. 245; cf. Enos E. Dowling, *An Analysis and Index of the Christian Magazine, 1848-1853* (Lincoln, IL: Lincoln Bible Institute, 1958), p. 215.

[35]Enos E. Dowling, *Analysis*, pp. 229f.

[36]*Christian Magazine*, Vol. 5 (1852), p. 115; reprinted in *Millennial Harbinger*, 1852, pp. 313f.

[37]*Campbell-Rice Debate*, Lexington, 1844, p. 797.

[38]Alexander Campbell, "Millennium, No. II," *Millennial Harbinger*, 1830, p. 145.

[39]Alexander Campbell, "The Christian Magazine," *Millennial Harbinger*, 1852, p. 392.

[40]Alexander Campbell, "A New Discovery," *Millennial Harbinger*, 1852, p. 322.

[41]Alexander Campbell, "Our Visit to Nashville," *Millennial Harbinger*, 1855, pp. 96f.

[42]*Ibid.*, p. 98.

[43]Alexander Campbell, "Reasons For Not Immediately Responding To The Posi-

tions Of Elder Ferguson," *Millennial Harbinger*, 1852, p. 535.

[44]Alexander Campbell, "The Christian Magazine, No. 1," *Millennial Harbinger*, 1852, p. 390.

[45]"The Attack of the *Millennial Harbinger* on the Christian Magazine," *Millennial Harbinger*, 1852, pp. 499f.

A PORTRAIT GALLERY OF THE STONE-CAMPBELL MOVEMENT

Portraits included in the first edition
original artwork by Robert Ferro
and by Bruce Hill (N.B. Hardeman).

Additional portraits in the revised edition
from the collection of the
Disciples of Christ Historical Society.

Photograph of Reuel Lemmons from
Abilene Christian University.

Thomas Campbell (1763–1854)

If the movement has a "patron saint" it would be the father of Alexander Campbell, who gave it its most famous quotation, "The Church of Christ upon earth is essentially, intentionally, and constitutionally one." His *Declaration and Address*, a magna charta of Christian liberty, is the Movement's most famous document. He excellently combined the virtues that John Wesley said are rarely found together, piety and scholarship. The love of God was his constant theme.

Lith. of P.S.Duval, Philadª

Alexander Campbell (1788–1866)

Unlike other portraits which depict the reformer as stern and forbidding, this lithograph by P.S. Duval reveals him as the gracious, magnanimous person that he was. He was at this time in his prime, "the showcase of the Movement," and as well-known and widely traveled as anyone on the American frontier. That after nearly two centuries he remains the dominant figure in the Movement's history speaks to his unique leadership.

James A. Haldane (1768–1851)

Along with his brother Robert he conducted a reformatory effort in Scotland that influenced Thomas and Alexander Campbell. Disillusioned with the formalism of the state church of Scotland, he withdrew in 1799 and launched an evangelistic effort that swept over Scotland and Ireland. Greville Ewing, who conducted the Haldanes' seminary in Glasgow, had lasting influence on Alexander Campbell. Haldanean practices included congregational polity, immersion, and weekly communion.

Barton W. Stone (1772–1844)

Though his own movement had priority and he was 15 years older, he happily conceded the leadership of the Movement to Alexander Campbell, its rightful architect. An ecumenist of the first order, he called for "fire unity" rather than a book or water unity, which was a unity created by the Holy Spirit. He considered his role in the Stone-Campbell union (Lexington, 1832) "the noblest act of my life." His "Let Christian unity be our polar star" remains a challenge to the Movement.

Elias Smith (1769–1846)

Along with Abner Jones he formed a "Christian Church" from among the Baptists in New England in about 1801, totaling some 12 congregations. Robert Richardson referred to it as "the Eastern branch of the Christian Connection," the others being the Stone and O'Kelly movements. These were forerunners of the Campbell movement. He was editor of the first American religious newspaper, the *Herald of Gospel Liberty*, which published the recently discovered pamphlet by Rice Haggard.

Abner Jones (1772–1841)

Along with Elias Smith he formed a "Christian Church" from among the Baptists in New England in about 1801. Alexander Campbell corresponded with this group and concluded that they and he had little in common as reformers, even though both were immersionists. While there were several groups of "Christians" before Stone and Campbell, they were not dedicated to unity and a restoration of the ancient gospel as was the Stone-Campbell Movement.

Raccoon John Smith (1784–1868)

At the union of the Stone and Campbell movements he urged, "Let us be no longer Campbellites or Stoneites, New Lights or Old Lights, or any other kind of lights, but let us come to the Bible, and to the Bible alone, as the only book in the world that can give us all the Light we need." He rode horseback among the churches, along with John Rogers, to effect the union that took place in Lexington in 1832. His humor and repartee gave balance to a life smitten by tragedy.

Walter Scott (1796–1861)

"The voice of the Golden Oracle" so magnificently glorified Christ in his oratory that he once brought Alexander Campbell out of his seat praising God. His "new evangelism," popularized by the five-finger exercise of faith, repentance, baptism, remission of sins, and the Holy Spirit, led thousands to baptism. He died at the outbreak of the Civil War. The two events crushed Campbell, who wrote of Scott, "Next to my father my most cordial and indefatigable fellow-laborer in the origin and progress of the present Reformation."

Samuel Rogers (1789–1876)

Reared in poverty and ignorance, he braved the rigors of the frontier in a ministry spanning 60 years, adding 7,000 converts and scores of churches to the Movement. Suffering incredible hardship, he was but the second man to bear the "ancient gospel" into Missouri. Baptized under the preaching of Barton W. Stone, he traveled horseback across prairies where great cities now stand. This volume tells the story of how he was caught in a dreaded prairie fire and what he did about it.

Sidney Rigdon (1793-1876)

One of the most enigmatic leaders of the early days of the Movement, he was once a popular preacher on the Western Reserve and worked alongside Alexander Campbell. Once he defected to the Mormons, he was credited with producing the Book of Mormon, a theory Campbell never accepted, believing the new Bible to be the brainchild of the Mormon prophet, Joseph Smith. After leading a Mormon splinter group for a time, Rigdon died a disillusioned old man.

Emily H. Tubman (1794–1885)

While her wealthy husband was an Episcopalian, she became a Disciple in 1828. A widow for 50 years and a slaveholder, she was one of the greatest philanthropists in the Movement's history, generously supporting educational and missionary causes. She sent young men from the South to study at Bethany and supported a black evangelist for the state of Georgia. She often tendered Alexander Campbell aristocratic hospitality at her Augusta plantation.

John T. Johnson (1788–1856)

His brother a vice-president of the U.S. and himself a congressman, his political career seemed certain until Alexander Campbell urged him to preach the gospel. Known as "the evangelist of Kentucky," he baptized 12,500 during a 25-year ministry, and started many churches. He was largely responsible for the union of the Stone-Campbell movements in Lexington in 1832. Campbell identified the secret of his success as "evident sincerity, honesty, and great earnestness."

John Rogers (1800–1867)

Baptized by Barton W. Stone in 1818, he preached the gospel in Kentucky for 40 years. He rode with Raccoon John Smith among the churches, consolidating the union that took place in Lexington in 1832. He wrote of that union: "The importance of that Union has never been appreciated, and perhaps cannot be yet. It will be hereafter, when we who were the actors in it shall have passed away." Like many of the pioneers, he was also a hymnologist.

Robert Richardson (1806–1876)

As a physician riding horseback in top hat and tails, he was a common and welcomed sight in the village of Bethany. Coming from an aristocratic Episcopalian family, he became Alexander Campbell's alter ego and the Movement's most articulate spokesman. His *Memoirs of Alexander Campbell*, much of which he dictated while blind, is still in print and remains the richest resource of the Movement's history.

B.F. Hall (1803-1873)

Ordained by Barton W. Stone, he did much of his preaching in the South, winning Tolbert Fanning for the Lord. While reading Campbell's debate with Maccalla on baptism for remission of sins he found "the keystone of the arch" he had long sought. A dentist by profession, he largely supported himself as he bore the plea far and wide, and became one of the best proponents of "the new reformation." He was such as powerful, effective preacher that some of his contemporaries said it affected his pride.

John Thomas (1805-1871)

A gentle, scholarly physician, it was hardly predictable that he would be one of the Movement's early defectors. He caused considerable controversy over rebaptism, insisting that one must understand that it is for the remission of sins for it to be valid. Alexander Campbell tried for years to dissuade him. He founded the Christadelphian sect.

David S. Burnet (1808–1867)

Scion of a famous political family in Cincinnati and a gifted leader, he was the natural successor to Alexander Campbell, but he survived him only two years. Recent research of his life work has hardly removed his "undeserved obscurity." As the father of the Movement's cooperative efforts, he was largely responsible for the creation of the missionary society in 1849.

Tolbert Fanning (1810–1874)

As founder of the *Gospel Advocate* and Franklin College in Nashville, he was the prince of the church in the South during the first generation of the Movement. Disturbed by the northern church's attitude toward the South, he nonetheless worked for the peace of the Movement. When the Civil War forced him to close his journal, he wrote "Brethren, we are one and have but one work to perform." A pacifist, he suffered great privations during the war.

Benjamin Franklin (1812–1878)

Following the death of Alexander Campbell, he was one of the most popular preachers and his strongly conservative *American Christian Review* the most widely-read journal. His mantle fell on Daniel Sommer, who fathered the Church of Christ in the North. The "anti" position of the *Review* led to the founding of the more moderate *Christian Standard*, edited by Isaac Errett. While Franklin was anti-organ, he, like McGarvey, would not make it a test. "Declare non-fellowship with no one," he advised.

Pardee Butler (1816-1888)

While most of the pioneer preachers were only moderately anti-slavery, he was a radical abolitionist, which caused him to be "rafted" in "bloody Kansas." Highly respected for his personal life, he
left his mark upon the history of the church in Kansas and the West, organizing seven new churches.
But he had his problems with the newly organized missionary society that did not want to support his
work unless he preached the gospel and ignored the slavery issue. He would not compromise.

Jesse B. Ferguson (1819–1870)

As minister of the Church of Christ in Nashville, 1846-56, he was one of the most popular preachers in the Movement. As an editor and pastor he promoted spiritualism and necromancy, becoming one of the church's first heretics. When Alexander Campbell came to Nashville to confront him, he refused to see him, claiming that William Ellery Channing, a departed spirit, warned him to have nothing to do with Campbell. Campbell wrote of being thwarted by a ghost. Ferguson died a broken recluse.

Eliza Davies (1819-1888)

A native Scot, she heard Alexander Campbell when he visited Scotland in 1847. Persuaded to join his movement, she followed him to America and became a "ministering angel" to the Campbell family in a time of adversity. She eventually served as a missionary teacher in Australia, taking the Movement's plea for unity with her.

Moses E. Lard (1818–1880)

Known both for his piety and rigidity, he was the only man during the organ controversy that made it a test of fellowship. Learning to read after he was grown, he became a respected scholar, and Campbell called on him to write a book in response to the Movement's bitter critic, J.B. Jeter. An ardent premillennialist, he allowed for freedom of opinion in some areas. He mellowed in his later years, saying that if he had his life over he would preach the same gospel, but in a different spirit.

Isaac Errett (1820-1888)

He became the founding editor of the *Christian Standard* the same year Alexander Campbell died, 1866. Always a reconciler, he is credited with preserving the Movement's unity in the uneasy years following Campbell's passing. The most influential Disciple at the time of his death, he is also credited with saving the Movement from fundamentalism.

J.W. McGarvey (1829-1911)

"Little Mac" served the College of the Bible for 46 years as professor and president. Widely respected for his conservative scholarship, he took the offensive in the onset with Biblical criticism. While adamantly anti-organ (but *pro* society), he never made the issue a test of fellowship, though he left his home church in Lexington when the organ was introduced. He remained a Disciple when the Churches of Christ became a separate fellowship.

David Lipscomb (1831–1917)

The catalyst for the emergence of Churches of Christ in the South, he has come to be appreciated for his role in the Movement's history only in recent years. Earlier historians did not even mention him. At first resolved that he would never divide the church, he at last yielded and said, "Division must come," thus lending his influence to the Church of Christ as a separate church. He was editor of the *Gospel Advocate* for 46 years, and was more concerned for social issues than most early editors.

T.B. Larimore (1843–1929)

Next to David Lipscomb he was the most influential leader in the South during the first generation of the Church of Christ. Uniquely gifted as an evangelist, he baptized thousands and formed churches all across the South, and he conducted a popular school at Mars Hill, Alabama. Even though pressured to do so, he never made societies and the instrument a test of fellowship. So exemplary was his life that it was said that one could not be in his presence without being made better.

Daniel Sommer (1850–1940)

In prophesying, "In a few years the Church of Christ will be as separate from the Christian Church as the Christian Church is from the denominations," he signalled the Movement's first open split. In adding *Hallelujah!* he voiced the conservative conviction that "purity of doctrine" justifies division, which contravened the motto, "We are free to differ, but not to divide." So the Church of Christ can be dated from his *Address and Declaration* (Sand Creek, IL, 1889), a withdrawal document.

Archibald McLean (1850–1920)

"Wherever the beer keg can go, the Bible must go," he would say as he led the Movement into missionary activity. As secretary of the Foreign Christian Missionary Society, he was a pastor to each missionary, praying for him daily and writing him regularly. A bachelor, he gave his time and money to what he believed to be the greatest work on earth, preaching the gospel to all nations. He would carry the bags of his missionaries to the depot, insisting that he was honoring an ambassador!

N.B. Hardeman (1874–1965)

Regal in his bearing and always meticulously dressed, he was an educator, evangelist, debater, orator, and horseman, and one of the builders of the Church of Christ in the South. He helped to initiate one of the first breaks from the Christian Church, in Henderson, TN, where he built one of the most influential colleges associated with Churches of Christ, one that has educated thousands of ministers. He probably preached to more people than any other Church of Christ minister.

Peter Ainslie (1867–1934)

Insisting that division is "the scandal of Christianity," he became the Movement's prophet of ecumenicity. One of the founders of the Council of Churches and Faith and Order, he led the Disciples of Christ in forming the Council on Christian Unity, the first ecumenical office of any denomination. Pastor of Christian Temple in Baltimore (he eschewed *any* sectarian name), his constant theme was the equality of Christians.

P.H. Welshimer (1873-1957)

With the formula, "Let's disagree without being disagreeable," he sought to avoid division between Disciples of Christ and Christian Churches. Yet he chaired the committee that formed the North American Christian Convention and he was a catalyst in the creation of the Christian Church. His church in Canton, OH, was the Movement's largest at the time, with over 5,000 members. He was a great believer in the Sunday School as a means of evangelism.

Marshall Keeble (1878-1968)

A living legend among Churches of Christ, it would be difficult to find anyone in that church that has not heard of this renowned evangelist, and most of the older ones have heard him preach. He is the only black preacher within the Movement that ministered on a national basis. While some of the new generation of blacks thought of him as a "Tom," he takes his place as one of the great princes of the church, white or black. He ran Nashville Christian Institute on a pittance of support.

James DeForest Murch (1892–1973)

More than any other Christian Church leader, he initiated efforts for unity within the Movement, especially with Churches of Christ. The Murch-Witty unity meetings were pioneering efforts. Always a reconciler, he served on the Restudy Commission and led Christian Action, which was an effort for spiritual renewal among feuding brethren. He was also a historian of the movement, authoring *Christians Only*.

Winfred E. Garrison (1874–1969)

Living to be 94, he was an influential Disciple leader for two generations. Son of James H. Garrison, founding editor of *The Christian-Evangelist*, Winfred became an editor, author, poet, sculptor, educator, and historian. One of U. of Chicago's first PhD's, he had two careers as a professor, first at Chicago and then at Houston. A dean of Disciples historians, he was also an ecumenist, representing the Disciples at the World Council of Churches.

Frederick D. Kershner (1875–1953)

Founding dean of the Butler School of Religion (now Christian Theological Seminary) he exercised considerable influence as a popular professor and theologian. He also served as an editor and columnist of *The Christian-Evangelist*, where his facile pen moderately addressed every brotherhood issue. Along with P.H. Welshimer, he sought to avert an open split between the Disciples and Independents.

G.C. Brewer (1884-1956)

One of the most respected ministers in the Church of Christ during the first half of the 20th century, he served its largest churches. As an orator, writer, and critic, he greatly influenced his people, appearing on the prestigious ACC lectureship more than any other. He was often critical of his church, such as its exclusive use of the name, "Church of Christ." He was founding editor of *Voice of Freedom*. Both Harding and Abilene Christian conferred on him a doctoral degree.

Edwin R. Errett (1891-1944)

Editor of the influential *Christian Standard* from 1939-1944, he served on the continuing committee that formed the second North American Christian Convention, as well as on the Commission for Restudy, which sought to preserve the unity of the Movement. He took part in the World Council of Churches and the World Faith and Order Convention, though he resigned from the latter when he concluded it was too political. As an editor he insisted that issues troubling Disciples should not be made a test of fellowship.

W. Carl Ketcherside (1908–1989)

A protégé of Daniel Sommer and "a wing commander of a faction," as he put it, he repudiated his sectarian past when he invited Jesus into his heart while on a mission in Ireland. Insisting that "Wherever God has a child, I have a sister or brother," he moved freely among all three churches of the Movement, "agreeing with none but loving them all." He edited *Mission Messenger* for 37 years in which he pled for a unity based on love.

Reuel Lemmons (1912–1989)

Longtime editor of the *Firm Foundation*, he was the Isaac Errett among Churches of Christ in that he sought a middle ground of unity for the disparate persuasions. He was also helpful in unity efforts with Independent Christian Churches. In his latter years he was the founding editor of *Image*, a more open Churches of Christ journal, and a promoter of World Bible School. He was many years an elder of the Westover Hills Church of Christ in Austin, Texas.

Don DeWelt (1919–1991)

As founder and publisher of College Press he made available a veritable gold mine of Restoration reprints, including all 41 volumes of Alexander Campbell's *Millennial Harbinger* and Walter Scott's *The Evangelist*. Known as a "Doer," he also pioneered in unity efforts between Churches of Christ and Christian Churches, helping to create the Restoration Forums. He founded *One Body*, a journal calling for unity among all believers.

12

DAVID STAATS BURNET
THE MOVEMENT LEARNS TO COOPERATE

We are true catholics.

By 1841 the Movement had matured to the point that simple solutions were no longer effective. It could no longer function as a group of radically independent frontier churches. There were now upwards of 2,000 congregations representing most all the states and several foreign countries. Could such a farflung, growing community function without some semblance of organization?

It was in that year that Alexander Campbell began a new series of essays on church organization in which he made a surprising judgment: "Our organization and discipline are greatly defective, and essentially inadequate to the present condition and wants of society." He went on to correct a fallacy that had deterred the churches in their work, which was that all "a church founded upon the Bible," a cliche among Disciples, needs is a Bible.[1]

"A book is not sufficient to govern the church," he daringly concluded. Since no book ever governed any community, whether political or religious, one cannot simply hand a Bible to a congregation and leave it to its own devices, he observed. Laws are not self-enforcing, but are executed through duly authorized agents, he reasoned. This is why the Lord placed apostles, prophets, evangelists, and pastors in his church. Likewise, if these churches act in concert, if they cooperate in any way at all, it must be through some agency.

He wrote of the "necessity" of a more intimate organization and cooperation than then existed. After 28 installments on the subject he rested his case on five arguments: (1) We cannot distribute the Bible abroad without cooperation; (2) We can do but little in the great mission fields without cooperation; (3) We cannot improve the Christian ministry without cooperation; (4) We cannot check and remove the flood of imposture and fraud without cooperation; (5) We cannot have thorough cooperation without a more ample, extensive church organization.[2]

Early Cooperative Efforts

When the Mahoning Association dissolved itself back in 1830, leaving the nucleus of "Reformed Baptist" churches with no cooperative arrangement, it left Campbell asking in bewilderment if they were never going to meet again. He saw then the necessity for some kind of cooperation. He gave an example of what might be done when he encouraged the churches in his own area to assemble in Wheeling and form a "cooperation" of churches, the term that came generally to be accepted. He served as its president and Dr. Richardson as secretary.[3]

From the outset the founders of the Movement showed no disinclination toward cooperative structures. We have seen that Thomas Campbell wanted his first church at Brush Run to be a part of some denominational cooperative. After being turned down by the Presbyterians he was accepted by the Redstone Baptist Association. When Alexander Campbell started their next church in nearby Wellsburg, it promptly became a part of the Mahoning Baptist Association.

When the Stone-Campbell forces united in 1832, a miniature agency was created, with John T. Johnson as the secretary, to raise and disperse funds for the two evangelists who went out among the churches to consolidate the union. This was the forerunner of the Kentucky Christian Missionary Society, which began in 1849.[4]

By the 1830's the Movement was edging toward county, district, and state cooperatives. In Indiana four churches cooperated in sending out an evangelist as early as 1833, and by 1839 representatives from 115 churches gathered for their first state convention. Churches in eastern Virginia began cooperative meetings in the mid 1830's. A letter to Campbell reveals that by 1839 they had "messengers and communications" from 20-25 congregations.[5]

Some of Stone's Christian Churches and "Reformed" Baptists in Ohio had cooperative meetings years before the 1832 merger. There were statewide meetings as early as 1833. Even in Tennessee cooperative efforts began by 1842.[6]

While Campbell had some negative things to say about missionary societies and Sunday schools during his *Christian Baptist* days, it is evident that he favored both by the time his efforts began to flower in the 1830's. Word came to him from Ohio in 1835 that the churches in two counties had met with their "messengers," the term preferred by Campbell instead of delegates, for the purpose of raising funds and sending out evangelists. The correspondent revealed that some were opposed to what they were doing.

In response Campbell gave a resounding approval to such efforts. "There is too much squeamishness about the *manner* of cooperation," he said, and went on to identify a problem that was to stalk the Movement to this day: "Some are looking for a model similar to that which Moses gave for building the tabernacle." He complained that those who make such demands hold an impossible position, for they may as well demand a model in the Scriptures for translating the Bible or for even printing the Bible as to demand a model for churches cooperating.

The model, he argued, is that the first churches did all they could in sending out and supporting evangelists, and *they did it in the best manner they could.* Let us do likewise, he urged, rather than to spend our time talking about ways and means and doing nothing.[7]

He was later to write that he definitely wanted cooperative enterprises for the churches, and again complained of those who "do nothing right lest they should do something wrong." And he told of a letter he had received from Barton W. Stone, who was grieved that so many preachers were leaving the field for lack of support, due to a lack of cooperative effort of the churches.[8]

Campbell's Support of Agencies

When the missionary society became a divisive issue following the Civil War, effort was made to show that Campbell, now deceased, really opposed the societies, as he had as a young editor, and that his endorsements in later life were those of a man with declining mental powers who was unduly influenced by the younger men around him.

No less a leader than David Lipscomb, editor of the *Gospel Advocate* in the South, contended that after his journey to Europe in 1847, at which time he suffered imprisonment and the tragic death of his little boy, Campbell was never the same. Had he been his old self he would have opposed the national missionary society when it was organized only two years after his return from Europe, and would not have allowed himself to be elected its first president, the argument went.[9]

Lipscomb based this upon the report of Tolbert Fanning, who, when he visited Campbell in 1857, was shocked to find him so senile, an old man who had to be coached by his wife in order to carry on a conversation.[10] The Nashville editor also drew upon a statement coming from the Campbell family, as reported in the preface to Campbell's *Familiar Lectures on the Pentateuch*, to the effect that Campbell was never the same after the death of his son.[11] This is the only way that Lipscomb could account for Campbell's approval of missionary societies.

That Campbell was pro-society has continued to be an embarrassment to the anti-society wing of the Movement that has remained true to the tradition of David Lipscomb, which understandably prefers to have Alexander Campbell on its side. That he approved of the American Christian

Missionary Society, served as its first president for sixteen years, and helped to support it financially are facts that some of the anti-society persuasion have chosen to ignore.

But one of their respected historians, Earl Irvin West, has no problem accepting the facts. After both describing and rejecting the Lipscomb thesis, he concludes quite candidly: "We feel no particular embarrassment for taking this position. Campbell is not our authority. He was a great man, but withal, a man, with the same tendency to err as others. That he was wrong in advocating these organizations, we believe most deeply, but that he nevertheless was friendly to them is a fact against which we cannot argue."[12]

One is left to wonder why one of Lipscomb's stature would choose to resort to such a tactic. Perhaps it was because the advocates of the society were invoking the magic name of Alexander Campbell in its support, and Lipscomb felt constrained to temper the effect by information that he considered reliable. But the fact remains, as West points out, that Campbell was an advocate of such agencies long before the tragic year of 1847, and that he never criticized them. He served as an officer of such societies both at the local and national levels.

As for Fanning finding a worn-out old man who could not converse without being coached by his wife, we have to conclude that he either exaggerated what he saw or was not duly sensitive to the power of an over-solicitous wife. After all, Selina was known to hang a sign at the gate near her husband's study, instructing any callers to see her first!

The basic motivation for the cooperatives was evangelism. Along with the union of all believers, there was the passion to win souls and to blend them into congregations "built upon the Bible alone."

However much the Disciples needed to cooperate, it was a lesson they were slow to learn, with or without the encouragement of Alexander Campbell. Had it not been for David Staats Burnet the lesson might not have been learned until much later. W.T. Moore was right when he wrote in 1896 that "the present system of societies among the Disciples owes its origin to his efforts more than to those of any other man."[13]

David Staats Burnet

"The future is born of the past."

D.S. Burnet has been described by his only biographer as "an all but forgotten Disciple," and as one who deserves a place alongside the Campbells, Stone, and Scott as "the father of organized cooperative benevolence, missions and education among Disciples of Christ."[14]

He was more than that, for he achieved a number of "firsts," one being the formation of the first strictly Disciples of Christ church. He served as president of the first Disciples college. He was also the first resident pastor, edited the first Disciples journal, wrote the first book published cooperatively by the Disciples, and was president of the first cooperative organization, which was the American Christian Bible Society. He was often described as the most eloquent pulpit orator of his day.

Born in 1808 in Dayton, Ohio, he grew up amidst the splendor of wealth and political influence. Two of his uncles were U.S. Senators, and his father served six terms as mayor of Cincinnati. He clerked in his father's law office, but not for long, for he turned to religion at an early age and was soon known as "the boy preacher." He came to the Disciples through the Baptists. Disenchanted with creeds, he searched the Scriptures for the lowest common denominator for Christian fellowship. He came up with Rom. 10:9, 10, which became the central theme of his ministry, and when W.T. Moore put together *The Living Pulpit of the Christian Church* in 1869, his first selection was "The Good Confession" by D.S. Burnet.

Burnet saw that confession, "If thou shalt confess with thy mouth the Lord Jesus, and shalt believe in thine heart that God hath raised him from the dead, thou shalt be saved," as the only test of Christian fellowship. One is to be accepted on this basis only, apart from all the demands of party creeds, and should then request baptism by immersion.

He thought the good confession should be the heart of Disciples preaching, just as it was with the New Testament preachers. He saw the apostolic message as centered in a Person more than doctrine: "They preached a person, Jesus, made of a woman, as human as his mother, and having been declared to be the Son of God with power, as divine as his Father."[15]

While still hardly more than a boy preacher, he began his periodic travels with Alexander Campbell. In his funeral oration for Campbell he recalled when the two of them first crossed the Ohio together back in 1827. He told how Campbell pointed to a New Testament and said: "I have but one object in this world, and that is to know and enjoy the meaning of that book."[16]

Richardson reveals that Campbell and Burnet were still working together in 1853, when Campbell had a big meeting going in Mount Vernon, Ohio. The town did not have a large enough facility to accommodate the crowd, not even the railroad depot, which they finally resorted to, which held 3,000. When Campbell had to go elsewhere, Burnet continued the meeting, with many converts.[17]

When he was only 20 he became pastor of the Baptist church in Dayton, Ohio, where he had been born, and doubled its membership the first year. His views of reform transformed this church into the Central Church of Christ, or, as it was known after a few years, the Central Christian Church. In 1829 this church passed a resolution to reject all creeds and to withdraw from the Baptist association to which they belonged. A small dissenting group challenged the steps taken by court action, hoping to retain the property.

The Ohio Supreme Court finally settled the matter in favor of Burnet's followers. Since this was a year or so before the dissolution of the Mahoning Baptist Association, the Dayton congregation has the honor of being the first of the Baptist churches to become a Disciples church. If Burnet were given the place in history that Keith desires for him, then McAllister and Tucker, official historians for the Disciples of Christ, could date the beginning of that denomination from 1829, when a Baptist church in Dayton, Ohio officially became a Church of Christ, rather than in 1830 when a group of Baptist churches did the same thing in dissolving the Mahoning Baptist Association.[18]

Or the beginning date could go back still another year, to 1828, at which time Burnet and James Challen organized the Eighth and Walnut Streets Christian Church in Cincinnati. In this case the Baptist church, with whom the men had been working, did not change *en masse*, though it did furnish the nucleus for the new Christian Church. This church has often been called "the first church of the Disciples of Christ."[19] This assumes, of course, that the first Campbell churches, which were much earlier, were really "Reformed Baptist" churches and not yet of the new denomination, for they belonged to Baptist associations.

But this can be questioned, for Thomas Campbell is on record as having dismissed 32 members from his first church at Brush Run in 1823 "to constitute a church of Christ" at Wellsburg, Va., which was to be overseen by his son Alexander.[20] This reveals what he conceived his churches to be, and he did not think of them as Baptist churches, not even *reforming* Baptist churches just because they were affiliated with Baptist associations.

This being the case the Disciples of Christ, Christian Churches, or Churches of Christ should be dated from 1811, the year the Brush Run church was organized, for this church soon had all the characteristics of a Disciples church. And this is to refer only to the Campbell movement. As we have noted in previous chapters, still earlier dates must be considered in the light of the Stone and O'Kelly movements.

But Keith's point that D.S. Burnet deserves a place as "a founding father" is nonetheless well made. Influenced as he was by Campbell, he turned a Baptist church into a Christian Church and started still another Christian Church from scratch, and so named them, at least a year before the Mahoning Baptist churches did something similar. This alone should spare him the "undeserved obscurity" which concerns his biographer.

As if it were not enough to have senators, mayors, and judges in his family, Burnet married a general's daughter, who became important in her own right in the Movement's history. She became co-founder, along with Mrs. James Barclay, wife of the missionary to Jerusalem, of the first organized women's missionary work. Mary Burnet also helped her husband in publishing the *Evangelical Enquirer*, 1830-31, which is considered the first Disciples publication. Again this regards papers by Stone and Campbell, as prefatory to the Disciples era.

Burnet went on to publish at least four other journals, one with John T. Johnson as a co-editor and another with Elder Benjamin Franklin. He also edited the 50-volume set of the *Sunday School Library*, which consisted of 32-page booklets ideal for serious study. He published *Jerusalem Mission*, which told of the Disciples' first missionary venture, and edited a one-volume edition of the *Christian Baptist*, which he considered Campbell's best work.

First Organized Effort: A Bible Society

While Burnet was aware all along of the need for organized effort, he got his chance to act when Campbell began to write along this line in the early 1840's. Burnet wanted a publication agency that would distribute Bibles, tracts, and books, as well as a missionary society for the purpose of evangelism at home and abroad. He was sensitive to the criticism that God's power is not in societies but in the gospel, and he agreed. While societies are not the generators of God's power, they can be the distributors of it, he insisted, and they can insure the efficiency and success of the means that God has given.[21]

While he had Campbell on his side in theory, he was to have difficulty when it came to putting it into practice. Even though Campbell had complained that "We can do comparatively nothing in distributing the Bible abroad without cooperation," he was critical when Burnet organized the American Christian Bible Society.

Realizing that his beginning had to be humble, Burnet started the Bible society through the cooperation of four Cincinnati churches. He laid the society before the Movement at large in "An Address to the Churches of God in the United States, and to our fellow-citizens generally, in behalf

285

of the American Christian Bible Society, organized in Cincinnati, January 27, 1845," which appeared in Campbell's *Millennial Harbinger*. It deserves a place among the more significant documents of the Movement.

"We desire to put into the hands of every human being the Bible, without note or comment," he said, "that he may read in his own tongue the wonderful doings of God." He went on to lay down the challenge: "The world expects it, we expect it of each other, and our God expects it of us all." He concluded with a reminder that the church is the light of the world and is to sound forth the word of the Lord. He also observed that the church, having no light of its own, must reflect the light of God's holy word.[22]

It was the first time in the Movement's history that it had been called upon to accept and support an organized agency. Burnet hoped to gain national acceptance for a society started locally. There was hardly any other way to do it.

Campbell's criticism was that it was improper for any institution to be set up without in some way getting the approval of the whole brotherhood, and insisted that "This is always essential to its claims upon them." This left him open for Burnet's incisive response: "Was there a convention of the churches to establish Bethany College, the claims of which must now be heard, and until they are the Society must die in despair? The Society, composed of some hundreds, cannot ask aid of their brethren; but Bethany College, called into being by one brother, may."[23]

Campbell replied that he had not named his college the *American* Christian College, and that if the Cincinnati folk had named their venture the *Cincinnati* Bible Society that he would have had no objections, which must have appeared as rather lame to Burnet. But Campbell had other objections, which may have been the real ones. The colleges, even if started by one man, were languishing for support, and there is not now enough for any other agency. Besides, the Baptists already had an effective Bible society and another one was not needed. Burnet *could* have replied that the Baptists also had effective colleges when Campbell started his!

This exchange reveals the beginning of a leadership crisis, not only between Campbell and Burnet but between Bethany and Cincinnati. While the two men were the best of friends, they were becoming rivals in the leadership of the Movement. Henry K. Shaw, the Ohio Disciples historian, tells how a solicitor of Bethany College revealed that the real reason why "the Bishop" opposed the American Christian Bible Society was that he feared that Cincinnati would become the Jerusalem of the Reformation instead of Bethany.[24]

Noel Keith finds support for this kind of tension in Campbell's absence from Cincinnati when the American Christian Missionary Society was organized. At the time Campbell gave his blessings to it and excused his absence on the grounds of impairment of health. But Keith finds evidence that there was more to it than that, that Campbell felt that Burnet's efforts were a slight to his own, and so he refused to attend.[25]

Be this as it may, it is to Campbell's credit that in time he supported Burnet's Bible agency not only in word but in deed. He consigned the profits of the sale of the *Campbell-Rice Debate* to the society and not to Bethany College![26]

Formation of a National Convention

Shortly after organizing the Bible society in 1845, the Cincinnati churches, led by D.S. Burnet, also formed a Sunday School and Tract Society. To Burnet these were means of applying the power of the Movement's newly-discovered truths, but they were not enough. A cooperative center was needed from which people with various talents could be sent forth to share the Disciples plea with the world. He wanted therefore a *general* convention that would have the capacity to do many things, made up of representatives from all the churches.

Burnet and Campbell both believed that a cooperative agency, involving a commitment from all the churches, could be both efficient and scriptural without infringing upon the independency of any congregation. They believed that radical independency is foreign to the New Testament, that churches are obligated to pool their resources and do in concert what they could not do separately. Messengers or delegates must be duly authorized to represent their congregations and not be self-appointed.

When Campbell began his series on church organization in 1843, there was much discussion on how the churches might organize. Campbell himself chaired a gathering in Steubenville, Ohio on the subject, and in his journal he asked for suggestions.

During the Rice debate that same year there was an *ad hoc* gathering of 67 people in the basement of the Church of Christ in Lexington to discuss the prospects of some kind of national meeting. Though Campbell was not present, there were such notables as L.L. Pinkerton, John T. Johnson, Raccoon John Smith, Jacob Creath, Sr., and D.S. Burnet. While nothing came of the meeting, it shows that the Disciples were feeling their way toward some kind of national agency.

It was Campbell who finally called for a general convention, naming both the place (Cincinnati) and the time (November, 1849), but it might never have been but for the work already done by Burnet's earlier societies. It was in fact the annual meeting of the Bible Society that final-ized plans for the Convention.

Campbell had already in a previous announcement promised the brethren that he would be present at such a Convention, whether in Cincinnati or elsewhere, and he was vigorously supportive of the proposal. He deemed it absolutely essential to the future of the work. He was careful to urge that every church, or at least each district, have a duly selected messenger present, and that it not be a convention of publishers and editors.[27]

The Convention held promise of being the most significant gathering in the history of the Movement. Enthusiasm for it spilled forth from all the papers. One correspondent pointed out that its success would be assured if the leading brethren were there, and he named some of them: Campbell, Shannon, Fanning, Fall, Pinkerton, Kendrick, Hall, Mathes, Franklin, Howard, Ferguson. "We all seem to see the necessity of such a meeting," he added.[28]

It was incongruous for Campbell to be absent, and one would suppose that only illness could keep him away, which is the reason he gave. He sent W.K. Pendleton, who was twice his son-in-law and a professor at Bethany, in his stead. It was he who is reported to have revealed, years after Camp-bell's death, that it was his feelings toward Burnet that kept him away, and that he would accept the presidency of the Convention only if Burnet's publication society were dissolved.[29]

He was elected president in his absence, and D.S. Burnet, who was vice-president, presided over the Convention in his place. When Pendleton returned with his report of what happened, the old reformer seemed delighted: "Our expectations from the Convention have more than been realized. We are much pleased with the result, and regard it as a very happy pledge of good things to come."[30]

American Christian Missionary Society

Campbell and Burnet got more than they asked for, a missionary soci-ety as well as a convention. When the 156 messengers from about 100 churches gathered for the first Convention in 1849, they organized a missionary society. To put it another way, what was intended to be only a general convention became a missionary society, having the same officers.

John T. Johnson, whom we have found to be a man of action, placed a resolution before the Convention that "a missionary society, as a means to concentrate and dispense the wealth and benevolence of the brethren of this reformation, in an effort to convert the world, is both scriptural and expedient." He further resolved that a committee be appointed to prepare a constitution for said society. The society soon became a reality and its constitution adopted.

The constitution made membership a matter of money, allowing delegates to become life members for $20.00 and life directors for $100.00. The response was immediate and enthusiastic. While the society was destined to have a stormy future, it was hardly predictable at that time that it would ever become a divisive issue. It not only emerged out of the will of the people, but it had the support of virtually all of the leaders.

After all, its two top executives were Alexander Campbell and D. S. Burnet. Its vice-presidents included Walter Scott, John T. Johnson, Tolbert Fanning, and W.K. Pendleton. Managers included J.B. Ferguson, Elijah Goodwin, T.J. Melish, and P.S. Fall.[31] Burnet could speak of the society as a monument to the devotion and sacrifices of the pioneers since those men were a vital part of its makeup.

At the outset there was but minimal objection to the society. Even the staunch conservative Benjamin Franklin was an enthusiastic supporter, though he later turned against it, as did Tolbert Fanning, as we have seen. Jacob Creath, Sr. was almost alone among the leaders who opposed the society in the beginning, and but for his opposition there might have been a missionary society as early as 1843.[32]

Burnet served as the society's first corresponding secretary. He received calls for missionaries "from Boston to Texas" that he could not fill for lack of both funds and personnel. He went out among the churches raising funds for the society. He could hardly have believed that the society, which he saw as a uniting force, would one day divide the Movement. It is just as well that he did not live to see it.

The society's first work was to send Dr. James T. Barclay and his family to Jerusalem, but it was destined to be an abortive effort. He returned home after a few years with little to show for his efforts, finding the populace hardened to the gospel and some who were willing to "sell themselves to the highest bidder in the ecclesiastical market," as Burnet described them. But Barclay's mission fired the churches with missionary zeal, and it enabled the Disciples to publish their first book as an organized effort, *Jerusalem Mission*, prepared by Burnet.

The society's next mission was to send J.O. Beardslee to Jamaica, which also brought only modest results. Alexander Cross was sent to Liberia, and this also was soon aborted due to his death in the field.

These three missions serve to show how the slavery issue among Disciples was a matter of "In opinions, liberty," even in the years just before the Civil War. Barclay, a Virginian, owned slaves when he served as a missionary, while Beardslee was an abolitionist. Cross was a slave that the society bought, freed, and educated. These three missions were all that the society attempted in foreign lands. The inactivity that followed eventually led to the Christian Women's Board of Missions in 1874 and the Foreign Christian Missionary Society in 1875, which were more successful.

The evidence indicates that all of Burnet's enterprises were pursued for the good of the Movement, and that he was not self-serving. Yet his efforts were only moderately successful, if not failures. The Bible society, which was dearest to his heart, floundered from lack of support and was finally dissolved by the missionary society, largely because of opposition from Bethany. The publication society, which issued books, tracts and a Sunday School library, was also unable to survive, partly because it was seen as a challenge to the Bethany enterprises. Even the American Bible Union, which he launched as an interdenominational effort to provide a fresh translation of the Scriptures for the American church, came upon hard times, and again it was because of bad press from Bethany, this time in the person of W.K. Pendleton, writing in the *Millennial Harbinger*.

The exchanges between Burnet and Pendleton became so serious that Campbell had to intervene, and the two men finally signed statements not to air their differences publicly. This was after Pendleton had accused the Cincinnati agencies of misappropriating funds, which was unfounded. Campbell even takes Burnet to task for allowing his name to appear on a program sponsored by the Masons, and Burnet had to explain that his name was used without his permission.[33]

Burnet's biographer refers to the "teeming rivalry" between Cincinnati and Bethany, and he accounts for Burnet's failures on the grounds that "the Bethany leader had signaled thumbs down." He sardonically adds: "It was not long before both Bible and Publication Societies were out of existence. Only the Missionary Society remained, and Alexander Campbell was president of it."[34]

But some men's failures are more significant than the successes of others. D.S. Burnet taught the Disciples the power of organized effort, and he showed them that they did not have to be a multiplicity of separated entities, disjoined by an extreme congregationalism. With Campbell's help he taught them that they were obligated to do some things that they could do only together. Whatever virtues organized efforts came to have among Disciples, the debt to Burnet was substantial.

W.T. Moore, who knew him well, remembered his marvelous power in the pulpit, estimating that his ability to control an audience was unsurpassed by any preacher in the ranks of the Disciples. He tells how the business men in Paris, Missouri closed their shops each day at the appointed hour so that the people could hear Burnet preach.[35]

Burnet was a true ecumenist. "We are true Catholics," he would say, "and are laboring to restore the true Catholic Church of God, by restoring the true and primitive grounds of faith and fellowship." As Campbell often asserted, Burnet told his hearers that the Disciples hold no sentiment, adopt no formula, observe no ordinances, and practice no duties that are not agreed to by all evangelical denominations.[36]

He loved Alexander Campbell to the end. He barely lived long enough to deliver his memorial sermon in Bethany in 1866, dying himself the following year at only 59. In his eulogy of Campbell he told of that night in Richmond, Virginia in 1833 when the two of them shared the same pillow, only to be awakened to see "the heavens falling." The owners and their slaves were in the streets watching the grandest sight since the deluge, a great storm of meteors filling the heavens. He told how Campbell "stood tranquil" as he witnessed the grand display, finally giving his explanation of the phenomenon.

He was sure that Campbell could have won laurels in any field, and he thought the secret of his success was his familiarity with the Bible. He may have had more in mind than met the ear when he assured the audience that the Campbell of the last fifteen years did not compare with the earlier Campbell.

At last he challenged the students by telling them how Lyman Beecher once asked Campbell how he managed to know so much. Campbell replied, "By studying sixteen hours per day." Then he said to them, "The future is born of the past. Follow the light of this brilliant example till you accomplish a similar glorious destiny!"[37]

The future is born of the past. So spoke David Staats Burnet, the obscure pioneer of the Movement who served the future by being a catalyst for change in the present.

The imperative for organized effort which Burnet sought to bequeath to the Movement has had difficulty in taking hold, for two wings of the Movement have consistently remained anti-organization. In a recent address at the North American Christian Convention, Henry E. Webb observed that both the Independent Christian Churches and Churches of Christ have paid a dear price for their rejection of organized work. The price has included not only ineffective and overlapping missionary efforts but also the creation of a haven for irresponsible and unscrupulous independent missionaries. The problem is traceable, Webb asserted, to the same mentality that plagued Burnet's effort: Organization is wrong because it cannot be found in the New Testament.[38]

The Disciples of Christ, the original wing of the Movement, have had no problem organizing, even to the point of a "proliferation of agencies," as Mark G. Toulouse puts it. It took them more than a hundred years to create the kind of delegate model that Campbell and Burnet thought necessary. Toulouse notes that from 1849 to 1967 the Disciples had an impressive record of cooperative endeavors, but they were all the work of an "association of interested individuals." Even when in 1967 they restructured themselves into a delegate model that could speak officially for the whole church, the question of authority was not completely resolved, Toulouse concedes.[39]

An oddity in all this is the apparent corollary between accepting denominational status and organized church work. The Independent Christian Churches and Churches of Christ are as adamant about not being a denomination as they are anti-organization. They choose to prostitute such biblical terms as brotherhood and fellowship ("Our brotherhood," etc.) rather than to admit to being a denomination, as did Alexander Campbell.

The Disciples of Christ also shunned being a denomination (They were "The Brotherhood," as Toulouse notes) until they restructured themselves into an official denomination. As their perception of denominational status grew so did the effectiveness of their organized work.

It was the same with Burnet and especially with Campbell. Early on Campbell was radically independent, opposing organized agencies. It was only when he could admit that he had created another denomination that he began to call for organized work and a delegate convention.

The Movement in Canada

"We have been a voice crying in the wilderness."

This is as good a place as any to point out that the Movement started in Canada as early, or almost as early, as it did in the United States, and from independent sources.

The heirs of the Movement in the United States today are prone to overlook the history of their counterparts to the north as not all that significant. They are to be informed that the basic history of the Canadian movement, *The Disciples of Christ in Canada Since 1830* (Toronto, 1949), by Reuben Butchart, with its 700 pages is longer than most American histories and is filled with exciting stories of how the work began and grew, with only minimal contact with the American movement.

The Canadians have their own heroes and pioneers, many of whom never heard of the Campbells or Stone or Scott or Burnet, and they have had their own publications, institutions, and cooperative enterprises. Butchart, even in his preface, emphasizes this independence. Comparing

Canadian and "American" origins, and he prefers to put that term in quotes since Canadians are also Americans, he says: "Disciple history, written in the U.S.A., has exhibited mostly the 'American' origins . . Canada has other and earlier sources as well."

In fact, David Oliphant, Jr., one of the second generation Canadian pioneers, tells how when he graduated from one of Bethany's first classes, Thomas Campbell made him a gift of a published *Address*, explaining that if he had come upon it as a young man it would have spared him forty years of study. It was written by John McKellar of Scotland, who began a reformation in his native land some fourteen years earlier than Thomas Campbell began his in this country.

When McKeller migrated to Canada in 1818 he brought with him ideas very similar to those of the Campbells. He soon joined forces with David Oliphant, Sr. and James Black, also from Scotland. They had more churches more quickly than their American counterparts, who were slow getting started.

McKeller, Oliphant, and Black, pioneers in Ontario, were Scottish Baptists, as the Scots would call them, though they claimed to be simply believers or disciples. The Scotttish Baptists, who broke from the state church of Scotland, had a chapel in Glasgow as early as 1769, and their practice of immersion was at that time viewed with such scorn that some of their leaders were forced to leave the city.

In Ontario these men rejected human creeds, accepted the Bible as the only rule of faith, and made the Lord's Supper central in their assemblies each first day. And they had the oddity of taking not one but three offerings, one of which was at the door as the people entered. Butchart explains that virtually all the Scottish Baptists that migrated to Canada became Disciples.

But this had a negative influence and probably explains why the Movement did not continue to grow in Canada as it did in America. The Scottish Baptists were exclusivists, and their demand that others conform to their interpretation of the "ancient order" was offensive. They were rigid and legalistic, periodically dividing among themselves over such matters as to who may serve the Supper. It is another instance of how the notion of restoring a fixed pattern has been divisive.

A Maritimes historian identifies the church in River John, Nova Scotia as the first in all Canada among Disciples, dating it from 1815, a congregation that still exists. It started when John Murray, another Scottish Baptist, immersed two persons amidst the jeers of his neighbors and went on to break bread with them and others that same day.[40] It should be noted that the first Campbell church, Brush Run, had begun only four years earlier. But Butchart finds the church in Roads, Queen's Co., P.E.I., even older than Brush Run, having been organized by John R. Stewart, another Scot of Haldanean background, in 1810.

Like Brush Run, they were not at first immersionists, but became so when Alexander Crawford, another Haldanean from Scotland, joined them in 1815. Crawford, well educated and effective, eventually had several churches on the Island, but most of them became Baptists instead of Disciples.

There were some influences radically different from that of the Scottish Baptists. Dr. John Knox, a physician, came from Scotland to Canada in 1841 as a missionary of the Church of England. Educated in Edinburgh and London, he became a tutor at both Cambridge and Edinburgh, but was still a young man when he migrated to Canada. He was destined to minister for forty years on little Prince Edward Island for the cause of reformation. Immersed by a Baptist, he soon became a Baptist minister and served a group of churches that eventually became identified with the Stone-Campbell Movement, whose influence had begun to reach into Canada. In 1859-60 he was sent out by the still young American Christian Missionary Society to evangelize in the Maritime provinces.

Knox represents the best tradition of the Movement in Canada. His liberal education and magnetic personality made him an attractive minister in the pulpit and out. Much more open and tolerant than his counterparts of Scottish background, he preached for various denominations on the Island, including the Anglicans. But his message had a "Campbellite" ring. "I formed a church last Lord's day, Jesus Christ being the chief cornerstone," he reported in 1846, "a church which is connected with no association but the universal brotherhood; no bond of union but Christian love; no ground of union but obedience to the whole truth as it is in Jesus."[41]

Like Thomas Campbell, Knox was blind in his latter years, but still "his ringing voice and commanding presence were unimpaired." Once he was gone, a fellow minister said of him that he left a name behind that will be forgotten only when Islanders cease to think. His lovable disposition had won him the confidence and friendship of many.

The Campbell influence exerted itself in a strange way. A Baptist minister, David Wiers, was walking by an auction sale in Lewiston, N.Y., just across the Niagara from Canada, and heard the auctioneer cry out, "How much am I bid for these books?" Weirs had never heard of the seven bound volumes of the *Christian Baptist* or their author, Alexander Campbell, but he nonetheless kept bidding until the books were his. Not only did the books change his life, but also that of his friend with whom he shared them, another Baptist minister. The two of them planted churches along the lake shore in Lincoln County, Ontario.

Butchart also found evidence of the Barton W. Stone influence in

Canada by 1830. In time the Stone Christians had 1,200 members in twenty congregations and about that many preachers in Ontario. While they and the Disciples have had contact through the years, and occasional efforts at union, they have remained separate communions.

Aware that the rigid Scottish influence was not as strong in the Movement in the States, Butchart explains the impact of the American movement upon Canada: "The Campbells and Barton W. Stone enlarged, qualified, and to a large extent developed what had already begun. Especially did they add soul and breadth to what was sometimes rigid, legalistic, and literalistic." The tradition from Scotland, he notes, emphasized restoration, while that from the States stressed unity.[42]

By the end of what Butchart calls "the pioneer period" (1869) the Movement had 71 churches in four of Canada's nine provinces with a total membership of about 5,000. Their first journal was issued from Halifax, Nova Scotia in 1836, and there was one from two other provinces by 1839. Their first cooperative, with delegates from sixteen churches, was reported in Campbell's paper in 1846.[43]

James Black, another Scottish immigrant, was their D.S. Burnet, and by 1849, the same year the American Christian Missionary Society was organized, he presided over the Provincial Cooperation in Ontario that sent out two evangelists. Their full-blown missionary society, the Ontario Cooperation of Disciples of Christ, did not come until the 1880's, but it was James Black that led the way. They had no colleges during the pioneer period. Preachers were trained by traveling with the more experienced, and there was an occasional evangelist that would have a school in his home. Until they had their own institutions a number of their people went to Disciples colleges in the States, the Canadian churches maintaining funds for such a purpose.

Campbell visited Ontario in 1855, with Selina at his side, and his travel letter about that trip tells of his contact with some of the pioneers herein named, James Black, and David Oliphant, Jr. in particular. Butchart tells how one pioneer preacher from Lobo Township, Ontario, Dugald Sinclair, heard Campbell in London, Ontario and returned to his congregation that up until then was known as "Scotch Baptist" and announced that they would henceforth be known as Disciples of Christ. In his report Campbell urged the Canadian churches to be less concerned with mere order or discipline and apply themselves more to faith, hope, and love, complaining that they were not as cooperative as they should be.[44]

The Canadian churches, however small, were doomed to suffer the same divisions that were to afflict the Movement in the States. They divided over societies, instrumental music, and other issues, just as they did in the U.S., and for the same reasons, a subject that will concern us in later chapters.

The divisions saddened Reuben Butchart, who wrote his history as an old man who could look back over seventy years in the Churches of Christ in Canada. He wrote of the tragic effects of the "needless divisions that have been perpetuated, all because of narrow thinking in the long ago." His irenic spirit is evident in a chapter on the non-instrument Churches of Christ in Canada. He lists their churches, and, in behalf of the people he represents, expresses "cordial and Christian greetings to our sister Churches in Canada."[45]

Reuben Butchart himself, as a quiet, unassuming historian who thought of himself only as a compiler, exemplifies the best of the Movement in Canada. Being at least a third generation Disciple (Campbell traveled in Canada with a "Brother Butchart"), he tells how he first began as a boy dipping into Disciples history in books he found in his father's attic.

In his old age Butchart expressed regret that his people had never united with anybody, even though their plea was unity. He indicated that his people had become so engrossed in "restoring the primitive church" that they had well nigh forgotten their heritage of Christian unity. The history of the Movement reveals that this judgment has much broader application than just Canada.

But Butchart still believed that the Movement's plea had had some salutary effect upon the church at large in Canada. "We have been a voice crying in the wilderness," he wrote, "often without the austere sincerity that accompanies such a herald."[46]

Since Butchart's time the Movement in Canada, torn by internal strife and separated by long distances, has struggled for survival. The Disciples have made controversial efforts to unite with Presbyterians and Methodists in the United Church of Canada. It failed, due in part to the fear that they would have to compromise their position on believer's baptism, and resulted in a loss of churches to the Independents. Today there are only about 40 Disciples churches with a membership of fewer than 4,000.

The Independents, with some 70 churches and 6,000 members, have been more successful. The oldest college, Alberta Bible College (1932), has nobly served the churches in Canada. Though lines have not been strongly drawn, the Independents list it as one of their Bible colleges.

The Movement in Great Britain

"The passion for Christian unity has never been lost."

The Movement's beginnings and early history in Great Britain is remarkably similar to that in Canada. The British also were strongly influenced by the Scottish Baptists, who impeded its growth there as they did in Canada. The first church seems to have been the one in Dungannon, Ireland that was influenced by their reading of the Bible more than anything else. An independent congregation, they began in 1804 to break bread each first day. Knowing nothing of Baptist churches, they resolved to be immersed, but, like Barton W. Stone in America at the same time, they had no one to immerse them.

In 1810 one of them, Robert Smyth, asked an old man living in the country of Armagh, a Baptist, to immerse him. He in turn immersed others. They took the name Church of Christ and in 1825 came to know Alexander Campbell and to correspond with him.[47]

Another early Church of Christ was in Auchtermuchty, Fife, Scotland that became independent of the state church in 1807, influenced as it was by the Glasites. Thirteen of their number were immersed into Christ in a small river near the town. Two brothers, John and George Dron, former Presbyterians, ministered to the group. Though immersionists, they did not identify with the Baptists. They had interest in all reform efforts at home and abroad, including the Stone-Campbell Movement, which they did not hear about until 1830. John Dron visited Campbell in America in 1834.

The most important pioneers in the British story were William Jones and James Wallis. A bookseller and historian of some reputation in Liverpool, William Jones later became minister of a Scottish Baptist church in London. He was unaware of the reformation in America until a visitor from there told him of it one Sunday in 1833. Sensing that the American movement had an order of service similar to the Scottish Baptists, he asked for names and addresses.

Jones recognized the name of Alexander Campbell, for he had read his debate with the infidel Robert Owen. But he was unaware of Campbell's "powerful advocacy of the cause of primitive Christianity," as he later put it in his journal. This led him to do an unusual thing. After corresponding with Campbell and receiving his publications, he began a journal in England the purpose of which was to reproduce the writings of Alexander Campbell for British readers. He named it The *Millennial Harbinger and Voluntary Church Advocate*, its first issue being in 1835.

While the journal enjoyed a ready circulation among the Scottish Baptists throughout Britain, Jones may have overacted. He soon realized that Campbell was not as much like the Scottish Baptists as he had supposed, especially in reference to the Holy Spirit. After sixteen months he was disenchanted and closed down the paper.

Since Jones eventually deserted the Movement, returning to the Baptists, he was not a continuing pioneer. He nonetheless laid the groundwork for a number of his churches becoming Churches of Christ. What happened in the U.S. happened in England. The Baptists drove out the Reformers, leaving them to start their own churches, but sometimes the Baptists were such a small minority that they left, leaving the Reformers the building. In this way Jones was inadvertently responsible for the emergence of some twelve Churches of Christ.

One of these was in Nottingham, England where a group broke away from the Baptists in 1836 and started a Church of Christ. Their pastor, James Wallis, began a journal in 1837, *The Christian Messenger and Reformer*, which was intended to resume the work begun by Jones, and he stayed with it, serving as an editor among British Churches of Christ for a quarter of a century. From the first year there were notices in the journal of new congregations beginning, including London. By 1842 there were 50 churches and 1,300 members, and by 1847, the year of Campbell's visit, there were 80 churches with 2,300 members, which was very modest alongside the statistics on American growth.

Wallis met with Campbell during his 1847 visit. He afterwards wrote to him, identifying what he considered to be the essence of the Campbell plea, which he referred to as "that all important truth":

> It is to you, Bro. Campbell, under the providence of a gracious God, that myself and others in this place are indebted for a more clear and correct knowledge of that all important truth, which in those days of darkness is kept so much out of view, viz., that the religion of Jesus is founded altogether upon the knowledge and belief of FACTS, instead of abstract influences and mystic operations.[48]

Wallis here identifies what became basic to "the Plea," that unity can be realized only by a mutual acceptance of the facts of the gospel, apart from all the theories and opinions about those facts. All believers may therefore be united upon the facts of what God has done through Christ. "All the means of grace are, therefore, only the means of impressing this seal upon the heart, of bringing these moral facts to make their full impression on the soul of man," Campbell wrote.[49]

Even though Campbell had more influence upon British beginnings than Canada's, the work progressed slowly. Inheriting the Scottish Baptist suspicion of theological education, the British had no college at all until 1920. By 1840 they had but one journal and only one evangelist in the field. The non-evangelistical outlook of the Scots influenced the British churches, leaving them content with modest growth. While they raised funds for Campbell's visit and urged him to find them a suitable American evangelist to preach among them, nothing ever came of it.

Instead of an approved evangelist, they got Dr. John Thomas, whose story is told in the previous chapter, who came on his own, and they were the worse off for it. Since he could not moderate his speculative views, he caused trouble in a number of churches. He was credited with causing seven churches in Scotland to disband.[50]

Now and again in those early years they asked their American brethren for evangelists, but none was sent. But by 1870 the British churches were finding their own way and it was deemed "a foolish enterprise" when the American Foreign Christian Missionary Society presumed to send missionaries to Great Britain.[51]

David King was the Alexander Campbell of the British churches. A powerful personality, he was an editor, publisher, debater, teacher, and evangelist, a kind of "Bishop" over the 76 churches that he either founded or consolidated. An editor for 35 years, he produced material equal to the best that came from America. He conducted at least seven public debates, mostly with secularists in defense of the Christian faith, but also with a Swedenborgian and an Anglican on baptism. But his greatest work was as an evangelist.

With J.B. Rotherham, one of their scholars who translated *The Emphasized Bible*, at his side, King went to Birmingham where they built a church of 500 members. Then to Piltdown, England where they turned an entire Adventist Church of 150 members into a Church of Christ. Suspicious of colleges for preachers, King was successful in training evangelists in the churches, one of whom was Lancelot Oliver, who became one of their most progressive editors. Like Campbell, King's ministry extended over half a century, and he gave the churches everything from their hymns to their theology.[52]

Unlike his U.S. counterparts who started new churches and left them to struggle the best they could, King taught the British evangelists to stay and nurture those they baptized. Once a church was "set in order" with duly appointed elders, the evangelist moved on. This explains why some British churches of the Movement have a tradition of opposing the professional ministry, which by 1870 was current in the American churches.

When Timothy Coop, an American whom the British described as one who had the misfortune of being rich, sought to introduce "the pastor" in the British churches, he had to deal with David King. Coop was accused of seeking to influence the churches through the power of the dollar. He influenced at least fourteen churches to adopt the minister system. This caused a breach that was not healed until 1917.

Open membership was another issue on which the British churches differed from the American. They kindly seated the unimmersed separately, believing that Communion is only for the baptized. Still later the British churches were disturbed by other Americanisms, such as a plurality of Communion cups, instrumental music, and confederation of churches. Today there are at least three divisions within the Movement in Britain.

William Robinson, who became principal of Overdale College in 1920, was the theologian of the British churches. He wrote one of the best apologetics on what the Movement stands for. In reviewing the history of the British churches, he concluded that they were too anti-clerical and anti-professional, going beyond the more moderate position of David King. While King always insisted that only able expositors address the assembly, the churches, as Robinson saw it, practiced a radical mutual ministry that allowed the unqualified to speak.

Robinson also saw the churches as anti-intellectual and indifferent to modern scholarship. They were also intolerant, which he attributed to their zeal for their interpretation of "the primitive faith."

Noting that they began cooperative meetings by 1842 and overseas missions by 1892, Robinson was pleased to report that the Movement's success in Australia and New Zealand, where it had 35,000 in 1959, is due to British efforts. Writing in 1959, he counted 123 churches and 9,000 members in Great Britain.

What then are the positive contributions of the Movement according to Robinson? He names six:

1. An unflinching testimony to the New Testament as the sacred record by which all Christianity must be judged.

2. It has witnessed to the centrality of Christ in Christian discipleship.

3. It has insisted on the divine nature of the church and its two great sacraments of baptism and the Lord's Supper.

4. It has witnessed to a weekly corporate worship centering in the Lord's Supper, and it has held up baptism as the badge of discipleship, rejecting the baptism of unconscious infants.

5. By its aversion to creeds and confessions it has combined liberty with order and orthodoxy.

6. With an undying passion it has witnessed to the unity of Christ's church.[53]

He reminds his readers that the Movement started, whether in Britain or in America, with a passion for Christian unity. He insists that that passion has never been lost.[54]

While British churches in general have been in a state of decline since World War I, the Movement has enjoyed modest growth, at least until the 1930's when membership reached some 17,000. But decline set in following World War II and by the 1960's the numbers were cut in half. Probably due to this decline and the popularity of ecumenicity, 54 of the British

Churches of Christ in the 1970's voted, on a congregational basis, to unite with the United Reform Church. There were 24 churches that opted to remain independent, forming the Fellowship of Churches of Christ. Today these churches number about 40, and they are considered by some as the remnant of the original Movement in Britain, the other churches having lost their identity through merger.

The Independent Christian Churches in America have been able in recent years to serve these remnant churches through what came to be known as the British-American Fellowship. C. Robert Wetzel of Milligan College found American resources for the founding of Springdale College, now accepted as part of the Selly Oak consortium of colleges in Birmingham. Springdale may be seen as replacing Overdale College, long served by the renowned William Robinson, which closed in 1976. Christian Missionary Fellowship, an Independent agency, is committed to supplying some ministers for both old and new churches.

The non-instrument Churches of Christ have also been at work in the United Kingdom in recent decades, with some 3,600 members in 95 churches. The Boston Church of Christ in London appears to be the most successful of all recent efforts. Overall, the outlook for the Movement's churches in Britain is encouraging.

The Movement in New Zealand and Australia

Like the Canadian churches, the churches in New Zealand and Australia trace their origins not to the American movement but to the British. In 1994 the Associated Churches in New Zealand celebrated the sesquicentennial of its beginning. Today a plaque on Rutherford St. in Nelson commemorates the occasion back in 1844 when Thomas Jackson, a Scotsman, preached the same gospel Peter preached on Pentecost and began the work of Churches of Christ in New Zealand.

In subsequent years there were several migrations of Scots, laypeople, who planted congregations in various parts of this two-island nation. Early on they too were called Reformed Baptists as well as Christians and Disciples, and there was a strong Scottish Baptist influence. Their common bond was freedom from sectarianism. They broke bread together each Lord's day in homes or rented halls. Growth was slow and mostly by immigration in the early years. Beside Nelson, Dunedin was an early stronghold and the site of the first church building. An American evangelist, T.H. Bates, rented a 1000-seat tabernacle in Dunedin and preached to capacity crowds. His labors led to several new congregations.

By the 1870's there were congregations in Christchurch and Wellington, the nation's capital. By 1885 there were about 1200 members in some 35 churches and chapels. Today the Associated Churches of Christ of New Zealand have about 2500 members in approximately 45 congregations. The non-instrument Churches of Christ have in recent years organized an additional 23 churches with about 1,080 members. In neither Australia nor New Zealand is there a Disciples/Independent division.

Growth has always been modest and the churches small. But their smallness has made for a rich fellowship, and for the most part they have been spared the internal strife that has afflicted the Movement as a whole.

The most eminent name in the history of New Zealand churches may well be that of Arthur L. Haddon, an Australian. He came to Dunedin in 1927 to serve as principal of the only Bible college the churches ever had. The college served the churches nobly for some 40 years before it closed for lack of students. But Haddon was also editor of *The New Zealand Christian*, which continues to serve the churches.

As both teacher and editor Haddon was a recognized leader of ecumenism both at home and abroad, and he served as a delegate to the World Council of Churches in New Delhi in 1961. He was one of the first anywhere to offer a college course in ecumenics, a course that inspired students to be unity-conscious. Haddon's irenic spirit is part of the heritage of the New Zealand churches and one reason why they have had relative internal peace.

In the best tradition of the Movement, New Zealanders make room for liberals and conservatives alike in the same fellowship. And for the most part they have preserved their own identity by resisting any merger with a union of denominations, which has been an issue now and again through the years.

A famous son of the New Zealand churches is R. Garfield Todd, who served as a missionary to Southern Rhodesia (now Zimbabwe). A lifetime missionary, he eventually became that nation's prime minister and a world renowned churchman/statesman.

While the Movement in Australia has enjoyed greater growth than in New Zealand, the former owes its origin to the latter. Thomas Magarey, another Scottish Baptist, migrated from North Ireland to Nelson, New Zealand, and in 1841 was converted to New Testament Christianity by Thomas Jackson. When Magarey moved on to Adelaide in Australia he worked with Scottish Baptists who were influenced by the writings of Alexander Campbell. Division ensued, with the Scottish Baptists opting for orthodoxy and the "Reformers" eventually becoming a Church of Christ. In 1847 Jackson came from New Zealand to help Magarey in the new work.

Other churches were started in various parts of Australia by immigrants from Scotland and England, prompted in part by a gold rush in the 1850's. The churches came to have a strong British influence, not only because of migration but from the impact of the *British Millennial Harbinger*, edited by James Wallis, who was strongly influenced by Alexander Campbell. The British influence came to be seen in the practice of closed Communion. Members only took Communion on Lord's Day morning; outsiders were invited to an evangelistic service in the evening. Mutual ministry was also common, led by the "rule of elders," with evangelists working among the unchurched.

But the greatest growth came with the help of educated preachers from America who introduced the protracted revivals that ran for weeks. They were more aggressive in presenting the uniqueness of "the Plea" and made it easier for converts to join the Movement by simple confession and baptism.

The American influence had its problems as it did in Britain. It challenged mutual ministry by placing a professional minister in the pulpit, and it called for open Communion and an end to the practice of separating members and non-members and allowing only members to contribute. There was friction over the American influence, but in time the Australians yielded to it better than their British counterparts.

But unlike the American churches the Australians have not been as suspicious of organizations, and have thus had cooperative agencies almost from the outset. Today they have area and national conferences, agencies for the needy and elderly, three Bible colleges, and a national journal, *The Australian Christian*, edited by Chris Ambrose, which is one of the better edited journals of the Movement. Today the Affiliated Churches of Christ number some 37,000 members in about 450 congregations. In recent years the growth has been encouraging, especially in Queensland and New South Wales.

While sometimes controversial, depending on the state, women have long served at all levels of ministry in the Australian churches, not only as an occasional pastor but as a state president. A woman can graduate from one of the Bible colleges and become ordained just as the men. But in keeping with the Movement's tradition, one can become a minister from the laity, apart from theological education.

At the national level the churches have home missionary outreach to the aborigines and an overseas mission board that has long had missionaries in Africa, India and New Guinea. Beside the national conference there are six state conferences, each with its own organization and programs. Unlike their American counterparts, neither the Australians nor New Zealanders have had serious controversy over such organizations. Even when instruments were introduced early on, there was no division.[55]

Australians from the outset had a vigorous interest in the writings of Alexander Campbell, not only in the form of the *British Millennial Harbinger* but also in Campbell's own *Millennial Harbinger* from Bethany. His debates, books, and hymnals also circulated widely.

When Eliza Davies went to Australia from Bethany in 1857, she took a trunk full of Campbell's writings. When these were quickly exhaused she took orders for more. Eliza found a small band of "Primitive Christians" in Newton, near Sydney, who also called themselves "Campbellites." She says they gloried in this name. For the sake of the record, this is the only known church in the Movement's entire history that gladly wore the name that others considered an opprobrium. But Eliza did not think they were good Campbellites, mainly because they berated those in other churches.[56]

In both New Zealand and Australia the Movement has always been identified as "Churches of Christ." It is understandable that members in both countries, where there is a general unawareness of the American divisions, are puzzled when non-instrument missionaries come to start a "Church of Christ" where there have been Churches of Christ for 150 years. Besides the 23 non-instrument churches in New Zealand, there are 85 in Australia, mostly tiny, with 2,100 members. It is another tragic example of how the Movement's divisions have compromised its plea for unity.

When in 1926 Jesse M. Bader visited both New Zealand and Australia and urged the churches to take part in a world convention of Disciples, he received an enthusiastic response. Since the first gathering of the World Convention of Churches of Christ in 1930 in Washington, D.C., these two countries have been vigorous participants. Meeting only every four years, the WCCC has assembled twice in Australia (Melbourne in 1952 and Adelaide in 1970) and in New Zealand once (Auckland in 1988), and is scheduled for Australia (Sydney) again in 2000.

Several from these two countries have served as officers of the WCCC, and presently two New Zealanders, Lyndsay and Lorraine Jacobs, serve jointly as general secretary, a fulltime staff position with offices at the Disciples of Christ Historical Society in Nashville. If all the thirty nations where the Movement is represented entered into the WCCC with the commitment of the delegations from these two countries it would indeed be an enriched world fellowship of disciples of Christ.

ENDNOTES

[1]Alexander Campbell, "The Nature of Christian Organization, No. 1," *Millennial Harbinger*, 1841, p. 532.

[2]Alexander Campbell, "Five Arguments for Church Organization," *Millennial Harbinger*, 1842, p. 532.

[3]W.E. Garrison and A.T. DeGroot, *The Disciples of Christ: A History* (St. Louis: Christian Board of Publication, 1958), p. 236.

[4]Quoted in Garrison and DeGroot, *op. cit.*, p. 237.

[5]Thomas M. Hensley, "Co-Operation Meeting," *Millennial Harbinger*, 1840, p. 37.

[6]Herman Norton, *Tennessee Christians* (Nashville: Reed and Co. 1971), p. 47.

[7]Alexander Campbell, "Co-Operation," *Millennial Harbinger*, 1835, p 121.

[8]Alexander Campbell, "Co-Operation," *Millennial Harbinger*, 1838, p. 269.

[9]See an extensive account of this in Earl I. West, *The Search for the Ancient Order*, Vol. 1 (Nashville: Gospel Advocate, 1974).

[10]James. R. Wilburn, *The Hazard of the Die* (Austin, TX: Sweet Pub. Co.), p. 199.

[11]C.V. Segar, *Familiar Lectures on the Pentateuch*, Cincinnati, 1871, p. 371.

[12]West, *Search for the Ancient Order*, Vol. 1, p. 195.

[13]W.T. Moore, *The Living Pulpit of the Christian Church*, Cincinnati: 1869, p. 44.

[14]Noel L. Keith, *The Story of D. S. Burnet: Undeserved Obscurity* (St. Louis: Bethany Press, 1954), p. 8.

[15]W.T. Moore, *The Living Pulpit*, p. 50.

[16]D.S. Burnet, "In Memoriam," *Millennial Harbinger*, 1866, p. 304.

[17]Robert Richardson, *Memoirs of Alexander Campbell*, Vol. 2 (Cincinnati: Standard, 1897), p. 598.

[18]Lester G. McAllister and William E. Tucker, *Journey in Faith, A History of the Christian Church (Disciples of Christ)* (St. Louis: Bethany Press, 1975), p. 15. Note their Timeline.

[19]Noel L. Keith, *The Story of D.S. Burnet*, p. 35.

[20]Richardson, *Memoirs*, Vol. 2, p. 69.

[21]Noel L. Keith, *The Story of D.S. Burnet*, p. 70.

[22]D.S. Burnet, "Address to the Churches of God in the United States," *Millennial Harbinger*, 1845, p. 369.

[23]D.S. Burnet, "American Christian Bible Society," *Millennial Harbinger*, 1845, p. 453.

[24]Henry K. Shaw, *Buckeye Disciples* (St. Louis: Bethany, 1952), p. 155.

[25]Noel L. Keith, *The Story of D. S. Burnet*, p. 115.

[26]W.E. Garrison, *Religion Follows the Frontier* (New York: Harper, 1931), p. 185.

[27]Alexander Campbell, "Convention," *Millennial Harbinger*, 1849, p. 419.

[28]*Ibid.*, p. 418.

[29]Noel L. Keith, *The Story of D. S. Burnet*, p. 115.

[30]Alexander Campbell, "The Convention of Christian Churches," *Millennial Harbinger*, 1849, p. 694.

[31] The constitution may be found in *Millennial Harbinger*, 1849, pp. 690f.

[32]See McAllister and Tucker, *Journey in Faith*, p. 172.

[33]Alexander Campbell, "Elder D.S. Burnet and Elder Clark," *Millennial Harbinger*, 1848, p. 646.

[34]Noel L. Keith, *The Story of D. S. Burnet*, p. 128.

[35]W.T. Moore, *The Living Pulpit of the Christian Church*, p. 44.

[36]Noel L. Keith, *The Story of D. S. Burnet*, p. 143.

[37]D.S. Burnet, "In Memoriam," *Millennial Harbinger*, 1866, p. 319.

[38]Henry E. Webb, "Our Restoration Movement: Heritage and Destiny," (Address) North American Christian Convention, St. Louis, 1993 (Tape).

[39]Mark G. Toulouse, *Joined In Discipleship: The Maturing Of An American Religious Movement* (St. Louis: Chalice Press, 1992), p. 212.

[40]W.H. Harding, "Beginning of the Churches of Christ in the Maritimes," in Reuben Butchart, *The Disciples of Christ in Canada Since 1830* (Toronto: Canadian Churches of Christ, 1949), p. 96.

[41]Reuben Butchart, *Disciples of Christ in Canada*, p. 123.

[42]*Ibid.*, pp. 61f.

[43]"News from the Churches," *Millennial Harbinger*, 1843, p. 376.

[44]Alexander Campbell, "Notes on a Tour to Canada West, No. 1," *Millennial Harbinger*, 1855, p. 532.

[45]Reuben Butchart, *Disciples of Christ in Canada*, p. 268.

[46]*Ibid.*, p. 279.

[47]A.C. Watters, *History of British Churches of Christ*, Indianapolis, 1948, p. 16.

[48]*Christian Messenger*, Vol. 10 (1845), pp. 98f.

[49]Alexander Campbell, *The Christian System* (Cincinnati: Standard, n.d., orig. pub. 1835), p. 90.

[50]A.C. Watters, *History of British Churches of Christ*, p. 491.

[51]Garrison and DeGroot, *Disciples of Christ*, p. 450.

[52]Louise King, *Memoir of David King* (Joplin: College Press Reprint, n.d., orig. pub. c. 1898), pp. 1-45.

[53]William Robinson, *What Churches of Christ Stand For* (Birmingham, England: Berean Press, 1959), p. 99.

[54]*Ibid.*, p. 69.

[55]For a helpful recent summary of the New Zealand and Australian churches see Henry E. Webb, *In Search of Christian Unity*, Chap. 19.

[56]Eliza Davies, *Story of an Earnest Life* (Cincinnati: Central Book Concern, 1881), p. 348.

13

THE EDITOR BISHOPS
THE MOVEMENT IN CONTROVERSY

Why contend so much about a mere matter of opinion?
— "A Sister" in 1880

The Movement's greatest strength may have proved to be its greatest weakness. Its churches were "founded upon the Bible" and the Scriptures were its only rule of faith and practice. From the outset "the primitive faith" was its model and a restoration of "original Christianity" its goal. While the unity of all believers was its passion, it was a unity based upon the authority of the Bible.

The determination to speak where the Bible speaks and to be silent where the Bible is silent, enunciated early on by the Campbells, had its potential for controversy as well as for harmony. When rigidly applied it became a motto that backfired. It was a Pandora's box that was sure to be opened sooner or later.

It was partly opened in the struggle to form a missionary society. The more conservative thinkers wanted to know where the Bible authorizes a missionary society. Campbell, who at first opposed such societies on the same grounds, had to explain that the Bible is not a rule book that anticipates all contingencies for all time to come. One may as well ask where the Bible speaks of a printing press or a publishing house, he argued. That at least meant that the motto that had helped to launch the Movement was not to be taken all that literally.

But there was more than a motto. In his *Declaration and Address* Thomas Campbell laid down one of the Movement's most crucial principles of applying the Bible to differences between Christians. "Nothing is to be admitted of Divine Obligation but what is expressly enjoined by the authority of our Lord Jesus Christ and his apostles upon the New Testament Church, either in express terms or by approved precedent."

This was taken to mean that any new practice or method had to be expressly authorized in the New Testament or there had to be a precedent (example) for it. In time a conservative hermeneutics emerged that was to be a problem: The Bible authorizes by direct command, necessary inference, and approved example.

The youthful Alexander Campbell may have sensed a flaw in the principle when he first read his father's document back in 1809, questioning as he did the import of the phrase "by approved precedent." But he did not or could not take the necessary steps to avoid the damaging controversies that would erupt once he was absent from the scene, stemming from that flaw.

The Movement's historians have recognized all along that the divisions that eventually came were caused more by disagreements over methods than over theology, methods that lacked "approved precedent." They had had their disputes with their heretics, whether spiritualists or Mormons, which were theological in nature, and these they could handle since they were clearly departures from "what is written." But now they were in controversy with each other, not over theology, but how to do what they agreed needed to be done.

They agreed that the gospel is to be preached in all the world, but is there to be a missionary society for such purpose? The Scriptures are to be expounded in church, but may a minister be hired for this purpose? The Bible is to be taught to children, but is there to be a Sunday school? The church is to sing praises to God, but is an instrument to be used? May there be agencies for benevolence and for the publication and distribution of Bibles?

On all such issues there were those who asked for a biblical precedent. Where is there an example in Scripture? Some made a valiant effort to comply by finding a precedent for every detail, whether meeting houses or lighting.

While there was some controversy over these and other things almost from the beginning, they were kept at bay so long as Alexander Campbell lived. His influence for a united movement was so thorough that "the period of controversy" is usually dated from his death.

Instrumental Music

The issues differed in their effect upon the Movement, and there were some oddities along the way. The two most serious issues were missionary societies and instrumental music. The latter was the more critical, for while some who opposed the instrument favored the society, all those who opposed the society also opposed the instrument. The instrument proved to be the most divisive, perhaps because of its visibility in church. A society was something far removed, while an instrument was a strange, imported box that stood in the corner and made sounds. To many it was a symbol of apostasy, while to others it was a sign of progress. But the conservatives had the leverage in that they only needed to ask, in good Campbellian tradition, *What church in the New Testament had instrumental music?*

We have noted that these were differences over methods, not theology, but there was one theological issue, which persists to this day, open membership. Oddly enough, while it has been persistent it never became critical and was never as divisive as societies and the instrument. It had the advantage of being something that could be practiced without admitting it!

In this chapter we deal with the instrument controversy in particular in that it led to the Movement's first major split, albeit the question remains as to whether it was the prime cause. We shall see that the instrument was first introduced in 1849 and slowly made its way into many churches in the decades that followed. In all these years, even into the late 1880's, there was no open division over the practice. Some churches had an organ for decades before they divided over it! In such cases was it really the instrument that at last divided them?

Another fact that runs counter to subsequent practice is that the most adamant opponents of the organ, J. W. McGarvey and Benjamin Franklin, insisted that it should not be made a test of fellowship. In fact, from 1849 until the 1880's there was only one prominent leader in the Movement that called for non-fellowship over the instrument, and that was Moses E. Lard.

There is reason to conclude, therefore, that they could have absorbed this controversy without an open split, just as they did the question of open communion. For decades the Movement had both instrument and non-instrument churches without schism, a difference but not division. This could have continued but for other factors.

Leadership proved to be the difference. Once Campbell left the scene in 1866, a leadership began to emerge, particularly "editor bishops," that was willing to divide churches by forcing its interpretation of "approved precedent" upon others. What happened in Henderson, Tennessee, which is the most prominent Church of Christ city of its size in the world, is a case in point.

Earl I. West, noted Churches of Christ historian, says that "the most important struggle over the instrument" took place in Henderson. Founded in 1878, the Christian Church in Henderson adopted the instrument in 1884. While it was the source of some disagreement, the church grew and flourished in comparative peace for the next 18 years, *with the instrument.* It divided in 1902 when an editor bishop from Nashville came to town for a revival, conducting his services in the Baptist Church. Following the revival the Church of Christ became a separate church, noninstrument.[1]

If the musical instrument divided the Henderson church, why did it take 18 years? We may be compelled to conclude that it is not *things* that divide churches as much as *men.*

L. L. Pinkerton: The First Liberal

"The New Testament is not a code of cast-iron laws for trembling slaves,
but a rule of life for loving children."

For a man to have this view of the New Testament in the early decades
of the 19th century was enough for him to be tagged a *liberal*, a label not
altogether undeserved. Not only was he the first preacher in the Movement
to espouse open membership, but he also questioned biblical inerrancy and
plenary inspiration, views that caused him to be seen as "worse than a
drunkard." He was one of the Movement's first settled pastors, in Lexington in 1841. He served in the Union army as both a surgeon and chaplain.
After the war he worked with an agency that rehabilitated slaves.

Besides practicing medicine, Pinkerton was a professor at Kentucky
University for a time, but there was always that call to be a preacher.
Baptized by Alexander Campbell, he became a minister of reputation, able
and well-educated. His ministry at Midway, Ky. included a school and an
orphanage as well as a church. On one occasion when imploring a church
on behalf of his orphans, only for the plates to return empty, he closed the
service with an unusual benediction, "May the Lord have mercy on your
poor, stingy souls."

He was also an abolitionist in a slave state, insisting on the equality of
the black people. As was common among churches in slave states, the
blacks attended Pinkerton's church with their masters, albeit seated separately. They were taught and baptized, but they could take no further part.
Pinkerton led his church into building a separate facility for the slaves so
that they could conduct their own services and call their own minister.
This was not done generally until after the Civil War. He shamed the
nation and church alike for treating people as if they were cattle.

It is understandable that William H. McDonald in a recent study would
describe Pinkerton as "the Disciples' first liberal."[2] It is not, therefore,
surprising that in 1849 he would be the first in the Movement to introduce
a musical instrument into the worship of his church. His reason was unambiguous: *The singing was so deplorable that it scared the rats away!*

As the story goes, the instrument (a melodeon) in the Midway church
was short-lived, for one of the elders who opposed the innovation arranged
for his slave to purloin the helpless intruder under the cover of darkness
and stash it away in the elder's barn for safekeeping. The dubious relic is
on display at Midway Christian College, serving as a grim reminder of the
beginning of the end of the unity of the Movement.[3]

Pinkerton was consistent with the genius of the Movement in his views
on unity, which allowed for such differences as instrumental music. "The

church will never be united in doctrines of any kind," he said. "She must be one in Christ Jesus, or divide still more, and remain divided until the Lord comes."[4]

By 1871 the Main Street church in Lexington tried to get Pinkerton's home church to bring him to trial for heresy. When he first saw the long list of charges, he said he'd rather plead guilty than to have to read it! Once he started reading, he found it so interesting that he regretted its brevity, though he opined that he could make up a more damaging list of negatives against himself.[5]

But a trial was not necessary, for he was already so widely rejected that his ministry was confined to black churches. All white churches, in Kentucky at least, closed their doors to him. When Benjamin Franklin, one of the editor bishops, called him "an ape" for introducing the instrument, Pinkerton replied that if the editor's fulminations represented the true character of "the Reformation," then the world should be rid of it.

Pinkerton had a way of saying "Whatever others might do . . ." he had to be true to his convictions. Before he died on his 62nd birthday in 1875 he forgave all personal matters without surrendering the principles for which he had fought. Many of his estranged friends called during his last hours, and his funeral was held at the church that once branded him a heretic. And today in the Christian Church in Midway, Ky. the likeness of L.L. Pinkerton gleams from a stained glass window that looks out upon the church that bore witness to his indominable spirit. Accepted at last!

The introduction of an instrument in one church had no widespread effect at the time. No one wanted to draw the line on the Midway church. Gradually other congregations as they grew larger and more prosperous, especially those in the cities, began to use an instrument. It was controversial in some places and not in others. It was generally treated as an opinion and a matter of congregational preference. The majority in many churches opted for an instrument, but deferred to the conscience of the minority, at least for a time.

By the 1870's it was common for congregations to be labeled "organ" or "non-organ," but there was yet no division. It was common for preachers to ride along together on horseback to their appointments, kidding each other about being "organic" or "nonorganic," with no break in fellowship. Many simply ignored the issue.

It was not until well into the 1880's that a different spirit began to emerge. By this time J.S. Lamar, associate editor of the *Christian Standard*, was writing about what he considered the greatest peril confronting the Disciples. This was the emergence of an intolerant, sectarian spirit, on the part of men of "comparatively small calibre" who through the years had been elevated by chance to positions of prominence.

Lamar charged them with betraying the truths and principles that had brought the Movement into existence by making incidentals a test of soundness. Looking back over the events a generation later, Lamar was amazed that some of the leaders could have been so petty and trivial in their concerns, as if Christ had died to prevent the formation of societies and to keep organs out of churches.[6]

There may well have been men of small caliber involved in the organ controversy, as Lamar charged, but this was hardly the case with much of the opposition, for some of the ablest minds of the Movement were involved in the dispute. These were men who would have been bishops in other churches while only editors among the Disciples.

Since the music controversy came mostly after his time, Alexander Campbell himself made only oblique references to it, albeit these were negative, such as "brazen organ" or "like a cowbell in a concert." But these were hardly more than anti-institutional remarks characteristic of a reformer, such as his denunciation of "beautiful literary compositions called sermons."

There were, however, men who were valedictorians among their peers who spoke with no uncertain sound when it came to instrumental music.

Moses E. Lard
"No preacher should enter a church where an organ stands."

It was hardly predictable that Moses E. Lard would attain academic honors at any college, for at 17 he was illiterate. But native ability and a passion for education were on his side. He taught himself to write, not from books, but from advertisements that were more available to him in his humble circumstances. His widowed mother, left with six children, was in such dire poverty that she had to separate her family for the sake of their survival.

All his mother had to give him in their separation was a small New Testament. In later life he was to see himself as wealthy at that moment and not poor, for he had his mother's love and the words of Jesus. It was a typical judgment for the pious Moses E. Lard.

It was also unlikely that he would be a preacher, even if he did have a New Testament and an inclination toward religion, for the problems of early manhood drove him to infidelity. He heard preachers of various parties to no avail, but his life was turned around when he heard J.P. Lancaster of the Christian Church preach the simple gospel. Within a year he was preaching, but only after careful preparation. His first protracted meeting, which was conducted in his hometown, resulted in a new congregation. He always preached without notes.

He advised young preachers that they would not have to refer to notes if they made sufficient preparation. "Think of your subject," he urged, "think of it till your head aches and your heart is clear; think of it till you cannot make a blunder; think till every point is transparent." He further insisted that "Heaven furnishes you the matter, but thinking alone can make it yours."[7]

Lard apparently learned how to think, for he not only won valedictory honors at Bethany College but went on to become "one of the most distinguished writers and speakers in the cause," as Robert Richardson described him. When Campbell found himself too busy to respond to a book published by his old antagonist, J.B. Jeter, entitled *Campbellism Examined*, he asked the youthful Moses E. Lard to do the honors. Published in a full-length book in 1857, Richardson credits Lard for handling Jeter's arguments skillfully, but criticizes him for sometimes being more ingenious than correct in his handling of Scripture and for the severity of some of his language.[8]

But another historian, while recognizing that Lard as an editor often came across as caustic, vouches for his "heart power" and his sympathy with all kinds of suffering, which those who read him might miss. He referred also to his impassioned eloquence that audiences often found irresistible.[9]

Lard gained an important place in the history of the Movement through his influential *Lard's Quarterly*, which began in 1863, and his successful work as an evangelist in Missouri and Kentucky. He served for one year as president of the College of the Bible in Lexington, and in 1875 published a commentary on Romans which reflects his ability as a critical interpreter of Scripture.

J.J. Haley, a historian who heard him personally, said that he had never heard a better preacher than Lard, and that he and W.H. Hopson were the two greatest preachers among the Disciples of their generation. Haley said Lard could move an audience to the point of virtually paralyzing it, and that frequently someone else would have to extend the invitation so as to bring the people back to a consciousness of their ability to step forward and make the good confession. He also reveals that Lard was a gifted storyteller, which he sometimes demonstrated in his *Quarterly*. The *New York Ledger*, which published material from Henry Ward Beecher, offered him $5,000.00 a year to write stories for it, which he declined.

Despite his high appraisal of Lard, Haley described him as "the prophet of radicalism, literalism, and conservatism in the second generation of the reformation movement." Haley says that his "bald literalism" not only led him to literalize even the Apocalypse, but to assume an intolerant and dogmatic position on instrumental music and closed communion. In recalling the fierce intolerance of this period, Haley was amazed that one of Lard's stature could be as bitter and dogmatic as he was in his writings.

Haley observed in retrospect, as he reread some of Lard's reasoning: "We can hardly help wondering that a great man under any conditions or combination of circumstances, should fail to see the difference between secondary and insignificant matters and the loftiest fundamentals in the religion of Christ."[10]

In one essay Lard drew upon Thomas Campbell's doctrine of "approved precedent," by insisting that "the smallest point of doctrine and the most trivial feature in practice" must be supported by the New Testament either by being actually asserted, necessarily implied, or positively backed by some divinely approved precedent. Since instrumental music lacks such support it is "criminal and wrong." This exemplifies the hermeneutics that became the Achilles heel of the Movement, handed down by the well-meaning Thomas Campbell.

Such use of Scripture led Lard to further charge that any church that would introduce an organ would suffer its Bible to be torn in shreds before it would part from its pet. Such a church forsakes the example of the primitive church, condemns the authority of Christ, and resorts to will worship.

Now resolved to make the instrument a test of fellowship, Lard laid down three rules to follow in disfellowshipping such churches: 1. No preacher should enter a church where an organ stands, and this should be an unalterable rule; 2. No one taking a letter from one church should ever unite with one using an organ, for it is better to live out of the church than to go into such a den; 3. When an organ is introduced those who oppose it should remonstrate gently and kindly, and if this goes unheeded they should leave without even asking for letters and unite elsewhere.

He predicted that "these organ-grinding churches" would in due time be broken down or else go into complete apostasy, and "the sooner they are in fragments the better for the cause of Christ."[11]

Haley concludes that Lard is to be understood not only in the light of the controversial age in which he lived, but in terms of his volatile personality. He saw him as "a person of marked individuality, great intensity of conviction, and feelings so strong as to be easily fanned into a flame." He graciously conceded that Lard was right about most things and that it is one of God's precious providences that a person's heart can be right and his central message can have its saving power even when he is wrong about some things.

He also tells how old age sweetened Lard's attitude. "If I had my life to live over," he quotes him as saying as the shadows lengthened, "I would not preach another gospel, but I would preach the same gospel in a different spirit. I would not allow myself to be stranded on the desert of dogmatism and a narrow construction of the love of God."[12]

Lard's last days may have been his finest, but the fact remains that the disfellowshipping rules he laid down on instrumental music would one day be accepted by enough Disciples to cause a division. But not in his own day, for there were few who then took such a hard line.

In a recent study, Kenneth Van Deusen notes that in these last years Lard called on his liberal counterpart, Isaac Errett, with whom he had engaged in controversy but barely knew. By sitting down together they saw qualities in each other that they didn't know existed. Errett afterwards reported to his readers that he found Lard sweet-spirited and that it was impossible not to admire his manliness, downright honesty, and unfeigned piety.[13] This was not the image that Lard had projected in his younger years as an editor bishop.

It is interesting that Lard allowed for diversity of opinion in other areas. He insisted that missionary societies were not wrong in themselves, and he supported both the national society and especially the Kentucky State Missionary Society, even when they did not meet his criteria of biblical authority.

He was also an ardent premillennialist when many of the Movement's leadership, including Alexander Campbell, were postmillennialists. He wanted segregated seating in the churches, with males and females separated, and he did not want baptistries in the buildings. But he did not press these notions. It was only on the organ, and, as we shall see later, open communion, that he was "stranded on the desert of dogmatism."

It was to his credit that in his old age he had a different spirit and regretted the trail of dogmatism he left to posterity. That may be his greatest contribution.

John W. McGarvey
"Alex, stop that thing!"

When in the 1890's it was evident that a division within the Movement was imminent, caused in part by the controversy over instrumental music, editors in Nashville looked to J.W. McGarvey in Lexington to take an uncompromising position, as he did on most questions. They were disappointed. While he was the first to contend that the instrument in worship was a sin and not merely inexpedient, he did not want it to be an occasion of division and was unwilling to make it a test of fellowship.

While he would not hold membership in an instrumental church, if he could avoid it, or serve as the pastor of such a church, he would not sever fellowship. Unlike Moses Lard, who was a close friend, McGarvey continued to visit and preach among instrument churches until his death, insisting that they not silence the instrument in deference to him.

This caused the editors in Nashville, who had begun to draw the line of fellowship, to chide McGarvey, reminding him that he should be grateful for their efforts. Except for their opposition to the instrument he would have no place to hold membership or contract to preach![14]

This was characteristic of McGarvey's ambivalence on the instrument question. After being adamantly opposed to the instrument in the earlier years of the controversy, he said little about it in the afteryears, leading some to suppose that he no longer objected to it, which was not the case. For forty years he kept the organ out of the Broadway church in Lexington where he served as preacher and elder, and yet he sanctioned the use of pianos in its Sunday School.

One year at the Kentucky state convention when McGarvey was the speaker and the organ was being used, he was heard to say to his friend, Alexander C. Hopson, who was presiding, "Alex, stop that thing!"[15] And yet it was common for him to insist that an "organ church," as they were coming to be called, not change its practice just because he was present. It is ironic that a quiet little man, of less than average size, who had a passion for playing the flute, should become the Movement's champion anti-instrument man.

Variously described as an ecclesiastical lawyer and a scribe of the ancient law, McGarvey was unquestionably a leading spirit among the second generation pioneers. To W.T. Moore he was "one of the safest and truest men in the Church of Christ," and Alexander Campbell, remembering him as a student at Bethany, where he delivered a Commencement oration in Greek, hailed him as "one of our best and most gifted students" and one with an enviable reputation.[16]

J.J. Haley knew McGarvey as a teacher at the College of the Bible where he served for forty years, sixteen of them as president. He described him as "a great and most influential factor in the making of Disciple history."[17]

Haley's account of his teacher, whom the students called "Little Mac," would hardly pass the test of modern pedagogy. Each class began with the students reciting the lecture of the previous class, all by memory. The learning was by rote. The students were inundated with notes that they were required to memorize and repeat to the teacher. Another of McGarvey's students, Colby Hall, confirms that the students had little incentive to think for themselves or to raise those questions that would be taken for granted in a seminary classroom today. He charges that McGarvey did more telling than teaching and that not once did he ever refer a student to any book except the Bible or to his own *Lands of the Bible*.[18]

But McGarvey is not without high marks, even from his most critical students. Even though he held to an unyielding and absolute view of verbal inspiration and inerrancy, even to being accused of asserting that Balaam's ass spoke good Hebrew (probably apocryphal), he had no equal when it came to communicating the Scriptures in simple, vital English. His prodigious industry was contagious, and his devotion to the Bible was evident in the preaching of his students who filled leading pulpits all across the Disciples brotherhood.

Haley concedes that by the time McGarvey finished with him he knew much of the Bible by memory, which gave him an advantage over other preachers. Morro contends that his teacher's work is not to be judged in terms of his methods as much as by the whole of his life, which was noble and exemplary.

McGarvey wrote for some twenty years, beginning in 1893 when he was 64, a column in the *Christian Standard* on "Biblical Criticism" in which he sought to expose what he considered the fallacies of the higher critics. Usually covering a full page, it was popular with the readers even if it was often technical and tedious and sometimes irrelevant. It was written for the readers rather than the scholars who were often caricatured as dishonest and reprehensible.

He became so sharp and sarcastic toward such significant people as President Harper of Chicago that his own colleagues at the College of the Bible urged more moderation, or at least to refrain from name-calling, all to no avail. His friends generally observed that it was unlike him to be so caustic in print, being the genial and humble soul that he was. But to McGarvey it was a matter of defending the Bible "through thick and thin," as he put it.

It is probable that this column, popular in part because of its vitriolic name-calling, both marred the good name of McGarvey and contributed to the division that eventually came. His own brethren, who were sympathetic with new approaches to biblical study, did not escape his wrath.

Young liberals, associated with Yale and Chicago, particularly H.L. Willett and W.E. Garrison, frequently clashed with him in the columns of the *Christian Century*. There was an extended confrontation between McGarvey and the more experienced J.H. Garrison of the *Christian-Evangelist*, which was often bitter. McGarvey saw Garrison as soft with the liberals, while Garrison described McGarvey as one who sought to regulate the brotherhood. Morro, for one, saw all this as a dividing factor.[19]

One Churches of Christ historian claims that the instrument controversy has been "symptomatic of an attitude toward the scriptures,"[20] which is a typical viewpoint in that wing of the Movement. The implication is that the anti-organ position is reflective of a stronger allegiance to biblical authority.

But the story of J.W. McGarvey does not support the view that those who disagreed with him about the instrument had a different attitude toward the Scriptures than he had, though there was obviously a difference in interpreting the Scriptures. For 19 years, off and on, McGarvey ministered to the Bethlehem church out from Lexington, which gave its people ample time to understand his argument against the organ. They nonetheless decided to use an instrument.

It is not likely that they had a different attitude toward the Bible than he, but simply that they did not agree with his conclusion. So with the Broadway church, which remained non-instrumental for forty years, mostly out of deference to him. When an organ was finally introduced in 1902, it was hardly because the church had changed its attitude toward Scripture, but because it did not believe, as did McGarvey, that the Bible condemned it as sinful.

A parallel may be seen in McGarvey's opposition to a plurality of cups for Communion, which began to be introduced sometime after the instrument. That most of his brethren did not go along with him in opposing this innovation did not mean that they viewed the authority of the Scriptures differently. It only meant that they disagreed with him on that point.

Even more significant is that McGarvey's position was opposed by some of the stalwarts of the Movement who did not favor the instrument, but who believed it was going too far to make the innovation a sin. A.S. Hayden, the Ohio pioneer who authored *A History of Disciples of Christ on the Western Reserve* and whose fidelity to the reformation cannot be questioned, challenged McGarvey's "argument from silence" by calling for positive proof that "the Holy Spirit reprobates the use of instruments in worship," as McGarvey claimed.

In all the history of law, morals, and science silence had never been a witness, Hayden insisted, and yet this was the essence of McGarvey's argument against instruments, the *silence* of the New Testament. McGarvey argued that since the likes of incense, priestly robes, anointing oil, and instrumental music were ordained under the old law, their absence in the New Testament implies God's disapproval.

Hayden surprised McGarvey when he questioned this premise, denying that instruments were ever ordained under the old law but were always a matter of expediency. When McGarvey sought to prove his point by a reference to Psalms, Hayden chided him for surrendering his premise by passing from Moses the lawgiver to David the poet. He went on to press McGarvey for proof that God ever required instrumental music of the Jews. His point was that instruments have never been a matter of legislation but of propriety, and so their *presence* in the Old Testament and their *absence* in the New Testament proves nothing.

It was on grounds of propriety that Hayden opposed instruments in worship, but he suggested that each church be left to decide the matter for itself. And he urged McGarvey to realize that since God has never legislated in reference to instruments he might do great harm in attempting to do so. If McGarvey kept on insisting that instruments are condemned by God, Christ, and the Holy Spirit, it will bring "blazing coals of fiery strife" upon the churches, Hayden predicted.[21]

W.K. Pendleton, now in Campbell's editorial chair, published the McGarvey-Hayden exchange but did not believe that instrumental music would be a serious problem among the churches. Less than enthusiastic about the innovation, he hoped that the churches would have a better place to invest their money than upon such a "wind doctrine"!

He urged the brethren to keep cool and to cultivate the musical powers that God had given them so that mechanical aids would be unnecessary. But if there must be aids, he went on, they should be pipe organs and not melodeons, for the Lord should be given nothing cheap. Still trying to be funny, he granted that the melodeon would be the smaller sin, measured in cubical feet, and not so noisy.[22] But if the music question could be laughed off, it was only for the present.

The controversy for the next decade or so was for the most part congenial and brotherly, if not breezy. C.L. Loos, a Bethany professor and one of the Movement's brightest minds, opined that man should speak to God without any artistic medium, but that if he must have instrumentation it should be in the form of trumpets as in Solomon's temple.[23] Another writer contended that if one opposes either the melody of the voice or instruments in praising God he sets himself against nature, against the elements of man's constitution, and against the pious men of all ages.[24]

It was also a time for making fine distinctions. When the anti-society folk contended that the New Testament is as silent on societies as on instruments, and therefore unlawful, McGarvey, who strongly favored societies, responded that societies are only a method while the instrument is an "act of worship."[25]

A writer in Lard's journal set forth what would one day be a common claim of anti-organ forces: that an instrument was not used during the first three centuries of the church's history and it was introduced then only because Christianity had become corrupt.[26] But some anti-organ folk were ambivalent, like John F. Rowe, who thought an organ would be all right if it were used strictly to aid the singing, but not "those little wheezing, grunting instruments."[27]

J.S. Lamar, on the other hand, was neither pro or con, but saw the instrument simply as the inevitable consequence of growth and culture. He was convinced, however, that the intemperate outcries against the instrument on the part of a few editors were contrary to the spirit that gave rise to the Movement. Such opposition tended to increase rather than decrease the number of instruments in the churches, he concluded.

Lamar granted that such men as Lard and McGarvey were sincere and dedicated, but their influence was stronger than their arguments. As he saw it, they made one fatal error in their vigorous opposition to the instrument: to mistake natural and normal growth for an illicit and reckless innovation.[28]

It was the moderate pen of the influential Isaac Errett in the *Christian Standard* that kept the music controversy from dividing the Movement at this time. He was inclined toward the conservative side, publishing for several years hardly anything that was not critical of instrumental music. Except for some responsible essays by Dr. Robert Richardson, he found the anti-organ rhetoric distasteful. When he at last in 1870 addressed the issue himself, he reminded his readers that years before in the *Millennial Harbinger* he had warned the churches that if they did not do something about their woeful singing they would one day have to face the question of instrumental music.[29]

Like Lamar, Errett saw a corollary between the extreme opposition to instruments and the increase of their acceptance by the churches. It would have been different, he surmised, if their zeal had been directed toward the cultivation of vocal music. As it was, the bitterness of anti-organ forces, which included threats to crush instrument churches and preachers, caused folk to overact in their determination to be free of a "tyrannical oligarchy."

The *Standard* editor, who had the respect of both sides of the controversy, chided the opposition for such extreme remarks as to say the organ "corrupts the worship," for an organ is no more a part of the worship than a tuning fork. He urged both sides to realize that the dispute was a matter of opinion and not of faith, and that "no man has the right to make it, on either side, a test of fellowship." He further urged that for the sake of peace the instrument should be discarded and never be allowed to be a cause of division among the churches.

Lamar says that Errett's plea influenced hundreds of churches to yield on the organ question, even when only a small minority objected to its use, but in many instances, in the face of such kindly consideration, the opposition would acquiesce and an organ would be introduced after all. Even in the late 1880's there continued to be "a great many" churches that remained non-instrumental, Lamar estimated. Apart from a few exceptions, where a factious spirit prevailed, the churches accepted Errett's moderate position and open division was averted. Some churches had the instrument and some did not, and this diversity appeared to be generally acceptable.[30]

The "great many" non-instrument churches that Lamar referred to eventually became the separated Churches of Christ. It would be interesting to know how much "good vocal music" had to do with these congregations remaining acappella. Errett would be pleased with today's Churches of Christ, not for making acappella music a test of fellowship, but for the relatively high quality of their music. One is left to wonder if the first churches that remained non-instrument did so as much out of a lack of need for such an aid as out of conviction that it was wrong. In other words, was it the vigorous *singing* churches that remained non-instrument?

McGarvey through all these years worked quietly and humbly at his teaching post at the College of the Bible and his ministry with Lexington churches, saying less and less about the organ, though he was always ready to state his position. The churches for the most part did not accept his conclusion that instrumental music in worship is *per se* sinful, including most of those who remained non-instrument. The acceptance of his "argument from silence" by an appreciable number had to await another generation.

When McGarvey at last prepared some autobiographical notes he conceded that nearly all the congregations and preachers took the side of "the party for the innovation," and that it was useless for him to continue repeating arguments that went unheeded. He expressed keen disappointment in not even being able to keep the organ out of the church he had ministered to for forty years.[31]

But there was ample glory left in McGarvey's ministry, and when he died in 1911 he was one of the most respected and influential leaders among the Disciples. He was not and did not consider himself a part of a separated group.

It is ironic that at McGarvey's funeral, which was held at his old Broadway church, the organ played for all three hymns that were sung by the congregation. But insofar as we know he never said, "Not over my dead body."

Benjamin Franklin
"Declare non-fellowship with no one."

If printer's ink could be found in the veins of these editors, it must have flowed abundantly in the veins of Benjamin Franklin, for he edited not one or two papers, but as many as five. He sometimes had two going at one time, papers that enjoyed substantial circulation. Among the second generation leadership he was probably the best known and the most widely travelled, and perhaps the most influential editor among the Disciples since Campbell himself.

He was widely regarded as an effective and powerful evangelist, as 8,000 baptisms and numerous new churches would suggest. Born in Ohio in 1812, he never knew any church except the Disciples, which he served with uncommon industry for 42 years, having begun his ministry at age 24 under the influence of the inimitable Samuel Rogers.[32]

That Franklin was given to controversy is evident not only from the 25 public debates he had with preachers of various persuasions, but also from the continual in-fighting with his fellow editors among the Disciples. W.T. Moore, himself an editor, admitted that one might suppose that Franklin delighted in controversy, but he would only say that he was not particularly adverse to it!

J.S. Lamar was not as guarded, accusing Franklin not only of writing in "a slapdashing sort of style," but of using his *American Christian Review*, at one time the most influential journal among the Disciples, to discredit Isaac Errett of the *Christian Standard* and such other editors as Robert Richardson, W. K. Pendleton and C.L. Loos. Lamar notes that Franklin not only rebuked Errett for allowing himself to be called *Reverend*, but that he could not abide any editor that was disposed to be charitable toward other Christians and churches. He viewed any editor as "unfaithful" if he did not make his paper as harsh, exclusive, and condemnatory as he made the *Review*.

While Lamar recognized Franklin as a uniquely gifted man, he saw him as the leading agitator of such issues as instrumental music and as one who would have made the Disciples a narrow, bigoted sect. Lamar accounts for the birth of the *Christian Standard* as a reaction to Franklin's *Review* "going too far" in the direction of dogmatism and exclusivism.[33]

And yet Franklin was ambivalent in regard to some of the controversial issues. Having worked with D.S. Burnet in the earlier years as an editor, he strongly favored cooperative societies for the churches, serving for a time as secretary for the missionary society. When its opponents asked for a "Thus saith the Lord" for such a society, Franklin insisted that it is justified on the same ground as building meetinghouses or translating the Bible.

When he later changed his mind, he almost killed the society through long years of opposition. The society imposed itself upon the freedom of the churches, he argued. He also supported the colleges at the outset, but again changed his mind. They had forsaken the Campbellian ideal by becoming theological schools and preacher training centers. The "anti-college" persuasion, prominent in Churches of Christ in the twentieth century, is therefore traceable to Benjamin Franklin through Daniel Sommer, his protege.

While he was never ambivalent about instrumental music, he at first treated the question as of little importance, supposing that instruments would never make their way into more than an occasional church. His first editorial against the instrument in 1860, directed against Pinkerton's melodian in Midway, Ky., did not suggest that it was anti-Scriptural, but that it might be appropriate if the church wanted to be a mere place of entertainment or wanted "a plaything in the church."

By the mid 1870's a portable organ was in many homes and the young people were clamoring for it in the churches, at least in the Sunday school. Some even refused to sing without an organ!

As the churches began to use an instrument in increasing numbers, Franklin began to "Cry out and spare not" in typical prophetic fashion.[34] He was so adamant in his position that he would not even publish a suggestion from John F. Rowe, a fellow editor, that an instrument might be all right if it were kept in the choir so that the elders could control both the organ and the choir![35]

Even though Franklin viewed the instrument as a departure from the ancient order and contrary to the Disciples plea, he was nonetheless so endowed with the Movement's passion for unity that he would not cause division over it or make it a test of fellowship.

When in 1876 the church in Charleston, Illinois elected to use an organ, the dissenters asked him what to do. His answer called for separation, if need be, without a breach of fellowship, which illustrates how strongly the Disciple leadership believed what W.T. Moore stated as an epigram, "We are free to differ but not to divide."

Confessing that he himself had used immoderate language in opposing the instrument, Franklin cautioned the Charleston people to be careful and not wound the feelings of anyone, lest it affect relationships once the organ question is resolved. While they were to be firm in their opposition, they were not to denounce anyone or be severe and should look to the Lord for an answer. Nor were they to stay at home or talk about starting another church. "Declare non-fellowship with no one," he advised, "say nothing about refusing fellowship, or leaving the church, or withdrawing from it."

Rather they were to meet quietly in another place and worship according to the Scriptures, though they were not to organize as a separate church. If in time the issue could not be resolved, they could then proceed to set the church in order with its own elders and deacons. This was separation without division.

This was the editor's way of placing the responsibility upon those who would impose the instrument upon others. Some years earlier he had made it clear that he would not only not worship with an instrument but that he did not want to be invited to minister to any church that used one while he was there. "If brethren will introduce the instrument in worship, they shall themselves be held responsible. We shall not be."[36]

That Franklin was the catalyst for a strong conservative persuasion — or "a non-progressive policy" as some editors were then calling it — is evident from W.H. Harding's account of the Movement in Canada. In explaining why the cause had not progressed in the Maritimes, he points to the influence of Franklin's *American Christian Review*, which circulated widely in those provinces. Preachers were willing to sacrifice their pay to support its circulation.

Writing in 1939, Harding says that no preacher, before or since, ever had such influence in those parts as Benjamin Franklin, which he saw as non-progressive and debilitating. "The plea for New Testament Christianity was turned into a hard and fast legality about methods of work rather than the work itself," he laments. He tells how in 1869 when Franklin came to the Maritimes that he was received with great ovation. The services were held in the groves since the churches could not accommodate those who crowded to hear him. The Movement in the Maritimes was at the crossroads, Harding notes, and Franklin led them in the wrong direction, into "anti-ism" as he puts it.

Instrumental music was but part of a larger package, the historian observes, for Sunday schools and the missionary society were also issues. Women had to be silent and preachers were not to have salaries but simply trust in the Lord. Not only did Franklin castigate sectarian churches as harlots, but even Isaac Errett was an anti-Christ and his new *Christian Standard* in anyone's house was a sign of heresy.[37]

Isaac Errett

"Let the bond of union be Christian character."

One of the Movement's earliest historians, W.T. Moore, described Isaac Errett as "preeminently among the most distinguished" of the 19th century leaders, while Mark G. Toulouse, a contemporary historian, sees him as "the premier leader of the second generation." He is generally credited with saving the Movement from legalism and sectarianism during its most controversial era. This was largely due to his being selected as the editor of the new *Christian Standard*, a journal that was launched in 1866 in hopes of combating the negative impact of Benjamin Franklin's *American Christian Review*.

It was a striking coincidence that the first issue of the *Standard* reported the death of Alexander Campbell. It was a turning point in the history of the Movement. Campbell's passing left a vacuum. While Franklin had become the most influential editor in Campbell's waning years, many now looked to Errett to provide the balanced leadership that appeared to be beyond Franklin's capacity.

Born in New York City in 1820, Errett had been a Disciple since 1832. After clerking and teaching in his late teens, he became a pastor at age 20. At a young age he knew Walter Scott and travelled with Alexander Campbell. He served as one of Campbell's co-editors, secretary for the American Christian Missionary Society, and president of the Foreign Christian Missionary Society. As a prominent minister in Detroit he did some daring things, such as allowing his admirers to give him a doorplate that read "Rev. Isaac Errett," and issuing "A Synopsis of the Faith and Practice of the Church of Christ," which his critics condemned as a creed.

Always a man of action, he applied for a commission to organize a regiment during the Civil War. As an editor, he supported an Inter-Denominational Congress in 1885 and generally encouraged his people to cooperate with other churches. He favored open Communion and disagreed with Moses Lard when he insisted that Martin Luther, if unimmersed, was not a Christian. He also made J.W. McGarvey unhappy when he would not say that the Bible is "absolutely free from error." While he admitted the fact of inspiration, he could hardly see Scripture as wholly inerrant, the problem of human communication being what it is.[38]

Errett set the tone for an irenic approach to controversial issues when he wrote in the *Standard*: "Let the bond of union among the baptized be Christian character in place of orthodoxy, right doing in place of exact thinking; and, outside of plain precepts, let all acknowledge the liberty of all, nor seek to impose limitations on their brethren, other than the law of love."[39]

This is what J.S. Lamar called "the broad Catholic ground" that had characterized the Movement from the outset. He thinks Benjamin Franklin also theoretically embraced this view but became increasingly uncomfortable with it and eventually repudiated it and all who upheld it.[40]

This ultraconservative element, which found its most persuasive voice in Franklin, was present in the Movement from the beginning. Had it not been for Isaac Errett the Franklin mentality might well have set the course for the Movement's future. It is understandable that historians Garrison and DeGroot would credit Errett and his *Christian Standard* with saving the Disciples from becoming "a fissiparous sect of jangling legalists."[41]

In an address in 1886 in which he reviewed 59 years of Disciples history, Errett granted that there were many who would make the use or non-use of organs, societies, and lesson-leaves a test of fellowship, and while this threatened the peace of the church he did not see it as leading to an open split.

They had to be watchful, he urged, lest they make the kingdom of God a matter of organs and societies and thus violate the law of Christian liberty on one hand and the law of Christian love on the other, thus negating their plea of Christian union.

In that address Errett urged upon his people a solution to the problem that well nigh prevailed through the nineteenth century: "Let every man be fully persuaded in his own mind as to his opinions, but let him not attempt to force them on others, or to erect them into tests of fellowship."[42]

This he wrote at a time when organs were being stolen from buildings or attacked with hatchets, and being imposed upon churches against their will. One church attempted to solve the problem by erecting a building with the door too narrow for an organ! But the Presbyterians were not behaving all that much better over the issue. A visiting evangelist concluded a sermon in a sardonic tone, certainly for a Presbyterian: "We will now stand, sing and *fiddle!*"

If, therefore, this era of Disciples history, had a hero, it would be Isaac Errett. Or it could be said the way historian T. W. Grafton put it, one who lived much closer to the period: "As the war clouds gathered and passions ran high, Mr. Errett, perhaps, did more than any other man to keep the good ship Zion from stranding and going to pieces."[43]

Did the Instrument Divide the Movement?

The evidence hardly allows the conclusion that the Movement divided over instrumental music, *per se*, either in the post-War years or later. While numerous congregations quarreled over the issue, there were few actual splits. Decades after the instrument (and other things) became a problem the Disciples of Christ were still one church or movement. We learned from J.S. Lamar that "many churches" did not use the instrument, but they remained in fellowship with those that did.

We have also seen that some churches had the instrument for years before it was made a divisive issue. Equally impressive is that the preachers on both sides of the issue ministered among all the churches, organ and anti-organ alike, without drawing lines. Even such anti-organ stalwarts as McGarvey and Franklin did not call for disfellowship.

Only Moses E. Lard demanded exclusion, and even he rejoiced that the Civil War had not divided the Disciples as it had other churches, and he predicted that nothing would ever divide the Movement if the War had not. "Never!," would the Movement divide, he emphasized. For the moment at least he seemed indifferent to what he had written about instrumental music.[44]

Legalism and exclusivism appear to be the culprits, along with a misunderstanding of the nature of the Movement. Lancelot Oliver, a British editor, identified as well as anyone the problem the Disciples faced during this controversial period.

> We have never held that a return to New Testament Christianity and acceptance of what we think constitutes it are necessarily one and the same thing; and at needed moments the fact has been recalled that we must ever be ready to diminish or enlarge as further truth breaks forth from God's word.[45]

Oliver named it. The Movement's leaders have often failed to distinguish between a plea for a return to the ancient faith and their opinion as to what constitutes such a return. There has been little latitude to "diminish or enlarge" even in the area of methods. Any given leader was inclined to confuse "the ancient order" with his own interpretation of what that meant.

An illustration of this is seen in a story out of Australia, which took place apart from the American controversy. By the time of their annual meeting in 1886 the churches had long been disturbed over the use of instruments in worship. Due to the way some interpreted "the primitive faith," a resolution was made that the organ be removed from those churches that had adopted it. Leaders with a different view of the nature of the Movement offered a counter resolution to the effect that it was inconsistent with what the Disciples stood for in reference to liberty of opinion to pass any such judgment. The matter was tabled, only to be debated at the next meeting.

What one side saw as a matter of faith the other side saw as a matter of opinion. Australian historian H.R. Taylor explains that the organ issue in his country was no storm in a tea cup, but was a serious hermeneutical problem. It had to do in particular with how the silence of the Bible is to be interpreted. "Brethren were concerned because instrumental music is not mentioned in the New Testament as an accessory to the worship of the primitive church."[46]

The instrument was therefore but the occasion of the Australian churches dividing. The cause was twofold: a different view of the nature of the Movement (restorationism vs. unity in diversity); a different view of the nature of the New Testament (patternism vs. progressiveness). Or as Lancelot Oliver put it, a confusion between what the norm is, which might be expanded or diminished, and what one thinks it is. When people make "what they think it is" a test of fellowship and thus become exclusivists they cause division.

This is further illustrated in the churches in Canada dividing over instrumental music in the 1880's, again apart from the American onset. Reuben Butchart explains that respected leaders were on both sides of the issue. It was again a matter of rigid patternism versus a catholic plea for unity rather than instruments as such.[47]

These instances show that the instrument question was not uniquely American, and that it was not that one side respected the authority of Scripture and the other side did not. It shows that while both sides respected the authority of the Bible they differed as to how marginal issues are to be resolved, and they allowed their differences to divide them. They had difficulty seeing what was clear to Stone and Campbell, that in a plea for unity such differences are permissible so long as they are not made tests of fellowship.

In a review of the Movement's first half-century, Thomas Munnell provided the first objective treatment of the instrument question. He revealed that it was not a unique problem with the Disciples. He could have mentioned that both Zwingli and Calvin were anti-organ and that Peter Cartwright condemned it on the basis of luxury and Thomas Aquinas on the grounds of Judaizing. Zwingli was not only anti-organ but opposed any singing in church, arguing that the melody is to be "in the heart" like the Bible says.[48]

Munnell further observed that other frontier churches adopted the instrument only after considerable conflict. They argued about the organ the same way the Disciples did, some insisting that it "corrupted the worship" while others saw it as an expediency. As for the controversy among his own people, Munnell was slow to cast blame, for both sides were sincere. He concluded that all judgments must be withheld until there is a more reliable way of interpreting such issues. "If this cannot be satisfactorily done," he wrote, "it must be left to each one to stand or fall to his own master."[49]

Several editors of that period wrote of the controversy as if there had been no open split over the organ. As late as 1880 the *Apostolic Times*, though anti-organ, was reluctant to say anything further on the question, insisting that "it has been thoroughly discussed without the accomplishment of good." While restating its opposition to the organ, it nonetheless declared that "We cannot hate, or disfellowship, or even cease to love a brother because he may differ from us in opinion." Desiring that his brethren be "thoroughly united" on the question, the editor did not write as if the Movement was about to rupture over the matter.

While F.G. Allen, editor of the *Old Paths Guide*, thought the organ issue should continue to be discussed, he agreed that it should not be made a test of fellowship. Three decades after the first organ was introduced, Allen was able to write: "This is not a question as to whether we shall fall out with and disfellowship those who differ from us on opinion." While he believed the organ was working evil in the churches and therefore inexpedient, he did not imply that it had or was about to divide the Movement.[50]

One historian outside the Movement observed that the instrument was a problem in several frontier churches by 1823, but it did not become critical until after the Civil War. But no denomination divided over it, he noted.[51]

We can draw the same conclusion in reference to the Disciples. They quarreled over the issue, as much or perhaps more than any other church, but it did not cause open division among them either, due in part to the irenic spirit of Isaac Errett. But in time there would be editor bishops with a different spirit, and then organs and societies would be good excuses for dividing the Movement.

Another ingredient to the division that eventually came was identified by "A Sister" who wrote to the *Old Paths Advocate* in 1880. After reading what the editors had said on the music question, she no doubt said what many were thinking. She was sick and tired of it all. "Why contend so much about a mere matter of opinion?," she asked. She went on to say,"Life is too short for fault-finding, and we 'pass this way but once,' therefore let us enlarge the mantle of love so that it will smoothly cover our neighbor as well as ourselves."[52]

We could say, therefore, that it was not instrumental music that eventually divided the Movement as much as a failure to enlarge the mantle of love to which this sister referred. We repeat that it is men who cause divisions, not things or issues.

ENDNOTES

[1]Earl Irvin West, *The Search for the Ancient Order*, Vol. 3 (Indianapolis: Religious Book Service, 1979), pp. 41, 42; Herman Norton, *Tennessee Christians* (Nashville: Reed and Co., 1971), p. 214.

[2]William H. McDonald, "Whatever Others Might Do: A Look At The Principles of L.L. Pinkerton," *Discipliana*, Vol. 53, No. 2 (Summer, 1993) p. 41.

[3]Earl Irvin West, *The Search for the Ancient Order*, Vol. 1 (Nashville: Gospel Advocate Co., 1974), p. 312.

[4]William H. McDonald, "Whatever Others Might Do," p. 41.

[5]John Shackleford, Jr., *Life of Dr. L. L. Pinkerton*, Cincinnati, 1876, p. 104.

[6]J.S. Lamar, *Memoirs of Isaac Errett*, Vol. 2, Cincinnati, 1893, p. 4.

[7]Moses E. Lard, "My First Meeting," *Lard's Quarterly*, Vol. 1 (1863), p. 217.

[8]Robert Richardson, *Memoirs of Alexander Campbell*, Vol. 2 (Philadelphia: Lippincott, 1868), p. 624.

[9]W.T. Moore, *Living Pulpit of the Christian Church*, Cincinnati: 1869, p. 230.

[10]J.J. Haley, *Makers and Moulders of the Reformation Movement*, St. Louis, 1914 (College Press Reprint), p. 114.

[11]Moses E. Lard, "Instrumental Music in Churches and Dancing," *Lard's Quarterly*, Vol. 1 (1864), pp. 330f.

[12]J.J. Haley, *Makers and Moulders of the Reformation Movement*, pp. 109, 115.

[13]Kenneth Van Deusen, *Moses Lard: That Prince of Preachers* (Joplin: College Press, 1987), pp. 259f.

[14]*Gospel Advocate*, Vol. 39 (1897), p. 529.

[15]W.C. Morro, *Brother McGarvey* (St. Louis: Bethany, 1940), p. 148.

[16]Alexander Campbell, "Notes of Incidents in a Tour through Illinois and Missouri," *Millennial Harbinger*, 1853, p. 130.

[17]J.J. Haley, *Makers and Moulders of the Reformation Movement*, p. 136.

[18]W.C. Morro, *Brother McGarvey*, p. 253.

[19]*Ibid.*, p. 203.

[20]Earl I. West, *The Search for the Ancient Order*, Vol. 2 (Indianapolis: Religious Book Service, 1950), p. 72.

[21]For the McGarvey-Hayden exchange see *Millennial Harbinger*, 1864, pp. 510f.; 1865, pp. 38f., 182f.

[22]W.K. Pendleton, "Instrumental Music in Churches," *Millennial Harbinger*, 1865, p. 40.

[23]C.L. Loos, "Music in Churches," *Millennial Harbinger*, 1865, p. 92.

[24]R. Salisbury, "Instrumental Music in Churches," *Millennial Harbinger*, 1865, p. 117.

[25]J.W. McGarvey, "Instrumental Music in Churches," *Millennial Harbinger*, 1864, p. 513.

[26]Dr.H. Christopher, "On Instrumental Music in Churches of Christ," *Lard's Quarterly*, Vol. 4 (1867), p. 363.

[27]W.E. Garrison and A.T. DeGroot, *The Disciples of Christ: A History* (St. Louis: Bethany, 1958), p. 344.

[28]J.S. Lamar, *Memoirs of Isaac Errett*, p. 29.

[29]Garrison and DeGroot, *Disciples of Christ*, p. 345.

[30]J.S. Lamar, *Memoirs of Isaac Errett*, Vol. 1, p. 41

[31]J.W. McGarvey, *Autobiography of J. W. McGarvey* (Lexington: College of the Bible, 1960), p. 44.

[32]W.T. Moore, *Living Pulpit of the Christian Church*, Cincinnati, 1869, pp. 339f.

[33]J.S. Lamar, *Memoirs of Isaac Errett*, pp. 279f.

[34]J. Franklin and J. A. Headington, *Life and Times of Benjamin Franklin*, St. Louis, 1899, p. 409.

[35]*Ibid.*, pp. 412f.

[36]Earl Irvin West, *The Search for the Ancient Order*, Vol. 2 (Indianapolis: Religious Book Service, 1950), p. 82.

[37]W.H. Harding, *Beginnings of the Churches of Christ in the Maritimes*, St. John, 1939, pp. 19f.

[38]Isaac Errett, "Inspiration," *Missouri Christian Lectureship* (St. Louis: John Burns, 1883), p. 167. Quoted in Tucker and McAllister, *Journey In Faith*, p. 365.

[39]Garrison and DeGroot, *Disciples of Christ*, p. 358.

[40]J.S. Lamar, *Memoirs of Isaac Errett*, Vol. 1, Cincinnati, 1869, p. 279.

[41]Garrison and DeGroot, *Disciples of Christ*, p. 358.

[42]Isaac Errett, *59 Years of History: An Address*, New Lisbon, Oh., 1886, p. 25.

[43]T.W. Grafton, *Men of Yesterday* (St. Louis: Christian Pub. Co., 1899), p. 176.

[44]Moses E. Lard, "Can We Divide?," *Lard's Quarterly*, Vol. 3 (1866), p. 336.

[45]Quoted from *Bible Advocate* (1910) in A.T. DeGroot, *Detour From Unity: Church of Christ Number Two*, Ft. Worth, n.d., p. 1.

[46]H.R. Taylor, *The History of the Churches of Christ in Australia*, Union, South Australia, 1959, p. 43.

[47]Reuben Butchart, *The Disciples of Christ in Canada Since 1830*, Toronto, 1949, p. 513.

[48]Even Karl Barth considered the organ "out of place in divine worship," preferring wind instruments. See Karl Barth, *Letters 1961-1968* (Grand Rapids: Eerdmans, 1981), p. 307.

[49]Thomas Munnell, "Fifty Years of Religious Reformation," *Christian Quarterly*, Vol. 8 (1876), p. 308.

[50]F.G. Allen, "Thumb Screws and Loose Screws," *Old Paths Guide*, Vol. 2 (1880), p. 147.

[51]J.W. Wells, *History of Cumberland County, Kentucky*, University of Kentucky Press, p. 76.

14

THE EDITOR BISHOPS: SLAVERY AND THE CIVIL WAR
THE MOVEMENT AT THE BRINK OF DIVISION

This spectacle of divided unionists is the most obvious indication
that somewhere in the program of the Movement
is to be found a cause for schism.
— A.T. DeGroot[1]

While the Stone-Campbell Movement had in its genes a proclivity to
divide, as A.T. DeGroot suggested, it nonetheless remained a *united* unity
movement through its first several decades. This chapter begins the story
of how a movement "to unite the Christians in all the sects" itself became
"a spectacle of divided unionists." Writing in 1940 and looking back on
several divisions, DeGroot found the flaw in the restoration principle itself,
which he saw as inherently schismatic.

DeGroot's abrasive term "spectacle" may not be too strong when
applied to a people who preached unity but could not practice it. They
professed to have discovered principles that would resolve the problem of
division and yet could not escape division themselves. Wherever they took
their plea they also sowed seeds of schism. They not only divided in their
own country but in Canada, Australia, and Britain as well. They have
continued to divide into the 20th century, again and again, often enough
to create at least one new faction each decade.

This divisiveness is, moreover, traceable to the Movement's forerunners, the Anabaptists and their Scottish heirs, the Haldanes and the Sandemanians. Divided unionists! It is a cruel verdict that other churches escape,
even when they too are divisive, for they do not claim to have a unity
heritage.

To its credit, however, the Movement continued united through its first
two generations. It even remained one church through the Civil War when
other churches divided. Alexander Campbell insisted that his people would
never divide if they remained true to their principles. We may conclude
that they did not have to divide, that they could have remained a united
unity movement, continuing to witness their oneness to the divided Christian world. If, as Campbell put it, they had remained true to their principles.

We have already indicated that the editor bishops, as W.T. Moore chose to call them, must bear a large part of the blame for departing from the principles to which Campbell referred. It was the editors who marshalled forces for fratricidal combat. Even so, the churches often enjoyed peace, in spite of the editors.

We have seen that while the editors made lots of noise over the instrument question, the churches endured it with a measure of tranquility and without extensive division. Up to this point, it could be concluded, the Movement for the most part had been faithful to the principles that gave it birth.

The slavery-Civil War issue was a much more serious problem, one that brought the Movement to the brink of an open split. It was again the editors who were at center stage of the drama. The churches generally desired peace, and they wanted to keep religion separate from politics. They chose to think of slavery and war as political issues. In some communities, even during the war, soldiers from both sides of the conflict sat side by side in church.

Following the war, Confederate soldiers in an Alabama church gladly listened to a Union general, James A. Garfield, a preacher destined to be President. Many a pulpit was filled by preachers from the North and South alike, and it was understood that they would preach the gospel and not politics.

And yet the Movement, like the nation, was deeply scarred. The story that follows shows how it was brought to the brink of division and yet survived as one church, one people.

Slavery and the Movement

"Slavery is wrong, both politically and morally." – *Barton W. Stone*
"I have always been anti-slavery, but never an abolitionist."
– *Alexander Campbell*

Even if Barton W. Stone believed slavery to be wrong, a position he took in his journal as early as 1828, he was hardly ready to emancipate the slaves. Should slaves be turned loose suddenly upon society, he told his readers, he would move out at once to a distant land to escape from them. But he did emancipate his own slaves and did not send them away empty. He still owned a few, "a curse upon my children," willed to him by a relative, but they were not under his control.

Even in 1828 he had been advocating liberty for the slaves for thirty years, but he was not a typical abolitionist. He wanted the slaves transported to Africa through the American Colonization Society. By 1825 he had helped organize a chapter for this society in his home in Georgetown, Ky. which sent about 30 slaves to Liberia, "the land of their fathers."[2]

Stone's anti-slavery sentiment is further revealed by his biographer, who tells us that it was generally understood among his close friends that the reason he moved to Illinois in 1834 was to escape the slavery environment of Kentucky.[3] This was not unusual, for there was a substantial exodus from the slave states during those years of leading citizens with anti-slavery convictions. Entire congregations sometimes made this exodus, which weakened the cause of emancipation in the South.[4]

One such emigrant from the South was David Purviance, who had signed *The Last Will and Testament* with Stone, and who eventually served in the Ohio legislature and as a trustee of Miami University. He worked for "gradual emancipation" all his life,[5] a position strongly current in the Movement both North and South, as well as among politicians from Thomas Jefferson to Henry Clay. It was generally the position of the Christian Church preachers of the Stone movement.

We observed in chapter 7 that Alexander Campbell championed the cause of gradual emancipation while a delegate at the Virginia Constitutional Convention in 1829. In his maiden issue as an editor in 1823 he condemned "a system of the most cruel oppression" that separates a wife from the loving embrace of her husband, and holds a man guilty because his skin is a shade darker than others.[6]

When he began the *Millennial Harbinger* seven years later, he stated his intention to deal with the way slaves were being treated, preparatory to emancipating them from their degraded condition. In that same issue he raps the state of Georgia for passing a law that made it a crime to teach a Negro to read or write. He scored the wise men of Georgia for not having heard that black men also have souls, which had recently been discovered by Virginia legislators![7]

As the slavery issue deepened in intensity, Campbell's moderate anti-slavery position became increasingly unsatisfactory to those he sought to influence. In 1835 he complained that he was being assailed from every quarter for not "coming out" for immediate emancipation. A few years later he wrote to his friend P.S. Fall in Nashville that he was surprised that his people were putting him through "an ordeal of calumny, jealousy, and rivalry," that he expected more liberality "for services rendered."[8]

By 1845, Campbell felt it necessary to present to the public an extended series of thirteen articles on "Our Position to American Slavery," and even here he had readers to reprimand him for not calling the series "*My Position . .*" The first installment, written by his father when he was 78, is the essence of the Campbell position, which is, that according to Scripture, slavery is not *per se* sinful, even if a social evil.

Thomas Campbell, whom Alexander spoke of as "pure a philanthropist as breathes," concluded from Scripture that one man might be the property of another so long as there is no infringement upon his inalienable rights. But he conceded that the nature of American slavery is such that "no Christian can either approve or practice it" and that it must and will be destroyed.[9]

The Campbells really had two positions on slavery, one theoretical and one practical. Both men made much of the scriptural injunction that masters are to render unto their slaves what is just and equal. Alexander believed that if slaveholders honored this principle that most of the evils of the system would disappear. They theoretically held a *beau ideal* view of what slavery could be, such as between Abraham and Eliezer, where the slave was both part of the household and an heir.

Theoretically, the Bible recognizes the system and lays down principles for its control. Practically, the Campbells always opposed what they saw in slave states and nations. "I am neither the advocate nor the apologist of American or any other kind of slavery," Alexander wrote in his series, but he added, "I have always been anti-slavery, but never an abolitionist."[10]

This moderate position, which advocated a gradual solution to the slave problem through legal and moral means was not sufficient to spare the Movement of the strain and stress of severe clashes between its leaders. Campbell's *Tract to the People of Kentucky* was a plea that they rid themselves of the blight of slavery in their upcoming constitutional convention, and while this may have been his best essay on slavery, it stirred the ire of some southern readers. Some cancelled their subscriptions and advised him to mind his own business — just as he had recounted in the *Tract* how he had given that advice to northern abolitionists![11]

The *Tract* to Kentuckians is important because it reveals some of his socio-economic and political thinking about slavery as well as some personal glimpses into his experience with the system. He argued that Kentucky would be much better off financially as a free state, comparing her economic record with the free state of Ohio. He went on to tell why he freed his own slaves. Impressed with the biblical principle that a master is to render to the slave what is just and equal, he concluded that a slaveholder is morally obligated to view his slave as "coequal and co-eternal" rather than as a mule.

The master should therefore provide for the slave religion, culture, and education. "It was such reasoning as this," he told his Kentucky readers, "and not the absolute Scriptural unlawfulness of Slavery, that constrained me to emancipate and set free from Slavery, not my slaves only, but myself."

He candidly added, "I hesitate not to add that emancipation was much more enjoyed by me than by them; and hence, from that day till now the emancipation of masters is full as much an object near to my heart as the emancipation of slaves." He concluded with a pungent line that pointed up the tragedy of the system: *But, alas! masters sometimes, as well as slaves, hug the chains that enslave them.*[12]

Campbell's notion that the slaveholder was also in need of emancipation is appreciated by Robert O. Fife who describes the master-slave relationship as "mutual bondage." He observes that "While the Negro was held in bondage of a very clear and obvious nature, the white master was bound with him by a yoke equally real although, perhaps, less obvious."[13] Masters who believed that they only owned the slave's labor, not his person, were less bound than the others. That must be what Thomas Campbell meant by preserving the slave's inalienable rights.

Even if Campbell's basic philosophy of social justice was, as expressed to the Kentuckians, "I desire to see every human being intelligent, virtuous, and free,"[14] he was nonetheless enmeshed in a controversy that plagued his church as well as his adopted country. If he were iconoclastic in his earlier years, he was now a peacemaker, stating explicitly that "To preserve unity of spirit among Christians of the South and of the North is my grand object."[15]

This he did by contending that the slavery issue is, after all, a political opinion, one upon which Christians may differ and still be united. Dr. Richardson, his biographer, concluded that Campbell realized his grand object, that while his moderate position brought animosity upon him from many quarters, he did save the Movement from division.[16]

Instances of Schism

It was, however, an uneasy peace, as the following data indicates, especially as it relates to the Civil War that followed the slavery controversy:

1. *They were divided as pacifists and combatants.* While both Stone and Campbell were confirmed pacifists, as were J.W. McGarvey, Benjamin Franklin, Moses E. Lard, Tolbert Fanning, and many others, there were those who took up arms against each other. Stone and Campbell both had a son in the Confederate army. James A. Garfield, destined to be President, was a Union general, while J.H. Garrison was a colonel.

Some were fiercely belligerent. A minister in Des Moines advocated hanging the Confederate leaders, while B.F. Hall denied that the Yankees in the Christian Church were even his brothers, and if there was any opportunity to shoot them with his trusty rifle, he wanted first chance.[17]

Pacifism was not sectional, for the war produced peace documents in both North and South. Fourteen ministers in Missouri issued a "Circular" that they would not take up arms against their brethren, the peace of the church being one reason. J.W. McGarvey was one of them.[18] In Tennessee leaders of ten to fifteen churches, including David Lipscomb, wrote to the president of the Confederacy, asking to be relieved of military service.[19]

Generally, however, the sectional feelings were bitter. One writer of the period notes that even the preachers would not attempt to mitigate the horrors of war or to soothe the fierce passions that were aroused, but actually strove to increase the horrors and further inflame the passions.[20]

2. *Fellowship in many churches was wrenched.* With 600,000 casualties in the conflict between the states, more than in all other wars of this nation combined, it would follow that the relationship between churches would be strained to the breaking point. Some would not break bread with slaveholders, while others would not fellowship abolitionists. Some made the war a test of fellowship. Campbell saw the abolitionists as the source of much of the problem.

One John Kirk, for example, wrote to Campbell from Ohio objecting to his moderate views, telling him that the brethren generally in the Western Reserve would not support anyone who was not "strictly anti-slavery." Furthermore, he told the editor, the church should deal with slaveholders the same way it would a horse thief. Campbell in turn likened him to a pope and the witch hunters of Salem.[21] Such exchanges, in churches and journals alike, were common.

3. *The societies were in turmoil.* When the American Christian Missionary Society met in Cincinnati in 1861, the war had already begun, hindering the attendance of the southerners who were usually there. Those present passed a resolution committing the society to loyalty toward the Union. Two years later the society passed a stronger resolution: "*Resolved, that we tender our sympathies to our brave and noble soldiers in the field, who are defending us from the attempts of armed traitors to overthrow our Government, and also to those bereaved, and rendered desolate by the ravages of war.*"[22]

When the news of these resolutions reached the South, a sizable number in the Christian Church went out angrily and joined the Confederate army.[23] Tolbert Fanning fumed, charging that the society was approving of wholesale murder and enforcing political opinion with the sword.[24] The news spread widely among the churches. The South was hurt.

It was the abolitionists, however, who posed the greatest threat to the unity of the Movement. They called an antislavery convention in Cleveland in 1854, and they created the rival Christian Missionary Society in

Indianapolis in 1859.[25] The convention was billed by some as "Trouble Among the Campbellites," but Campbell insisted that it was of no moment, for it was arranged by a handful of "factionists" and attended by only 33 people.[26]

But the rival missionary society, inspired by Pardee Butler, the militant abolitionist whose story we have recounted, was more significant than Campbell admitted. Its call to convene garnered over 800 signatures, and with Butler as president it attracted some of the Movement's ablest men. While it lived only four years and did little more than to sponsor Butler in Kansas, it served as a symbol of the factional spirit that prevailed during the war. The churches that supported it were labeled "abolitionist," and it put pressure on many of the preachers who were divided in their loyalties between the welfare of the church and the cause of abolition.

Some of the leading editor bishops saw the society as factional. Isaac Errett charged that the new society made it clear that the abolitionists were willing to divide the church over a difference of opinion, while Benjamin Franklin sought to curb the society's influence by urging his readers to have nothing to do with it.[27]

4. *There was tension between journals and schools.* Not satisfied with the pacifistic stance of the Movement's leading journals, the abolitionists started their own paper, the *North-Western Christian Magazine*, edited by John Boggs, in Cincinnati in 1854. This journal and its successor, the *Christian Luminary*, were explicitly abolitionist and carried on a crusade against the more moderate publications. While Campbell hailed Boggs as "a good and honorable man," he questioned both the name and the intent of the new journal, this being one of the rare occasions that he showed editorial pettiness. He objected to the use of *North-West* as sectional bias and to the use of *Magazine* as contradictory to *Christian*, since no magazine could be Christian! Moreover, the journal had a political mission, which was to teach its views on slavery to people of the North, which was needed in neither North or South, Campbell charged.[28]

But the journal had its constituency, for, as Henry K. Shaw has noted, the majority of Ohio Disciples were sympathetic to abolitionism, as were many in northern Indiana, though not southern Indiana. The historian observes that North-Western Christian University, founded in 1855 in Indianapolis with a pronounced anti-slavery bias, floundered financially for lack of support from southern Indiana churches. They objected to what Benjamin Franklin called the school's "hobbyism and ultraism."[29] Boggs' editorial efforts sparked a radical anti-slavery campaign that brought moderates and abolitionists into serious conflict. The conflict was intensified by the founding of North-Western Christian University, which was in tension with Bethany College from the outset. Ovid Butler, its founder, frankly told Campbell that Disciples of his persuasion felt that Bethany favored the South in both politics (meaning the slavery issue) and religion.

He further charged that this sectionalism was evident in the pattern of Campbell's travels, which nearly always took him south and never as far west as Indiana, despite repeated invitations. Campbell's reply to the latter criticism probably did not help matters: He had not yet ventured into Indiana because it has fevers in the autumn and bad roads in the winter![30]

This conflict, along with others we have noticed, cannot be appreciated without realizing Campbell's obsession for Bethany College as a necessary adjunct of his reformation, "essential to its progress and prosperity" as he once put it. Even though it was "a continual incubus and trouble" to him personally, he was perplexed that his people had responded to it with such apathy.

He saw Bethany as *the* college, even the only college if need be, of the Movement, for it was centrally located, "not a provincial affair," and serving impartially all sections of the nation. It was not a theological school, but "a literary and scientific institution built upon the Bible." While it served "the greatest cause pled by man," it still went begging for funds and students. He left it with the brethren to decide if it would pine away and die or go forth and do its work.[31]

It is understandable, therefore, that his response to a new college as near as Indianapolis would be less than enthusiastic. Campbell told the Indiana brethren that another college was not as appropriate and necessary as they supposed and that their efforts were sectionally and politically inspired, as well as ill-begotten. But it was left to his junior editor and son-in-law to reveal how strongly they both thought. "Northwestern Christian University is too much tinctured with the fanatical sectarianism of politico-religious abolitionism," wrote W.K. Pendleton, "to be of any service to the Christian church or cause."[32]

A student protest at Bethany College in 1855 served to illustrate what was happening on a large scale. While Bethany was then in the slave state of Virginia, it was in a free county, and Campbell boasted of the fact that there was not one slave in the entire county. The college nonetheless seemed to have a southern bias, for most of its students and its support came from the South. In 1855 only 30 of its 130 students were from free states. Though the school had a policy that "strictly scientific, literary and moral" subjects should be pursued and "sectional" controversies should be avoided, slavery nonetheless was now and again debated by the students.

Those from the North felt that they were put upon by the southern majority. A ministerial student from Canada sought to atone for this by preaching against slavery on a Sunday evening at the village church. Campbell described the student's behavior as "unjustifiable and rude" since it was generally understood that "the much vexed question of slavery" was not to be aired behind the sacred desk.[33]

The student's discourse against slavery was met with hissing and rustling of feet. Campbell conceded that 20 to 30 in the audience got up and walked out, "making lots of noise, both with their feet and canes." The reference to canes alludes to the practice that was common in those days of using them to cope with Bethany's hills.

This led the northerners to strike, vowing that they would attend no more classes until debate on slavery was allowed and the offending students were reprimanded by the faculty. The faculty was incensed by such insubordination and ruled that the students should return to their classes forthwith or be expelled. Five students were eventually dismissed and five others voluntarily left with them.

But Campbell thought it noteworthy that two-thirds of the northerners stayed, and he insisted that a congenial spirit prevailed among the remaining student body. He was ready to pass the incident off as one more disciplinary problem, common to all schools, especially when some come as patriots and reformers rather than as students. It is interesting that one of the dissenting students was Barton W. Johnson, who was destined to join the ranks of the Movement's editor bishops.[34]

The affair might have ended here had not radical antislavery forces taken advantage of it. Some of the expelled students proceeded to apply for admittance to North-Western Christian University. While it was customary for one school to honor the disciplinary actions of another, the Indianapolis school deemed it appropriate to make an exception in this case and thus accepted the students, as did the Indianapolis church. This added fuel to the Indianapolis-Bethany feud and set in motion a controversy that hardly has a parallel in the Movement's educational history.[35]

These two colleges, with so much in common, embarked upon a vendetta that appears incredible. Their exchange of letters only intensified the tension. North-Western requested from Bethany an accounting of why they had dismissed the students, implying that the reason was sectional bias. Bethany responded that they were not responsible to others for their decisions, but that the students, who were "under the wicked spirit of a politico-religious fanaticism," would have been expelled regardless of where they came from.

Using the columns of the *North-Western Christian Magazine*, whose editor, John Boggs, was for sometime in the North thought to be a "nigger," the Indianapolis college leveled insinuations against Campbell.

The Bethany faculty in turn charged that North-Western's motives were wanton, and that it was with poor grace for a young faculty, themselves educated at Bethany, to become "public revilers of the fathers in Israel." It was clear to Bethany that the abolitionists in Indianapolis were out to do them in and that the issue was slavery.[36]

This is indicated by what others were making of the Bethany affair, some as far away as Scotland where Campbell had been, as he saw it, jailed for his views on slavery. Two newspapers in Glasgow headlined the Bethany onset as "Campbellite Proslaveryism" and "Slavery Intolerance." To an Indianapolis newspaper it had become "The Bethany Riot." Even the *New York Tribune* gave what Campbell called "a dissertation of its own peculiar type." He was pleased that the *Louisville Journal*, the one paper that took Bethany's side, "unanswerably" responded to it.[37]

Further Tensions

The Bethany episode serves to reveal the intensity of the slavery issue both in and out of the church. It was a time when, according to Indiana pioneer Elijah Goodwin, leaders in the Movement spoke in terms of *We* and *They* even when they decried division.[38] Name-calling was now common. James A. Garfield would complain to Isaac Errett of an effort "to throw the abolition stench around us," while Errett, who moved from a strong anti-slavery stance to a more moderate position, was labeled by John Boggs as "the pliant tool of slave-holding aristocracy."[39] The tension even came to affect the way innovations were described, such as "niggers and organs."

It should be noted, however, that the tension was not as much North and South as one might think. The Indianapolis-Bethany feud was between northerners, as was the struggle between the editor bishops. The abolitionists within the Movement focused their attack on the moderates, such as Errett in Cincinnati and Campbell who was even farther north in Virginia's "free" panhandle, not on the editors or churches in the South. Not only were the radicals who caused all the trouble, such as John Boggs and Pardee and Ovid Butler, northerners, but so were their antagonists.

The only editor in the South that was even mildly proslavery was John Howard of the *Christian Pioneer*, but he was so irenic that he managed to avoid strife even in a few exchanges with John Boggs. Howard, in fact, from his perspective in the slave state of Missouri, saw the Movement as still united the very year the war started. Howard responded to an article in the *Missouri State Journal*, written by an outsider who theorized that the Christian Church had avoided sectional strife because it had never allowed political dogmas to be taught in the pulpit. He agreed that his people had remained united, while others had not, because they adhered closely to the Bible, "which leads us to ignore all speculations and political dogmas."[40]

While the friction was severe it was mostly in the North and in the border states, and agitated by the abolitionists, who were comparatively few. The vast majority of the leadership, North and South, was moderate, even inclined toward pacifism, and this helps to explain why the Movement survived in spite of all the strife.

The deep South was protected from extensive schism because of this moderation. John Boggs, looking back on those trying years two decades later, observed that while the slavery question was "peculiarly perplexing" it did not lay as heavily upon the southern church as it might have. This is because the leaders opposed slavery "only in the abstract," even suggesting that the relation of master and slave was not necessarily sinful.[41]

The moderation of Tolbert Fanning, editor of the *Gospel Advocate* in Nashville during those turbulent years, is a case in point. While he was a witness to the injustices of slavery, he realized that two-thirds of the white people of the South had no involvement whatever with the system, including himself. He hated slavery, as did most southerners, not only for what it did for the Negro but to the white man as well. Furthermore it was divisive, and long before the Civil War it had divided the leading denominations. As his biographer puts it: "Fanning waged a relentless war, however, aimed both North and South, to stave off this same division in the Churches of Christ.[42]

The Nashville editor worked and worshipped with Negroes for decades before the war, his church in the state capital being half-white and half-black. After the war he expressed regret that this could not continue. All through those years he kept busy as a peacemaker, instilling trust and understanding between brethren North and South.

Fanning visited Negro churches in the North and returned home convinced that the black brother had a better way of life in Nashville than in any other city. And, as we have seen, he also went North to attend the American Christian Missionary Society in 1859 with his perennial message, *We are one people!* Above all, Tolbert Fanning did not want to quarrel with his brethren, North or South, over slavery and the war, and he can be seen as the alter ego of the southern church.

Belles-Lettres of the Frontier

While slavery and the war were, as John Boggs said, "perculiarly perplexing," the Movement responded to the pressure with grace, and survived as a force for unity and reformation as intended by its founders.

This can be seen in the belles-lettres of the frontier, the thousands of reports from the field written by various leaders in the church both North and South. Some were written by preachers who moved back and forth across the Mason-Dixon line as if there were no sectional strife.

These letters not only in some instances qualify as fine literature, but they mirror the mind of the churches and the spirit of the people in time of great peril.

One surprising element in these reports, which were sent to the various journals and especially to Campbell's *Millennial Harbinger*, is that they so often make no reference at all to the war. They tell of extensive travel of the evangelists among the churches in both North and South, numerous baptisms and additions to the church, the victories and defeats common to church life, and generally reflect the well-being of the Movement.

Some of the reports from the South disarm the researcher who expects to find most southern churches in a bad way. This one from Richmond, Va. is an example, written the year the war ended by one of the abler preachers, W. H. Hopson: "A few, and only a few, of our churches, were demoralized by the war. These few we feel fully confident of being able soon to reconstruct."[43]

Hopson reports in the same letter that "We lost many of our brethren — especially the young — during the war," but goes on to say that as an evangelist among the churches he had gained 1,000 new additions in Virginia in the past six months. In the same context Justus M. Barnes, the foremost leader in Alabama, wrote from the capital of the Confederacy that he was disgusted with politics and never intended even to cast another vote, for he had voted for peace and it had failed. But he believed that future generations would take note of the fact that "the prominent men of the Reformation both North and South" had in time of strife preached the gospel of peace and goodwill.

Barnes conceded that "Internal commotions indeed trouble us," which he attributed to the liberation of uneducated and uncultured slaves. Still he was confident that "Primitive Christianity never saw a brighter day in this section of the country than at this time." He went on to tell Campbell that their people had suffered greatly and that they had not even sold what little cotton they had, but that "the Christian is always rich without a cent in his pocket." He also reported upwards of 150 additions to the churches in the area since the federal army had taken over.

A random survey of some of the letters written the year the war ended reveals a Movement that was very much alive. One from Philadelphia reports that the church was increasing and the people encouraged. W.T.

Moore, who was later to write his monumental history of the Disciples, tells of 50 additions to his Detroit church within three months, insisting that no field could be greater.

An Ohio preacher reports 28 converts in the best meeting they ever had, while an evangelist from Kentucky tells of 500 additions among the churches over a period of fifteen months. An obscure preacher from southern Virginia writes of 192 additions and says, "I have never found the public ear more open to conviction." One from Decatur, Illinois not only told of 20 immersions, but added that he was having large audiences and no abatement of interest. Another report from W.H. Hopson in Richmond revealed that a move was underway to unite the Baptists and Disciples.

While a preacher in Alabama makes no reference to the war, he makes use of military language: "The old Jerusalem doctrine, which is the Sword of the Spirit, is becoming a formidable weapon here. We have recently made a push at the King's enemies — 78 were slain, and many wounded. The Captain of our salvation, Jesus, is braver than death."

Another from the deep South writes: "Never was there such a spirit of inquiry among the people as now. . We have ten or a dozen preaching brethren in the State, unsurpassed for intelligence and devotion to the cause, whose efforts are almost entirely paralyzed on account of *poverty and nothing else!*"[44]

A pattern emerges from the mountain of correspondence: Northern churches were growing with prosperity; southern churches were growing in poverty. W.K. Pendleton, while at Bethany in the year that Campbell died, launched an effort to help the poor brethren in the South. He tells how a southern brother reported on the poverty in the South to the Indiana State Missionary Society and of the tearful response of that body.[45]

Pendleton also refers to the prospects of a restoration of political harmony between North and South and the "close fellowship of our Christian union."[46] The contributions continued for some two years, and while the amount forwarded to southern churches was not great, it served to bear witness to the fact that brethren in the North still cared. Sisters in the Bethany church made 400 garments for their counterparts in the South.

T.M. Allen: The Movement's Correspondent

The most illustrious instance of frontier belles-lettres was the correspondence of T.M. Allen of Missouri, whose letters to various papers over a period of 40 years serve as a miniature chronicle of the Movement. Campbell referred to them as a model for collecting information about their community, and Pendleton said that his letters read like those of a patriarch. Having come up through the Christian Connection, Allen's earliest reports from the field were to editors Elias Smith and Barton W. Stone.

He reported also to Benjamin Franklin, John R. Howard, Tolbert Fanning, and Alexander Campbell. The 145 letters he sent to Bethany are a veritable storehouse of historical data. One editor refers to him as "the most accurate and voluminous correspondent." All this should lend credence to the judgments he made about the Movement during the war crisis.[47]

More than any other reporter from the field, Allen made reference to the "political excitement and feeling in the country" and its effect upon the reformation. From Columbia, Missouri in 1861 he told of 64 additions, mostly from students at the state university and the Christian college there, and then added: "May the good Lord carry on his good work, and save us from division and ruin." Later that year he reported from St. Louis that he had immersed "two very intelligent Presbyterian ladies" among others, and he said he believed that "The spirit of Christian union is evidently on the increase, and the brethren are greatly strengthened."[48] Ever since he had helped to solidify the merger of the Christians and Reformers in Lexington in 1832, the preservation of the union of those people had been his constant concern.

After Fort Sumter was fired upon, Allen reported to Campbell that "the war spirit had been high in the country" and that some of the brethren had gone off to war with implements of death in their hands. When they asked him if he did not arm himself during such perilous times, he replied that he was indeed armed, with the sword of the Spirit, the word of God, and that he would carry no other weapon. "I would sooner go to the grave being killed for not killing my brother," he told Campbell, "than to go to the tomb with my brother's blood on my hands," which was a common view among Disciples preachers.

Still he reported more additions and noted that the work continued to be encouraging.[49] In July of 1861 he wrote from Audrain county, Missouri and told of fighting between "the U.S. and State troops" in the adjoining counties, which created excitement in his meetings that continued to attract large crowds and bear abundant fruit.[50]

Shortly after the outbreak of the war he wrote to Campbell from St. Louis: "It is pleasing for us to know that notwithstanding the defection, troubles and afflictions that prevail in our land, we are yet a united people; and God grant that we may continue with one heart and soul to contend for the faith once delivered to the saints."[51]

At last, in the midst of the war, Campbell writes to Allen and tells him how Bethany is reduced to only a shadow of what it once was, that military glory was being canonized, and that their brethren were more interested in saving their country than in saving their souls. And Campbell pays tribute to the old warrior of many seasons, applying Psa. 92:12-14 to him, which promises that the righteous will flourish like the palm tree, and that in old age it will bear fruit when others fade. He reminded his worn-out colaborer that there is a reward that God gives that eclipses all the honors and glories of this world.[52]

It is noteworthy that one of T.M. Allen's knowledge of the Movement would express gratitude to Campbell that *We are yet a united people*. It is incredible that the Movement could at this time have been divided, as some historians now conclude, and T.M. Allen not know it!

Did the Civil War Divide the Movement?

The foregoing data indicate that slavery, the Civil War, and their socio-economic aftermath did not divide the Disciples as they did other churches, but this thesis has been vigorously challenged by recent historians. The thesis is as old as Disciples history itself. Back in 1899, W.T. Moore, the first to prepare a definitive history, insisted that the Disciples were "neither practically nor formally" divided during the war, though he conceded afterwards in his chronicle of the Movement that the war "put a heavy strain on fellowship."[53]

W.E. Garrison and A.T. DeGroot, the deans of Disciples history, have especially argued for the continued unity of their people during the Civil War. In their *Disciples of Christ: A History* they feature a sub-heading that reads "Through Civil War without Division," noting that the first-generation leaders were still alive during the war and that they had too strong a passion for unity to allow division to occur.[54]

In a separate study DeGroot cites the ruptures that occurred within Baptist, Presbyterian, Methodist, and Episcopal churches because of war issues, and then claims that "the Disciples of Christ remained unique in their solidarity."[55]

James DeForest Murch in a more recent study has also said: "The Christian churches were the only major Protestant body having sizable numbers of constituents in both North and South that did not divide."[56] In other studies by Earl I. West, Oliver Read Whitley, and Robert O. Fife, who represent all three major wings of the Movement, the same thesis is defended.[57]

Henry K. Shaw in 1966 was the first to question this, stating there was "a *de facto* division among the Disciples over slavery and the war." The war deprived the church of the will to remain united, he says, and division finally came over issues that would have been ignored before the war. While this *de facto* division continues to be ignored by Disciple historians, he insists that it contained the seed that led to the separation of Churches of Christ in 1906.[58]

In another challenge to the common Disciples interpretation, David E. Harrell, Jr. adds a new dimension, contending that statistics of the sectional distribution of Churches of Christ (non-instrumental) in the South demonstrates a socio-economic cause for a division that did indeed take place.

Harrell finds the statistical evidence overpowering, for nearly two-thirds of the 156,658 members of Churches of Christ in the 1906 census were in the eleven former states of the Confederacy, while most of the rest were in the border states. Only one state north of the Ohio had as many as 5,000 members. This led him to pose the pertinent question: "Why did such a large number of Southern Disciples oppose 'innovations' while most northern Disciples believed the Scriptures authorized them?"[59]

The rejoinder of Shaw and Harrell have had some effect in altering the "official" position on Disciples unity during the Civil War. In a history commissioned by the Christian Board of Publication, William E. Tucker, chancellor of Texas Christian University, departs from the Garrison-DeGroot thesis to concede that the Civil War must now be seen as a watershed for the Christian Church (Disciples of Christ).[60] Henry Webb of Milligan College in a recent essay supports Harrell's thesis.[61]

But the case for the Movement's unity during the Civil War is not yet overturned. Harrell's position has serious difficulties, one being that the strongholds of conservatism during this period were not in the South but in the North, a fact we shall deal with later. As for his question as to why southerners rejected innovations while the northerners accepted them may beg the issue, for the dichotomy was not all that sharp.

There are numerous instances in both North and South where the organ, for instance, was *both* received and rejected, with no evidence that sectional bias was a factor. As Forrest Read concluded in his incisive study of this period, "The conservatist-liberal or the fundamentalist-modernist controversy is not confined exclusively to any section of the country and never has been."[62]

Even so, the great conservative bloc in the South that eventually became Churches of Christ may be accounted for on the same basis as so many other things in Disciples history, the incredible influence of its editor bishops. There is no way to minimize the strong conservative influence of those indomitable leaders in Nashville, Tolbert Fanning and his protege David Lipscomb. They were the southern church and gave it its vigorous conservative character.

But more than all this, those who find the Movement's first rupture in some kind of social determinism must account not for one division but many. Why has the Movement continued to divide, again and again, not only in the U.S. but abroad as well? How is the divisive pattern that reaches back to the Haldanes, the Sandemanians, and finally to the Anabaptists to be explained? The answer appears not to lie as much in socio-economic forces as in the nature of restorationism itself.

Restorationists or primitivists who find in Scripture a fixed pattern for the church are tempted to impose their interpretation of "the true church" upon others. This is a good description of legalism, which has divided the church into *hundreds* of warring sects. The Plymouth Brethren are a case in point. As restorationist-legalists, they have divided into at least six sects, each claiming to be the true church. This kind of restorationist legalism appears to be what happened to the Stone-Campbell Movement, which stemmed in part from an unfortunate application of Thomas Campbell's call for "an approved precedent," as we have noted.

But this legalism did not gain dominance in the Movement by the time of the Civil War, or as long as Alexander Campbell lived, though it was at work. There was not, therefore, what W.T. Moore chose to call "a real division" for another generation.

Equivocating terms that keep coming up in this context like *practical* division, *formal* division, *de facto* division, and *real* division suggest that this is partly a semantic problem.

If by "divided" one means there were local schisms and widespread conflict, then the Movement divided during the Civil War. But if "divided" means it was at first united as one church and afterwards became two or more, then it did not divide. We agree with Robert Fife's research, as noted above, that while there were local schisms resulting from the war, there was "general unity." The time came, however, when they *did* divide into two churches, then three. But this was long after the Civil War and for other reasons.

Can A Movement Be Divided And Not Know It?

It hardly figures that a people could be divided and not know it. Both Harrell and Tucker quote Moses E. Lard's answer to the question *Can we divide?*, in which he said the fierce ordeal of a terrible war did not cause a single rent in Disciples ranks. It may have caused tensions, he granted, but "still it effected no division." *We can never divide!*, he insisted.[63]

Harrell calls this premature and Tucker says it was exuberance, as if Lard's was a lonely, sanguine voice among a people who surely knew better. But this was hardly the case, for we have already seen that such seasoned leaders as T.M. Allen and Robert Richardson saw themselves as still a united people. Allen rejoiced with Campbell that "We are yet a united people," while Richardson said it was Campbell's moderate position on slavery that kept the Disciples from dividing.

Moreover, David Lipscomb in the South pled with his brethren in the North for financial aid for their poor southern brethren on the basis that they were a united people:

> Christian union won't let the preachers North of the Ohio and Cumberland rivers dress fine, receive 1,000 dollars, live in ease and plenty, while their preaching brethren just across the State line are driven from the field of evangelical labor, to save their families from starvation and nakedness, while thousands equally as poor in this world's goods are crying at their doors for the bread of life.[64]

The Nashville editor really laid it on: Brethren, *such a union as this is not of God.* Lipscomb would not have argued this way if the war had made them a northern and southern church, but he clearly saw something lacking in the unity that prevailed, which is often the case, in any age of the church, when alms are solicited.

In 1868, when dealing with a dissident group of Disciples who were saying "the Reformation is a failure," to the delight of the critics of the Movement, W.K. Pendleton insisted it was a case of their enemies making a mountain of a mole hill. This led him to add: "The fact is there is no such 'party,' nor is there any sign or fear of division among us. There never was a more united and indissoluble people than we are."[65]

One Disciples historian sees the schisms recounted in this chapter as testimonials to the Movement's basic unity during this period. She cites Benjamin Franklin's assertion that there was general unity in spite of two little factions, those who were the hobbyists on both sides of the slavery question. Franklin called it only a "schism in feeling," though he was aware it could have become a schism in practice.

Quoting John Boggs to the effect that "Slavery has divided us," the historian shows that this was hardly the case, for even a second missionary society was allowed to exist without any serious difficulty. It was only a tiny minority, even from the North, that answered the call for an anti-slavery society, she observes, and these were allowed their opinion. She says it was their passion for unity that kept them together, and yet she concludes that the Disciples too would probably have divided as did the other churches if they had had a similar ecclesiastical structure.[66]

Another Disciples historian, Ronald E. Osborn, sees his people still united during the slavery-Civil War controversy only because of the charismatic leadership of Alexander Campbell. The magnitude of the implications of Campbell's death in 1866, he says, has scarcely been suggested by historians.

The ills that followed, leading to the eventual separation of Churches of Christ, are due to the fact that there was no one to take Campbell's place who could hold the opposing forces together, Osborn concludes. Even though the Movement grew in those years following his death, it nonetheless began to fall apart, for upon Campbell's death "the bankruptcy of the plea became evident,"[67] a judgment that does not necessarily follow even if division did come.

A spate of seminary and university theses have weighed the question of just when and why the Movement divided, so many in fact that still another thesis could be prepared analyzing their conclusions! W.O. Harrison (Chicago, 1936) sees the legalism of the radicals as the basic cause of division, though cultural and social factors were contributing causes. Edward Coffman (Vanderbilt, 1930) does not see the war as a cause, but, like Osborn, concludes that Campbell's death set in motion a power struggle among the editors that eventually led to schism. He pinpoints the time of division to David Lipscomb's leadership in the South in the 1890's. Ernest Ford (Lexington, 1922) traces the split to a conservatism that has always been present in the Movement.

One of the more influential theses, that of historian Howard E. Short (Hartford, 1932), cites three isms, legalism, literalism and anti-ism, as the culprits. James B. Major (Vanderbilt, 1966) sees sectionalism as the real cause of the eventual fission, while the non-cooperation issue was the presumed cause. Billy Joe Humble (Iowa, 1964) accepts sectionalism and the war as causes, but, like DeGroot, sees the restoration principle as the basic cause. Arthur V. Murrell (Vanderbilt, 1972) rejects both Garrison's thesis, that the war had no divisive affect at all, and Harrell's, that the war divided the Disciples, and concludes that while the war certainly worked havoc, it was the exclusivism of those who became the Churches of Christ that caused the split.[68]

We can only conclude that all these factors played some part in the divisions that finally came. In all of life's tragedies, whether the breakup of a marriage or the fracture of a unity movement, there are many forces at work. What is noticeable in these studies, however, is a lack of emphasis upon the Civil War as the major cause. There is general agreement that the Movement did not divide until the Churches of Christ separated from the rest of the Movement long after the Civil War.

The historian has to decide the degree to which he yields to the claims of social determinism. If socio-economic factors related to the Civil War *caused* the Stone-Campbell Movement to divide, then the schism was determined by forces beyond the moral responsibility of those involved. If the Christian historian sees sin in the events of history, then blame is to be laid at someone's door. If social forces beyond his control are to blame, then man is only victimized by his environment and has not sinned.

The pioneers who launched the Movement rediscovered the sinfulness of a divided church. Their passion for unity was predicated upon the proposition that division is "a horrid evil fraught with many evils." Their conviction that the church by its very nature is one made them reluctant to start another church or to be separatists.

Once they were a denomination *in protest*, they remained a unity movement, and they were determined never to become a divided people. Campbell was persuaded that his people would never divide if they remained faithful to the principles they had embraced.[69] To divide would not only be a betrayal of their mission, but a sin against heaven.

The determinist sees socio-economic forces as the cause of the effect in question. When these forces are present, the effect is inevitable. That is why some of these historians tell us that the Movement *had* to divide. If a secular historian is oblivious to the effect of sin in human history, the Christian historian should not be. He sees that some things that happened did not have to happen, and that it was wrong when they did happen. He presents the facts so that people may learn from the mistakes of their forebearers, and "Go and sin no more."

The story of the first major rupture in the Stone-Campbell Movement will be told in chapter 16. Our conclusion at this point is that the Movement was still one church, North and South, as it faced the post-Civil War era, though it had been brutally assailed. Its integrity as a unity movement had been severely tested, but it passed the test, even if bruised and bloodied by the ordeal.

Or, as suggested by our chapter title, the Movement was brought to the brink of division. While the times were indeed precipitous, the Movement had not yet fatally sinned against its own principles. It was at the brink, and, as some historians have suggested, if someone could have taken Alexander Campbell's place, it might have retreated from the brink and never divided. But this was not to be.

ENDNOTES

[1]A.T. DeGroot, *The Grounds of Divisions Among the Disciples of Christ,* Chicago: Privately published, 1940.

[2]Barton W. Stone, "An Humble Address to Christians, etc.," *Christian Messenger,* Vol. 3 (1828), p. 298f.; "Georgetown Colonization Society," *Ibid.,* Vol. 4 (1829), p. 236.

[3]John Rogers, *Biography of B. W. Stone,* Cincinnati, 1847, p. 293.

[4]W.H. Yarbrough, *Economic Aspects of Slavery in Relation to Southern and Southwestern Migration,* Nashville, 1932, p. 8f.

[5]Levi Purviance, *Biography of Elder David Purviance,* Dayton, 1848, p. 111.

[6]Alexander Campbell, "Christian Religion," *Christian Baptist,* Vol. 1 (1827), p. 18 (Gospel Advocate Edition).

[7]Alexander Campbell, "Prospectus," *Millennial Harbinger,* 1830, p. 1; "Georgia Slaves," *Ibid.,* p. 47.

[8]Alexander Campbell, "Abolitionism," *Millennial Harbinger,* 1836, p. 282; Letter of Campbell to Fall see footnote in D.E. Harrell, Jr., *Quest for Christian America* (Nashville: DCHS, 1966), p. 105.

[9]"Elder Thomas Campbell's Views on Slavery," *Millennial Harbinger,* 1845, p. 8.

[10]Alexander Campbell, "American Slavery," *Millennial Harbinger,* 1845, p. 355f.

[11]Alexander Campbell, "Letter from Brother Smith," *Millennial Harbinger,* 1849, p. 413.

[12]Alexander Campbell, "A Tract for the People of Kentucky," *Millennial Harbinger,* 1849, p. 249.

[13]Robert O. Fife, *Teeth on Edge* (Grand Rapids: Baker, 1971), p. 25.

[14]Alexander Campbell, "A Tract for the People of Kentucky," *Millennial Harbinger,* 1849, p. 243.

[15]Alexander Campbell, "Our Position to American Slavery," *Millennial Harbinger,* 1845, p. 195.

[16]Robert Richardson, *Memoirs of Alexander Campbell,* Vol. 2, Cincinnati, 1897, p. 534.

[17]Herman Norton, *Tennessee Christians* (Nashville: Reed, 1971), p. 93.

[18]"Circular from Preachers in Missouri," *Millennial Harbinger,* 1861, p. 583.

[19]Earl I. West, *Life and Times of David Lipscomb* (Henderson, TN: Religious Book Service), p. 87.

[20]William Baxter, *Pea Ridge and Prairie Grove* (Reprint, 1957, Arkansas Historical Series) Orig. publ. 1864, p. 113.

[21]Alexander Campbell, "Our Position to American Slavery," *Millennial Harbinger,* 1851, pp. 49f.

[22]See Norton, *Tennessee Christians,* pp. 105-108 for an account of the resolutions and their effect on the South.

[23]Earl I. West, *Life and Times of David Lipscomb*, p. 82.

[24]Norton, *Tennessee Christians*, p. 107.

[25]See Eileen Gordon Vandergrift, *The Christian Missionary Society*, Unpublished M.A. thesis, Butler, 1945.

[26]"Trouble Among the Campbellites," *Millennial Harbinger*, 1854, p. 173.

[27]David E. Harrell, *Quest For A Christian America* (Nashville: DCHS, 1966), p. 119.

[28]Alexander Campbell, "North-Western Christian Magazine," *Millennial Harbinger*, 1854, p. 474.

[29]Henry K. Shaw, *Buckeye Disciples* (St. Louis: Christian Board of Pub., 1952), p. 142. See also his *Hoosier Disciples* (St. Louis: Bethany), p. 170.

[30]Alexander Campbell, "The North-Western Christian University," *Millennial Harbinger*, 1850, pp. 329f.

[31]Alexander Campbell, "Letter to B.F. Perky," *Millennial Harbinger*, 1851, pp. 715f.

[32]W.K. Pendleton, "Our Progress and Prospects," *Millennial Harbinger*, 1859, p. 713.

[33]For Campbell's lengthy description of this interesting episode see "Disturbance at Bethany College," *Millennial Harbinger*, 1856, pp. 54f.

[34]B.W. Johnson was co-editor of *Christian Evangelist* with J. H. Garrison and was known as liberal on social issues. He authored the popular *Johnson's Notes on the New Testament*.

[35]For an objective description of this incredible story see Henry K. Shaw, *Hoosier Disciples*, pp. 163f.

[36]"College Etiquette and the Faculty of the North-Western University," *Millennial Harbinger*, 1856, pp. 226f.

[37]"Reported Troubles in Bethany College," *Millennial Harbinger*, 1856, p. 111.

[38]Henry K. Shaw, *Hoosier Disciples*, p. 158.

[39]J.S. Lamar, *Memoirs of Isaac Errett*, Vol. 1 (Cincinnati: Standard, 1893), p. 217.

[40]John R. Howard, "The Christian Church," *Christian Pioneer*, Vol. 1 (1861), p. 130.

[41]John Boggs in R.B. Hastings, *Personal Recollections of Pardee Butler* (Cincinnati: Standard, 1889), p. 318.

[42]James R. Wilburn, *The Hazard of the Die* (Austin: Sweet), p. 207.

[43]"Good Words from Our Correspondents," *Millennial Harbinger*, 1866, p. 46.

[44]*Ibid.*, p. 384.

[45]W.K. Pendleton, "Aid for the Suffering Brethren in the South," *Millennial Harbinger*, 1866, p. 525.

[46]"Contributions for Churches in the South," *Ibid.*, p. 383.

[47]Alvin Jennings, *T. M. Allen: Pioneer Preacher of Kentucky and Missouri* (Ft. Worth: Star Bible and Tract Corp., 1977), pp. 153f.

[48]"Progress of Reform," *Millennial Harbinger*, 1861, pp. 175f.

[49]*Ibid.*, p. 478.

[50]*Ibid.*, p. 539.

[51]*Ibid.*, p. 360.

[52]Alexander Campbell, "Response," *Millennial Harbinger*, 1862, p. 83.

[53]W.T. Moore, "Reformation of the 19th Century," *Christian Evangelist*, Vol. 36 (1899), p. 680; W. T. Moore, *Comprehensive History of the Disciples of Christ*, New York: Revell, 1909, p. 150.

[54]W.E. Garrison and A. T. DeGroot, *The Disciples of Christ: A History* (St. Louis: Bethany, 1948), pp. 333-337.

[55]A.T. DeGroot, *The Grounds of Division Among Disciples of Christ*, pp. 73-75.

[56]James DeForest Murch, *Christians Only* (Cincinnati: Standard, 1962), p. 151.

[57]Robert O. Fife in his *Alexander Campbell and the Christian Church in the Slavery Controversy*, Unpublished Ph.D. thesis, Indiana University, 1960, says "general unity" was maintained, but lists several instances of division among churches, especially in Illinois and Ohio.

[58]Henry K. Shaw, *Hoosier Disciples* (St. Louis: Bethany, 1966), pp. 155-163.

[59]David E. Harrell, *The Social Sources of Division in the Disciples of Christ 1865-1900* (Atlanta: Publication Systems, 1973), pp. 324-326.

[60]Lester G. McAllister and William E. Tucker, *Journey in Faith: A History of the Christian Church (Disciples of Christ)* (St. Louis: Bethany, 1975), pp. 207,208.

[61]Henry E. Webb, "Sectional Conflicts and Schism Within the Disciples of Christ Following Civil War," *Essays on New Testament Christianity*, Edited by C. Robert Wetzel (Cincinnati: Standard, 1978), pp. 115-127.

[62]See Forest F. Reed, *Background of Division Between Disciples of Christ and Churches of Christ* (Nashville: DCHS, 1968), p. 13.

[63]Moses E. Lard, "Can We Divide?," *Lard's Quarterly*, Vol. 3 (1866), pp. 330-336.

[64]David Lipscomb, "Christian Union," *Gospel Advocate*, Vol. 18 (1866), p. 200.

[65]W.K. Pendleton, "Strife and Division among the Campbellites," *Millennial Harbinger*, 1868, p. 152.

[66]Eileen Gordon Vandergrift, *The Christian Missionary Society*, p. 781.

[67]Ronald E. Osborn, "Dogmatically Absolute, Historically Relative," *The Reform of Tradition* (The Renewal of the Church, Vol. 1, Ed. by W.B. Blakemore) (St. Louis: Bethany), pp. 278, 279.

[68]Arthur V. Murrell, *The Effects of Exclusivism in the Separation of the Churches of Christ from the Christian Church*, Unpublished Ph.D. thesis, Vanderbilt, 1972. See pp. 155-159 for a survey of the theses referred to above.

[69]Alexander Campbell, "Our Position to American Slavery," *Millennial Harbinger*, 1845, p. 51.

15

ARCHIBALD MCLEAN AND PETER AINSLIE
THE MOVEMENT IN MISSIONARY
AND ECUMENICAL OUTREACH

A divided church is the scandal of Christianity
— Peter Ainslie

While the decades following the Civil War were among the most controversial in the Movement's history, they were also the period of its greatest numerical growth. In 1820 the Campbell wing had 400 members in four churches. By 1857 the Movement as a whole had grown to 200,000, according to Campbell's estimate,[1] and by the turn of the century it had multiplied to "almost a million," according to C.L. Loos. One Disciples journal in 1899 quoted an outside source as giving the number in the Movement as 1,085,615.[2] This reflects a phenomenal growth for a frontier reformation effort, several times that of the population.

A.W. Fortune is probably right that the Movement during the post-Civil War decades not only grew rapidly but also enjoyed reasonable peace. He says the deep sectional animosities were soon forgotten. This is suggested also in F.G. Allen's description of Kentucky churches in the post-war years. He says they anticipated the war's end by insisting that those who filled the pulpits, from North and South alike, "preach the gospel and not politics."

Allen tells how one church in particular, where both Union and Confederate soldiers were frequently in the community, conducted itself as if no war was going on so that they would be able to minister to both sides when the war was over. He says of them: "When the war was over they had no alienations to adjust, no broken down walls to rebuild, no breaches to close up. They needed no reconstruction. Their history demonstrates that even cruel war need not necessarily alienate the people of God."[3]

As the Movement moved into the post-war decades and towards a new century, it faced the question of its own mission and destiny. Would it remain a separatist group or would it become ecumenical in practice as well as in its plea, by cooperating with other churches?

And would it become truly missionary by taking the gospel to regions beyond? Or would it remain simply an *American* church, one whose growth had come partly by proselyting those from other churches?

Two men in particular were prominent in determining the answer to those questions, Archibald McLean and Peter Ainslie, neither of whom has yet gained his proper place in history. Their work is the concern of this chapter, but before we turn to the first of these, Archibald McLean, who gave his life to the *foreign* missionary society, which began in 1875, it is important that we understand the controversy over the American Christian Missionary Society, which began in 1849.

Missionary Society

"The whole earth is yet, indeed, one grand missionary field," Alexander Campbell said in his address at the 15th anniversary of the American Christian Missionary Society in 1863. "We would send to them missionaries," he went on to say, "as far as in us lies, with the Bible, and the Bible alone, in their hands, announcing to them the same gospel which Peter and Paul preached."[4]

He said nothing about the intense opposition to the society that had prevailed since the mid-1850's. A decade earlier, at the society's fifth annual gathering, he greeted them as "Beloved brethren in the cause of Christian missions" and urged them to take the gospel to the great capitals of the world.[5]

Having been elected president in absentia at its initial assembly, a position he held until his death in 1866, Campbell was always an enthusiastic supporter of the society. This included such financial aid as the royalty from the sale of his hymnal, which was substantial.

Moreover, his notices of the proposed convention that created the society reveal that he was involved from the start: he gave his blessing to the idea, stated his intention to be present, proposed the time and place, suggested that each church send a messenger, and described it as "all important to the cause of Reformation."

While Campbell was unable to attend due to illness, he reported what happened, publishing the procedures and resolutions, including the constitution of the new organization, the American Christian Missionary Society. He stated that the results were more than he had hoped for, and he regarded it as "a very happy pledge of good things to come."[6]

In spite of this data anti-society advocates have suggested that Campbell did not really favor the missionary enterprise, for he had always opposed any organization beside the church itself, and, after all, he was elected president in his absence. This notion was stated as early as 1906 by G.W. Rice, co-editor with the society's most influential critic, Benjamin

Franklin, to the effect that the presidency of the society was forced upon Campbell "in opposition to his own convictions." Rice said he had good reasons for believing this, but he did not say what they were.[7]

As we have seen, this view continues to circulate in anti-society circles today, even if lamely, which is reflective of the incredible influence of Alexander Campbell in the Movement, now as well as then. There is a reluctance to stand at a distance of where Campbell stood on most any issue.

The effort to place Campbell against the society, or at least lukewarm towards it, goes back to the post-Civil War years when the controversy was most intense. W.K. Pendleton, who was the closest to Campbell outside his immediate family, succeeded him not only as president of Bethany College but also as president of the missionary society.

When Pendleton addressed the society the year of Campbell's death, he took pains to show that the old reformer had always favored the society, describing it as "a grand auxiliary to the churches in destitute places," quoting Campbell himself. As for Campbell's opposition to societies in his earlier days, Pendleton put this down as "a sort of bibliolatry toward the *Christian Baptist*," insisting that even in those days Campbell did not oppose societies *per se* but the sectarian character of them.[8]

It hardly figures that there would ever have been such a furor over the missionary society, the "hot spot in the controversies," as W.E. Garrison put it. It not only had Campbell's support from the outset, but it also had the blessing of virtually all the renowned pioneers. Among the delegates to the first convention were Walter Scott, Tolbert Fanning, John T. Johnson, D.S. Burnet, J.W. McGarvey, Benjamin Franklin, Elijah Goodwin, John O'Kane, and T.M. Allen. Most of these held some office.

Walter Scott addressed the society in 1855 and said, "Let us remember that our Reformation is eminently synthetical in its aims — reconstruction," and went on to show that local and state efforts must be crowned by efforts "in behalf of a common humanity," and saw the society as a place where all Disciples could take their stand for a world outlook.[9]

Another reason for supposing the Disciples would have readily accepted a general missionary society is that they already had several state societies. Indiana had a state society as early as 1842 and Tennessee began state cooperative efforts in 1844. Kentucky and Illinois had societies before objections were ever raised against the national society.

All this shows that the Disciples did not at first object to societies *per se*, as most of the initial objections would indicate, but the controversy had to do more with abuse of power than with the idea of a society as such. But this is not what the anti-society position eventually came to be, which is that the society is *per se* sinful, being without scriptural warrant — no "approved precedent" in the New Testament.

In spite of the endorsement of the pioneers and the precedent set by state societies the A.C.M.S. was soon in trouble, which appeared at first to be no more than apathy. Ironically, the hope of the society lay with Benjamin Franklin, the most influential leader in the Movement following the passing of Campbell, who made some early efforts to get it generally accepted and supported, but who eventually turned against it and became its most devastating critic.

The Church of Christ in Connelsville, Pa. was the first to go on record against the society, and its objections were the ones that crystallized into a mountain of opposition in the following decades. The church is the only scriptural organization for missions, they argued, and they therefore could support no society "apart from the church." Campbell published their statement in 1850, and urged upon them patience, reminding them that those who formed the society were hardly the kind as would be easily deceived. Such things were, after all, a matter of human judgment, he allowed, and so differences could be expected.

But the Connelsville church raised the question that had to be answered: *If the church is the only organization through which to do God's work on earth, then why a missionary society, which is apart from the church?* They insisted that this was against the principles that their Reformation had always stood for. Campbell realized that this was a question that had to be answered.

He agreed with the principle of the sufficiency of the church, but pointed out that no one congregation is the church, but all of them together, and that while each congregation is independent it is not independent of all others in every respect.

> It is competent to the *church of Christ* to consult and cooperate with all the individual communities called churches of Christ, which enter into her constituency, in whatever state, nation or empire, they may be found, in each and every matter beyond their own individual duties to themselves and their localities.[10]

Campbell thus argued that a local church has responsibilities that reach beyond its own community, and that these can be met only by cooperative effort on the part of the church as an aggregate of congregations.

This question of what constitutes *the church* has been an issue from the early days of the Movement. This has resulted, on the one hand, in the restructure of the Christian Church (Disciples of Christ) in the 1960's, which interprets the church as something even more than the totality of congregations, and, on the other hand, a radical congregationalism, which allows for almost no cooperative, organizational effort between local churches, as evident in Christian Churches and Churches of Christ.

The Connelsville contention would not die easily, in spite of Campbell's response. Over two decades later, at the height of the controversy, a pioneer preacher in Kentucky, wrote to the *Gospel Advocate*, which was adamantly anti-society: "I do believe with all my heart, that an individual church of God is the highest ecclesiastical authority on earth, and that when we as a people surrender this ground, we give up one of the main pillars of our cause."[11] This was a common view. In 1866 the missionary society in California adjourned *sine die* for lack of scriptural precedent for a delegate convention.[12]

Before Benjamin Franklin turned against the society in 1866, he made some effective responses to those who were asking for a "thus saith the Lord" for the new organization. He told them they find authority for the society in the same place they find authority for building a meeting house, or for a baptistry or for translating the Scriptures.[13]

Franklin was an enigma. He vigorously defended the society for thirteen years and served as its corresponding secretary and leading fundraiser. When he turned against the society with equal vigor, it surprised everyone, especially the anti-society folk. In Nashville, Tolbert Fanning rejoiced that Franklin was now "making war upon all human organizations as substitutes for the church of God," but still thought he ought to repent of the "side cuts" he had taken at good brethren and ask God to forgive him of his "bushwhacking experiment."

David Lipscomb, now Fanning's junior editor for the *Gospel Advocate*, congratulated Franklin in being delivered from "the vanishing institutions of man's device."[14] Others saw him as a turncoat.

W.K. Pendleton could hardly believe that Franklin would bushwhack his way through the society while one of its vice-presidents. Sensing that Franklin felt that Campbell's mantle had fallen upon him, Pendleton wondered if he had now "turned against the work of Barton W. Stone, Alexander Campbell, Walter Scott, John T. Johnson, John Rogers, and other illustrious servants of God," all of whom supported such enterprises.[15]

C.L. Loos responded by placing Franklin against Franklin, juxtaposing his arguments *for* and *against* the society, suggesting that the ones *for* were more impressive. He recalled the time when Franklin, chairing procedures for the society, brushed off someone's effort to defend the society as a waste of time, insisting that the society's rightful place had been unquestionably established. Granting that any man has the right to change his mind, Loos wondered why the change in Franklin was so sudden and what new argument could have persuaded one so thoroughly convinced.[16]

Franklin's response to Loos was that he had been harboring doubts about the scripturalness of the society for sometime. That was the essence of his attack, that the society was not authorized in Scripture. It had now become an "outside society with laws and names unknown to God."[17]

It is not clear what precipitated Franklin's change, but it is noteworthy that he did not make it public until shortly after Campbell's death. Pendleton supposed that the society's war resolutions, recounted in the previous chapter, had impressed Franklin as inappropriate and unwise, just as it had alienated brethren in the South.

These two factors, the war resolutions, which made the society appear to be as politically minded as missionary, even to some northerners, and the disaffection of Benjamin Franklin, the most popular editor in the Movement, brought the society upon hard times. Something had to be done to save it from ruin. The convention of 1868 selected a committee of 20 prominent Disciples, Franklin being one of them, to draw up a plan for the society that would satisfy the critics. It was called the Louisville Plan since it was adopted in that city when the convention met there the following year.

It was an elaborate arrangement of district, state, and general boards, with each board having its own officers and fiscal policy. There would be a hierarchy of conventions centered in the general convention, to which two delegates would be sent from each state plus one delegate for each 5,000 members. Money pledged by churches would be divided at district, state, and national levels.

It is surprising that Franklin ever approved of such a plan, even if it was partly his creation, and even more surprising that he again changed his mind and condemned it as a human invention. But with or without his blessings the plan was doomed, for it was too cumbersome to get off the ground, gaining the support of neither the friends nor the enemies of the old society. There was no way, in fact, to appease the critics except to bury the society, for the issue was now clearly theological. *The society was unscriptural!*

This is evident from the numerous efforts of "society men" to appease their critics. They twice changed the constitution that charged for membership, lest it be a "moneyed aristocracy," but this only reduced the income of the society. They changed the structure and name of the society, lest the society be a sin *per se*. They exercised great caution not to interfere with the autonomy of churches, lest it be "an oppressive ecclesiasticism." But nothing satisfied the opposition. It had to survive without their help, which it did.[18]

The missionary society, as much if not more than the organ, thus became a symbol of apostasy to the conservative Disciples. Tolbert

Fanning, who did not object to societies as such, could not forget the war resolutions. He insisted that the society had committed "a great wrong against the Church" and called for its repentance, and he continued to describe it as "a fixed purpose to substitute other organizations in the place of the Church of Christ."[19]

It was Fanning who told Campbell in 1854 when he came to Nashville, according to one story, that when he allowed the society to elect him president he was shorn of his strength just as Samson was when he allowed Delilah to cut his hair.[20] The society gradually became a cause for exclusivism among the conservatives. Earl I. West relates that in the 1890's James A. Harding, an editor with Lipscomb for the *Gospel Advocate* and head of the Nashville Bible School, refused Hall L. Calhoun a place on the Bible school faculty because he would not publicly renounce the society and the organ, even when he would privately express his opposition.

West also reveals that T.B. Larimore declined the superintendency of the Bible school because he realized that his moderate views on the society and the organ would invite conflict with Lipscomb, who was now the editor bishop of the southern church.[21] But Lipscomb was not at first an exclusivist, and the dramatic story of how he gradually became one and thus separated the conservatives into Churches of Christ will be told in the next chapter. It is enough to say here that the missionary society became one of the issues that led to that separation.

The intense opposition to the society in the South does not mean that it was a sectional issue. We have noted that the society was first questioned by a church in Pennsylvania and that its severest critic, Benjamin Franklin, was a northerner, and he was succeeded by Daniel Sommer, another northerner, who, like Lipscomb, made the society a test of fellowship.

Neither was there any theological consistency in reference to these "innovations." J.W. McGarvey, as we have seen, was adamantly opposed to the organ, and yet he, with others, started the *Apostolic Times* in defense of the society. John F. Rowe, another northern editor, opposed the organ but supported the society. And most surprising of all, Moses E. Lard, the only one in the early days to make the organ a test of fellowship, was equally aggressive in his *defense* of the society! But there was no one among the editors, apparently, who was *against* the society and *for* the organ!

When one reaches the bottom line of this controversy, he might agree with the conclusion drawn by J.M. Mathes, a lesser known editor from Indiana:

The controversy about Missionary societies has not borne much good fruit. Brotherly love has not been promoted, nor the liberality of the churches increased by it. But, on the contrary, it has rather been calculated to divide and distract the minds of the brotherhood, and thus hinder them, for the time being at least, from doing a tithe of what they are fully able to do in the Lord.[22]

Archibald McLean
"Wherever the beer keg can go, the Bible must go."

In 1895 Archibald McLean, secretary for the Foreign Christian Missionary Society, which was organized in 1875, circled the globe in order to visit the mission stations recently set up by the Disciples. He spent time with missionaries of other denominations as well, having versed himself on the history of their work that dated back a century or more and was replete with examples of great courage and sacrifice.

In Hawaii he visited the graves of Congregational missionaries who brought Christ to those heathen islands fifty years before, the converts then numbering 50,000. He looked upon the graves of some who had died as martyrs. In the museum he leafed through Bibles translated by old missionary linguists into the vernaculars of the natives, realizing the debt of his own people.[23]

In Japan and China McLean visited with veteran missionaries of various denominations, as well as independent Disciples efforts, in order to learn as much as possible for the benefit of his own missionaries. A true ecumenist, he was always an example to his people in relating to the broad spectrum of missionary activity. In Japan he went with his missionaries to the grave of Bishop Reginald Heber, who was among the first to bring light to that dark empire, and who wrote the old hymn *From Greenland's Icy Mountains the Son of God Goes Forth.*

He also stood at the grave of Christian Swartz in humble appreciation of his one-half century of labor among Moslems and Hindus, who respected him even when he pointed to errors in their faith. Swartz was one missionary to India who was respected by all the warring political parties, from the king to the humblest peasant. Amidst their wars they would allow "the Christian" to pass unhindered, for they realized that his only cause was Christ. McLean learned from the life of Swartz, who died in 1797, that "the most honorable and blessed service in which any human being can be employed in this world" is the work of a missionary.[24]

McLean's call to missions seems to have been as clear as any of the renowned missionaries that he wrote about. He was born in Prince Edward Island in 1850 and trained as a carriage maker. In 1867 he left the Scottish Presbyterian faith of his family and accepted the principles of the reformation, first proclaimed in Prince Edward Island by Alexander Campbell himself. McLean shared the Reformers' conviction that they were not really a church, even if they had local congregations, but "a movement within the church for the union of all Christians."[25]

Archibald was deeply committed to Christ and the Scriptures, and he soon entered Bethany College as a ministerial student. Arriving in Bethany in 1870, only four years after Campbell's time, he was especially impressed by the teaching talents of W.K. Pendleton, Robert Richardson, and C.L. Loos. It was Loos' Greek classes that led him to the lifelong habit of reading daily a chapter from the Greek New Testament.

Once he graduated from Bethany with honors, he became pastor of the Mt. Healthy Christian Church in the suburbs of Cincinnati, where he served for eleven years. Never marrying, he gave his life to the church with uncommon dedication, and was known for his dedication and piety. Never a great speaker, he was nonetheless a power in the pulpit. His power was rooted in his dependence upon the word and his ability to speak to the conscience of his audience. While he had an infectious love for people in general, he related especially well to children.

The pulpit at Mt. Healthy was between two front doors, causing late comers to pass by the preacher. Once a lad blurted out as he walked by the preacher, "I got a new cap." McLean stopped his sermon to give the boy's remark the attention he thought it deserved, which illustrates his lifelong concern never to hurt anyone's feelings. This was his attitude toward his most bitter critics once he became secretary and later president of the controversial foreign missionary society.[26]

It was amidst uneasy times that the Disciples attempted organized foreign missions. The American Christian Missionary Society had celebrated its silver anniversary in 1874, though it was hardly a celebration since it was viewed by many as virtually dead. The missions to Jerusalem and Jamaica, short-lived and ineffective, had been deserted. An effort in Liberia might have been fruitful but for the sudden death of the black missionary that was sent there. Many Disciples were willing to write off foreign missions as a failure, and, besides, they hurt the work at home.

W.T. Moore was one who believed otherwise, insisting that foreign missions had not really failed in that they had not really been tried. He tells how he prayed in the basement of the Richmond Street Church in Cincinnati that his people might catch a vision for missions, and then called a meeting of 25 or 30 leaders who organized the Foreign Christian Missionary Society.

Moore tells how he was moved by a speech given at the convention of 1874 by Joseph King, who chastised the Disciples for being the only people who were doing nothing to carry out the great commission. He brought both humiliation and anger when he charged that they did not seem even to care for foreign missions. It gave birth to a new day for Disciples, especially in 1882 when McLean was appointed secretary.[27]

McLean was to explain later that it was not the new society's intention to establish missions in strongholds of Protestantism, though that was the direction first taken. This was due perhaps to the underlying conviction among Disciples that their message was to the Christian world. Due to financial help from Timothy Coop of England, the society's first work was in Southampton (1876), and then to other cities of England until there were 2,400 members in 15 churches by 1900.

Efforts in France (1878) proved less successful, while a mission to Turkey (1879) resulted in 434 members in 17 churches. A chapel in Smyrna bore the name of the society's first president, the Isaac Errett Memorial Chapel. Other programs were set up in Norway, Sweden, Italy, Germany, and Mexico with modest results, but all this was among other believers.[28]

By 1880, the society was asking itself about the true nature of foreign missions. A committee on new missions reported that its function was not to change believers from one Protestant faith to another, but to Christianize the heathen. "It is to plant congregations of Christian believers in lands distinctively and admittedly pagan, idolatrous and heathen," said the committee in identifying the society's mission. The report went on to concede that the society's work thus far was not done for "the salvation of men and women from idolatry, with all its abominations."[29]

The Disciples thus began a gradual break from the provincialism and exclusivism of American frontier religion. Missions it now seemed, especially foreign missions, should be among those who had never heard of Christ and who were steeped in idolatry. Foreign missions had to be more than proselyting believers from other churches.

The resolution to preach Christ to the heathen rallied the Disciples to increase dramatically their financial support. J.H. Garrison, editor of the *Christian-Evangelist* and an avid supporter of missions, told the 1880 convention that his two little boys and another child had given him their savings of $1.13 with the request that it be spent on sending the gospel to children who had never heard of Jesus. This tender story moved the Disciples to ask the Sunday schools to devote one offering each year to foreign missions, which came to be known as Children's Day. It doubled the society's income in one year.[30]

The foreign society began in 1875 with less than $2,000. By 1900, due in part to Children's Day, receipts totaled $180,000. In 1882 the first missionaries were sent to India. The next year a station was opened in Japan. Then came China, Panama, the Belgian Congo, the Philippines, Cuba, and Hawaii, all by 1900. In that year, the silver jubilee of the society, there were 111 missionaries in nine countries using 146 native assistants. Medical missionaries treated 40,000 annually in four fields. There were upwards of 6,000 converts in 79 churches and 113 stations.[31]

Recent Disciples historians, looking back on this story, give the credit to "a remarkable man, Archibald McLean," and then say: "The name 'A. McLean' literally became a household word while his leadership in the development of a missionary consciousness among the Disciples and in the developing structure of the brotherhood was a contribution of great importance."[32]

When F.M. Green, an associate editor of the *Christian Standard*, published a book in 1884 on Disciples missions, he presented data supporting the view that the formation of a foreign missionary society was anticipated by the best minds among the pioneers. Alexander Campbell, John T. Johnson, David S. Burnet, James Challen, and Walter Scott were all called as witnesses that foreign missions are consistent with the Movement's ideal.

Referring to James T. Barclay's mission in Jerusalem, which was the Disciples' first foreign effort, Campbell described it as "our first foreign mission in the identical city where our Lord was crucified" and went on to insist that their foreign efforts should take them to Asia and Africa as well.

As early as 1849 Johnson called for a society that would involve "the brethren of this reformation in an effort to convert the world." Burnet saw the first mission in Jerusalem as a step toward "the preaching of the gospel to the representatives of the world." Challen said he looked forward to the day when the hearts of 300,000 Disciples would throb with "the divine impulse of sending the gospel of salvation to the perishing heathen."

In calling for Disciples to carry out the great commission, Scott said it like a poet: "Leave your footprints on the snows of the frozen north. Trace out pathways in the flowery pampas of the balmy south. Seek the setting sun, the far west, the wild prairies, and the wilder men that inhabit them." He went on to make it clear as to how broad the mission should be:

> Go to those who water their steeds in the Rhine; to those who drink from the Seine, or who bathe in the Nile and the Niger, the sacred Ganges, Indus, Brahmaputra, and Irrawaddi. Go to the ends of the earth, for your success will be in the ratio of your mobility.[33]

While the Disciples have always differed on methodology more than on principles, and, as we have seen, this included societies, there was nonetheless substantial support for organized foreign missions. It was at first a problem of apathy. Isaac Errett, the foreign society's first president, described the Disciples as "alarmingly rich," implying that their failure in missions was a lack of will.

There was nothing in their heritage or in the ideals of their pioneers that would preclude an enthusiastic response to missions or to a society as the means. In those uneven decades following the Civil War they needed a catalyst, and this was the role of Archibald McLean. When he first raised his voice in behalf of foreign missions, he sadly reminded his people that in that world destitute of the gospel "we do not have a single herald of the cross."[34]

A half century later, with his work done, the Disciples had 185 missionaries, assisted by 926 native workers, in 13 nations, supported by $625,522.73 from 3,173 churches and 3,859 Sunday schools.[35]

McLean was always a pastor at heart. While he served a short while as president of Bethany College, he was clearly more suited for the shepherd's staff than an academic gown. As head of foreign missions he did, of course, have administrative responsibilities, but it was his pastoral concern for his missionaries that accounts for his unique influence. He prayed for every missionary every day, even when this involved scores of them. For many years, until there were too many, he wrote a personal letter at least once a month to each one in the field. A missionary in Japan preserved 129 letters from him over seven years, many written on trains and in hotels.

His missionaries were his parishioners. He knew their problems, how they lived, and he shared their joys and sorrows. He realized the loneliness of a Christian worker in a pagan land, and he was always sending books and other unexpected gifts to help ease the burden. Each missionary was constantly reminded of his deep respect and fatherly solicitation. He would carry their bags to the railroad station. When they complained, he would say, "Would you do me out of the honor of escorting an ambassador?"[36]

McLean's tour around the world, referred to above, was not only to visit his missionaries, but to learn as much as possible about the world in which they lived. He made copious notes and gathered huge funds of information, learning as much in a single year that would have ordinarily required several years.

So impressed was he with the opportunities of the little mission in China, planted amidst the world's oldest and most populous civilization, that he doubled his efforts, even to the point of exhaustion, to discover better ways of preaching the gospel. He had great admiration for the Chinese, whether mandarin or coolie, and saw in them infinite possibilities if they only had the gospel. He eagerly sought to learn their habits, religion, government, and every aspect of their lives.

Always a preacher, he preached at the various stations around the world through interpreters, one of his favorite texts being, "This is life eternal, that they should know thee, the only true God, and Jesus Christ whom thou didst send." He deeply impressed his hearers as one who truly cared for their souls. While his reports referred to various baptismal services, it was only in the letters from the missionaries that one learns that McLean did the baptizing.

While he made every effort to cooperate with other churches and to visit their mission stations, he never failed to preach the gospel as he understood it, and to immerse converts according to his convictions. One of his favorite preachers must have been the old sage of Bethany himself, for he published *Alexander Campbell As A Preacher*, in which he stated that it is a calamity that so few of his sermons were preserved.[37]

That McLean touched the hearts of the natives is suggested in a story out of India. Ten years after the secretary's visit, a missionary called on a Christian woman in a remote Hindu village, where he found to his surprise a single picture on the wall, that of Archibald McLean. She highly prized the picture because it was given to her after she had been immersed, while an orphan girl, by brother McLean. But the natives also impressed him, as did the missionary tour as a whole. He came to see missions as a tremendous enterprise. "It is the most colossal task ever undertaken by men," he was convinced, "More workers should be sent out and thoroughly furnished for the work."[38]

While he was generally a man of prayer, there was the main prayer of his life, that the Lord of the harvest would send forth laborers into his harvest. One missionary observed that it is the only prayer Jesus ever commanded his disciples to pray, and yet one they never do offer. But McLean prayed it constantly, fervently, and confidently, and he believed that every missionary he enlisted was the work of God.[39]

Beside the usual objection to societies, the one complaint he always had to cope with was "We have too many heathen at home to be sending missionaries abroad." To combat this he published the *Missionary Intelligencer* and set up missionary rallies over the country, having 21 of them in one year alone. He endeavored to show that a vigorous program abroad would improve the work at home. He also contended that foreign missions were important to the Disciples plea, for cooperation among Christians in reaching the heathen promotes unity.

McLean had a passion for souls everywhere, at home as well as abroad. He was impressed with the vastness of this country, that Texas is larger than Germany, California than Turkey, and Oregon than England, Scotland, and Wales. There is room for a thousand million, he noted, and the resources are unlimited. But still it is righteousness that exalts a nation, and only the gospel can redeem a nation. "The Gospel must be carried into every city and hamlet of this broad land," he demanded. *Wherever the beer keg can go the Bible must go.*[40]

Like Isaac Errett who was persuaded that missions "powerfully promote" Christian unity, McLean was convinced that there is no way for believers to be one without cooperating in carrying out the great commission. In his mind unity and missions were inseparably connected, and sectarianism at home is an unconscious but efficient ally of heathenism abroad.[41]

Attending the World Missionary Conference in 1910, which brought together the missionary leaders of all the denominations, he reported that the need sounded most frequently was the need for union. Nearly every speaker, he said, referred to the loss incurred by the unhappy divisions, and missionaries from the field begged the churches at home to respond to the Lord's prayer for the oneness of his followers. It was McLean's conviction that the unity sought by Disciples must first be realized in the mission field.[42]

Beside being an exemplary pastor and preacher and a highly respected Christian gentleman, McLean's significance in the Movement's history is twofold. He demonstrated that a society, which continued to be suspect by many Disciples, could be both Christian and effective. It was due to his influence that agencies generally gained their place in the life of the Movement. His effective programs made it evident that such results could hardly have been realized without such a cooperative enterprise as the Foreign Christian Missionary Society.

Equally significant was McLean's leadership in moving the Disciples into the ecumenical movement, however unintentional this may have been. He made foreign missions something far more than having missionaries in foreign lands, for they became the opportunity for making constructive contact with other churches. Rather than seeking to "convert" Protestants, which was still a common goal of many Disciples in his day, McLean sought to work with them in reaching those that had never heard of Christ.

McLean thus became the first Disciple to sit in an official capacity in ecumenical conferences, in London (1888), New York (1900), and Edinburgh (1910). In London he enjoyed fellowship with 1,494 representatives from all the societies of the Christian world, who had upwards of 6,000 missionaries in the field with an annual outlay of ten million dollars. Most of his brethren back in America did not know that such a world existed.

By the time of the Edinburgh ecumenical conference, McLean was serving on the general committee. There were now 159 societies with 19,280 missionaries, expenditures totaling nearly $25,000,000. Here McLean was with such world missionary leaders as John R. Mott (Y.M.C.A.), Robert E. Speer (Presbyterian Church, U.S.A.), and S.M. Zwemer (Editor, *Moslem World*). Business leaders from around the world were among the delegates. McLean was one of the founders of the Foreign Missions Conference of North America, which was set up in 1893 to foster more intimate cooperation among the societies.[43]

Unity and Missions

McLean's conviction that cooperative missions fosters love and fellowship is supported by the story of A.L. Shelton, whom the Disciples sent to Tibet as a medical missionary. He was captured by Chinese bandits and held for ransom, which Shelton would not allow his friends to pay. No one worked for his release more than a veteran French Catholic missionary. Shelton survived the ordeal and returned home half dead. Returning to Tibet, he was this time killed by bandits. This mercifully came after McLean's own death, sparing him the pain he always shared with missionaries in trouble.[44]

The Catholic missionary's gracious efforts in behalf of Dr. Shelton further confirmed McLean's assurance that unity can come only through a mutual love for Jesus Christ. He wrote a chapter in one of his books on "Christian Unity and World-Wide Evangelism," in which he urged that the Disciples plea can be realized only by this combination. "Christ himself is the only basis of unity," he wrote, "We can unite on him: we cannot unite on a theory of the atonement or of inspiration, or upon the five points of Calvinism or on the five points of Arminianism."

Like Thomas Campbell before him, he went on to say, "It is not necessary for us to have complete and exact knowledge about Christ and the method of salvation. It is necessary that we put our trust in him and do his commandments." He stood firmly within the best tradition of the Movement when he insisted, "Our ground of unity is in him and not in our opinions or in our reasoning processes."[45]

The difference that Archibald McLean made was in placing this plea for unity within the context of foreign missions.

Peter Ainslie

"We acknowledge the equality of all Christians before God."

Edgar Dewitt Jones referred to Peter Ainslie as "a flaming apostle of

371

Christian unity" and George G. Beazley, Jr. credited him with being one of the founders of the ecumenical movement.[46] He might also be described as one of the first within the Movement to advocate open communion. His church in Baltimore was among the first to adopt the practice and he one of its staunchest defenders.

He was a bitter critic of sectarianism among his own people, such as a reluctance to accept all other Christians as equals. For these reasons he was the most controversial leader within the Movement in the first three decades of the 20th century.

Beazley reveals that Ainslie absented himself from the floor of the International Convention Assembly for years because he did not want to cause an uproar, for there were always vituperative attacks when he was present.[47]

This means that he was always fair game for the editor bishops, one of whom was Daniel Sommer of the *Octographic Review*, whose opposition provides an insight into Ainslie's character. Ainslie invited Sommer to Baltimore to spend a week as his guest, giving himself to his guest with utter abandon and sweet reasonableness. Since Sommer was anti-organ, Ainslie kept the instrument silent when his guest addressed the Temple congregation, and he listened all week to Sommer's endless arguments, which appeared to him as inconsequential. Ainslie apparently won the mind of the belligerent editor with his gracious patience, for Sommer returned home declaring that he could no longer dispute with so good a man.[48]

Ainslie's most effective years were during the time that the Independents began their break from the Disciples. He was in the eye of the storm of controversy. But he always loved the heritage that had brought him to Christ, which is a mark of a true ecumenist. A. Dale Fiers tells how Ainslie expressed his loyalty to the Movement at a gathering of the Campbell Institute, insisting that if the Disciples should kick him out that night he would come back the next morning begging to get in.[49]

Another anecdote that reveals the man's character was his appointment to preach the annual sermon for the Army of the Republic. Born in Virginia in 1867 and always a southerner, Ainslie considered it a compliment to be invited. But his hosts did not realize they had invited a "rebel" until he arrived, his southern accent betraying him.

When his hosts learned that his relatives had fought on the southern side, they would have cancelled his appointment had they not feared the consequence to such stern action. After much ado they decided that the lesser evil would be for him to go on and speak, even if the colonel *was* running for Congress! While Ainslie graciously offered to withdraw, he reminded them that he was born after the war, and now after nearly three decades would they extend their animosities to the southerners of his generation?

That night when a storm blew down the tabernacle where he was to speak, some interpreted it as God's wrath for having a southerner on the program! Repairing to a church, the Army heard Ainslie speak of unity, love, and brotherhood. He said he would place a flower and drop a tear on the graves of the blue and gray alike, for they were all brave men and brothers of American blood.

He made no apology for his southern heritage, for "from her defeated battlefields arises a fragrance sweeter than the fragrance of a crushed flower." He asked them, "Will you permit the prejudice of war to be kept alive in the hearts of the conquerors when it has died in the hearts of the conquered?"[50]

So moved were they by his sermon that they requested that he stay over and address the entire community in the largest auditorium in town.

While Ainslie was then still in his 20's, that incident anticipated not only the continual confrontations of his precipitous life, but also the loving candor with which he entered into every situation. Beazley explains that he had a way of being "a very prickly burr under everybody's saddle," and he was a man absorbed by causes, especially the unity of Christians.

He was a champion of social justice and pacifism as well as ecumenicity. While his biographer recognized his rare tenderness in all relationships, applying the biblical "a bruised reed he would not break" to him, he sees him as an incensed prophet in the face of grave inconsistencies, such as the church's involvement in war.

In a speech in Washington, D.C. in 1925 before a confederation of churches, where many chaplains were present, he scored the practice of "a minister of the gospel of the Galilean becoming a paid officer of the army," and called upon the churches to recall all their chaplains. Many clergy were irritated and the New York *Herald Tribune* called it blatantly outrageous, preposterous, and insulting.[51] As prophets usually are, Ainslie was undaunted. He was courageously committed, sometimes to the point of recklessness, to any cause he espoused.

His greatest commitment was to the unity of the church. He became the conscience of the Disciples in reference to their original plea, his credentials being unimpeachable. His grandfather (Peter Ainslie I) was a Haldanean back in Scotland who joined the Movement when he migrated to this country. His father (Peter Ainslie II) studied under Campbell at Bethany and was a minister in Virginia.

While intensely devoted to his tradition, Ainslie insisted that the Movement had digressed from its earliest mission, the unity of believers, and had become preoccupied with gaining denominational converts. He called upon Disciples to return to their true heritage as set forth by Thomas Campbell in the *Declaration and Address.*

In his presidential address before the Convention in Topeka in 1910 he rebuked his people for forsaking the cause that brought them into existence, exchanging a passion for the unity of the church for a desire to build up their own ranks by winning converts from other churches. A people born to be cooperative with other believers, they had become legalistic, sectarian, and exclusivistic. They had become mere guardians of a noble conception, with little understanding of what the pioneers intended.

While some approved, accepting his rebuke as that of a prophet among them, many saw him as a traitor to the cause. Ministers and layman alike vied with each other in crying out against him, some standing in their chairs to shout their denials. Ainslie stood in the pulpit dumbfounded, asking himself, *Are these my brethren?*[52]

He nonetheless gained sufficient support to spearhead the founding of the Council on Christian Unity in 1910, which still functions as part of the restructured Christian Church (Disciples of Christ), though for a time it was called the Association for the Promotion of Christian Unity.

Serving as its first chairman, Ainslie gained immediate support both from his own people and from other churches. The Disciples generally gave both money and approval, and large numbers attended his meetings for the promotion of unity. It was only when he began to advocate open membership by recognizing members of other churches as Christians that he became the center of a long and sometimes bitter conflict.

He was now a "heretic" who was attacked by the editor bishops, and many churches were closed to him. After serving the association for 15 years, Ainslie resigned, explaining that he had too much contact with other believers to please his brethren. He noted that the announcement of his retirement before the Convention met with general applause! He responded irenically: "We must be patient with each other. It is so hard for us Christians to be gentlemen like Jesus."[53]

Ainslie challenged the Disciples as few leaders have, perhaps because he knew their history so well. Knowing how diverse and individualistic they had always been, why should they not grant the same liberty of opinion to other Christians? If they continue to manifest an air of self-satisfaction, he charged, they can never make any large contribution to Christian unity. They do not really stand for unity, he prodded, except by absorption, by converting other Christians, which is the position of most denominations.

As for open membership, which was the stick in the craw, he insisted that it logically followed open communion, which was the general practice throughout the Movement. "To have a Christian sit with me in the inner sanctum at the Lord's supper and for me to deny him membership with me because he had not been baptized by immersion seemed to me an anomalous proceeding," he argued.[54]

While he always believed and practiced baptism by immersion, he was convinced that unity among Christians could not be realized apart from an open pulpit, open communion, and open membership. To close any of these is to set up a barrier to unity.

One of his prodding phrases was "the scandal of Christianity," the title of one of his books, which he saw as foremost among all the world's scandals, the flagrant circumstance of Christians being ugly toward one another. He lamented the fact that in most cities of the world it was impossible to get Christians together to discuss the possibilities of brotherhood.

He believed that the scandal of a divided church can be corrected only by experimentation, as in science. He rejoiced over the adventures in brotherhood that had led to the union between Presbyterians in Scotland, Methodists in England, and the Congregationalists and Christians in the United States. He lamented the fact that his own church did not join three other denominations in forming the United Church of Canada.

The need for experimentation in unity led him to publish the *Christian Union Quarterly*, a modest publication with a worldwide circulation, reaching all divisions of the church and deposited in hundreds of university and seminary libraries. It also led him to be a part of the Federal Council of Churches from its inception. He was offered the presidency, but declined because he felt he would not have the support of his own denomination. At this the stated clerk of the Presbyterian Church offered to make him a Presbyterian, but he would not desert his people, saying of them, "They are mine and I love them, but how they do bungle things up."[55]

The Pact of Reconciliation

Ainslie's ventures in brotherhood led him to conclude that the Movement's unity plea was more theoretical than practical. The problem of a divided church is neither theological or ecclesiastical, but ethical, an ethic that reflects the mind of Christ in practical efforts.

Tired of endless theological discussions he heard as part of the World Conference on Faith and Order, he dared to issue the Pact of Reconciliation, which was a practical, no-nonsense way to unity, stated in less than 200 words. It was appropriate that it was issued by an heir of the Stone-

Campbell Movement, for it deplored a divided church as opposed to the spirit of Christ and as a hindrance to winning the world, as did Thomas Campbell.

But it called for transcending denominationalism that few were ready to accept, such as: "We acknowledge the equality of all Christians before God and propose to follow this principle, as far as possible, in all our spiritual fellowships," and "We pledge, irrespective of denominational barriers, to be brethren one to another in the name of Jesus Christ, our Lord and Savior, whose we are and whom we serve." It called for an open pulpit, open communion, and open membership among all churches.[56]

It was sent to a hundred leading churchmen, Protestant and Roman Catholic, two-thirds of whom signed it, some enthusiastically. Others feared it went too far and would prove offensive. But when the *New York Times* gave it a three-column spread, letters poured in from ministers of various churches offering to sign it. A group of New York ministers held a unity conference based on it.

Apart from this, it reveals something about its author. Peter Ainslie was restive and impatient in a divided church, and he was not content to leave things the way he found them. As a Christian he was ashamed of the divisions in the church, and he was reluctant to have his name listed with the ministers of any denomination.

He called his church in Baltimore the Christian Temple, lest it bear any denominational tag. On the ceiling he inscribed the names of 42 religious leaders, including Abraham and Moses, Paul and Peter, Augustine and Wycliffe, Chrysostom and Moody, Origen and Tolstoy, Cyprian and Campbell, Francis of Assisi and Wesley. They well represented the far-ranging mind of the church's pastor.

After Ainslie, the Movement could not be as exclusive as it had become during the decades following the Civil War. Ronald E. Osborn, Disciples historian, observes that his people were not known even to be courteous to other Christians, not to speak of cooperative efforts, until Peter Ainslie began to lead them in ecumenical concerns.[57]

Ainslie challenged his people to consider their origins as *a unity people*. He led them out of the wilderness of separatism and gave them new vision of their mission in a divided Christendom. His mission went well with that of Archibald McLean. With McLean the Disciples learned to reach out to pagan lands, while with Ainslie they learned to reach across denominational lines and accept other Christians as equals.

Ainslie also gave the Movement a loftier view of its future. "Some day the spirit of Jesus will find its outlet in the world through a real brotherhood among his disciples," he assured them. "I can help a little toward it, as can every one of his disciples, by being unafraid to make experiments in love of the brethren and I propose to work at it as long as I live."[58] He spoke assuringly of a new epoch finer and freer than anything before, "a more understandable interpretation of Jesus, marked by simplicity and brotherhood."[59]

So radiant was his hope that it is understandable that the crusty old journalist H.L. Mencken would hail him as the only real Christian he had ever met.[60]

While interpreters of the Movement will view him differently, it is evident that Peter Ainslie, who died in 1934, did for the Disciples something like what Immanuel Kant said David Hume did for him. *He awoke them from their dogmatic slumbers.*

ENDNOTES

[1]Alexander Campbell, "A Loud Cry to Our Brethren," *Millennial Harbinger,* 1857, p. 646.

[2]D. S. Burnet, "The Good Confession," *The Living Pulpit of the Christian Church,* Edited by W. T. Moore, Cincinnati, 1869, p. 47; C.L. Loos, *Christian Evangelist,* Vol. 37 (1899), pp. 75, 200.

[3]Robert Graham, Editor, *Autobiography of F. G. Allen,* Cincinnati, 1887, p. 87.

[4]Alexander Campbell, "Missions and Missionaries," *Millennial Harbinger,* 1863, pp. 496-506.

[5]Alexander Campbell, "An Address," *Millennial Harbinger,* 1853, pp. 601-615.

[6]See *Millennial Harbinger,* 1849, pp. 419, 453, 475, 689, 707; cf. F.M. Green, *Christian Missions and Historical Sketches of Missionary Societies Among the Disciples of Christ,* St. Louis, 1884, pp. 68-71, 101-108 for details of Campbell's support of the society.

[7]G.W. Rice, *Biographical Sketches and Writings of Elder Benjamin Franklin,* Indianapolis, 1906, p. 38.

[8]W.K. Pendleton, "Address," *Millennial Harbinger,* 1866, pp. 497, 498.

[9]F.M. Green, *Christian Missions,* p. 121.

[10]Alexander Campbell, "The Christian Missionary Society," *Millennial Harbinger,* 1850, pp. 282-287.

[11]"Pioneer Preachers No. 2," *Gospel Advocate,* Vol. 15 (1873), p. 8.

[12]W.K. Pendleton, "Missionary Movement," *Millennial Harbinger,* 1866, p. 144. Pendleton notes that the anti-society element exulted in this report from California, including David Lipscomb in Nashville, who saw this move against the society as the trend.

[13]Garrison and DeGroot, *The Disciples of Christ,* p. 353.

[14]W.K. Pendleton, "Missionary Movements," *Millennial Harbinger*, 1866, p. 146.

[15]*Ibid.*

[16]C.L. Loos, "Bro. Franklin's Argument for the Missionary Society," *Millennial Harbinger*, 1867, pp. 241-244.

[17]Earl I. West, *The Search for the Ancient Order*, Vol. 2 (Indianapolis: Religious Book Service, 1950), pp. 48,49.

[18]See Archibald McLean, *The History of the Foreign Christian Missionary Society* (New York: Revell, 1919), pp. 22-32 for a summary of charges against the ACMS and the efforts to appease them.

[19]Tolbert Fanning, "I Did Wrong," *Gospel Advocate*, Vol. 8 (1866), pp. 170, 119.

[20]A.V. Murrell, *The Effects of Exclusivism in the Separation of Churches of Christ*, Unpublished Ph.D. thesis, Vanderbilt, 1972, pp. 70, 71.

[21]Earl I. West, *The Search for the Ancient Order*, Vol. 2, p. 375.

[22]J.M. Mathes, "Missionary Society," *The Christian Record*, Vol. 1 (1867), p. 196.

[23]William R. Warren, *The Life and Labors of Archibald McLean* (St. Louis: Bethany Press, 1923), p. 143.

[24]Archibald McLean, *Modern Makers of Modern Missions* (New York: Revell, 1912), pp. 65-70.

[25]William R. Warren, *Life and Labors*, p. 51.

[26]*Ibid.*, p. 78.

[27]Garrison and DeGroot, *The Disciples of Christ*, p. 367.

[28]Archibald McLean, *The History of the Foreign Christian Society*, pp. 51-60.

[29]*Ibid.*, p. 79.

[30]Garrison and DeGroot, *The Disciples of Christ*, p. 370.

[31]Archibald McLean, "The Foreign Christian Missionary Society," *Christian Evangelist*, Vol. 37 (1899), p. 1447.

[32]L.G. McAllister and W. E. Tucker, *Journey in Faith: A History of the Christian Church (Disciples of Christ)* (St. Louis: Bethany Press, 1975), p. 267.

[33]F.M. Green, *Christian Missions and Historical Sketches of Missionary Societies Among Disciples of Christ* (St. Louis: Burns Pub. Co., 1884), pp. 197-203.

[34]J.H. Garrison, *The Reformation of the 19th Century*, St. Louis, 1901, p. 378.

[35]*History of the Foreign Christian Missionary Society*, p. 431.

[36]William R. Warren, *Life and Labors*, p. 227.

[37]Archibald McLean, *Alexander Campbell As A Preacher* (Grand Rapids: Baker, 1955, reprint: Revell, 1908), p. 9.

[38]William R. Warren, *Life and Labors*, p. 157.

[39]*Ibid.*, p. 224.

[40]Archibald McLean, *A Circuit of the Globe* (St. Louis: Christian Pub. Co., 1897), p. 15.

[41]Warren, *Life and Labors*, p. 182.

[42]*Ibid.*, pp. 182-183.

[43]*Ibid.*, pp. 296, 297.

[44]Tucker and McAllister, *Journey in Faith*, p. 322.

[45]William R. Warren, *Life and Labors*, p. 213.

[46]*Discipliana*, Vol. 27 (1967), pp. 22-28.

[47]*Ibid.*, p. 25.

[48]Finis S. Idleman, *Peter Ainslie: Ambassador of Goodwill* (Chicago: Willett, Clark and Co., 1941), p. 103.

[49]*Discipliana*, Vol. 27 (1967), p. 25.

[50]Peter Ainslie, *Some Experiments in Living* (New York: Association Press, 1933), p. 4.

[51]Idleman, *Peter Ainslie*, pp. 153, 154.

[52]*Ibid.*, pp. 124, 125.

[53]*Ibid.*, p. 127.

[54]Peter Ainslie, *Some Experiments in Living*, p. 116.

[55]Idleman, *Peter Ainslie*, p. 135.

[56]Peter Ainslie, *Some Experiments in Living*, pp. 120, 121.

[57]Ronald E. Osborn, "Dogmatically Absolute, Historically Relative," *The Reformation of Tradition* (The Renewal of the Church, Vol. 1, W. B. Blakemore, Editor), (St. Louis: Bethany Press, 1963), p. 279.

[58]Idleman, *Peter Ainslie*, p. 135.

[59]Peter Ainslie, *Some Experiments in Living*, p. 138.

[60]*Discipliana*, Vol. 27 (1967), p. 25.

16

MORE EDITOR BISHOPS:
DANIEL SOMMER AND DAVID LIPSCOMB
THE MOVEMENT DIVIDES

We will no longer consider them our brothers.
— Sand Creek Declaration

A story circulates in Texas of a man in Dallas who makes a hobby of collecting cornerstones engraved Church of Christ: A.D. 33. Be he friend or foe to the Churches of Christ, his hobby is not without its resources, for it was not uncommon in the early decades of this century for this wing of the Stone-Campbell Movement to affirm its origin in this manner. After all, A.D. 33 is an acceptable date for the beginning of the New Testament church, and these people were persuaded that they were that church duly restored.

One well-known spokesman for these people, Leroy Brownlow, puts it simply: "I am a member of the Church of Christ because Christ is the Founder of only one church."[1] While that proposition in itself is as ecumenical as Thomas Campbell's *Declaration and Address*, it would be interpreted by many as sectarian in that the writer is referring to "the Church of Christ" as something less than the church universal.

Another spokesman, David E. Harrell, leaves no doubt as to how he views the church universal: "The group to which I belong is the church universal." Sharing in the Reed Lectures in Nashville with a scholar from both the Christian Church and Disciples of Christ, Harrell went on to say that as a "radical legalist" he had nothing in common with the other two. "Reconciliation is inconceivable," he told them, referring to himself as a biblical literalist whose aim is "the exact restoration of the ancient order of things."[2]

While Harrell concedes that he and his "peculiar" group of Churches of Christ are not mainline and that many in the mainline churches are making a feeble effort to break away from the old dogmas, he believes he is consistent with the historic Churches of Christ position, now a century old. Even the Churches of Christ members admit, some of them regretfully, that they are generally known for two things especially, that they do not believe in instrumental music and that they think they are the only ones going to heaven.

Tracts issued by their publishing houses have often identified themselves with the New Testament church itself, claiming identity in origin, name, organization, and worship. Their polemicists once affirmed in debate, if not still, that their church was scriptural "in name, doctrine, and practice," implying that no other church was.

Even though they use the name Church of Christ exclusively, usually with lower case "c" for church, they are adamant about not being a denomination. One publication, whose title, *The True Religion and the Religion of Others*, is itself revealing, repeats a conversation that is typical:

> Some time ago I was asked, "What denomination are you a member of?" I answered, "I am not a member of any denomination." Then I was asked, "Well, do you just take up with all of them?" I affirmed then, as I do now, "I'm not a member of any of them. I'm a member of the church of Christ, the church we read about in God's word and do not apologize for the statement."[3]

This view is not, of course, unique to Churches of Christ but characteristic of restorationist groups in general. Referring to the role of Daniel Sommer in Churches of Christ beginnings, which we are presently to consider, Steve Wolfgang observes that "one who can understand him has taken a major step toward an understanding of the conservative religious psychology generally and of the Churches of Christ in particular." He admits the "divisive nature" of his own group and concedes that "any ecumenical position is unthinkable."[4]

There is a mysterious "psychology" to religious exclusivism, whatever be the church. Logan J. Fox, himself a psychologist and once a professor in Churches of Christ colleges both in California and Japan, looks at this phenomenon in his own church in terms of "the power of Nashville," the magisterial city of Churches of Christ:

> In few places is the church so dominated by a few men, yet as I seek now to understand how I was taught that the Church of Christ is the "one and only true church" I find no particular name coming to mind. Rather does this central dogma of our brotherhood so thoroughly permeate the area that its source cannot be discovered. Like the myth of white supremacy, or the sacredness of the Bible, or the existence of God, it is taken for granted and never questioned.[5]

Fox goes on to say that in Nashville they played at having an open mind, but no one *really* questioned whether the Church of Christ was the one true church. "To do so is taboo, unthinkable," he says, "And the few who seriously question are first laughed off, then gently warned, and finally ruthlessly cut off as dangerous and beyond hope."

Exclusivism has always been a force to be dealt with in the Stone-Campbell Movement. A.T. DeGroot describes those decades following Campbell's death as a period when the Movement was in danger of going the way of all restorationist groups by succumbing to exclusivism. Pointing to the journal and the editor who made the difference, he says: "It was to the *Christian Standard* and Isaac Errett that the Disciples were indebted for being saved from becoming a fissiparous sect of jangling legalists."[6]

In a study in a Baptist journal, William D. Carpe, a Disciple, recognizes that the coupling of unity and restorationism has always caused much controversy in the Movement. "The more firmly one held to restorationism, the more difficult it was to maintain relationship with churches whose order, doctrine, and practice, especially baptism, were regarded as unbiblical," he says.

Carpe notes that the catholic concern for unity, always dominant since the time of Campbell, was threatened by "the sectarian force of rigid restorationism." He concludes that two branches of the Movement, the Churches of Christ and Christian Churches, resolved the tension between restorationism and ecumenical concern by opting for restorationism, while the Disciples of Christ have resolved the tension by favoring ecumenical relationships. He recognizes that a church can hardly be both restorationist and ecumenical.[7] As to whether he is right would depend on how those terms are defined.

Stephen England, longtime Disciples analyst, is severer in his judgments of the left and right wings than is Carpe. He agrees that the left wing (Disciples) are the unitists but says they have abandoned the basis of unity as set forth by the Campbells, while the right wing (Churches of Christ/Christian Churches) as restorationists have been true to the *method* of the Campbells but have forsaken the goal, which was unity. The power of the Campbell plea, he figures, is that it reduced the essentials for unity to a minimum, such as the seven unities of Ephesians 4.

The divisions that came, England concludes, are traceable to a "multiplying of essentials." He observes that "Everything in the New Testament became essential," pointing out that the real issue became one of what to do with the silences of Scripture. Like DeGroot, England dates the controversies from the death of Campbell and says they "seethed beneath the surface for four decades" before they erupted into an open split. It was then a matter of a postal address being a sign of orthodoxy![8]

The controversy that hung as an albatross about the Movement's neck and eventually led to open division was the question of whether there are Christians in the sects. While the epigram *Christians only!* was of early origin, there were always some Disciples who presumed they were the only

Christians. This was and is the basis of the open membership question. If one's doctrinal position excludes other believers as Christians, it would not be appropriate for them to commune with those who are. It was also the basis of the other disputes, whether societies, organs, or rebaptism, for if one had to be *right* on such matters to be a true Christian, he would have to be excluded if he did not convert to the correct position.

Lunenburg Letter

It is not easy to account for the exclusivism that seems to have always been more or less present in the Movement, however inconsistent this was to its plea for unity. It may be traceable to the Reformers becoming a separatist group and finally another church. Coupled with this was the question that soon emerged as to whether there are Christians in the sects. If one can be a Christian among the sects, then why leave and become part of the Movement? Had not the Reformers discovered the truth?

It is understandable, therefore, that one of Campbell's readers expressed "surprise" in reading his journal that he "finds in all Protestant parties Christians." This letter and Campbell's reply, known as "the Lunenburg Letter," is the most famous exchange within the history of the Movement. It came to have enormous implications.

The intense debate that followed reveals an exclusivism within the soul of the Movement that helps to explain the emergence of the Churches of Christ as a separate church. The dichotomy is still evident, for the liberal/ecumenical persuasion is forever quoting the Lunenburg Letter, while the exclusivistic/restorationist element appears to be embarrassed by it.

The reader from Lunenburg, Va., bolstered by the high estimate Campbell placed on the female character, made her question pointed: "Are there any Christians except those who believe the gospel, repent, and are buried by baptism?"

Campbell's answer was an unequivocal yes. "There is no occasion for making immersion, on a profession of the faith, absolutely essential to a Christian," he wrote, and added, "He that infers that none are Christians but the immersed, as greatly errs as he who affirms that none are alive but those of clear and full vision." He supposed his correspondent belonged to that class that believes that the value of an institution is compromised the moment one admits the possibility of anyone being saved without it.

The reformer was to learn that that class was larger than he imagined. But he was clear as to his position: "I cannot, therefore, make any one duty the standard of Christian state or character, not even immersion." He went on to insist that it is the image of Christ that counts, not in being exact in a few items but in general devotion to the whole truth as far as known.

Finally he said, "I should sin against my own convictions should I teach any one to think that if he mistook the meaning of any institution, while in his soul he desired to know the whole will of God, he must perish forever."

It was in this letter that Campbell gave his oft-quoted definition of a Christian: "But who is a Christian? I answer, Every one that believes in his heart that Jesus of Nazareth is the Messiah, the Son of God; repents of his sins, and obeys him in all things according to his measure of knowledge of his will."[9]

As the dispute over this question intensified, Campbell equivocated in reference to this definition. He was soon to contend that Christian has various meanings and that the "scriptural" definition is "one who has first believed in Jesus as the Messiah, repented of his sins, and been immersed in water into the name of the Father, the Son, and the Holy Spirit, and who follows Christ in all his appointments."[10]

The controversy did intensify. Campbell was inundated with letters of protest from his brethren who insisted that he had neutralized all that he had taught on baptism. His critics taunted him, claiming that he had surrendered the one vital point, that immersion is not essential to being a Christian. He bleakly concluded that one thing was evident from the experience, that there were very few "Campbellites" in the country!

In a follow-up to the Lunenburg Letter, Campbell filled two essays with affirmations that there was nothing new in what he had said, that he had believed and taught that there were Christians in the sects since his early *Christian Baptist* days. "What could mean all that we have written upon the union of Christians on apostolic grounds had we taught that all Christians in the world were already united in our own community?," he asked his readers. He again rejected the notion that immersion is absolutely essential, and warned his people against being "ultraists on the subject of Christian baptism." He expressed uneasiness over any view that would make a pagan of a man who would die for Christ simply because he had a mistaken understanding of baptism.[11]

But the issue was not allowed to rest. Campbell conceded that some of the most respected men in the reformation disagreed with him, which may be why he allowed one Christianos to publish in his journal an extended series of ten learned essays on "Christians Among the Sects," a persuasive defense of the position Campbell had taken.

While some able respondents gave Christianos a hard time over his thesis, his identity was never revealed, not even in Robert Richardson's detailed biography of Campbell. Over a half century later historian W.T. Moore identified him as one of Campbell's brothers-in-law, a probable reference to Archibald McKeever, who conducted a girl's school near Bethany. The controversy got so hot that Campbell stopped the series with an ambiguous statement of his own.[12]

As for the question of whether an unimmersed person is an acceptable worshiper, Christianos laid down a proposition that challenged the legalistic mind: *The man whose heart is bowed to the Divine will is accepted.* "Our heavenly father estimates men according to the state of their affections and passions," he insisted, "not according to the state of their understandings or the amount of their knowledge." He thus contended that sincerity before God is the standard of acceptance, and yet he saw *wilful* ignorance as sinful as wilful disobedience.

"The man of a weak and uncultivated mind may have many faults and fall into many errors, and yet cordially hate sin and sincerely love the Lord," he said to the consternation of some of his readers, and then added: "on the other hand the man of a refined and philosophical mind may be free from any external fault, whilst his heart is as cold and as hard too, as an adamant stone." There are saints in Babylon and sinners in Jerusalem, he ventured.

For those who demanded scriptural precedent for his thesis, Christianos submitted the case of Cornelius in Acts 10. "Thy prayer is heard," the angel said to him and this was before he was immersed. Conceding that Acts 11:14 says that Cornelius was not yet saved, he concludes that "Cornelius certainly needed more light in order to his *enjoyment*, but not in order to his acceptance with God."

Christianos made much of the principle laid down in 2 Cor. 8:12: "For if there be first a willing mind, it is acceptable according to what a man hath, and not according to what he hath not." The *willing mind* was his definition of sincerity and the basis of acceptance with God. The passage shows that God demands no more than a person is able to give, and this applies to knowledge as well as money. "Can any one suppose," he asked, "that our Divine Father has one rule for money matters and another for moral matters?"

He insisted that a distinction must be made between the person who travels an open highway and perversely turns aside, and the one who in darkness of night loses his way and is earnestly endeavoring to find it again. The sincere man, he said, is willing to bring his head, his heart, his life to the examination of light, whether he is yet immersed or not.[13]

Roots of Schism

This was offensive to the Movement's more conservative minds. Dr. M. Winans, a physician of Jamestown, Ohio who was baptized by Thomas

Campbell during the Campbell-Owen debate, was one of the disturbed ones. He was known for his keen intellect, and his interesting and perceptive letters to Editor Campbell were a delight to the readers.

Winans agreed with Christianos that one can be right in heart and wrong in head, or right in practice and wrong in theory, but he was unable to perceive how one could practice a theory without a knowledge of it. A servant may know his master's will without doing it, the doctor allowed, but he cannot do his master's will without knowing it. Heart religion apart from head religion would have to be a religion of ignorance, he avowed. The doctor insisted that there was no way for Christianos to deal with commands like baptism without "cutting his own throat," for his theory is not worth a fig if it is true that knowledge has to precede those commands.

Winans went on to chide Christianos with: "To talk or write about 'Christians' who do not know what it requires to make a man a Christian is like talking or writing about chickens without eggs or butter without milk."[14]

Thomas M. Henley, a highly respected Virginia minister and a personal friend of the Campbells, also took Christianos to task in a series of responses. "If they can be Christians through a perversion of baptism, why not Christians without faith and repentance? He who gave one command gave all." Henley, who had suffered persecution at the hands of his former associates for joining the reformation, told Christianos that it was reasoning like his that indoctrinated him in Calvinism, and that he was thankful for having found *the truth*, which he had obeyed to the plain letter of the word, implying that anyone could do likewise if he wanted to be a Christian.

In making an unimmersed person an acceptable worshiper, Henley protested, Christianos makes an alien a citizen of the kingdom without obeying the prescribed conditions for citizenship, which no kingdom allows. To talk of obeying in spirit without the letter is to separate what God has joined. "How does Christianos know a man obeys in spirit, *without the letter*, these positive and absolute commands of heaven?," he asked with telling force.[15]

This controversy, which continued through three years of Campbell's journal, reveals that a large and respectable part of the community that Campbell had helped to create was more conservative and exclusivistic than himself. Moderation was his only recourse. He did not approve of all that Christianos had said, he told those who were eager for his reaction, even though he had said some excellent things. But those good things were improperly placed, he said, without being specific. He promised to be more specific at a later date, but never got around to it.

He did opine that if perfection in knowledge and obedience was necessary to being a Christian, then there are no Christians in the sects or out. Again revealing his preference for "disciples of Christ" as the name for believers, he went on to argue that since the disciples were called Christians (Acts 11:26) it would surely be conceded that there were "disciples of Christ" among the sects. He closed the controversy until "a more convenient season," but he was too wise a leader to allow that season to become convenient.[16]

Campbell obviously did some retrenching during the three-year controversy. His unambiguous stand in the Lunenburg letter in behalf of the unimmersed believer was not now unambiguous. It is not that he had changed his mind, but that he had a unity movement on his hands that had reactionary elements stronger than he had supposed. He did not want it to blow up in his face through internal disputes. Like his friend Henry Clay, he was the great pacifier who held the Movement together as long as he lived.

In this "Christians in the Sects" controversy one can see the roots of the open split that eventually became the Churches of Christ. Stephen England was right that it "seethed beneath the surface for four decades" before it divided a people that had been called to be a unity movement. If the sister in Lunenburg who started the whole thing with her letter was "surprised" that Campbell found Christians in the sects, the reformer must have been equally surprised to discover that his Movement had such strong exclusivistic elements, including some of his most trusted colleagues.

They insisted that Campbell's own logic excluded the unimmersed from the fellowship of the church. He saw there was no way to win through argument, so he preserved the Movement through appeasement. Some of those who succeeded him chose to do otherwise, allowing the *logic* of restorationism to produce an exclusivistic party within the Movement. It explains why the Churches of Christ have all along been the most rationalistic of all the wings of the Movement — and the most successful on the polemic platform!

Daniel Sommer

"The Church of Christ will be entirely separated
from the Christian Church. Hallelujah!"

Daniel Sommer, at 89, was on a train when he suddenly became blind. Undeterred, he proceeded to his preaching appointment in Pittsburgh, and, due to a remarkable memory, filled the pulpit as usual. From there he went to his next appointment in West Virginia where he preached for several days, all in a world of darkness. His friends persuaded him to cancel his other appointments and return home. Returning to Indianapolis, he took a taxi to his home, deposited his luggage in his upstairs bedroom, washed up, went to the kitchen and greeted his family.

He movingly thanked God for the food before him. It was only when his hands groped for the silverware that his family realized that he was blind! He was such a frequent traveler that he knew his way by rote, and porters and taxi drivers, who knew him well, provided what help he needed.

That anecdote alone, which is but a tithing of what could be told, reveals a man of indomitable will, one toughened by fourscore years of poverty and hardship. He was no ordinary man by any count. Burly as an ox, he could lift with one hand what most men could not lift with two. Poverty-stricken and ignorant, he gained the respect of his professors at Bethany College, even when he was poorly equipped for what was demanded of him.

Confident that he was the best woodsman in his native Maryland and fearful of nothing, he was nonetheless always uneasy in the pulpit, even after 70 years as a preacher. His most joyous and confident years were in early manhood with ax in hand and a forest of trees for a challenge. He was in the ministry a long time before he made as much money preaching as he did cutting cord-wood at 75 cents a cord![17]

As men cut from large molds often are, he was full of bold contradictions, even a "schizophrenic doctrinal personality," if one of his biographers is correct. The biographer sees him as an inexplicable mixture of tolerance and intolerance, affirmance and negativism, broadmindedness and dogmatism. He was both an ardent unionist and a theological axman. He was praised as tolerant and fairminded and yet damned as vengeful and hateful.[18]

The inconsistencies *are* glaring. While he himself was bitterly opposed to societies, Bible colleges, the pastor system, and instrumental music, he was grossly impatient with those who opposed other innovations of which he approved, such as Sunday schools and multiple cups (for Communion). He was ready to debate the "innovations," in behalf of some and against the others. If he used one document, the *Address and Declaration*, to withdraw fellowship from the Christian Church, thus creating what some called "Sommer's Church of Christ," he used another document, called "The Rough Draft," in an effort to restore unity within the Church of Christ.

Even though he publicly disfellowshipped the Disciples, he probably had more fellowship with them than any Church of Christ leader of his day, especially with Dean Frederick D. Kershner and the Butler School of

Religion, where he often appeared in cooperative efforts.

Kershner's estimate of the man, which has to be respected, was that while Sommer was at "the very tip of the right wing," he was the last of the great pioneers. Not only did he find no bigotry in Sommer, but esteemed him as "one of the most tolerant and fair-minded men we have ever known." It impressed Kershner that Sommer would go anywhere and work with anybody, no matter how much he disagreed, and that even though he never had more than a bare living money was never a consideration.[19]

Joseph Franklin, longtime pastor of the Christian Church in Bedford, Indiana, which changed its name to First Church of Christ when Sommer started "The Church of Christ" in the same town, had a different estimate of the man. Sommer's unfairness was "a public scandal," and his new church, which he ruled with an iron hand, was narrow and bigoted.

It rankled Franklin that Sommer considered as Christians those who left the Christian Church to join his, but not those who remained. Actually, the two churches agreed on all positive matters, Franklin wrote, differing only in that Sommer's group was *anti*. Even so, Sommer insisted that his folk were the only Church of Christ in town.[20]

A similar story came out of Winchester, Indiana, where "Daniel Sommer's Church of Christ," sued the original Church of Christ for the property. James Vernon, who described the episode as "a Daniel come to judgment," told how Sommer did not do as well in a court of law as among untutored brethren.

After sitting in court all morning and seeing the weakness of his case, he did not appear for the next session that afternoon, leaving it to his lawyer to suggest that the case be dropped. Vernon, who thought one of Sommer's problems was his ignorance of Disciples literature (such as saying that Thomas Campbell was a Baptist when he wrote the *Declaration and Address!*), told how Sommer left town, leaving the *antis* holding the bag.

Sommer may have lost in court that time around, but his antagonist was hardly right when he went on to say: "Since Sand Creekism failed miserably in court, and with such speed, I am satisfied that the final overthrow of this piece of opinionism is in sight."[21] Vernon was indulging in wishful thinking. Not only was Sand Creekism nowhere near dying, it was about to burst forth into a fellowship all its own and become the conservative Churches of Christ, the Movement's first major open split.

Sand Creekism and Churches of Christ

Sommer's long life, 1850-1940, touched every generation of the Movement's history. He was 16 years old when Campbell died and was a student at Bethany only three years afterward. He heard David S. Burnet as a boy and Benjamin Franklin as a student. He lived long enough to associate with such Disciples leaders as Dean Kershner and such Churches of Christ leaders as N.B. Hardeman and G.C. Brewer. But his were turbulent years and trouble seemed to follow him wherever he went.

Even while a student at Bethany he caused an uproar over a "Mite Society," created by the sisters of the congregation. He took it up with them from the pulpit when C.L. Loos took the risk of putting an inexperienced student preacher in the Bethany pulpit on a Sunday evening.[22]

He preached his way across Maryland, Pennsylvania, and Ohio, and settled in Indianapolis where he spent most of his life. Since those decades following Campbell's death were the most controversial in the Movement's history, the times were right for his leonine disposition. He was indeed *Like A Lion*, as Matthew C. Morrison entitled his study of this enigmatic preacher. He was advised by his mentor, Benjamin Franklin, who bestowed his mantle upon young Sommer, to occupy "the most radical ground" possible, and to oppose the "departures" as they appeared.[23]

Faithful to that charge, Sommer aggressively pursued "innovationism" throughout the midwest, entering towns with the express purpose of challenging Disciples to debate and starting rival churches. He admits in his autobiography that he had given over 60 years to "saving a residue of the disciples of Christ" from apostasy, which accounted for his controversial life. Such internecine struggles not only found him on the polemic platform, brother against brother, but in courts of law as well, church against church, again and again.[24]

Sommer gradually came to refer to those loyal to his plea as "The Church of Christ," while the others were the "So-called Christian Church." When one respected leader of the Movement saw what was going on, he complained to the *Christian Standard*: "Daniel Sommer is trying to get control of some of our congregations, and form a distinct religious body. He would thus start a new sect. Its bond of union would be its opposition to certain methods of Christian work done by us."

He went on to repeat what the Movement had always insisted upon, that opinions concerning methods should not be made a test of fellowship. He pled with the "anti brethren" to see the error of their way.[25]

Sommer was not to be deterred. He was by now editor of the *American Christian Review*, founded by Benjamin Franklin and the most influential journal in the Movement in the post-Civil War years. With the *Review* at his disposal he was in a position to issue a call to arms and summon the "So-called Christian Church" to judgment. He chose Sand Creek, Illinois as the battleground, and urged Peter P. Warren to draw up a document that would draw the line against the innovators, which Sommer named "An Address and Declaration," an obvious play on Thomas Campbell's *Declaration and Address* of an earlier day. If the first document had launched the Movement, the second would save it.

At least 6,000 conservative Disciples gathered for the occasion, and Sommer discoursed at length against the innovations. Warren read the document, which named choirs, societies, and preacher-pastors as culprits, but, oddly enough, did not mention instrumental music, except in the catch-all phrase "and other objectionable and unauthorized things." It was the conclusion that set a new direction for conservative Disciples:

> In closing up this address and declaration, we state that we are impelled from a sense of duty to say, that all such innovations and corruptions to which we have referred, that after being admonished, and having had sufficient time for reflection, if they do not turn away from such abominations, that we can not and will not regard them as brethren.[26]

We cannot and will not regard them as brethren! For the first time in its history a substantial segment of the Stone-Campbell Movement made a test of fellowship and a bond of union over issues that had generally been considered matters of opinion. The document was signed by representatives of five churches, and it may be assumed that it was generally agreed to by many conservative Disciples, at least in the North.

It was immediately responded to by others as divisive and as a betrayal of the spirit of Thomas Campbell and the *Declaration and Address*. The date was Sunday, August 18, 1889, and while it is risky to attempt to pinpoint the origin of any church, this would be a suitable date for the beginning of the Churches of Christ.

Within only three years Daniel Sommer was confident that a new church was in the offing:

> The Sand Creek Declaration is being adopted, and those who will not do right are purged out as old leaven. In course of a few years the Church of Christ will be entirely separated from the Christian Church. Then there will be no more fellowship between them as there now is between the Church of Christ and any other branch of sectarianism. Hallelujah.[27]

By 1895 there were 200 to 500 Sommerite churches in the North, according to Joseph Franklin, which, he believed, should have been called "the Church of the Antis" rather than the Church of Christ. He said the Movement had 9,000 churches, called alike Christian Churches and Churches of Christ, that the names meant the same, and that if Sommer wanted a separate "Church of Christ," he insisted that it be called "A Sectarian Church of Christ."[28]

The Disciples fought back, sometimes in like kind, to the Sommerite onslaught. A letter in the *Christian Standard* from Odon, Indiana told how the Sommerites stole through the window in order to take over a church that had been denied them, and how they were no longer considered "communicates proper" in the Church of Christ. They are like cuckoos, said the writer, for all over southern Indiana they were taking over other birds' nests and using them.[29]

Russell Errett, in a *Standard* editorial, was outraged, insisting that Sommer was no more a Disciple than was Sidney Rigdon, and he called upon John F. Rowe, editor of the *Christian Leader* in the North, and David Lipscomb, editor of the *Gospel Advocate* in the South to "let it be known that they have no sympathy with Sommerism and Sand Creekism." He was incensed that Sommer would do a schismatic work with shouts of hallelujah, assuming himself to be the "supreme and infallible judge."

To Errett it was a divisive movement that would destroy the work of Campbell, Stone, Scott, Isaac Errett, and Franklin but he was confident that while Sommer might "form a cave of Adullam and fill it with malcontents and with silly men and women laden with sins, but he can not build a church or even a respectable sect on that foundation."[30]

But Errett's anger blinded him to the facts. Sommer would emerge from the "cave" with more than Errett supposed. Within 18 years of Errett's prediction the Census Bureau would list the Churches of Christ separately, with 159,658 members in 2,649 churches, served by 2,100 ministers. The first of these were Sommer's churches in the North. While the majority was in the South and led by others, as we note below, they were of the same exclusivistic persuasion.

Sommer lived another half-century beyond Sand Creek, solidifying the work he had begun, and, surprisingly enough, trying to keep the peace in a church that had inherited from Sand Creek a proclivity to divide. Time brought new issues, especially when Churches of Christ began to build colleges in good Campbell tradition. Sommer was as opposed to Bible colleges as he was to societies and the organ.

This brought more debates and more division, so that in time the "Sommerite churches" in the North became a separate fellowship from the Churches of Christ in the South, commonly referred to as "anti-college churches." Too, there were disputes within the Sommer segment, due in part to whether Sommer himself had remained true to his own position, and part of this, tragically, was within his own family. One of his sons, D. Austin, started a rival publication, disfellowshipping his own father. And since Sommer's publication was a family enterprise, his wife gained control and as editor would not even allow her husband to write for it![31]

The thing that turned many of his own people against him, including some of his family, may well have been the noblest act of his volatile life. It was the publication of a unity document after the order of Haggard, Stone, and Thomas Campbell, called "The Rough Draft." Its theme was: "If we can search out the things we can agree on, and unite on them, and work together, we'll have unity!" In listing the items "necessary to a New Testament Church," Sommer now, at 83, showed an attitude far different from Sand Creek. He made Bible colleges, orphan homes, Sunday Schools, and several other issues matters of individual opinion.

He drew the line only on instrumental music and missionary societies, and this less belligerently. While the Rough Draft was not an overture for peace to the Christian Church, it was an effort to unify the splintering Churches of Christ. Realizing that people have little interest in "the finer points" of the disputes, he called upon the leaders and the rank and file alike to respond to his plea for unity.[32]

There was not much of a response, except that Sommer had "surrendered" his position on the college question. The president of David Lipscomb College in Tennessee sent a qualified endorsement, but it was largely ignored by the Churches of Christ as a whole. Either they were suspicious of him or did not know how to handle gestures toward unity, or both. It is, after all, difficult for a lion to assume the role of peacemaker.

Sommer's "unfriendly friends," as he called them, were forever scrutinizing his life and motives, even charging that his objection to the colleges was based upon his failure to gain the presidency of one. Even though he always denied it, it can be documented that Sommer was offered a professorship in two new Bible colleges and in each case held out for the presidency.[33] This was before the turn of the century and prior to his anti-college campaign.

Since he was blind the last months of his life, he dictated to his son Allen a final statement to his brethren in which he stated that his chief concern in life had been "the disciple brotherhood." He now grieved over its divisions and the part he had played. Jesus' prayer for unity was now his concern.

Sommer expressed similar feelings in the last lines of his life story. He blamed "a divided and disgraced brotherhood" on those who strained certain scriptures. His last line provided an ominous epitaph to his own life: *The strainers have all come to grief sooner or later.*[34]

One of his last public appearances was at the Murch-Witty unity meeting in Indianapolis in 1939, which was a positive effort to promote better understanding within the Movement's divided ranks. Daniel Sommer was asked to pray. Both frail and blind, he stood before the audience *leaning on the piano*, which was kept locked, covered, and silent during the proceedings. Someone observed, "How the mighty have fallen."[35]

We have learned that Russell Errett, owner of the *Christian Standard*, called upon the church's editors, including David Lipscomb in the South, to renounce Daniel Sommer and Sand Creekism. James H. Garrison of the *Christian-Evangelist* in St. Louis was among those who unequivocally did so. Errett waited in vain for a similar judgment from Lipscomb in Nashville, insisting that "silence is shame."

Lipscomb had little use for Sommer, whom he considered a sectarian. In an 1893 letter, Lipscomb told him plainly, "You turn me off," which may have been triggered by Sommer's opposition to Nashville Bible School, which Lipscomb had opened in 1891. Sommer's refusal to allow free discussion in his journal also rankled Lipscomb, who always had an open policy in the *Gospel Advocate*.[36]

While David Lipscomb at first resisted any move to separate from the Disciples, he eventually did in the South what Sommer did in the North. Even though there was little contact between the two, Matthew C. Morrison is correct in calling Lipscomb "Sommer's conservative counterpart in the South."[37]

Those who look for southern origins for the Churches of Christ are to note that it had its beginning in the North, not the South, and that the first divisive conflicts involved northerners with other northerners rather than northerners and southerners. But despite Sommer's role in the North, the Churches of Christ would never have made it without Lipscomb and the South, for it was in the South that it gained its greatest strength.

The Churches of Christ therefore have two founding fathers, one in the North and one in the South. Daniel Sommer and David Lipscomb both planted. Many watered. God gave the increase.

David Lipscomb

"Division must come."

It is not often that a kiss makes its way into church history, especially one between a Baptist and a Campbellite. But there is the impressive story of young David Lipscomb getting a whipping in school for kissing "a cherry-lipped Baptist lass," as he described her. Telling the story gave him a chance to say: "I have always cherished the kindest feeling for the Baptists and earnestly prayed for the time to come when we could be one people."[38]

Lipscomb was by nature a peacemaker. He applauded an effort in Pittsburgh in 1896 to unite with the Baptists, and opposed rebaptizing them when they joined the Disciples, which was insisted upon by Austin McGary in Texas, who started the *Firm Foundation* to promote this exclusivistic practice.

In the reconstruction years following the Civil War, Lipscomb raised funds to feed and clothe the deprived of both North and South. When the great Chicago fire struck in 1871, he asked the readers of the *Gospel Advocate* in the South to help their brothers in the North. He was far in advance of his time in advocating integration in the churches, deploring separate congregations for the races, and he always supported "Negro work."[39]

His irenic nature was so pronounced that he was led to conclude: "We have never seen a circumstance arise in which we were willing to advise division . . . in a church of Christ." He went so far as to say: "The Spirit of God, so far as we have learned, never saw a church of God so corrupted as to advise withdrawal from it."

Citing these references, A.V. Murrell, in a Ph.D. thesis at Vanderbilt, says this strong irenic position on the part of David Lipscomb is one of the principle reasons the Disciples did not divide before 1906. He observes that Lipscomb criticized a meeting called in 1882 by John Rowe, editor of the *American Christian Review*, for the purpose of dealing with innovations, for he saw it as divisive.

This conservative effort to polarize the Movement, which was also above the Mason-Dixon line rather than in the South, came to naught. But Murrell notes that men and events around Lipscomb in the ensuing years caused him to do what he could not conceive of himself ever doing — divide the church. Seven years after Rowe's aborted effort, Daniel Sommer did his thing at Sand Creek, and this time Lipscomb offered no protest.[40]

If ever there was a son and a sire of the Movement it was David Lipscomb. Born in Tennessee in 1831, his father was disfellowshipped by a Baptist church for Campbellism. Educated by Tolbert Fanning at Franklin College, he became both an editor and an educator, founded Nashville Bible College (now David Lipscomb University), and served for 46 years as editor of the *Gospel Advocate*.

Lipscomb's admirers in the Churches of Christ through the years have hailed him as the church's most outstanding man in the South and even as "greater than Campbell." During the Bicentennial year the Tennessee Historical Society named him the 14th most important man in the state's history.

While Lipscomb would easily qualify as the editor bishop of the Movement in the South in the last quarter of the 19th century, it is remarkable that the earlier Disciples historians could have ignored him so completely. W.T. Moore's "Comprehensive" history (1909) does not even mention Lipscomb. Nor do the histories by J.H. Garrison, B.A. Abbott, and Errett Gates. Even the able work by Garrison and DeGroot (Revised, 1958) barely mentions him. These also, except the latter, ignore or neglect the schism that led to separation of Churches of Christ.

More recent research has changed this. McAlister and Tucker (1975) recognize the "enormous influence" that Lipscomb and the *Gospel Advocate* had in the South, and a study by David E. Harrell on social sources of the Movement's divisions (1973) has no less than 74 references to the Nashville editor. And our footnotes point to two recent biographies and several theses that give Lipscomb substantial treatment.

The neglect of the earlier historians may be attributed to their hope that the problem of schism, which was such a contradiction to the Movement's plea, would go away. Now that the Churches of Christ have long since come into their own as a church, there are efforts to explain their beginnings, and from this perspective there is no way to ignore David Lipscomb.

We have noted that Lipscomb was slow to adopt the exclusivistic posture of Daniel Sommer. It was common for him to preach in churches that had an organ, and he defended a church's right to use pro-organ ministers. While Austin McGary in Texas was after him for "shaking in the Baptists" without rebaptism, other editors badgered him for being "too soft" on the innovators. When "digressive" preachers came to Nashville to preach at the "organ-society" churches, Lipscomb would honor them with his presence and entertain them in his home. Most of his colleagues at the *Advocate* office and Nashville Bible School would not do this, such as James A. Harding, John Poe, and E.E. Sewell.

This may have made it easier for those same editors to rebuff him for criticizing the "moneyed societies" in the North while rich himself. While once very poor, Lipscomb became wealthy through farming and printing.

While the men around Lipscomb talked division and identified the innovators as the enemy, he was still saying, as late as 1888, only a year before Sand Creek, "We have never been able to reach the point when we would say, 'Let us divide the Church of Christ.' "[41]

A decade later, however, he was saying something different, and he admitted it was painful: "Division must come until we are all willing to be led by God."[42] That which caused Lipscomb to change his mind is what gave the Churches of Christ its unique character: *He became an exclusivist.*

He did not separate the Churches of Christ over the organ question, even if this was a contributing factor, for he had tolerated the organ for decades. The missionary society was a more serious issue with him, but even here he was sufficiently tolerant to hire F.D. Srygley to the *Advocate* staff, one who opposed his views on the society question, and this in the face of much criticism from southern radicals. These two issues, the hallmark of Churches of Christ loyalty in generations to come, were important to Lipscomb, even crucial, but hardly the reason why he eventually chose division.

Disciples historian Herman Norton is impressed that while those around Lipscomb during the controversies of the 1890's were making the organ a test of fellowship, he was not willing to take that position.[43] But Earl I. West, Churches of Christ historian, observes that it was about that time that James A. Harding, colleague to Lipscomb, affirmed in a debate with J.B. Briney, Christian Church, that instrumental music was such a serious sin that it justified "withdrawal of Christian fellowship by those who oppose from those who use it."[44]

West tells how pressure was put on Lipscomb to state whether or not he agreed with Harding. Lipscomb hardly equivocated, stating that a church that introduces the organ rejects God and that a Christian cannot fellowship or build up such a church without disloyalty to God. This did not satisfy one inquirer who wanted Lipscomb to say whether it was sinful to use an organ to assist in the song service. This time Lipscomb did equivocate, insisting that instruments are not used in the service in that manner.

The organ issue now shifted from the question of it being scriptural to the question of fellowship, or as to whether the non-organ persuasion would become exclusivists, rejecting those who differed with them.

West also tells of the pressure put on such men as T.B. Larimore and Hall Calhoun, preachers highly esteemed by the southern church, who remained noncommittal on "the issues." The editor of the *Christian Standard* understood from what Larimore wrote in the *Advocate* that he disagreed with those who would make organs and societies tests of fellowship. Lipscomb conceded that the *Standard* had accurately read Larimore, and he insisted that his southern colleague should come down on one side or the other and not be neutral. This he did after conceding that Larimore's position was simply to favor "what is written" and to oppose what is not. He pressured Larimore to be an exclusivist. It was a new role for Lipscomb.

Hall Calhoun, the first Churches of Christ minister to take a Ph.D. at Harvard, was also pressured to become an exclusivist. Even though he was opposed to both the organ and societies, and would say so privately, James A. Harding would not allow him on the faculty at Nashville Bible School because he would not take a hard line. Harding cancelled a series of lectures when Calhoun told him he did not know what the Bible said about organs and societies.[45]

There was a medley of circumstances that contributed to Lipscomb's journey to exclusivism. While his sectional bias was moderate, he could not forget the war resolutions of the American Christian Missionary Society that denounced the South. It was the South that was maltreated, as Lipscomb saw it, and the main reason he got the *Advocate* going again was to give southerners something to read that would not hurt their feelings. To some extent he also associated innovations with the North, especially the missionary society, even though he had it in the South as well.

His opposition became more intense when the society organized in his own state and had its first convention in Nashville in 1891. He brutally assailed it as "the invention of the devil," which brought strong rebuke from the northern press. When the national society held its convention in Nashville the following year, Lipscomb was deeply resentful, charging that it was an attempt to embarrass the non-society churches.[46]

Another factor in Lipscomb's move toward exclusivism was a division in the Woodland Street Christian Church in Nashville over the organization of state missionary work, 1891. The anti-society folk who left started the Tenth Street Church of Christ. Herman Norton selects this event, along with the organization of the state society in Chattanooga, as the date, October, 1891, that the Christian Church and Church of Christ became separate churches in Tennessee.[47]

This was a time of numerous divisions in the churches, in and out of Tennessee, which must have influenced Lipscomb's eventual separatist posture. The first division in the state over the organ was in Chattanooga in 1897, when the anti-organ group walked out and started over. In Newbern, Tennessee the anti-organ group sued for the property when an instrument was installed.

Even though Lipscomb championed their cause by frequently testifying in a trial that lasted two years, the court ruled that "the things complained of were not of sufficient importance to justify the intervention of the court," which meant the anti-organ side lost. Smitten by the decision, Lipscomb rehashed the trial in the columns of the *Advocate* for some time.[48]

In McGregor, Texas in 1898 it was the "progressives" that sued the conservatives who had locked them out of the building, for making tests of fellowship over instruments, societies, and the rebaptism issue, which, they claimed, was contrary to the original plea of the Movement. When the organ-society people won, the decision was appealed all the way to the Texas Supreme Court, which upheld the decision.[49] In San Marcos, Texas in 1887 the pro-organ group managed to keep the property without going to court, even though "Grandma" Driskill demolished the organ with a hatchet, which was one way to solve the instrument question![50]

During these years Lipscomb witnessed scores of divided churches all over the brotherhood, from Texas to Missouri and from Alabama to Illinois, and even to Canada. By the time of U.S. Census of 1906, he conceded what was obvious, that the group known as Churches of Christ was a separate church, distinct from the Christian Church. Two other factors caused him to conclude that it was irrevocable.

One was the work of A.I. Myhr, who for 20 years directed the missionary society in Tennessee. While he organized 150 churches in the state during that time, many of them resulted from bitter in-fighting with Lipscomb-influenced churches. Herman Norton says that Myhr "engendered a bitter partisan spirit in almost every congregation in the state." When Myhr issued a partisan Yearbook of the churches, Lipscomb retorted that it listed Christian Churches and not "the Churches of Christ in Tennessee."[51] It reveals how he was thinking by 1901.

Equally disturbing to Lipscomb was the "rationalism" in Missouri, which is where Myhr came from, especially in the persons of James H. Garrison, editor of the *Christian-Evangelist*, and R.C. Cave, minister of the Central Church of Christ in St. Louis. While Garrison's "liberalism" consisted of an acceptance of modern biblical criticism, Cave went so far as to deny the virgin birth and the inspiration of the Bible. He was also one of the first to practice open membership.

Lipscomb saw these men as guilty of treason against the basic truths of the Christian faith. James A. Harding had predicted that the organ-society folk would be accepting the unimmersed into their churches within a decade, and Lipscomb was impressed that the prophecy was beginning to be fulfilled in just two years. These were the days when Garrison wrote to Lipscomb and asked that his name be removed from the *Advocate*'s mailing list.[52]

When therefore Lipscomb received a letter from S.N.D. North, director of the U.S. Census Bureau, in 1906, asking if the Churches of Christ should be listed separately, he was not unprepared. He and J.W. Shepherd had already begun to form a list of faithful churches, and by 1904 a list of approved preachers appeared.

Citing instrumental music and societies as the cause of the division, Lipscomb told North that his people had remained true to the original intent of the Movement. "There is a distinct people," he told the Census director, "taking the Word of God as their only rule of faith, calling their churches 'churches of Christ,' or 'churches of God,' distinct and separate in name, work, and rule of faith from all other bodies or people."[53]

It is odd that he would have told the Census director that the churches were called "churches of God" as well as "churches of Christ," for the latter name has always been the exclusive name of these people, from the beginning, whether in the North or South.

In any event the division that had been developing for a quarter of a century was now as "official" as one could make it. This is why it is not inappropriate to date the Churches of Christ from 1906, though, as we have seen, the Sand Creek episode in 1889 provides an earlier date of origin.

We have shown that congregations had differences over the organ and societies long before there was an open split. For a time there was peaceful coexistence within such diversity, with some congregations anti-society/organ and others not. Preachers often moved freely from one persuasion to the other, with no breach of fellowship, as in the case of Lipscomb himself in his earlier years. At the outset of the disputes the two most influential conservative leaders, Lipscomb and J.W. McGarvey, insisted that the issues should not be made tests of fellowship. McGarvey did not change his mind like Lipscomb did.

Grounds For Division

The separation of Churches of Christ is to be accounted for on theological and hermeneutical grounds more than any other factor. The conservatives, influenced by the restorationist point of view, could not find the society and organ in the New Testament. The more liberal interpreters, not bound by patternistic hermeneutics, were more progressive in accepting change. It was the mentality of "multiplying the essentials," as Stephen England noted. Even the silences of Scripture were made essentials.

It is to the credit of hundreds of congregations that they weathered the crisis without rupture, some adopting the innovations and others not, but always preserving peace. But this was not sufficient to prevent open division.

There were of course other divisive influences at work, including sectional and cultural differences. But these alone cannot account for the fact that these disputes did their deadly work in North and South alike and even in Canada. Divisions in Texas do not reflect sectional bias, for the disputes, including legal battles, involved only southerners, while those in Indiana and Ohio were quarrels between northerners, with no evidence of sectional influence. The Canadian divisions were not caused by influences from the States, but because their own people interpreted the Scriptures differently and therefore responded to the changes differently.

Socio-economic change forced such issues as instrumental music on the Disciples as it did other churches. But differences did not necessitate division. They could have continued as an undivided unity movement, with some churches adopting the innovations and some not, which was the case for decades. It became a question of whether the leaders would become exclusivists by making such things a test of fellowship, thus proclaiming themselves the only faithful church. When such a leadership emerged division came.

Robert E. Hooper, a historian at David Lipscomb College, in his study of David Lipscomb concludes that the "apostasy" was caused by "the failure to adhere closely to the Bible." He quotes Lipscomb to the effect that the Disciples must interpret the Bible strictly or apostatize completely.[54]

We have learned, however, that no one in the Movement was any stricter about the Bible than J.W. McGarvey, who spent much of his life opposing higher criticism. And McGarvey was a "society man," to the consternation of Lipscomb, who could not understand how a man like McGarvey, who opposed the organ and held to a strict interpretation of the Bible, could support the missionary society. In describing the two men, Hooper provides a revealing insight on what divided the Movement: "The one thing dividing them was McGarvey's acceptance of the missionary society and his willingness to fellowship those whom he (Lipscomb) considered to be in error."[55]

McGarvey did not break fellowship over such differences while Lipscomb, finally, did. Lipscomb always admired McGarvey's scholarship and respected his devotion to the Bible. He was disappointed that he would not write for the *Advocate*, which may be attributed to Lipscomb's exclusivism, which McGarvey could not abide. So, the division was hardly due to a lack of biblical loyalty. The difference between Lipscomb and McGarvey serves to explain the separation of the Churches of Christ.

When division came, the two men were on opposite sides, even though both opposed the organ. Lipscomb became a part of what he came to call "the church of Christ," non-instrument. McGarvey remained in the mainstream of the Movement, refusing to be a separatist. Lipscomb became an exclusivist, McGarvey did not. It is ironic that today McGarvey is one of the most honored of the pioneers among Churches of Christ, with scholarships named for him, though he was never a part of the separated Churches of Christ.

Perhaps it was the men around Lipscomb who nudged him toward exclusivism, such as John Poe, who, when J.W. Caldwell urged through the *Apostolic Times* that they all realize that no body of believers has a monopoly on truth, wrote in the *Advocate*, "Get out, J.W.C., and go to your own. You are not one of us."[56]

And when J.W. McGarvey indicated that he would have no problem in calling on those in other churches to lead prayer, James A. Harding, another of his colleagues, rebuked him by noting that if they should fraternize with such people "we make the impression upon others that we regard them as Christians, and that we consider their churches branches of the church of Christ."[57]

This was the mindset of Churches of Christ leadership in its founding years. The old controversy over whether there were Christians in the sects, which began in the 1830's with the Lunenburg Letter, continued to be a divisive issue. The main body of the Movement gradually became more inclusive, recognizing other Christians as equal to themselves.

Those who insisted that they had restored the true church and saw themselves as the only faithful Christians not only divided the Movement but continued to divide among themselves, again and again. This "spectacle of divided unitists," to quote DeGroot once more, questioned the integrity of the Movement that presumed to have discovered principles for the unity of all Christians.

Another way of putting it is that division came when the leaders of the Movement lost the vision of their founding fathers, capsuled in the slogan, "In essentials unity, in opinions liberty, in all things love." Not only were opinions transformed into essentials, but they lost the love they had at first, the love that preserves the unity of the Spirit in the bond of peace.

Two editors, one in the North and one in the South, led the way. The coming years would bring other issues and other editors. It would happen again.

ENDNOTES

[1]Leroy Brownlow, *Why I Am a Member of the Church of Christ* (Fort Worth: Published by author, 1945), pp. 22-27.

[2]David E. Harrell, "Peculiar People: A Rationale for Modern Conservative Disciples," *Disciples and the Church Universal*, The Reed Lectures for 1966 (Nashville: Disciples of Christ Historical Society, 1967), pp. 34-44.

[3]Leslie L. Spear, *The True Religion and the Religion of Others*, n.p., n.d., p. 147.

[4]James Stephen Wolfgang, *A Life of Humble Fear: The Biography of Daniel Sommer, 1850-1940*, Unpublished M.A. thesis, Butler U., 1975, pp. 142, 143.

[5]Logan J. Fox, "Destiny or Disease?," *Voices of Concern: Studies in Church of Christism*, Edited by Robert Meyers (St. Louis: Mission Messenger, 1966), p. 14.

[6]W.E. Garrison and A. T. DeGroot, *The Disciples of Christ: A History* (St. Louis, Bethany Press, 1948), p. 358.

[7]William D. Carpe, "Baptismal Theology in the Disciples of Christ," *Review and*

Expositor, Vol. 77 (1980), pp. 89-100.

[8]Stephen England, *We Disciples* (St. Louis: Christian Board of Publication, 1946), pp. 61-76.

[9]Alexander Campbell, "Any Christians Among Protestant Parties?," *Millennial Harbinger*, 1837, pp. 411-414.

[10]"Review of Christians Among the Sects," *Millennial Harbinger*, 1840, p. 164.

[11]"Christians Among the Sects," *Millennial Harbinger*, 1837, pp. 506-508, 561-567.

[12]*Christian Evangelist*, Vol. 20 (1901), p. 491.

[13]For the series by Christianos, see Index to *Millennial Harbinger*, 1838-40. For above quotations: "Christians Among the Sects," *Millennial Harbinger*, 1838, pp. 567-570; 1839, pp. 43-45, 168-173.

[14]M. Winans, "Christians Among the Sects," *Millennial Harbinger*, 1839, p. 547.

[15]Thomas Henley, "Christians Among the Sects, No. 2," *Millennial Harbinger*, 1839, p. 125.

[16]Alexander Campbell, "Remarks on the Above," *Millennial Harbinger*, 1840, pp. 127, 128.

[17]Daniel Sommer, "A Record of My Life," in typeset in Disciples of Christ Historical Society, has been included in William E. Wallace, *Daniel Sommer*, n.p., 1969.

[18]Matthew C. Morrison, *Like A Lion: Daniel Sommer's Seventy Years of Preaching* (Murfreesboro, TN: DeHoff, 1975), p. 159.

[19]F.D. Kershner, "Daniel Sommer," *Christian Evangelist*, Vol. 59 (1940), p. 290.

[20]Joseph Franklin, "Franklin's Reply," *Christian Standard*, Vol. 31 (1896), p. 1274.

[21]James Vernon, "A Daniel Come to Judgment," *Christian Evangelist*, Vol. 36 (1901), p. 416.

[22]William E. Wallace, *Daniel Sommer*, p. 92.

[23]Matthew C. Morrison, *Like A Lion*, p. 87.

[24]William E. Wallace, *Daniel Sommer*, p. 254.

[25]T.J. Holloman, "Sectism and Anti-ism," *Christian Standard*, Vol. 30 (1895), p. 1029.

[26]William E. Wallace, *Daniel Sommer*, p. 305.

[27]Daniel Sommer, "Publishers Paragraphs," *Octographic Review*, Vol. 35 (May 24, 1892), p. 1.

[28]Joseph Franklin, "A Sectarian Church of Christ," *Christian Standard*, Vol. 30 (1895), p. 923.

[29]A.B. Cunningham, "A Schismatic Work," *Christian Standard*, Vol. 25 (1892), p. 542.

[30]Russell Errett, "A Divisive Work," *Christian Standard*, Vol. 28 (1892), p. 521.

[31]Matthew C. Morrison, *Like a Lion*, p. 163. Story about Sommer's wife,

personal interview, W. Carl Ketcherside, longtime associated with family.

[32]William E. Wallace, *Daniel Sommer*, pp. 289-292.

[33]The schools were a new Bible college, Ellettsville, IN (a Mr. Krutsinger) and Potter Bible College, Bowling Green, KY (J. A. Harding). See "About Face," *Christian Evangelist*, Vol. 60 (1941), p. 867.

[34]William E. Wallace, *Daniel Sommer*, p. 267.

[35]"Leaning on the Piano," *Christian Evangelist*, Vol. 60 (1941), p. 23.

[36]Robert E. Hooper, *Crying in the Wilderness* (Nashville: David Lipscomb College, 1980), p. 315.

[37]Matthew C. Morrison, *Like A Lion*, p. 105.

[38]Lloyd Cline Sears, *The Eyes of Jehovah: The Life and Faith of James Alexander Harding* (Nashville: Gospel Advocate Co., 1970), p. 126.

[39]A.V. Murrell, *The Effects of Exclusivism in the Separation of the Churches of Christ from the Christian Churches*, Unpublished Ph.D. thesis, Vanderbilt U., 1972, pp. 174f.

[40]*Ibid.*, p. 167.

[41]David Lipscomb, "Can Two Walk Together Except They Be Agreed," *Gospel Advocate*, Vol. 30 (1888), p. 821.

[42]Robert E. Hooper, *Crying in the Wilderness*, p. 297.

[43]Herman Norton, *Tennessee Christians* (Nashville: Reed and Co., 1971), p. 162.

[44]Earl Irvin West, *The Life and Times of David Lipscomb* (Henderson TN: Religious Book Service, 1954), pp. 244f.

[45]Earl Irvin West, *The Search for the Ancient Order*, Vol. 2 (Indianapolis: Religious Book Service, 1950), p. 375.

[46]Robert E. Hooper, *Crying in the Wilderness*, p. 283.

[47]Herman Norton, *Tennessee Christians*, p. 193.

[48]*Ibid.*, pp. 213-214.

[49]C.D. Hall, *Texas Disciples* (Ft. Worth: TCU Press, 1953), pp. 149f.

[50]S.D. Eckstein, *History of the Churches of Christ in Texas* (Austin: Firm Foundation, 1963), p. 133.

[51]Herman E. Norton, *Tennessee Christians*, pp. 225, 212.

[52]Robert E. Hooper, *Crying in the Wilderness*, pp. 252, 253, 262.

[53]David Lipscomb, "The Church of Christ and the Disciples of Christ," *Gospel Advocate*, Vol. 49 (1907), p. 457.

[54]Robert E. Hooper, *Crying in the Wilderness*, p. 298.

[55]*Ibid.*, p. 284.

[56]A.V. Murrell, *Effects of Exclusivism*, p. 213.

[57]J.A. Harding, "Brother McGarvey's Reply Reviewed," *Gospel Advocate*, Vol. 29 (1887), p. 351.

17

PAPERS, PREACHERS, PROFESSORS
THE MOVEMENT DIVIDES AGAIN

Church of Christ Number Two
— A.T. DeGroot

The separation of Christian Churches-Churches of Christ, often referred to as Independent Christian Churches, during the first half of the twentieth century signaled the second major division within the Movement. It is cruel irony that a movement born of a passion to unite the Christians in all the sects should within a few decades suffer two major splits. But one historian sees it as more than ironic. He says that it is an indication that the Movement had failed even to control its own divisive forces, let alone to unite the larger Christian community.

> The "Christian Churches and Churches of Christ" claim to stand squarely in the great tradition of Stone and the Campbells. So do Disciples and Churches of Christ. Yet the existence of three distinct communions, sharing a common past, provides vivid testimony that the Stone-Campbell movement itself failed to overcome the forces of divisiveness, let alone lead a fragmented church into a new day of unity.[1]

It is important to identify "the forces of divisiveness" that made havoc of one of the most dramatic experiences in the history of the modern church. That a unity movement of some moment, launched by men of substance and rallied to by hundreds of thousands, should be compromised by the very evil it sought to overcome is a phenomenon we seek to explain.

When Did The New Church Begin?

There are several dates that one might choose in pinpointing the beginning of the Independent Christian Church, all the way from the first North American Christian Convention (NACC) in 1927 to the restructuring of the Disciples of Christ in 1968. Independent historians tend to date their beginnings with the origin of the NACC, which dramatized their differences with the Disciples and their convention. But Disciples historians see the Independents as still part of them in the 1960's, and were not officially separated until the the Christian Church (Disciples of Christ) became a restructured denomination.

The difficulty with the NACC (1927) date is that its beginning reflected no break of fellowship. There had been similar gatherings beside the International Convention (Disciples) for two decades before the NACC began. Once it began, many in good faith attended both conventions, and they continued to do so for at least two decades. The first president of the NACC, P.H. Welshimer, had also been president of the Disciples' convention. It began as a preaching convention with no intention of being competitive with the International.

The fact is that from the late 1920's until the 1950's there was no Independent Christian Church, separated from the Disciples. Fragmentation was at work, but there was no clear-cut distinction (two separate churches) until well into the 1950's.

Disciples historian A.T. DeGroot suggests a probable date of origin, if it is to be pinpointed to a particular year. After naming this second division in the Movement as "Church of Christ Number Two," he points to 1955. In that year for the first time a directory of ministers was published by one of the leaders of the "Undenominational Fellowship of Christian Churches and Churches of Christ."[2]

But this date too can be challenged since the directory was the work of only one man. Too, it could have been done anytime during the half century of dispute between the two groups that stubbornly remained one church.

Another Disciples historian, William E. Tucker, refers to this reluctance to accept division by noting that it was not until 1971 that the *Yearbook of American Churches* was asked, presumably by the Independents, to list the Christian Churches separately. He points out that this ambiguity of relationship might have gone on indefinitely but for the restructuring of the Disciples of Christ into a *de jure* denomination in 1968. Restructure, therefore, minimized the ambiguity to the point that the Christian Churches expressed their separate status in a formal way in the Yearbook of 1971, as Tucker sees it.[3]

This provides an interesting parallel with the Churches of Christ being listed separately in the 1906 Census. Both serve only as outside dates since the separations actually came many years earlier.

Even Independent historian James D. Murch could not avoid being ambiguous in that he juggles with dates covering at least three decades. He refers to two episodes in the 1940's that may well mark the *de facto* separation of the more conservative wing of the Disciples. In 1944 the International Convention of Disciples for the first time elected as president an outspoken advocate of open membership, and in 1948 the Commission on Restudy, created in hopes of avoiding an open split, made its final report to the convention and disbanded with a sense of failure.[4]

All these dates point to issues and events that help explain the Movement's second major division. The NACC may not have been provocative at the outset, but in time it became the alter ego of the Independents. Open membership, long a disputed issue, became a dividing wedge in 1944 when the Disciples by majority vote forced a Convention president of that persuasion upon the dissenting minority. And when conditions are such that one sees it as appropriate to draw up a separate list of ministers, or when a commission set up to avert a split gives up and goes home, it is reasonable to conclude that division is a reality.

Open Membership: The Basic Issue

It was the old issue of "Christians in the sects" all over again, appearing in different dress that led to the separation of the Independents. It now bore the dubious description of "open membership," which meant simply that believers were received as members of the church without being rebaptized by immersion. This referred to people who came from other churches and had been baptized by a mode other than immersion. Open membership has never implied an indifference to baptism, but only that believers may be received regardless of how they were baptized.

All segments of the Movement have always baptized by immersion and never by any other mode. At issue was whether other believers who were baptized in other churches by a mode other than immersion, even in infancy, were also Christians. In the Lunenburg Letter, Alexander Campbell allowed that the "pious unimmersed" were Christians. He never, however, actually advocated open membership.

Since Campbell's day there were those within the Movement who reasoned that if the unimmersed believers are Christians they should be accepted as members without rebaptism. While the leaders during the pioneer period differed on the matter it did not become a serious issue. Even when it was granted that there were "Christians in the sects," new members were received only by immersion and open membership was not practiced.

By the time of Isaac Errett, founding editor of the *Christian Standard*, which began in 1866, a general position had crystallized. According to Errett, the unimmersed believers, while Christians, were "Christians in error" who should not be officially received as members without being immersed. But this did not preclude fraternity and cooperation with other churches.[5]

Until well into the 20th century this was the practice. Beginning in

1917 reports began to filter in from the mission fields, particularly China and the Philippines, that some missionaries were practicing open membership. This issue, along with others, ignited a bitter and acrimonious feud the like of which the Movement had never seen, and so persevering that Stephen J. Corey could write of it as *Fifty Years of Attack and Controversy* (1953).

The fratricidal nightmare *did* seem to reach its climax in 1944, as Murch suggests, when the International Convention boldly elected an open membership man as president, thus ending decades of equivocation. The majority of Disciples had serious misgivings about open membership during the early decades of this century. It is therefore understandable that the most liberal leaders would minimize the significance of the reports from China and the Philippines, even to the point of denial, lest the support for such missions be in jeopardy.

For decades the Disciples had moved toward open membership, at home if not abroad, furtively if not openly. The data indicates that while in 1929 only 19 churches were avowedly open membership, many times this number practiced it clandestinely.[6] This would figure, for open membership was consistent with the emerging liberal theology of the times, which Disciples leaders were accepting.

The selection of an avowed open membership president in 1944, therefore, indicates that the Disciples realized it was not only time for candor but also a symbolic acknowledgement that there were *de facto* two churches within the fellowship.

Commission on Restudy

Equally significant to understanding the beginnings of the Independent Christian Church was the Commission on Restudy of the Disciples of Christ, created by the International Convention in 1934 in hopes of restoring peace to a fragmenting fellowship. The resolution read, "In view of the passion for unity which gave birth to the brotherhood of Disciples of Christ, and in view of the need of an aroused passion for unity among ourselves," and went on to charge the Commission as follows:

> It is hereby recommended that after a century and a quarter of history the convention, by its regularly constituted methods, appoint a commission to restudy the origin, history, slogans, methods, successes and failures of the movement of the Disciples of Christ, and with the purpose of a more effective and a more unified program and a closer Christian fellowship among us.[7]

That the Commission was a serious effort to preserve internal unity is indicated by the excellence of its makeup, its members being those who were prominent in their respective churches, once their efforts failed and division finally came. Among those that served were Edward Scribner Ames, R.M. Bell, F.W. Burnham, J.H. Dampier, Stephen J. England, Edwin R. Errett, A.W. Fortune, W.E. Garrison, Edgar DeWitt Jones, F.D. Kershner, C.E. Lemmon, C.C. Morrison, James D. Murch, M.E. Sadler, W.E. Sweeney, Robert S. Tuck, Dean E. Walker, L.N.D. Wells, P.H. Welshimer. The list of names of those given the task of saving the brotherhood could in retrospect be viewed as an honor roll of leaders in both churches.

After more than a decade of study and consultation the Commission delivered to the Convention one of the most remarkable documents in the Movement's history. It was a unity document in that after explaining the divergent viewpoints within the controversy it went on to appeal for unity and fraternity on the basis of what all parties believed as Disciples.

The unifying center is Jesus Christ and his word, the Restudy group reported, and it urged all within the fellowship to examine their position in the light of that center. It further recommended "That we all seek opportunities of expressing our conviction that diversity of methods in Christian activities is no barrier to the fellowship of Christian men."

Seeking to understand what was dividing them, the Commission concluded that their differences were matters of opinion, methods, and theology, while their agreements were in the area of fact, faith, and doctrine. "The differences touch only the periphery," it insisted, "but the agreements are at its center." It concluded its report with *We therefore sound a call to all Disciples:*

> That we sink into oblivion the particularisms which divide us as a people and rally ourselves to a supreme and common effort for the realization of Christian unity, beginning each one with himself . . .

> That we evaluate our differences by treating them for what they really are, opinions which are subjects for free and open discussion, and which all are free to accept or to reject, answering only to Christ. To make these divergences from our central agreements more than this is to fall into the sin of sectarianism . . .

> That we rise to a new sense of our mission to the Church and our mission to the world, noting their essential interdependence; for only if the Churches hear our Lord's prayer for unity may we expect the world to believe.

"Let us remember the holy purpose calling our movement into existence," the Commission went on to say, drawing upon its rich history. "How can we today, standing under the impending world tragedy, do less than throw ourselves unreservedly into the one divinely commissioned

411

business of the Church," the report concluded, calling upon the Disciples to cease their divisive ways and do what they had done so well in the past, evangelize: "using whatever means and methods may commend themselves to our Christian intelligence to reach all this generation's unreached with the Gospel."

It was a stirring appeal that closed with the prayer that their souls would find no rest until "the Church is united for the world's redemption."

One would suppose that if anything would revive a sagging unity movement such an appeal from its most respected leaders would. They had declared in their report that "We are embarrassed in our testimony and humbled in our hearts by the divisions that have already occurred in our own fellowship, and by the present tensions which gave rise to the creation of our commission." They were hopeful for a groundswell of intolerance of divisiveness at the grass roots level and that their report would be studied and discussed across the brotherhood.

But the Commission did not receive the support it deserved. While the 1949 Convention received the Report with appreciation and agreed to a Restudy Extension Committee, the support was inadequate for proper follow-up. There was no money for the study and discussion groups. The leading journals on both sides either ignored the Report or labeled the Restudy Commission as "ineffective." If the two sides were interested in reconciliation when the Restudy group was formed, they were clearly indifferent now.

It was a turning point in the Movement's history. Neither the conservative nor the liberal elements showed any real interest in preserving their unity heritage, even when appealed to in a dramatic and forceful manner by their own respected leaders. It was clearly a decision to divide and become two churches rather than to be conciliatory and preserve the Movement. Murch sums it up: "Conditions within the brotherhood apparently had deteriorated to the point where it was impossible to rally a strong concern for internal unity.[8]

Even though Disciples historian W.E. Garrison as late as 1958 referred to the Churches of Christ as "the only split among Disciples that has become clearly explicit."[9] we may conclude that for all practical purposes the Independent Christian Church was a separate fellowship by 1948. The ambiguity that Garrison referred to is due to the fact that for sometime to come many of the dissenters continued to call themselves Disciples and to list themselves and their churches in the same yearbook. For decades it was not uncommon for a minister to be listed by both churches, a practice that the Disciples discouraged once they officially became a denomination. Even today a few are listed in both yearbooks.

Reasons For the Separation: Federation

As in the breakdown of a marriage or a business, the reasons for a church split are usually complex. The apparent reasons are not always the real reasons. It is as marriage counselors sometimes put it: *The issue is not the issue!* We have seen that open membership was very controversial during this period, but it had been around since the days of Barton W. Stone and L.L. Pinkerton and hardly had the potential *per se* to divide the Movement.

The Restudy Commission came up with what it believed to be a basic reason for both the Churches of Christ and Christian Church divisions:

Our study of the history and ideals of our people has led us to the conclusion that a basic cause of our divisions and our more serious dissension, both past and present, lies in a difference of understanding with respect to the fundamental purpose of our movement.

Some believe that unity and restoration are "held together in a parity of mutual dependence," the Report stated, while others are persuaded that the two concepts are not necessarily coordinate and that restoration is often interpreted in such a way as to hinder unity. One interpretation thus makes restoration the means to unity, while the other holds that unity must always be the goal, even if this means a compromise of restoration. The restorationist, therefore, sees no way to unity except through the restoration of primitive Christianity.

No one has said this more pointedly than P.H. Welshimer, nor has anyone been more qualified to represent this position:

While unity is desirable, restoration of the church of the New Testament is more desirable, and in place of spending so much time in talking about unity we had better be about the business of having in every community, the restored church of the New Testament, and when we have that we will have unity, and we will never have it without it.[10]

Referring to Welshimer's position, Stephen J. Corey notes that it has never brought the Movement any unity, and in fact has led to division over what constitutes the restoration of the primitive church. "No other religious body has ever approached us for unity on this proposition and very likely no group ever will," he goes on to say, observing that in Welshimer's own city of Canton, Ohio, where he had the largest congregation in the brotherhood, the churches were probably no closer together because of his plea for restoration.[11]

While the Restudy group may have identified restorationism as a major cause for the separation of Churches of Christ, it is not evident that it figured substantially in the Christian Church division. The Restudy Commission recognized that there were those that sought a synthesis between restoration and unity, avoiding the dogmatic extremes of claiming that they alone had restored the New Testament church on the one hand, and on the other "an indifferentism that regards the restoration concept as irrelevant to Christian unity."

From the outset the Christian Church generally has been of this persuasion, avoiding the exclusivism of radical restorationism. It rather represents those that have sought a synthesis between unity and restoration. While restorationism figured substantially in the separation of Churches of Christ, as we have seen, it was not a major factor in the second division. We can properly identify other causes.

In responding to Stephen J. Corey's extensive treatment of the half-century controversy, Edwin V. Hayden, who later became editor of the *Christian Standard*, lists four causes, "digressions" he calls them, for the split: (1) Federation in interdenominational activities; (2) The acceptance of "the conclusions of historical criticism advanced by modern scholars"; (3) Open membership, sheltered and condoned if not actually practiced; (4) The limitation of missionary fields and activities through comity agreements.[12]

The main point of Hayden's response to Corey is that these causes for separation were indeed *digressions* from the course traditionally taken by the Movement, which Hayden insisted were acknowledged in Corey's treatment. Corey saw the digressions as changes that must come as a church progresses and matures. We have seen that open membership was clearly a departure from traditional Disciples practice, and it had the potential to be divisive in that it was tied to a theology of baptism that was crucial to the Movement's mission and message.

Of the four causes named by Hayden federation is the most significant, for it reveals more than any other development the direction the Disciples were now resolved to go, a direction that many conservatives (who did not go with the Churches of Christ) were not willing to follow. Federation, first proposed by the Presbyterians back in 1891, was simply a matter of fellowship and cooperation with other churches.

This eventually led to the formation of the Federal Council of Churches of Christ in America in 1905, which Disciples leaders helped to develop, working on an *ad hoc* basis. The federation principle came before the 1902 International Convention and was adopted by a large assembly with only minimal opposition. This was because the Disciples generally had come to believe their witness for unity was hindered by their lack of contact with others they considered Christians.

The battle was joined from the outset, for at the 1902 Convention J.A. Lord, editor of the *Christian Standard*, expressed fear that federation would be a recognition of the denominations, which many Disciples believed to be a compromise of their non-denominational position. W.E. Garrison, in his first Convention speech as a young man, responded to Lord that federation merely recognized that the denominations existed and that there were Christians in them, not that they ought to exist.[13]

For decades federation, which came to be closely tied to open membership, was a bone of contention. To many of the conservatives it was a trap for unwary Disciples, while to the liberals it was the only escape from being an exclusivistic sect. The oddity of it was that most of them believed in cooperating with other churches. It was a question of whether they could *agree* to cooperate! Some insisted that this was the only difference between cooperation and federation. But the real issue was baptism, for federation was seen as fellowship with the unimmersed.

David Filbeck of the Independent persuasion names baptism as the cause for the division. Explaining that the Churches of Christ withdrew over instrumental music and the missionary society, he goes on to say: "This in effect left only the Disciples of Christ to fight over the question of baptism and its role in Christian unity. Unfortunately it wasn't long before a division occurred among the Disciples of Christ over the matter."

He observes that the liberal Disciples had to choose between the traditional position on baptism for the remission of sins and thus maintain unity within by appeasing the conservatives, and a more liberal position on baptism (open membership) which would enable them to relate more effectively with those outside the Movement.

He dates the beginning of the Christian Church with the formation of the North American Christian Convention in 1927, noting that the controversy over baptism raged until then. He is surprisingly candid in summarizing the *raison d'etre* of his own people: "For the conservatives it was more important to maintain a strong position on baptism, but for the liberals it was more important to downplay baptism in order to open up the way for unity with other groups."[14]

The burden of his essay is to warn of still another controversy over baptism (its essentiality) among his own conservative Christian Churches, which further shows that the Movement has never really agreed on baptism and has never ceased arguing about it.

While Filbeck's evaluation of the division may be too simplistic, he recognizes an important difference between the first and second splits. The

Churches of Christ separated over methodology, while the Christian Church withdrew over theology. While a theology of baptism was not the only area of concern, as we shall see, it was a crucial part of the problem, and this explains why federation was one of the main causes for the division. The conservatives rejected federation, not because it took cooperation with other believers more seriously, but because, as they saw it, it compromised the Movement's position on baptism and consequently its restoration plea.

A.T. DeGroot also names federation as one of the basic causes of the division, charging that the *Christian Standard*'s unrelenting attack on "recognizing the denominations," beginning in 1902, led to the creation of "Church of Christ Number Two." Noting that the Disciples never recognized denominationalism as the ideal, he goes on to give a summary similar to that of Filbeck's:

> This is the principle that has led Disciples of Christ to work *from within* the existing larger Christian community to reform it to New Testament principles. The Independent position, on the other hand, is to stand apart from the existing Christian world and to show by its life and deeds so superior a type of character that all others will join them in unconditional surrender. The difference between the two bodies is clear.[15]

Liberalism

As significant as federation (along with open membership) was in all this, historian William E. Tucker (Disciple) is correct in concluding that there is no way to understand the separation of the Christian Church without taking into account the impact of American liberal theology upon the Disciples of Christ. By the turn of the century the "higher criticism," as it came to be called, of German universities was making its way into virtually every American denomination, working havoc among people who believed the Bible to be "the inspired word of God." There were heresy trials in some of the leading denominations, and some of the leading seminaries divided into rival institutions over what was commonly called "modernism."

While we have identified L.L. Pinkerton as the first Disciples "liberal," he could hardly hold a light for Robert C. Cave (1843–1923) who had to resign his pulpit at Central Christian Church in St. Louis for denying the virgin birth and the bodily resurrection of Jesus. He was even sympathetic with the Christ-myth theory, then current among radical German liberals. Even though he formed an independent church of Disciples, he had little impact upon the Movement since his views were so radical. But he did signal the beginning of liberalism among the Disciples, which not only moved them in a different theological direction but was a prime cause in the separation of the Christian Church.

The key figure among the liberals was Herbert L. Willett, who took one of the first Ph.D.'s from the new University of Chicago. Tutored by W.R. Harper, the president of the university and an able exponent of higher criticism, Willett became something of a crusader for historical criticism of the Bible among Disciples. An unusually gifted writer, teacher and speaker, he not only wrote regularly for the *Christian-Evangelist* but conducted seminars throughout the brotherhood, popularizing a new approach to biblical studies. He was credited with bridging the gap between the higher critics and the lay folk in the churches that feared them.

Willett, who served as the first dean of the controversial Disciples Divinity House, a cooperative of the University of Chicago, was the object of continual attack from the conservatives, some of it abusive. He nonetheless went on to do more than anyone else in liberalizing the Disciples. He was encouraged by James H. Garrison, editor of the *Christian-Evangelist*, who, while himself only moderately liberal and uneasy with some of the conclusions of the critics, wanted the Disciples to be an open and informed people. Willett was especially effective in writing the weekly Sunday school lessons for Garrison, in which he demonstrated to a growing number of readers that he was not only devoted to the Bible but true to the Stone-Campbell heritage.

In a recent study on Willett, M. Eugene Boring points out that he was always a popularizer rather than an elitist. He wrote for the church, not the scholars, which sets him apart from most Disciples scholars today. Willett was no research scholar who sought to expand the frontiers of knowledge in the academic community, Boring explans, but a scholar whose intent was the growth of the Disciples.[16]

But his efforts were not always appreciated. A dramatic moment came when Willett was billed to address the Centennial Convention in Pittsburgh in 1909, the most significant gathering of Disciples during their first century. There was a concerted effort by the conservatives to keep him off the program, even if it broke with the tradition of not making theological diversity a test of fellowship at the Convention. The *Christian Standard* ran a series of articles against Willett, charged that his theology was at variance with the fathers of the Movement, and published many letters protesting his participation.

Willett nonetheless appeared and addressed an overflow audience. The *Standard* found no objection to what he said, but that it was he who said it, a man "notorious for public utterances that conflict with the plain teaching of the Scriptures."[17]

While hardly any of the liberals of this period were radical after the order of Cave, their number grew and their influence was substantial, especially at the Disciples Divinity House in Chicago and the College of the Bible in Lexington. At Chicago Willett was succeeded as dean by W.E. Garrison and Edward Scribner Ames, men who trained many seminarians in a hermeneutics far different from what many leading Disciples had learned from the renowned conservative scholar J.W. McGarvey.

Generally the new approach was appreciated, and it turned Disciples ministerial education in a new direction, especially when the College of the Bible, after an extensive baptism of fire, also became liberal. Once McGarvey was gone, the Lexington institution sported a new faculty of progressive thinkers, including W.C. Bower, A.W. Fortune, G.W. Henry, and E.E. Snoddy.

The liberals may have captured the learning centers, but they hardly had a journal equal to the influence of the *Christian Standard*, which had become increasingly conservative since the death of Isaac Errett in 1888. To be sure, the *Christian-Evangelist* was supportive of what it believed to be progressive, but it was not strongly liberal. W.C. Morrison temporarily filled the void with his *Christian Century*, but after a few years it became "an undenominational journal of religion," one of the most exciting and widely-read journals in the nation, but no longer Disciples oriented.

Nonetheless Morrison, working out of Chicago, joined with Willett, Garrison, and Ames in forming a vanguard of liberalism that profoundly influenced the thinking of many Disciples, especially with help from the College of the Bible in Lexington. Ronald E. Osborn gives these men credit for saving the Disciples from the isolation that had long handicapped them by bringing home the currents of contemporary thinking and the full impact of liberalism.[18]

The liberal organ was *The Scroll*, published in Chicago by the Campbell Institute, the most notorious of liberal agencies, especially when it eventually sponsored "midnight sessions" during the national conventions. The Institute was a fellowship of the better educated ministers and other leaders and its purpose was threefold: a scholarly spirit, quiet self-culture, contributions of permanent value to the literature and thought of the Disciples of Christ.

Encouraged by "the Chicago liberals," Yale seminarians who went to the Disciples Divinity House for further study started the Campbell Institute in 1896 with a charter membership of fourteen. It had a substantial influence for over a half century, with membership sometimes reaching several hundreds, which says something for the growth in ministerial education since a college degree was required for membership. It was more a school of thinkers than a school of thought.

Since the Campbell Institute and *The Scroll* flourished during the rise of liberalism, they came under relentless attack, causing James H. Garrison to suggest that some of his good brethren would reject the Ten Commandments should they be issued by the Campbell Institute![19] The *Standard* called it a clique whose members dominated the agencies, and noted that in 1939 six of the last eight presidents of the International Convention were members of the Institute.

The editor went on to charge that the Institute "has nothing but contempt for what is called 'external authority' and commands that come down to us from Jesus." "Those who still believe in the Great Commission," the editor warned, must "rid ourselves of the incubus before it completes the wreckage of every constructive work the churches of Christ possess."[20]

It was judgments of this sort on the part of papers, preachers, and professors on both sides that figured substantially in the Movement's second major split.

No one realized the seriousness of the differences more than Herbert L. Willett, which led him to write a book (1901) on the crisis the Disciples faced. He wrote of those who eventually became the Christian Church as "another section of our brotherhood" that supposes that all Christians besides ourselves are hopelessly wrong, if they can by an extraordinary stretch of charity be called Christians at all. To cooperate with such people, who are indiscriminately called "the sects," is disloyalty to Christ, and to save a soul from the bondage of the Methodists or Presbyterians is as much a cause of rejoicing as the conversion of a sinner from a godless life.

Willett doubted that brethren of such an attitude could be counted on for any move toward federation. He saw this as clannish indifference and hostility to any united effort. The real tragedy, however, is "when we become a narrow, suspicious sect with all the exclusiveness and intolerance of the Plymouth Brethren or Auld Licht Presbyterians, and yet pleading for union."

In the best tradition of the Movement, Willett was not one to settle for division. Despite the differences, separation could be avoided by an appeal to the principles that gave birth to the Movement, which he summarized as:

1. Loyalty to Christ and his teaching. This can never be compromised.

2. The right to private judgment that one demands for himself concede to others. Because they differ he has no right to impugn their loyalty to Christ. In some cases he may see that their spiritual life outweighs his own correctness on Biblical teaching.

3. It is not necessary for us to agree on all points before we can cooperate in actual service to Christ. A Disciples group in a given town should be

closer to other churches in the same town than to another Disciples group in another town and should find ways to work together.

4. Things we can do together: exchange preachers, union services.

5. Unity comes through actual cooperation, not by pacts and agreements by denominational leaders.

6. The task of the new century for the Disciples is to assist in the practical realization of Christian union.

Willett saw two possible directions for point six. One would be for the Disciples to become a denomination with all of the usual machinery. In that case they would continue to grow until they lose the vital impulse of their youth and sink "into a mere denomination like the rest." The other direction is to take up seriously the problem of Christian unity with which they started.

To do this the Disciples must be willing to give up anything which stands in the way, "including ourselves, our denominational standing, our machinery, and merge ourselves in the great united Church of Christ." He insisted that "We shall not have to give up a single principle for which we have contended, but only our divisive attitude. By this means we lose ourselves, but we save our plea, and thus ourselves, in the largest way."[21]

These two directions identified by Willett are strikingly similar to "A Fork in the Road" faced by the Disciples of Christ during their critical period of restructure, as identified by W.E. Garrison in a 1964 address, which is discussed in the next chapter.

There was one man who epitomized the principles set forth by Willett, even though he was a catalyst in the separation of the Independents. P.H. Welshimer was not a founder of the Independent Christian Church in the same way that Daniel Sommer and David Lipscomb were of the Churches of Christ, but he was as important to its beginnings, or nearly so.

P.H. Welshimer
"Let us disagree without being disagreeable."

There was something special about P.H. Welshimer in that he was a protagonist in the drama without being a factionalist. He stood on the conservative side of all three of the divisive issues that were at work — open membership, federation, liberalism — and yet he was a peacemaker or sought to be. He deserves special attention in that if his attitude had prevailed division might have been averted.

When the preachers in Canton, Ohio wanted to bring Billy Sunday to the city for an extended revival, it was P.H. Welshimer who met with the famed evangelist and worked out details, and it was he that raised the

$12,000 to pay for it. Then when Sunday left town he conducted a revival of his own at the First Christian Church and added 1,032 to its membership, many of them being Sunday's converts!

Born in 1873, he was soon known simply as P.H. rather than Pearl Howard. Educated at Hiram College, he always remembered the words of its president E.V. Zollars: "Young men, as you go into communities to save souls, remember that you, too, have a soul to save. Don't do anything to lose it." That well summarizes Welshimer's long, fruitful life in the ministry. He lived as one who had a soul to save, his own. As the pastor of the Movement's largest church, he was never sidetracked from his lifelong mission: "To the best of my ability I am preaching the gospel of my Lord Jesus Christ."[22]

P.H. was always there to serve his church. When Will Rogers came to town, P.H. had him in his pulpit the next Sunday, overflowing the building, which was his delight. But he could fill his own church without outside help, and he eventually had a membership of 5,500. Always cooperative with other churches, he was a leader in the ministerial association and active in most every community project, even to riding in police cars behind picket lines to minister to those who chose to work. It was said of him that he made more calls in a single day than most preachers did in a week.

Hardly ecumenical in the usual sense, he had no qualms about converting other Christians to the restoration plea. He immersed the Episcopal priest who ministered just across the street, one who went on, after resigning his position, to serve Christian Churches. And when Aimee Semple McPherson came to town P.H. opposed her from the pulpit and in the press, even when other ministers in the city supported her, and he was undaunted when she threatened to sue him. If need be, he would defend his cause on the polemic platform, as he did in a debate on baptism with the Lutheran pastor in his city. He even took on Clarence Darrow, the atheist.

The doughty criminal lawyer was taken aback when P.H. based his faith upon the testimony of prophecy. When the two met for a second debate, Darrow asked P.H. to suggest books he might read, explaining that he had never known anyone to base his faith on prophecy![23]

P.H., who was known about town as "Mr. Canton," built his great church by making the Sunday School an agent for evangelism. He would recruit parents along with their children as he walked the neighborhoods. He baptized people at almost every service, and he conducted his own revivals that would run for weeks, wherein hundreds would be added to the church. He became known as one of the most powerful preachers in the brotherhood. His simplicity confused the more sophisticated. He was without apology a very doctrinal preacher and a forthright restorationist. During his 56-year tenure in Canton his influence spread far and wide, and he was in constant demand as a speaker at state and national conventions.

When the issues detailed in this chapter emerged, P.H. was among the first on the firing line for the conservative cause, but always as irenic as forthright. He believed the reports that open membership was being practiced abroad and countenanced at home, so in 1920 his Canton church was among the first to withdraw financial support from the United Christian Missionary Society. But two years later when the society ruled that contributions could be designated for particular causes, P.H. led his church to resume its support.[24]

We have already stated that Welshimer was a member of the Restudy Commission, and it was in part his influence that gave its conclusions both an irenic tone and a strong restorationist viewpoint. His biographer notes that his preaching in churches and at conventions was to point out positively that there was "a church pattern clearly discerned in the New Testament."[25]

We have quoted him as saying that restoration is more desirable than unity, and it was easy for him to say, quite naively, when deploring the tragedy of division: "The solution will be found when we all get back to the position of the church in New Testament days, and that is the only hope of a divided church."[26] But P.H. never lost what many others seemed never to have had, a loving and conciliatory spirit.

As much as they admired P.H.'s graciousness, most of the Disciples leaders did not agree with him on how unity is to be attained and preserved. They held that unity cannot be predicated upon a restorationism that assumes a "clearly discerned pattern" in the New Testament for the church, and then assumes that the Disciples had restored such a church. An incident in Welshimer's own experience points up the charge made by Corey, which we have referred to, that P.H.'s restorationist approach did not work even in his own city, as successful as he was otherwise.

In one of the meetings of the ministerial association in Canton, a fellow preacher accused Welshimer of "stealing sheep" from other churches. While P.H. nobly defended himself, noting that folk came to his church on their own accord, the incident revealed that the growth of the First Christian Church in Canton did not necessarily promote unity.

Welshimer chaired the committee that gave birth to the North American Christian Convention in 1927, and he served as its first president. He eventually served as president three times, the only man ever to do so.

Since the NACC in time became inseparably connected with the new division, P.H. became a catalyst, whether intentional or not, for the formation of the Independent Christian Church. He had also served as president of the International Convention, and he continued for years to attend both conventions in an effort to preserve the peace.

While there was at first no intention of starting another fellowship, the NACC provided programs more in keeping with conservative interests. P.H. probably expressed the sentiments of many conservatives who sought to avert division when he described the International Convention as "the fellowship was wonderful but the program lousy."

Welshimer was not only loyal to both conventions, but in 1938 the International selected him to be its representative to the convention of British churches. He continued to address the International even after it was evident that he and the NACC were moving in a different direction. He was something of a mediator between the two groups, and he often called for a more conciliatory spirit on the part of both sides.

One such appeal was in 1940, when as president he announced the NACC's first gathering since 1937. It is no place for "the grumbler, fault-finder, the murmurer, nor the apostate," he avowed. "We are brethren and will give a demonstration of 'how pleasant it is for brethren to dwell together in unity.'" He concluded with: "Whether we agree or disagree, we will have the good sense to disagree without being disagreeable."[27]

Disagree without being disagreeable. It was an attitude that impressed Dean Kershner of the Butler School of Religion, who served as president of the International Convention and on the executive committee of the NACC. He too sought to be a peacemaker amidst the storm. He assured the brotherhood that the NACC was not schismatic, and he could not find better proof than that P.H. Welshimer was president of it. Throughout the controversy Kershner had hopes of averting division, which to him would be nothing less than disaster:

> Nothing could constitute a greater tragedy for our people than for another open schism to be catalogued in the U.S. Census reports. Two divisions in our original movement for Christian union are bad enough, but three would be little short of calamitous. The fact is we should be trying to pull the two together instead of creating a third.[28]

As late as 1948 the editor of the Disciples' leading journal, the *Christian-Evangelist*, referred to Welshimer's "disagree without being disagreeable" and expressed hope for peace between the two conventions. He unequivocally accepted those of the NACC as "part of the brotherhood designated as Disciples of Christ," and pointed out that "Many of their speakers and their messages have been and will be welcome on state and International Convention programs."[29]

But only two years later, in 1950 when the NACC decided to assemble every year, the *Christian-Evangelist* asked, "Does This Mean Division?" The editor feared that a permanent NACC would accelerate "this protest movement and eventually divide the brotherhood," despite the best intentions. While he hoped that the disaster could be avoided, he feared the inevitable. It may already be too late, he told his readers.[30]

These three issues — open membership, federation, liberalism — continue to be named by Independent historians as the reasons for their separation from the Disciples, as in the resourceful work of Henry E. Webb of Milligan College, recently published by *Christian Standard*.[31] But it is arguable that these issues, at least two of which had been present in the Movement all along, are not what further divided the Movement.

They could have remained united on the principles that gave birth to the Movement, which allowed for liberty of opinions. This was impressively exemplified in P.H. Welshimer. As critical as Stephen J. Corey sometimes was towards the Independents in his account of the long controversy, he commends P.H. in terms that deserve emphasis in any serious effort to understand what really caused the division: "We could have and should have remained united if we had followed the appeal of P.H. Welshimer, of Canton, Ohio, to "disagree without being disagreeable."[32]

In the best tradition of the Movement the Welshimer approach could have prevailed. The real cause for the division, therefore, was more than "issues" upon which sincere people will always differ. It was the vindictive spirit and unbrotherly attitude of certain papers, preachers, and professors. They were not of the mind to disagree agreeably, and thus chose to effect what Dean Kershner considered both a tragedy and a calamity, a unity movement now divided, not only two ways but three ways.

Papers, Preachers, Professors

"You can't trust a Disciple!"

The Welshimer plea for unity in diversity came upon hard times, especially from some of his own Independent brethren. To Robert E. Elmore, editor of *Restoration Herald*, P.H. Welshimer was a traitor to the conservative cause, "a UCM$ fraternizer," the dollar mark being part of his description of the United Christian Missionary Society. That was a mild epithet in comparison to others he used: *betrayers, infidels, false teachers, wolves,* and *fakes.*

Elmore criticized Welshimer for speaking at Bethany College, which was a member of the "Disciple Board of Higher (infidel) Education," and for allowing a Bethany professor to preach at his church. And when P.H., who edited the *Canton Christian*, included the Disciples as part of the brotherhood, Elmore avowed that they were "not the brotherhood to which this writer belongs."[33]

The editor really wound it tight, referring to a subscriber who had sent him a donation as one who "follows her New Testament, which forbids Christians to have any fellowship with the UCMS works of darkness." He did not fellowship the society, he explained, "not because it is an organization, but because it is corrupt." To him open membership was the work of "Promoting Perverters" and is "one concrete example of their flagrant denial of Christ and nullification of His Word and repudiation of His church."[34]

The *Restoration Herald* was published by the Christian Restoration Association, one of its purposes being to oppose "all moves, whether by individuals or organizations, which are against the gospel," with special attention to the activities of the United Society and the International Convention of the Disciples of Christ and their affiliated agencies.[35] The association was a missionary agency for the conservatives, sometimes assuming the support of missionaries terminated by the United Society, and it exported its feelings toward the "UCMS Octopus" as far as the Philippines where division resulted in churches because the conservatives denounced the UCMS as untrue to the faith.[36]

Elmore also edited *The Touchstone*, a journal started by the *Standard* Publishing Co. to expose further the doings of the UCMS. At one time in the 1920's there were three journals at war with the United Society: *Restoration Herald*, *The Touchstone*, and the *Christian Standard*, which sometimes reproduced material from *The Touchstone*.

While the apparent issue was open membership, with the liberals denying its practice and the conservatives crying "whitewash," the real issue was "the infidel administration" that the editors were eager to oust. This appears to have been a typical struggle for power in the church.

Both *The Touchstone* and the *Christian Standard* ran Elmore's essay calling for "Out With This Divisive Thing." They looked to the Restoration Congress in Memphis in 1926 (which laid the ground work for the NACC) as the opportune time to "mark the final overthrow of the coterie of dissensionists that have been disturbing our convention life and sowing seeds of discord among brethren and churches for nearly thirty years."[37] While the likes of P.H. Welshimer may have had other ideas, it appears that these editors had division in mind from the outset.

It may seem incongruous for the name of John D. Rockefeller, Sr. to be part of the story of a church split, but his gift of $25,000 to the Foreign Christian Missionary Society, 1905-07, became part of the controversy. The *Standard* charged that it was "tainted money" and should be returned to the donor. It became a bitter and personal harangue between Editor J.A. Lord and Archibald McLean, president of the FCMS.

Lord called upon Thomas W. Phillips, a competitor of Rockefeller in the oil business as well as a preacher, to expose Rockefeller as unscrupulous. McLean, who submitted rebuttals to the *Standard* that the editor would not publish, rejoined that Editor Lord himself had profited from Standard Oil, being a stockholder in one of its auxiliaries, and that the *Standard* itself ran ads for the company's products. He also quoted from J.W. McGarvey, who said he would take money from the devil for use in Christ's service.[38]

The Rockefeller fiasco, which was resolved when the Convention elected almost unanimously to keep the money, was but a symptom of what really ailed J.A. Lord. His role in the dispute over federation was so intense that A.T. DeGroot credits him with fathering Church of Christ Number Two.[39]

Lord opposed any fellowship or cooperation with other churches as a repudiation of the Movement's plea, insisting that "Federation is not a union in Christ, but union in denominationalism, union in an order of things which Christ and his apostles condemn as carnal and as an enemy to Christian union or the union in Christ."[40] When the *Standard* drew this hard line against federation, which most Disciples now accepted, it lent inevitability to the break that eventually came.

J.D. Murch rightly describes this controversy as deteriorating from a discussion of principles to "base political jockeying and personal insults and diatribe" on both sides. He recalls how one Disciples editor referred to his conservative counterparts as "Theological Tomcats."[41]

There were instances during the long controversy when *Standard* editors, especially Edwin R. Errett (his father was a nephew of Isaac Errett), sought peace and tried to neutralize the influence of such strong leaders as Robert E. Elmore. When Elmore persisted in referring to the UCMS in such language as *infidelity* and *jesuitism*, Errett warned that there was as much danger in "an anti-United Society denomination" as in the kind Elmore feared. He put the *Standard* on record as recognizing all sincere believers as brethren and as refusing to make the United Society a test of fellowship.[42]

This irenic spirit in the *Standard*'s editorial chair was, unfortunately, short-lived. Following Editor Errett's untimely death in 1944, the *Standard* began an editorial policy that was equivalent to making "the issues" a test of fellowship, as the following developments indicate.

1. The *Standard* was not merely indifferent toward the Commission on Restudy's effort to preserve unity, as were the Disciples journals, but went so far in 1948 as to say: "Its very existence is an attempt to perpetuate the fallacious assumption that believers and unbelievers can be joined in a 'Brotherhood.'"[43] If those the *Standard* opposed were now *unbelievers*, fellowship was hardly a possibility. This was not the attitude of the late Editor Errett, who served on the Restudy Commission.

2. By 1947 the *Standard* was calling for an "Honor Roll of the "Faithful" ministers and churches, those who have "thrown off the shackles of a sectarian leadership." "Let us hear from you. Just a postcard or letter will do," an editorial urged, promising a weekly listing of the faithful. For the first time in the long controversy the paper called for "a listing separate from the Disciples' yearbook," noting that brethren had been demanding it. Here it is, said the *Standard*, while conceding that the list was not yet a yearbook.[44] Hardly anything promotes separatism as much as the creation of "a list of the faithful."

3. While a 1946 editorial was entitled "The UCMS is Not a Test of Fellowship," it was hardly the tolerant position that Errett had taken earlier, for it had reference to the support or nonsupport of the UCMS on the part of those who might not have known that their money was used for the "enslavement of the churches." As for the "faith-denying and faith-destroying liberals" who controlled the society, the *Standard* repudiated them, insisting that they "cannot be part of the brotherhood."[45]

4. In the same year the *Standard* issued "An Open Letter" to the Disciples' Convention in assembly in Columbus which was based on Matt. 18:16-17, which sets forth the procedure for withdrawing fellowship. The "final urgent" appeal was for the Disciples to renounce their leaders who had "attacked the authority of the Bible." The open letter appeared in the public press as well as the *Standard*, and it was stated that it would be duplicated 2,000,000 times and sent to every member of the Christian Church.[46]

The papers had help from some of the colleges and seminaries that had begun during these years as part of the protest of Disciples' liberalism, particularly the Cincinnati Bible Seminary. While Editor Elmore accused the liberals of stealing conservative churches, the liberals accused the conservatives, especially young preachers from Cincinnati, of stealing their churches.

There were several lawsuits that were long, bitter, and divisive, sometimes caused by a minister dividing the loyalties of a congregation and fomenting litigation. Unlike the lawsuits over organs and societies, which the instrumentalists always won, the issues this time were more theological and more difficult for a court to decide, the decisions often being ambiguous and two-sided.

Cincinnati Bible Seminary's renowned professor, Rupert C. Foster, who was educated at both Yale and Harvard, led the opposition. According to *Restoration Herald* C.B.S. was the "school of the prophets" that taught its students "how to meet the enemies of Christ that are now infesting every corner of the field."[47] Prof. Foster was the foremost teacher who impressed upon the young prophets that the UCMS was the enemy and that a Disciple cannot be trusted. There is evidence that the prophets got the message.

While Foster used inflammatory rhetoric like Elmore, he went further than the editor in his opposition to the UCMS in that he questioned the organization *per se*, which Elmore did not, insisting that it was the *corruption* of the society that he opposed.

To Foster the UCMS was "A towering super-organization unknown alike to the founders of our movement and to the New Testament." The Disciples leaders were not simply mistaken, but dispensers of "a deadly poison virus in the system of the brotherhood" and guilty of "deception" and "idolatrous fetishism." He mocked the UCMS by restructuring an old motto: "In all things, trust the UCMS officials; in support of the super-machine, unity; in opinions, liberty." As early as 1923 he saw the situation as "absolutely irreconcilable."[48]

Foster's impassioned attacks appeared even when writing on other subjects. In an essay on the believer's liberty in Christ, he referred to his brethren in Kentucky as "abject slaves of an infidel ecclesiasticism with headquarters at Lexington," a reference to the College of the Bible, which was "a branch office of Chicago, Indianapolis, and St. Louis." He found an infidel behind every Disciples bush, the Campbell Institute being "an infidel organization" and the United Society "an infidel oligarchy which has betrayed and divided the movement." He made these judgments as late as 1946 before the Congress on Evangelism, when the likes of Dean Kershner and P.H. Welshimer were suing for peace.[49]

Like Welshimer, Foster was a rigid restorationist, believing that "the restoration of His church is the only means of uniting a divided Christendom," but unlike the Canton minister he was intolerant of those who disagreed with him. He called them "shrewd and aggressive men who have abandoned the truth and authority of the word of God" and manufactured "a modern, human basis of union through fellowship and benevolent compromise with our religious neighbors."

The professor's attacks in the *Standard* reflect what he said in the classroom, the essence of which was *You can't trust a Disciple!* They "play fast and loose with facts and funds" and "keep people in darkness and run recruits in from radical colleges." Moreover, they practice "subterfuge and camouflage," and "compass sea and land to propagate skeptical theories and swing the Restoration movement over to radical interdenominationalism."[50] He influenced many of his ministerial students to share his attitude as they served the churches, further polarizing the brotherhood.

The most revealing of all the professor's essays was his extended review of W.C. Morro's *Brother McGarvey*. While Foster conceded that Morro, who had studied under and taught with McGarvey, had said many good things about McGarvey, the book was nonetheless an attack on McGarvey, as Foster saw it, a "very able and very subtle piece of propaganda for modernism." This strikes a reader of Morro's book as incredible. Dean Kershner also reviewed the book and concluded that Morro had esteemed McGarvey too highly, placing him above Isaac Errett![51]

It is evident, therefore, that the second major split within the Movement was a reality by the 1950's, if not by the 1940's. And that papers, preachers, and professors on both sides, who were less than charitable in attitude, must bear a substantial part of the blame for the separation.

While such issues as federation, open membership, and liberalism were contributing causes, it was a vindictive spirit and a lack of brotherly love on the part of the leadership of both sides that was the real cause. Like the editor bishops among Churches of Christ who hastened the first split, they could tolerate only a diversity that they themselves prescribed.

Thomas Munnell, one of the early secretaries of the International Convention, anticipated the problem back when the first division was developing:

> The chief difference of all arises from our unwillingness to grant toleration and fellowship to a mistaken brother long enough to admit of his growth in knowledge . . Each one is very willing to admit the fallibility of his neighbor, but not his own . . It is better even to tolerate some mistakes in theory, and even in practice for a time, if some grander good is to be accomplished.[52]

James H. Garrison, editor of the *Christian-Evangelist* long enough to experience something of both of the divisions, referred to these controversies in a personal note: "The years immediately preceding it (the Centennial Convention in 1909) were marked and marred by some controversies which we would be glad to forget. But they are history, and it is dangerous to forget history."[53]

These seventeen chapters are history, some of which the heirs of the Movement, now three churches rather than one, would be glad to forget. But those heirs would do well to heed the wisdom of one of their pioneer editors. It is dangerous to forget history.

ENDNOTES

[1]Lester G. McAllister and William E. Tucker, *Journey in Faith: A Journey in Faith* (St. Louis: Bethany Press, 1975), p. 386.

[2]A.T. DeGroot, *New Possibilities for Disciples and Independents* (St. Louis: Bethany Press, 1963), p. 24.

[3]McAllister and Tucker, *Journey in Faith*, p. 386. Also personal interview with William E. Tucker.

[4]James DeForest Murch, *Christians Only* (Cincinnati: Standard, 1962), p. 277.

[5]Isaac Errett, "The Grounds of Christian Fellowship," *Missouri Christian Lectures* (Cincinnati: Standard, 1888), pp. 38-63.

[6]W.E. Garrison and A. T. DeGroot, *The Disciples of Christ: A History* (St. Louis: Bethany Press, 1948), p. 439.

[7]James DeForest Murch, *Christians Only*, p. 263.

[8]*Ibid.*, p. 271.

[9]Garrison and DeGroot, *The Disciples of Christ*, p. 405.

[10]P.H. Welshimer, "Unity Is Desirable: Restoration More So," *Christian Standard*, Vol. 79 (1943), p. 629.

[11]Stephen J. Corey, *Fifty Years of Attack and Controversy* (St. Louis: Special Committee, 1953), p. 184.

[12]Edwin V. Hayden, *50 Years of Digression and Disturbance* (Joplin: Published by author, 1955), p. 6.

[13]Garrison and DeGroot, *The Disciples of Christ*, p. 408.

[14]David Filbeck, "The Coming Second Controversy Over Baptism," *Christian Standard*, Vol. 116 (1981), p. 519.

[15]A.T. DeGroot, *New Possibilities*, p. 33.

[16]M. Eugene Boring, "The Crucial Third Generation," *A Case Study of Mainstream Protestantism*, Edited by D.Newell Williams (St. Louis: Chalice Press, 1991), p. 40.

[17]Stephen J. Corey, *Fifty Years of Attack and Controversy*, p. 33.

[18]McAllister and Tucker, *Journey in Faith*, p. 374.

[19]*The Scroll* (July 1924), p. 285.

[20]Edwin R. Errett, "Campbell Institute," *Christian Standard*, Vol. 75 (1940), p. 271.

[21]Herbert L. Willett, *Our Plea for Union and the Present Crisis* (Chicago: Christian Century, 1901), pp. 26-31.

[22]Francis M. Arant, *"P.H." The Welshimer Story* (Cincinnati: Standard, 1958), p. 65.

[23]*Ibid.*, p. 57.

[24]*Ibid.*, p. 87.

[25]*Ibid.*, p. 88.

[26]*Ibid.*, p. 58.

[27]P.H. Welshimer, "A Reunion to Honor the Plea," *Christian Standard*, Vol. 75 (1940), p. 735.

[28]Frederick D. Kershner, "The North American Christian Convention Is Not Schismatic," *Christian Standard*, Vol. 75 (1940), p. 545.

[29]Raphael H. Miller, "The North American Convention," *Christian-Evangelist*, Vol. 86 (1948), p. 492.

[30]Lin D. Cartwright, "Does This Mean Division?," *Christian-Evangelist*, Vol. 88 (1950), p. 551.

[31]Henry E. Webb, *In Search of Christian Unity* (Cincinnati: Standard Publishing, 1990), pp. 249f.

[32]Stephen J. Corey, *Fifty Years of Attack and Controversy*, p. 257.

[33]Robert E. Elmore, "Bethany Booster," *Restoration Herald*, Vol. 34 (Sept. 1948), p. 10; "Brotherhood Week," *Ibid.* (Dec. 1948), p. 2.

[34]Robert E. Elmore, *Restoration Herald*, Vol. 34 (1948), p. 6; "Promoting Perverters," *Ibid.* (March 1948), p. 11; "Open Membership," *Ibid.* (April 1948), p. 8.

[35]Leon L. Meyers, "The Christian Restoration Association Reaffirms Its Established Policy," *Restoration Herald*, Vol. 16 (Feb. 1938), p. 1.

[36]Stephen J. Corey, *Fifty Years of Attack and Controversy*, p. 109.

[37]*Christian Standard*, Vol. 62 (Oct. 9, 1926), Supplement, p. 2.

[38]Stephen J. Corey, *Fifty Years of Attack and Controversy*, pp. 19f.

[39]A.T. DeGroot, *New Possibilities*, p. 29.

[40]J.A. Lord, "Compromise Christian Union," *Christian Standard*, Vol. 29 (1894), p. 386.

[41]James DeForest Murch, *Christians Only*, p. 251.

[42]Stephen J. Corey, *Fifty Years of Attack and Controversy*, p. 172.

[43]Editorial, *Christian Standard*, Vol. 84 (1948), p. 220.

[44]Editorial, *Christian Standard*, Vol. 83 (1947), p. 402.

[45]Editorial, *Christian Standard*, Vol. 82 (1946), p. 611.

[46]*Christian Standard*, Vol. 82 (1946), pp. 561-563.

[47]Leon L. Meyers, *Restoration Herald*, Vol. 16 (Jan. 1938), p. 4.

[48] Rupert C. Foster, "Current Tendencies of the Brotherhood," *Christian Standard*, Vol. 59 (Oct. 27, 1923), p. 77.

[49]Rupert C. Foster, "The Scriptures Require Christians to Maintain Their Liberty in Christ," *Christian Standard*, Vol. 82 (1946), p. 851.

[50]Rupert C. Foster, "An Analysis of Our Present Situation," *Christian Standard*, Vol. 57 (1922), p. 3637.

[51]Rupert C. Foster, "Interpreters of McGarvey," *Christian Standard*, Vol. 75 (1940), p. 1115.

[52]Thomas Munnell, "The Union Movement, What Will Come of It?," *Christian Quarterly*, Vol. 1 (1909), p. 115.

[53]James H. Garrison, *Memories and Experiences* (St. Louis: Christian Board of Publication, 1926), p. 120.

18

THE MOVEMENT WITH THREE FACES
CHURCHES OF CHRIST

Church of Christ, Founded in Jerusalem, A.D. 33.
This building erected in 1953.
— Cornerstone, Southside Church of Christ, Springfield, MO.

In recent years Churches of Christ have been in search of their identity, which has involved them in the throes of self-discovery. Among other phenomena this has produced a unique denominational directory titled *Churches of Christ in the United States* (1991), responsibly compiled by Mac Lynn of David Lipscomb University.

The uniqueness of this directory is that while it includes Churches of Christ of all persuasions, it dares to categorize them according to genre. There is a "Key to 'Character' Abbreviations" that identifies some churches as Ch (Charismatic), some as NC (Non-Class), some as NI (Non Institutional). Others are NBHS (Oppose ownership of building, baptize in the Holy Spirit), OC (One-Cup), OCc (One-Cup, with fermented fruit of the vine), PM (Premillennial), etc.

There are 37 churches labeled E (Ecumenical). Interestingly, those that are unlabeled are considered mainline. Lynn found that most of the non-mainline groups (91%) fall into three categories (see below).

All categories total 13,174 congregations with a membership of 1,284,056. This represents a 3.5% growth over the past decade. There are only eight congregations with a membership of 2,000 or more, three of these being non-mainline "Boston" or "International" churches, described below.

Unity In Diversity

In view of the foregoing it might appear odd to describe these churches as united, for they are known to be divided into many factions, a circumstance that they admit. Noting the divisiveness that Mac Lynn referred in his directory, Joe R. Barnett, formerly of the Broadway Church of Christ in Lubbock, Texas, pointed to "at least 27 factions (splits) in the Restoration Movement,"[1] most of these being within his own church.

C.W. Zenor, a fourth generation member of the Churches of Christ, in a doctoral thesis found "approximately two dozen other groups of the same name" beside the "mainstream Church of Christ." These are churches that wear only the name Church of Christ, he notes, which distinguishes them from Disciples of Christ and Christian Churches, who also use the name.[2]

A subtle unity nonetheless pervades these churches, for they all believe and practice things that set them apart from the rest of the Christian world, despite their differences on subordinate issues.

1. *The name Church of Christ.* While they teach that the church has numerous names in Scripture, they all wear only the name Church of Christ. It is a question among some of the more "open" churches as to whether they should wear this name exclusively. All who do not are suspect.

2. *Acappella singing.* This is an absolute among these churches. Any church that uses instrumental music is not considered a Church of Christ, whatever it may call itself.

3. *"Only true church" concept.* While there are exceptions, such as the premillennial group, these people believe that their church is the only true New Testament church. When the *U.S. Catholic* informed its readers of these people it correctly represented them as believing that "they alone represent the church of Christ as it existed in the first century."[3]

4. *An exclusivistic posture.* These motifs make separatists of these people. Only they are "undenominational," while all others are sects or denominations, with whom they can have no fellowship. Other churches do not expect any cooperation from a Church of Christ.

While there is considerable reaction today against these ideas within Churches of Christ, especially the last two, they continue to mark all these churches as "a peculiar people" and to give them commonality, despite their differences. Most members of Churches of Christ are fairly comfortable in relating to any other Church of Christ so long as they can move either laterally or to their right, which is the case with the vast majority.

An interesting instance of this is when the Preston Road Church of Christ in Dallas lost all four of its school of preaching faculty in an airplane tragedy. It recruited a teacher from the non-Sunday School Church of Christ to help in the emergency, with whom there is usually no working fellowship. This is the subtle unity that we speak of. They would not have considered calling on a Disciples or Christian Church teacher.

There are other basic doctrines and practices that the Churches of Christ share with other groups of the Movement, such as congregational autonomy, the rule of elders, baptism by immersion for remission of sins, and weekly Communion. While they practice closed membership, sometimes reimmersing those who come from other immersionist churches, they are open Communion, following Alexander Campbell's dictum of "We neither invite nor debar."

Clusters of Churches of Christ

As Mac Lynn has indicated, it is misleading to refer to "two dozen" divisions within Churches of Christ, for this includes tiny dissident groups that hardly qualify as separate churches. It is less confusing to think in terms of clusters of churches that have at least one hundred congregations and are promoted by their own journals and schools, and that sponsor their own missions. Besides the mainline group these are:

Conservative or Non-Cooperative Churches of Christ

This group of some 2,000 congregations, mostly small, is both the latest and largest division, if the Boston group is excepted (see below). It emerged during the 1950's over the issue of organizations preempting the function of the local congregation, particularly the Herald of Truth, a radio-TV program supported by thousands of churches and administered by a "sponsoring church."

The dissenters insist that there is no more Scripture for this arrangement than for instrumental music or a missionary society. Often called "Anti's" by the mainline, these people are particularly strong in the deep South. They have 222 churches in Alabama, 23 of them being in the small city of Athens. They have been particularly missionary in recent years and now have churches in 34 foreign countries, where they have about 200 churches, 23 of them in South Africa, 20 in Nigeria, and 12 in Australia.[4]

This group is served by Florida College in Tampa, which, like other Churches of Christ colleges, has a strong, reputable liberal arts program. Its leading journals are *Guardian of Truth* and *Christianity Magazine*.

As is often the case with a sub-group within a larger fellowship, many of these churches are struggling for survival. The fear was expressed some years back by Yater Tant, one of their veteran editors, that their churches were on "a steady progress toward extinction." This was evident, he noted, in that their once strong churches are "reduced to a handful of faithful brethren."[5] Since they continue to be wracked with internal dissension over such issues as divorce and remarriage their situation has not improved in recent years.

Non-Sunday School (Non-Class) Churches of Christ

There are more than 1,000 congregations that are oppposed to the organized Sunday school or the practice of dividing the assembly into classes, but they are divided amongst themselves into several factions, including the One-Cup (for Communion) group.

One finds the labels confusing. Generally, the non-Sunday School churches that use multiple cups for Communion are referred to as Non-Class (or non-Sunday School), while the other non-class churches are designated "One-Cup." There is little or no fellowship between them due to a flaw that has long afflicted the Movement: the distinctive characteristic is made a test of fellowship.

The Non-Class churches (as opposed to the One-Cup), with some 559 congregations, are the most progressive of all the separatist groups. In several west Texas towns, where they are especially strong, one will find impressive edifices, with a suite of offices for the staff, fellowship hall, library, etc., but no classrooms! It saves a lot of money! Their church in Farmers Branch, Texas (Dallas area) has one of the most elegant edifices in the area and some 900 members. They are perceived to be a more "open" church than the mainline church that is less than a block away!

They have two Bible institutes, both in Texas, that are open to both sexes. These days their student preachers (men only) are encouraged to pursue a secular education at nearby colleges while studying at the institute.

In their early days they produced a roster of great debaters who debated the mainline churches on the Sunday school and always won since they held the more conservative position. In those days mission work consisted of planting a "faithful church" not far from "a class church." This has changed radically in recent decades in that "the old issue" is no longer debated and no longer made a test of fellowship, albeit their non-class conviction remains the same. A much more brotherly spirit now prevails.

They are now vigorously involved in foreign missons, particularly in Africa. They have had a substantial work in Malawi for 40 years, and more recently have been in Kenya, with plans for Uganda and Nairobi. They also have missions in Mexico and India. They bring orphans from India for adoption, and they have an orphanage in Louisiana. They issue well-edited, colorful journals in *Gospel Tidings* and *Christian Appeal*, which often deal with social and ethical problems and rarely refer to the Sunday School question.

When they do state their case on the Sunday School, it is often as reasonable and persuasive as that made by Thomas Langford, a Ph.D. from TCU and a dean at Texas Tech University in Lubbock. He explains that his church does not have a Sunday School for the same reason it does not have instrumental music: "The Bible is utterly silent on the subject of

Sunday Schools and we would be out of place deciding for God in such matters." Like most all other leaders in the Movement, he appeals to "the Restoration Ideal." These churches are a good example of how sincere Christians see that ideal differently.

Realizing this, Langford goes on to say: "We could be mistaken, of course, and for this reason we will not judge our brethren who obviously do not reach the same conclusions as we .. they are still our brothers and we will seek to treat them as such, asking only for liberty to follow the truth as we understand it."[5]

This irenic spirit has long pervaded these churches. While N.L. Clark, who is described as "the father of the non-class churches," vigorously opposed the Sunday School, he was a man of peace who never made his position a test of fellowship.[6]

G.B. Shelburne, Jr., who was recently honored at ACU for more than a half century of service to the church, has carried on the Clark tradition by advocating tolerance for the "Sunday School brethren." This brought him into conflict with some of his own people. In the introduction to Shelburne's autobiography, Langford remembers "a campaign of criticism and villification" directed against him back in the 1950's because of his tolerance toward those who differed with him. Langford credits Shelburne with doing more than anyone else among these churches "toward greater peace and unity."[7]

Some of Shelburne's critics who insisted on more rigidity eventually broke away and formed another cluster of non-class churches. At one time there may have been as many as a hundred of these churches, led by Paul and Leland Knight, both now deceased. Their paper, the *Church Messenger*, is now defunct and the group continues to decline.[8]

One-Cup Churches of Christ

Since it is fractured five ways, this cluster of churches is the most difficult to identify. The main group may have as many as 30,000 members in upwards of 530 churches, most of which have 30-60 members.[9] Homer King, Stockton, Ca., now deceased, was the old editor bishop, and his *Old Paths Advocate*, which began in 1928, has long been what the old-timers call "the standard." It is now edited in Lebanon, Mo. by his son, Don King. There is also the *Christian Expositor*, a quarterly, edited by Smith Bibbins, in Buffalo, Mo.

Like Alexander Campbell who donated three chalices to the Bethany church, these people believe that more than one container might be used if the size of the congregation requires it. It is *individual* cups, which hinders the communal value of drinking together, that these people have opposed. This goes back to J.W. McGarvey, the most renowned one-cup advocate, who spoke disdainfully of those "tiny little individual cups."[10]

They are fractured into (1) the "wine group," those who insist on wine for the Supper rather than grape juice; (2) the "bread breakers," those who break the loaf (near the middle) at the table before it is served; (3) the anti-divorce group that believes there is no reason at all for divorce and remarriage, while others hold to the "fornication only" position; (4) the "order of worship" group that holds to Acts 2:42 as providing the only order for worship, a practice that goes back to the Glasite churches in Scotland.

Even though all these are One-Cup, they usually make these peculiarities a test of fellowship. Each of the four sub-groups are tiny fellowships, some of them having no more than eight or ten churches. Of all the One-Cup churches no more than one-third are growing and many are threatened with extinction. The "liberals" among them, such as J. James Albert and Ervin Waters (see below), continue to hold to the One-Cup persuasion, but no longer make it a test of fellowship.

Premillennial Churches of Christ

Even though this cluster has fallen below 100 congregations in recent years (now 76), it is included here because of its influencial role in the history of Churches of Christ. Unlike the other marginal groups, the "premills" did not choose to be separated, but were excluded by the mainline for its prophetic views. This was a gradual development, fueled by feuding editors, that was complete by the late 1930's.

The late R.H. Boll, the pious and scholarly patriarch of these churches, was the popular front-page editor of the mainline *Gospel Advocate* when the vendetta began. Premillennialism has been believed by leaders of the Movement since Barton W. Stone and Moses E. Lard without any issue being made of it. Moreover, Boll was known to have held the position long before any lines were drawn. For these reasons his surviving friends are convinced that it was resentment of Boll's growing popularity as a writer on the *Advocate* staff, which included essays on prophetic themes, that caused the altercation and eventual separation.

Premills were among the pioneer missionaries for Churches of Christ, and these churches today support missions in Africa, Japan, the Philippines, Hong Kong, and Greece. They have several elementary schools, a high school, and until recently a college. Louisville has always been their stronghold, where *Word and Work*, always a well-edited journal (presently by Alex Wilson), has been published for 60 years, R.H. Boll being its founding editor. They seek unity with all groups of the Movement and have more fellowship with other denominations than any other segment of the

Churches of Christ.[11]

Since the days of Foy E. Wallace, Jr. this group, perhaps the most spiritual of all, has been cruelly rejected by the mainline churches. The anti-premillennial posture imposed on Churches of Christ during the Wallace era created a theological oddity for a conservative church, an amillennial position on prophecy. In this respect Churches of Christ departed radically from its heritage, which is millennialist. Stone was premill and Campbell post-mill (the difference was never an issue), while the doctrine of "no millennium" did not exist.

Besides these clusters of Churches of Christ, which, as Mac Lynn observes in his directory, make up the vast majority of the non-mainline churches, there are two other separatist groups that should receive special attention, the Black churches and the so-called Boston (International) Movement.

Black Churches of Christ

In his directory Mac Lynn included black Churches of Christ, some 1,218 in number with 160,570 members, as part of the mainline, but there is *de facto* separation, as with our society in general. They have their own journal, annual lectureship, and college. Their churches, while in close proximity in both distance and doctrine to white churches, are so thoroughly separated that a leading black minister writes: "The cold truth is that black and white churches of Christ represent two distinct fellowships."[12]

They have 15 churches in Los Angeles, two of which have more than 700 members. There are nine in Detroit, three of which have over 300. Dallas has 17 black churches; four have 400 or more. But the vast majority are tiny, especially in the South. Alabama, for instance, has 109 black churches, but only 16 have as many as 100 members. Most have less than 50 and many report no more than 10 to 15 members. Five congregations, however, in five different states, have more than 1,000 members.

Their journal, *Christian Echo*, founded by pioneer G.P. Bowser in 1902, is the third oldest paper among Churches of Christ. It was edited for many years by R.N. Hogan, one of the great preachers in the black church. Hogan founded the Figueroa Church of Christ in Los Angeles in 1938, an historic and influencial church, and one of their largest. It helped in forming 22 other black churches in the greater Los Angeles area, and Hogan's long evangelistic ministry accounts for many of the black churches across the country.[13]

Apart from a few "closet liberals," the churches are, like most white churches, strongly conservative and exclusive. They were cool toward Martin Luther King, Jr., both for being liberal and a Baptist. In one public meeting in Miami black leaders were offended by the suggestion that King was even a Christian.[14]

When Floyd Rose left the Churches of Christ in Detroit and started his own Family Baptist Church, his own father, also a Churches of Christ minister, barred him from his pulpit, avowing that no Baptist would preach in his church, not even his son. But Rose insists that he preaches the same gospel. Hogan, referring to Rose's defection, insisted that no one can preach the truth in a Baptist church, which is reflective of the old-line Church of Christism that is alive and well in the black church.

Rose's story began when he was one of "Keeble's boys," being one of the hundreds of preachers trained by traveling with famed Marshall Keeble, the father of the black church, and studying at his institute in Nashville. Preaching to whites as well as blacks, Keeble segregated his audiences by placing a rope across the center of his tent. Young Rose would ask his mentor why this had to be, especially when the rope stayed up when sinners were called upon to repent. "Brother Keeble, do they have to come to Christ with a rope between them?," he would complain tearfully. "You don't understand," Keeble would always say.

He cautioned his boys never to talk back to a white man, and "Don't dress too nice" in their presence. While Keeble came to be seen as a "Tom" by some of his boys, his memory is held sacred by the black church, and he gained a noble place in Churches of Christ history as one of its most dedicated princes, white or black.[15]

In years past white churches have often been patronizing toward black churches, helping them erect modest buildings "beyond the tracks" and giving them their used hymnals and old pews while they built elegant buildings for themselves and furnished them lavishly. White Churches of Christ in the South were as cool toward civil rights and integration as other white denominations, and the church's white colleges were among the last to give up segregation.

The indignities have sometimes been gross. G.P. Bowser (died 1950), the father of education among the black churches, walked away from a new school built in Nashville by Churches of Christ, refusing to teach when his students were required to enter by the back door. Floyd Rose was refused admittance to Abilene Christian College in those days, being told that "you people" have a college of your own.

Unlike the other churches in the Movement, the Churches of Christ have a substantial brotherhood of black churches, with a long and impressive history, "tolerated but not wanted," to quote Rose, "separate but *not* equal."

Boston (International) Church of Christ

On Oct. 15, 1993 the 20/20 TV program had a segment on the Boston Church of Christ, just as the British Broadcasting Company had given major coverage earlier in the year. Through interviews with former members, who referred to being brainwashed and manipulated, the church was depicted as a cult. Some had been so affected as to commit suicide. While the church had grown rapidly in only a few years, spreading to countries all over the world, 20/20 presented it as seductive and dangerous, even rehearsing some of its mind-control tactics with former members.

But it did present the other side, allowing current members to tell how the church had saved them from everything from drugs to crime. A major league baseball player testified that in the Boston church he had found spritual direction for the first time in his life. In an interview Al Baird, one of the elders of the Boston church, denied that the church used cultish methods, pointing out that the criticisms were from disenchanted dropouts. The church asked its members to write 20/20 and give their own verdict.

Jon Stossel, 20/20's investigative reporter, told of receiving 4,000 letters in a matter of a few days, with impressive testimonials. He concluded his report with "I don't know what to believe." Hugh Downs, one of the anchors of 20/20, was careful to explain that the Boston Church of Christ was to be distinguished from the denomination also known as Church of Christ.

In this episode one finds all the confusion and contradictions of the Boston movement. While the Boston church and Churches of Christ generally disown any connection with each other, Mac Lynn includes them in his directory of Churches of Christ, listing 52 "B" (Boston) churches. He notes that many of the larger churches are "B" churches, with the flagship church in Boston having the largest in attendance of any Church of Christ (4,250).

The Boston churches are the only Churches of Christ whose attendance consistently runs considerably higher than its membership. This is a characteristic of fast-growing churches of all persuasions.

In the light of the four unique marks of Churches of Christ, listed above, the Boston church is a legitimate offspring of Churches of Christ. It always wears that name, though it has recently added "International" to the name. It is acappella, exclusive, and believes itself to be the only true church. The Churches of Christ should be slow in rejecting the Boston group, for it is consistently carrying out, with much more success, what the Churches of Christ have always believed but not practiced with Boston's zeal.

But the mainline church, in an effort to disassociate itself, has leveled two main criticisms of the Boston church, both of which appear to be peripheral. Flavil R. Yeakley refers to its "ecclesiastical hierarchy," which calls for several key congregations to serve as "pillar churches," which in turn control "capital city churches." Then comes "small city churches" which in turn supervise "countryside churches." The Boston church, with its elders and Kip McKean as "world evangelist," is atop the pyramid of oversight.[16]

While Yeakley says this kind of structure is contrary to the New Testament, Boston responds that congregational autonomy, the polity of Churches of Christ, is also contrary to the New Testament. Some observers have noted that the Boston plan is similar to any number of pyramidal structures used by big sales organizations. It is apparent that Boston had to go beyond the ineffective polity of "no organization but the local church" in its goal of world evangelism.

The other objection is to the "one-on-one discipleship" in which a more experienced member appears to have "authority" over a less experienced. Indeed, all members of the Boston church are required to have a "discipler," even the evangelists. Bad press describes this as coercive and manipulative, but Boston sees it as members watching out for each other in love, which is not exactly contrary to the spirit of the New Testament.

When Boston opened its church in Atlanta in 1987, 27 mainline Churches of Christ ran a full-page ad in a local paper titled "An Open Letter To The Boston Church of Christ," in which they said, "We stand opposed to the strategies and practices presently advocated by the Boston congregation." Among the listed offenses were disciple-discipler relationship, multiplying ministries, and a hierarchial system of church organization.[17]

The mainline churches could level more serious charges, such as being legalistic on baptism (Boston baptizes or rebaptizes all new members, even those coming from mainline Churches of Christ!), neglecting grace in its emphasis on works, subjugation of women, and its sectarian view of the church. But such criticism would get too close to where the Churches of Christ have been all these years.

Boston's bad press has reached far beyond criticism from the mainline church, for it has been presented in an unfavorable light in big city newspapers all across the country. *The Indianapolis News*, for instance, in a 1990 feature story quotes the Chicago-based Cult Awareness Network as saying the Boston church meets the criteria for a destructive cult. But the newspaper told of other traits that make the church unique: it meets in rented halls, attracts those under 40, conducts lively worship, and is racially mixed.

A missionary in the Independent Christian Church, after an intensive investigation, found more to praise than to criticize in the Boston church. He is impressed that a church only a few years old could send missionary teams to such difficult fields as Hong Kong, Bombay, Bangalore, Sao Paula, and Johannesburg, not to mention the chief cities of the Western world. He notes that they baptize several hundreds in each mission within a few years, and by using rented halls on Sunday and homes through the week, they are not bothered with acquiring property.

While he points to such weakness as trying to mold all members into one type, the "extrovert evangelist," he concludes by comparing Boston with his own church: "They have a concern for reaching the lost, which most of us lack. They actually believe that the whole world can be reached in this generation."[18]

Against all the criticism hurled against them, the Boston people have an ace card to play. Elder Al Baird played it when 20/20 asked him why they receive so much criticism. "We're growing!," he said. They are growing when others are not. It is not easy to badmouth a winner. If they are as bad as their critics say, why would so many joyfully join them, including many young professionals?

Starting with a church of 30 members in Lexington, Mass., in 1979, Kip McKean had 4,000 meeting in the Boston Garden a few years later. By 1989 he had upwards of 25,000 in 65 churches in 27 nations around the world. By 1992 the church had 40,920 members in 102 churches. In 1992 alone there were 23,000 baptisms. But like all fast-growing churches they lose a large percentage of their converts, and some leave disenchanted.

When one sees their zeal and commitment (and success!) in preaching the gospel to all nations, he could well pause and say after the order of another who was slow to judge, "Let him who has like commitment cast the first stone."

Call for Renewal from the Right

Before we look at what is happening in the mainline Churches of Christ, we will do well to notice a phenomenon in the ranks of the marginal groups, the church's right wing, even the far right wing. While one would expect calls for change to come from liberal ranks, the earliest and most vigorous calls for reform among Churches of Christ have come from these conservative groups. They have pled for a renunciation of partyism and a return to the Movement's mission as a unity people, beginning with a healing of divisive wounds within each of the separated groups.

An impressive feature of these reformers is that they have not left the

443

group they seek to change, nor have they asked their people to surrender their convictions or practices. They have only asked that they not be sectarian and to accept all other Christians as equals.

From the ranks of the One-Cup cluster, which might be viewed as the farthest to the right, comes voices with no uncertain sound in their call for change. For many years James W. Russell issued *Outreach* from Fresno, Ca., a paper that went into 1500 homes monthly, encouraging those who seek to overcome the factious spirit in their churches. He learned to love those he once rejected and urged his people to do likewise. Russell, now deceased, believed that one-third of his people are seeking a more open fellowship.[19]

Ervin Waters, longtime champion debater, editor, and eloquent orator for this group (who never lost a debate!) startled his people by repudiating his factious past. "I have been a hatchet man for factionalism long enough, and I am weary of serving as a sectarian battle-ax" he told them as he proceeded to engage in unity forums with others of the Movement. A changed man, he often told his people: "I seek now to tear down the walls that I once helped build." While many of all persuasions were moved by his eloquent plea for peace, especially in unity conferences where he often spoke, he has been largely rejected by his own party, but still he has refused to leave and remains One-Cup in conviction.[20]

J. James Albert is another voice among the One-Cup group who insists that only love can heal the wounds of party strife. In a crude one-page newsletter, which he has mailed to his people for many years, he has consistently said things like: "Brethren are fearful of a personal relationship with God through Jesus Christ and are equally fearful of an intimate relationship with their brethren in Christ that is based upon love."[21] While he stays within his party, he refuses to be a party man. Like Waters, he has made some headway in freeing his people from a divisive spirit, but most see him as a liberal and a heretic.

We have seen that the Non-Sunday School brethren have had peacemakers from the outset, men who could be true to their scruples and yet reach out in brotherly love to those who differed with them. They continue to have many of such spirit, so that today they are probably the most irenic of all the marginal groups. But unlike the other groups, they have a church in Lubbock, the Quaker Ave. Church of Christ, that is particulary avant-garde in healing broken relationships. It recently issued a peace document that reflects the spirit of the *Last Will and Testament* and the *Declaration and Address*.

It was in the form of a letter addressed to the elders of the Broadway Church of Christ in the same city, a "Sunday School church" with which there had been no fellowship. It referred to the "animosities of the past" and the "settled divisions among us," along with all the debates and hard feelings. Without trying to cast blame for all the division and without surrendering their own convictions, the Quaker elders sought peace and unity between their churches.

They conceded that while they had not caused the division that reaches back many years, they had perpetuated it, and for this "We repent and seek the forgiveness of God and all our brethren." They went on to say in the best tradition of their heritage: "We believe that honest differences need not divide us, and that we can enjoy sweet fellowship in all that we mutually hold dear while allowing for some diversity in interpretation and practice."[22]

One can imagine how surprised, if not shocked, the more liberal church was to receive such a letter from an "anti" church. But they responded with like grace. The two congregations had a joint meeting that filled to overflowing the large Broadway church. It proved to be a healing experience for all concerned.

The would-be reformers among the conservative, anti-institutional churches have had more difficulty working within the system. They report that they would have stayed and worked for renewal from within, but they soon found themselves on the outside looking in, summarily kicked out!

It does appear that these churches are inordinately averse to dissident voices, particulary on "the issues" that give them their *raison d'etre*.

Arnold Hardin, for instance, has been issuing a modest two-page mailout from his Dallas church, originally anti-institutional, for 27 years, pleading for a Campbellian view of unity and fellowship. In what he calls *The Persuader*, Hardin has scored his brethren as being sectarian, legalistic, and grace-less. He explains that he would have stayed with his party, working for peace and renewal, but he found it impossible. He tells of a visit to an "Anti" church in the Dallas area to hear a prominent guest preacher of that persuasion.

When the guest preacher saw Hardin in the audience, he told the host minister that if he called on Hardin to lead the prayer, he would close the meeting and go home. The host minister, an old friend to Hardin, told him afterwards, with tears in his eyes, that he wanted to extend him fellowship but could not. He knew he would be ostracized by the party for fellowshiping a heretic.[23]

That sad story not only points up the difficulty of working for change within a sectarian system, but it illustrates how the heirs of the Movement have often been their own worst enemy by forsaking a basic principle of their heritage, liberty of opinion.

445

Edward Fudge has faired no better among the anti-institutional brethren, even though he has enjoyed international acclaim for his controversial study, *The Fire That Consumes*. The book, which questions the doctrine of endless punishment, has been published and republished on both sides of the Atlantic, and it has opened doors for Fudge to speak in many and sundry churches. It is an unlikely ending for one brutally rejected by his own people for calling for a change in direction.

Even though a second-generation "Anti" and an associate editor of their leading journal, he was eventually fired and rejected when he showed interest in the "Ketcherside unity movement" and a broader view of fellowship. Now an elder in a mainline Church of Christ in Houston, Fudge has for two decades advocated an unsectarian faith in the church at large. When he was asked by one outside the Church of Christ how he managed to get along so well with other believers, he gave an impressive list of how to handle differences.

Fudge's acceptance of diversity reflects an understanding of the principles of the Stone-Campbell Movement: (1) By making Jesus Christ the center of our faith and the basis of our unity; (2) By maintaining balance in doctrine and avoiding being one-sided; (3) By assuring the contentious person that he does not have to agree with you, but you ask him in love to consider another point of view; (4) By remaining teachable yourself; (5) By putting loving ministry first and allowing doctrine to fit in naturally.[24]

These voices of concern from the right wing are significant in that they have served to influence change in mainline churches as well as their own segments. This is because the mainline hears better with its right ear than with its left.

Inside the Mainline Churches of Christ

Back in 1979 Flavil R. Yeakley, Jr., in his statistical study of the mainline Churches of Christ, found the decline of membership so serious as to report: "It is clear that if the 1965-1980 trend were to continue unchanged, the church of Christ would cease to exist in this nation in just a few years." He said at the time that this was unlikely, and he was of course right.

By 1990 the figures were more encouraging, for while the number of congregations had declined from 10,165 to 9,600 there was about a 3.5 increase in membership, from 918,206 to 950,201. This does not include the 3,400 marginal churches referred to above. Allowance has to be made for improved census-taking from one decade to the next, a new experience for these churches.[25]

Yeakley's and Mac Lynn's research is a reflection of the church's growing awareness of principles of church growth and missiology. Its universities are offering graduate degrees in these fields and its scholars are taking doctorates in these areas. The missions faculty at Abilene Christian University issues *Mission Strategy* for studies in depth, and there are numerous church growth seminars among the congregations.

Now more than a century old, the Churches of Christ have moved steadily on the continuum from sect to denomination. If it was once a sect with some denominational traits, it is now a denomination with some sectarian traits, which is the case in the history of most all churches. Or to use Samuel S. Hill's four categories of southern evangelical churches (truth-oriented, conversion-oriented, spiritually-oriented, service-oriented), the Churches of Christ was once largely confined to the first category, but is now becoming more balanced in all four categories.

The directory lists 12 colleges and universities, several of which are highly respected institutions. There are nine schools of preaching, which have an uneasy relationship with the colleges in that they are suspected of being more doctrinaire than academic.

The church has four full-fledged, accredited seminaries (or the equivalent), though for traditional reasons it avoids calling them that. They are the Harding Graduate School of Religion in Memphis, which is part of Harding University in Searcy, Arkansas; the College of Biblical Studies of Abilene Christian University in Abilene, Texas; the Department of Religion of Pepperdine University in Malibu, California; and Southern Christian University in Montgomery, Alabama, which is a misnomer since it is more of a seminary than a university, and it is independent of Faulkner University, also Churches of Christ, in the same city.

Harding, the oldest of the church's graduate schools of religion, offers the M.Div., the traditional 3-year seminary degree, as well as the lesser Doctor of Ministry (D.Min.), and two master's (one to two years) in religion. It had 213 students in 1994, 13 of them women, who will go mostly into counseling. The school conducts extension programs in other cities as well.

In 1994 ACU had 283 enrolled in graduate religious studies, pursuing approximately the same degrees offered at Harding, including the 3-year M.Div. What is surprisingly new at Abilene in recent years is that among the 774 undergraduate "ministry students" 21% are female. This does not mean that these women are studying for the "pulpit minstry," which is not yet possible among Churches of Christ. They are rather ministers' wives, student ministers' wives, or women preparing for the mission field.

In recent years Pepperdine has also offered the 3-year seminary degree (M.Div.) with some 15 students enrolled in 1994, several of them women who hope to be teachers if not preachers. Still more take the Master of

447

Science in Ministry that Pepperdine offers in extension centers in such places as Portland and Fresno.

Southern Christian has an enrollment of about 150, with some 15-20 of them women. Besides undergraduate work in religion, it offers an M.A. and D.Min. at the graduate level, as well as the traditional 3-year M.Div., all accredited by the Southern Association. The small faculty holds several doctorates, including two from Emory. Unlike the other schools, some of SCU's women are themselves pulpit ministers, coming from various denominations, as do a number of the male students. Surprisingly, this "seminary" in the deep South, the bastion of Church of Christ conservatism, with its substantial outreach to students of other churches, may well be the most "open" of the four institutions.

The courses offered and the degrees conferred in all these graduate schools are comparable to those of other seminaries. And for a church with a history of being anti-intellectual the faculties are surprisingly well qualified, with most professors having doctorates from leading seminaries and universities.

In one instance at least the faculty appears over-qualified. While the Institute of Christian Studies in Austin is not a graduate seminary but a college offering courses only in Bible and religion, it has an experienced faculty made up of Ph.D.'s from Vanderbilt, Emory, and Yale. Ensconced as it is, European-like, between a university and the church that sponsors it, it is one of the most impressive institutions of its kind in the nation.

The church has some of the largest conventions of any denomination, but again they do not call them that. The largest are the International Soul Winning Workshop in Tulsa with some 12,000 in attendance each year; Nashville Jubilee, which attracts a similar number to the city's Convention Center, and the somewhat smaller Abilene Christian University Lectureship, the oldest and still the one to attend to see and be seen. It is the historic "flagship" lectureship of Churches of Christ, annually displaying hundreds of exhibits under a big tent.

But rumor has it that the Pepperdine University Bible Lectures, while smaller in attendance is of the highest quality. That would figure, for Pepperdine always goes first class, as its elegant campus in Malibu, Ca. would indicate.

There are 19 Churches of Christ colleges (now often called universities), and most of them have an annual "lectureship" (euphemism for convention), as do some congregations. The lectures tend to reflect the theological perspective of the sponsor. The Freed-Hardeman University Lectureship in Tennessee, for example, has historically been concerned with liberal-conservative issues, often in the form of debates and open forums.

Journals are prolific, ranging from the "Old Reliable" *Gospel Advocate*, the oldest (1855) and somewhat to the right, to *Wineskins*, the newest (1992) and an advocate of "change without chaos." The *Firm Foundation*, the second oldest (1888), had its "middle-of-the-road" era under longtime editor Reuel Lemmons, but in recent years has represented the church's right wing, which is not to be confused with the non-mainline churches listed above. In his emeritus years Lemmons founded and edited *Image*, which, under the editorship of Denny Boultinghouse, continues to provide the church with what has been all too rare, responsible journalism free of sectarian bias.

The Christian Chronicle, published by Oklahoma Christian University of Science and Arts and edited by Howard W. Norton, is unique in that it is "An International Newspaper For Members of Churches of Christ." Along with news of the churches, a calender of events, and feature stories, it has extensive editorials on current problems and issues that are usually well-balanced. Its readers' column reflects a healthy diversity of viewpoint. In its October, 1993 issue it even dared an extensive study of homosexuality.

Upreach is an attractive journal that congregations can use to person-alize an evangelistic message in their community in mailouts of 1,000 or more. Unlike mass mailouts of decades past, it enphasizes grace and compassion in its presentation of the gospel. *The Christian Woman* is another journal that deserves high marks both for its attractive format and its inspirational articles and Bible studies. These journals present the Churches of Christ at their best.

Ad Hoc Outreach

It is nothing less than phenomenal that the Churches of Christ get so much done without any centralized planning or structure. Everything is *ad hoc*. Most programs emerge from the inspiration and commitment of a single congregation or even a single person. Worthwhile projects survive and pros-per by the voluntary cooperation of other individuals and congregations.

There are impressive outreach programs that cost millions and calcu-lated to reach millions. A single church in Cookville, Tn. under the aegis of "One Nation Under God" undertook to raise $10 million from thousands of sister congregations in order to place a gospel brochure in every home in America, almost 102 million. The mission was accomplished, even if the *Wittenburg Door* named it as a classic example of how churches waste money.

The Herald of Truth TV/radio program has for 42 years been one of the church's most effective ministries. It is today reaching into the former Soviet

Union with televised gospel programs. A dynamic radio ministry of more recent origin (1983), World Christian Broadcasting, emanating from Alaska, preaches the gospel to every major city of the former USSR. It also reaches China, Japan, and the Pacific Basin countries in the nation's own language.

The World Bible School, which teaches through correspondence courses, was the inspiration of the ubiquitous Jimmie Lovell (died 1984), probably the most active and dedicated layman in Churches of Christ history. In his day the school enrolled two million students in 107 nations. It pleased Jimmie that two-thirds of the students were black and were taught by 43,000 white members of the Churches of Christ, two-thirds of which were women. Following Lovell's death the work was carried on by Reuel Lemmons and now by Tex Williams. The school today has some 50,000 American teachers supplying lessons for about one million students in 140 of the 188 nations of the world. It results in some 50,000 baptisms each year, making it one of the church's most fruitful missionary efforts.[26]

The White's Ferry Road Church of Christ in Monroe, La. took the lead in raising $2.5 million in relief to Poland in just two years, 1981-82. The following year White's Ferry joined the Richland Hills church in Ft. Worth in raising $4 million for African relief. It is estimated that various congregations gave $50 million in cash and goods for relief around the world in a single decade.

The World Bible Translation Center in Fort Worth is one of the church's most impressive ministries. Now 20 years old, it has issued 20 different translations, ten of which are complete New Testaments and/or Old Testaments. It has recently translated the complete Bible into Russian, and over a million copies have already been printed and are making their way into that country. The Center's "Easy To Read" English version was first for the deaf, but it has made its way into many nations around the world for the sake of the less literate. The Center has published a total of three million Bibles.

Even before the fall of Communism the Bammel Road Church of Christ in Houston sponsored efforts that resulted in the smuggling of 400,000 Bibles into the Soviet Union. Now that Eastern Europe has opened up, various ministries are sending even more Bibles and other relief. The Prestoncrest Church of Christ in Dallas, for example, has raised $3.5 million for ministries in Eastern Europe.

While missionary activity declined for a time, there has been growth in recent years, with 660 missionaries serving in some 121 countries. Mac Lynn in his *Churches of Christ Around the World* finds 747,568 members in 13,908 congregations in these 121 nations. Some efforts have been especially fruitful.

The Minter Lane Church of Christ in Abilene, Tx., for instance, sponsors the work of Stephen and Reba Bilak who have labored in the Ukraine for 34 years in effective radio outreach. They have a new congregation in Ternopil that is helping the needy in that Ukrainian city.

All of this is hardly more than a sampling of what is going on in Churches of Christ, all *ad hoc*. It leaves one to wonder what the church could do if it were better organized for cooperative, long-range planning. While there is of course some overlapping of effort and some fiscal inefficiency, there is no assurance that it would be more effective if they were better organized.

A Past That Is Changing

We observed in chapter 16 that the Churches of Christ were born of exclusivism in the choices made by David Lipscomb and Daniel Sommer, but the church's ensuing history shows that a more open view has always been prevalent, championed by some of its noblest sons. It was a matter of which would dominate, inclusivism or exclusivism. Thus far the Churches of Christ generally have been exclusive, but there is evidence that this is changing. We will only briefly review this history.

T.B. Larimore

Next to David Lipscomb, T.B. Larimore was the most significant of the Church of Christ pioneers. His biographer, F.D. Srygley, credits him with starting more churches in the South than any other man and as being the most widely known preacher, albeit in 1889 he was calling him a "Disciple," which shows that Larimore, who lived until 1929, belongs to that period when the Churches of Christ were becoming a separate church.[27]

Larimore was under great pressure to take sides and be an exclusivist. Each party of the organ-society dispute wanted him on its side, but he would go on preaching to great crowds, refusing to take sides and insisting that "No man has a right to make a test of fellowship of anything which God has not made a condition of salvation,"[28] a saying that appears now and again in the thinking of the more liberal minds of the Movement. He was nonetheless viewed as a conservative, and once division came he was identified with Churches of Christ.

C. Leonard Allen sees in Larimore's attitude a way to deal with divisive issues in any age, that is, by not taking sides. He notes that when Larimore was asked what "wing" of the church he belonged to, he responded with "I propose never to stand identified with one special wing, branch, or party of the church."[29]

In a Ph.D. thesis on this divisive period of the Movement's history, Douglas A. Foster notes that Larimore did not take sides on the organ and society issues because he considered them opinions. While one has the right to his opinions, Larimore believed, he does not have the right to impose them on others.

In another study Foster notes that Larimore conducted his Mars Hill College in Alabama for 17 years, giving one half of the year to the school and the other half to evangelism. "Larimore and his Boys," as they came to be called, founded hundreds of churches in northern Alabama and middle Tennessee, which explains the concentration of Churches of Christ in that area to this day. Foster observes that Larimore sought to hold back the tide of division by his irenic spirit, but was unable to do so.[30]

Larimore was among the first of a long line of preachers and scholars among Churches of Christ who had a broader view of fellowship. Some of these of the generation following Larimore were George Klingman, Walter Sikes, R.H. Boll, T.H. Cooper, W.W. Freeman, H.L. Olmstead, S.P. Pittman, Hall Calhoun, W.F. Ledlow, and, in his later years, R.C. Bell.

George Klingman, who was among the first in the Churches of Christ to take a doctorate, which itself made him suspect, was known as "an apostle of love" who deplored division and freely crossed lines of fellowship. This, along with being accused of being premillennial, caused him to be fired by Abilene Christian College in 1923. W.W. Freeman, another ACC "modernist" with a doctorate, was fired shortly afterwards. Besides being ecumenical, Freeman was "written up" for saying the Bible is inerrant only in doctrine, not in science and other areas.[31]

This set a pattern for the way "liberals" were treated in Churches of Christ for long years to come. Some scholar would do well to do a thesis on these free spirits in early Churches of Christ history. It would serve to show, since there were so many "liberals" through the years, that the church also has a non-sectarian side to its heritage. It would provide the church today a greater selectivity to draw from out of its past. It is significant that while these leaders suffered abuse for their more open views they always loved the church and did not leave.

If the spirit of Larimore and these men had prevailed, the history of Churches of Christ would have been different. To understand why an exclusive, sectarian spirit at last dominated, one has to look at the kind of leadership the church had during the second quarter of the 20th century.

Era of N.B. Hardeman, G.C. Brewer, and Foy E. Wallace, Jr.

These three men were largely responsible for charting the course taken by Churches of Christ into the second half of the 20th century. Their era was a time not only of extensive growth for the church but of the crystal-lization of exclusivism.

N.B. Hardeman (1874-1965) made an important contribution to the Churches of Christ as an educator as well as preacher, promoting the Campbellian ideal of teaching the Bible in a framework of liberal educa-tion. He educated thousands of preachers in two colleges in Henderson, Tenn. for half a century. He was also a debater of reputation, including confrontations with the Christian Church over the use of instrumental music. He not only built a tradition of strong biblical teaching but of Church of Christ exclusivism as well.

Hardeman's young preachers went forth from Freed-Hardeman College prepared to defend, in a style not unlike Hardeman himself, the proposi-tion that only the Church of Christ was right "in name, origin, organiza-tion, doctrine and practice." The elegant patriarch, always charming and meticulously dressed, would emphasize his absolutes with, "Boys, that's not nearly it, that's it!" The boys went forth with the same absolutes. I know, for I was one of them. I always loved and admired brother Harde-man; he was my friend as well as my mentor; I was a guest in his home and we corresponded for many years; and I treasure his memory. While in many ways he was a great blessing, I regretfully add that he helped to make a sectarian of me in my youth.

Tragically, Hardeman's own students eventually rebelled against what they saw as a tyrannical attitude, staged a college-wide strike that drew national attention, and was so effective as to force Hardeman's resignation as president in his latter years. But his eminent place in Churches of Christ history is nonetheless secure.

When C.W. Zenor wrote his doctoral thesis on biblical interpretation in the Churches of Christ he selected G.C. Brewer (1884-1956) for special study because he was "one of the most influential leaders in the Church of Christ during the first half of the twentieth century."

Zenor noted that in his day Brewer was the most frequent speaker for the prestigious Abilene Christian College lectureship. He often had public debates with preachers of other churches, including Christian Church ministers on instrumental music. He insisted that the Church of Christ is not a denomination but "the one true church." Brewer summarized his long ministry as "defending the truth and exposing error," which was inter-preted to mean that the Church of Christ has the truth and "the denomina-tions" do not.[32]

While Brewer was a gracious and tolerant man, and relatively free of a sectarian view of the church, insisting on "undenominational Christianity," he never quite liberated himself from Church of Christ exclusivism. But his was more of a benign exclusivism that simply ignores the church at large, a mindset that continues to permeate the Churches of Christ.

Both Hardeman and Brewer were pulpit orators of great persuasion. The former conducted the largest revival meetings in the church's history, while the latter served as minister of the largest churches of his time. Their influence upon Churches of Christ was monumental. While they are to be credited for making great sacrifices in the growth of the church, they must also bear some of the blame for its exclusive and sectarian posture.[33]

While Foy E. Wallace, Jr. (1897-1979) was younger than Brewer and Hardeman, he joins them in forming a triumvirate of leadership that substantially influenced the Churches of Christ in the 1930s and 1940s. Equally charismatic and persuasive, he also had the advantage of being an editor, which included the editorship of the influential *Gospel Advocate*, beginning in 1930, as well as his own papers later on.

Robert Hooper, historian at David Lipscomb University, concludes that Wallace must be seen in the light of the depression of the 1930s. Times were hard, and those that were "down and out" needed a winner. This set the stage for demogogues such as Huey Long and Father Coughlin. Hooper sees in Wallace "every characteristic of a demogogue." While other demogogues used social and political issues to their advantage, Wallace used religious issues, particularly premillennialism, which he dubbed "Bollism," named for R.H. Boll, who became the father of the premillennial churches.

He found a "Bollite" in every college and behind every editor's desk, and even in the person of G.C. Brewer with whom he carried on a prolonged feud, accusing him of being "soft on the issues." Always good at humor in the pulpit, he would charge Brewer of being the only person who could strut sitting down! Brewer in turn (in an Abilene lecture without calling his name) criticized Wallace as having zeal without love, assuring his auditors that "a radical never converted anybody."

Wallace not only called for "militant preaching," which included castigating "the denominations" by name, but he denounced his own brethren who would "call on sectarians to lead prayer." He even made an issue of using "Great Songs of the Church" in that it had premillennial hymns, and in his latter years "the modern versions" was the issue, insisting on the use of the King James Version only.

Hooper sees Wallace's influence on the Churches of Christ as "very detrimental," and his journal, the *Bible Banner*, as "rank." He says Wallace "set a direction for the Church of Christ that we have not to this day rid ourselves of."[34]

It remains to be said that Brewer and Hardeman were moderates in comparison to Wallace. But few men sacrificed more for the cause of Christ than Foy E. Wallace, Jr. When I interviewed Tillet S. Teddlie, the church's great singer and hymnist, near his 100th birthday, I asked him to name the greatest preacher he had sung for in revivals, for there had been many. "Foy Wallace," was his immediate response.

Teddlie told of working with Wallace in towns across Texas, planting churches that today owe their existence to him. It was tiring work in hard places. Teddlie told of Foy's love for the hymn "Millions in heaven are singing it now," which Teddlie had composed. As people came forward during the invitation, Wallace would cry out to his singer, "Sing it again, Tillet!" As Wallace himself would say (I have heard him say it), "Those were great days for the church!"

Wallace's virtues extend to the way he cared for his invalid wife for 28 years. Brethren who might otherwise be critical of him were touched when Wallace would drive up to the church for a preaching appointment, take his invalid wife into his arms and bear her to a place in the church. This became a common scene all across the country, for he always wanted her along.

In research on preaching "The Core Gospel" in the first four generations of the Movement, Bill Love came up with some startling conclusions on the preaching of Brewer, Hardeman, and Wallace, along with others. He found that Brewer preached the Cross more than anyone since the first generation of Stone and Campbell.

Love analyzed 100 of Hardeman's sermons and found references to the Cross in only three. He found that Hardeman had a "defective theology," for even in a sermon on "The Blood-Bought Institution" he did not even mention the Cross while giving a lengthy discussion on the church. Love concluded from a study of Hardeman's many sermons: "The church was his main message."

He concluded from a study of Wallace's sermons that "preaching the gospel meant preaching baptism." He preached "first principles" that had little reference to the Cross. Wallace saw in Acts 2 "the hub of the Bible," but even here it was Peter's reference to baptism more than to the atonement of Christ. He concludes with a fearful indictment on Wallace's preaching, which may go far in explaining what happened to Churches of Christ during this era: "The church was everything in his preaching, the Cross almost nothing."[35]

Love could have added that in the Hardeman-Brewer-Wallace era preaching on the church meant that "The Church of Christ" is the one and only true church, and all others are sects or denominations. He found that from the days of Stone and Campbell preaching the Cross progressively gave way to preaching the church, which was in fact a sectarian view of the church.

Hooper points to the "attitudinal change" that occured from the 1920's (Larimore's time) to the 1930's (Wallace's time). If the openness of the Larimore era had prevailed and had not been displaced by the sectarianism of the Hardeman-Brewer-Wallace era, the Churches of Christ would not likely be the isolated church it is today.

Today the Churches of Christ face a new era, a time of crisis some of their leaders call it, for it is being told that change is imperative. While it is described as "change without chaos," there is fear that if change can be without chaos it cannot be without pain. While many of the rank and file do not want to be what the church was in the 1930's and 1940's, they are reluctant to turn loose of their absolutes.

Such ones would find solace in an essay by Lynn Mitchell, a professor at the University of Houston and an elder in Churches of Christ, which was presented at David Lipscomb University. He persuasively argues that his people can abandon their claims to absolute truth and still not lose their reason for existence. They can believe that absolute truth exists without presuming to know absolute truth absolutely. He challenges them with the frightening prospect of acknowledging one's finitude.[36]

Hardly anyone among Churches of Christ deals with the need for change as well as veteran minister James S. Woodroof in his book, *The Church In Transition*. He says it is a matter of self-examination: "There must be a change of attitude toward ourselves, toward our brethren, and toward the world." His diagnosis is that the church is not in good health with all its factions, its declining membership, and its waning interest in missions. He is especially concerned that the church has lost the Movement's vision of a united church: "The scriptural call for unity is so clear and our need so urgent we can no longer afford the luxury of ignoring the divisions among us or rejecting out of hand any genuine attempt to bring about unity."

Woodroof levels some severe criticisms: the church is interested in debate, not dialogue; it is critical of others but not of itself; it has overemphasized baptism; it is not a church in transition but a church in isolation; it is inflexible in allowing for differences of opinion. He is frank to say that "somewhere along the way we took a wrong turn."

He does not leave his readers without a cure: "A Christ-exalting restoration will restore unity where there has been division, mercy where there has been judgment, freedom where there has been bondage." He is convinced that the answer is for the Churches of Christ to know Jesus, not just know about him, "see with his eyes, feel with his heart, serve with his hands."[37]

Cecil Hook, who wrote a self-deprecating essay on "The Lamentations of a Mediocre Preacher," has probably reached as many of the rank and file among the Churches of Christ in his "renewal books" as any writer of this generation. The titles reveal his mission: *Free In Christ, Free To Speak, Free As Sons, Free To Change, Free To Accept.* He learned something of the meaning of freedom when he lost his preaching job in a Church of Christ in New Braunfels, Tx. for being a liberal. He opted to settle for the next best job offered, the church's janitor!

In a humorous and inoffensive way Hook has challenged every sacred cow and every pious platitude with such vignettes as "We have been building a lot of pie-shaped church buildings and trying to fill them with pie-shaped religion." His publication ministry has been phenomenal. Without a publisher or promotional techniques, and mostly by word of mouth, he has upwards of 50,000 of his books in circulation.[38]

Even the scholars are speaking out and calling for change. Three professors from as many Churches of Christ institutions issued a controversial book on *The Worldly Church: A Call For Biblical Renewal* in which they charge that their church is impacted more by the world than it is impacting the world. The church is, in fact, selling out to the secular world, they charge, seeking to satisfy what the world supposes it needs rather than offering the world what it really needs. Their call for change challenges Churches of Christ to be "a community of the Cross" and "a fellowship of the Spirit." They might well be speaking of the American churches in general as well as Churches of Christ when they say: "The immediate problem is not so much the unbelief of the world outside the church as it is the insidious presence of the world *inside* the church."[39]

The significance of all this is more than what is said, but that it is said at all. Such soulful self-criticism could not have taken place in the Churches of Christ a few years back.

A View From the Right Wing

One learns as much or more about what is going on in a church from its right wing than from its "establishment" critics. After all, as a Harvard professor once assured me, it is the liberals who create the conservatives, not the other way around. And it is the conservatives in their impassioned concern for orthodoxy who know what the liberals have been up to.

The Churches of Christ, like other churches, has its vocal right wing. While still *de jure* part of the mainline, it has its own papers, lectureships, and "loyal" churches and ministers. Thus, there is *de facto* separation between the two. One able representative of this persuasion is Goebel

Music who recently authored a 660-page volume entitled *Behold the Pattern* in which he laments the departures from the faith taking place in the "disloyal" churches.

One can learn more about what is going on in Churches of Christ by reading this well-researched book from the right wing than from most any other source. Perhaps this is because it is a voice of concern, a sincere conviction that the changes taking place are going too far. It it evident that the changes that disturb Music reflect a church far different from the Churches of Christ of the recent past.

Of first concern to Music are the "strange and uncertain sounds" coming from Max Lucado, minister of the Oak Hills Church of Christ in San Antonio. In recent years Lucado has ventured outside traditional Churches of Christ circles so far as to become one of the most popular religious writers in America with several best sellers. This has brought invitations to speak in various "denominational" churches, including a Roman Catholic group where he spoke on "Getting to Know Jesus Personally." If that were not incredible enough for a faithful gospel preacher, Music notes, Lucado also joined the Catholics in an Easter service and called the priest "Father." He even referred to Chuck Swindoll as a Christian!

It also disturbed Music that Stephen Taylor, lesser known but still a professor at Abilene Christian, could so easily leave Churches of Christ to become the pastor of a United Reformed Church in England. But it is Larry James, minister of the East Richardson Church of Christ in Dallas, who has done the unthinkable in questioning his church's position on instrumental music, insisting that it is an opinion and should never have been a cause for division. James compounded his offense by joining the First Christian Church in a unity service. Music concludes that these incidents point to "perilous times" for Churches of Christ.

But Music goes on, chapter after chapter, with a litany of departures from "the pattern." Rich Atchley of the Richland Hills Church of Christ in Ft. Worth grieves Music for asking such questions as: "If we're the only Christians, and we've only been around since the early 1800's, where were all the Christians the first 1800 years of the church?" And he doesn't like for Atchley to refer to their church in such terms as: "we who make up what we call the church of Christ." Music understands "church of Christ" to be a divine name.

Randy Fenter, minister of the MacArthur Park Church of Christ in San Antonio, also got Music's attention. In a lecture at Oklahoma Christian College, Fenter questioned some fundamentals of his church's hermeneutics, particulary the use made of the silence of Scripture. In an essay in *Image* he also questioned approved example and necessary inference as valid hermeneutical rules even though long advocated by Churches of Christ. He rejected the notion that the New Testament is a "constitution" for the church, along with the "pattern theology" advocated by Music and church tradition.

Rubel Shelly, minister of the Woodmont Hills Church of Christ in Nashville, is given special attention by Music, perhaps because he was once of the right wing persuasion. He takes exception to Shelly saying "There are sincere, knowledgeable, devout Christians scattered among all the various denominations," and "We have shown a sectarian spirit through our attitudes and speeches and papers." He even told a joke about Church of Christ folk thinking they were the only ones in heaven.

Shelly's other deviations include his own astonishment that he could ever have believed that the only place God was at work on this earth was in "our narrow little .0012% of the world's people." Nor did it help him with the author of *Behold The Pattern* to say that "Pattern theology has been our undoing," or when he insisted that instrumental music should never have been made a test of fellowship. In one lecture Shelly made it clear that he had had enough of the Churches of Christ of the 1940s. "The church has got to change," he told the Richland Hills Church of Christ in Ft. Worth, "If it doesn't change my kids are not going to stay with it."[40]

If it is "the way things were" in yesteryears that Goebel Music desires for Churches of Christ, then he has blessings to count, for all these voices that disturb him are yet a minority. But they do reveal that there is a serious and substantial move toward change.

If these men are digressives to Music, they are the fruit of the "Progressive Period" to Richard Hughes, which began back in the early 1960's and was pioneered by Carl Ketcherside and Leroy Garrett. In his forthcoming history of Churches of Christ, Hughes traces present-day changes to "a virtual host of aspiring scholars from Churches of Christ" that were educated at prestigious institutions of higher learning. His honor roll includes Roy Bowen Ward, Harold Forshey, Thomas Olbricht, and Don McGaughey.

Hughes also names "LeMoine's boys" (those that the late Prof. LeMoine Lewis of ACU nudged toward Harvard), Abraham Malherbe, Pat Harrell, and Everett Ferguson, who conceived a new scholarly journal, *Restoration Quarterly*, that would "create a community of scholarly discourse" among Churches of Christ. These "Progressives" also started *Mission*, a journal that focused on social issues and questioned sectarian dogmas.

Hughes explains that Ketcherside and Garrett, always more conservative, were not actually a part of the "growing network of biblical and theological scholars who emerged within mainstream Churches of Christ." They led the way, however, in that their publications, *Mission Messenger* and *Restoration Review*, appealed to the same people, "a more educated clientele," especially in their appeal for unity and a broader fellowship for Churches of Christ.

What Is New?

When historian Edwin S. Gaustad, an outsider, wrote about the Churches of Christ back in 1969, he noted change taking place in a church long enslaved by its legalism:

> While, therefore, the old cliches are still heard, the petty legalisms still urged, and the assured superiority still cherished, none of them goes unchallenged and none seems in the best of health. For the most fascinating and exciting facet of life in the churches of Christ today is not what's happening to the old but what's happening that is new.[41]

The things that are new that impressed Gaustad in 1969 are even more evident today, and even more fascinating and exciting.

A New Ecclesiology Or A "Sect to Denomination" Transition

The voices of concern referred to above, along with other impressive evidence, indicate that the Churches of Christ are moving toward a new doctrine of the church, one far more catholic in its scope. While it cannot yet use the term, it is beginning to accept itself as a denomination among denominations. It is now well along in the transition from sect to denomination and is behaving accordingly. To put it another way, it is moving away from being churches to being "Church," even though it yet lacks the structure to do this effectively.

An interesting indication of this is a quiet rejection of an oddity that has long been an unwritten law: the lower case "c" is to be used in the church's name, as in "the churches of Christ." The rationale for this has been that this witnesses to the undenominational character of the church, the proof-text being Rom. 16:17, "the churches of Christ salute you."

James S. Woodroof in his book referred to above explains why he opted to use "Church of Christ" rather than "church of Christ," realizing it might prove offensive to the readers. While all his life he had used the lower case "c," he now realizes it is unrealistic to do so.[42]

Several books have been published by the ACU Press in recent years in which the upper case "C," as in "the Churches of Christ," is consistently used without apology or explanation. Equally impressive is that the church's directory, referred to above, consistently uses "the Churches of

Christ." But, surprisingly, in his new book on the history of the church Robert Hooper reverts to the use of "the church of Christ."[43]

Long years ago G.C. Brewer wrote of the folly of this distinction: "Some unthinking brethren seem to hold that to spell the church with a small 'c' avoids making a title or proper name of the phrase 'church of Christ.' This is laughable." He went on to say that it was "both unscriptural and ungrammtical."[44] His point was that when the church is given a distinctive name such as the Church of Christ it makes it a denomination, whether "c" or "C."

It may appear to be a small thing, but for the Churches of Christ to refer to itself as this sentence does, thus breaking with entrenched tradition, is a herculean step in a different direction. Brewer said it prophetically: "to consent to wear a denominational name is to consent to be a denomination."[45]

A Renewed Concern For History

Not until 1993, after it was more than 100 years old, did the Churches of Christ have a history of itself written by one of its own, referred to above. Still another by a historian at Pepperdine University is soon to be published.[46] Various other research projects are in the works, and scores of articles on the church's history have been published in recent years.

But the church has a growing interest in history in a much larger sense. The history of the church through the centuries is begining to matter. Recent publications by the ACU Press, particularly *Discovering Our Roots: The Ancestry of Churches of Christ*, a study that goes back through the centuries, are instances of this. The time was that the church was so ahistorical that not only did Calvin and Luther not matter but even Stone and Campbell did not matter. Now there is interest not only in the church's immediate roots in Stone-Campbell, but in its deeper roots in the church at large.

This has to mean that the Churches of Christ will become less restorationist in its thinking, for restorationism is ahistorical. It "leaps the centuries" in its obsession for the "purity" of the primitive church. The Churches of Christ will come to see that if it has restorationist roots, it is of a different sort, for Stone and Campbell were not ahistorical.

A New Position On Instrumental Music

For several decades the Churches of Christ have been moving from an anti-instrument position that made the use of an instrument a sin and a test of fellowship to a non-instrument position that makes it a preference or tradition. While it was once vigorously debated, it is today no longer an issue in most congregations. One may attend a typical mainline Church of Christ for years and never hear the subject raised. To debate the issue would now be almost unthinkable.

But still the church is for the most part adamantly "acappella only" in its singing. When one veteran preacher was advocating some needed changes, he said, "But I don't want any piano!" Few do, but that is not the issue with those who seek change. They are willing to remain acappella but for different reasons than the traditional ones. They insist that instrumental music should not be made a test of fellowship and never should have been.[47]

They also say that the old arguments against it should be forgotten if not repudiated. Even the more conservative concede that while it would be a sin for them to worship with an instrument, it is not necessarily a sin for others.

A few congregations, however, are going beyond "acappella only" in that they opt for an in-and-out portable instrument, such as a guitar, for special music. Or they have multiple song leaders accompanied by an instrumental sound track. A church in Dallas uses portable instruments in its special praise services. To my knowledge there is not a single Church of Christ that has a visible, permanent piano or organ. So ingrained is the non-instrument dogma that a congregation virtually surrenders its identity as a Church of Christ if it "moves in" an instrument.

If and when this happens, it will likely be in the wedding chapel. For the foreseeable future the Churches of Christ will remain acappella in its congregational singing, along with some use of instrumental sound tracks. One reason for this is that it usually sings so well without instruments while many other churches sing so poorly with instruments.

The most avant-garde congregation on this issue is the Southern Hills Church of Christ in Tulsa which has issued an in-depth study of the music question in which it repudiates the old position. Naming the study "The Acappella Myth," Terry Bell, minister and elder at Southern Hills and formerly minister with some of the largest congregations, rejects the traditional argument that *psallo*, the Greek word for sing, meant "acappella only" in its use in New Testament times.

After garnering the evidence, including the arguments made in M.C. Kurfees' *Instrumental Music in Worship*, the old textbook for the case against instruments, Bell concluded that the evidence supports the opposite of what Kurfees claimed. *Psallo* (and its attendant *psalmos* for "psalm") does not exclude but includes instrumentation. Even so, Southern Hills will continue to be "primarily acappella" and will use instrumental soundtracks for special music.[48]

Instrumental music in worship is such a traditionally-rooted and emotionally-laden issue in the Churches of Christ that the most modest change may be viewed as substantial, and these changes are more than modest. One thing is certain: in mainline Churches of Christ instrumental music is a dead issue. It may not be buried, but it is nonetheless dead.

Toward More Freedom For Women

In one of his studies of the Movement, Ronald E. Osborn described it as "a cardinal commitment to freedom" that was determined "to break the chains holding it captive to sectarianism and a preoccupation with non-essentials."[49] The description fits the changing face of the Churches of Christ today. The time was that an errant minister or congregation could be "written up" as "liberal" and it would serve as an effective boycott, but it does not work anymore.

Women were once expected to be quiet and were, but today they are beginning to ask questions about their rights as priests of God. And thousands of them are venturing beyond the Churches of Christ for contacts previously unavailable to them, such as the nationwide Bible Study Fellowship, some serving as leaders. The stigma of "fellowshipping the denominations" no longer works and is seldom used. Now better educated, members generally are thinking more boldly, reading more extensively, and circulating more widely.

This newly-realized freedom includes the freedom to question. Jack R. Reese, a professor at Abilene Christian, quotes one of the church's ministers as saying, "We need to reconsider everything, including women's public role and the use of instrumental music."[50] This kind of questioning is new for the Churches of Christ.

Only one congregation to my knowledge, the Brookline Church of Christ in Massachusetts, is on record as making no sexual distinction whatever in ministry. Women may perform any ministry and hold any office. What has impressed Robert Randolph, a minister to the church, is that when visitors from the South hear a woman in the pulpit they appear to be as pleased as surprised! This is of course very rare, for women are not yet in the pulpits of the Churches of Christ except to read Scripture in a few congregations.

The change is that the ministry of women is now on the table for discussion. It is frequently on the study agenda at college lectureships, and there are several recent books that take a more open view of the subject.

Fellowship With Other Churches

Freedom to enjoy fellowship with other churches still eludes nearly all

Churches of Christ. The dogma of exclusivism is so entrenched that progress is very slow. Most members of the Churches of Christ have never heard any minister of another church speak in their pulpit, not even once in a lifetime. But there is some progress. Philip Yancey, editor of *Christianity Today*, recently spoke at Pepperdine, and Fred Craddock, noted Disciples minister, is scheduled for ACU. A few avant-garde churches invite ministers who are "not of us" and a few daring ministers join the ministerial alliance. But generally Churches of Christ remain isolated from the rest of the Christian community.

Nonetheless, a group of Baptist and Churches of Christ professors and ministers, seven from each church, have been meeting quietly on an annual basis in Nashville since 1992. Two professional women, one from each church, take part in the discussions. The subjects discussed thus far have been hermeneutics and baptism, with the Holy Spirit the next topic. They are looking for ways to share their rich experience in brotherhood with others in their churches. That both sides have to be careful about revealing what they have been up to shows that a sectarian spirit is not the problem of just one church. A student at Southern Baptist Seminary in Louisville recently told me that he had to keep it quiet if he even visited a Church of Christ.

Other Changes

There is hardly an end to the list of changes. Many congregations have a renewed concern for worship, and, oddly enough for the Churches of Christ, this has much to do with music in worship. Music is "the coin of the realm," says Lynn Anderson of the Preston Road Church of Christ in Dallas, and if the Churches of Christ are going to be "a church that connects" it is going to have to have music that connects with the world of the 1990's. As we have noted, the most visible sign of "connecting" is multiple songleaders (men and women), called "praise teams," singing "heart" songs. In the Boston (International) churches they resemble cheerleaders!

The most fearsome issue is "the new hermeneutics," even if no one seems to know just what that is. It at least questions the way the Churches of Christ have treated the Bible, not only proof-texting but what some call "pattern theology." A Ph.D. thesis by one of the church's young scholars, Michael Casey, questions the "rationalistic Restoration hermeneutic," especially the rule of "command, example, and necessary inference," which has long influenced Churches of Christ. He insists that hermeneutics is the most serious challenge facing Churches of Christ today. "A failure to address this question," he concludes, "means that the tradition is dead, having rejected its purpose and goals."[51]

All this means that a basic attitudinal change is taking place. Where it will lead is a question weighed by Robert H. Rowland in a study on the ministry of women. He looks into the future and sees women ministering in Churches of Christ alongside men, and even baptizing. While he primarily has the role of women in mind, his conclusion applies to the future of Churches of Christ in general.

After concluding that change can come only through "a never-ending quest for truth," Rowland goes on to express a confidence held by many in the Churches of Christ: "Truth will win out. The bars of our prison cells will be stripped away."[52]

An outsider who took a critical look at the Churches of Christ gives his view of the church's future. "These, then, are the evidences of a new drum beat heard within the marching ranks of the churches of Christ," wrote Edwin S. Gaustad, referring to the signs of change he found, and then concluded:

> This brotherhood-sect-denomination-church-movement-wing is an energetic youngster among America's ecclesiastical bodies. It has idealism and good health – along with some of the awkwardness of adolescence. Puberty can be a painful, lonely time, but on its other side the creative possibilities of maturity beckon.[53]

ENDNOTES

[1]Joe R. Barnett, "Off the Cuff," *Broadway Bulletin*, Vol. 35, No. 11 (March 19, 1978), p. 1.

[2]C.W. Zenor, *A History of Biblical Interpretation in the Church of Christ: 1901-1976*, an unpublished Ph. D. thesis, Iliff School of Theology, 1976, pp. 2-3.

[3]William J. Whalen, *U.S. Catholic* (Feb., 1976), p. 36.

[4]*Directory of Churches of Christ* 1994 (Bowling Green, KY: Guardian of Truth Foundation).

[5]"Mirror of a Movement," *Firm Foundation*, Vol. 94 (1977), p. 610.

[6]Thomas Langford, "No Sunday Schools?," *Gospel Tidings*, Vol. 63 (1978), p. 124.

[7]G.W. Shelburne, Jr., *A Providential Journey*, (Englewood, CA: Gospel Tidings, 1991), p. vii.

[8]For further study of non-SS churches see Larry Hart, "Brief History of a Minor Restorationist Group," *Restoration Quarterly*, Vol. 22, (1979), pp. 212-232; Larry Branum, "Those Anti-Non-Sunday School Churches," *Mission*, Vol. 10 (July 1976), pp. 8-11. Hart notes that while N.L. Clark was "the father of the non-class movement in Texas" he never made it a test of fellowship.

[9]*Where the Saints Assemble: A Directory of Churches of Christ*, Compiled by Ronny F. Wade, Springfield, MO, 1993. Interview with Ronny F. Wade.

[10]See Victor Knowles, *The One Cup Faith*, n.p., 1976, p. 79.

[11]H.E. Schreiner, "Of Love and Labels and the Thousand-Year Reign," *Mission*, Vol. 10 (April 1976).

[12]Andrew J. Hairston, "Deterrents to Being One Church," *Mission*, Vol. 4 (June 1971), p. 5.

[13]Personal interview with R.N. Hogan.

[14]Witnessed by the author.

[15]Interview with Floyd Rose; on Keeble see J.C. Choate, *Roll Jordan Roll* (Nashville: Gospel Advocate Co., 1968); Robert E. Hooper has an informative chapter on black Churches of Christ in his *A Distinct People* (West Monroe, LA: Howard Pub. Co., 1993).

[16]Flavil R. Yeakley, Jr., "The Hierarchy of Discipling Churches," *Gospel Advocate*, (Nov. 5, 1987), p. 643.

[17]*Firm Foundation* (Dec. 8, 1987), p. 725.

[18]David M. Bayless, "Look Out! The Bostonians Are Coming!," *Christian Standard* (July 2, 1989), p. 597.

[19]Interview with James W. Russell; see also his "The 'One Cup' Segment in American Church History," *Mission*, Vol. 9 (1976), pp. 180-183.

[20]Ervin Waters, "The Odyssey of Division," *Restoration Review*, Vol. 13 (1971), p. 39.

[21]*California Letter* (August, 1993).

[22]Letter available from Quaker Ave. Church of Christ, 1701 Quaker Ave., Lubbock, TX 79416; see also *Restoration Review*, Vol 34, No. 10 (1992), p. 393.

[23]Interview with Arnold Hardin.

[24]Interview with Edward Fudge; see also Edward Fudge, "Preserving Fraternal Relations," *Restoration Review*, Vol. 33, No. 5 (May, 1991), pp. 96f.

[25]Flavil R. Yeakley, Jr., Why Churches Grow, Third Edition (Broken Bow, OK: Christian Communications, Inc., 1979), p. v.; cf. *Churches of Christ in the United States*, Compiled by Mac Lynn (Nashville: Gospel Advocate Co., 1991).

[26]Bill Youngs, *The Man of Action: The Story of Jimmie Lovell*, Austin: (Sweet Pub. Co., 1969), pp. 117-127; Letter from Tex Williams, director, World Bible School, Austin, TX, 1994.

[27]F.D. Srygley, *Larimore and His Boys* (Nashville: Gospel Advocate Co., 1956), p. 7.

[28]*Ibid.*, p. 151.

[29]Leonard Allen, *Distant Voices* (Abilene, TX: ACU Press, 1993), p. 156.

[30]Douglas A. Foster, *The Struggle for Unity During the Period of Division of the Restoration Movement, 1875-1900*, Ph.D. Thesis, Vanderbilt U., 1987, p. 294; "Holding Back the Tide: T.B. Larimore and The Disciples of Christ Division," *Discipliana*, Vol 53, No. l, pp. 3f.

[31]W.W. Freeman, *A History of the Campbell Movement*, M.A. Thesis, Southern Methodist U., 1933, p. 710. Also interview with Mrs. Jean Bly, Denton, TX, daughter of W.W. Freeman, who has data on her father and George Klingman being fired at ACC. See also Michael W. Casey, *The Interpretation of Genesis One in the Churches of Christ, etc.* (M.A Thesis, ACU, 1989).

[32]C.W. Zenor, *History of Biblical Interpretation*, pp. 119-173.

[33]See G.C. Brewer, *Autobiography of G. C. Brewer* (Murfreesboro, TN: DeHoff Publications, 1957): J.M. Powell and M.N.H. Powers, *NBH A Biography of Nicholas Brodie Hardeman* (Nashville: Gospel Advocate Co., 1964).

[34]Bob Hooper, "The 1930's: Attitudes That Will Not Go Away," Tape recorded, Woodmont Hills Church of Christ, Nashville, TN, (Aug. 15, 1993).

[35]Bill Love, *The Core Gospel: On Restoring the Crux of the Matter* (Abilene, TX: ACU Press, 1992), chap. 3 & 4.

[36]Lynn E. Mitchell, *Does Abandoment of Exclusive Truth Claims Mean the Loss of Reason for Existence*, Typeset of presentation at David Lipscomb College, 1991.

[37]James S. Woodroof, *The Church In Transition* (Searcy, AR: The Bible House, 1990), pp.17, 21, 27, 33, 38.

[38]Cecil Hook's titles are available through him at 1350 Huisache, New Braunfels, TX 78130.

[39]C. Leonard Allen, Richard T. Hughes, Michael R. Weed, *The Worldly Church* (Abilene, TX: ACU Press, Second Edition, 1991), p. x.

[40]Goebel Music, *Behold the Pattern* (Colleyville, TX: Goebel Music Publications, 1991), chap. 6-8.

[41]Edwin S. Gaustad, "Churches of Christ in America," *The Religious Situation 1969* (Boston: Beacon Press, 1969), p. 1022.

[42]James S. Woodroof, *The Church In Transition*, p. 6.

[43]Robert E. Hooper, *A Distinct People* (West Monroe, LA: Howard Pub. Co., 1993).

[44]G.C. Brewer, *Autobiography of G.C. Brewer* (Murfreesboro, TN: DeHoff Publishers, 1957), p. 138.

[45]*Ibid.*, p. 135.

[46]Richard T. Hughes has written a history of Churches of Christ for the Greenwood Press series on American denominations, not yet published.

[47]A professor at Abilene Christian University recently said this in a well-received presentation before the faculty, and was tape recorded.

[48]Terry Bell, *The A Cappella Myth*, mimeographed notebook with cassette tapes, Southern Hills Church of Christ, 5150 E. 101st St., Tulsa, OK 74137, 1993.

[49]Ronald E. Osborn, *Experiment in Liberty* (St. Louis: Bethany Press, 1978), p. 116.

[50]Jack Reese, "Worship In Transition," *Image*, Vol. 9, No. 4, (July/August), 1993, p. 13.

[51]Michael William Casey, *The Development of Necessary Inference in the Hermeneutics of the Disciples of Christ*, Ph.D. Thesis, U. of Pittsburgh, 1986, p. 389.

[52]Robert H. Rowland, *I Permit Not A Woman To Remain Shackled* (Newport, OR: Lighthouse Pub. Co., 1991), p. 165.

[53]Edwin S. Gaustad, "Churches of Christ," p. 1029.

19

THE MOVEMENT WITH THREE FACES
CHRISTIAN CHURCHES

The "Independent" Church

This segment of the Movement, as with the Movement in general, has had a problem naming itself. It seems willing to wear any name associated with the Movement except Disciples of Christ, which goes back to the tragic division we have recounted. If there is an "official" name it is "the undenominational fellowship of Christian Churches/Churches of Christ," but its signboards and letterheads usually read simply "Christian Church" or "Church of Christ."

To distinguish itself from the Churches of Christ, who use the same name, it identifies them as "Churches of Christ (Non-instrumental)," but never itself as "Instrumental." And there is no way to know if the "First Christian Church" in any given locale is of this group or a Disciples church, which also uses "Christian Church." In recent years the latter has removed much of the confusion by designating its churches as "Christian Church (Disciples of Christ)," causing some to dub it "the parenthesis church."

While "the undenominational fellowship of Christian Churches/ Churches of Christ" itself often uses the term "Independent" to describe itself, it is not used with enthusiastic approval. While not exactly the church's nickname, it is its pragmatic name. "Independent Christian Church," therefore, identifies these people in a fairly acceptable way, both by themselves and others. It has never had a pejorative connotation, but it does have historic implications.

The church became "independent" in its separation from the Disciples of Christ and particularly in its disassociation from the United Christian Missionary Society. It was missions and missionaries that first became "independent" of the United Society (while they were all still Disciples of Christ). The "independent" missionaries were supported by "independent" churches who eventually became a separate church known as "Independent Christian Churches/Churches of Christ."

While therefore "independent" historically meant "independent of the United Society and its agencies," it now has a broader meaning in that it refers to the free exercise of the entire ministry of the church. David Filbeck, a veteran missionary, sees "Independent" or "Direct-Support" missions as the work of a "free" church: "In Direct-Support missions, we recognize the freedom to create forms and organizations in addition to the local congregations by which to carry out the Great Commmission."[1]

We therefore look at this church from its "Independent" perspective, which is an important way to see it as a whole.

Independent Missions

In a chapter in his book on the history of the Movement entitled "The Widening Gulf," Henry E. Webb give a long list of missionaries who became "independent" from the United Society in the decade from 1919 to 1929. Sometimes they were recalled by the United Society for "incompatibility," a reference to the theological confrontation going on between liberals and conservatives. Some missionaries went "Independent" because, as they saw it, the Society did not leave them free to preach the gospel. Comity and open membership were areas of dispute.

Upwards of a dozen missionary couples were recalled (or their terms not renewed) from Mexico, South Africa, the Philippines, China, Tibet, India, and Japan. In the 1930's and 1940's there was a substantial growth in "Independent" missions that had no original connection with the United Society.

In his history of "The Direct-Support Missionary Movement" David Filbeck shows the parallels between the beginning of Independent missions and the origin of the Independent Christian Church. Two crucial events set the stage for both. One was the "Sweeney Peace Resolution" which was voted on by the International Convention of 1925. It sought to resolve the open membership dispute by allowing no one to serve as a UCMS missionary who believed in open membership, and those already employed who so believed were to resign, including the Society's officials.

After a stormy session where both sides allowed tempers to flare, the resolution overwhelmingly passed, which meant that the rank and file of a still united church was conservative. But the UCMS leadership, which was more liberal, interpreted the resolution to apply not to those who only favored open membership but to those who were contentious about it. The conservatives saw this as a way for the liberals to ignore the resolution. It helped to set the stage for a new convention the next year, a new method for missions, and in time a new church. All three could properly be called "Independent."

The other event, also in 1925, which confirmed the conservatives in their conviction that the United Society was beyond reform, was the Society's recall of Leslie Wolfe, from the Philippines. The charge was incompatibility with fellow missionaries, along with personal problems, but Wolfe's conservative friends saw the recall in terms of his opposition to open membership, which they believed the Society wished to promote.

It turned out to be an ugly story. There were bitter exchanges in the journals, and the 1926 Convention, where some effort was made to resolve the issue, was "like a boiling caldron," as Filbeck describes it, and "A Convention of Bad Faith," as the *Christian Standard* put it. The Society proceeded to dismiss Wolfe and the dissenters resorted to a "Direct-Support" method to return him to the Philippines.[2]

All this led not only to a new convention and a new method of doing missions but eventually another division. They are "Independent," not only because they are free of what Filbeck calls "centralized ecclesiasticism," but also because congregations and individuals alike are at liberty to be creative in their response to the Great Commission.

The Independent Christian Church was thus born amidst a passion for missions, and missions has been its constant concern. Painful controversy resulted in a "Direct-Support" method. Its leaders acknowledge that this method has some serious weaknesses as well as impressive strengths.

While the church had fewer than 100 foreign missionaries before World War II, it now has some 2,000 in 71 nations. Special effort has been made in Brazil where there are 21 missions and 55 missionaries, and in Japan with its 26 missions and 64 missionaries.

Hundreds of churches maintain these people on a "Direct Support" basis, with no missionary society *per se*, though there are such agencies as the Christian Missionary Fellowship. The CMF has 35 missionary couples in Kenya, Brazil, Indonesia, and Mexico. Committed to "preaching the Gospel and planting indigenous churches among the receptive people of the world," it works with churches in recruiting, supervising, and funding missions.

Filbeck notes that the church can have such cooperative agencies without compromising the autonomy of the local congregation. This solves, he believes, what he calls "the Campbellian Dilemma," the problem Alexander Campbell had of preserving the integrity of the local congregation on one hand and responding to the imperative for extra-congregational cooperation on the other.[3]

Independent Convention

The same events that led to Independent missions led to an Independent convention. Conservative Disciples disillusioned with what they considered "the treacherous official maneuvering" of the UCMS formed the

Committe for Future Action, chaired by P.H. Welshimer. Meeting in Memphis in 1926, it called for a new convention to assemble in Indianapolis the next year. The purpose was not schismatic. It was to be a preaching convention and would assemble only occasionally with no intention of permanency. For the first 23 years it met only nine times and did not become permanent until 1950.

In time the North American Christian Convention (NACC) became the alter ego of the Christian Church, reflecting all that the new church stood for. From the outset, before it served as a catalyst for the new church, it provided conservative Disciples with what the International never did, strong biblical preaching and joyous fellowship. Too, it was both conservative and independent. It ruled early on that a "liberal" would never be on its program, a rule that has been honored all through the years.

From the outset there was opposition to the NACC becoming permanent. Even the conservative *Christian Standard* editorialized: "The *Christian Standard* will not allow itself to be made party to the development of the NACC into a permanent institution. This we asserted a year ago and we repeat it now." One of its readers commended this decision, fearing that a permanent convention would develop into another denomination like the Church of Christ, "refusing to have fellowship in any broad and inclusive way with other Christians."[4]

In the early years when many attended both conventions there was hope for compatibility. The Disciples leadership was cautiously optimistic: "It seems to us that this convention," wrote the editor of the *Christian Evangelist*, "which was at first feared as being divisive, is being managed in a way to help instead of to hinder cooperation in the Brotherhood."[5] Dean Kershner saw it as a new experiment for Disciples that proved that folk will still listen to good preaching. His only regret was that the two conventions could not unite.[6] It was appropriate that Kershner, always a Disciple and always irenic, was the first on the program of the first NACC.

In 1942, a war year, the Disciples suggested a joint convention, but the NACC declined, causing the editor of the *Christian Evangelist* to suspect that there were implications of disunity that "cannot be concealed from ourselves or from others."[7] But when the editor attended a later convention he was moved by "the refreshing and transforming power of gospel preaching at the North American Convention," though he felt that it did not deal with contemporary issues.[8]

In 1950 the Religious News Service broke the news that the NACC had resolved to be a permanent convention. It went on to say that this was viewed as "preliminary to the establishment of an independent Disciples denomination which would eventually sever all connections with the International Convention of the Disciples of Christ." The NACC denied that its permanent status implied a new church.

The *Christian Evangelist*, noting that the NACC was now to be a permanent institution, asked if this meant division.[9] The *Standard* had already answered that question years earlier: "The NACC is intended to be a unifying factor among all those who believe in the unique character of Jesus Christ, the Son of God, and the unique character of the Scriptures as divinely inspired and authoritative. It cares nothing about unity with anyone else." It added, "If this be division, make the most of it!"[10]

Churches usually create conventions, but in this case it was a convention that created the church. The congregations came to be described, especially by the Disciples, as those "affiliated with the NACC."

Mark Collis, a member of the Committee for Future Action, observed that the convention would discuss "matters of vital interest to those who love the Lord," and for this reason no modernist would be on the program. It was not to be a "fundamentalist convention," he explained, though such issues would be discussed. Above all it would be a real, old-time *preaching* convention.[11]

The first gathering in Caudle Auditorium in Indianapolis set the tone for the future: there were nine sermons a day on biblical topics! The founding committee called for sermons on the deity of Christ, the integrity of the Scriptures, the New Testament church, and gospel evangelism. The first NACC also featured a sermon on the Restoration Movement.

From the outset the convention met with phenomenal success, its most serious problem being a place to meet that would accommodate the thousands that gathered. It was successful because the people loved it, or as W.R. Walker put it, "the yearning for faith-strengthening preaching explains the demand for the convention."[12]

The first NACC was described by the *Standard* as "a convention where no one has an ax to grind."[13] And it is more recently described as providing "a platform for the preaching of the pure gospel of Jesus Christ; giving special emphasis to the restoration of the church to the plan revealed in the New Testament."[14]

The NACC today, with an attendance of 18,000-20,000, is one of the largest conventions of all American denominations. With an annual budget of some $850,000 it is big business. It is a "family convention" with something for everyone, whether in Babyland, Kiddieland, forums for educators, teenage sessions, college career, or scores of workshops of great diversity, besides the preaching sessions. While the purpose and spirit may be the same, the NACC today hardly fits the description of its first president, P.H. Welshimer, who likened it to "a yearly county meeting in the grove."[15]

In more recent years the NACC has been criticized as "clergy controlled." It is true that the "Committee of 120" that charts the programs is nearly all preachers, and the convention president is nearly always a preacher. One observer complained that it is too political, describing a recent convention as "a gathering of right wing Republicans." Others say it has the "big church" mentality of trying to please everyone, which tends to make it pragmatic, shallow, and irrelevant. When others see the displays of more than 500 agencies, all without any centralized organization, they wonder why there cannot be more efficiency.

The Convention's most serious problem may be that in more recent years its appeal has been more to the church professionals and their families than to the rank and file members. The most encouraging sign may be that in recent years a few women have been elected to "The 120," at first as non-voters but now with full voting rights. But it is likely to be awhile before a woman serves as the Convention president!

Many see the NACC as a place to see and be seen, a season of great fellowship for all the family, and a place to hear great music and preaching. It may be fair to conclude that if the NACC is known more for its great music and fine preaching and fellowship, it is known less for its prophetic character and its sense of the urgent, which may be the case with church conventions generally.

The NACC is not the the church's only convention. The National Missionary Convention (1951) gives an emphasis to missions that is absent in the NACC. There are also several state conventions that attract thousands annually, as well as youth conventions.

Independent Bible Colleges

The Christian Church could also be described as "the church of Bible colleges," perhaps more than any other denomination in America. The Bible colleges serve a twofold purpose in that they are both educational and evangelistic agencies of the church. This report from Dallas Christian College is not atypical: "Over the years DCC has been greatly involved in helping start new congregations, reopening closed ones, and supplying leadership to the churches in our service area."[16]

There are 33 of these schools in the U.S. and three in Canada. Since they are mostly small and financially deprived, many struggle to survive. Six have closed since 1980, some of which had survived for 40 years. Only two of the schools, Johnson Bible College and Northwest Christian College, date from the last century. Only two others, Minnesota Bible College and Kentucky Christian College were also originally Disciples schools in that they predate the division between the Independents and Disciples.

It is generally conceded that Cincinnati Bible College, which began in 1924, was in protest to the liberalism of the Disciples colleges, especially the College of the Bible. One should note that this date parallels the other "Independent" developments noted above. Counting Cincinnati, there were 15 Bible colleges started between 1924 and 1949, the same years that foreign missions and the NACC were becoming "independent." We may conclude that most of these schools were also "independent" protests.

This is the explanation given by Howard Hays in his response to Colby D. Hall of TCU who complained about "a veritable rash of new schools." These schools began, Hays says, because the Disciples had sabotaged the schools and pulpits with German rationalism. "Once strong schools repudiated the 'faith of our fathers' a group withdrew and started what is now the largest school among us," he explains, referring to Cincinnati. And if one wonders why the schools continue to proliferate, he answers: "Rebellion and apostasy in once-loyal halls still compel this 'rash' to continue."[17]

If this explanation applies to some of the earlier colleges, it hardly accounts for more than half of them that have begun since 1950. Rather than being protest institutions, they are part of the *modus operandi* of the Christian Church. Vernon Newland, for instance, who pioneered in starting several of these colleges, believed the Bible college to be a means of establishing and strengthening churches. Iowa Christian College, one of Newland's schools, which is not far from other Bible colleges, was justified on the ground that it was needed for the evangelization of that state. In his analysis of these colleges C.J. Dull referred to them as "regional centers for evangelism."[18]

By using church property for a campus and nearby preachers as faculty, the schools were easier to start than they were to maintain. And Newland did not bother with accreditation, not even those agencies that accredit Bible colleges, for if they were "God-accredited" that was good enough for him. For this and other reasons many of these schools have had a poor academic image. There is concern that the majority of ministers in the Christian Church who have "only a Bible college education" is not adequately prepared for ministry.

This history explains why the Independent Christian Church did not follow the Campbellian tradition of building liberal arts colleges as did both the Disciples and the Churches of Christ. While the Churches of Christ have in recent years started several schools of preaching, which also have a problem being academically acceptable, it is known more for its outstanding liberal arts colleges, particularly Abilene and Pepperdine, which rank among the better colleges in the nation.

It remains to be said that at least four of the Bible colleges are accredited and others are moving toward accreditation. It is interesting that several of them have in recent years renamed themselves "Christian College," and they are becoming more liberal arts in their offerings. Milligan College in Tennessee is the only liberal arts school among the Independents, but, having begun in 1881, it was originally associated, albeit loosely, with the Disciples.

Johnson Bible College, one of the four that have gained accreditation, is the most renowned, mainly because of its long, sacrificial history of educating outstanding ministers. Founded in 1893 by Ashley S. Johnson as the School of the Evangelists, it has always been open to any young man who wanted to preach the gospel, however poor he might be.

Under R.M. Bell and David Eubanks the college has attained academic excellence and broad acceptance in the church. Even though it is now "Independent" it somehow stood apart from the fratrical strife that divided the Disciples. Many Disciples ministers, some of whom are still living, were "Johnson men" who prized their heritage. Some would applaud Johnson for not changing its name to "Christian College," and for being content to be a "Bible college" *par excellence.*

Northwest Christian College in Eugene, Oregon (founded 1895) has a tradition similar to Johnson's in that it is as much "Disciples" as it is "Independent." James D. Murch, an Independent, in his *Christians Only* (1962), listed Northwest as an Independent college, while Henry C. Webb, also an Independent, in his *In Search of Christian Unity* (1990) listed it as a Disciples college! It is historically either or both (or neither!) in that it reflects a distinctive characteristic of the Oregon churches, who have never drawn the line of fellowship as sharply as have churches in other states, especially in the Midwest. Like Johnson, Northwest has long educated ministers for "both sides" and done it well.

Some of the smaller Bible colleges may not have the resources for accreditation, but they nonetheless have dedicated, well-trained faculty who make incredible sacrifice to educate young people. I have personally witnessed this as an adjunct teacher at Dallas Christian College where a caring faculty and a responsive student body of less than a hundred create a family-like atmosphere and an impressive esprit de corps. It reminds me of the (then) tiny Church of Christ college (now Freed-Hardeman University) that I attended in the late 1930s. We had not even heard of "accreditation" and it would not have mattered. We had a camaraderie that blessed us for life, and this must be considered when evaluating schools.

The Independents have three graduate seminaries, and, unlike the Churches of Christ, are willing to call them that, namely Cincinnati Bible Seminary and Lincoln Christian Seminary. The newest one (1961), however, and the most progressive, is named Emmanuel School of Religion. Nestled in the hills of east Tennessee and across the road from Milligan College, it has an impressive "state of the art" facility, a roster of Ph.D.'s from top universities, and is accredited by both the Association of Theological Schools and the Southern Association of Colleges and Schools.

Other Independent Agencies

Some of the church's most effective outreach is in the 78 campus ministries that serve students in state universities. These are usually supported by congregations in the general area of the university served. While a campus ministry usually works closely with a sponsoring congregation in the same city, it will have its own staff, led by the campus minister. It will usually have it own meetings through the week and its own Sunday service, sometimes on campus.

The *Directory of the Ministry* lists over 1,000 such agencies! These range all the way from 39 children's homes to 85 camp sites that minister to thousands of youth each summer. There are 28 homes for the retired, 86 day schools, and 15 nursing homes. For home missions there are 123 evangelistic associations in 44 states and two Canadian provinces.

The Christians' Hour is in its 39th year, and is now on about 75 radio stations with a potential audience of 50 million. It presents "undenominational Christianity, its doctrines, its ordinances, and its fruits." There are 111 other gospel programs on radio, and there are upwards of a dozen TV programs and several agencies that encourage the use of this media. There are 34 publications that are mailed regularly on a second-class permit and two major publication houses.

The Standard Publishing Company in Cincinnati has an outreach far beyond the Christian Church in that it supplies materials for Sunday and vacation Bible schools for many denominations, one of the largest in the business. Its most important contribution to the Christian Church is its publication of the *Christian Standard*. It was founded by Isaac Errett in 1866 and "Devoted to the restoration of New Testament Christianity, its doctrines, its ordinances, and its fruits." Now in its 128th year and ably edited by Sam Stone, it is easily one of the most significant journals in the history of the Movement.

College Press in Joplin, Missouri has specialized in providing reprints of both journals and books out of the Movement's history, In 1981 Emmanuel School of Religion honored the publisher, the late Don DeWelt, for making available once again such works as Alexander Campbell's *Millennial Harbinger* and Walter Scott's *The Evangelist*. That the company has in recent years published more than a million books says something for the church's interest not only in Bible study but in its heritage as well.

While the *Directory* reveals that the Christian Church has grown by only 12,000 members in the past decade, it has long been concerned about church growth. Edwin V. Hayden in a 1980 survey of 49 growing churches found that most of them emphasized strong Bible teaching and evangelism, involving as many members as possible. The Johnson County Christian Church in Overland Park, Kansas, for example, gave first priority to evangelism and sought to make every member a soul-winner. While some churches credited their growth to improved facilities, an enlarged professional staff, a lively youth ministry, and even an efficient secretary, Hayden concluded that "growing churches enjoy the enthusiastic involvement of the total membership in evangelism."[19]

"The Undenomination"

The church's claim to be "The Undenominational Fellowship of Christian Churches and Churches of Christ" did not go unnoticed by *Christianity Today* who editorialized it as "the Undenomination." While some in the church saw this as a criticism, others used it as an occasion for self-examination. It led Robert O. Fife to remind his people that other churches remain unconvinced when they are told that the Christian Church is not a denomination, for "we looked like one and seemed to act like one." He went on to ask, "Is it any wonder they did not understand us, when we had not adequately understood ourselves?"[20]

To be undenominational or an *undenomination*, a term that he does not find offensive, Fife says his people must not say to the denominational world, "Come *to* us," but "Come *with* us." It is an obligation to be reformable, he says. He raises a question appropriate for any church: what is meant by "We"? There is the lesser "we" of a Christian college or of a convention that cannot be allowed to modify, define, or obscure the grand "We" in Jesus.

True to the Stone-Campbell heritage, Fife thinks in terms of *movement*: "If we can show that the 'we' which roots in the effort of nineteenth-century pioneers is but a community for witness within the *We* of that community which roots in Pentecost, we shall demonstrate an alternative to denominationalism." He envisions his people as "a community of understanding and concern within the church." And so he concludes that they should not be content with an undenominational plea, for this is not enough. "Let our plea be for Christ and the church!"[21]

John Greenlee, pastor of a Christian Church in Thousand Oaks, Ca., sees the designation of *undenomination* as a "recognition of our separate but equal identity," and asks whether his people are a sect, denomination, movement, or church. He concludes that there is a sense in which they are all four. He regrets that "there is much sectarian attitude among our people," some supposing that the Christian Church is the church to the exclusion of all other believers. Like some concerned ones in the Churches of Christ, he is puzzled that "some of our brethren seem unable to stand firmly in the position of New Testament Christianity without denouncing everyone else in Christendom, to disagree without being disagreeable." But he does not find this a dominant view.

Greenlee concedes that sociologically his people are a denomination and will obviously be seen as such by others, but it is more important to him for the Christian Church to be *Church*, as well as a *movement* within the church at large. Not *a* church or *the* church, he cautions, but simply *Church*, filled with the Spirit of Christ, the only thing that will make it Christ's church.

Being eminently Campbellian, Greenlee, like Fife, wants his people to be a movement, which he sees as an identifiable group within the church that is "consciously endeavoring to bring about reform" without separating itself from the structures within which it moves.

He speaks like a prophet when he tells his people that as a movement they do very little moving: "We have purposely cut ourselves off from meaningful conversations with Christians outside our own people and seem rather content, for the moment at least, to talk to ourselves." Speaking at the NACC, Greenlee proposed that "this free convention" select someone to represent it before other Christian gatherings. Sensing his people to be in "the grip of an amnesia of purpose and plea," he urged them to be a unity people and thus return to the purpose to which they were called. Fearing that they have become "a walled-in denomination" that holds the truth only for themselves, he pled with them to bear the restoration plea to others.[22]

It was this kind of vigorous self-analysis in the Churches of Christ that impressed Edwin S. Gaustad. He was amazed to find a young Ph.D. writing about the Pharisaism in his own church: ". . . we of the Church of Christ have killed the spirit of New Testament Christianity! Yes, the sin of Pharisaism is on our hearts."[23] If one does not find as much confessional preaching in the Christian Church, it may be because it is not as badly needed. Not having a distinctive left-wing as have the Churches of Christ, any meaningful self-analysis has to come from those considered orthodox.

Henry E. Webb, historian at Milligan College, has served as a keen observer of his church through the years. Back in 1981 he expressed concern that acculturation had affected the Christian Church as much as other churches. While his people were once doctrinaire and dogmatic, especially in restoration theology, he found that the students in the Bible colleges were no longer interested in these things.

He also concluded that "a semirural mentality" had affected the role of the Christian Church in today's society, such as its absence in the inner-city and its apparent inability to reach blacks and ethnic groups. Rather than to try to understand social change and the plight of the urban poor, the churches relocate in the suburbs, providing little support for the organizations that are working for social change. "In terms of social concern," Webb said, "Independent Christian Churches largely reflect the attitude of the evangelical community at large."[24]

While Webb has remained an alert student of his people through the years, his recent diagnosis is more critical. In the Dean E. Walker Lecture for 1993 at the NACC he repudiated as ineffective the "radical independency" of the Independent Christian Churches. Pointing to the "heavy price" exacted of the Churches of Christ for their non-instrumental mentality, he avowed that his people pay as great a price for their "radical independent corporate methodology." An example of this, he noted, was the numerous instances of abuse of trust in the independent missionary enterprise.

Webb quoted Max Ward Randall as saying "Independent missions can become the refuge for scoundrels." He probably surprised some of his Independent colleagues in stating what has long been the position taken by the Disciples, reflected first in the writings of Alexander Campbell: "The dogma that the church exists only in the local congregation is defective and not faithful to the teaching of the New Testament."

Citing another example of Independent ineptness, Webb told of the noble evangelistic enterprise called Double Vision, which was projected as a brotherhood-wide program. "It sputtered and failed," he said, "because we do not have the means of projecting a brotherhood-wide program." He added that if his people are to succeed they must move beyond the *ad hoc* way of doing things.[25]

However the term "the undenominational fellowship" fits the Christian Church, such robust self-examination as the foregoing is a sign of spiritual growth. In saying it is "undenominational" the Christian Church could mean that if it has to be a denomination it is one in protest. That in itself is a witness for New Testament Christianity. How many denominations are there that do not want to be a denomination? Not wanting to be a denomination may be the essence of being "an undenominational fellowship," or an *undenomination*, if they please.

The Christian Church and Fundamentalism

One of the most interesting descriptions of the Christian Church comes from the late Joseph H. Dampier, one time president of the NACC and longtime professor of Emmanuel School of Religion. He explained to me in an interview that the Christian Church is not only evangelical, as Webb does above, but also Fundamentalist. He pointed out that the Independents began to break with the Disciples during Protestantism's crisis over modernism, and that the Independent opposition to the Disciples was similar to the general hue and cry against modernism.

It was opposition to modernism that gave birth to the Fundamentalist movement, which eventually failed to win mainline Protestantism, perhaps because it did not give proper place to the great doctrines of the church, as did the Protestant reformers, Dampier reasoned. But the Fundamentalist mentality lived on, which Edward J. Carnell describes as rigid, intolerant, and doctrinaire, and dominated by ideological thinking.

Fundamentalism wages holy wars, Carnell says, without acknowledging the elements of pride and personal interest that prompt the call to battle. He points to the crusade against the Revised Standard Version, which did not stem from the conviction that the version offends Hebrew and Greek idioms, but that the translators were modernists. He notes also that various agencies among the denominations were opposed because modernists were on their staffs. Fundamentalists presume that the way to purify the church is to withdraw fellowship from all modernists, Carnell observes.[26]

One can therefore see the logic of Dampier's interpretation, for the Independents responded to the Disciples modernists in much the same way Fundamentalists opposed modernists in general. Dampier recalled that his people's Bible college movement was a protest against the modernism of Disciples colleges, causing them to move away from the Campbellian stress on liberal arts to a rigid biblical program. Moreover they became doctrinaire on Fundamentalist's issues, such as the inerrancy of Scripture.

Dampier saw the Disciples moving from a restorationist-unity posture in their early history to a liberal theological-ecumenical position today, while the Churches of Christ moved to a restorationist-legalistic position. The Christian Church, in reaction to the direction taken by the Disciples, moved to a restorationist-Fundamentalist emphasis, Dampier concluded.

He noted that the Independents did not become a part of the Fundamentalist movement as such, for they were restorationists who believed in baptism for the remission of sins. For this reason other Fundamentalists would not accept them.

Dampier believed that this explains why all three churches of the Movement have to an appreciable degree compromised the original plea for unity. The Disciples rejected restoration as irrelevant to unity in their interest in ecumenicity. The Churches of Christ rejected unity by demanding conformity. The Christian Church compromised unity by supposing that Fundamentalist restorationism is the way to unity.[27]

This insightful viewpoint is surprising since the Movement appears to be largely untouched by Fundamentalism. The Disciples from the days of Campbell, who did not believe in biblical inerrancy, have always had both an ecclesiology and a hermeneutics that are the antithesis of Fundamentalistism, even when strongly biblical. Even when sectarian and divisive the Movement has not been Fundamentalist.

William S. Banowsky concluded in a study of the Churches of Christ that even though they grew up in a Fundamentalist environment and were rigidly biblical they have never been Fundamentalist, one reason being their exclusivism. The Churches of Christ did not become Fundamentalists because they would not have anything to do with Fundamentalists! But Banowsky also found doctrinal reasons why his people rejected Fundamentalism.[28]

Since Dampier, a scholar of rare historical insight, saw the Independents as the only Fundamentalists in the Movement, we may conclude he had information that escaped others. Recent developments indicate that there has indeed been an incipient Fundamentalism in the Christian Church. Henry Webb, in fact, in his recent history, names "the doctrine of Biblical inerrancy," the *sine qua non* of Fundamentalism, as a "potentially divisive" issue among Christian Churches.[29]

In a similar vein John W. Wade, professor of Atlanta Christian College, insists that the "inerrancy" issue among Independents is so serious that unless they broaden their theological consensus they will face division. He sees no solution except that they start talking *to* one another rather than *about* one another.[30]

C.J. Dull traces Fundamentalism among the Independents to the reaction against liberalism at the College of the Bible back in the 1920s. He finds it mostly, if not exclusively, at Cincinnati Christian Seminary, the largest and most conservative of the church's three seminaries, and such satellite undergraduate schools as Ozark, Roanoke, and Central Florida.[31]

Cincinnati stands alone among the seminaries in requiring a Fundamentalist oath of its faculty, which includes an affirmation that the Bible is "infallible and inerrant in its entirety." The requirement dates from the school's founding in 1924 and is kept updated as terms in the oath become obscure. The original oath, for instance, used the term "infallible" but not "inerrant." The latter term was recently added.

While Dull assures us that the doctrinal concerns at Cincinnati are more issue-oriented than person-oriented, the chief spokesman of what he calls "Independent Fundamentalism" appears to be Jack Cottrell, professor of theology at CCS. Cottrell holds a doctorate from Princeton Seminary, which once divided over Fundamentalism and is today far from that ideology. He also holds a degree from Westminster Seminary, which resulted from the Princeton split and today is Fundamentalist. So Cottrell, who is seen by some of his peers as a Fundamentalist rather than a restorationist, is not without credentials when he speaks on this subject.

Cottrell is disturbed by the fact that "a growing number of our brotherhood teachers and preachers are unashamedly denying the inerrancy of the Bible." Equally disturbing is that some are denying the historicity of the early chapters of Genesis. He holds that the Genesis record cannot have meaning as God's word if it is myth or "story," as some of his brethren believe, but must be actual history.

But Cottrell does not write as one who wants to cause trouble or be divisive over the issue. While he finds a denial of inerrancy "false doctrine and a dangerous doctrine," he does not make it a test of fellowship nor does he believe it separates one from Christ. He sincerely believes that affirming inerrancy, which he defines as the Bible being wholly without any mistakes or errors in its original form, is "the only way to be true to the Bible's teaching about itself."[32]

This position not only sets Cottrell at variance with many of the scholars in the Christian Church, but with such scholars as C.H. Dodd, who, noting that the Bible contains some sub-Christian material, said that the dogma of verbal inspiration or complete infallibility "does less than justice to the Bible itself, in the interests of a theory about the Bible."[33] But Cottrell is on familiar and nostalgic ground when he says, "I believe it *because* it is in the Bible," even if such an affirmation must be made with some reservation.

Fundamentalists generally have left the impression that "If you do not believe in inerrancy you don't believe the Bible," and have gained the reputation of being rigid, intolerant, and divisive. Some of Cottrell's own brethren see him as this way, and that he is raising an issue that has nothing to do with our present Bible, but only with the autographs.

If those who embrace this ideology in the Christian Church can avoid this attitude and show the spirit of P.H. Welshimer's "agree to disagree," the spectre of another division can be avoided.

In What Sense Restorationists?

While most all Independents adamantly claim to be restorationists and almost unamimously refer to their heritage as the Restoration Movement, they are not agreed on what restoration should mean.

A common view, which is described in Chapter 1, was presented in an NACC workshop by Robert W. Green, pastor of the South Side Christian Church in Springfield, Il.: "The Restoration Movement is simply the attempt to return to the original pattern of Christianity as found on the pages of the New Testament Scriptures." It is like the game of baseball, he says. Should it become extinct, and someone found a book of rules on how to play the game, it could be restored in exactly the same way it was played originally. So it is in restoring primitive Christianity, the New Testament serving as the pattern.[34]

It is interesting that this baseball illustration has long been used in both Churches of Christ and Christian Churches, and not often questioned. In recent years it is being questioned if the New Testament is really like a rule book that serves as a detailed pattern for the church, or whether it is a composition of documents quite different from that and not so simple to interpret.

W. Dennis Helsabeck, Jr. of Northwest Christian College is one that takes a different view: "Unfortunately, there has been a well-intended but counter-productive tendency to think of this restoration in blueprint or patternistic terms." It is not "a legalistic blueprint," he says, but a return to our source. He thinks the attitude that "We are the restored New Testament Church" does discredit to the plea. While the New Testament does not provide a detailed pattern, it does provide "apostolic teaching of testimony and ordinances that can still leave Christians the freedom to transcend barriers of time, culture, nation, or ethnic circumstances."[35]

E. Richard Crabtree, pastor of the Academy Christian Church in Colorado Springs, Co., is also uncomfortable with *blueprint* or *pattern* as descriptive of the New Testament's role in restoration. He rather believes that there is "the divine order" that provides "universal elements which would be applicable to any time and culture," a position reminiscent of Robert Richardson's "general Christianity."[36]

While warning his people not to confuse the *advocacy* of an objective with the *achievement* of the objective, Fred P. Thompson, Jr., former president of Emmanuel School of Religion, is nonetheless convinced that the restoration plea is valid. There is a standard against which the church is to measure itself, he insists, and that is "the apostolic description of the church as the body of Christ, agent of reconciliation and redemption in the world."

Restoration does not mean that there was once a perfect church that serves as a model, Thompson notes. It rather points to "the true character of the church disclosed in apostolic testimony." The mission of the Christian Church, he says, "is nothing less than the restoration of humanity to fellowship with God."[37]

If the Independents were able to listen to their most eminent theologian as to the place of restoration, the late Dean E. Walker, there might be less confusion. In a study of Walker's doctrine of the church, William J. Richardson observed that he was always committed to the restoration plea but insisted that it must be better articulated. Walker was uncomfortable with the assertion that "We have restored the New Testament church."

The restoration movement did not begin in America, Walker insisted, but in Eden where God sought to restore man to His own image. Restoration thus refers to the whole mission of God, and it consists in "measures to recover whatever has been distorted or lost." He believed that the emphasis on restoration should be to restore one to the fellowship of God.

It does not mean "a return to the first century to identify the church's nature and forms within that past culture." It is rather an appeal to origins to find the genius of the church in the mind of Christ, to recover the mind of Christ respecting the church. Restoration, to Walker, was thus "a plea to occupy catholic ground."[38]

If the Independents could heed these voices and make a mid-course correction in their view of the nature of both the church and Scripture, it would position them for a more viable witness in the 21st century. It would also help solve some of the issues threatening internal unity, such as the inerrancy conflict, for history demonstrates that restorationist/patternistic hermeneutics tends not only to be divisive but a hindrance to free Bible study.

Conversations With Church of God

Like the Churches of Christ, the Christian Church has historically not only eschewed the term ecumenical, but has avoided doing anything that resembles ecumenicity. It is therefore significant that it has of late entered into serious dialogue with the Church of God (Anderson, In.). Leaders of both churches met in a forum on "Christian Holiness Today" at the 1993 assembly of the NACC in St. Louis.

They discovered early on that the two churches have a great deal in common, historically and theologically. Both were born of American 19th century restorationist movements, with rationalistic and revivalistic roots. Both were originally unity movements that sought to call the faithful out of the denominations into the one true church. Both have pioneers who had an aversion for organizations and ecclesiasticism. Both insist that they are not a denomination, and have stood apart from other churches. Both are strongly biblical, baptize by immersion, and believe strongly in the integrity of the church. And yet both have grown up in a context of division and sub-division.

While the two churches have their differences, their forums have been mainly for fellowship and conversation. Since this is the first serious ecumenical venture for either church, the most important thing about it is that it happened at all. But they have learned from each other along the way. As one Church of God participant put it: "We can learn something from you about baptism and the Lord's supper, while you may learn something from us about holiness." He was referring to his church's *raison d'être* as a "holiness" movement. As restorationists the Church of God sought to restore the true church through "entire sanctification" as "the second work of grace," while the Christian Church has emphasized a restoration of right ordinances.

The forums have caused some of the Christian Church participants to be circumspective. When asked why he met in such forums, Wayne Shaw, professor at Lincoln Christian Seminary, answered that they gave him an opportunity to practice what he had been taught all his life – "our restoration plea for Christian unity." He explained that the forums were in the spirit of dialogue rather than the spirit of debate, and to the Church of God folk he said, "Our emphasis is more cognitive; yours is more heartfelt."

Shaw named several things that he had learned from the Church of God. First, he had made a new set of friends, listing them by name and saying, "I have learned to love these guys." He went on to say that he had learned that it is more important to understand than to be understood. He appreciated the Church of God's ministry among ethnics, and was impressed with their black leadership. He also said he thought the two churches could help each other since they had so much in common in reference to what really matters. He thought he had also learned something about personal worship.[39]

Barry L. Callen, professor at Anderson University, spoke for the Church of God when he said that his people had been "newly sensitized to the central importance of Baptism and the Lord's Supper." Referring to what the Christian Church might have gained from them about "the sanctifying work of the Spirit of God,' he posed a question that should weigh heavily on all heirs of the Movement: "Is a 'holy' church primarily one that is practicing the right 'primitive' things or one that is the holy, true church by virtue of the grace and power of God?"

Callen also challenged the Stone-Campbell tradition when he observed that to be "holy" implies more than a mere change of status before God, as when one is baptized. It means a change in our very nature and our relation to the world, and it means to be a new creation that is different from the world. So, he noted, we must move beyond the important question "What must I do to be saved?" to the second important question "What must I be and do now that I am saved?" Callen adds: "To avoid the demands of the second question surely is to reflect negatively on the accomplishment of the first."[40]

Such penetrating questions as these, which we might not ask of ourselves, illustrate the importance of the churches of the Movement involving themselves more in dialogue with other churches. And when one sees the spirit shown in the forums between the Independents and the Church of God, where participants expressed love and brotherhood toward each other, he is left to wonder if the Movement would ever have been fractured if that spirit had prevailed all along. Those involved in these dialogues are persuaded they will continue, and from these others may come with other churches.

Doing Theology

Since the days when Alexander Campbell wrote into the charter of Bethany College that theology could never be taught, the Movement has had an uneasy relationship with theology. But when one sees how theological Campbell himself was, he may conclude that it was the theologians that Campbell did not like! Not only did Campbell do theology but the Movement has always done theology, even if it has not always admitted it.

In any event all three churches of the Movement have begun to take theology more seriously in recent history. The Independents are doing serious biblical theology on all fronts, whether in the conventions, the colleges, the publications, and even the pulpits. The NACC has long featured a theological forum, and the publication houses are issuing books that treat substantive issues.

College Press has issued upwards of two dozen titles on the general subject of "What the Bible Says About." These books, which run on average about 500 pages, include such subjects as God, Christ, Holy Spirit, Covenant, Grace, Kingdom, Miracles, Salvation, Sin, as well as such practical issues as Growing Old, Leadership, Ministry of Women, and Marriage and Divorce. They are responsibly done and suitable for the rank and file as well as professionals.

For example, Mont W. Smith's *What the Bible Says About Covenant* has an informative chapter on the Hebrew word *hesed*, the word most used in the Old Testament to describe the nature of God. He shows how it relates to covenant. Virgil Warren, who did his doctorate at Southern Baptist Theological Seminary on systematic theology, authored *What the Bible Says About Salvation*, and in 621 pages covers every conceivable aspect of the subject, including an extended treatment of "Eternal Security." He includes a glossary of terms that lists the likes of forensic justification, liberation theology, monergism, and sublapsarianism.

One only needs to thumb through College Press' catalogue to sense the interest in theology. What is new is publications by authors outside the Stone-Campbell tradition. A new title for 1993 is *Why Believe? God Exists!* by two honored professors at Oxford. The blurb notes that the book tells why many scientists are becoming Christians and why God allows pain and evil. Other new titles deal with worship, creation, discipline, and sin.

One serious theological study done by the Christian Church was issued by Standard Publishing back in 1978 entitled *Essays On New Testament Christianity*, which was a festschrift in honor of Dean E. Walker and edited by C. Robert Wetzel. The leading essay by Frederick W. Norris is an impressive analysis of the genius of the Stone-Campbell tradition. Norris sees his heritage as a search for "the catholic interpretation of Scripture offered by the consecrated and qualified interpreters of each age," and he emphasizes that the church is both catholic and apostolic. It is not likely that many in the Christian Church see themselves as catholics!

But Norris does more in reinterpreting the heritage when he notes that the founding fathers could not have meant by "the Bible alone" that each person is to sit in his closet and interpret the Bible for himself, a view that has created endless sects. They rather meant that the Bible is to be interpreted within the church, "interpreted by the ages of study and living of the gospel." He says that is what Campbell meant by "the consensus fidelium."[41]

This festschrift does theology in the kind of critical way the Movement has long needed, such as in Toyozo W. Nakarai's essay on Old Testament theology. He shows that all the major doctrines of the New Testament are anticipated in the Old, and that "the Old Testament is the indispensible background to the New Testament." He refers to the Old as "the immediate parent" of the New, and insists that the God of the Old and of the New are the same God.[42] It is an appropriate emphasis for a people captive to the New Testament.

In doing theology Independent scholars are not only probing basic doctrines but doing so in the light of their heritage. In 1991 the Westwood Christian Foundation in Los Angeles began an annual series of "Restoration Lectures" for this purpose. The first four lectures of the series, all by Ph.D.'s, have drawn upon some of the most seminal thinking in the Movement's history in order to relate them to current needs.

The first lecture by William J. Richardson was an impressive analysis of Alexander Campbell's teaching on grace. He noted that Campbell saw God's grace as both conditional and unconditional. In being bestowed or in its origination grace is unconditional, the initiative being wholly on God's part. But for its appropriation and enjoyment grace is conditional, requiring a response on man's part. To put it another way, Campbell referred to both antecedent and consequent blessings. Grace is an antecedent blessing, which is wholly sovereign favor, but the remission of sins and our adoption into the family of God are consequent blessings that require faith and obedience.

Richardson found no idea of human merit in Campbell's view of grace and man's response to it. Man is to believe and obey, but this is not merit; it is a response to God's pure grace. Grace and works are incompatible, Campbell insisted, but grace and baptism are not. Richardson concluded that Campbell did not only not teach "water regeneration," as he was accused of doing, but that the idea was repugnant to him.

In relating all this to the present, Richardson concludes that modern preaching should focus more upon the "indicatives of grace" and less upon the "imperatives of obedience." He also considers serious the current tendency to see grace as having no imperatives at all. Even more serious is the view, long current in the Movement, that we achieve acceptability from God by our obedience. God does not love us because we obey him; we obey him because he loves us.[43]

Another Westwood lecturer, Byron C. Lambert, probed British theologian William Robinson's sacramental view of the Lord's Supper. Robinson held that in the Movement's development of the Eucharist there were two stages, the prescriptive tradition which makes it a duty, and the sacramental view, which sees Christ as present in the observance. The prescriptive view, which sees the Supper as prescribed by the apostles, has dominated, while the sacramental view, which calls for fellowship with Christ, has been neglected. Robinson saw the Eucharist as more than "in remembrance," for that term could mean that in the Supper we make Christ our contemporary by "recalling" his presence, not simply remembering him.[44]

Further evidence of a growing interest in theology is seen in such substantial publications as *The Collected Works of Dean E. Walker* (1992) by Emmanuel School of Religion. This tome, reflecting the thought of the church's most eminent theologian, could serve as a base for much more serious theological reflection, particularly on the nature of the church. *The Seminary Review*, published quarterly by Cincinnati Christian Seminary, also does theology seriously.

Challenge Of The Future

As for the future of the Christian Church, historian Henry E. Webb was cautiously optimistic back in 1981. Noting that the future of all Protestant churches would be significantly influenced by the nation's economy, he rightly predicted that among his own people economic necessity would not only curtail the feverish building activity of recent decades, but would close some Bible colleges and consolidate others.

He may have been overly optimistic in seeing the Christian Church of the future as "possessed with a dynamic that if skillfully brought to bear on the problems that loom ahead could make for an exciting and I hope useful contribution to American religious life."[45] The numerical growth over the past decade has not been exciting, and if some recent analyses are reliable there is a question about the general well-being of the church.

There was a forum held at the 1993 NACC on the future of the Christian Church. Attended by 150 leaders, it raised the question of where "Our Movement" should be headed, and along with it was an examination of the status quo. The conclusions were less than sanguine.

Victor Knowles, editor of *One Body*, opined that his people had gone so far in being "independent" that it had made them anti-organization. And in being locally autonomous they had ceased being a movement. In fact, he said, his people reminded him of a rag tag band where each member "plays what he wishes and goes where he wants." He was unhappy with what was going on in the churches, all the way from biblical illiteracy that included elders and preachers to a subjectivism that is "slowly supplanting Scripture." But he was pleased about the forums with the Church of God and was hopeful of joint efforts with other evangelicals, especially with those invading the former Soviet Union with the gospel.[46]

The forum on the future must have paid special attention to Leonard G. Wymore, for he is not only a veteran minister but formerly director of the NACC. He reminded the forum that the Movement was originally a unity movement and that this should be its future, though, he conceded, "There are those who couldn't care less about Christian unity." The church, he said, must discuss the role of women and become more involved in ethnic evangelism. "As white people," he said, "we must overcome our isolationist attitude." The church's ministry must be seen in terms of servanthood that involves all members. He also insisted that the future must bring new church plantings.

Wymore, who took part in the discussions with the Church of God, also told the forum that the goal of unity must be mission rather than merger. He indicated that his people might be ready to take unity seriously, especially in terms of reaching out to other churches, and he asked if the NACC should not be used for such contacts. Quoting William Robinson, the British interpreter of the Movement, he told his people that they should be a "bridge church" mediating between Christians in other churches. Finally, he said, the Movement has been about a restoration of relationships, and "Let us practice what we preach."[47]

E. Richard Crabtree, longtime minister in some of the largest churches, focused on his people's future by drawing a parallel between the ending of the Cold War between East and West, which calls for new challenges, and the cessation of the tragic conflict between the Independents and the Disciples of Christ, which was also a cold war, the end of which brings new responsibilities. The Independents early on found their identity in opposing the Disciples, which brought new conventions, new colleges, new missionary apparatus, new parachurch organizations.

Just as the West might say of the Cold War,"We won!," the Independents might say the same in reference to their struggle with the Disciples, Crabtree claims, but he sees no cause for boasting. He finds some comfort in the fact that while the Christian Church is growing only modestly it is not declining, while the Disciples are a dying denomination, a risky conclusion.

Crabtree sees his church facing a new era of secularism, one dominated by passion more than reason; it is a post-modern culture, even superstitious. While 95% of the people claim to believe in God, it does not matter. We can no longer preach logic and reason as we once did, he says.

He concludes from all this that the Christian Church must return to its original plea of Christian unity, a principle too long neglected. Since surveys indicate that people are in search of undenominational Christianity and are no longer interested in dogma, he believes "our plea" should be more relevant than ever. His own participation in forums with both the Churches of Christ and the Church of God has left him "very encouraged," and he is confident that there are other churches with whom his people can confer.

After displaying such ecumenical openness, Crabtree surprisingly finds no reason for further contact with Disciples. Due to their "low view of Biblical authority" he finds "no common basis for appeal" as he does with Churches of Christ and Church of God. He does, however, think his church would have common ground with the "Disciple Renewal," a conservative movement among the Disciples.[48]

There is evident in Crabtree's distinctions a mentality that has long adversely affected the Movement: conservatives can hope for unity only with other conservatives. And the reason is always the same: liberals have a "low view" of the Bible. This is what the Churches of Christ said about the Independents, but now they are talking to each other. It may be the opposite approach that makes for true unity: creative tension in a fellowship of forbearing love between liberals and conservatives.

Too, it is unlikely that any substantial segment within the Movement has a "low view" of biblical authority as Crabtree supposes. Anyone who hears or reads the likes of Fred Craddock, Roger Carstensen, Michael Kinnamon, or Anthony Dunnavant, to name just a few "mainline Disciples," would be surprised to hear that they have a "low view" of the Bible. Anyone who can talk with leaders in Churches of Christ and the Church of God ought to be able to talk with such men as these.

In considering the future of Christian Churches as well as the Movement as a whole this is the place to start, *a restoration of trust in each other.*

ENDNOTES

[1]David Filbeck, *The First Fifty Years* (Joplin, MO: College Press, 1980), p. 307.

[2]*Ibid.*, pp. 93f.

[3]*Ibid.*, p. xiv.

[4]"The Significance of Canton," *Christian Standard*, Vol. 64 (1929), pp. 970, 1093.

[5]"The North American Convention," *Christian Evangelist*, Vol. 66 (1929), p. 1222.

[6]"A New Experiment," *Christian Evangelist*, Vol. 64 (1927), p. 1329.

[7]R.H. Miller, "The North American Convention," *Christian Evangelist*, Vol. 80 (1942), p. 476.

[8]*Ibid.*, Vol. 84 (1946), p. 507.

[9]"Does This Mean Division?," *Christian Evangelist*, Vol. 88 (1950), p. 551.

[10]"If This Be Division," *Christian Standard*, Vol 72 (1937), p. 416.

[11]"The Convention Proposed for This Fall," *Christian Standard*, Vol. 62 (1927), p. 269.

[12]*Christian Standard*, Vol. 75 (1940), p. 521.

[13]*Christian Standard*, Vol. 62 (1927), p. 323.

[14]Leonard G. Wymore, "These Made It Possible," *Christian Standard*, Vol. 102 (1977), pp. 775-776.

[15]P.H. Welshimer, "The Indianapolis Convention," *Christian Standard*, Vol. 62 (1927), p. 483.

[16]"Churches and DCC," *Dallas Christian College Visitor*, (Dec. 1978), p. 1.

[17]Howard Hays, "A Look at Bible Colleges," *Christian Standard*, Vol. 86 (1950), p. 28.

[18]C.J. Dull, "Intellectual Factions and Groupings of the Independent Christian Churches," *The Seminary Review*, Vol 31, No. 2 (June 1985), pp. 91f.

[19]Edwin V. Hayden, "How Does Your Congregation Grow?," *Christian Standard*, Vol 105 (1980), pp. 195f.

[20]Robert O. Fife, "Maintaining the Undenominational Plea," *Christian Standard*, Vol. 104 (1979), p. 309.

[21]*Ibid.*, p. 310.

[22]John Greenlee, *Who Are We — Movement or Church?*, NACC Forum, Seattle (July 9, 1980); pp. 1-13; mimeographed by NACC.

[23]Edwin S. Gaustad, "Churches of Christ in America," *The Religious Situation 1969* (Boston: Beacon Press, 1969), p. 1022.

[24]Henry E. Webb, "The Christian Church ('Independent') — Where From Here? Looking to the Future," *Lexington Theological Quarterly*, Vol. 16, No. 1 (Jan. 1981), pp. 26-32.

[25]Henry E. Webb, "Our Restoration Movement: Heritage and Destiny," European Evangelistic Association's Dean E. Walker Lecture, NACC, 1993 (Tape).

[26]Edward J. Carnell, *The Case for Orthodox Theology* (Philadelphia: Westminster, 1959), pp. 113-115.

[27]Interview with Joseph H. Dampier.

[28]William S. Banowsky, *Mirror Of A Movement* (Dallas: Christian Publishing Co., 1965).

[29]Henry E. Webb, *In Search of Christian Unity*, p. 431.

[30]John W. Wade, "A Candid Look At Some of Our Problems," *Christian Standard*, Vol. 70, No. 30 (1985), p. 668.

[31]C.J. Dull, "Intellectual Factions," p. 104.

[32]Jack Cottrell, "Dedicated to Scriptural Inerrancy: The Biblical/Theological Implications," *The Seminary Review*, Vol 30, No. 3 (September 1984), pp. 93f.

[33]Quoted in J. Philip Hyatt, *The Heritage of Biblical Faith*, St. Louis: Bethany Press, 1964, p. 326.

[34]Robert W. Green, *Keeping Leadership Tuned into the Restoration Movement*, NACC Forum, Seattle (July 11, 1980), pp. 1-4; mimeographed by NACC.

[35]W. Dennis Helsabeck, Jr., *An Apologetic For the Restoration Movement*, NACC Forum, Seattle (July 1, 1980), pp. 1-7; mimeographed by NACC.

[36]E. Richard Crabtree, "Restore the Divine Order," *Unleavened Bread*, Vol. 2, No. 1 (Jan. 1977), pp. 11-12.

[37]Fred P. Thompson, Jr., "Restore What?," *Envoy*, Vol. 10, No. 11 (Nov. 1978), pp. 1, 3.

[38]William J. Richardson, *The Nature of the Church in the Thought of Dean E. Walker*, Typeset, Theological Forum, NACC, 1991.

[39]Wayne Shaw, *What I Have Learned From the Anderson Church of God*, Typeset, Lincoln Christian Seminary, Lincoln, IL.

[40]Barry L. Callen, *The Quest for Holiness: Our Continuing Imperative*, Typeset, NACC: St. Louis, 1993.

[41]Frederick W. Norris, "Apostolic, Catholic, and Sensible: The *Consensus Fidelium*," in *Essays On New Testament Christianity*, C. Robert Wetzel, Ed. (Cincinnati: Standard Publishing Co., 1978), pp. 20, 29.

[42]Toyozo W. Nakarai, "The Old Testament Background of the New Testament" in Wetzel, *Essays*, p. 88f.

[43]William J. Richardson, *The Role of Grace In The Thought of Alexander Campbell* (Los Angeles: Westwood Christian Foundation, 1991).

[44]Byron C. Lambert, *The Restoration of the Lord's Supper And The Sacramental Principle* (Los Angeles: Westwood Christian Foundation, 1992).

[45]Henry E. Webb, "The Christian Church ('Independent') — Where From Here? Looking to the Future," *Lexington Theological Quarterly*, Vol 16, No. 1 (Jan. 1981), p. 32.

[46]Victor Knowles, *Focus On Our Future: Where Should Our Movement Be Headed?*, Typescript, Workshop, NACC, July 8, 1993.

[47]Leonard G. Wymore, *Focus On Our Future: Where Should Our Movement Be Headed?* Typescript, Workshop, NACC, July 6-9, 1993.

[48]E. Richard Crabtree, *Focus On Our Future: Where Should Our Movement Be Headed?* Typescript, Workshop, NACC, July 8, 1993.

20

THE MOVEMENT WITH THREE FACES
CHRISTIAN CHURCH (DISCIPLES OF CHRIST)

Restructure was inevitable.
— Mark G. Toulouse

On September 26, 1968 the Christian Churches (Disciples of Christ) officially became the Christian Church (Disciples of Christ). The change from churches to church was a significant one, reflecting a new theology of the church, and it was a monumental turning point in the history of the Disciples of Christ.

The occasion was an annual meeting in Kansas City of what had been since 1919 the International Convention of Christian Churches but was now the Provisional Assembly of the new church. Ronald E. Osborn, veteran scholar and minister, was presiding. The move had been made that the assembly give final approval of "The Provisional Design," which had been recommended by the Commission on Brotherhood Restructure. It would transform over 4,000 loosely connected congregations into an official restructured denomination. It passed overwhelmingly.

With the assembly standing in reverence, Bill Guthrie, at Osborn's request, led the newly-created church in the singing of the doxology. For the first time in its history the Disciples of Christ could corporately see itself as a bona fide denomination, one among others, "within the universal body of Christ," as the Provisional Design put it. The parenthesis in the new name made it evident that the new denomination saw itself as only part of the universal Christian church, thus Christian Church (Disciples of Christ). The name also points back to 1832 when two movements, one called Christians and the other Disciples of Christ, became one church.

A. Dale Fiers, the first to serve as General Minister and President of the restructured church, referred to the experience as one of the most creative and turbulent periods in the Movement's history. He noted that it required eight years of intensive study, research, and debate.[1]

But according to Independent historian Henry E. Webb there was not all that much "debate" and the "research" was one-sided in that those opposed to restructure never received a fair hearing. Moreover, as Webb sees it, the Kansas City vote in 1968 had already been assured by partisan tactics at the Detroit and St. Louis conventions in 1964 and 1967.

In the Detroit convention a motion passed, after harsh and bitter debate, to make the convention a delegate assembly in which only delegates could vote. This left out many congregations who feared that if they sent certified delegates they would not be free to oppose other matters in future conventions. So, as Webb puts it, "Many were unable to vote because of the 1964 action limiting voting to certified delegates." Webb goes on to say that this action plus a change in bylaws that gave agency officials heavy voting representation assured a victory for restructure in the convention's initial vote in St. Louis in 1967.[2]

Restructure had to be approved by two-thirds of the states and area associations (but not congregations) and two-thirds of the agencies as well as two-thirds of the delegates at the convention. All this was in place when the final vote was taken in Kansas City in 1968. The dissidents were clearly disillusioned. Webb appears amazed that President A. Dale Fiers could suggest in his report that the restructure plan would be as significant to the Disciples' future as was Thomas Campbell's *Declaration and Address*.

Four years earlier at the 1964 International Convention, Winfred E. Garrison had given his "Fork In The Road" address, which became a momentous incident in the church's move toward restructure. The occasion was the Oreon E. Scott Ministers' Breakfast, sponsored by the Pension Fund of Christian Churches. Since 1930 it had been a significant event at the Convention. Some of the nation's most famous clergyman had addressed it, including Daniel Poling, George W. Truett, and Elton Trueblood.

Garrison, then 90 years old, was the church's esteemed patriarch, as well as historian, philosopher, and poet. He was, as William E. Tucker described him, "widely respected and venerable." The speech was billed as "a penetrating analysis of decisions facing Disciples."

As son of the renowned James H. Garrison, longtime editor of the *Christian-Evangelist* (now *The Disciple*, the church's official organ), Garrison was uniquely qualified to make such an analysis. In the address he reminisced about his 80 years as a Disciple, including his apprenticeship in his father's editorial office and his exposure to the great leaders in the church of yesteryears. That he was always seen as a leader among the liberal Disciples makes the address all the more significant.

The Disciples were at this time already in the process of restructure, but it was not yet determined what form this would take. Garrison was persuaded that the decision soon to be made would affect the Disciples' witness in the decades ahead. He therefore urged his people to "prepare for the year 2000" by realizing that they then stood at "a fork in the road."

One fork, he observed, leads to "a more closely organized denomination, oriented toward efficiency, institutionally unified, structurally integrated, with our numerical boundaries and our doctrinal position clearly defined." This would enable Disciples to deal on terms of parity with other denominations in such places as the World and National Councils of Churches. It would also give them a united voice representing the whole body of Disciples, he allowed.

The other fork would be an enhancement of what the Disciples had always been, which was, as Garrison put it: "that the Disciples of Christ should be, as nearly as possible, a pilot project for a completely united church." To take this fork, he noted, the Disciples would not seek to base their own unity upon either an integrated ecclesiastical structure or on a formulation of theological doctrine." He thought this followed since "the whole church cannot conceivably be united in these ways."[3]

When McAllister and Tucker refer to this speech in their discussion of the controversy over restructure (after Garrison's death) they say, "Garrison implied that if they were not careful the Disciples would choose the wrong 'fork in the road.' He was not explicit, however, as to which fork was wrong."[4]

Friends of Garrison, particularly the late A.T. DeGroot, who joined him as author of *Disciples of Christ: A History*, chided the historians for making this statement, telling them that they knew very well which fork Garrison believed to be wrong. The historians conceded that they had erred and agreed to make the correction in future editions,[5] which they did, conceding that "He later indicated the wrong fork had been taken."

While the momentous event of 1968 described above makes it evident that the Disciples took the first fork Garrison described, Robert O. Fife, an Independent historian, says there is a sense in which they took both forks. His analysis helps to explain the separation of the Independent Christian Churches.

As Fife put it: "Some opted for a denomination whose fellowship would be clearly delimited by institutional relationships of the common American Protestant variety," while others, referring to the Independents, chose to continue "as a movement bearing witness to the Church, and seeking to exhibit that witness in a corporate life, whose bonds of unity could be commended to the whole Church of Christ on earth."

Those who took the first fork, Fife observes, in effect made agency participation a test of fellowship in that they changed what were voluntary agencies into administrative units of the church.[6] Garrison would apparently agree, but he would question whether the Independents, either before or after 1968, have created "a corporate life" that is sufficiently effective to commend itself to the whole Church of Christ. In his address Garrison called for an "enhancement" of the corporate structure that then existed.

The misgivings expressed by Garrison and Fife have to do with a new doctrine of the church that has emerged with restructure. Since the days of Stone and Campbell the Disciples have believed that the unity and catholicity of "the Church of Christ on earth" is expressed in "the Christians in all the sects" and in congregations everywhere. They thus saw the essence of the church in the local congregation.

Almost from the outset the Movement had cooperative agencies that were entered into on a voluntary basis. These agencies were not the church, but servants to the church, and were never made tests of fellowship, or, as Garrison put it, never used to determine who was a Disciple of Christ and who was not. Restructure presented a new way of looking at the church.

The Case For Restructure

Leading Disciples have seen restructure not only as a significant development in their history, but as necessary to a viable and effective witness. Virgil A. Sly, onetime executive in the agencies, saw it as "a new valid reason" for their existence as a church. While restructure made them an official denomination, the reasons for it were far weightier than that. It not only enhanced the ministry of their own church, but it is also a means of ecumenical outreach. To Sly restructure was a *must* if the Disciples were serious about "a united world witness and strategy involving our sharing in the total world evangelistic enterprise of the Church as one organic movement."

In their ecumenical efforts the Disciples had not been able to deal with other denominations *as a church*, but as the International Convention, and even this was not an official representation (by delegates) from the churches. Restructure enables them, Sly noted, to "speak as one within the ecumenical movement" and as an equal with other denominations.

To Sly restructure was more than a means to greater efficiency. He saw it as the call of God: "We will fail if we are interested only in building a bigger, more efficient denomination. This is a God-given opportunity to be something more than that."[7]

The concept of restructure was first proposed in 1958 by Willard Wickizer, a chairman within the UCMS, before the Council of Agencies. Granville Walker, a prominent pastor, took it before the general convention, and in 1961 a committee was formed that created the Commission on

Brotherhood Restructure, consisting of 126 leading Disciples.

The issues were soon identified. Congregational autonomy, long held sacred, was to be examined in the light of the interdependency and unity of the church as revealed in the New Testament. Rather than a leadership of dominant persons, which tends to be the way of conventions, the church would be led by the "principle of polity." A new "sense of the church" was emerging, rather than an assumed fellowship of 8,000 congregations, a figure that then included those that soon became the Independent Christian Churches.

This gave rise to the idea of a delegate convention, which had been considered since the days of Campbell. They now opted for an organization based on official representation from the churches rather than an *ad hoc* one made up of self-appointed individuals. Greater efficiency was of course an issue, and it was anticipated that restructure would enable the brotherhood to "fulfill its mission as part of the whole church of Christ."[8]

The Disciples have now had more than 25 years to test restructure. Mark G. Toulouse, a professor of history at TCU, looking back on the trauma of the ordeal, is persuaded that it was all along more of a pragmatic issue than theological. Referring to the "hopelessly entangled" efforts of the various agencies of the UCMS, including conflicts over territory and finances, he asks a telling question: "How could accountability be established for agencies, educational institutions, and congregations without resorting to ecclesiastical coercion?" Restructure met that need. Conditions being what they were, Toulouse sees restructure as inevitable. He thinks the leaders should have argued for it "purely from a pragmatic perspective."[9]

The dissidents of that day, like W.E. Garrison, would remind Toulouse that they were aware that mid-course corrections were in order, and that, yes, something needed to be done. But did it have to take the form of the Provisional Design, which many committed Disciples conceived as contrary both to their own tradition and the biblical doctrine of the church? To them it was theological.

But Toulouse is not unmindful of the theological implications of restructure, citing the three thesis set forth by Ronald Osborn during the debate: (1) Since no doctrine of the church can dictate the particulars of any structure there are theological limits to the decision process; (2) Any doctrine of the church calls for some form of structure; (3) Since theology has its limits, the pragmatic decision has to be based on "common sense and practical experience."[10]

Toulouse concludes that the 50-year history of the UCMS, which he sees as the most important development in Disciples history, laid the necessary groundwork for restructure. If there had been no UCMS, which provided the glue that held the loosely-related congregations together, there would have been no restructure. The end result is a more effective denomination, and he sees it as amazing that his people were able to restructure the church in only about six years.[11]

But, again, what Toulouse sees as strength the dissenters see as weakness. Restructure was hurried in that there was not sufficient discussion. The price paid for "a more effective denomination" was too great in that in the end the restructured church lost over one-third of its congregations, and many of these were faithful churches not numbered among the Independents that were already deemed a separate group.

Had there been more patience and more acceptance of diversity, observers ask, could a less costly structure have been found? In fact, when Charles H. Bayer, regular columnist for *The Disciple* lists the divisions among Disciples he names three, not two. The first was over music (Churches of Christ), the second over open membership, etc. (Independents), and the third over restructure. He was weighing the possibility of a fourth.[12]

Was another division part of the price of restructure — by a people called of God to be a unity movement?

The Provisional Design: Pros and Cons

At the heart of the Provisional Design ("Provisional" was dropped at the 1985 General Assembly) was the levels of authority assigned to three "manifestations of the church." One wonders if they could not have found a better word, for as one "outsider" put it: "Manifestations? Sounds like poltergeist!" To their credit the architects of the Design purposely avoided using "levels," which might have implied an hierarchy of authority. So, they came up with three "manifestations," each equal to the others: the local church, the regional church, the general church.

One of the articulate creators of the Design, Loren E. Lair, explained it this way: "This means that there is a local congregational church, a regional church, and a general (national-international) church." He conceded that this represented "a fundamental shift in thinking for the brotherhood." But he insisted that the plan was not set in concrete: "There can be no final conclusion to restructure. It is an ongoing process and must remain fluid and flexible. It is subject to change as situations warrant and as the corporate judgment of the church is expressed on structure."[13]

Since by tradition the Disciples are freedom-oriented and uncomfortable with authoritative structures, they sought a different theological base for their administrative levels and for restructure as a whole. The theological base was described by Ronald E. Osborn as "the community of the covenant." Drawing upon the idea of covenant in Scripture all the way from Adam to Jesus, he concluded: "It is altogether appropriate that in the process of restructure we should develop this concept more fully by devising a declaration of our covenant in Christ, by which our congregations may bind themselves to one another in the common life and mission of the Christian Church (Disciples of Christ) for the service of God."[14]

Theologically, therefore, restructure is a covenantal relationship more than an authoritative one. Or to put it another way, authority is expressed in covenantal relationships, as in a marriage. The local congregation has a covenant relationship not only within itself but with all others in its Region, which makes up the regional manifestation of the church. The regional minister is thus "a leader among equals" based on covenant. The Region in turn has a covenantal commitment to the General Church, which in turn has covenantal responsibilities to the whole church. The General Minister and President (GMP), presiding over the General Church, is the servant of all, covenantally bound, and again "a leader among equals." The "levels of authority" are thus parallel rather than pyramidal.

The Design presently calls for a representation of two delegates from each congregation for the first 500 members or less, plus one delegate for each additional 500 members. This number, which has the potential of being unwieldy, constitutes the General Assembly. The congregations, now some 4,000 in number, are divided into 36 Regions and have their own organization led by the regional minister. They make up the regional manifestation of the church.

A few Regions, where churches are more numerous, also have Areas. The Christian Church (Disciples of Christ) in the Southwest, for example, is within the Texas-New Mexico Region, but it has its own office in Dallas with a full-time staff, and its own budget and programs. It too is autonomous and is funded by its Area churches, which it serves in numerous ways.

The North Texas area has existed from pre-restructure times and was not part of the Design. This further illustrates the traditional role of local churches, which have always had a way of doing what they please. These churches in fact relate more practically to the Areas than to the Region. This means that there are actually four manifestations of the church, not three, in at least one Region. When one Disciples leader referred to the manifestations as "the three autonomies," he could have said "the four autonomies." Autonomy is of course what he was emphasizing, and this appears to be the case throughout the church.

The General Assembly meets every other year. Voting is restricted to the delegates from the congregations and the regions, all recognized ministers of the denomination, the General Board members, and officials of the colleges and administrative units. Any other Disciple may attend the Assembly and even take part in the discussions, but he cannot vote.

The general manifestation is made up of the General Assembly, the GMP, eleven administrative units, and the General Board, a deliberative body of some 170 elected by the Assembly. The Board, after due deliberation, makes recommendations to the Assembly. But the sheer weight of numbers in the Assembly makes meaningful debate impossible. The GMP is purposely designated a minister, for that is his or her intended role rather than that of a mere church executive.

Theoretically, the Assembly accepts or rejects the Board's recommendations, but it is seldom that an issue is resolved that way. It appears that the process is not as democratic as the Design implies since most decisions are actually made by the Board.

This led Charles H. Bayer to write: "Disciples might talk about representative government, but the rhetoric is window dressing for what turns out to be a closed system." He goes on to say that Southern Baptists and Unitarians do a better job of practicing what the Disciples preach. He concludes that it would be the better part of candor for the Disciples "to give up the illusion that the General Assembly has any power, and simply recognize that the General Board really makes all the decisions."[15]

Other informed Disciples disagree with this assessment of the power of the General Assembly. It was at least the case in 1991 when the Assembly rejected the Board's recommendation that Michael Kinnamon be named as GMP. But this was an unusual situation involving the highly emotional issue of homosexuality. Conservatives, led by Disciple Renewal (see below), mounted a drive to reject Kinnamon because he was considered too liberal on gay issues. His lack of pastoral experience was also a concern. Even so Kinnamon barely missed receiving the two-thirds vote required.

It would be expected that there would be conflict between the "autonomies." It is sometimes the case that the right hand does not approve of what the left hand does, such as when the GMP wrote to President Clinton that the Christian Church (Disciples of Christ) approved of his policy of gays in the military. Many out in the churches thought that if the GMP wrote such a letter at all it should say that he, not the church, approved of the President's policy! Apparently the churches did not approve.

Recent research reveals that the Disciples clergy are far more liberal than the laity. On the homosexual issue, for instance, 79% of the ministers favored gay rights while only 34% of the members did. The survey revealed about the same percentage (80%) of Presbyterian clergy favored gay rights, while 57% of their laity did. Only 14% of Disciples ministers believe the Bible to be inerrant, but 48% of the members do. This makes the Disciples laity much more conservative than the Presbyterians (32%) and much more liberal than the Baptists (70%).[16]

This "in house" problem of having a liberal clergy and a conservative laity weighs heavily on the Disciples. It works havoc on the "autonomies" of the church, "covenantal relationships" or not.

It appears that the authors of the Design never took seriously the criticisms made against it. It was not enough to label all opposition as from Independents who had never cooperated anyway, for the most responsible opposition came from eminent leaders who had always been loyal and cooperative Disciples. Beside W.E. Garrison there was Robert W. Burns, pastor of the Peachtree Christian Church in Atlanta and former president of the International Convention, who served on the Restructure committee. Others included A.T. DeGroot and Frank N. Gardner, professors at TCU and Drake.

These men, except Garrison, formed the Atlanta Committee that issued in 1967 the "Atlanta Declaration" in which they stated their case against the Design: (1) It threatens our freedom in Christ by being authoritarian; (2) The proposals are so complex that no immediate action should be taken; (3) The effect will be to exclude many who have been cooperative in the past. It went on to state that it favored restructure, but only of the agencies, leaving congregations unrestricted. The document was widely distributed, but was never a part of formal discussion. It expressed the concerns of many congregations and thousands of Disciples.

Burns, who served as secretary of the Atlanta Committee, made a special appeal to the Campbell Institute at the 1967 Convention just prior to the initial vote. He told the Institute, which included a number of Disciples leaders, that he was not trying to change their minds but only wanted "dialogue with dignity, and in brotherhood, with equal time allowed for the various differences to be expressed and with access to our magazines." He asked the group to make room for "those of us who cannot accept the narrow confines of the Provisional Design."[17] He did not get his way.

The interesting thing about all this is that the fears expressed by the dissenters seemed never to have materialized. Congregational freedom, so prized and defended by the Atlanta Committee, appears to be alive and well in Disciples churches today. My inquiry of numerous pastors indicates that Restructure has made no discernible difference in their autonomy. If anything they are freer in that they have more resources to draw on, but yet chart their own course.

The First Christian Church in my hometown of Denton, Texas is over 125 years old and has always been cooperative, supporting the agencies. It still does and in about the same way. Its own board decides how much the church gives and to which manifestations of the church. In its support it favors its own Area (to be distinguished from the Region as noted above), for which one of its pastors serves as moderator.

There are no mandates and no pressures from Indianapolis. If it chooses, the Denton church could send no money at all. It hires its own ministers. The area and regional ministers serve only in an advisory capacity and have no authority over the congregation; neither does the GMP in Indianapolis. The Denton church sends two delegates to the General Assembly who are free to vote as they will, though some churches instruct their delegates. When I asked one board member what difference restructure had made, she could not name anything in particular.

The First Christian Church (Disciples of Christ) in New Kensington, Pa. recently effected a union with a neighboring United Church of Christ. The united church now calls itself the Trinity United Christian Church, but is still a Disciples church. This was effected largely by the dynamic Disciples pastor who grew up and was educated as an Independent at Johnson Bible College!

Even though the leadership of both denominations have talked union for decades, they were less than enthusiastic about what happened at New Kensington. The two churches did not know better than to practice what their leaders have been preaching! It was premature, the leaders of both denominations said. But there was nothing they could do about it. The two churches opted to do it, and all is well. If that is not congregational freedom, what is?

There are also a number of congregations in the *Year Book* that are multi-denominational, such as the United Christian and Presbyterian Church in Coleman, Texas. While such churches may or may not financially support the Christian Church (Disciples of Christ), they are listed as Disciples churches.

There are numerous churches in the *Year Book 1993* that do not now send any money to the General Church and have apparently never supported the agencies. While they are mostly small, they have the character of being "Independent," but they have not been dropped as Disciples churches. They may not be good "covenant" churches but no one bothers them. They might not send delegates to the Assembly, but they could if they chose to.

This indicates that the fear of congregations losing their freedom, as expressed by the Atlanta Committee, has not materialized after 25 years of restructure. The facts indicate that the Disciples churches are as free as they choose to be. It also shows that the Independents left because they wanted to and not because they had to, a fear expressed by W.E. Garrison. But some left for conscience' sake, which is what Garrison hoped to avoid, believing that the nature of the Movement allows for such diversity.

This does not mean, of course, that the Disciples are immune to the power plays that affect any large organization, but for those who supposed the Disciples were headed toward a heavy-handed eccleciasticism just the opposite appears to be the case. If power runs in any direction, it is from the local church up or down or across, and this includes finances. This is reflective of the Movement's long and strong tradition of the autonomy of the local church, so inbred that it has been a problem. It has left much of the Movement without any organizational structure at all beyond the local church.

One wonders if Ray Lindley, who served on the Panel of Scholars that laid out the theological basis for restructure, did not have a point when he charged that "the sin of the Disciples has been to impute to the local congregation an authority that properly belongs to the whole church." He reminds us that Alexander Campbell insisted that "the church" is more than the sum total of the congregations.[18]

The question that sought the final word on all this was posed by W.A. Welsh, a former president of the International Convention. As a member of the restructure committee he asked: "Will restructure really serve to strengthen our 'spirit' as a brotherhood, thereby making us more effective in evangelism, stewardship, etc., or not?"[19] He then feared that it would not, but it was too soon to make that judgment back in 1963. In 1994 he still had reservations about restructure, noting that there were too many questions left unanswered, especially at the regional level. "They were in too big a hurry," he recalled with regret.[20]

But the younger generation, who are the heirs of what their fathers did back in 1968, may have a more objective view of the effects of restructure. Richard L. Harrison, Jr., now president of Lexington Theological Seminary, looks back with an historian's eye and sees restructure as "painful" to those who went through it, and even a cause of division. But still he says, "The alternative was to become marginalized, to have little or no impact on the ways of the world, which, ultimately, would have been a giving up on the third ideal of mission."[21]

In a book written by two laymen, Robert L. Friedly and D. Duane Cummins, restructure is looked back on as the time when Disciples could at last call themselves a Church. They would no longer have to use such euphemisms as "brotherhood" or "fellowship." They had moved from being a group of churches to being Church. It was an end to 119 years of frustration of "trying to carry the gospel to the world without an adequate vehicle." Friedly and Cummins see the 4,000 churches and one million Disciples that made restructure a reality as making an important statement: *They needed each other in mission.*[22]

While there are of course dissenting voices to these appraisals, they show that there are responsible voices among the younger generation who not only know what happened back in the 1960's, but consider it important to their heritage as Disciples of Christ.

Authority

Ray Lindley's indictment that the Disciples have throughout their history imputed too much authority to the local congregation points up a problem that continues to plague them even as a restructured church: *Can a denomination with autonomous levels really have a definable authority?* Is there an ultimate authority in the three (or four) manifestations of the church?

In 1957, well before restructure, Hampton Adams, late pastor of the Park Avenue Christian Church in New York, stated plainly that the ultimate authority of the Disciples of Christ is the congregation itself.[23] It appears that restructure has not appreciably changed that. No one can really speak or act for the whole church. This was a weakness that restructure intended to correct.

The question of authority has troubled the Movement since the days of the pioneers who complained of the "wandering comets" that no one had sent and none could control. In more recent history the infamous Jim Jones affair illustrates the problem, for both he and his People's Temple enjoyed official standing with the Christian Church (Disciples of Christ) at the time of the Guyana mass suicides. The GMP issued a pastoral letter to the churches concerning the incident, but neither he nor the regional minister seemed to have authority to enact disciplinary measures.

While the architects of restructure refer to local authority (the Official Board of the local church), regional authority (the regional assembly) and general authority (the General Assembly), they do not identify *ultimate* authority. It is of course an age-old problem, which the Roman Catholics have resolved in the office of the pope, the Methodists in their college of bishops, and the Presbyterians in their general assembly. Both the Independent Christian Churches and the Churches of Christ hold that authority stops at the level of the local church, as do the Disciples even after restructure.

Michael Kinnamon, the dean of Lexington Theological Seminary who narrowly missed being elected the GMP, reminds Disciples that "The ultimate authority in the life of the church is the presence of God expressed to us in Christ." The Bible has authority, he went on to say, in that it bears witness to the presence of God in Christ. He concedes that the Bible has to be interpreted, and since this cannot be done infallibly there will be tensions in differences of interpretation.

"For Disciples," Kinnamon says, "the authority of the church must be understood in terms of covenant." This calls for trust, compassion, and forgiveness toward each other, for that is the way God deals with us, and it makes us accountable to each other. God's authority, he says, is expressed in the church in two ways, charismatic (persuasion) and institutional (conferred by office). These must find balance, for an overemphasis of the first risks losing the truth of the gospel and an overemphasis of the second risks quenching the Spirit.[24]

Kinnamon made these observations, which were not intended to be practically definitive, in the context of a conference held at Lexington Theological Seminary on "Christians Only But Not the Only Christians; Reappraising the Disciples Tradition for the 21st Century." It was a gathering that attracted far more than was expected, including several from the Independents and Churches of Christ, including me. Authority was one of the questions discussed. Kinnamon, who directed the conference, stated that no consensus was reached on the issues raised about authority.

In his own working paper at the conference Kinnamon made some practical proposals on how the Disciples might escape the mentality of "We don't know what we believe," which he sees as a threat to their self-identity. One suggestion was to nurture the concept of the regional minister as "authoritative teacher of the faith." This means the regional minister would function more as an authoritative teacher than as an efficient manager. Another was that "church-wide study" might cultivate the concept of the General Assembly as an "authority-in-community" for the whole church. It should be able to speak for the whole church on such matters as false ideologies which threaten the integrity of the faith. He gives no suggestion on how such an assembly, composed of thousands, could make such *ex cathedra* pronouncements.[25]

The prospect that the Assembly might speak for the whole church on matters of faith is dim, especially since the trauma of the Kinnamon nomination in which issues relative to homosexuality proved to be bitterly divisive within the Assembly itself. The Assembly has recently taken steps to avoid voting on social and theological issues and confine itself to procedural matters, or at least avoid divisive issues.

Dale and Mary K. Patrick brought their conclusions from a study on authority in the church before the same conference. Their first discovery, they revealed, was that out there in the churches is the prevalent mentality that "nobody – and I mean nobody – is going to tell me what to think," or what to do or how to vote or even when to sit down and shut up. They indicate that this anarchy might be as much toward God and the Bible as toward people. They are also concerned that "The liberal wing of the church has embraced critical scholarship at the expense of Scripture's authority to teach the church."

On the other hand, they see the conservative wing as "isolated from secular culture, critical scholarship, and denominational structure of power" while adhering to biblical authority. While the liberal wing has prevailed in Disciples centers of power, it is in an awkward, vulnerable position, for "The erosion of the authority of Scripture erodes the church's authority as well." When the Bible ceases to be the authority, they avow, authority is transferred to the "conscience" and "reason" of the interpreter, which has the effect of rendering the church and its ministry superfluous. Those growing up in such a mindset see their church as standing for nothing of consequence and drop out at an alarming rate.

The Patricks disagree with "A Word to the Church on Authority" which was issued by the Commission on Theology and Church Union. This document redefined authority to mean "servanthood which wins compliance through persuasion rather than coercion," thus rejecting the common understanding of authority as defined in Webster. As the Patricks see it, persuasion and coercion are partners and the church must have both. The partnership fails when the clergy fear to offend the sacrosanct individual conscience of laity lest unemployment result. They conclude by charging that "our radically democratic polity has confused and undermined authority within the body," and that "A little coercion at the right place promotes the persuasion God intends."[26]

Mark G. Toulouse disagrees in that he believes the Disciples must find a way to speak "in the name of an authoritative gospel without practicing coercive forms of authority to go along with it." The church's authority must be like Christ's, persuasive rather than coercive. It must also be broadly participatory and widely dispersed throughout the denomination. It must respect the claims of diversity.

While Toulouse sees a trend toward "a teaching office," perhaps at the regional level, as having general teaching authority, he concludes that among Disciples authority will have to remain informal. He says Disciples will accept authority so long as it is not formalized! And it must always honor and not demean "the congregation as the most basic expression of the church in human history."[27]

In a perceptive piece at the Indianapolis conference, Richard L. Harrison, Jr. notes that most movements that last more than a generation develop conflicting sources of authority. For the Disciples the competing ideals of unity and restorationism "provided grist for the mill of division." They agreed that the Bible was authoritative but not on how it was to be interpreted or by whom.

That cost "one and a half divisions," he goes on to say, and the move from personal authority to institutional authority, which was necessary if there was to be "accountable authority," cost the completion of the second division. The significance of this analysis is that Harrison sees an accountable institutional authority in the restructured Disciples church, however costly the price may have been.[28]

James O. Duke, a theologian at TCU, is not as definitive in his explanation of Disciples polity in a study guide for the laity. "It is a new mix," he tells them, and he might have confused them when he added, "In lieu of a centralized organ of administration, a web of interlacing relationships — shared commitments, interdependent functions, and mutual accountability — are to hold the church together."

After showing that this depends on "covenantal relations," Duke goes on to insist that individuals in any manifestation of the church cannot be "captains of their own ships, with liberty to chart any course they please." But he does not say what the church is to do when people decide to be "captains" instead of covenanters and act in such a way that the church is not held together.[29]

Neither does the "A Word to the Church on Authority" issued by the Commission on Theology and Christian Unity. While it notes that the Disciples have lived for decades without "a clearly defined statement on authority," it concludes after a lengthy statement that authority in the Christian Church (Disciples of Christ) is "a shared authority" between the three manifestations of the church, based on covenant. It does not address the problem of conflict within the shared authority.[30]

A veteran Disciples leader was telling me recently of the problems some regions create for the whole church. One such region took it upon itself to build an elaborate regional facility, going into heavy debt to do so — and cannot now pay the debt! It is pressuring its congregations for more money. When I asked if the General Church could not step in and correct such abuse of power, the answer was no. This is the "shared authority" of "autonomous manifestations"!

But he went on to say that the churches could do something about it — by withholding the money! This goes back to what Hampton Adams said about the ultimate authority for the Disciples being the local church. It is arguable that in most any institution "authority" or "power" is in the hands of those who control the money. The 4,000 Disciples churches had offering receipts in 1992 totaling 288 million dollars. They kept 88.5% of this for their own local ministries, giving 11.5% (33 million) to Disciples Outreach in the other manifestations of the church.

So, the churches have the "power" until it leaves their hands. Once the churches give the money to the Area (where these exist), their particular Region, and the General Church (some given to the General Church is distributed to Regions), the churches have little control over it, if any. This means the "Boards" at various levels have 33 million to allocate to numerous administrative units and various ministries, all of whom compete for what they are certain they need. The decisions are made, as would be expected, by a comparatively small number of people. At that point it is a long way from Indianapolis to Peoria!

Disciples ministers will tell you that their members, who give their share of the 33 million, know little about what goes on in Indianapolis and care less. They may hear or read about this or that program, but what interest they have is confined mostly to the local church. And some charge that Indianapolis doesn't know much about what is going on in the local church, though Richard L. Hamm, the current GMP, is trying to correct this.

The Disciples tradition of congregational freedom and suspicion of ecclesiastical power means that it will continue to grapple with the question of authority. This is as it should be, for they are Disciples, not Presbyterians or Episcopalians. In the meantime we may conclude that "authority," if that is the term to use, is tilted toward the local church. In the future this is more likely to grow stronger than to grow weaker.

The local church has control of its own money and property. It formulates its own programs and calls its minister. It does not have to get approval from anyone for anything it wants to do. While the Region approves candidates for ordination and can remove their "Standing," no one can be ordained except by a local church.

A quarter-of-a-century after restructure the fact remains that no one in the Christian Church (Disciples of Christ) can issue any authoritarian ruling to a local Christian Church. If there is such a thing as "ultimate authority" (on earth) among Campbellites, the local church has it. That is the way it was in the days of Stone and Campbell.

Disciple Renewal Rift

The Disciples of Christ have always been blessed by not only having a right wing, as most denominations have, but a highly visible and vocal right wing. Thus far this has resulted in two major divisions. Some see a third division in the making in the attitude and activities of the Disciple Renewal movement. The leaders of this organization vigorously deny any intention to be divisive. It began in 1985 with the concern of three Disciples ministers and a laywoman, and in 1990 became a full-time ministry for renewal within the Christian Church (Disciples of Christ) with the hiring of a full-time executive director, Kevin D. Ray.

In a presentation before other conservatives, the Independent Christian Church at its 1991 North American Christian Convention, Ray spoke candidly about the concerns of the Renewal movement. He told his Independent brethren that "We are a dying denomination," and that if the present rate of decline continues the Disciples of Christ will cease to exist by 2027. One reason for this, he ventured, is that "we are in a fog doctrinally."

The Disciples, Ray charged, no longer view the Scriptures as authoritative and no longer accept Jesus Christ as the only Savior. "We are a church where subjectivity rules," he said. While the Renewal movement is not intentionally divisive, he sees a "falling away" as inevitable if the Disciples continue their present course of merging with the even more liberal United Church of Christ.

Division can be averted, he allowed, only by conservative Disciples standing up and speaking out. The purpose of his organization is to encourage them to do this. He urged the Independents to seek fellowship with the conservative Disciples, who often feel isolated and rejected.

In a statement titled "Our Witness," Disciple Renewal affirms loyalty to the Christian Church (Disciples of Christ) and insists that it desires "to work within the church rather than seeking to create further division." Its journal, *Disciple Renewal*, which circulates widely among the churches, has the stated purpose of "working and praying for a change in the theology and policies of our denomination" and "to see our beloved church reclaim the vision from which it came." The two basic issues are the authority of the Bible and Jesus Christ as the only Lord and Savior.

The Renewal agenda is more doctrinaire than Disciples usually are, not only affirming loyalty to Christ as Savior but to the Bible as the inspired Word of God and "pure truth without error." But they stop short of making their agenda either a creed or a test of fellowship. They in fact allow for differences and state their willingness to work with all those who affirm the Saviorhood of Christ and the authority of the Bible.[31]

Even though the Preamble to the Design says first of all that "As members of the Christian Church, we believe that Jesus is the Christ, the Son of the living God, and proclaim him Lord and Savior to the world," the executive director of Disciple Renewal implies that the Disciples leaders do not believe this. In a form letter from his office in Lexington, Illinois, Ray emphasized the claims of Jesus as Lord and Savior. He urges his readers "to join Disciple Renewal in this battle to keep Jesus in the center of our faith as the one and only Savior of the world."

The crux of the issue is in the phrase "one and only Savior." The implication is that if one does not believe that Jesus is the only Savior he does not believe that he is Savior. It is an odd kind of doctrinal issue in that the church through the centuries has made it its creed that Jesus is Lord and Savior. That may have implied that Jesus is the only Lord and Savior, but it has never been stated that way, not even in Scripture.

In the same letter Ray pinpoints his concern: "This brings me to the main reason for writing. Lately — surprisingly — sadly, some of our denominational leaders have been assenting to the saving value of all religions." The Disciples leaders are saying that one might be saved in any of the great religions, Ray charges, which can only mean that Jesus is not the only Savior.[32]

At the urging of Disciple Renewal, this obscure and explosive issue was introduced as a resolution to be debated in the 1987 General Assembly. While Resolution 8728 called for a vote on whether Jesus is the only Savior, the Assembly was able to avoid a bitter showdown by an alternate vote that referred it to the Commission on Theology for study. After two years of deliberation the Commission issued its "Report of the Commission on Theology: 'Salvation in Jesus Christ.'"

The battle was joined as the issue became clearer. The conservatives saw the Assembly's reluctance to affirm Jesus as the only Savior as a repudiation of the faith. The liberals saw the resolution as an effort to put God in a box by placing parameters on his sovereign grace to save whom he pleases. It was a "no win" situation from the outset.

If the Commission could not state explicity that Jesus is the only Savior, which it apparently was unprepared to do, it would be accused of "Apostasy in Full Bloom," as one minister wrote across his copy of the Report. The conservatives only needed to point out that the Commission wrote 13 pages about salvation in Christ but could not plainly state that Jesus is the world's only Savior, which was the intent of the resolution before the Assembly.

And never mind how eloquently and unambiguously the Report made Jesus Christ central to the faith of the Disciples of Christ. In a cover letter

to the Report that was sent to all the congregations, Paul Crow, Jr. pointedly stated that the church confesses boldly that "Jesus Christ is Lord and
Savior of the world." The Report itself was unequivocal: "Tbe words 'Jesus
is Savior' expresses a truth fundamental to the faith of the church." It also
said: "The church must confess to itself and the world that its life is
centered on God's revelation in Christ." And yet it demurred from the
implication of Resolution 8728 by adding, "The church must confess its
faith humbly, leaving final judgment in the hands of God."

The Report was saying, perhaps too obliquely, that God is the ultimate
Savior, and he will save whom he will, whether in reference to faith in
Christ or not, which is not all that far out theologically. It is the old
doctrine of "available light" which goes back to Alexander Campbell
himself, who insisted that God judges in reference to the light one has.
Campbell noted that the Bible never condemns the unbeliever, only the
disbeliever. He considered the distinction crucial.

This means that the issue implied in Resolution 8728 is not the real
issue. The real issue is the vast chasm that separates conservatives and
liberals. They are at an impasse so serious that it is questionable that they
can coexist in the same church, especially in reference to the nature of
Scripture. The liberals are as intractable as the conservatives.

An editorial in *The Disciple* recognizes this when it concedes that the
conservatives have been excluded from "the inner sanctum of the Disciples
of Christ," naming in particular the church's theology commission and the
General Board — 170 members but no conservatives! It also admits that
there is no mechanism for minority reports and that conservatives have
been denied a fair public hearing. The editorial urges those in "the seat of
power" to be wary of the temptation to believe they have a corner on truth.
Listening carefully to the voice of truth is crucial, it concludes. It also
warns Disciple Renewal against boasting of being guardians of the "true
faith," implying that others are not.[33]

The Renewal movement, on the other hand, behaves in a manner that
causes Disciples leaders to conclude that another division is in the offing.
The same editorial in *The Disciple* lists recent Renewal activity that it finds
disturbing: a move to establish its own national and regional assemblies, its
own seminary ties, its own link with missionaries, its own pastoral place-
ment process, its own congregational resources. But still the Renewal
people insist that "This Is Not A Split," to quote the title of one of their
pieces written by Douglas A. Harvey. Harvey says his organization only
desires to provide frustrated Disciples with "alternative" ministries, and
that these will not lead to the formation of another denomination.[34]

But Anthony Dunnavant observes that a similar conservative

movement among Disciples that eventually became the Independent Christian Church insisted that it had no divisive intention when it started the North American Christian Convention back in 1927. He refers to the two major divisions thus far as "the chief irony of Disciples history," and then asks, "Are we to become more and more 'ironic'?" alluding to Disciples Renewal as possibly still another division.[35]

That most Disciples are more conservative than their leaders works to the advantage of the Renewal movement, especially when the leaders unnecessarily involve the church in controversial social issues. Beside sending a letter to President Clinton in support of gays in the military, the GMP wrote to the governor of Colorado threatening to boycott the state (by removing the church's 1997 Convention from Denver) if it did not reverse its ruling that denies special rights to gays.

Kevin D. Ray of Disciples Renewal seized the opportunity when he wrote the governor an off-setting letter in support of the state's position. He probably spoke for a majority of Disciples when he told the governor that "official letters from Disciple church leaders often reflect views that very few in the denomination would affirm."[36]

Disciple Renewal saw it as incredible that Disciples leaders would be so insensitive to conservative feelings as to allow condoms to be sold (at 25 cents each!) at the General Assembly in St. Louis in 1993. Even teenagers could buy condoms, complete with instruction sheets, at an AIDS research booth. This was, however, a project of the United Church of Christ and was offensive to Disciples in general. The incident has caused tension between the two churches.

The Renewal people also speak for the majority, if recent surveys are reliable, when they criticize what they see as the Disciples' ultra-liberal stand on abortion, even to the support of the controversial abortion pill known as RU-486, which is illegal in this country.

When Dr. Mike McConachie, pastor of the First Christian Church in Paris, Mo., recalled his distressful experience at the 1993 Assembly, he wrote, "From supporting special rights for homosexuals, to advocating RU-486, to supporting an end to the embargo against Cuba, the liberal viewpoint carried the day." He went on to say, "I cannot think of a single thing that either conservative or moderate Disciples could take comfort in."[37]

It remains to be seen what inroads Disciple Renewal will make in the main body of the church. A number of leaders from the recent past are encouraging them. Their journal occasionally lists congregations that join their ranks, always with a view of renewing the church from within and without leaving.

They might be dismissed as malcontents, as a former GMP seemed to think, or as "dissidents" as Anthony Dunnavant more accurately refers to them. But they could be viewed as the church's wake-up call. A wake-up to the fact that the denomination's leadership is simply too liberal for its own people. The call for unity in diversity is in order, but how diverse can a church be and still be united? To his credit, Richard L. Hamm, the present GMP, is sensitive to the concerns of Disciple Renewal, even appearing on its program.

Passion for Unity: Ecumenicity

In 1952 when W.E. Garrison, at 78, stood before the Third World Conference on Faith and Order, a unit of the World Council of Churches, in Lund, Sweden, he became one of the only two Disciples that have ever had such an honor of addressing this elite ecumenical assembly. Peter Ainslie, one of the founders of the order, had read a paper at the first conference in Lausanne in 1927. He made the unusual recommendation that all the participants celebrate the Lord's Supper together as a testimonial of their oneness and to signify "the equality of all Christians before God." While this was then in advance of the possibilities, it has since been practiced.

Garrison's speech set forth what the Disciples believed to be both desirable and possible for a united church. It would be unity based upon "loyalty to Christ with full freedom of opinion in regard to doctrines and ordinances." He set forth specific characteristics of a united church, the first of which was that members would love one another and have a sense of brotherhood. It also called for an interchangeable ministry and membership, and it urged that "Jesus is Lord" be the only doctrinal test.[38]

The passion for a united church evident in Garrison and Ainslie remains undiminished in current Disciple thought. Ronald Osborn supported restructure on the ground that it might lead to greater ecumenical involvement,[39] and Hampton Adams referred to the Disciples as "a denomination that wants to die" so that it may live more fully in "the universal church of the Lord Jesus Christ."[40] More than either of the other churches of the Movement it insists that "Christian unity is our business."

The Disciples were charter members of what is now the National Council of Churches of Christ, having taken this step at their Omaha convention in 1902. They passed a resolution in support of the federation "as the best means of promoting that complete unity for which our Lord prayed," and they offered to cooperate with any movement that had for its object the unification of believers.[41]

They have not only been participants but leaders in ecumenical efforts since then. They were the first of the denominations to have an ecumenical office in the form of what is now the Council on Christian Unity and their *Christian Union Quarterly* was the first journal on ecumenical studies ever published.

They have also been involved in the World Council of Churches from its first conference in Edinburgh in 1910, even though in that gathering they were virtually ignored. J.H. Garrison, who was present in Edinburgh, called it an unintentional injustice caused by the world churches not knowing anything about the Disciples. "The remedy," he said, "is a more whole-souled participation in all union efforts at home, and greater consecration to the work of missions." They would compel recognition, he avowed, by the place they would win for themselves in ecumenical service.[42]

This proved to be prophetic, for in the decades that followed the Disciples were credited with having helped create the Faith and Order conferences, and Peter Ainslie was hailed by the World Council president as one of the seven apostles of the ecumenical movement. They helped organize the National Council of Churches, and two Disciples have served as president. When the important work, *History of the Ecumenical Movement* (Westminster Press, 1954), was published it was dedicated to the Disciples of Christ for their "untiring ecumenical spirit." And the late general secretary of the World Council, W.A. Visser T Hooft, stated that "The Disciples of Christ have played a very considerable role in the launching, and later on in the development, of the ecumenical movement."[43]

The Council on Christian Unity has led the Disciples into a variety of ecumenical concerns. In 1946 they joined eight other denominations in forming COCU (Conference on Church Union), which has attempted to form a United Church for the U.S.A. The basic plan was the work of C.C. Morrison, a Disciple hailed by John A. Mackay, late president of Princeton Seminary, as "a crusading ecumenist who lived and fought for the kingdom of God."

In more recent years there have been bilateral talks with both the Roman Catholic Church (1977-78) and the Russian Orthodox Church (1987). While in Rome Dr. Paul Crow, Jr. president of the Council on Christian Unity, presented Pope John Paul II with a copy of Thomas Campbell's *Declaration and Address*. He told the pope that "The Disciples of Christ is a unique Church that bears witness to Protestant principles of the Biblical faith and the Catholic principle of the unity of Christ's Church centered in the celebration of his Eucharist."[44]

In the dialogue in Rome the two churches reached an interesting consensus on baptism: "In baptism our sins are forgiven, we become a new creation and we enter into a new relationship with God as his children and as brothers and sisters with each other in Christ." And a Roman Catholic sister, writing of her experience at the conference, went beyond her own church's tradition to say, "It deepened our convictions that the Lord calls us insistently to 'visible ecclesial unity'; that he is himself the Way by which we journey toward the completion of the oneness that is already ours."[45]

Canadian Disciples have not been unmindful of their heritage in ecumenicity. They have been in a three-way union dialogue with the United Church of Canada and the Anglicans, which are thus far unsuccessful. But in a recent analysis on the progress of the ecumenical movement Michael Kinnamon points out that while ecumenical leaders once viewed dialogue as a means to union they now see it as an end in itself. He notes that dialogue is fellowship whether it leads to consensus or not.[46]

All this might confirm what Walter A. Sikes said back in the days of restructure. All such efforts are reflective of "the catholic impulse and intention" inherent in the Movement, but it was necessary to be freed from "the incubus of restorationism" before there could be meaningful dialogue.[47]

Since 1961 the Disciples have talked merger with the United Church of Christ, which is itself a union of four denominations, one of them being, like the Disciples, of Barton W. Stone background. It was supposed that the merger would be a reality before now, but it is presently as unlikely as ever, perhaps because there is not sufficient support for it at the grassroots level in either church.

But the two churches did enter into an "ecumenical partnership" in 1985, the practical effect of which at least means that the Disciples can lend the UCC money! They also share administrative work in education and missions. Officially the partnership means "we wish to express our unity in Christ by doing nothing alone which can be done together." They are "Partners for the Glory of God."[48]

It is not surprising that the conservative Disciples are offended by the UCC partnership, mainly because, as the Disciple Renewal puts it, the UCC is arguably "the most apostate denomination in the United States." Their main concern is that the UCC ordains gay and lesbian ministers, and they do not want this imposed on Disciples through a mutual recognition of ministers, which is one goal of the partnership.[49] They seem unaware that the Disciples have already ordained gays!

However any one project may fair, it is evident that what Howard E. Short said long ago continues to be fundamental in the heritage of the Disciples of Christ — "Christian unity is our business." Mark G. Toulouse put it this way only recently: "When Disciples assert that the 'church of Christ is one,' they also assert their responsibility to work toward the natural expression of that unity."[50]

The State of the Church

When C. William Nichols, interim GMP, reported to the General Board at its 1992 meeting in St. Louis on the state of the Disciples of Christ, he said that there was good news and bad news. The good news was that the church had been given a gospel of wholeness to preach to the whole world. The bad news was that the church proclaiming that gospel is, in itself, anything but whole.[51]

While the GMP did not list specifics, some of his colleagues have sought to identify the "bad news" in reference to the state of the church. One thing, according to Friedly and Cummins, is that the membership is graying and the church has failed to appeal to the current generation of young adults, a problem not unique to Disciples. "Fully 62% of the Disciples of Christ in the mid-1980s were 55 years or older," they noted, and then added, "Yet 40% of the U.S. adults were in the 18-34."

Friedly and Cummins point out that for its first 133 years the church's growth was a "given," but beginning in 1965 it has been in a constant "decline of membership," ranging from 1% to 3% a year. They note that the continual decline has rallied the conservatives in their call for more effective evangelism, and has put the leadership in Indianapolis on the defensive.[52]

Paul Crow, Jr., in explaining why the progress toward merger with the United Church of Christ has been so slow, named a more basic weakness in today's Disciples of Christ. While there is "a diminished commitment to Church unity" in both denominations, he blames his own church for a "silence about Christian unity" in both congregations and seminaries that is "surprising, even shocking." He says his people are too concerned for their own "denominational strategies and structures" to give more than lip service to unity with other churches. He predicts that if a passion for unity does not once again become "central to our self-identity" ecumenical concerns will be "marginal."[53]

There is much concern about Disciples today "recovering their identity," as suggested in the title of the study by Friedly and Cummins, *The Search for Identity*. When Clark M. Williamson, professor at Christian Theological Seminary in Indianapolis, wrote along these lines he said that "If Disciples today are to recover their identity as a people witnessing to the all-inclusive love of God" they must free themselves from "the embarrassing legalisms and moralisms that vitiate our witness to Christian unity."

Williamson is saying that the Disciples, even after two major divisions, still have a hermeneutical problem. He wishes that Alexander Campbell's liberal rules of interpretation were better known among Disciples. He fears that the church has ceased to think theologically, and when this happens it loses its ecclesial existence and becomes "a privatistic, alienated association of people providing such services as the relief of psychic distress and institutional maintenance."[54]

The professor indirectly points to a problem that we have already referred to, which may be the most serious that the Disciples face, the dilemma of a church that has a liberal leadership and a conservative membership. This involves far more than the old liberal/conservative differences over biblical criticism, which, when treated with sensitivity, pose no serious threat. It is rather the more emotionally-charged social and moral issues that are causing rift among Disciples.

Beside the differences on gay rights and biblical inerrancy referred to above, there are other astounding findings: 72% of Disciples clergy allow abortion for any reason, while only 25% of the laity does; 83% of the clergy favor more welfare spending, while only 10% of the laity does.

When compared to Presbyterians and Baptists, who were included in the survey, the Disciples clergy was comparable to the Presbyterian clergy but much more liberal than their Baptist counterparts. The Disciples laity was considerably more conservative than the Presbyterian laity and only slightly less conservative than the Baptist laity, which is less conservative than the Baptist clergy!

The research also revealed that 91% of Disciples laity believes that homosexual sex is always wrong and 83% believe that pornography corrupts, 66% insisting it should be outlawed; 85% believe that extramarital sex is always wrong and 48% that premarital sex is always wrong; 73% believe divorce should be more difficult. Again, the Disciples laity was more conservative than the Presbyterians and slightly less conservative than the Baptists.

The rift is equally serious on theological issues. The average Disciple would likely be surprised that only 46% of his clergy believes that Jesus is the only way to salvation in comparison to 97% of the Baptists and 65% of the Presbyterians. Nearly all Baptist ministers believe the devil actually exists and half of the Presbyterians do, but only one-third of Disciples do. And only 38% of Disciples ministers believe that Jesus will return to earth someday, while virtually all Baptists do and over half of the Presbyterians do.[55]

These figures are misleading if they imply that the Disciples ministers do not believe anything much. But this is precisely the Disciples' problem, the impression that they are so extremely liberal that they do not really believe anything substantial. This led one prominent pastor to preach on "Do We Believe Anything?" While he concluded that they do indeed believe "plenty," such as that God is at work in Christ healing broken relationships, he conceded that because of the church's great diversity and its avoidance of creedal absolutes the question is appropriate. He concluded his sermon with an appeal to Disciples to "find our mission and our fulfillment in being the people of God and in living out this vocation toward Christian unity."[56]

In response to the research on the liberal/conservative rift, Charles H. Bayer concedes that because of "radically different world views" the rift may be "essentially unfixable." He says that "we liberals" are not going to retreat to a Baconian mentality that holds to biblical inerrancy, nor will they abandon 200 years of biblical scholarship.

It is not the conservatives that are the problem, he insists, but that "We clergy have abandoned, practically, our vocation of teachers of the faith, and have become directors of small businesses and keepers of the institution, marketers, and public relations experts."

The problem, Bayer goes on to say, is that "we clergy have abdicated our teaching task." The liberal church, he avows, has not lost large numbers to fundamentalism but to secularism. "When the line between the church and the world becomes so fuzzy," he concludes, "why bother to get up and go to church? If we have not heard the thunderous footsteps of those who have voted with their feet we have not been listening." Secularism in the church is the problem, he says, not how to accommodate the gospel to the fundamentalists so that they will be comfortable enough to stay with us.[57]

The response of D. Newell Williams is more conciliatory to the conservatives. He concedes that in their theology modern Disciples have been "remarkably vague," and they have left the impression that any theological position is acceptable so long as unity is a possibility. Moreover, he insists that liberals must start listening to the conservatives. Like Bayer, he calls on ministers to become teachers in the churches, as well as the academicians, who have too long been aloof from the congregations.

And churches must free the preachers to study more so that they can improve their sermons, which are so often irrelevant. Too, the Disciples need to undertake a fresh appraisal of their history so that they can see that they have a theological heritage.

As for the liberal/conservative gap, Williams says that the Disciples must continue to be a church that accepts diversity, and to obstruct the role of either liberals or conservatives would be a violation of Disciples identity. They must therefore find their unity, not in a particular approach to the Bible, but in the glorious gospel of Jesus Christ, a distinction he boldly makes after the order of Alexander Campbell, who insisted that it is the gospel that unites us, not the Bible.

Williams further notes that the most rapidly growing "religious" sector is not the conservatives but the nonaffiliated sector of highly educated younger adults. These, he says, are closer to where Disciples ministers now are than the present active members. The church must be in a position to reach this sector, which it cannot do if it sacrifices diversity to become either liberal or conservative.

While he is at it, Williams speaks to what the Disciples mission should be. The church must do more than to accept diversity. If it reaches the nonaffiliates and other Americans they must stand for positions that are "theologically and morally plausible." They must also speak a word that adds "a quality to human existence that cannot be found outside the Christian community." This word is nothing other than "the gospel of God's gracious love for all made known in the apostolic witness of Jesus Christ."[58]

Williams' view of the Disciples future is reminiscent of what W.E. Garrison said a generation earlier, "That destiny as I see it is to become a strong body of devoted and intelligent Christians, carrying their share of the common responsibility that rests upon all Christians, united by such ties as may hereafter unite all Christians."

Garrison went on to echo what Barton W. Stone envisioned at Cane Ridge back in 1804 when all this first began: "and in a future beyond our calculation but not beyond our faith and hope, losing their distinctive identity by 'sinking (or I would say rising) into union with the Body of Christ at large."[59]

ENDNOTES

[1]A. Dale Fiers in Loren E. Lair, *The Christian Church and Its Future* (St. Louis: Bethany Press, 1971), p. 7.

[2]Henry E. Webb, *In Search of Christian Unity* (Cincinnati: Standard Publishing Co., 1990), pp. 365f.

[3]Winfred E. Garrison, *A Fork in the Road* (pamphlet) (Indianapolis: Pension Fund of Christian Churches, 1964).

[4]Lester G. McAllister and William E. Tucker, *Journey in Faith* (St. Louis: Bethany Press, 1975), p. 445.

[5]Private interview with Lester G. McAllister.

[6]Robert O. Fife, *Ecclesiological Issues in the Restructure of the Christian Church (Disciples of Christ)*, pamphlet (Los Angeles: Westwood Christian Foundation, 1981), pp. 1-10.

[7]Virgil A. Sly, "The Importance of Brotherhood Restructure," *Mid-Stream*, Vol. 3, No. 1 (Sept., 1963), p. 67.

[8]Loren E. Lair, "Our Present Organization and the Issues the Commission Must Face in the Task of Restructure," *Mid-Stream*, Vol. 3, No. 1 (Sept., 1963), pp. 42-57.

[9]Mark G. Toulouse, *Joined In Discipleship: The Maturing of a Religious Movement* (St. Louis: Chalice Press, 1992), p. 208.

[10]*Ibid.*, p. 211.

[11]*Ibid.*, p. 214.

[12]Charles H. Bayer, "A Response," *Disciples Theological Digest*, Vol 7, No. 2 (1992), p. 28.

[13]Loren E. Lair, *The Christian Church and Its Future*, pp. 134, 231.

[14]Ronald E. Osborn, *Toward the Christian Church* (Louisville: Commission on Brotherhood Restructure, 1964), p. 37.

[15]Charles H. Bayer, *The Disciple* (Jan. 1984), p. 38.

[16]D.Newell Williams, "Disciples and the Liberal/Conservative Divide," *Disciples Theological Digest*, Vol 7, No. 2 (1992), p. 19.

[17]Quoted in Henry E. Webb, *In Search of Christian Unity*, pp. 371f.

[18]D.Ray Lindley, "The Structure of the Church," *The Reformation of Tradition* (Ronald E. Osborn, editor) (St. Louis: Bethany Press, 1963), p. 191.

[19]W.A. Welsh, "What Restructure Means to Me," *Mid-Stream*, Vol. 3, No. 1 (Sept., 1963), p. 103.

[20]Personal interview, Dallas, Texas, Jan. 12, 1994.

[21]Richard L. Harrison, Jr., "Places of Authority in the Disciples of Christ: An Historical Reflection," *Reappraising the Disciples Tradition for the 21st Century* (Lexington, KY Lexington Theological Seminary, 1987), p. 323. Reprint from *Mid-Stream*, Vol 26, No. 3 (July 1987).

[22]Robert L. Friedly and D. Duane Cummins, *The Search For Identity: Disciples of Christ: The Restructure Years* (St. Louis: CBP Press, 1987), pp. 9f.

[23]Hampton Adams, *Why I Am A Disciple Of Christ* (New York: Thomas Nelson, 1957), p. 136.

[24]Michael Kinnamon, *Disciples of Christ In The 21st Century* (St. Louis: CBN Press, 1988), pp. 16f.

[25]Michael Kinnamon, "Authority: Reflections on the Future of Disciples Tradition," *Reappraising the Disciples Tradition for the 21st Century*, p. 336. Reprint from *Midstream*, Vol 26, No. 3, (July 1987).

[26]Dale Patrick and Mary W. Patrick, "Fundamental Issues of Authority in the Church Today," *Ibid.*, pp. 324f.

[27]Toulouse, *Joined In Discipleship*, pp. 215f.

[28]Richard L. Harrison, Jr., "Places of Authority in the Disciples of Christ: An Historical Reflection," *Ibid.*, pp. 317f.

[29]James O. Duke, *What Sort of Church Are We?*, (Study Series 1) (St. Louis:

Council on Christian Unity, n.d.), p. 28.

[30]This report appears as Appendix B in William Baird, *What Is Our Authority?*, Study Series 2 on *The Nature of the Church* (St. Louis: Council on Christian Unity, n.d.)

[31]Kevin D. Ray, *Fellowship With Disciple Churches In Renewal*, NACC (July 12,1991), Denver CO, Typeset.

[32]Kevin D. Ray, Letter (Nov. 5, 1993), Disciple Renewal, Box 109, Lexington, IL.

[33]Editorial, "Sowing Seeds of Schism?," *The Disciple*, (Nov. 1993), p. 58.

[34]*The Disciple*, (Nov. 1993), p. 22.

[35]Anthony Dunnavant, "Diagnosing Disciples Divisions," *The Disciple*, (Nov. 1993), pp. 19f.

[36]*Disciple Renewal*, Vol 8, Nos. 8&9 (Aug/Sept 1993), p. 17.

[37]."Reflections on St. Louis," *Ibid.*, p. 12.

[38]Paul Crow, Jr., "The Christian Church (Disciples of Christ) in the Ecumenical Movement," *The Christian Church (Disciples of Christ): An Interpretative Examination in the Cultural Context* (St. Louis: Bethany Press, 1973), pp. 268-269.

[39]Ronald E. Osborn, *Toward the Christian Church*, p. 37.

[40]Hampton Adams, *Why I Am A Disciple of Christ*, p. 109.

[41]W.E. Garrison, *Christian Unity and the Disciples of Christ* (St. Louis: Bethany Press, 1955), p. 124.

[42]*Ibid.*, pp. 178f.

[43]In letter to W.E. Garrison, *Christian Unity*, p. 265.

[44] *Disciples of Christ-Roman Catholic International Commission for Dialogue* (mimeographed), Alverna Retreat Center, Indianapolis (1977), Instituto Ravasco, Rome (1978).

[45]Agnes Cunningham, "A Continuing Pilgrimage: Disciples-Roman Catholics in Dialogue," *Mid-Stream*, Vol. 17, No. 2 (April, 1979).

[46]Michael Kinnamon, "Does the Ecumenical Movement Have a Future?," *Lexington Theological Quarterly*, Vol. 28, No. 1 (Spring 1993), p. 28.

[47]Walter W. Sikes, "The Disciples' Hope for Christian Unity," *Ecumenical Studies Series*, Vol. 4, No. 1 (Sept., 1958), pp. 54-55.

[48]*Business Docket and Program: Partners for the Glory of God*, General Assembly/Synod, A Common Gathering of Christian Church (Disciples of Christ) United Church of Christ, St. Louis, 1993, p. 440.

[49]*Disciple Renewal*, Vol 8, Nos. 8&9 (Aug/Sept), pp. 7,17.

[50]Toulouse, *Joined in Discipleship*, p. 193.

[51]*Yearbook and Directory*, 1993, p. 111.

[52]Friedly and Cummins, *The Search For Identity*, pp. 15f.

[53]Paul A. Crow, Jr., "The Lure and Languishing of Disciples-United Church of Christ Unity," *Mid-Stream*, Vol. 32, No. 3 (July 1993), p. 6.

[54]Clark M. Williamson, "Theological Reflections and Disciple Renewal," *Disciples of Christ in the 21st Century*, Michael Kinnamon, Ed. (St. Louis: CBP Press, 1988), pp. 96, 101.

[55]For this extensive research see *A Case Study of Mainstream Protestantism: The Disciples' Relation to American Culture, 1880-1989*, D. Newell Williams, Ed., (Grand Rapids: Eerdmans, 1991), pp. 363-415. Cf. D. Newell Williams, "Disciples and the Liberal/Conservative Divide," *Disciples Theological Digest*, Vol. 7, No. 2 (1992), pp. 5f.

[56]Dan P. Moseley, "Do We Believe Anything?," *Disciples Theological Digest*, Vol. 7, No. 1 (1992), pp. 33f.

[57]Charles H. Bayer, "A Response," *Disciples Theological Digest*, Vol 7, No. 2 (1992), pp. 27f.

[58]D. Newell Williams, "Future Prospects of the Christian Church (Disciples of Christ) *A Case Study of Mainstream Protestantism*, D. Newell Williams, Ed. (Grand Rapids: Eerdmans, 1991), pp. 561f.

[59]Winfred E. Garrison, *Heritage and Destiny* (St. Louis: Bethany Press, 1961), p. 156.

21

THE THREE CHURCHES OF THE MOVEMENT
THEIR RELATION TO EACH OTHER

These churches today exhibit only faint family resemblances.

Back in 1850 one of Alexander Campbell's antagonists, Heman Humphrey, one-time president of Amherst College, predicted that upon Campbell's demise the community he had begun would "dissolve, scatter, and be absorbed in the great Babel that now is,"[1] a prophecy that was made now and again through the years in one form or another. He must have been a better college president than a prophet, for by the turn of the century Campbell's people numbered a million, and today they total some three million in some 20,000 congregations, even if divided into three separate churches. The first fact would no doubt have shocked Humphrey, the second fact, Campbell.

Even when faced with the divisive problem of slavery in 1845, Campbell was convinced that "We are the only religious community in the civilized world whose principles (unless we abandon them) can preserve us from such an unfortunate predicament" as fission.[2] Other pioneers were as hopeful, if not as certain, as Campbell for the continued unity of their unity movement. Referring to the union that was effected between the Stone and Campbell forces in Lexington in 1832, John T. Johnson exulted: "Thus out of two, making one New body, not Campbellites nor Stoneites, but Christians; and so making peace. May it long continue to bless our land!"

Responding to this hopeful outlook, Barton W. Stone said, "From our heart we say with brother Johnson, we trust in God that no such disaster as that of division shall ever befall us." He ventured to add that if the principles set forth by Campbell were adhered to division can never come.[3] We have already noted that even in the aftermath of the bitter Civil War that Moses E. Lard insisted that "We can never divide."

It is tragic enough for any church to split, but for one born of a passion for the unity of all believers to divide is indeed a disaster, as Stone put it. Or so it seems. But one prominent Disciple, Howard E. Short, editor emeritus of *The Disciple*, sees it otherwise: "The two complete breaks that have befallen the Stone-Campbell movement may be stages of growth. It is possible for all three existing groups, as they pursue their chosen ends, to contribute something to the kingdom of God on earth. In fact, it is almost a certainty."[4]

But if there must be three separate churches, each pursuing its own mission for the kingdom of God on earth, must there be no fellowship between them, no common missions, no cooperative efforts? Must the historians of today have to chronicle that "the three main groups deriving from the Stone-Campbell movement are seldom in contact with one another"?[5] Are there no advantages to a common heritage?

Back in 1976, when James L. Merrell, then editor of *The Disciple*, responded to an article in the *U.S. Catholic* on the Churches of Christ he explained that while the Disciples and Churches of Christ are "miles apart," they do have common roots that are important to recall from time to time. He went on to tell the Catholic editor that the Disciples can have more meaningful dialogue with the non-instrumental group than with the Independents. "After there has been a definite break in fellowship for a period of time," he says, "we then have opportunity to talk with one another on a different plane." Now that a clear split had come from the Independents, he adds, he looks forward to similar opportunities for discussion with them, in another decade or so.[6]

One is left to wonder when all those conversations took place between Disciples and Churches of Christ that Merrell refers to, except perhaps on an individual basis. There has in fact been no bilateral conversations between these two churches since their separation a century ago. It is as if they had no common heritage whatever. The exclusivism of the Churches of Christ and the more ambitious ecumenical endeavors of the Disciples make any meaningful dialogue unlikely for the foreseeable future.

Another Disciple, W. Clark Gilpin, not only saw "only faint family resemblances" between the three churches, but recognized that their disparate development has insulated them from each other and that any contact between them will be rare. Accounting for the break with the Independents as well as the Church of Christ, Gilpin concluded that the Disciples chose unity and critical biblical scholarship while the other groups opted for restorationism and doctrinal conservatism.

Since the three churches have appropriated their history differently, they will come up with different answers to their problems, Gilpin noted. While deploring "the disfellowshipping mania" and an "intolerant exclusivism" in Churches of Christ, he was encouraged that some leaders were calling for a "unity in diversity" that may well make a difference in the future for this group.[7]

Marginal Contacts

One might conclude from all this that there is no good news in reference to possible dialogue between the three churches. The fact is that in recent decades there has been some meaningful contact, even if only marginal.

There are at least three institutions that serve all three churches equally. The European Evangelistic Society sponsors the Institute for the Study of Christian Origins in Tübingen, Germany, which invites scholars from all wings of the Movement to teach and do research at one of the great learning centers of the world. Founded in 1942 by Ludwig von Gerdtell, who once had a public debate with Adolf Hitler, it is a missionary outreach to the academic community in Tübingen.

While listed in the Disciples *Yearbook* as a "reporting unit" of that denomination, its board, staff, and officers have been mostly Independents, including Dean E. Walker who served as president. Several scholars from Churches of Christ have done research there and some serve on its executive committee. It has in fact suffered criticism from ultra liberals and ultra conservatives alike for serving what it calls "the total heritage of this movement."[8]

The Disciples of Christ Historical Society in Nashville, though a legal child of the Disciples, is open to all three churches, and all three are represented on the board. The Churches of Christ use it the most and support it the least, while the Disciples support it the most and use it the least!

While much of the society's operational expense is paid by the Disciples, the elegant Gothic library, named for pioneer Thomas W. Phillips, was funded by the Phillips family of Butler, Pa., of the Independent Christian Church. The family did this with the understanding that the following provision of the constitution would always be honored, which says that the society

> . . . shall concern itself impartially with the total heritage of the movement embracing Disciples of Christ, Christian Churches, Churches of Christ, and related groups; shall render services impartially to all such groups, and shall seek support from all such groups, and shall commit itself to no particular interpretation of the movement or its history.[9]

The society publishes books written by scholars of all three churches, issues *Discipliana*, a 50-year old research journal, and sponsors the Reed Lectures, which are usually given by professors from institutions representing all three wings. The library is the largest depository of literature on the Stone-Campbell tradition, and it attracts hundreds of scholars annually, providing rare opportunities for personal and academic fellowship for those who influence the thought of the Movement.

Aware that there were eight worldwide church families with world gatherings but none for Disciples of Christ, Jesse M. Bader complained that the Disciples were so preoccupied with contact with other denominations that they neglected fellowship within their own family. This led to his organizing the World Convention of Churches of Christ in 1930. There have been conventions every four years since 1930 in eight different nations, attended by thousands from most every country where there are Disciples.

Americans may dominate the conventions in number, but not necessarily in service or influence. The current president, Marj Black, is a Canadian, the executive director, Lyndsay A. Jacobs (fulltime) is a New Zealander, and on the executive committee are people from Australia, New Zealand, Canada, Puerto Rico, Belize, and Zimbabwe as well as the U.S.A., and they represent all three churches of the Movement. There is always a large delegation of Australians and New Zealanders at the conventions to the delight of the Americans, with whom there are close ties.

Recent conventions in Honolulu (1980), Jamaica (1984) New Zealand (1988), and Long Beach (1992) have realized Jesse Bader's hopes of providing rich fellowship for "Disciples" from around the world. The next one will be in Calgary (1996) and Sydney is scheduled for 2000. Anyone interested in the "heart" of the Movement from a world perspective would do well to attend. There is always someone special to give the endowed "Bader Lecture." At Long Beach it was Fred Craddock, who practiced unity in the presence of a very diverse group as well as preached it.

The international office of the WCCC is in Nashville. Its new logo specifically names "Christian, Churches of Christ, Disciples," and its mailouts explicitly state that it is a global fellowship for all heirs of the Stone-Campbell Movement. A recent newsletter stated, "World Convention has continued to make good contacts with Church of Christ people in Nashville and elsewhere. We are hoping for a significant number of Church of Christ people at Calgary."[10]

Another area of marginal contact is in recently published books that encourage those in the three churches to a greater awareness and understanding of each other. An instance of this is the first edition of this book, which circulated widely in all three wings and was generally accepted as a nonpartisan account of the Movement. A physician in California and a member of the Independent Christian Church was so persuaded that a reading of this book would provide insights into the true nature of the Movement that he offered to send a copy free of charge to any Church of Christ minister who would promise to read it. Some 2,000 of them made the promise by returning a signed card.

It was a unique circumstance for a layman of one church to fund a project at considerable expense to send a history book to 2,000 clergy of another church. The results of the project were, insofar as we could determine, generally encouraging.

One noble effort that had great promise was the publication of *Fellowship*, which began in 1974 and whose board was composed of some of the ablest and most dedicated men in both churches, with some from Churches of Christ also involved. There were three editors of the quarterly, one from each of the fellowships, and its purpose was "to encourage a deeper sense of unity and fellowship among Disciples of Christ (Christian Churches), Christian Churches and Churches of Christ, to foster open and free discussion, and to rediscover the principles of our cherished heritage in reference to our present task."

While it lived but three years, the journal was a depository of numerous essays that spoke to the vital issues confronting the Movement, such as Dean E. Walker's essay in which he said, "I affirm my conviction that we cannot create unity of Christians, nor construct unity, nor 'find' it in political or sociological devices. But we can receive it from its Author, that gift Christ brought to us in His incarnation, that unity for which He prayed on our behalf . . ."[11]

That the journal did not survive when it had so much going for it says something of the lack of substantial concern in the 1970's for the internal unity of the Movement. There is evidence that this is changing in the 1990's, as we shall see.

The ACU Press in Abilene, Texas, serving Churches of Christ in particular, has in recent years published books that tend to breakdown the old barriers. In C. Leonard Allen's *Distant Voices* Churches of Christ people read of heroes and heroines that they did not know they had, some being women preachers! And in Allen's *Discovering Our Roots*, which he co-authored with Richard T. Hughes, these people see that they are not the restored or transplanted first-century church, as they have been told all these years, but a 20th century church with roots in the Lutheran Reformation, the Puritans, and the Disciples of Christ.

This is to say that the various branches of the Movement are having some dialogue by way of historical studies. The Disciples of Christ Historical Society regularly brings together historians from all three churches to share in research projects. Its recent publication of *Cane Ridge in Content* (1992) is an instance of this. In this book historians from all three churches present essays on their common heritage in Barton W. Stone.

The Westwood Christian Foundation in Los Angeles has now published three Restoration Lectures, one from each of the three wings of the Movement. The atmosphere created by all these dialogues has impressive unifying effect, not only on those who take part but on those that read the material.

Especially significant is the proposed publication of *An Encyclopedic Dictionary of the Stone-Campbell Movement* which will briefly but accurately define or interpret names, groups, dates, places, and organizations within the life of the Movement. There will be three general editors, one from each of the churches, and 15 to 24 associate editors, as well as a number of advisers, again from all three churches. Already some 2,400 titles have been identified. This one-volume publication of some 1,000 pages, due off the press by 1996, proposes to cut across all lines and divisions within the Movement, treating all subjects in an open and nonpartisan manner.

That a project of this dimension, requiring the cooperation and sacrifice of many leaders in all three churches, could be realized in our time reveals that there is a measure of "practical" unity within the Movement. Such journalistic fellowship, as it might be called, would have been impossible only a few years ago.

This journalistic fellowship has reached such maturity as to generate some responsible criticism and evaluation of each church's role in the Christian world. W. Clark Gilpin, a Disciples historian, did a comparative study on the Disciples and Churches of Christ in a book edited by Martin Marty. They have common roots but have taken divergent paths, he told the readers. He explained that the Disciples, with considerable difficulty, were able to move "from movement to Church," whereas the Churches of Christ, because of its "restorationist repudiation of denominational Christianity," has isolated itself from the Christian world.

Gilpin went on to say that the Churches of Christ has concerns that are "nearly incomprehensible" to the outsider. But he was impressed with the signs of change he saw, such as editors and ministers calling for unity in diversity. He read with interest *Voices of Concern* (1966), edited by Robert Meyers, a compilation of essays by talented and well-educated members of the Churches of Christ, tired of all the sectarianism, calling for "a more charitable tomorrow." Gilpin finds sufficient reasons to conclude that that "charitable tomorrow" is dawning for the Churches of Christ.[12]

C. Leonard Allen, on the other hand, has offered some critical evaluation of the Disciples from the perspective of a Churches of Christ scholar. He sees three tensions afflicting the Disciples, all growing out of their obsession for the church: freedom and conformity, church and world, past and present. He suggests ways these tensions might be eased. He warns that the passion for freedom, which has always dominated Disciples thought, can prove to be an insufficient cord to bind a church in community. There must also be a structured and responsible theology, which early Disciples found in Alexander Campbell.

While Allen deplores the sectarian restorationism in his own church, he cautions the Disciples that to reject the ideal of restoration is to lose a powerful source for maintaining Christian identity in the world. He appeals to the "restorationist impulse in its highest form" as a way to say No to the world. Disciples suffer from an acute antitraditionalism in its rejection of conformity (restoration) and its desire to be modern. The illusion of historylessness has made it difficult for Disciples to come to terms with their own history. If the restorationist Churches of Christ risk seeking a naive utopian past, the Disciples risk seeking a naive utopian future. Both thus have an identity crisis. Allen urges both churches to grapple seriously with their past, "living out of the past," as he puts it.[13]

Equally penetrating as an analysis of the Disciples of Christ and the Churches of Christ, even if more subtle, is an essay by M. Eugene Boring of TCU on J.W. McGarvey and Herbert L. Willett. While he never mentions the two churches, it becomes evident to the reader that the Churches of Christ stand in the tradition of McGarvey while the Disciples are after the order of Willett. These two men represent two schools of thought in what Boring calls "the crucial third generation" of Disciples history.

McGarvey was rural, regional, status quo. Willett was urban, cosmopolitan, progressive. McGarvey was absolute and exclusive. Willett was relative and inclusive. While both were effective, informed teachers, McGarvey taught by indoctrination, even memorization, while Willett taught by education. McGarvey opposed modern biblical criticism, Willett supported it. McGarvey shared the third generation's restorationist myth of a pure first-century church, while Willett viewed history as progress. To McGarvey the book of Acts was the core gospel, to Willett it was the gospels.

And yet, as Boring notes, the two men were in the same church, both loved the Bible and Disciples tradition, and both were able, sincere scholars. While McGarvey stands within Churches of Christ tradition, it is ironic that he never left the Disciples to join the new church, a product of the third generation, even though he adamantly opposed instrumental music. Boring tells us that the church can accept such diversity as McGarvey and Willett without division.

But he also observes that those Disciples in the crucial third generation who could not follow McGarveyism "lost their grip on the Bible," which became a factor for the statistical decline in the generation that followed. Willett, however, as liberal and modern as he was, never lost his hold on Scripture. This is an example of how the past helps us to understand where we are today.[14]

While the foregoing survey of relationships might be viewed as only marginal in terms of internal unity, it is possible to see things the way Howard E. Short does:

> We no longer fear or fight one another. Individuals among us have never found it necessary to break the bonds of friendship. In the Disciples of Christ Historical Society and in the World Convention of Churches of Christ we maintain fellowship in mutual concerns. Thus, a new kind of unity – the recognition of one another as bearers of a common load – is possible. Indeed, it is in existence.[15]

The Irenic Spirit
"Wherever God has a child, I have a brother or sister."

Just as the Stone-Campbell Movement had its pioneers in bearing the plea for union to the Christian world, it has also had its pioneers in calling for the internal unity of the Movement, once the divisions had taken their toll.

One such was Ernest Beam, minister of the Lakewood Church of Christ in Long Beach, Ca. in the 1950's. With a passion for unity between Christian Church people and his own non-instrument church, his congregation adopted the plan of alternating services, one without the instrument and one with it. This church also became the focal point of a one-man attack upon what it considered a sectarian spirit in Churches of Christ, led by Beam, who published *The Christian Forum*, a monthly journal that insisted it was "Undenominational-Unsectarian."

Beam laid the blame for "twenty plus divisions" in the Churches of Christ at the feet of the editors of the *Gospel Advocate* and *Firm Foundation*, the church's leading journals, and the leaders of the Christian colleges. He called them the "new digressives" in that they preach "another gospel" when they make matters of human judgment the law of God. In a most unique document that he called "Manuscript C," Beam addressed an open letter to these leaders who had "promoted, permitted, and perpetuated" these divisions. He solicited their help in encouraging the brethren to "receive one another as the unsectarian gospel requires."

He told them that for 25 years he had preached that "there is the realm of faith where God speaks and we are bound; and there is the realm of necessary judgment where God has not spoken, but where we must speak, and wherein we are not to bind one another." He went on to say that as much harm is done to the church by making God speak when He has not spoken as to ignore Him when He does speak.

This was the essence of Beam's appeal in his journal. Men make parties, he insisted, and beget perverted gospels by binding their opinions on other men's consciences. Sometimes he spoke with prophetic wrath: "How ugly are the feet of those who preach the bad news of hate and division and leave in their wake leanness of soul and hungry hearts and confusion upon confusion." He complained that "we have promoted a new party" when instrumental music, Sunday schools, and millennial views are made tests of loyalty.[16]

Beam offered to bring his message of reconciliation to the colleges, but he was never invited. He pled for space in the leading journals, but was turned away, even though others were allowed to criticize his views. His church was viewed with suspicion. But his plea for unity ended only with his death in 1957. While he apparently had little impact upon the leadership that he sought to influence, he aroused many from the rank and file who had a passion for unity and were prepared to follow others who were soon to appear, taking up where he left off.

An irenic voice among Christian Churches in the 1940's was J.D. Murch who worked with Church of Christ leaders in conducting unity conferences of some moment. While addressing a Christian Church on unity, Murch was approached by an elder of a non-instrument congregation who expressed hope that the spirit he manifested would promote unity among their divided people. This brought Murch into contact with Claude E. Witty, minister of the West Side-Central Church of Christ in Detroit, with whom he launched the Murch-Witty unity meetings, a pioneering effort that had a hard time of it.

While Murch was supported by his church generally and the *Christian Standard* in particular, Witty was unable to sell the idea to his people. The leading Church of Christ papers either ignored or opposed the effort, and while he was able to bring such eminent leaders as H. Leo Boles to the forums, they were not as irenic as he, sometimes using language that was counter productive.

Boles, for instance, told the forum: "Brethren, put away the organ and you will be where the pioneers stood when the unity of God's people was enjoyed . . . if you think there will be a compromise or surrender by the churches of Christ on this point you are mistaken," and went on to accuse the Christian Church of binding its opinions upon others.[17]

Murch nonetheless called the effort "an adventure in unity," for he and Witty believed that "something should be done about the scandal of division in the ranks of the Restoration movement." They created an "Approach to Unity" that called for prayer, study, and discussion, which brought small groups together in several cities, and issued a *Christian*

Unity Quarterly, edited by the two men, and gave wide distribution to a tract, *Christian Unity: Churches of Christ and Christian Churches*.[18]

Murch concluded that the meetings, which brought some 50 key men together from the two churches, were helpful in cultivating acquaintances and clarifying issues, but there is no hard evidence that the adventure was any less frustrating or more fruitful than Beam's efforts a few years later. The important thing about the Murch-Witty gatherings is that they happened at all, for they demonstrated that divided brethren can get together, giving hope to some that sooner or later something substantial might happen.

In 1969, three decades later, Murch, along with Reuel Lemmons, who as an editor bishop encouraged unity efforts among Churches of Christ, brought a new generation of leaders of the two churches together in Memphis and St. Louis, but these were on a much smaller scale than the meetings with Witty, which sometimes attracted a thousand people.

The Murch-Lemmons gatherings were of the top echelon, being editors, college presidents, professors, and leading ministers. When asked why he called such a group, Murch replied: "For many years I have had the conviction that the churches of Christ (non-instrument) and the Christian churches and churches of Christ were brethren committed to a common faith and practice in all matters essential to salvation." He went on to explain that his earlier efforts with Witty encouraged him to join with Lemmons in these new dialogues.[19]

When Lemmons, editor of the *Firm Foundation*, was asked if he saw instrumental music as the main roadblock to fellowship with the Christian Church, his answer was no. "The thing that really separates these two great groups of the brotherhood," he said, "is their respective position regarding the scriptures." He explained that the Churches of Christ speak where the Bible speaks and are silent where the Bible is silent, while the Christian Churches speak where the Bible speaks and "where the Bible is silent we are free to choose."[20]

It was left to Robert O. Fife of the Chistian Church to respond to Lemmons' implication that his people should give up the instrument because of the silence of Scripture. Fife said that the suggestion was a reasonable one, but that his people would take the proposal more seriously when the Churches of Christ that have the Sunday school are willing to give it up for the sake of unity with the hundreds of Churches of Christ who believe it to be wrong, and for the same reason, the silence of the Scriptures. He observed that we all feel "free to choose" where the Bible is silent, only on different things.[21]

If there was a prophet for Christian unity among these churches for this generation, it was W. Carl Ketcherside, who died in 1989. A protégé of Daniel Sommer, one of the founders of the Churches of Christ (see chap. 16), Ketcherside spent the first half of his ministry as a "wing commander," to use his term, of the "Sommerite" Church of Christ, sometimes called "Anti-college."

Benjamin Franklin, the champion of the arch-conservatives in the pioneer period, told Sommer that Franklin's mantle of leadership should fall upon him, a behest that Sommer militantly assumed. In his last years Sommer told young Ketcherside, who was conducting revivals at age 12, that his mantle should fall upon him. The charge was not taken lightly, for Ketcherside was soon the sect's editor bishop and champion debater, his foes including no less than G.C. Brewer of the mainline church.

The turning point in Ketcherside's ministry came while he was a missionary to Ireland, where he was exposed to a larger fellowship of believers. Finding that the sectarianism he had brought with him from America was not the answer, he was tossed upon a sea of despair and uncertainty. He found his answer on a wintry night in a little frame Church of Christ in Belfast. Alone and cold, he set his mind upon the promise of Rev. 3:20, and while he had been a preacher for three decades and had baptized thousands and was a "bishop," he did what he had never done before. He invited Jesus into his heart.[22]

Resolving never again to be a party man and seeking to undo his sectarian past, Ketcherside began to work for peace and unity throughout the Movement, using his *Mission Messenger*, with a circulation as high as 8,000, as an instrument to remove walls of separation rather than to build them. Though largely rejected by his own sect, his ministry of reconciliation has had a tremendous impact upon all three churches.

He crossed lines of fellowship with abandon, avowing that he "loves them all while agreeing with none." Whether before the NACC, the World Convention of Churches of Christ, or one of virtually all of the Movement's colleges that he visited, his plea was that fellowship cannot be restored by confrontation and debate but only by the dynamic of love. "Wherever God has a child, I have a brother or sister," he avowed, and "Nothing should be made a test of fellowship that God has not made a condition for going to heaven."

Through scores of books and 37 years as an editor he cried out like a prophet that "the dynamic of love is the only power in the universe which can ever make whole that which has been broken." Applying this principle to a divided unity movement, he went on to say:

Love is the only power which can span the gaps of a broken fellowship. It alone can batter down walls, remove barriers, and open gates of access.

535

Argument will not do it. Debating will not do it. Neither will conferences, committees, creeds or concordats. Nothing will do it but love.[23]

Ketcherside spent the last years of his life in an inner-city ministry in St. Louis, which had been his home for over a half-century. His ministry gave thousands the hope for a more loving, responsible, and united brotherhood. Hundreds of leaders, young and old alike, are now persuaded that "Nothing will do it but love!," and are turning their churches in new directions.

The dreams of the irenic pioneers of an earlier day are being realized, at least in part, those of Ernest Beam, J.D. Murch, Claude Witty, Reuel Lemmons and Carl Ketcherside.

Internal Unity Meetings

Further efforts like those of the Murch-Witty unity meetings had to await another generation. Beginning in 1966 at Bethany College and ending there in 1975 there was a decade of unity meetings called the Annual Unity Forum. Unlike the earlier effort which involved only Churches of Christ and Christian Churches, these not only brought all three churches together but several sub-groups within Churches of Christ. Since the forum was especially for educators, it was usually held on college campuses, including Milligan College, Atlanta Christian College, and Lubbock Christian College.

The idea originated with Perry Gresham and Leroy Garrett when they worked together at Bethany College, and it was implemented by irenic people from all three churches, including Thomas Langford of the Churches of Christ and Charles Gresham of the Christian Church. The forum was the occasion for highly responsible papers that spoke to the issues, which were published in various journals and circulated on tapes all over the country. This gave it considerable exposure among the rank and file.

Two anecdotes growing out of this forum well illustrate its role as pathfinder. When Perry Gresham, then president of Bethany College, spoke at the Fifth Annual Unity Forum in 1970 at Lubbock Christian College it was the first time some of the well-heeled west Texas ranchers, stalwart members of Churches of Christ, had ever heard "a Christian Church preacher."

They were captivated by Gresham's down-home manner and by the stories he told about pioneers they had barely heard of, whether the Campbells, Stone, Scott, or McGarvey. And they chuckled when he told of sometimes seeing Campbell's ghost about the Bethany campus. It was a relaxing and liberating experience for folk too long separated, provided by an orator of the old school.[24]

On a more sophisticated note but no less impressive was a presentation by Robert O. Fife, then of Milligan College, at the Ninth Annual Unity Forum in Nashville in 1974. In the presence of people from all three wings of the Movement, he posed the question "How close can we get to each other before our faith is compromised by another's error?"

Fife asked if the Christian Church could not support the work of Juan Monroy in Spain or the Herald of Truth, projects of Churches of Christ. And could not Churches of Christ support Christian Missionary Fellowship or the Institute of Christian Origins in Tübingen, programs of the Christian Church?

He went on to ask with telling effect: "Must we approve of everything before we do anything together?" Referring to possible cooperative efforts, he deplored the fact that they feel compelled to compete with each other in every suburb. He asked at last, "Can't we in spite of our differences join together in a common evangelistic thrust?"[25]

One can see that this forum not only brought people together for the first time, but it asked questions that had not been asked before. Since it was avant-garde and suspect, it was difficult to get influencial leaders to participate except the more daring, and the papers ignored them except perhaps to criticize.

This has changed in more recent years with a new series of unity meetings, albeit it makes no effort to include the Disciples. These are called the Restoration Forum and had their beginning in 1984 at Ozark Christian College through the inspiration of Don DeWelt, Dennis Randall, and Alan Cloyd.

Except in 1985 when two forums were held, they are held on an annual basis and attract several hundreds. Unlike the earlier forums, these are sufficiently "kosher" that any Church of Christ leader can feel free to attend without criticism, except from the far right, and the papers carry notices. By the time of his death in 1991, Don DeWelt, one of the founders, had attended the first seven forums. Shortly before his death, he reported that the progress in brotherhood even since 1984 was nothing less than amazing. He ventured that the two churches were poised to do world evangelism together.[26]

Seth Wilson, a professor at Ozark Christian College and a veteran of internal unity efforts, sees these forums as having significant results. "They bring us opportunity to know each other and to care more for one another," he says, and he is impressed with the friendships that are made. He also noted that influencial leaders of both churches sit down together and study the nature of both unity and division.[27]

William Pile described Restoration Forum VIII (Tulsa, 1991) as "They

Had a War but Nobody Came," a reference to the irenic spirit that pervaded the sessions. The format, as in all the forums, allowed for keynote speakers, panel, and group discussions of 15-20 people each. Pile was impressed with the liberating remarks of various speakers, such as those of Thomas Langford of the non-class Churches of Christ: "We ought to quit making tests of fellowship out of anything the Lord doesn't make a requirement for salvation." Pile also quotes Rubel Shelly, Churches of Christ, as saying: "Let's stop the intramural bloodbath," and Ben Merold, Christian Church: "The more we evangelize the less we build walls and make tests of fellowship."[28]

Don Browning, minster to the Singing Oaks Church of Christ in Denton, Texas, who attended Restoration Forum XI (Ozark Christian College, 1993) considers a presentation made by Mike Armour, minister to the Skillman Avenue Church of Christ in Dallas and a perennial leader of the forums, as setting the tone for meaningful unity between Churches of Christ and the Christian Church. It is not a matter of either church trying to change the other, Armour insisted, but a matter of accepting each other as they are and working together in every way that conscience allows.[29]

While there is an occasional voice to the contrary, such as the old bromide that the Christian Church must give up instrumental music if there is to be unity, the prevailing attitude at these forums appears to be like that of Mike Armour's, that unity is a matter of accepting diversity rather than of demanding conformity.

To quote William Pile again, who has attended most of the forums: "The Forums have moved from excercises in academics, logic, and polemics to exercises in love, grace, and relationship. We spent far more time as brethren than competitors." As if that were not enough, he added, "Argumentation lost to amiability. Being right gave way to being real."[30]

The publication *One Body*, also begun by Don DeWelt in 1984, is now the only publication with the explicit purpose of promoting the internal unity of the Movement. Victor Knowles now serves as the full-time editor. The publication, a 24-page quarterly out of Joplin, Mo., is attractively edited and gives vigorous support to the annual Restoration Forum.

The editor never misses a chance to pass along any good news of improved relations between the churches. A case in point is when Denny Boultinghouse, editor of *Image*, urged Churches of Christ leaders to invite speakers from the Christian Church to their college lectureships, which they never do, even though they are invited by the Christian Church. That was newsworthy![31]

In an earlier day of the divided Movement, two preachers in Louisville, one of the Christian Church and the other of the Churches of Christ, met regularly to pray together for the unity of their people. They could then only hope for such an eventuality as the Restoration Forum. They produced a hymn that expressed their desire, M.C. Kurfees writing the words and A.C. Hopkins doing the music.

When the Annual Unity Forum first gathered at Bethany in 1966, the old Campbell church, long boarded up, was opened for the Lord's day assembly where six or eight segments of the Movement worshiped together. The theme was unity and the Lord's supper, with a speaker from each of the three main groups: Carl Ketcherside, Seth Wilson, and J.J. Hamilton, pastor of the Disciples church in Bethany. When the story was told of the Hopkins-Kurfees hymn, the diverse gathering stood and sang it together.

> How blest and how joyous will be the glad day,
>> When heart beats to heart in the work of the Lord;
> When Christians united shall swell the grand lay,
>> Divisions all ended, triumphant his word!
> Oh! shout the glad work, Oh! hasten the day,
>> When all of God's people are one.

Someone remarked from the floor that those gathered in that historic room that day were already one in Christ in spite of differences, and that "the spirit of Bethany" should be taken back with them to their churches. It was a fine hour in the history of the Movement.[32]

ENDNOTES

[1]Alexander Campbell, "Response to Dr. Humphrey's Letters," No. 4, *Millennial Harbinger*, 1850, p. 429.

[2]Alexander Campbell, "Our Position to American Slavery," *Millennial Harbinger*, 1845, p. 51.

[3]John Rogers, *Biography of Elder Barton W. Stone*, Cincinnati: 1847, p. 347.

[4]Howard E. Short, "Still Some Problems to be Solved," *The Disciple*, Vol. 3 (Oct. 17, 1976), p. 20.

[5]Lester G. McAllister and William E. Tucker, *Journey in Faith* (St. Louis: Bethany Press, 1975), p. 459.

[6]"Churches of Christ," *U.S. Catholic* (June, 1976), p. 46.

[7]W. Clark Gilpin, "Common Roots, Divergent Paths: The Disciples and the Churches of Christ," *The Christian Century* (Dec. 20, 1978), pp. 1234-1238.

[8]Ron Nutter, *The European Evangelistic Society: The Establishment of an Institute in Europe*, (Pamphlet, n.d.,n.p.)

[9]Claude E. Spencer, "Not Wholly Separated," *Christian Standard*, Vol. 113 (1978), p. 172.

[10]*Christian Friends*, Newsletter of World Convention of Churches of Christ (3rd Quarter 1993), 1101 19th Ave. S., Nashville, TN 37212-2196.

[11]Dean E. Walker, "Restoration?, Unity?, Mission!," *Fellowship*, Vol. 1 (1974), p. 14.

[12]W. Clark Gilpin, "The Disciples and the Churches of Christ: Common Roots, Divergent Paths," in Marty Marty, Ed., *Where The Spirit Leads*, pp. 180-183.

[13]C. Leonard Allen, "Congregational Life and Discipline," in *Reappraising the Disciples Tradition for the 21st Century*, (Midstream, Vol. 26, No. 3, July 1987), pp. 379f.

[14]M. Eugene Boring, "The Disciples and Higher Criticism: The Crucial Third Generation," in D. Newell Williams, Ed., *A Case Study of Mainstream Protestantism* (Grand Rapids: Eerdmans, 1991), pp. 29f.

[15]Howard E. Short, "Still Some Problems to be Solved," p. 20.

[16]Ernest Beam, "An Open Letter," *The Christian Forum*, Vol. 1 (1950) pp. 2-5.

[17]H. Leo Boles, *The Way of Unity Between "Christian Church" and Churches of Christ* (Mimeographed), Indianapolis, 1939, p. 5.

[18]J.D. Murch, *Christians Only* (Cincinnati: Standard, 1962), pp. 274-75.

[19]"Two Dialogues About Unity," *Christian Chronicle*, Vol. 27, No. 3 (1970), p. 1.

[20]*Ibid.*, p. 6.

[21]Personal interview with Robert O. Fife.

[22]Personal interview with W. Carl Ketcherside; see also W. Carl Ketcherside, "A Knock At The Door," *Restoration Review*, Vol. 20 (1978), pp. 152-156.

[23]W. Carl Ketcherside, "The Dynamic of Love," *Mission Messenger*, Vol. 28 (1966), p. 203.

[24]Leroy Garrett, "Report on Unity Forum in Lubbock," *Restoration Review*, Vol. 12, No. 7 (1970), pp. 128-131.

[25]Robert O. Fife, "What Will the United Church Be Like?," 9th Annual Unity Forum, Nashville, July 5, 1974 (Tape recording).

[26]"One Body Interview," *One Body*, (Winter 1991), p. 12.

[27]"A Visit With Seth Wilson," *One Body*, Vol. 10, No. 3 (Summer 1993), p. 5.

[28]William Pile, "Restoration Forum VIII," *One Body*, (Winter, 1991), pp. 8-11.

[29]Interview with Don Browning.

[30]William Pile, "Restoration Forum VIII," p. 10.

[31]"An Observation," *One Body*, Vol.10, No.1 (Winter 1993), p. 9.

[32]Leroy Garrett, "The Bethany Meeting," *Restoration Review*, Vol. 8, No. 7 (1966), pp. 122-125.

22

THE MOVEMENT FACES THE 21ST CENTURY

I have no light to illuminate the pathway of the future save that which falls over my shoulder from the past. — Patrick Henry

Serious concern for renewal of the Stone-Campbell Movement as it faces a new century calls for an honest appraisal of the past. What went wrong? What mistakes might the pioneers have made? In what ways might succeeding generations have failed the ideals of the founding fathers? What did the pioneers do that was right, and what can we take with us into the future?

This was, as we have seen, Justin's view of history: hold up for censure what was wrong; preserve and commemorate what was noble. The pioneers themselves would want us to be discriminating in drawing upon their labors. Such a selective use of history should serve us well as we move on toward God's tomorrow.

What Went Wrong

Alexander Campbell himself realized as early as 1835 that "this glorious struggle for the restoration of ancient and primitive Christianity" had some serious problems. He referred to them as "The Crisis" that threatened the progress and prosperity of the Movement, which he then numbered at 150,000. His analysis of the crisis includes some surprises, not the least of which was that the Movement had come to be seen as "a sort of family quarrel among the Baptists."

He admitted that some of his own people who "have a peculiar controversy with the Baptists" are partly responsible for the misconception. And a misconception it was, Campbell insisted, for the Movement really emanated from the Presbyterians, not the Baptists, and that "the reformation of no one party in christendom was the original intention of the first advocates of the original gospel and order of things."

Beside being viewed as a fuss among Baptists, the Movement was also seen as having a strong "anticalvinian character," as Campbell put it, which he thought was misleading. Again he saw some of his own people partly to blame, those who "glory in its anticalvinistic attributes." But Campbell insisted that his reformation was no more anti-Calvinistic than it was anti-Arminian. Speaking for himself, he said there was more of John Calvin in him than James Arminius. In any event he had no interest in fighting over again the battles between the two. "Let none of our brethren," he urged, "represent this good cause as antiarminian or anticalvinian – as making cause with any sect or party in christendom." He opted for "Bibleism," he avowed, and "against all other *isms* ancient and modern."

Campbell also complained that because of some of the speculations of his people the Movement had been tagged as "antitrinitarian." He rejected the description, especially when applied by the Unitarians who saw "a large class of Reformers in the West" as on their side. Campbell insisted that if his Movement was antitrinitarian it was even more antiunitarian. He wanted his people to hold fast to the apostles' doctrine and to be neutral toward all parties and systems.

Another problem Campbell cited was the "liability to extremes," some because of youth and inexperience, some from age and obstinacy. Some read too little, he complained, and some too much! Even more serious was "the phlegmatic temperament," which, when coupled with speculative issues, causes much mischief. He emphasized once more that they all knew the bond of union – one Lord, one faith, one baptism – and that speculation must be kept in its place as opinion.

The thing that seemed to bother him the most, however, was "the dogmatical, unfeeling, and snarling temper" of those who were content to denounce error rather than preach the gospel. He insisted that "the white horse that carries the message of peace" should not be burdened with declamations against societies, cooperatives, and "the saddlebags of party politics and political aspirants."[1]

It is to Campbell's credit that he was not blind to the Movement's weaknesses, and that he moved early on to correct them. But the weaknesses he named continued to plague his reformation and finally contributed to the divisions that came.

We have the advantage of a century and a half later as we look at what went wrong and what went right. But it is in the best tradition of Alexander Campbell himself to do this. In placing the weaknesses alongside the strengths we allow history to serve rather than to deter.

1. *It was a unity movement that itself divided again and again, led by separatists.*

It was always an embarrassment to the pioneers that they pled for unity as separatists. Even on his deathbed Campbell expressed regret that they had separated from the Baptists, and Stone equivocated as to whether he had really left the Presbyterians. O'Kelly and Haggard made it clear they were not breaking fellowship with the Methodists. And old Raccoon John Smith insisted he would never leave the Baptists even though they wanted him to!

The fatal irony is that for whatever reasons they were not able to be what they intended: a unity movement within the church at large and not become another denomination. They eventually created an oxymoron, a divided unity movement.

Could they have remained within their churches and worked more effectively for unity? It can be argued, as this book does, that they were forced out and really had no choice. But even if forced out, could they have remained a movement only and not added three more denominations, as they initially were as the Christian Association of Washington?

The fatal tragedy remains that the Movement launched to unite the Christians in all the sects itself divided over and over again. Its heirs must keep this painful fact on the table for study and prayer as they face the future.

2. *An overemphasis on doctrinal particulars to the neglect of universal truths, and making those particulars (opinions) tests of fellowship.*

When Robert Richardson wrote his series on "Reformation" back in the 1840's he named this as a weakness of Protestantism that the Movement sought to correct. An overemphasis on doctrinal details divided Protestantism into warring sects, he charged, and it is "general truths" that unite. While noble efforts were made to overcome this weakness, the Movement nonetheless failed to heal the divisions and added even more.

We could have borne particular differences, which, as W.E. Garrison noted, have had more to do with methods than doctrine, if they had not been made tests of fellowship. We could have churches that sing acappella only and those that use instruments, churches that support the agencies and societies and those that do not, those that have Sunday schools and those that do not, those that serve Communion in one chalice and those who use multiple cups, etc., etc. and still be a united people, "holding to the Head" who is Christ, bonded by "general Christianity" as Richardson put it. It was not to be.

Such differences are not only not sinful, they are inevitable. It is in building walls and dividing over differences that is sinful. Overcoming this sin, inherited from our Protestant forbearers, has always eluded us.

3. *They fell prey to the common fallacy that there was a golden age of the church, "the primitive church," that was a pattern for all time to come.*

While always resisted by some, there was the naive assumption that there is an indisputably inspired and authoritative pattern of organization (polity), doctrine, worship, and practice. Still more fatal to the Movement's effectiveness was the implication that others must conform to our understanding of that pattern or "ancient order" if there is to be unity. Our undoing has been that even our own leaders could not interpret "the pattern" alike, much less the church at large.

Recent biblical research has shown that primitive Christianity was far more diverse than the Movement has allowed, and that the early churches were not united in the sense of being copies of each other. It is a myth that there was ever "the ideal pristine church" in the first century that can be restored or transplanted in the 19th or 20th centuries. While our pioneers may have eventually realized this, the Movement was never able to free itself of this fallacy.

4. *A failure to balance the tension between two basic motifs of their plea, unity and restoration.*

While the pioneers emphasized unity in their plea, there was the implication, at least early on, that unity is possible only through "a restoration of the ancient order of things." If this was eventually modulated, especially by Alexander Campbell as noted below, it was not sufficent to remove the tension between the two concepts.

This tension is reflected in the divisions that exist today. Those who emphasize restoration tend to neglect unity, while those who stress unity have all but denounced restoration. When the Restudy Commission made its report to the International Convention in 1949 (Chapter 17), it named this tension as a basic cause of divisions within the Movement.

The tension is due in part to a difference in interpreting the genius of the Movement. If both motifs have validity, as most leaders have believed, it has been a failure of finding proper balance between the two. A lack of critical examination of the meaning of both unity and restoration has also been part of the problem.

5. *An undue fear of organization.*

In the earliest days of the Movement it was possible to be indifferent to structure and organization, but with age and growth the need for cooperative effort became apparent. We have seen that by the 1830's Campbell considered it imperative to call for cooperation, insisting that the church is more than the total of congregations. He met with opposition that never subsided. Even the loosely-structured missionary society almost died aborning. Conservatives have always been suspicious of all organization, presuming it to be without biblical authority. This has been an Achilles Heel to the progress of the Movement throughout its history.

6. *An unwarranted suspicion of theology.*

It was somehow supposed that theology made creeds and creeds created division. Wiser heads came to see that theologians might create sects, by being pushy, but not theology as such. Nonetheless the Movement became "anti-theological," however theological it actually was. Campbell put a "creed in the deed" when he mandated in the charter of Bethany College that theology could not be taught. They taught "Christian Doctrine" instead!

This "anti" posture has made the Movement less theologically responsible than it might have been otherwise. We have felt justified in skirting such weighty issues as the sovereignty of God and election on the grounds that they are "theology." We have thus run the risk of not taking "biblical theology" seriously. Does this account for so much biblical illiterarcy in our churches today? Why do our people have to go to such parachurch organizations as the Navigators and Bible Study Fellowship for serious Bible study? Our pioneers, of course, cannot be blamed for all this. While we have always been a biblical people, we have not been encouraged to think theologically.

7. *A failure to distinguish between a plea for New Testament Christianity and their conception of what that constituted.*

We observed in Chap. 13 that Lancelot Oliver, the British editor, warned against this fallacy, which he thought the Movement had largely avoided. But we have too often left the impression that we draw no distinction between a call for restoration or reformation and our idea of what that means. Oliver noted that we must be ready "to diminish or enlarge as further truth breaks from God's word." That is far different from supposing we already have all the truth and that there is no reason to invite others to join us in the search.

8. *The practice of starting churches and leaving them unnurtured and unattended.*

In the early days the Movement may have grown too fast. Churches were planted at a rapid pace, often with many baptisms. Evangelists felt the need to move on to other fields, leaving new congregations to survive the best they could. This problem was compounded by the absence of organization and lack of longterm planning. This failure to consolidate gains proved costly in that it created too many ill-prepared leaders and undernourished churches.

9. *An uncanny inability on the part of the leaders to get along with each other.*

While this plagues all movements and churches to some degree, it has been particularly destructive among us. It is not clear why. We have pointed to the inordinate influence of editor bishops. If power corrupts, as the verdict of history indicates, the editor's chair in the Stone-Campbell tradition has been corruptive, especially in the early generations. It serves to warn all leaders to beware of positions of power.

At the same time we have had impressive overtures for peace from editors that were ignored. Both Isaac Errett and James H. Garrison, for instance, urged the churches not to dispute over societies and music, but for each side to show what method is most effective by excelling in that method. So, we have also had a penchant for ignoring the advice of our wisest minds to our own hurt.

While this may not complete the list of things that went wrong, it is sufficient to point up the wisdom of Cicero when he advised that "Any man may make a mistake, but none but a fool will continue in it."

A Flawed Plea?

Apart from the foregoing list of things that went wrong, there is the larger question as to whether "the Plea" for unity based upon a restoration of primitive Christianity was valid. The painful fact remains that it did not even work for the Movement itself. The following story points up this problem in a dramatic way.

It concerns a speech made by Peter Ainslie at an ecumenical conference at either Stockholm or Lausanne in 1925 or 1927. Before dignitaries of the World Council, Ainslie pled for unity on the grounds of all parties abandoning their creeds and ecclesiastical inventions and accept the New Testament as the sole authority in religion. With pride he told of belonging to a people who had abandoned human names and accepted only Christ and the Bible as the basis of union, and enjoyed freedom in matters of opinion. Ainslie earnestly invited all those that made up divided Christendom to unite upon a return to simple New Testament Christianity.

The story has it that the ecclesiastical dignitaries from around the world listened to Ainslie with rapt attention, admiring the sincerity and simplicity of his plea and the eloquence of his presentation. But at last a bearded patriarch broke the silence by asking Ainslie, "And you have never divided?" It was all the rebuttal that was necessary.[2]

The Disciples who tell the Ainslie story recall that in those days it did not occur to them that there was a flaw to the plea; they only blamed the dissidents for dividing the Movement. It should be evident that we have been naive and have oversimplified the problem by saying, "Ho, come and be like us and there will be unity." Respondents only need to remind us of our own divisions.

If the plea for unity that is based on "the restoration of New Testament Christianity" is valid, then why are we ourselves who make that plea divided umpteen different ways? If the plea has not worked for us, how do we figure it will work for others? No unity has ever been effected by such a plea, either for ourselves or for the church at large.

This calls for selectivity in drawing from our own heritage in our search for workable unity principles. From our earliest days there were those who based unity only upon faithfulness to Christ, according to one's own understanding. The Republican Methodists who in 1794 became the first Christian Church set forth "Christian character" as the only test for church fellowship and membership, as we saw in Chapter 3. Barton W. Stone likewise made loyalty to Christ the only basis of unity.

It was the Campbells, especially in their earlier years, who pled for unity on the basis of "the ancient order of things" and a restoration of primitive Christianity. In time, however, Alexander Campbell moved toward what he came to call "catholic grounds" for unity. By 1839 he stated that while unity had been a "darling theme" to him all along, "it was some time before we could see clearly the ground on which all true Christians could form one visible and harmonious union."[3]

What he now saw clearly as the basis of unity made no reference to restoring primitive Christianity, which, as he came to see, sincere believers interpret differently. He now defined "the rule of union" as: "whatever in faith, in piety, and morality is catholic, or universally admitted by all parties, shall be adopted as the basis of union." This he set forth as a resolution before a large audience in Lexington, Ky. in 1841. The audience overhelmingly approved the resolution by a standing vote. It reflects a dramatic mid-course correction in Campbell's theology of unity.[4]

He may, however, have taken back with one hand what he gave with the other when he went on to call for an abandonment of all tenets, forms, and usages not admitted by all as catholic. This may be an instance where we have to be selective, accepting Campbell's first resolution but not the second.

It is ecumenically sound to call for unity on what all believers hold and practice in common, but must they give up any doctrine or practice that is not catholic? The Churches of Christ, for example, should not insist on all other Christians singing acappella as a basis for unity, for this is not catholic, but must it abandon acappella singing in order to be a part of a united church? This would be true of countless "particulars" believed and practiced by all churches, which they need not be asked to abandon, but only not to make them tests of fellowship.

Campbell may have stated this revised doctrine of unity better two years later when he addressed an educators' convention in Clarksburg, Va. In this address he stated that irrespective of sectarian differences there is "a common Christianity" on which all Christian people can unite. This common faith, he indicated, was based upon common principles of piety and morality.[5]

Had this been Ainslie's plea before the World Council — a unity based upon our mutual faith in Christ — would not the response have been different? If this had been our only test for fellowship with each other — a unity based on what (or better still, *whom*) we hold in common — would we ever have divided? Is this not to be our plea for unity in the 21st century?

What Was Right?

There were things of "worthy action," to quote Tacitus again, that we should not only commemorate, as he advised, but take with us into the 21st century. However, if we have been inclined to repeat the mistakes of the past, the following list may reveal that we have erred even more in not preserving the noblest features of our heritage.

1. *Their passion for unity.*

Whatever failures they had, the pioneers undertook one of the noblest endeavors in the history of the church. They launched a movement to unite the Christians in all the sects. Richardson rightly described it as a movement "born of a passion for unity and unity has been its consuming theme." It was an experience in ecumenicity long before the modern ecumenical movement was born. If the heirs of the Movement fail in this aspect of their heritage, they fail in what was most important.

If Paul Crow is right that even the Disciples of Christ have lost their zeal for unity, as was noted in chapter 20, then it can be said that none of the three churches has that passion for the unity of all Christians that gave birth to the Movement. If in our hearts Christian unity is no longer our business it will affect our sense of mission as we enter a new century.

"Identity" is the word these days. All three churches are trying to discover or redefine their identity. This has led Independents and Churches of Christ to talk of getting "the Restoration Movement" back on track, while the Disciples speak of how to make "covenant" more meaningful in a restructured church. Is either of these emphases equivalent to once again being a unity movement, or are they calls for a particular ecclesiological identification?

Are we to identify ourselves the way Barton W. Stone identified our people in his day: "Let Christian unity be our polar star"?

Such recovery must begin with a renewed zeal for prayer for unity. Some years ago I was impressed with a notice on a wall in Westminster Abbey in London that read: "Prayers for Christian Unity in this Chapel each Tuesday at 2 p.m." If Anglicans set aside time to pray for unity, how much more a people whose heritage is a passion for unity! And yet in most of our congregations there is little said about unity either to people or to God.

2. *Their disdain for and repudiation of division among Christians.*

If we were "sick and tired of the bitter jarrings and janglings of a party spirit" as was Thomas Campbell, and if we believed as did he that "division among Christians is a horrid evil, fraught with many evils," we would be as prone to do something about it as he was. We must come to see what our forebearers saw, that our divisions are a sin. The awful truth is that not only does Christendom at large continue to be divided, but we, called to be a unity movement, continue to divide and sub-divide. In every decade of the 20th century we have added still another faction or have had one in the making.

If we could see as did Peter Ainslie that a divided church, especially our own divided Movement, is a "scandal" before the world, we would no longer accept it as tolerable. If in the 21st century we Americans solve the problem of crime in our streets and schools by treating it as intolerable, we who are heirs of the Stone-Campbell Movement will solve our internal divisions in the same way. We must be resolute that some things, like random crime and church splits, are intolerable. Campbell and Ainslie loathed division. We must be similarly impassioned.

So, along with praying more for unity we should repent more for our partisan behavior. If we did not create the factions we have been tolerant of them and have preserved them without serious concern. If there could be an occasional "Reconciliation Sunday," with participants from all our factions, in which we boldly confess our sin of being a divisive people, it might well set in motion the healing that must come.

3. *Their view of the church as inherently and essentially one.*

After all our study we may conclude that the most famous quotation outside the Bible in our history is Thomas Campbell's "The Church of Christ upon earth is essentially, intentionally, and constitutionally one." We learned in Chapter 5 that when Campbell wrote that in the *Declaration and Address* he did not yet have a congregation of his own, and yet he spoke of "the Church of Christ" as a reality upon earth.

He thus had no illusion of "restoring" the true church as if it did not exist. He was also well aware of, even incensed by, all the divisions among Christians, and yet he referred to the essential unity of the church, as if it cannot be divided.

It is well that we remind ourselves, in the light of Paul's "Is Christ divided?," that to speak of a divided church is a contradiction, an oxymoron. The church as the Body of Christ is by its very nature one. What then mean the divisions? They are encroachments upon the Body of Christ, not unlike carbuncles on a physical body or the surface of a ship. Divisions may be likened to the festering sores in a troubled marriage. The couple is still one in holy matrimony, but their oneness is not being realized.

That is the way Ronald Osborn once put it, "Unity is real but it is not realized." We can move into the 21st century with a better handle on the problem if we see, as did Campbell and Paul, that the church in the world is one and cannot be other than one. We must learn to behave as people who are one in Christ.

Our task therefore is not to achieve unity through various ecumenical exercises, but to realize the unity that is already ours. It thus becomes a matter of accepting the gift of the Spirit's unity. We might therefore better heal our divisions with a new approach, such as "Let's accept the gift."

4. *They were people of principles, not only moral but pragmatic.*

Our founding fathers were principled, not only in the exemplary lives they lived, but in that they thought in principles. They formulated principles of unity and fellowship and gave pragmatic expression to them in slogans. The founding documents are replete with principles, which have the advantage of transcending time and circumstance. They did not bother with rules, fads, or even theological deductions. They worked from principles wrought out of the long experience of the church.

The Campbellian view of the catholicity of the church, Stone's coupling of unity and evangelism, Scott's theme of the golden oracle, and Haggard's plea for unity in the name Christian are examples of this. Sometimes a principle was expressed humorously as well as pragmatically, as in *The Last Will and Testament*: "We will that preachers and people pray more and dispute less." That principle would serve us well for all time to come.

5. *Their concern for ordinances in the life and worship of the church.*

They had a sacramental view toward the ordinances — baptism, Communion, the Lord's day — in that they are not only commands but also means of grace. Alexander Campbell also viewed the Bible as an ordinance, for it too is someting the church does, through study and interpretation, in response to God's grace. The church not only gathers around the Lord's table on the Lord's day but also around an open Bible.

Baptism, which Campbell saw as a work of grace, inducts one into the fellowship, while Communion is a continual expression of that fellowship. They were not "church ordinances" as much as they were ordinances of God. If we are true to our heritage in this regard, we will not only always take the ordinances seriously but see them in reference to God's grace.

6. *In taking the Bible seriously, their preaching was biblical and authoritative.*

They unashamedly built congregations "upon the Bible," and their preaching was grounded in the authority of Scripture. They especially emphasized what they called "the facts of the Bible" rather than their own opinions and deductions. Authoritative, biblical preaching is thus our heritage.

Authoritative preaching may not be easily defined, but we all recognize it when we witness it. It has to do with making the Scriptures relevant, causing the hearer to respond with something like "This is about me and my world." It must also project the authority of God: *God speaks through the preaching.* There is a sense of urgency in such preaching. The preacher projects the truth of God, not himself or herself, and the truth, even when spoken in love, may have a bite to it. Authoritative preaching subdues and chastens as well as builds up and encourages. It always provides hope.

Such preaching is also direct and specific in its exposure of sin, such as sexism or racial injustice, and does not dally in generalities. It does not merely declaim eternal truths but makes them meaningful by placing them in their contemporary context. It speaks to the life experiences of the congregation.

In authoritative preaching the Bible is used to show that there *are* objective and personal moral standards, however contrary this may be to the mentality of today's Western society. Above all, it always proclaims the gospel of God's love in Christ for all people, and shows that in the gospel God demands justice for all.

In his study of Disciples preaching, Joseph E. Faulkner found few instances of this kind of preaching. Only 5% of the 208 sermons analyzed dealt with social justice in any forthright manner. There seemed to be little awareness of the complexity and moral ambiguity of the daily life struggles faced by the congregation. While he found the sermons overwhelmingly doctrinal in nature, there was more declamation than analytical explanation. There is a hunger for relevant, biblical interpretation that is not being met.

Faulkner found that the preachers largely ignored the Old Testament, showing little interest in its great narrative stories, and even less for the indignation at social injustice expressed by the eighth-century prophets. Even the illustrations, which often did little to enhance the theme, had little relevance to people's lives.[6]

There is no reason to suppose that the sermons preached in the other two churches of the Movement would be all that different if subjected to a similar analysis. In fact, in one recent publication Churches of Christ scholars concluded that "With the adoption of secular fads and the rush to meet an ever-expanding array of 'needs,' Churches of Christ are losing their biblical base and becoming confused about what human beings really need."[7]

If our churches have "lost their biblical base" we are ill-prepared to minister to the world of the 21st century. We must take theology seriously and be urgent in preaching the gospel if we are to reach the vast "unaffiliated sector" that is out there. This means we will have to know the needs of the world of the 21st century in all their complexity, and then address the word of God to those needs. Perhaps this is what Alexander Campbell meant at the outset when he talked about a church built upon the Bible.

7. *They connected with each other and with their world.*

They were a pioneer church on the American frontier, and they were part of that frontier, building a new nation as well as a new church. They were adventurers. In ideas, in principles, in unity. They not only launched a unity movement but effected a union between themselves. We have seen that Barton W. Stone considered the union of his movement with that of Campbell's as the noblest act of his life. It was also a noble example for the church at large, anticipating modern ecumenicity. They took the necessary pragmatic steps to make the union work.

They were involved with the issues of their day, whether slavery, politics, or business. They followed the frontier west, editing papers, organizing schools, and building colleges. They were the people, a people's church, an American church. Within a single generation they became from scratch a sizable and respected Christian denomination, involved in its world and the church at large.

If we are today an irrelevant and disconnected people, we are at odds with our own heritage.

Other Changes for a New Century

Leaders throughout the three churches speak of the need for change, some of which are deemed imperative for survival. Some are pragmatic in nature, matters of expediency rather than matters of faith. Since they threaten longstanding tradition they are controversial. Some are more serious, questioning the integrity of our faith. There is general agreement that we are in crisis and that we must meet the challenge of a changing world if we as Christ's church are to be the pillar and ground of truth.

1. *Spirituality.*

Our forebearers believed the church is to be holy as much as it is to be one. Thomas Campbell not only saw the church as essentially one, but as consisting of those who believe in and obey Christ, and that "manifest the same by their tempers and conduct." He insisted that "none else can be truly and properly called Christians." Alexander Campbell believed that reformation must first be personal, manifest in the heart and life of the believer, before it can be ecclesial. Barton W. Stone placed "fire unity" above either book, head or water unity, referring to the Spirit's presence in the life of the believer.

These were men of prayer and personal holiness. The old Scottish Presbyterian piety burned within them, expressing itself in the family circle. They saw education of the heart as important as education of the mind.

The dull, cold orthodoxy that characterizes so much of modern Protestantism, including many of our own churches, must be rejected as sub-Christian. In a day when in our own nation in the last 30 years there has been a 500 percent increase in violent crime and a 400 percent increase in illegitimate births, the church must take the lead in building moral and spiritual values.

2. *Biblical literacy.*

If the Stone-Campbell people were once known as "people of the Book" and grounded in "sound doctrine," there is a question whether it is still the case. Roger Carstensen found such abysmal ignorance of Bible basics among Disciples of Christ that he founded an agency whose mission it is to stamp out biblical illiteracy among those churches. Leaders among Christian Churches and Churches of Christ have long complained that their people, especially the youth, are almost as biblically illiterate as the unchurched. Serious Bible study in our churches is all too rare, which may help explain the success of parachurch organizations that have moved in to fill this need.

Our people must be grounded in sound doctrine, the basic truths of the Christian faith, and be able to articulate it and defend it. There are of course marginal issues where we will differ among ourselves, but upon the central issues there can be no compromise. If we believe that Christianity is true, we must be prepared to give honest answers to honest questions. We must once again be a people who believes something.

3. *Polity and organization.*

If the Disciples have better positioned themselves to do something as a church through restructure, it is not the case with the Independents and Churches of Christ, both of which are in crisis over ineffective organization or no organization at all. Both are hampered by rigid congregationalism. Even at the local level there is no clearly defined polity, and congregations are left to make policy as they go along. It is imperative that these churches rise above the mentality that organization is wrong.

Imagine some 17,000 congregations, mostly small, that make up these two denominations, that have no effective structure through which to pool their resources! Behind this incredible lack of responsibility is the myth that such radical localism is mandated in the New Testament.

4. *Ministry of women.*

This issue now imposes itself on virtually every denomination, including Roman Catholics, and there is no indication that it will go away. It is an issue of whether the whole church is to be involved in public ministry or whether there is to be a gender test. Throughout the Movement, especially among Independents and Churches of Christ, both leadership and public worship is male-dominated.

Some 60% of the congregation is barred to serve because of sex. Again, this is supposedly mandated by the New Testament, but one is forced to be very selective in his use of Scripture to conclude that gender is a test for ministry.

Some bold leaders are conceding that it is tradition pure and simple, drawn from sexism in our pagan culture. Many are persuaded that unless we get with it and implement the biblical principle that in Christ there is neither male nor female we will pay dearly for our parochialism in the complex world of the 21st century.

5. *Worship and Body Life.*

We must face the reality that our services are often boring, even to ourselves. Our people often attend out of duty or because they are good sports. Not only must there be more relevant biblical preaching, as noted above, but there must be a sense of urgency, excitement, and meaning in the entire service. Some congregations have innovative singing, interpretative readings, sharing time in which there is real Body life, and thus create an atmosphere of "the presence of the Spirit." They no longer neglect the emotional dimension of worship.

These churches must be looked to as leading the way rather than being ignored or criticized. When a church is growing because of an exciting, innovative program, others should "go and see" and be challenged to make similar changes. If we are to be around for the next century we must find ways to overcome our casual, matter-of-fact approach to religion.

6. *Instrumental music.*

This longtime controversial issue is no longer an issue, and the divisive debates are a thing of the past. But more needs to happen in order to lay the issue to rest once for all. It would be helpful if the Churches of Christ would go on record, preferably by public statements, that it has changed its longstanding position on this issue. Not that it is wrong not to use instrumental music, but to have made an issue of it all these years, even to the point of judging others as unfaithful Christians if they sing with an instrument.

If this position were publicly repudiated throughout the Churches of Christ, it would have a great healing effect, and it would encourage the present membership to believe that meaningful change is in the offing, most of whom see nothing wrong with instruments. We can take heart that some statements to this effect have been made.

It is not true, as some think, that Churches of Christ must become instrumental if it survives and grows, for some congregations are finding effective ways to improve acappella singing. When these changing churches have "special music" they sometimes use soundtracks in deference to those who would be offended by visible instruments. And some acappella singing is so innovative that it sounds as if instruments are being used!

7. *Sectarianism.*

After all these years the sectarian spirit continues to dog the Movement, with more divisions impending. We have seen that fundamentalism is threatening the peace of both the Independents and the Disciples. Churches of Christ, on the other hand, is far from overcoming "the only true church" mentality that has long tainted its witness, though progress has been made.

Sectarianism must be exposed for what it is, a sin against God and the church. The antidote is the longsuffering of Christ, that we accept each other on the same basis that Christ accepted us. As Christ accepted his own chosen disciples in spite of their differences, the church must accept all believers as equals, allowing for diversity. We as a people have a future only insofar as we resolve once for all to put sectarianism behind us.

8. *Modern biblical scholarship.*

This is certain to continue to be a lively issue among us in the upcoming generation, one reason being the progress we have made in recent years in coming to terms with the nature of the Bible. Since there can be no turning back there will be tensions. It helps to realize that every denomination has been affected by a liberal/conservative gap. We can bridge such a gap by not thinking of being either liberal or conservative, but in simply being honest with the Bible. If we are truly biblical we will not make claims for the Bible that it does not make for itself.

And if we follow Alexander Campbell's hermeneutics of interpreting the Bible by the same rules we interpret any other book, we will not ignore modern biblical scholarship. A truthseeker before an open Bible has nothing to fear from scholarship and much to gain.

9. Our destiny must be: to cease to exist as a church or denomination by sinking into union with the Body of Christ at large.

This is our heritage. It is who we are, a people hopeful of losing their identity as a separate denomination in a union with the church at large. We must leave it in God's hand as to what form such a unity will take or how long it will take. He will use us in answering the prayer of Christ for the unity of all believers.

This principle of "emptying ourselves" for the unity of the whole church is what gave us birth in the movement of Barton W. Stone. In Chap. 4 we learned that great line from *The Last Will and Testament of the Springfield Presbytery*: "Let this body die, be dissolved, and sink into union with the Body of Christ at large."

It is our calling to keep this dream alive, however remote it may seem. We must not "settle in" as a denomination or denominations, as if our own preservation were our mission. We must cultivate an "in the meantime" approach to ongoing history. In the meantime we are going to be what W.E. Garrison called "a pilot project for a completely united church."

In the meantime we will be intelligent and responsible Christians, cooperating with other believers in reaching out to a troubled world. In the meantime we will seek for meaningful growth through viable missions. In the meantime we will work and pray for unity among ourselves and others, seeking to become a model of what the united church would be like.

But we must remain conscious that this is all "in the meantime." Down the road, someday, in God's tomorrow and in God's own way, we will cease to exist as a separate people. We will gladly "Let this body die" so as to rise in union with the Body of Christ catholic. Beyond that is still a greater end, the conversion of the world, for according to the prayer of Jesus it is only a united church that will win a lost world.

Really believing this into the 21st century — praying and preaching about it, and holding it up as our mission — will not only make us true to our heritage but a blessing to the world.

This means we will be a cruciform church, a people formed by the Cross by being crucified with Christ. The Cross will be both our witness and the source of our unity. As we are drawn to the Cross we will be drawn to each other.

Now that this history is complete it is for the reader to judge as to whether we have fulfilled Alexander Campbell's expectations of such a history as expressed back in 1840:

> Whenever the history of this effort at reformation shall have been faithfully written, it will appear, we think, bright as the sun, that our career has been

marked with a spirit of forbearance, moderation, a love for union, with an unequivocal desire for preserving the integrity, harmony, and cooperation of all those who teach one Lord, one faith, and one immersion.[8]

A love for union? Bright as the sun? Indeed! The torch has been passed.

ENDNOTES

[1]Alexander Campbell, "The Crisis," *Millennial Harbinger*, 1835, pp. 595f.

[2]Ronald E. Osborn tells this story in *Disciples and The Universal Church* (Nashville: Disciples of Christ Historical Society, 1967), p. 59.

[3]Alexander Campbell, "Union of Christians — No. 1," *Millennial Harbinger*, 1839, p. 212.

[4]"Union Christian Meeting," *Millennial Harbinger*, 1841, p. 259.

[5]Alexander Campbell, "An Address," *Millennial Harbinger*, 1841, p. 445.

[6] Joseph E. Faulkner, "What Are They Saying? A Content Analysis of 208 Sermons Preached in the Christian Church (Disciples of Christ) in 1988," *A Case Study of Mainstream Protestantism*, Edited by D. Newell Williams (Grand Rapids: Eerdmans, 1991), pp. 416f.

[7]Leonard Allen, Richard T. Hughes, Michael R. Weed, *The Worldly Church* (Abilene, TX: ACU Press, 1991), p. 97.

[8]Alexander Campbell, "The Editor's Response to Mr. Broaddus," *Millennial Harbinger*, 1840, p. 556.

SUGGESTIONS FOR FURTHER READING

(Inasmuch as extensive bibliographies on the Movement are abundant, it may prove more helpful to the reader to provide a select, annotated list for further reading. These titles are mostly of recent date or reprints of old titles. All are in print or have recently been in print and should be readily available.)

Allen, C. Leonard and Hughes, Richard T., *Discovering Our Roots: The Ancestry of Churches of Christ*, Abilene, TX: ACU Press, 1990. One of several recent titles out of Abilene reflective of how the Churches of Christ have begun a critical examination of their past.

Allen, C. Leonard, *Distant Voices: Discovering A Forgotten Past For A Changing Church*, Abilene, TX: ACU Press, 1993. A Churches of Christ historian provides surprising discoveries from his church's past, from men and women pioneers alike.

Campbell-Rice Debate, Lexington: 1844. Republished by Religious Book Service, Germantown, TN. A debate on baptism and creeds, it also provides insights into the nature of the Movement.

Cochran, Louis, *The Fool of God*, New York: Duell, Sloan and Pearce, 1958; Reprint Edition, College Press, 1992. This historical novel based on the life of Alexander Campbell makes an excellent introduction to the Movement; both interesting and informative. Especially recommended.

Cochran, Louis and Cochran, Bess White, *Captives of the Word*, Joplin, MO: College Press, 1987. Highly recommended as one of the better studies of the Movement, dealing with all three churches.

Craddock, Fred B., *The Bible In The Pulpit of the Christian Church*, Claremont: Disciples Seminary Foundation, 1982. Shows that Disciples' pioneers believed in a "principle of clarity" in the Bible that all can generally understand.

Dunnavant, Anthony L., Ed., *Cane Ridge in Context: Perspectives on Barton. W. Stone and the Revival*, Nashville: DCHS, 1992. Represents the most recent research on Stone.

Fife, Robert Oldham, *Celebration of Heritage*, Los Angeles: Westwood Christian Foundation, 1992. A compilation of lectures by one of the Movement's most reliable interpreters. Especially recommended.

Fitch, Alger M., Jr., *Alexander Campbell: Preacher of Reform and Reformer of Preaching*, Joplin, MO: College Press, 1988. Important study that makes use of Campbell's earliest writings recently found.

Gerrard, William A., *A Biographical Study of Walter Scott: American Frontier Evangelist*, Joplin, MO: College Press, 1992. Reveals the significant role of one of the founders of the Movement and its greatest evangelist.

Gresham, Perry, Ed., *The Sage of Bethany: Pioneer In Broadcloth*, Joplin, MO: College Press, 1988. Significant essays on Alexander Campbell by Arthur Schlesinger, Jr., W.E. Garrison, Roland Bainton, Stephen J. England, Eva Jean Wrather, and Harold E. Lunger, as well as by the editor. Highly recommended.

Hooper, Robert E., *A Distinct People*, West Monroe, LA: Howard Pub. Co., 1993. An interesting and informative history of Churches of Christ.

Hook, Cecil, Ed., *Our Heritage of Unity and Fellowship*, New Braunfels, TX: Cecil Hook, pub., 1992. Selections from the writings of W. Carl Ketcherside and Leroy Garrett; numerous essays on pivotal historic persons and events.

Keene, Lawrence C., *Heirs of Stone and Campbell On The Pacific Slope: A Sociological Approach*, Claremont: Disciples Seminary Foundation,1984. A sociologist studies attitudes of leaders in all three churches of the Movement. Other essays trace the history of the Movement in western states. A rare and impressive analysis.

Kinnamon, Michael, Ed., *Disciples of Christ In The 21st Century*, St. Louis: CBP Press, 1988. Theological essays by leading Disciples; one by Clark M. Williamson on theology and renewal is especially recommended.

McAllister, Lester G., and Tucker, William E., *Journey In Faith: A History of the Christian Church (Disciples of Christ)*, St. Louis: Bethany Press, 1975. The rightful (and official) successor of the old Garrison/DeGroot history that is no longer in print.

Murch, James D., *Christians Only*, Cincinnati: Standard, 1962. Longtime the definitive history by an Independent; still worth reading.

Morrison, John L., *Alexander Campbell: Educating the Moral Person*, n.p., 1991. Points to Campbell's philosophy-theology as basically moral and his stress on educating the heart as well as the mind.

North, James B., *Union In Truth: An Interpretive History of the Restoration Movement*, Cincinnati: Standard, 1994. A well-documented and resourceful account from an Independent perspective.

Richardson, Robert, *Memoirs of Alexander Campbell*. Originally published in 1868 in two volumes; republished in one volume by Religious Book Service, Germantown, TN. If one chose but one book to read on the Movement, this should be it; a must for any serious student. Read it a second time!

Scott, Walter, *The Gospel Restored*, Cincinnati:1836. Republished by College Press, 1986; one of the important theological works in the history of the Movement.

Toulouse, Mark G., *Joined in Discipleship: The Maturing of an American Religious Movement*, St. Louis: Chalice Press, 1992. A brilliant but critical study by a Disciples historian that traces his people from church to Church. Martin E. Marty, an outsider, writes the introduction.

Tucker, William E., and McAllister, Lester G., *Journey In Faith*, St. Louis: Bethany Press, 1975. The authorized Disciples history, successor of Garrison-DeGroot; very well done.

Van Deusen, Kenneth, *Moses Lard: That Prince of Preachers*, Joplin, MO: College Press, 1987. Biography is an effective way to study the Movement, including this one.

Webb, Henry E., *In Search of Christian Unity: A History of the Restoration Movement*, Cincinnati: Standard, 1990. From the Independent viewpoint, responsibly critical and objective. Highly recommended.

Williams, D. Newell, Ed., *A Case Study Of Mainstream Protestantism: The Disciples Relation to American Culture, 1880-1989*, Grand Rapids: Eerdmans, 1991. A Lily grant made possible a study of declining mainline denominations, including the Disciples. The editor's essay on future prospects is especially informative.

Woodroof, James S., *The Church In Transition*, Searcy, AR: Bible House, 1990. A hard-hitting call for change in Churches of Christ by a veteran minister; he draws upon the church's unity heritage in calling for an end to division and sectarianism.

Yancey, Walt, *Endangered Heritage: An Examination of Church of Christ Doctrine*, Joplin, MO: College Press, Revised edition, 1991. A bold challenge of the church's position on instrumental music and other unique claims by a third-generation member; it draws liberally from the writings of the pioneers.

INDEX

359, 365, 368, 389, 424, 487, 536, 545

Bibbins, Smith, 437

Bilak, Stephen and Reba, 451

Black, James, 293, 295

Black, Marj, 528

Blakemore, W.B., 116, 237, 251, 355, 379

Boggs, John, 339, 341-343, 350

Boles, H. Leo, 7, 227, 533, 540

Boll, R.H., 438, 452, 454

Book of Mormon, 114, 258, 260-262

Boone, Daniel, 47, 56

Boring, M. Eugene, 417, 430, 531, 540

Bostick, Sarah Lue, 223

Boston Church of Christ, 301, 441-442

Boteler, Mattie, 224

Boultinghouse, Denny, 449, 538

Bowen, Celia Wilson, 74

Bower, W.C., 418

Bowser, G.P., 439-440

Branum, Larry, 465

Brewer, G.C., 391, 452-454, 461, 467, 535

Briney, J.B., 398

British Millennial Harbinger, 229, 240, 297, 303-304

Brodie, Fawn, 260

Brown, John, 151

Brown, Margaret, 125

Browning, Don, 538, 540

Brownlow, Leroy, 381

Brush Run Church, 3, 14, 125-129, 131, 138, 144-145, 157, 284

Bryant, David, 127

Buffalo Seminary, 132

Buley, R.C., 53

Burgess, O.A., 234

Burnet, David Staats, 141, 178, 212-213, 251, 282-284, 287-291, 295, 305-306, 322, 359, 367, 391

Burnham, F.W., 411

Burns, Robert W., 503

Butchart, Reuben, 292, 296, 306, 328

Butler, Ovid, 340, 342

Butler, Pardee, 198, 217, 220, 228, 339, 354

C

Caldwell, J.W., 402

Calhoun, Hall L., 363, 398, 452

Calixtus, George, 33

Callen, Barry L., 486

Calvin, John, 34-36, 40, 542

Calvinists, 5, 33

Campanus, John, 36

Campbell, Alexander, 2, 4, 6, 9-11, 14, 16, 21, 23, 29, 31, 33, 35, 40-41, 43-44, 48, 53-54, 61, 68, 70-71, 78, 82, 84, 86, 89, 92-94, 98-99, 104, 110, 113, 116-117, 119-120, 128-129, 133, 136, 140, 143, 146, 148, 151-152, 154-155, 161, 163, 167, 171-172, 174-175, 177-179, 189-192, 194-195, 197-199, 204-205, 207-211, 214, 216-218, 220, 224-227, 229, 232, 240-241, 247, 249-253, 255-256, 258, 260, 262, 269-270, 275-276, 279-283, 289-292, 294, 297, 299, 302-305, 308, 310, 312, 315-316, 325, 330, 333-335, 346, 349, 351-353, 355, 358-359, 361, 365, 367, 369, 378, 409, 435, 437, 471, 477, 480, 487, 489, 494, 505, 513, 518, 520, 525, 531, 541-542, 544, 547, 550, 552-553, 555-556

Campbell, Clarinda, 225

Campbell, Decima, 224

Campbell, Dorothea, 127

Campbell, Elizabeth, 73

Campbell, George, 162-163, 257

Campbell, Lavinia, 225

Campbell, Margaret, 132, 144

Campbell, Selina, 225, 268

Campbell, Thomas, 9, 13, 22, 25-26,

353, 355, 361, 363, 377-378, 393,
395-397, 402, 405, 438, 449, 454,
466-467, 532
Graft, Mary,   221
Grafton, T.W.,   326
Graham, Billy,   163, 231
Graham, Robert,   234
Great Awakening, The,   48-50, 75
Grebel, Conrad,   37
Greeley, Horace,   219
Green, F.M.,   367, 377
Green, Robert W.,   484
Greenlee, John,   479
Gresham, Charles,   536
Gresham, Perry,   29, 536, 559
Grotius, Hugo,   34
Guirey, William,   68, 70
Guthrie, Bill,   495

H

Haddon, Arthur L.,   302
Haggard, Rice,   4, 13, 47, 60-63, 65-
67, 69-71, 543
Hailey, Homer,   7
Haldane, James,   41, 120-121
Haldanes,   40-42, 120-121, 147-149,
333, 349
Haley, J.J.,   237, 251, 313, 316
Hall, B.F.,   178, 206-209, 337
Hall, Colby D.,   66-67, 198, 317, 475
Hamilton, J.J.,   539
Hamm, Richard L.,   510, 515
Hardeman, N.B.,   391, 452-453
Hardin, Arnold,   445, 466
Harding, James A.,   363, 397-398,
400, 403, 405
Harding, W.H.,   324
Harper, W.R.,   317, 417
Harrell, David E., Jr.,   348, 353, 381
Harrell, Pat,   459
Harrison, Richard L., Jr.,   505, 509
Harrison, W.O.,   351
Harrison, William H.,   174

Hart, Larry,   465
Harvey, Douglas A.,   513
Hastings, R.B.,   354
Hayden, A.S.,   318-319
Hayden, Edwin V.,   414, 478
Hayden, William,   218, 257
Hays, Howard,   475, 493
Hazelrigg, Clara,   223
Heber, Reginald,   364
Helsabeck, W. Dennis, Jr.,   484, 493
Henley, Thomas M.,   387
Henry, G.W.,   418
Herald of Gospel Liberty,   62, 66, 68
Herald of Truth,   435, 449, 537
Heretic Detector, The,   269
Hill, Samuel S.,   447
Hiram College,   224, 421
Hodge, William,   72
Hogan, R.N.,   439, 466
Hook, Cecil,   457, 559
Hooper, Robert E.,   402, 405, 466,
559
Hopkins, A.C.,   539
Hopson, Alexander C.,   316
Hopson, Winthrop H.,   203, 313,
344-345
Howard, John R.,   91, 346
Hudson, Winthrop S.,   48
Hughes, Richard T.,   92, 459, 467,
529, 557, 558
Hull, Debra B.,   223, 226, 228
Humble, Bill J.,   7, 91, 237, 351
Hume, David,   25, 30, 377
Humphrey, Heman,   252, 525
Hussey (Brother),   229

I

Image,   449, 458, 467, 538
Instrumental Music,   212, 295, 300,
308-310, 312, 314-315, 318-324,
326-330, 381, 389, 392, 394, 398,
400-401, 415, 434-436, 453, 458-
459, 461-463, 531, 533-534, 538,
554-555